AF574486

Syntax of Dutch
Adpositions and Adpositional Phrases

Comprehensive Grammar Resources

Editors:
Henk van Riemsdijk
István Kenesei

Syntax of Dutch
Adpositions and Adpositional Phrases

Hans Broekhuis

With the cooperation of:
Hans Bennis
Carole Boster
Marcel den Dikken
Martin Everaert
Liliane Haegeman
Evelien Keizer
Anneke Neijt
Henk van Riemsdijk
Georges de Schutter
Riet Vos

Amsterdam University Press

The publication of this book is made possible by grants and financial support from:
Netherlands Organisation for Scientific Research (NWO)
Center for Language Studies
University of Tilburg
Truus und Gerrit van Riemsdijk-Stiftung
Meertens Institute (KNAW)

This book is published in print and online through the online OAPEN library (www.oapen.org).

OAPEN (Open Access Publishing in European Networks) is a collaborative initiative to develop and implement a sustainable Open Access publication model for academic books in the Humanities and Social Sciences. The OAPEN Library aims to improve the visibility and usability of high quality academic research by aggregating peer reviewed Open Access publications from across Europe.

Cover design: Studio Jan de Boer, Amsterdam
Layout: Hans Broekhuis

ISBN 978 90 8964 601 9
e-ISBN 978 90 4852 225 5 (pdf)
e-ISBN 978 90 4852 226 2 (ePub)
NUR 616 / 624

Contents

Abbreviations and symbols

This appendix contains a list of abbreviations and symbols that are used in this volume. Sometimes conventions are adopted that differ from the ones given in this list, but if this is the case this is always explicitly mentioned in the text.

°XXX	Refers to the XXX in the glossary
A+section #	A3.2 refers to Section 3.2. in Hans Broekhuis (2013). *Grammar of* Dutch*: Adjectives and adjective phrases.*
Domain D	Domain of discourse
N+section #	N3.2 refers to Section 3.2. in Hans Broekhuis & Evelien Keizer (2012) and Hans Broekhuis & Marcel den Dikken (2012), *Grammar of Dutch: nouns and noun phrases*, Vol. 1 & 2.
QC	Quantificational binominal construction
V+section #	V3.2 refers to Section 3.2. in Hans Broekhuis & Norbert Corver (in prep). *Grammar of Dutch: Verbs and verb phrases.*

Abbreviations used in both the main text and the examples

AP	Adjectival Phrase	PP	Prepositional Phrase
DP	Determiner Phrase	QP	Quantifier Phrase
NP	Noun Phrase*	VP	Verb Phrase
NumP	Numeral Phrase		

*) *Noun phrase* is written in full when the NP-DP distinction is not relevant.

Symbols, abbreviations and conventions used in the examples

e	Phonetically empty element
Ref	Referent argument (external °thematic role of nouns/adjectives)
Rel	Related argument (internal thematic role of relational nouns)
OP	Empty operator
PG	Parasitic gap
PRO	Implied subject in, e.g., infinitival clauses
PRO_{arb}	Implied subject PRO with arbitrary (generic) reference
t	Trace (the original position of a moved element)
XXX	Small caps indicates that XXX is assigned contrastive accent

Abbreviations used as subscripts in the examples

1p/2p/3p	1st, 2nd, 3rd person	nom	nominative
acc	accusative	pl	plural
dat	dative	poss	possessor
dim	diminutive	pred	predicate
fem	feminine	rec	recipient
masc	masculine	sg	singular

Abbreviations used in the glosses of the examples

AFF	Affirmative marker
COMP	Complementizer: *dat* 'that' in finite declarative clauses, *of* 'whether/if' in finite interrogative clauses, and *om* in infinitival clauses
prt.	Particle that combines with a particle verb
PRT	Particle of different kinds
REFL	The short form of the reflexive pronoun, e.g., *zich*; the long form *zichzelf* is usually translated as *himself/herself/itself*
XXX	Small caps in other cases indicates that XXX cannot be translated

Diacritics used for indicating acceptability judgments

*	Unacceptable
*?	Relatively acceptable compared to *
??	Intermediate or unclear status
?	Marked: not completely acceptable or disfavored form
(?)	Slightly marked, but probably acceptable
no marking	Fully acceptable
%	Not (fully) acceptable due to non-syntactic factors *or* varying judgments among speakers
#	Unacceptable under intended reading
$	Special status: old-fashioned, archaic, very formal, incoherent, etc.

Other conventions

xx/yy	Acceptable both with xx and with yy
*xx/yy	Unacceptable with xx, but acceptable with yy
xx/*yy	Acceptable with xx, but unacceptable with yy
(xx)	Acceptable both with and without xx
*(xx)	Acceptable with, but unacceptable without xx
(*xx)	Acceptable without, but unacceptable with xx
.. <xx>	Alternative placement of xx in an example
.. <*xx> ..	Impossible placement of xx in an example
$\Rightarrow$	Necessarily implies
$\not\Rightarrow$	Does not necessarily imply
XX ... *YY*	Italics indicate binding
XX_i ... YY_i	Coindexing indicates coreference
XX_i ... YY_j	Counter-indexing indicates disjoint reference
$XX_{*i/j}$	Unacceptable with index *i*, acceptable with index *j*
$XX_{i/*j}$	Unacceptable with index *j*, acceptable with index *i*
$[_{XP}$ ...]	Constituent brackets of a constituent XP

Preface and acknowledgments

1. General introduction

Dutch is an official language in the Netherlands, Belgium-Flanders, Surinam, Aruba and the Netherlands Antilles. With about 22 million native speakers it is one of the world's greater languages. It is taught and studied at more than 175 universities around the world (source: taalunieversum.org). Furthermore, Dutch is one of the most well-studied living languages; research on it has had a major, and still continuing, impact on the development of formal linguistic theory, and it plays an important role in various other types of linguistic research. It is therefore unfortunate that there is no recent comprehensive scientifically based description of the grammar of Dutch that is accessible to a wider international audience. As a result, much information remains hidden in scientific publications: some information is embedded in theoretical discussions that are mainly of interest for and accessible to certain groups of formal linguists or that are more or less outdated in the light of more recent findings and theoretical developments, some is buried in publications with only a limited distribution, and some is simply inaccessible to large groups of readers given that it is written in Dutch. The series *Syntax of Dutch* (SoD) aims at filling this gap for syntax.

2. Main objective

The main objective of *SoD* is to present a synthesis of currently available syntactic knowledge of Dutch. It gives a comprehensive overview of the relevant research on Dutch that not only presents the findings of earlier approaches to the language, but also includes the results of the formal linguistic research carried out over the last four or five decades that often cannot be found in the existing reference books. It must be emphasized, however, that *SoD* is primarily concerned with language description and not with linguistic theory; the reader will generally look in vain for critical assessments of theoretical proposals made to account for specific phenomena. Although *SoD* addresses many of the central issues of current linguistic theory, it does *not* provide an introduction to current linguistic theory. Readers interested in such an introduction are referred to one of the many existing introductory textbooks, or to handbooks like *The Blackwell Companion to Syntax*, edited by Martin Everaert & Henk van Riemsdijk, or *The Cambridge Handbook of Generative Syntax*, edited by Marcel den Dikken. A recent publication that aims at providing a description of Dutch in a more theoretical setting is *The Syntax of Dutch* by Jan-Wouter Zwart in the *Cambridge Syntax Guides* series.

3. Intended readership

SoD is not intended for a specific group of linguists, but aims at a more general readership. Our intention was to produce a work of reference that is accessible to a large audience that has some training in linguistics and/or neighboring disciplines and that provides support to all researchers interested in matters relating to the syntax of Dutch. Although we did not originally target this group, we believe that the descriptions we provide are normally also accessible to advanced students of language and linguistics. The specification of our target group above implies that we have tried to avoid jargon from specific theoretical frameworks and to use as much as possible the *lingua franca* that linguists use in a broader context. Whenever we introduce a notion that we believe not to be part of the *lingua franca*, we will provide a brief clarification of this notion in a glossary; first occurrences of such notions in a certain context are normally marked by means of °.

4. Object of description

The object of description is aptly described by the title of the series, *Syntax of Dutch*. This title suggests a number of ways in which the empirical domain is restricted, which we want to spell out here in more detail by briefly discussing the two notions *syntax* and *Dutch*.

I. Syntax

Syntax is the field of linguistics that studies how words are combined into larger phrases and, ultimately, sentences. This means that we do not systematically discuss the internal structure of words (this is the domain of morphology) or the way in which sentences are put to use in discourse: we only digress on such matters when this is instrumental in describing the syntactic properties of the language. For example, Chapter N1 contains an extensive discussion of deverbal nominalization, but this is only because this morphological process is relevant for the discussion of complementation of nouns in Chapter N2. And Section N8.1.3 will show that the word order difference between the two examples in (1) is related to the preceding discourse: when pronounced with neutral (non-contrastive) accent, the object *Marie* may only precede clause adverbs like *waarschijnlijk* 'probably' when it refers to some person who has already been mentioned in (or is implied by) the preceding discourse.

(1) a. Jan heeft waarschijnlijk *Marie* gezien. [Marie = discourse new]
Jan has probably Marie seen
'Jan has probably seen Marie.'
b. Jan heeft *Marie* waarschijnlijk gezien. [Marie = discourse old]
Jan has Marie probably seen
'Jan has probably seen Marie.'

Our goal of describing the internal structure of phrases and sentences means that we focus on competence (the internalized grammar of native speakers), and not on performance (the actual use of language). This implies that we will make extensive use of constructed examples that are geared to the syntactic problem at hand, and that we will not systematically incorporate the findings of currently flourishing corpus/usage-based approaches to language: this will be done only insofar as this may shed light on matters concerning the internal structure of phrases. A case for which this type of research may be syntactically relevant is the word order variation of the verb-final sequence in (2), which has been extensively studied since Pauwels (1950) and which has been shown to be sensitive to a large number of interacting variables, see De Sutter (2005/2007) for extensive discussion.

(2) a. dat Jan dat boek *gelezen heeft.*
that Jan that book read has
'that Jan has read that book.'
b. dat Jan dat boek *heeft gelezen.*
that Jan that book has read
'that Jan has read that book.'

This being said, it is important to point out that *SoD* will pay ample attention to certain aspects of meaning, and reference will also be made to phonological aspects such as stress and intonation wherever they are relevant (e.g., in the context of word order phenomena like in (1)). The reason for this is that current formal grammar assumes that the output of the syntactic module of the grammar consists of objects (sentences) that relate form and meaning. Furthermore, formal syntax has been quite successful in establishing and describing a large number of restrictions on this relationship. A prime example of this is the formulation of so-called °binding theory, which accounts (among other things) for the fact that referential pronouns like *hem* 'him' and anaphoric pronouns like *zichzelf* 'himself' differ in the domain within which they can/must find an antecedent. For instance, the examples in (3), in which the intended antecedent of the pronouns is given in italics, show that whereas referential object pronouns like *hem* cannot have an antecedent within their clause, anaphoric pronouns like *zichzelf* 'himself' must have an antecedent in their clause, see Section N5.2.1.5, sub III, for more detailed discussion.

(3) a. *Jan* denkt dat Peter hem/*zichzelf bewondert.
Jan thinks that Peter him/himself admires
'Jan thinks that Peter is admiring him [= Jan].'
b. Jan denkt dat *Peter* zichzelf/*hem bewondert.
Jan thinks that Peter himself/him admires
'Jan thinks that Peter is admiring himself [= Peter].'

II. Dutch

SoD aims at giving a syntactic description of what we will loosely refer to as Standard Dutch, although we are aware that there are many problems with this notion. First, the notion of Standard Dutch is often used to refer to written language and more formal registers, which are perceived as more prestigious than the colloquial uses of the language. Second, the notion of Standard Dutch suggests that there is an invariant language system that is shared by a large group of speakers. Third, the notion carries the suggestion that some, often unnamed, authority is able to determine what should or should not be part of the language, or what should or should not be considered proper language use. See Milroy (2001) for extensive discussion of this notion of standard language.

SoD does not provide a description of this prestigious, invariant, externally determined language system. The reason for this is that knowledge of this system does not involve the competence of the individual language user but "is the product of a series of educational and social factors which have overtly impinged on the linguistic experiences of individuals, prescribing the correctness/incorrectness of certain constructions" (Adger & Trousdale 2007). Instead, the notion of standard language in *SoD* should be understood more neutrally as an idealization that refers to certain properties of linguistic competence that we assume to be shared by the individual speakers of the language. This notion of standard language deviates from the notion of standard language discussed earlier in that it may include properties that would be rejected by language teachers, and exclude certain properties that are explicitly taught as being part of the standard language. To state the latter in more technical terms: our notion of standard language refers to the core grammar (those aspects of the language system that arise spontaneously in the language learning child by exposure to utterances in the standard language) and excludes the periphery (those properties of the standard language that are explicitly taught at some later age). This does not mean that we will completely ignore the more peripheral issues, but it should be kept in mind that these have a special status and may exhibit properties that are alien to the core system.

A distinguishing property of standard languages is that they may be used among speakers of different dialects, and that they sometimes have to be acquired by speakers of such dialects as a second language at a later age, that is, in a similar fashion as a foreign language (although this may be rare in the context of Dutch). This property of standard languages entails that it is not contradictory to distinguish various varieties of, e.g., Standard Dutch. This view is also assumed by Haeseryn et al. (1997: Section 0.6.2), who make the four-way distinction in (4) when it comes to geographically determined variation.

(4) • Types of Dutch according to Haeseryn et al. (1997)
  a. Standard language
  b. Regional variety of Standard Dutch
  c. Regional variety of Dutch
  d. Dialect

The types in (4b&c) are characterized by certain properties that are found in certain larger, but geographically restricted regions only. The difference between the two varieties is defined by Haeseryn at al. (1997) by appealing to the perception of the properties in question by other speakers of the standard language: when the majority of these speakers do not consider the property in question characteristic for a certain geographical region, the property is part of a regional variety of *Standard Dutch*; when the property in question is unknown to certain speakers of the standard language or considered to be characteristic for a certain geographical region, it is part of a regional variety of *Dutch*. We will not adopt the distinction between the types in (4b) and (4c) since we are not aware of any large-scale perception studies that could help us to distinguish the two varieties in question. We therefore simply join the two categories into a single one, which leads to the typology in (5).

(5) • Types of Dutch distinguished in *SoD*
  a. Standard Dutch
  b. Regional variety of Dutch
  c. Dialect of Dutch

We believe it to be useful to think of the notions in (5) in terms of grammatical properties that are part of the competence of groups of speakers. Standard Dutch can then be seen as a set of properties that is part of the competence of all speakers of the language. Examples of such properties in the nominal domain are that non-pronominal noun phrases are not morphologically case-marked and that the word order within noun phrases is such that nouns normally follow attributively used adjectives but precede PP-modifiers and that articles precede attributive adjectives (if present); cf. (6a). Relevant properties within the clausal domain are that finite verbs occupy the co-called second position in main clauses whereas non-finite verbs tend to cluster in the right-hand side of the clause (see (6b)), and that finite verbs join the clause-final non-finite verbs in embedded clauses (see (6c)).

(6) a. de oude man in de stoel [word order within noun phrases]
the old man in the chair
b. Jan *heeft* de man een lied *horen zingen.* [verb second/clustering]
Jan has the man a song hear sing
'Jan has heard the man sing a song.'
c. dat Jan de man een lied *heeft horen zingen.* [verb clustering]
that Jan the man a song has hear sing
'that Jan has heard the man sing a song.'

Regional varieties of Dutch arise as the result of sets of additional properties that are part of the competence of larger subgroups of speakers—such properties will define certain special characteristics of the variety in question but will normally not give rise to linguistic outputs that are inaccessible to speakers of other varieties; see the discussion of (7) below for a typical example. Dialects can be seen as a set of properties that characterizes a group of speakers in a restricted geographical area—such properties may be alien to speakers of the standard language and may give rise to linguistic outputs that are not immediately accessible to other speakers of Dutch; see the examples in (9) below for a potential case. This way of thinking about the typology in (5) enables us to use the language types in a more gradient way, which may do more justice to the situation that we actually find. Furthermore, it makes it possible to define varieties of Dutch along various (e.g., geographical and possibly social) dimensions.

The examples in (7) provide an example of a property that belongs to regional varieties of Dutch: speakers of northern varieties of Dutch require that the direct object *boeken* 'books' precede all verbs in clause-final position, whereas many speakers of the southern varieties of Dutch (especially those spoken in the Flemish part of Belgium) will also allow the object to permeate the verb sequence, as long as it precedes the main verb.

(7) a. dat Jan <boeken> wil <*boeken> kopen. [Northern Dutch]
that Jan books wants buy
'that Jan wants to buy books.'
b. dat Jan <boeken> wil <boeken> kopen. [Southern Dutch]
that Jan books wants buy
'that Jan wants to buy books.'

Dialects of Dutch may deviate in various respects from Standard Dutch. There are, for example, various dialects that exhibit morphological agreement between the subject and the complementizer, which is illustrated in (8) by examples taken from Van Haeringen (1939); see Haegeman (1992), Hoekstra & Smit (1997), Zwart (1997), Barbiers et al. (2005) and the references given there for more examples and extensive discussion. Complementizer agreement is a typical dialect property as it does not occur in (the regional varieties of) Standard Dutch.

(8) a. As$_{sg}$ Wim komp$_{sg}$, mot jə zorgə dat je tuis ben.
when Wim comes must you make.sure that you at.home are
'When Wim comes, you must make sure to be home.'

b. Azzə$_{pl}$ Kees en Wim kommə$_{pl}$, mot jə zorgə dat je tuis ben.
when Kees and Wim come must you make.sure that you home are
'When Kees and Wim come, you must make sure to be home.'

The examples in (9) illustrate another property that belongs to a certain set of dialects. Speakers of most varieties of Dutch would agree that the use of possessive datives is only possible in a limited set of constructions: whereas possessive datives are possible in constructions like (9a), in which the possessee is embedded in a °complementive PP, they are excluded in constructions like (9b), where the possessee functions as a direct object. Constructions like (9b) are perceived (if understood at all) as belonging to certain eastern and southern dialects, which is indicated here by means of a percentage sign.

(9) a. Marie zet Peter/hem$_{possessor}$ het kind op de knie$_{possessee}$.
Marie puts Peter/him the child onto the knee
'Marie puts the child on Peter's/his knee.

b. %Marie wast Peter/hem$_{possessor}$ de handen$_{possessee}$.
Marie washes Peter/him the hands
'Marie is washing Peter's/his hands.'

Note that the typology in (5) should allow for certain dialectal properties to become part of certain regional varieties of Dutch, as indeed seems to be the case for possessive datives of the type in (9b); cf. Cornips (1994). This shows again that it is not possible to draw sharp dividing lines between regional varieties and dialects and emphasizes that we are dealing with dynamic systems; see the discussion of (5) above. For our limited purpose, however, the proposed distinctions seem to suffice.

It must be stressed that the description of the types of Dutch in (5) in terms of properties of the competence of groups of speakers implies that Standard Dutch is actually not a language in the traditional sense; it is just a subset of properties that all non-dialectal varieties of Dutch have in common. Selecting one of these varieties as *Standard Dutch in the more traditional sense described in the beginning of this subsection* is not a linguistic enterprise and will therefore not concern us here. For practical reasons, however, we will focus on the variety of Dutch that is spoken in the northwestern part of the Netherlands. One reason for doing this is that, so far, the authors who have contributed to *SoD* are all native speakers of this variety and can therefore simply appeal to their own intuitions in order to establish whether this variety does or does not exhibit a certain property. A second reason is that this variety seems close to the varieties that have been discussed in the linguistic literature on "Standard Dutch". This does not mean that we will not discuss other varieties of Dutch, but we will do this only when we have reason to believe that they behave differently. Unfortunately, however, not much is known about the syntactic differences between the various varieties of Dutch and since it is not part of our goal to solve this problem, we want to encourage the reader to restrict the judgments given in *SoD* to speakers of the northwestern variety (unless indicated otherwise). Although in the vast majority of cases the other varieties of Dutch will exhibit identical or similar behavior given that the behavior in question reflects properties that are part of the standard language (in the technical sense given above), the reader should keep in mind that this cannot be taken for granted as it may also reflect properties of the regional variety spoken by the authors of this work.

5. Organization of the material

SoD is divided in four main parts that focus on the four LEXICAL CATEGORIES: verbs, nouns, adjectives and adpositions. Lexical categories have denotations and normally take arguments: nouns denote sets of entities, verbs denote states-of-affairs (activities, processes, etc.) that these entities may be involved in, adjectives denote properties of entities, and adpositions denote (temporal and locational) relations between entities.

The lexical categories, of course, do not exhaust the set of word classes; there are also FUNCTIONAL CATEGORIES like complementizers, articles, numerals, and quantifiers. Such elements normally play a role in phrases headed by the lexical categories: articles, numerals and quantifiers are normally part of noun phrases and complementizers are part of clauses (that is, verbal phrases). For this reason, these functional elements will be discussed in relation to the lexical categories.

The four main parts of *SoD* are given the subtitle *Xs and X phrases*, where *X* stands for one of the lexical categories. This subtitle expresses that each part discusses one lexical category and the ways in which it combines with other elements (like arguments and functional categories) to form constituents. Furthermore, the four main parts of *SoD* all have more or less the same overall organization in the sense that they contain (one or more) chapters on the following issues.

I. Characterization and classification

Each main part starts with an introductory chapter that provides a general characterization of the lexical category under discussion by describing some of its more conspicuous properties. The reader will find here not only a brief overview of the syntactic properties of these lexical categories, but also relevant discussions on morphology (e.g., inflection of verbs and adjectives) and semantics (e.g., the aspectual and tense properties of verbs). The introductory chapter will furthermore discuss ways in which the lexical categories can be divided into smaller natural subclasses.

II. Internal syntax

The main body of the work is concerned with the internal structure of the °projections of lexical categories/heads. These projections can be divided into two subdomains, which are sometimes referred to as the lexical and the functional domain. Taken together, the two domains are sometimes referred to as the EXTENDED PROJECTION of the lexical head in question; cf. Grimshaw (1991). We will see that there is reason to assume that the lexical domain is embedded in the functional domain, as in (10), where LEX stands for the lexical heads V, N, A or P, and F stands for one or more functional heads like the article *de* 'the' or the complementizer *dat* 'that'.

(10) [$_{\text{FUNCTIONAL}}$ ... F ... [$_{\text{LEXICAL}}$ .... LEX .....]]

The lexical domain of a lexical head is that part of its projection that affects its denotation. The denotation of a lexical head can be affected by its complements and its modifiers, as can be readily illustrated by means of the examples in (11).

(11) a. Jan leest.
Jan reads
b. Jan leest een krant.
Jan reads a newspaper
c. Jan leest nauwkeurig.
Jan reads carefully

The phrase *een krant lezen* 'to read a newspaper' in (11b) denotes a smaller set of states-of-affairs than the phrase *lezen* 'to read' in (11a), and so does the phrase *nauwkeurig lezen* 'to read carefully' in (11c). The elements in the functional domain do not affect the denotation of the lexical head but provide various sorts of additional information.

A. The lexical domain I: Argument structure

Lexical heads function as predicates, which means that they normally take arguments, that is, they enter into so-called thematic relations with entities that they semantically imply. For example, intransitive verbs normally take an agent as their subject; transitive verbs normally take an agent and a theme that are syntactically realized as, respectively, their subject and their object; and verbs like *wachten* 'to wait' normally take an agent that is realized as their subject and a theme that is realized as a prepositional complement.

(12) a. Jan$_{\text{Agent}}$ lacht. [intransitive verb]
Jan laughs
b. Jan$_{\text{Agent}}$ weet een oplossing$_{\text{Theme}}$. [transitive verb]
Jan knows a solution
c. Jan$_{\text{Agent}}$ wacht op de postbode$_{\text{Theme}}$. [verb with PP-complement]
Jan waits for the postman

Although this is often less conspicuous with nouns, adjectives and prepositions, it is possible to describe examples like (13) in the same terms. The phrases between straight brackets can be seen as predicates that are predicated of the noun phrase *Jan*, which we may therefore call their logical SUBJECT (we use small caps to distinguish this notion from the notion of nominative subject of the clause). Furthermore, the examples in (13) show (a) that the noun *vriend* may combine with a PP-complement that explicates with whom the SUBJECT *Jan* is in a relation of friendship, (b) that the adjective *trots* 'proud' optionally may take a PP-complement that explicates the subject matter that the SUBJECT *Jan* is proud about, and (c) that the preposition *onder* 'under' may take a nominal complement that refers to the location of its SUBJECT *Jan*.

(13) a. Jan is [een vriend *van Peter*].
Jan is a friend of Peter
b. Jan is [trots *op zijn dochter*].
Jan is proud of his daughter
c. Marie stopt Jan [onder *de dekens*].
Marie puts Jan under the blankets

That the italicized phrases are complements is somewhat obscured by the fact that there are certain contexts in which they can readily be omitted (e.g., when they would express information that the addressee can infer from the linguistic or non-linguistic context). The fact that they are always semantically implied, however, shows that they are semantically selected by the lexical head.

B. The lexical domain II: Modification

The projection consisting of a lexical head and its arguments can be modified in various ways. The examples in (14), for example, show that the projection of the verb *wachten* 'to wait' can be modified by various adverbial phrases. Examples (14a) and (14b), for instance, indicate when and where the state of affairs of Jan waiting for his father took place.

(14) a Jan wachtte *gisteren* op zijn vader. [time]
Jan waited yesterday for his father
'Jan waited for his father yesterday.'
b. Jan wacht op zijn vader *bij het station.* [place]
Jan waits for his father at the station
'Jan is waiting for his father at the station.'

The examples in (15) show that the lexical projections of nouns, adjectives and prepositions can likewise be modified; the modifiers are italicized.

(15) a. Jan is een *vroegere* vriend van Peter.
Jan is a former friend of Peter
b. Jan is *erg* trots op zijn dochter.
Jan is very proud of his daughter
c. Marie stopt Jan *diep* onder de dekens.
Marie puts Jan deep under the blankets

C. The functional domain

Projections of the lexical heads may contain various elements that are not arguments or modifiers, and thus do not affect the denotation of the head noun. Such elements simply provide additional information about the denotation. Examples of such functional categories are articles, numerals and quantifiers, which we find in the nominal phrases in (16).

(16) a. Jan is *de*/*een* vroegere vriend van Peter. [article]
Jan is the/a former friend of Peter
b. Peter heeft *twee*/*veel* goede vrienden. [numeral/quantifier]
Jan has two/many good friends

That functional categories provide additional information about the denotation of the lexical domain can readily be demonstrated by means of these examples. The definite article *de* in (16a), for example, expresses that the set denoted by the phrase *vroegere vriend van Peter* has just a single member; the use of the indefinite article *een*, on the other hand, suggests that there are more members in this set. Similarly, the use of the numeral *twee* 'two' in (16b) expresses that there are just two members in the set, and the quantifier *veel* 'many' expresses that the set is large.

Functional elements that can be found in verbal projections are tense (which is generally expressed as inflection on the finite verb) and complementizers: the difference between *dat* 'that' and *of* 'whether' in (17), for example, is related to the illocutionary type of the expression: the former introduces embedded declarative and the latter embedded interrogative clauses.

(17) a. Jan zegt [*dat* Marie ziek is]. [declarative]
Jan says that Marie ill is
'Jan says that Marie is ill.'
b. Jan vroeg [*of* Marie ziek is]. [interrogative]
Jan asked whether Marie ill is
'Jan asked whether Marie is ill.'

Given that functional categories provide information about the lexical domain, it is often assumed that they are part of a functional domain that is built on top of the lexical domain; cf. (10) above. This functional domain is generally taken to have an intricate structure and to be highly relevant for word order: functional heads are taken to project, just like lexical heads, and thus to create positions that can be used as landing sites for movement. A familiar case is *wh*-movement, which is assumed to target some position in the projection of the complementizer; in this way it can be explained that, in colloquial Dutch, *wh*-movement may result in placing the interrogative phrase to the immediate left of the complementizer *of* 'whether'. This is shown in (18b), where the trace *t* indicates the original position of the moved *wh*-element and the index *i* is just a convenient means to indicate that the two positions are related. Discussion of word order phenomena will therefore play a prominent role in the chapters devoted to the functional domain.

(18) a. Jan zegt [dat Marie een boek van Louis Couperus gelezen heeft].
Jan says that Marie a book by Louis Couperus read has
'Jan said that Marie has read a book by Louis Couperus.'
b. Jan vroeg [wat$_i$ (of) Marie t_i gelezen heeft].
Jan asked what whether Marie read has
'Jan asked what Marie has read.'

Whereas (relatively) much is known about the functional domain of verbal and nominal projections, research on the functional domain of adjectival and prepositional phrases is still in its infancy. For this reason, the reader will find independent chapters on this issue only in the parts on verbs and nouns.

III. External syntax

The discussion of each lexical category will be concluded with a look at the external syntax of their projections, that is, an examination of how such projections can be used in larger structures. Adjectives, for example, can be used as °complementives (predicative complements of verbs), as attributive modifiers of noun phrases, and also as adverbial modifiers of verb phrases.

(19) a. Die auto is *snel*. [complementive use]
that car is fast
b. Een *snelle* auto [attributive use]
a fast car
c. De auto reed *snel* weg. [adverbial use]
the car drove quickly away
'The car drove away quickly.'

Since the external syntax of the adjectival phrases in (19) can in principle also be described as the internal syntax of the verbal/nominal projections that contain these phrases, this may give rise to some redundancy. Complementives, for example, are discussed in Section V2.2 as part of the internal syntax of the verbal projection, but also in Sections N8.2, A6 and P4.2 as part of the external syntax of nominal, adjectival and adpositional phrases. We nevertheless have allowed this redundancy, given that it enables us to simplify the discussion of the internal syntax of verb phrases in V2.2: nominal, adjectival and adpositional complementives exhibit different behavior in various respects, and discussing all of these in Section V2.2 would have obscured the discussion of properties of complementives in general. Of course, a system of cross-references will inform the reader when a certain issue is discussed from the perspective of both internal and external syntax.

6. History of the project and future prospects

The idea for the project was initiated in 1992 by Henk van Riemsdijk. In 1993 a pilot study was conducted at Tilburg University and a steering committee was installed after a meeting with interested parties from Dutch and Flemish institutions. However, it took five more years until in 1998 a substantial grant from the Netherlands Organization of Scientific Research (NWO) was finally obtained.

Funding has remained a problem, which is the reason that *SoD* still is not completed yet. However in the meantime financial guarantees have been created for Hans Broekhuis to finish all four main parts of *SoD* in the next few years. Due to the size of the complete set of materials comprising SoD, we have decided that the time has come to publish those parts that are currently available. In what follows we want to inform the reader of what has been done so far and what is to be expected in the near future.

I. Noun and noun phrases (Hans Broekhuis, Evelien Keizer and Marcel den Dikken)

This work, which was published in two volumes in 2012, discusses the internal make-up as well as the distribution of noun phrases. Topics that are covered include: complementation and modification of noun phrases; properties of determiners (article, demonstratives), numeral and quantifiers; the use of noun phrases as arguments, predicates and adverbial modifiers.

II. Adjectives and adjective phrases (Hans Broekhuis)

The volume, which was published in Spring 2013, discusses the internal make-up as well as the distribution of adjective phrases. Topics that are covered include: complementation and modification; comparative and superlative formation; the attributive, predicative and adverbial uses of adjective phrases. Special attention is paid to the so-called partitive genitive construction and the adverbial use of past/passive participles and infinitives.

III. Adpositions and adpositional phrases (Hans Broekhuis)

The present volume discusses the internal make-up and the distribution of adpositional phrases. Topics that are covered include complementation and modification of adpositional phrases, as well as their predicative, attributive and adverbial uses. A separate chapter is devoted to the formation and the syntactic behavior of pronominal PPs like *erop* 'on it', which also includes a more general discussion of the syntax of so-called R-words like *er* 'there'.

IV. Verbs and Verb phrases (Hans Broekhuis and Norbert Corver)

This work will consist of three volumes of about 600 pages each. The first volume is currently in the process of being prepared for publication, the second volume is now nearly completed, and the third volume is in progress. These volumes will be published before Spring 2016.

In addition to the three main parts in I-IV, we have planned a separate volume in which topics like coordination and ellipsis (conjunction reduction, gapping, etc.) that cannot be done full justice within the main body of this work are discussed in more detail. Furthermore, the *SoD* project has become part of a broader project initiated by Hans Bennis and Geert Booij, called *Language Portal Dutch/Frisian*, which includes similar projects on the phonology and the morphology of Dutch. We may therefore expect that the *SoD* will at some point be complemented by a *PoD* and a *MoD*. The Language Portal also aims at making a version of all this material accessible via internet before January 2016, which will add various functionalities including advanced search options. Finally, we want to note that Henk van Riemsdijk and István Kenesei are currently in the process of initiating a number of grammar projects comparable to *SoD*: languages under discussion include Basque, Hungarian, Japanese, Mandarin, Polish, Romanian, Russian, Swedish, and Turkish. For this reason, the volumes of SoD are published as part of the *Comprehensive Grammar Resources* series, which will bring together the future results of these initiatives.

7. Acknowledgments

Over the years many Dutch linguists have commented on parts of the work presented here and since we do not want to tire the reader by providing long lists of names, we simply thank the whole Dutch linguistic community; this will also safeguard us from the embarrassment of forgetting certain names. Still, we do want to mention a couple of persons and institutions without whom/which this project would never have been started or brought to a good end. First we would like to thank the members of the steering committee (chaired by Henk van Riemsdijk) consisting of Hans Bennis, Martin Everaert, Liliane Haegeman, Anneke Neijt, and Georges de Schutter. All members provided us with comments on substantial parts of the manuscript. Second, we should mention Evelien Keizer and Riet Vos, who discussed the full manuscript with us and provided numerous suggestions for improvement.

The pilot study for the project, which was performed from November 1993 to September 1994, was made possible by a subsidy from the *Center for Language Studies* and the *University of Tilburg*. This pilot study resulted in a project proposal that was eventually granted by *The Netherlands Organisation for Scientific Research* (NWO) in 1998 and which enabled us to produce the main body of work mentioned in Section 6, sub I to III, during the period from May 1998 to May 2001. The work could be prepared for publication in the period from April 2008 to October 2010 thanks to a subsidy to Hans Broekhuis from the *Truus und Gerrit van Riemsdijk-Stiftung*. Since November 2010 Hans Broekhuis continues his work on *SoD* as an employee of the *Meertens Institute* (KNAW) in Amsterdam. *SoD* has become part of the project *Language Portal Dutch/Frisian*, which is again financed by *The Netherlands Organisation for Scientific Research* (NWO). We gratefully acknowledge the financial and moral support of these institutions and thank them for the opportunity they have given us to develop *SoD*.

August 2013

Hans Broekhuis
Co-author and editor of Syntax of Dutch

Henk van Riemsdijk
Chairman of the steering committee

Introduction

Verbs (V), adjectives (A), nouns (N) and adpositions (P) constitute the four major word classes. The present volume deals with adpositions and their projections (adpositional phrases or PPs). The general introduction in Chapter 1 provides a survey of the most distinctive syntactic, semantic and morphological characteristics of adpositions. Like the other categories, adpositions can project: in other words, they select complements and can be modified, which will be discussed in Chapter 2 and Chapter 3, respectively. After this, we will have a closer look at the syntactic uses of the adpositional phrases in Chapter 4. This study will be concluded in Chapter 5 with a discussion of the formation of pronominal PPs like *er op* 'on it', which consist of a so-called R-word like *er* and a preposition, and the phenomenon that these pronominal PPs can be split by extraction of the R-word. We will also address the complicated issue of co-occurrence and conflation of different types of R-words, although, strictly speaking, this goes somewhat beyond the main theme of this work.

Chapter 1
Adpositions: characteristics and classification

Introduction

This chapter provides a more general discussion of adpositions and their projections (adpositional phrases). Section 1.1 starts by providing a general characterization of the category of adpositions. Section 1.2 and 1.3 continue by discussing two possible ways of classifying the adpositions. The first classification is based on the relative position of the adpositions with respect to their complement (if any), which results in distinguishing the following four subclasses: prepositions, postpositions, circumpositions and intransitive adpositions/particles. The second classification, on the other hand, is based on the meaning of the adpositions, which results in distinguishing the following three subclasses: spatial, temporal and non-spatial/temporal adpositions. Section 1.4 concludes with a discussion of a number of borderline cases, that is, elements that resemble adpositions in various respects, but for which it is nevertheless not entirely clear whether they should really be considered adpositions.

1.1. Characterization of the category adposition

This section provides a brief characterization of the category of adpositions. Section 1.1.1 discusses some characteristic properties of this category. Section 1.1.2 provides illustrations of the four basic types of adpositions: prepositions, postpositions, circumpositions and intransitive adpositions/particles. Section 1.1.3 concludes with a preliminary discussion of the syntactic uses of adpositional phrases. Since the purpose of the discussion below is to provide the necessary background for the remainder of our discussion on adpositional phrases, it is inevitably sketchy and far from complete; most issues mentioned here will be taken up again and discussed more exhaustively later in this study.

1.1.1. Properties of adpositions

There are several features that distinguish the class of adpositions from the other three main categories of words: verbs, nouns and adjectives. These are discussed in Subsection I. It is nevertheless difficult to design syntactic tests that single out the full set of adpositional phrases, although there are several tests that can be used in order to recognize certain syntactic or semantic subtypes. These will be discussed in Subsection II.

I. Differences from the other main categories of words

The subsections below discuss several respects in which adpositions differ from verbs, nouns and adjectives.

A. The set of adpositions is "closed"

Unlike verbs, nouns and adjectives, adpositions constitute a relatively small and more or less closed class in the sense that the set of adpositions can be nearly exhaustively listed; cf. Section 1.2. Despite this, it must be noted that it is not entirely impossible to introduce new adpositions in the language; Section 1.2.1 will discuss a number of relatively recent adpositions.

B. The form of adpositions is invariant

Whereas verbs are inflected for tense and agree with the subject of the clause in person and number, nouns are inflected for number, and adjectives are inflected in attributive position, inflection of adpositions does not occur in Dutch. Adpositions like *in* 'in' or *onder* 'under' have the same form in all syntactic environments. The property of invariance, of course, only holds as far as inflection is concerned; derivation and compounding are possible.

There are two exceptions to the general rule that the form of adpositions is invariant. The first involves the prepositions *met* 'with' and *tot* 'until', which change into *mee* and *toe* when R-extraction applies: *er ... mee/toe*; cf. Chapter 5. The second involves the preposition *te*, which can surface as *ter* or *ten* in certain fixed expressions (historical relics) like *ter wereld brengen* 'to give birth to' and *ten aanzien van iemand* 'toward someone'. The forms *ter* and *ten* must, however, be seen as conflated forms of the preposition *te* and the case-marked determiners *der* and *den*, just as present-day German *zum* is the conflated form of the preposition *zu* 'to' and the dative determiner *dem* 'the'.

C. Adpositions assign case to their nominal complement

Adpositions typically take a noun phrase as their complement, to which they assign non-nominative case. In present-day German, adpositions differ in whether they assign genitive, dative or accusative case. In Dutch, on the other hand, the case assigned by the adposition cannot be determined due to the lack of morphological case; the form of noun phrases like *de jongen* and *het meisje* in the primeless examples in (20) remains the same in all imaginable syntactic positions (subject, object, or complement of adposition). That adpositions do assign non-nominative case is clear, however, from the fact, illustrated in the primed examples, that they cannot be followed by the nominative forms of the personal pronouns.

(20) a. Jan zit naast de jongen
Jan sits next.to the boy
'Jan is sitting next to the boy.'

a′. Jan zit naast hem/*hij.
Jan sits next.to him/he

b. Jan zit voor het meisje
Jan sits in.front.of the girl
'Jan is sitting in front of the girl.'

b′. Jan zit voor haar/*zij.
Jan sits in.front.of her/she

D. Adpositions typically express a relation between two elements in the clause

Adpositions often express a relation between their complement and some other entity in the clause. In (20), for example, the adpositions *naast* and *voor* express a spatial relation between their nominal complement *de jongen*/*het meisje* and the subject of the clause *Jan*.

II. Tests to distinguish adpositions

The following subsections briefly discuss certain processes that typically occur with adpositions as well as certain constructions that typically contain an adposition. The occurrence of these processes or constructions is generally sufficient to argue that we are dealing with an adpositional phrase.

A. Pronominalization

Spatial and temporal adpositional phrases can be pronominalized. Example (21), for example, shows that the spatial adpositional phrase *in Amsterdam* can be replaced by the adpositional pro-form *er* 'there'.

(21) a. Jan heeft jarenlang in Amsterdam gewoond.
Jan has for years in Amsterdam lived
'Jan has lived in Amsterdam for years.'
b. Jan heeft er jarenlang gewoond.
Jan has there for years lived
'Jan has lived there for years.'

The spatial pro-form *er* is referential in the sense that it refers to some place known to the speaker and the addressee. Table 1 provides an overview of the other spatial pro-forms, which are generally referred to as R-WORDs because they all contain an /r/. Observe that this classification of spatial pro-forms is virtually identical to the classification of pronouns given in Section N5.2.

Table 1: Spatial adpositional pro-forms (R-words)

		R-PRONOUN	EXAMPLE
REFERENTIAL		*er/daar* 'there'	*Jan heeft er jarenlang gewoond.* 'Jan has lived there for years.'
DEMON-STRATIVE	PROXIMATE	*hier* 'here'	*Jan heeft hier jarenlang gewoond.* 'Jan has lived here for years.'
	DISTAL	*daar* 'there'	*Jan heeft daar jarenlang gewoond.* 'Jan has lived (over) there for years.'
INTERROGATIVE		*waar* 'where'	*Waar woont Jan?* 'Where does Jan live?'
QUANTIFI-CATIONAL	UNIVERSAL	*overal* 'everywhere'	*De boeken liggen overal.* 'The books lie everywhere.'
	EXISTENTIAL	*ergens* 'somewhere'	*Het boek moet toch ergens zijn.* 'The book must be somewhere.'
	NEGATIVE	*nergens* 'nowhere'	*Ik zie het boek nergens.* 'I don't see the book anywhere.'
RELATIVE		*waar* 'where'	*het huis waar Jan woont* 'the house where Jan lives'

The two referential pro-forms *er* and *daar* differ in the same way as the weak and strong referential pronouns: *er* is unstressed whereas *daar* is stressed. This is shown in the primed examples in (22) by means of topicalization, which is only possible with stressed phrases.

(22) a. Jan heeft mij/me gekust.
Jan has me/me kissed
'Jan has kissed me.'
a′. Mij/*Me heeft Jan gekust.

b. Jan heeft daar/er jarenlang gewoond.
Jan has there/there for.years lived
'Jan has lived there for years.'

b′. Daar/*Er heeft Jan jarenlang gewoond.

Since Table 1 shows that *daar* can also be used as a demonstrative pro-form, example (22b) is actually ambiguous: *daar* can be interpreted referentially and thus refer to some place known to the speaker and the addressee or it can have demonstrative force.

There are three temporal adpositional pro-forms, which differ in that they refer to different points on the time line: *toen* 'then' in (23a) refers to a point of time before the actual speech time: *dan* 'then' in (23b) refers to a point following the speech time; *nu* 'now' in (23c) refers to the speech time itself, and can be seen as the pro-form corresponding to an adpositional phrase like *op dit moment* 'at this moment'.

(23) a. Jan was_{past} in de vakantie/toen in Frankrijk.
Jan was in the vacation/then in France
'Jan was in France during his vacation/then.'

b. Jan zal_{future} in de vakantie/dan naar Frankrijk gaan.
Jan goes in the vacation/then to France go
'Jan will go to France during his vacation/then.'

c. Jan $is_{present}$ op dit moment/nu in Frankrijk.
Jan is at this moment/now in France
'Jan is in France now.'

B. R-pronominalization of the complement of the adposition

The complement of an adposition can often also be replaced by means of an R-word, a phenomenon to which we will refer as R-PRONOMINALIZATION. An example with the referential R-word *er* is given in (24b). The other R-words in Table 1 can also be used in this function; this is shown for the proximate demonstrative *hier* 'here' in example (24b′). For an extensive discussion of R-pronominalization, see Chapter 5.

(24) a. Jan speelt graag met de pop.
Jan plays gladly with the doll
'Jan likes to play with the doll.'

a′. Jan speelt graag met deze pop.
Jan plays gladly with this doll
'Jan likes to play with this doll.'

b. Jan speelt er graag mee.
Jan plays there gladly with
'Jan likes to play with it.'

b′. Jan speelt hier graag mee.
Jan plays here gladly with
'Jan likes to play with this.'

C. Placement within clauses and noun phrases

Just like clauses, but unlike nominal and adjectival phrases, adpositional phrases can often follow verbs in clause-final position without the need of a comma-intonation. This phenomenon, which is often referred to as °PP-over-V, is illustrated in (25) by means of an adverbial manner phrase.

(25) a. dat Jan met grote nauwkeurigheid/nauwkeurig werkte.
that Jan with great accuracy/accurately worked
'that Jan worked with great accuracy.'
b. dat Jan werkte met grote nauwkeurigheid/*nauwkeurig.

Example (26a) further shows that attributively used PPs are normally placed in postnominal position. In this respect they differ from attributively used APs like *aardige* in (26b), which normally occur prenominally.

(26) a. het <*met het rode haar> meisje <met het rode haar>
the with the red hair girl
b. het <aardige> meisje <*aardig(e)>
the nice girl

D. Modification

Modification by means of the adverbial phrases *vlak* or *pal* 'just/right' seems to be restricted to (a subset of) spatial and temporal PPs only.

(27) a. Jan stond vlak/pal achter Marie.
Jan stood close behind Marie
'Jan stood right behind Marie.'
b. Jan vertrok vlak/pal voor de wedstrijd.
Jan left just before the game
'Jan left just before the game.'

E. The XP met die NP! *construction*

In order to enter the *XP met die NP!* construction, XP must be directional in nature. Since directions are typically expressed by means of (a subclass of the) adpositional phrases, XP is an adpositional phrase in the prototypical case. Adjectival phrases like *dood* in (28c), for example, cannot enter the construction.

(28) a. [$_{\text{PP}}$ Naar buiten] met die man!
to outside with that man
'Throw that man out!'
b. [$_{\text{PP}}$ De klas uit] met jou!
the classroom out.of with you
'Get out of the classroom!'
c. *[$_{\text{AP}}$ Dood] met die schoft!
dead with that bastard
Intended meaning: 'Kill that bastard!'

F. Stress properties

Many adpositions may or may not be assigned stress depending on the complement they take. When they take a referential noun phrase or a strong pronoun, stress is generally assigned to the complement (although in contrastive contexts, accent may also be assigned to the adposition). When the complement is a weak pronoun, however, stress is assigned to the adposition itself. In the examples in (29), the stressed syllable/word is given in small capitals.

(29) a. met PEter 'with Peter' b. naast PEter 'next to Peter'
a′. met MIJ 'with me' b′. naast MIJ 'next to me'
a″. MET me 'with me' b″. NAAST me 'next to me'

Some non-spatial adpositions, however, require a stressed complement, and are thus not able to take a weak pronoun as their complement. Note that this has nothing to do with the stress properties of the adposition itself: both the spatial adposition *tegen* 'against' and the non-spatial adposition *namens* 'on behalf of' are assigned stress on the first syllable, but only the former is able to take a weak pronoun as its complement.

(30) a. TEgen PEter 'against Peter' b. NAmens PEter 'on behalf of Peter'
a′. TEgen MIJ 'against me' b′. NAmens MIJ 'on behalf of me'
a″. TEgen me 'against me' b″. *NAmens me 'on behalf of me'

Other adpositions behaving like *namens* are *dankzij* 'thanks to', *ondanks* 'despite', *vanwege* 'because of', *volgens* 'according to' and *wegens* 'because of'. Some non-spatial adpositions that do allow a weak pronoun as their complement are *met* 'with', *van* 'of' and *zonder* 'without'. See Sections 5.1 and 5.2 for a more extensive discussion of pronominal complements of adpositions.

For completeness' sake, note that whether or not a weak pronoun complement is possible may, of course, depend on factors other than the choice of the adposition. The PP *met me* in (29a″), for instance, is possible when it is part of a sentence, as in (31a), but not when it is used as an independent utterance in response to the question *Met wie heeft ze gisteren gedanst?* in (31b).

(31) a. Ze heeft gisteren met Peter/mij/me gedanst.
she has yesterday with Peter/me/me danced
'She danced with Peter/me yesterday.'
b. Met wie heeft ze gisteren gedanst? Met Peter/mij/*me.
with whom has she yesterday danced with Peter/me/me
'With whom did she dance yesterday? Met Peter/me.'

The fact that the answer to the question in (31b) requires the presence of a non-pronominal noun phrase or a strong pronoun is probably due to the fact that the complement of the preposition conveys the new/requested information, and must therefore be stressed. Support for this suggestion comes from the fact that the PP *naast me* in (29b″) can be used in the question-answer pair in (32a), where the full PP counts as new information, but not in the question-answer pair in (32b), where it is only the complement of the preposition *naast* that counts as new information.

(32) a. Waar wil zij zitten? Naast MIJ/NAAST me.
where want she sit next.to me
'Where does she want to sit? Next to me.'
b. Naast wie wil zij zitten? Naast MIJ/*NAAST me.
next.to whom want she sit next.to me
'Next to whom does she want to sit? Next to ME.'

1.1.2. Types of adpositions

Adpositions can be divided into four basic types on the basis of their position with respect to their complement. We can make the distinctions in (33), with apologies for the *contradictio in terminis* in the notion of intransitive adposition in (33d).

(33) • Formal classification of adpositions
- a. Prepositions: adpositions preceding their complement
- b. Postpositions: adpositions following their complement
- c. Circumpositions: discontinuous adpositions enclosing their complement
- d. Intransitive adpositions and particles: adpositions without a complement

Table 2 gives two examples of each type. Section 1.2 will provide a comprehensive discussion of these four syntactic subclasses.

Table 2: Formal classification of the adpositions

ADPOSITION TYPE	EXAMPLE	TRANSLATION	SECTION
preposition (P + NP)	***voor** het huis* ***tijdens** de voorstelling*	in front of the house during the performance	1.2.2
postposition (NP + P)	*het huis **in*** *het hele jaar **door***	into the house throughout the year	1.2.3
circumposition (P + NP + P)	***onder** het hek **door*** ***tussen** de lessen **door***	under the gate in between the lessons	1.2.5
intransitive adpositions and particles (P)	*De vakantie is **voorbij**.* *De kachel is **uit**.*	The holiday is over. The heater is off.	1.2.4

1.1.3. Syntactic uses of adpositional phrases

This section exemplifies the syntactic uses of adpositional phrases in order to provide the background information required for the more extensive discussion in Section 1.2 of the four classes of adpositions distinguished in Table 2. The final column of Table 3 indicates where these syntactic uses will be discussed in more detail.

Table 3: Syntactic uses of the adpositional phrase

<table>
<tr><th colspan="4">SYNTACTIC FUNCTION</th><th>SECTION</th></tr>
<tr><td colspan="4">Argument</td><td>4.1</td></tr>
<tr><td rowspan="4">Predicative</td><td rowspan="3">Complementive</td><td rowspan="2">spatial</td><td>(change of) locational</td><td rowspan="2">4.2.1.1</td></tr>
<tr><td>directional</td></tr>
<tr><td colspan="2">non-spatial</td><td>4.2.1.2</td></tr>
<tr><td colspan="3">Supplementive</td><td>4.2.2</td></tr>
<tr><td colspan="4">Attributive</td><td>4.3</td></tr>
<tr><td colspan="4">Adverbial</td><td>4.4</td></tr>
</table>

1.1.3.1. Use as an argument

Adpositional phrases that are used as an argument are typically selected by a verb, an adjective or a noun; only in a few cases can an adpositional phrase be the complement of an adposition. As an illustration we take the verb *wachten* 'to wait' in (34a), which may take a theme realized as a PP headed by the preposition *op*. The preposition does not seem to have a well-defined meaning, the choice being fully determined by accidental selectional restrictions of the verb *wachten*; the lexical entry of this verb in (34b) explicitly requires the preposition *op* to be present. That the choice of the preposition is a lexical, and not a semantic, matter is clear from the fact that its English counterpart, *to wait* in (34c), selects in this case the preposition *for*, which is normally translated in Dutch by *voor*.

(34) a. Jan wacht op zijn vader.
Jan waits on his father
'Jan is waiting for his father.'
b. *wachten*: NP, $[_{PP}$ *op* NP$]$
Agent Theme
c. *to wait*: NP, $[_{PP}$ *for* NP$]$
Agent Theme

Because of their lack of semantic content, we will refer to prepositions in argument PPs as FUNCTIONAL prepositions. A small sample of verbs, nouns and adjectives selecting a functional preposition can be found in Table 29 in Section 1.3.3.2.2.

1.1.3.2. Complementive use

This section discusses adpositional phrases that act as predicative complements (henceforth: °complementives); cf. Hoekstra (1984a/1987), Mulder and Wehrmann (1989) and Hoekstra and Mulder (1990) and many others. Complementives differ from arguments in that they do not necessarily saturate a slot in the lexical entry of the verb, but are themselves predicated of some noun phrase in their clause, for which reason they are also often referred to as SECONDARY PREDICATEs. The complementive adpositional phrases are generally spatial in nature, and we will therefore restrict our attention mainly to these; the discussion of the other cases will be postponed to the more extensive discussion of complementive adpositional phrases in Section 4.2.1.

1.1.3.2.1. General introduction

When an adpositional phrase is used as a complementive, it specifies a property of some noun phrase that occurs in the same clause. In example (35a), for instance, the adpositional phrase *in het zwembad* 'in the swimming pool' is predicated of the noun phrase *Jan*. Actually, the adposition can be considered as a two-place predicate that denotes a spatial relation between its complement and the argument the full adpositional phrase is predicated of. In other words, the semantic interpretation of example (35a) is as given in (35b).

(35) a. Jan is in het zwembad.
Jan is in the swimming.pool
b. IN (Jan, het zwembad)

Complementive adpositional phrases can either denote a location or a direction. The examples in (36) involve locational adpositional phrases, which are always headed by a preposition. The two examples differ in that in (36a) the PP simply refers a location, whereas (36b) also involves a change of location.

(36) a. Jan ligt in het zwembad.
Jan lies in the swimming.pool
b. Jan valt in het zwembad.
Jan falls into the swimming.pool

It seems reasonable, however, to not attribute the difference between the location and change of location reading to the PPs themselves. The PP *in het zwembad* is compatible with both readings, and it is the verb that determines which reading is most salient: when the verb is stative, like *liggen* 'to lie', the locational reading arises; when it is a verb denoting an activity or a process, like *vallen* 'to fall', the change of location reading may arise.

Directional adpositional phrases can be headed either by a preposition like *naar* 'to', a postposition like *in* in (37b), or a circumposition. These directional adpositional phrases always involve a change of location, and, as a result of this, they cannot be combined with stative verbs, as is shown in (37a).

(37) a. *Jan ligt het zwembad in.
Jan lies the swimming.pool into
b. Jan valt het zwembad in.
Jan falls the swimming.pool into

The semantic difference between change of location constructions like (36b) and directional constructions like (37b) is often not very clear: (36b) and (37b) seem nearly synonymous. The main difference between locational and directional adpositional phrases is, however, that the latter implies the notion of a PATH, whereas the former does not. The fact that the adpositional phrases in (36b) and (37b) differ in this way can be made clear by means of the *XP met die NP!* construction discussed in (28) above. For many (but not all) speakers, the XP must be a directional phrase; when the XP is a locational phrase, the construction gives rise to a marked result for these speakers. This accounts for the difference in acceptability between (38a′) and (38b′).

(38) a. We gooien die jongen in het zwembad. [change of location]
we throw that boy into the swimming.pool
a′. %In het zwembad met die jongen!
into the swimming.pool with that boy
b. We gooien die jongen het zwembad in. [directional]
we throw that boy the swimming.pool into
b′. Het zwembad in met die jongen!
the swimming.pool into with that boy

The semantic difference between locational and directional phrases can also be made clear by means of the examples in (39). In the location construction in (39a), it is expressed that Jan is involved in a jumping event as a result of which he obtains some position on the stairs; the perfect tense construction in (39a′) therefore implies that, after finishing the activity of jumping, Jan is on the stairs. In (39b), on the other hand, it is expressed that Jan is involved in the event of ascending the stairs, and that his path on the stairs is covered by means of jumping; the perfect tense construction in (39b′) does *not* necessarily imply that, after finishing the activity, Jan is situated on the stairs; this may or may not be the case. That (39b′) does not necessarily imply that Jan is situated on the stairs is clear from the fact that it is possible to add an adverbial phrase like *naar zijn kamer* 'to his room', which refers to the endpoint of the path covered by Jan; with this adverbial phrase added, (39b′) suggests that Jan is in his room. The addition of this adverbial phrase to (39a′), on the other hand, leads to a contradiction and therefore gives rise to an unacceptable result. The number signs in the (a)-examples indicate that they are acceptable with the *naar*-PP, but only if the PP is construed as an attributive modifier of the noun *trap* (*de trap naar zijn kamer* 'the stairs that lead to his room').

(39) a. Jan springt op de trap (#naar zijn kamer).
Jan jumps onto the stairs to his room
a′. Jan is op de trap gesprongen (#naar zijn kamer).
Jan is on the chairs jumped to his room
'Jan has jumped onto the stairs (to his room).'
b. Jan springt/rent de trap op (naar zijn kamer).
Jan jumps/runs the stairs onto to his room
b′. Jan is de trap op gesprongen/gerend (naar zijn kamer).
Jan is the stairs onto jumped/run to his room
'Jan has jumped/run onto the stairs (into his room).'

Note in passing that example (39a), but not (39b), can also be interpreted such that Jan is occupying a position on the stairs and that he is jumping up and down at that position. Under this interpretation, we are dealing with an adverbially used PP. For the moment, it suffices to note that under this interpretation the verb *springen* takes the auxiliary *hebben* 'to have' in the perfect tense (and not *zijn* 'to be' as in the primed examples in (39)), and that the PP can be omitted; cf. (40a). See Section 1.1.3.2.2, sub I, for more differences between adverbial and complementive adpositional phrases.

(40) a. Jan heeft (op de trap) gesprongen.
Jan has on the stairs jumped
'Jan has jumped on the stairs.'
b. *Jan heeft de trap op gesprongen.
Jan has the stairs onto jumped

We have suggested in our discussion of the examples in (36) that the actual interpretation of locational prepositional phrases is regulated by the aspectual properties of the verb: stative verbs like those in (41a) are only compatible with adpositional complementives denoting a location, whereas activity verbs like *springen* 'to jump' or process verbs like *vallen* 'to fall' require that the adpositional complementives denote a change of location or a direction. Some verb classes impose even more strict constraints on the interpretation of the adpositional complementive in that they are compatible with only one of the two interpretations available for *springen*/*vallen*: the verbs of change of location in (41b), which can be seen as the causative counterparts of the verbs in (41a), force a change of location reading on the adpositional phrase, and the verbs of traversing in (41c) are only compatible with adpositional phrases denoting a direction (change of location along a path).

(41) a. Verbs of location (monadic): *hangen* 'to hang', *liggen* 'to lie', *staan* 'to stand', *zitten* 'to sit'
b. Verbs of change of location (dyadic): *hangen* 'to hang', *leggen* 'to lay', *zetten* 'to put'
c. Verbs of traversing: *rijden* 'to drive', *fietsen* 'to cycle', *wandelen* 'to walk', etc.

The examples in (42) to (44) illustrate the restrictions imposed by the verb types in (41) on the interpretation of the adpositional complementive. In (42), the locational verb *staan* 'to stand' indicates that the car is situated on the hill; note in passing that the complementive adpositional phrase in this example differs from the adverbial phrase in (40) in that it is obligatorily present.

(42) De auto staat op de heuvel. [location]
the car stands on the hill
'The car is standing on the hill.'

In (43a) the car is also situated on the hill, but in addition it is claimed that a change of location is involved: the car ends up on the hill as a result of some activity by Jan. That the verb *zetten* is not compatible with a directional adpositional phrase is clear from the fact illustrated in (43b) that the prepositional phrase cannot be replaced by the postpositional phrase *de heuvel op*.

(43) a. Jan zet de auto op de heuvel. [change of location]
Jan puts the car onto the hill
'Jan is putting the car onto the hill.'
b. *?Jan zet de auto de heuvel op. [directional]

Example (44a) also indicates a change of location, but in addition it is expressed that the car is covering some path. That *rijden* preferably takes a directional adpositional phrase is clear from the fact that it is at best marginally compatible with the prepositional phrase *op de heuvel* in (44b).

(44) a. Jan rijdt de auto de heuvel op. [directional]
Jan drives the car the hill onto
'Jan is driving the car onto the hill.'
b. ??Jan rijdt de auto op de heuvel. [change of location]

It must be noted, however, that the acceptability of examples like (44b) also seems to depend on properties of the referent of the complement of the preposition. When that is a relatively small object, the result improves.

(45) a. Jan rijdt de auto de weeginstallatie op.
Jan drives the car the balance onto
'Jan drives the car onto the balance.'
b. ?Jan rijdt de auto op de weeginstallatie.

The verb of traversing *rijden* can be used not only as a dyadic verb, as in (43) to (45), but also as a monadic unaccusative verb: *Jan rijdt de heuvel op* 'Jan is driving onto the hill'. In the latter case, it has an intransitive counterpart that functions as a regular activity verb. As in the case of *springen* 'to jump', the activity verb differs from the verb of traversing in selecting the auxiliary *hebben* instead of *zijn*, and in that the adpositional phrase is optional and functions as an adverbial phrase indicating the location where the activity takes place; see the contrast between the perfect tense form of the unaccusative construction in (46a) and the perfect tense form of the intransitive construction in (46b).

(46) a. Jan is *(de heuvel op) gereden.
Jan is the hill onto driven
'Jan has driven onto the hill.'
b. Jan heeft (op de heuvel) gereden.
Jan has on the hill driven
'Jan has driven (on the hill).'

As was already mentioned above, motion verbs like *vallen* 'to fall' and *springen* 'to jump' are not specialized in the way the verbs in (41) are. This is clear from the fact that they can be combined with both a prepositional and a postpositional phrase, as has already been shown in (36b)/(37b) and (39). The same thing holds for the verbs *slaan* 'to hit' and *gooien* 'to throw' in resultative constructions like (47).

(47) a. Jan sloeg de spijker in de muur. [change of location]
Jan hit the nail into the wall
a′. Jan sloeg de spijker de muur in. [directional]
Jan hit the nail the wall into
'Jan hit the nail into the wall.'
b. Jan gooide de spijker in de doos. [change of location]
Jan threw the nail into the box
b′. Jan gooide de spijker de doos in. [directional]
Jan threw the nail the box into
'Jan threw the nail into the box.'

The following two sections will briefly discuss some of the basic properties of complementive locational and directional adpositional phrases. A more comprehensive discussion will be given in Section 4.2.

1.1.3.2.2. Locational adpositional phrases

Section 1.1.3.2.1 has shown that a complementive locational PP specifies a property of some noun phrase in the same clause. For example, the adpositional phrase *in het zwembad* in (48a) is predicated of the noun phrase *Jan*. In this respect, (48a) behaves just like the copular construction in (48b), in which the AP *aardig* is predicated of the noun phrase *Jan*.

(48) a. Jan is in het zwembad.
Jan is in the swimming.pool
b. Jan is aardig.
Jan is nice

Traditional grammar would not consider examples like (48a) to be copular constructions; the adpositional phrase is analyzed as an adverbial phrase. One reason for this is that assuming that (48a) is a copular construction would force us to assume that the set of copular verbs should be extended considerably by including the locational verbs in (41a) and motion verbs such as *vallen* 'to fall' and *springen* 'to jump' in order to account for the similarity between (48a), on the one hand, and examples like (36) and (39), on the other.

From the perspective of present-day theoretical linguistics, there is no compelling reason to assume that there is a principled syntactic distinction between the copular verbs and the verbs of location and motion, although they do, of course, differ in the semantic contributions that they make: copular verbs mainly express aspectual and modal meanings, whereas verbs of location and motion denote states, processes and activities. But from a syntactic point of view, these verbs can all be assumed to take a complementive adpositional phrase that, in turn, takes the subject of the clause as its °logical SUBJECT; in short, they are all °unaccusative verbs. In fact, this is precisely what is to be expected, given that complementive adjectives can also occur as complements of verbs other than the copulas, such as the verb *vallen* in (49b) or the verb *schoppen* 'to kick' in the resultative construction in (49c). Treating the locational PPs in the primed examples in (49) not as adverbial phrases but as complementives enables us to analyze them in the same way as the corresponding primeless examples, and thus to provide a natural account for the fact that the predication relations in the primeless and primed examples are identical: the AP *dood* and the PP *in het zwembad* are predicated of the nominative subject of the clause in the (a)- and (b)-examples, whereas they are predicated of the accusative object of the clause in the (c)-examples.

(49)				
a.	Jan is dood. Jan is dead	a′.	Jan is in het zwembad. Jan is in the swimming.pool
b.	Jan viel dood. Jan fell dead	b′.	Jan viel in het zwembad. Jan fell into the swimming.pool
c.	Marie schopte Jan dood. Marie kicked Jan dead	c′.	Marie schopte de bal in het zwembad. Marie kicked the ball into the swimming.pool

We therefore reject the traditional view that locational PPs always function as adverbial phrases in favor of the more subtle view that, depending on the syntactic context, locational PPs can be used both adverbially and predicatively.

Complementives are always predicated of either the nominative or the accusative argument within their clause, as illustrated in the examples in (49). Below, we will briefly discuss these two cases.

I. Adpositional phrases predicated of the nominative argument in the clause

Complementive adpositional phrases that are predicated of the (DO-)subject of the clause are generally the complement of a locational verb like *liggen* 'to lie' or a motion verb like *vallen* 'to fall' in (50).

(50) a. De baby lag in het zwembad.
the bay lay in the swimming.pool
'The baby was lying in the swimming pool.'
b. De baby viel in het zwembad.
the baby fell into the swimming.pool

We have claimed above that these verbs are unaccusative in constructions like (50). This is, however, not so clear for the locational verb *liggen* in (50a), given that it does not meet the conditions sufficient for assuming unaccusative status; the examples in (51a&b) show that the verb *liggen* does not take the auxiliary *zijn* in the perfect tense and that its past/passive participle cannot be used attributively. The only property that suggests unaccusative status for this verb is that the impersonal passive is excluded, but this is not sufficient to conclude that we are dealing with an unaccusative verb.

(51) a. De baby heeft/*is in het zwembad gelegen.
the baby has/is in the swimming.pool lain
'The baby has lain in the swimming pool.'
b. *de in het zwembad gelegen baby
the in the swimming.pool lain baby
c. *Er werd in het zwembad gelegen (door de baby).
there was in the swimming.pool lain by the baby

The verb *vallen* does meet the conditions for unaccusative status, but this is of course not very telling, because it also acts as an unaccusative verb when the locational PP is not present.

(52) a. De baby is/*heeft in het zwembad gevallen.
the baby is/has into the swimming.pool fallen
'The baby has fallen into the swimming pool.'
b. de in het zwembad gevallen baby
the into the swimming.pool fallen baby
'the baby that has fallen into the swimming pool'
c. *Er werd in het zwembad gevallen (door de baby).
there was into the swimming.pool fallen by the baby

More conclusive support in favor of the claim that addition of a complementive PP results in unaccusative status for monadic verbs can be obtained from motion verbs like *kruipen* 'to crawl'. This verb normally has all the properties of regular intransitive verbs: it takes the auxiliary *hebben* in the perfect tense, its past/passive participles cannot be used attributively, and it allows the impersonal passive.

(53) a. De baby kruipt al.
the baby crawls already
b. De baby heeft/*is al gekropen.
the baby has/is already crawled
c. *de gekropen baby
the crawled baby
d. Er werd gekropen (door de baby).
there was crawled by the baby

However, when we add a locational PP, as in (54a), the behavior of *kruipen* changes. First, the verb can then take either *hebben* or *zijn* in the perfect tense, where the choice between the two options is related to meaning. Example (54a) is actually ambiguous between two readings: on the first reading, the crawling event takes place at the location referred to by the PP *onder de tafel*; on the second reading, change of location is involved in the sense that the baby ends up under the table as a result of the crawling event. When the first reading is intended, the auxiliary *hebben* is used, but when the second reading is intended, the auxiliary *zijn* must be used.

(54) a. De baby kroop onder de tafel.
the baby crawled under the table
b. De baby heeft/is onder de tafel gekropen.
the baby has/is under the table crawled

The difference between the two readings is related to the syntactic function of the PP: when the PP just refers to the place where the event is taking place, we are dealing with an adverbial phrase; when change of location is involved, the PP is not an adverbial phrase. This claim can be supported by applying the VP °adverb test to the examples in (54b): when the auxiliary *hebben* is used, as in (55a), the clause can be paraphrased by means of an ... *en pronoun doet dat PP* '... and pronoun does it PP' clause, which shows that we are dealing with an adverbial PP modifying the VP; when *zijn* is used, this paraphrase is not possible, so that we can conclude that the PP does not act as a VP adverb.

(55) a. De baby heeft gekropen en hij deed dat onder de tafel.
the baby has crawled and he did that under the table
b. *De baby is gekropen en hij deed dat onder de tafel.
the baby is crawled and he did that under the table

In the change of location construction, the PP acts like a complementive, which is clear from the fact that, like adjectival and nominal complementives, the PP in (56b) must be left-adjacent to the verb in clause-final position. Example (a) show that the placement of the adverbially used PP is much freer.

(56) a. De baby heeft <onder de tafel> vaak <onder de tafel> gekropen <onder de tafel>.
the baby has under the table often crawled
b. De baby is <*onder de tafel> vaak <onder de tafel> gekropen <*onder de tafel>.
the baby is under the table often crawled

When we now consider the behavior of the examples in (54), it turns out that when the PP is used adverbially (that is, refers to the place where the event takes place), the verb behaves like a regular intransitive verb. However, when it is used as a complementive (that is, when we are dealing with the change of location reading), the verb acts as an unaccusative verb. This is shown in the first three rows in Table 4. The two final rows of this table summarize the data in (55) and (56).

Table 4: Adverbial versus complementive adpositional phrases

	EXAMPLE	ADVERBIAL USE OF PP	COMPLEMENTIVE USE OF PP
AUXILIARY SELECTION	*De baby heeft/is onder de tafel gekropen* 'the baby has/is under the table crawled'	hebben	zijn
ATTRIBUTIVE USE OF THE PAST/PASSIVE PARTICIPLE	*De onder de tafel gekropen baby* the under the table crawled baby 'the baby that crawled under the table'	—	+
IMPERSONAL PASSIVE	*Er werd onder de tafel gekropen* there was under the table crawled	+	—
ADVERB TEST	(55a&b)	+	—
"FREER" PLACEMENT OF PP	(56a&b)	+	—

Given that the PP can be used either as an adverbial phrase or as a complementive in (54a), we might expect the same uses to be possible with locational verbs such as *zitten* 'to sit', *liggen* 'to lie', *hangen* 'to hang' and *staan* 'to stand'. The difference between the two readings in (57) should be that under the adverbial reading of the PP, it is claimed that the sitting event takes place in the garden, whereas under the complementive reading, it is claimed that Marie is in the garden. Since the first reading logically implies the latter, it will be clear that it is difficult to distinguish these two readings. There is, however, evidence that PPs can be used as the complement of locational verbs, but to discuss this here would lead us too far afield. We therefore postpone discussion of this evidence to Section 4.2.1.1.

(57) Marie zit in de tuin.
Marie sits in the garden
'Marie is sitting in the garden.'

II. Adpositional phrases predicated of the accusative object in the clause

The previous subsection has shown that, like adjectival complementives, adpositional complements of locational and motion verbs are predicated of the subject of their clause; the primed and primeless (a)- and (b)-examples in (58) behave on a par. For that reason, we would expect that resultative constructions like

(58c), in which the adjective is predicated of the accusative object of the clause, have an adpositional counterpart as well, and example (58c′) shows that this expectation is indeed borne out. For completeness' sake, note that adjectival and adpositional predicates also alternate in the absolute *met*-construction; cf. Section 4.2.3.

(58) a. Jan is dood.
Jan is dead
b. Jan viel dood.
Jan fell dead
c. Marie sloeg de hond dood.
Marie hit the dog dead
a′. De bal ligt in het zwembad.
the ball lies in the swimming.pool
b′. De bal viel in het zwembad.
the ball fell into the swimming.pool
c′. Marie gooide de bal in het zwembad.
Marie threw the ball into the swimming.pool

Given that *slaan* and *gooien* are normally used as regular transitive verbs, the complementives in the (c)-examples of (58) are of course optional. There are, however, some verbs that are specialized in requiring a locational PP (or some other predicative complement). Some examples are the verbs of change of location *leggen* 'to lay', *hangen* 'to hang' and *zetten* 'to put' in the primeless examples of (59), which can be seen as the causative counterparts of the locational verbs *liggen* 'to lie', *hangen* 'to hang' and *zitten*/*staan* 'to sit/stand' in the primed examples; cf. (41) in Section 1.1.3.2.1.

(59) a. Jan legt het boek op de tafel.
Jan lays the book onto the table
'Jan puts the book on the table.'
b. Jan hangt de jas in de kast.
Jan hangs the coat into the closet
c. Jan zet de kleuter op het bed.
Jan puts the toddler onto the bed
d. Jan zet het boek in de kast.
Jan puts the book into the bookcase
a′. Het boek ligt op de tafel.
the book lies on the table
'The book is lying on the table.'
b′. De jas hangt in de kast.
the coat hangs in the closet
c′. De kleuter zit op het bed.
the toddler sits on the bed
d′. Het boek staat in de kast.
the book stands in the bookcase

The fact that the PP is optional in (58c′) shows that the SUBJECT of the PP can also appear as the direct object of the verb. This need not always be the case, however: the noun phrase *een gat* 'a hole' cannot be used alone as the theme argument of the transitive verb *slaan* 'to hit' in (60a), but gives rise to a fully acceptable result when the locational PP *in de muur* 'in the wall' is present. Similarly, adding the locational PP *onder het tafelkleed* 'under the table cloth' to the otherwise intransitive verb *blazen* 'to blow', licenses the introduction of the accusative argument *het stof*.

(60) a. Jan sloeg een gat *(in de muur).
Jan hit a hole in the wall
b. Jan blies het stof *(onder het tafelkleed).
Jan blew the dust under the table cloth

The primeless examples in (59) as well as the examples in (60) therefore show that, just as in the case of complementive adjectives, the accusative noun phrase is introduced in the sentence as an argument of the adpositional phrase, and not as an argument of the verb.

1.1.3.2.3. Directional adpositional phrases

The discussion of example (39) in Section 1.1.3.2.1 has already made clear that directional adpositional phrases involve the notion of a path. Directional adpositional phrases can be headed by pre-, post- and circumpositions; for our present purpose of illustrating the main properties of directional phrases, we will only use examples involving postpositions; see Section 1.3.1.2 for a list of directional prepositions. Directional adpositional phrases typically occur as the complement of motion verbs like *vallen* 'to fall' or *duiken* 'to dive'. They are not possible as the complement of a stative locational verb like *liggen*; the stative reading of these verbs is apparently not compatible with the path reading inherently expressed by directional phrases.

(61) a. *Jan ligt het water in.
Jan lies the water into
b. Jan viel/dook het water in.
Jan fell/dived the water into

Like the locational PPs discussed in Section 1.1.3.2.2, directional adpositional phrases trigger unaccusative behavior on the verb by which they are selected. This will become clear by comparing the primeless and primed examples in (62). The (b)-examples show that whereas *duiken* normally takes *hebben* in the perfect tense, it takes *zijn* when a postpositional phrase is present. The (c)-examples show that the attributive use of the past/passive participle also requires the postpositional phrase to be present. The (d)-examples, finally, show that the presence of the postpositional phrase blocks impersonal passivization.

(62) a. Jan dook
Jan dived
a′. Jan dook het water in.
Jan dived the water into
b. Jan heeft/*is gedoken.
Jan has/is dived
b′. Jan is/*heeft het water in gedoken.
Jan is/has the water into dived
c. *de gedoken jongen
the dived boy
c′. de het water in gedoken jongen
the the water into dived boy
d. Er werd gedoken.
there was dived
d′. *?Er werd het water in gedoken.
there was the water into dived

Example (63a) shows that the postpositional phrase exhibits complementive behavior in the sense that, like other complementive phrases, the postposition must be left-adjacent to the verb in clause-final position. It must be noted, however, that this does not hold for the complete postpositional phrase, as the complement of the postposition (viz. *het water*) need not be adjacent to the postposition but may occupy a position more to the left. This is shown in (63b).

(63) a. Jan is <*het water in> waarschijnlijk <het water in> gedoken <*het water in>.
Jan is the water into probably dived
b. Jan is < het water > waarschijnlijk < het water > in gedoken.
Jan is the water probably into dived

Like the locational PPs from Section 1.1.3.2.2, directional adpositional phrases can be used in resultative constructions. So alongside (49b′) and (60b) it is possible to have examples like (64). The fact that the accusative noun phrase *de asbak* in example (64b) is only possible when the postposition *in* is also present shows that this noun phrase is introduced into the structure as an argument of the postpositional phrase and not of the verb; cf. the discussion of (60).

(64) a. Marie gooide de bal het water in.
Marie threw the ball the water into
b. Jan blies het stof *(de asbak in).
Jan blew the dust the ashtray into
'Jan blew the dust into the ashtray.'

Finally, note that directional phrases cannot occur as the complement of the causative counterparts of locational verbs like *liggen* 'to lie'; the locational PPs in (59) cannot be replaced by directional adpositional phrases. This suggests that, unlike the verb *gooien* in (64a) and like locational verbs like *liggen* 'to lie' in (61a), the verbs in (65) are not compatible with the path reading inherently expressed by directional phrases.

(65) a. *Jan legt het boek de tafel op.
Jan lays the book the table onto
b. *Jan hangt de jas de kast in.
Jan hangs the coat the closet into
c. *Jan zet de kleuter het bed op.
Jan puts the toddler the bed on
d. *Jan zet het boek de kast in.
Jan puts the book the bookcase into

1.1.3.3. Supplementive use

The °supplementive is not a complement of the verb, but an adjunct. It can be predicated of either the subject or the object of the clause, and denotes a property that applies "simultaneously" with the event denoted by the clause. The supplementive use of adpositional phrases seems less common than that of APs. In (66), we give three examples. In (66a) the property denoted by the nominal complement of *als* is attributed to the subject of the clause: Brüggen is much beloved in his capacity of director (not necessarily in his capacity of flutist). In (66b), this property is attributed to the object (assuming, at least, that the speaker is not a director himself): the speaker admires Brüggen very much in the latter's capacity of director (not necessarily in his capacity of flutist). Example (66c) is ambiguous between two readings: the director Leonhardt may feel admiration for (the flutist) Brüggen, or (the harpsichordist) Leonhardt may feel admiration for the director Brüggen. Since the supplementive will not play an important role in this section, we postpone further discussion to Section 4.2.2.

(66) a. Als dirigent is Frans Brüggen erg geliefd.
as director is Frans Brüggen very beloved
'As a director Frans Brüggen is very beloved.'
b. Als dirigent bewonder ik Frans Brüggen erg.
as director admire I Frans Brüggen very
'I admire Frans Brüggen very much as a director.'
c. Als dirigent bewondert Gustav Leonhardt Frans Brüggen erg.
as director admires Gustav Leonhardt Frans Brüggen very
'Gustav Leonhardt admires Frans Brüggen very much as a director.'

1.1.3.4. Adverbial use

Adpositional phrases are perhaps most typically used as adverbial phrases modifying a VP or a clause. The two instances can be distinguished by means of the two °adverb tests in (67): clauses containing an adpositional phrase modifying the full clause can be paraphrased by means of the *Het is PP zo dat ...* 'It is PP the case that ...' frame, whereas clauses containing an adpositional phrase modifying only the VP can be paraphrased by means of the *... en doet dat PP* '... and does it PP' frame. Adverbially used adpositional phrases are always headed by a preposition.

(67) a. Clause adjunct: $[_{CLAUSE}$ ... PP ...$]$ ⇒ het is PP zo dat CLAUSE
b. VP adjunct: $[_{CLAUSE}$ subject ... PP ...$]$ ⇒ $[_{CLAUSE}$ $subject_i$ ...$]$ en $pronoun_i$ doet dat PP

Many adverbially used PPs are specialized for one of these two adverbial functions. This is illustrated in (68) for PPs headed by the prepositions *namens* 'in the name of' and *volgens* 'according to'; the (a)-examples show that the former can only be used as a VP-adjunct, and the (b)-examples show that the latter can only be used as clause adjunct.

(68) a. Marie verkoopt het huis namens haar familie. [VP adjunct]
Marie sells the house in.name.of her family
'Marie sells the house in the name of her family'
a′. *Het is namens haar familie zo dat Marie het huis verkoopt.
it is in.name.of her family the.case that Marie the house sells
a″. Marie verkoopt het huis en ze doet dat namens haar familie.
Marie sells the house and she does that in.name.of her family
b. Marie verkoopt volgens Jan het huis. [Clause adjunct]
Marie sells according.to Jan the house
'According to Jan, Marie will sell the house.'
b′. Het is volgens Jan zo dat Marie het huis verkoopt.
it is according.to Jan the.case that Marie the house sells
b″. *Marie verkoopt het huis en zij doet dat volgens Jan.
Marie sells the house and he does that according.to Jan

The examples in (69) show that clause adjuncts precede modal and frequency adverbs such as *waarschijnlijk* 'probably' and *vaak* 'often' (which themselves are also clause adverbs), whereas VP adjuncts follow them. Note that the direct object *het huis* can either precede or follow the modal adverb *waarschijnlijk* in (69), so that this does not interfere in the acceptability judgments.

(69) a. Marie verkoopt <waarschijnlijk> het huis <waarschijnlijk> namens haar familie <*waarschijnlijk>.
b. Marie verkoopt <*waarschijnlijk> volgens Jan <waarschijnlijk> het huis <waarschijnlijk>.

Spatial and temporal PPs can be used both as clause and as VP adjuncts; examples like (70a&b) are ambiguous between the readings in the primed examples. Note that, for some speakers, the preferred reading of (70b) is the one in (70b″) and that the reading in (70b′) is only readily available when the PP is followed by an adverb of frequency; cf. (71).

(70) a. Marie sliep tijdens de lessen.
Marie slept during the lessons
a′. Het was tijdens de lessen zo dat Marie sliep.
it was during the lessons the.case that Marie slept
a″. Marie sliep en ze deed dat tijdens de lessen.
Marie slept and she did that during the lessons
b. Marie sliep in de klas.
Marie slept in the classroom
b′. Het was in de klas zo dat Marie sliep.
it was in the classroom the.case that Marie slept
b″. Marie sliep en ze deed dat in de klas.
Marie slept and she did that in the classroom

The ambiguity of the primeless examples in (70) is consistent with the fact that adverbial PPs can either precede or follow clause adjuncts like the frequency adjective *vaak* ‘often’ in (71); when the PPs precede *vaak*, the resulting readings correspond to the singly-primed examples in (70); when they follow the frequency adverb, the resulting readings correspond to the doubly-primed examples.

(71) a. Marie sliep <vaak> tijdens de lessen <vaak>.
Marie slept often during the lessons
b. Marie sliep <vaak> in de klas <vaak>.
Marie slept often in the classroom

Section 1.1.3.2 has shown that spatial adpositional phrases function as predicates (and the same thing will be shown later for temporal adpositional phrases). The difference between the complementive use and the adverbial use of adpositional phrases is that in the former case the adpositional phrase is predicated of some argument in the clause, whereas in the latter case it is predicated of some projection of the verb. This goes hand in hand with a (sometimes subtle) meaning contrast. The contrast is clearest with temporal PPs: on the VP-adjunct reading, (71a) expresses that Mary often performed the activity of “sleeping during the lesson”; on the clause reading, (71a) expresses that, during the lessons, the event of Marie sleeping often took place. A similar contrast can be found in (71b); on the VP-adjunct reading, it is expressed that Marie often performed the activity of “sleeping in the classroom”; on the clause-adjunct reading, it is expressed that, in the classroom, the event of “Marie sleeping” often took place.

1.1.3.5. Attributive use

When an adpositional phrase is used as an attributive adjunct, its function is to delimit the denotation of the noun; the denotation of the noun *mannen* 'men' is larger than the denotation of the modified noun *mannen met baarden* 'men with beards'. Attributively used adpositional phrases are generally headed by prepositions, as in (72a), but occasionally post- and circumpositional phrases are possible as well, as in (72b&c). As in the case of predicatively used adpositional phrases, spatial prepositional phrases refer to a location, whereas the post- and circumpositional ones refer to a path.

(72) a. de weg op de berg
the road on the mountain
'the road on the mountain'
b. de weg de berg op
the road the mountain onto
'the road onto the mountain'
c. de weg naar de top toe
the road towards the top TOE
'the road towards the top'

1.2. A formal classification of adpositional phrases

This section discusses the four basic syntactic types of adpositions: prepositions, postpositions, circumpositions and intransitive adpositions. After a general discussion of the proposed classification, in which we also pay some attention to some more special instances of adpositions, we devote a section to each basic type.

1.2.1. General introduction

Adpositions can be divided into four basic types on the basis of their position with respect to their complement. Section 1.1.2 made the distinctions in (33), repeated here as (73).

(73) • Formal classification of adpositions
a. Prepositions: adpositions preceding their complement
b. Postpositions: adpositions following their complement
c. Circumpositions: discontinuous adpositions enclosing their complement
d. Intransitive adpositions and particles: adpositions without a complement

Table 2, which is also repeated from Section 1.1.2, provides some examples of each type and also indicates the subsections in which these types will be more comprehensively discussed; for reasons of exposition, the intransitive adpositions and particles will be discussed before the circumpositions.

Table 2: Formal classification of the adpositions (repeated)

ADPOSITION TYPE	EXAMPLE	TRANSLATION	SECTION
preposition (P + NP)	***voor*** *het huis* ***tijdens*** *de voorstelling*	in front of the house during the performance	1.2.2
postposition (NP + P)	*het huis* ***in*** *het hele jaar* ***door***	into the house throughout the year	1.2.3
circumposition (P + NP + P)	***onder*** *het hek* ***door*** ***tussen*** *de lessen* ***door***	under the gate in between the lessons	1.2.5
intransitive adpositions and particles (P)	*De vakantie is* ***voorbij****.* *De kachel is* ***uit****.*	The holiday is over. The heater is off.	1.2.4

However, before we start with the discussion of the four basic types of adpositions, we briefly want to say something about phrasal adpositions and compounds.

I. Phrasal prepositions

The prepositional phrase *in de richting van* 'in the direction of' in (74b) performs a function similar to that of *naar* 'to' in (74a). Therefore, we will call sequences like these PHRASAL PREPOSITIONs. Occasionally, phrasal prepositions tend to get reduced; the (originally nominal) element *richting* 'direction' in (74c) performs the same function as the complex phrase in (74b); cf. Loonen (2003). It is clear that this kind of reduction may result in extension of the class of prepositions, for which reason we cannot say that the prepositions constitute a fully closed class category.

(74) a. De bus gaat *naar* Amsterdam. [preposition]
the bus goes to Amsterdam
b. De bus gaat *in de richting van* Amsterdam. [phrasal preposition]
the bus goes in the direction of Amsterdam
c. De bus gaat *richting* Amsterdam. [reduced phrasal preposition]
the bus goes direction Amsterdam

The reduction of phrasal prepositions is not syntactically innocuous, given that phrasal and reduced phrasal prepositions may impose different selection restrictions on their complement. The phrasal preposition in (75a), for instance, takes a noun phrase that is obligatorily introduced by an article, whereas the reduced phrasal preposition in (75b) preferably takes a bare noun phrase.

(75) a. De bus gaat in de richting van *(het) centrum.
the bus goes into the direction of the center
b. De bus gaat richting (?het) centrum.
the bus goes in.the.direction.of the center

The examples in (76) show that the reduction requires various other modifications of the nominal complement: whereas (75a) takes two conjoined noun phrases as its complement, the complement in (75b) is juxtaposed.

(76) a. Jan woont op de hoek van *(de) Kalverstraat en de Heiligeweg
Jan lives on the corner of the Kalverstraat and the Heiligeweg
b. Jan woont hoek Kalverstraat-Heiligeweg.
Jan lives on.the.corner.of Kalverstraat-Heiligeweg

Many phrasal prepositions are historical relics. The preposition *te* in the examples in (77), for instance, is conflated with a case marked article resulting in the forms *ter* and *ten*, whereas overt case marking of the article is normally not possible in present-day Dutch. Another reason to assume that these phrasal prepositions are relics is that the "nominal part" is sometimes obsolete.

(77) a. ter benefice van 'in favor of'
b. ter ere van 'in honor of'
c. ter gelegenheid van 'on the occasion of'
d. ter grootte van 'with the size of'
e. ter wille van 'because of'
f. ten aanzien van 'with regard to'
g. ten bate van 'on behalf of'
h. ten behoeve van 'for the benefit of'
i. ten faveure/gunste van 'in favor of'
j. ten laste van 'at the expense of'
k. ten naaste bij 'approximately'
l. ten opzichte van 'with regard to'

In (78) examples are given of phrasal prepositions that are semantically transparent from a synchronic point of view. However, these phrasal prepositions are syntactically special in that the "nominal parts" in these expressions are often not preceded by a determiner.

(78) a. aan de hand van 'on the basis of'
b. in antwoord op 'in answer to'
c. in de geest/trant van 'in the spirit/way of'
d. naar aanleiding van 'referring to/on account of/in connection with'
e. met betrekking tot 'with relation to'
f. met het oog op 'in view of/with a view to'
g. met uitzondering van 'except'
h. onder verwijzing naar 'with reference to'
i. onder leiding van 'under the leadership of'
j. op basis van 'on the basis of'
k. op grond van 'on account of'

Furthermore, the "nominal part" of the phrasal prepositions in (78) categorically resists modification by means of, e.g., an attributive adjective. This can be illustrated by means of the examples in (79): in (79a), the absence of a determiner indicates that we are dealing with a phrasal preposition, and in accordance with this the "nominal part" *leiding* cannot be preceded by an attributive adjective; in (79b), on the other hand, we are dealing with a PP, which is clear from the fact that the noun *leiding* is preceded by a determiner and can also be preceded by an attributive adjective. These examples therefore strongly suggest that, although semantically transparent to the present-day speaker, the phrasal prepositions in (78) are also lexicalized.

(79) a. onder (*bezielende) leiding van Frans Brüggen
under inspiring leadership of Frans Brüggen
'directed by Frans Brüggen'
b. onder de (bezielende) leiding van Frans Brüggen
under the inspiring leadership of Frans Brüggen

In some cases, phrasal prepositions have been reanalyzed as single words. Some examples are given in (80). The complex forms in (80a&b) function as regular prepositions. In (80c&d) the case-marked pronoun *dien*, which seems to act as the complement of the prepositional part *aangaande/tengevolge*, has been reanalyzed as part of the complex form; in accordance with this, these adpositions are intransitive.

(80) a. niettegenstaande 'notwithstanding'
b. overeenkomstig 'in accordance with'
c. dienaangaande 'as to that'
d. dientengevolge 'consequently'

II. Compounds

This chapter will mainly discuss adpositions that are simple (at least from a synchronic point of view). It must be noted, however, that, in addition to these simple adpositions, Dutch has a large set of complex prepositions, which are mainly spatial in nature. As an example we give *bovenop* 'on top of' in (81). When used as prepositions, compounds like these can be easily confused with cases like (81b&c): example (81b) involves modification of the preposition *voor* by the adverb *vlak* 'just' and example (81c) is a case in which the preposition *voor* 'for' takes a PP-complement.

(81) a. Jan zat *bovenop* die auto. [compound]
Jan sat on.top.of the car
b. Jan stond *vlak voor* die auto. [modification]
Jan stood just in.front.of that car
c. De koekjes zijn *voor bij* de koffie. [complementation]
the biscuits are for with the coffee

The examples in (82) show that the three constructions can be easily distinguished by means of their behavior under °R-pronominalization: the compound *bovenop* must follow the R-word *daar*; when we are dealing with modification, the R-word *daar* can either precede the preposition or the modifier; and when we are dealing with complementation, the R-word must follow the preposition that selects the PP-complement.

(82) a. Jan zat <daar> boven <*daar> op. [compound]
b. Jan stond <daar> vlak <daar> voor. [modification]
c. De koekjes zijn <*daar> voor <daar> bij. [complementation]

This R-pronominalization test will be used in Chapter 2 on complementation and Chapter 3 on modification as a test to establish the status of prepositional phrases in unclear cases.

1.2.2. Prepositions

Prepositions precede their complements. Some examples, given in (83), also show that prepositional phrases may perform various semantic functions.

(83) a. Jan zwemt *in* de sloot. [spatial]
Jan swims in the ditch
'Jan is swimming in the ditch.'

b. Jan kletste *tijdens* de voorstelling. [temporal]
Jan chattered during the performance
'Jan was chattering during the performance.'

c. De winkel werd tijdelijk gesloten *vanwege* de brand. [other]
the shop was `temporarily closed because-of the fire

Table 5 provides an alphabetical list of simple prepositions that occur frequently in everyday speech and also indicates what semantic functions the PPs headed by these prepositions may perform; these three semantic functions will be the topic of Section 1.3. Note that the set of functional prepositions, that is, "semantically vacuous" uses of the prepositions heading PP-complements like *op zijn vader* in *Jan wacht op zijn vader* 'Jan is waiting for his father', are not subsumed under the three semantic functions distinguished in Table 5.

Table 5: List of simple prepositions (colloquial language)

PREPOSITION	SPATIAL	TEMPORAL	OTHER	REMARKS
aan 'on'	+			
achter 'behind'	+			
alvorens 'before'		+		introduces infinitival clauses
beneden 'below'	+			see remark below the table
bij 'near/close to'	+	+		
binnen 'inside/within'	+	+		
boven 'above'	+			
buiten 'outside'	+			
dankzij 'thanks to'			+	
door 'through/by'	+	+	+	causative/passive *by*-phrase
gedurende 'during'		+		
gezien 'in view of'			+	
halverwege 'halfway'	+	+		
in 'in(to)/within'	+	+		
langs 'along'	+			
met 'during/with'		+	+	instrumental/comitative
na 'after'		+		
naar 'towards'	+			
naast 'next to'	+			
namens 'in name of'			+	
om 'around/at'	+	+	+	purpose
omstreeks 'around'		+		
ondanks 'despite'			+	

PREPOSITION	SPATIAL	TEMPORAL	OTHER	REMARKS
onder 'under'	+			
ongeacht 'regardless of'			+	
op 'on(to)/at'	+	+		
over 'across/in'	+	+		
per 'as of/by'		+	+	see remark below the table
rond 'around'	+	+		
sinds 'since'		+		
tegen 'against/towards'	+	+		
tegenover 'across'	+			
tijdens 'during'		+		
tot (en met) 'until'	+	+		
tussen 'between'	+	+		
uit 'out (of)'	+			
van 'from'	+			
vanaf 'from'	+	+		
vanuit 'from out of'	+			
vanwege 'because of'			+	
via 'via'	+			
volgens 'according to'			+	
voor 'in front of/before'	+	+		
voorbij 'past'	+			
wegens 'because of'			+	
zonder 'without'			+	

Note that the preposition *beneden* has more or less the same meaning as *onder* but seems restricted to idiomatic expressions such as *beneden de grote rivieren* 'below the big rivers' (the southern part of the Netherlands), *beneden de zes jaar* 'under six years of age', *beneden de vereisten/verwachting blijven* 'to fall short of requirements/expectations' and *beneden mijn waardigheid* 'beneath my dignity'. In addition, it is used in nautical jargon as in, e.g., *beneden de wind* 'leeward'. The temporal use of the preposition *per* is formal; the more colloquial form that corresponds to this preposition is *vanaf*. The preposition *per* is common, however, in the more or less fixed combinations in (81). The complement of *per* generally refers to a means of transport like *post/auto* in (81b), or a measure noun phrase like *kilo* or *dozijn* in (81c).

(84) a. Hij verstuurde het manuscript per post.
he sent the manuscript by mail
b. Hij vertrok per auto.
he left by car
c. Hij verkoopt zijn appels alleen per kilo/dozijn.
he sells his apples only by kilo/dozen
'He sells his apples only by the kilo/dozen.'

Unlike the prepositions in Table 5, the prepositions in Table 6 are restricted to official language and writing. Because these prepositions will not play an important role in what follows, we will give an example of each of them. Observe that many of these prepositions have developed from a verbal source.

Table 6: List of simple prepositions (official language/writing)

PREPOSITION	EXAMPLES
aangaande	*aangaande deze zaak* 'regarding this case'
behoudens	*behoudens goedkeuring door ...* 'subject to ...'s approval'
benevens	*benevens een vergoeding voor* 'besides an allowance for'
betreffende	*betreffende deze zaak* 'regarding this affair'
bezijden	*bezijden de waarheid* 'far from the truth'
blijkens	*blijkens zijn rapport* 'according to his report'
gehoord	*gehoord de commissie* 'after hearing the commission'
getuige	*getuige het feit dat ...* 'witness the fact that ...'
hangende	*hangende het onderzoek* 'pending the inquiry'
ingevolge	*ingevolge artikel 16* 'in accordance with article 16'
inzake	*inzake uw opmerking* 'concerning your remark'
jegens	*jegens uw naaste* 'towards your fellow human being'
krachtens	*krachtens artikel 16* 'under article 16'
niettegenstaande	*niettegenstaande het feit dat ...* 'in spite of the fact that ...'
middels	*middels deze brief* 'by means of this letter'
omtrent	*omtrent deze tijd* 'by this time'
onverminderd	*onverminderd het bepaalde in ...* 'without prejudice to what is said in ...'
overeenkomstig	*overeenkomstig de afspraak* 'in accordance with the agreement'
sedert	*sedert haar overlijden* 'since her decease'
staande	*staande de vergadering* 'during the meeting'
te	*te Amsterdam* 'in/at Amsterdam'; *te negen uur* 'at 9 o'clock'
teneinde	*teneinde + infinitival clause* 'in order to ...'
trots	*trots de regen* 'despite the rain'

Other prepositions that are mainly restricted to official and juridical language are Latin loan words like the following: *à*, *ad*, *conform*, *contra*, *circa*, *cum*, *de*, *ex*, *pro*, *qua* and *versus*. The only Latin preposition that really made its way into colloquial speech is the spatial preposition *via* in Table 5. Borrowings from French are *inclusief* 'including/with' and *exclusief* 'excluding/without': observe that these formations are classified as adverbs in the Van Dale dictionary, which is probably due to their adjective-like morphological makeup. However, the fact that they *precede* their nominal complement *btw/verzendkosten* in (85) shows, however, shows that they behave like prepositions in these examples, given that Section A2.2 has shown that adjectives always *follow* their nominal complement. The fact that the phrases *inclusief btw*/*exclusief verzendkosten* must follow the noun they modify also suggests that they are prepositional, given that attributively used adjectives normally precede the noun: cf. *een redelijke prijs* 'a reasonable price'.

(85) a. De prijs inclusief btw is 15 euro.
the price including VAT is 15 euro
'The price including VAT is 15 euros.'

b. De prijs exclusief verzendkosten is 20 euro.
the price excluding shipping is 20 euro
'The price without shipping is 20 euros.'

Further, the archaic prepositions *lastens* 'on the account of', *luidens* 'according to', *nevens* 'on the side of', *nopens* 'about' should be mentioned. Although normally used as a temporal preposition, *omtrent* can occasionally also be used as a spatial preposition meaning "near" or be used in other functions: cf. *omtrent de vijftig euro* 'about 50 Euros' and *omtrent de moord* 'concerning the murder'.

1.2.3. Postpositions

The examples in (86) show that, next to the prepositions, there is a smaller set of postpositions, which follow their complement. A comparison of (83a) and (86a) will reveal that some adpositions can be used both as a preposition and as a postposition. Broadly speaking, the most conspicuous semantic difference between pre- and postpositions is that the former refer to a certain position in space or on the time line, whereas the latter refer to a path; see Section 1.3.1 for a more precise and detailed discussion.

(86) a. Jan reed de sloot in.
Jan drove the ditch into
'Jan drove into the ditch.'

b. Jan kletste de hele voorstelling door.
Jan chattered the complete performance through
'Jan was chattering throughout the complete performance.'

Table 7 provides a list of spatial postpositions. When we compare this set of postpositions to the set of spatial prepositions in Table 5, we see that the former is practically a subset of the latter; the only adposition that cannot be found in Table 5 is the postposition *af* 'off' (although the Van Dale dictionary mentions that *af* is used as a preposition in certain varieties of Dutch).

Table 7: Spatial postpositions

POSTPOSITION	EXAMPLE	TRANSLATION
af	*de berg af*	from the mountain
binnen	*het huis binnen*	into the house
door	*het hek door*	through the gate
in	*het huis in*	into the house
langs	*het huis langs*	along the house
om	*de hoek om*	around the corner
op	*de berg op*	onto the mountain
over	*het grasveld over*	across the lawn
rond	*het plein rond*	around the square
uit	*de auto uit*	out of the car
voorbij	*het huis voorbij*	past the house

In addition to the forms in Table 7, the adposition *onder* 'under' seems to occur as a postposition in the southern and Flemish varieties of Dutch (Liliane Haegeman, p.c.). Standard Dutch has constructions like (87), but there the noun *kopje* is clearly not the complement of the adposition; the adposition instead seems to have a cognate complement corresponding to *the water* in the English renderings. The phrases *kopje onder gaan* and *iemand kopje onder duwen* should be seen as fixed idiomatic expressions.

(87) a. Jan ging kopje onder.
Jan went head$_{dim}$ under
'Jan went under the water.'
b. Jan duwde Marie kopje onder.
Jan pushed Marie head under
'Jan pushed Marie under the water.'

Table 8 shows that the set of temporal postpositions is even smaller than the set of spatial postpositions. The set seems to be exhausted by the adpositions *door*, *in* and *uit*.

Table 8: Temporal postpositions

POSTPOSITION	EXAMPLE	TRANSLATION
door	*het hele jaar door*	throughout the year
in	*het nieuwe jaar in*	into the new year
uit	*dag in dag uit*	lit: into day out of day 'continuously'

Occasionally, the elements *geleden* and *terug* in (88) are also included in the set of temporal postpositions. These elements differ from *door*, *in* and *uit*, however, in that they do not express the notion of path (on the time line), but simply refer to some fixed position on the time line.

(88) a. Drie weken geleden is ze overleden.
three weeks ago is she died
'She died three weeks ago.'
b. Jaren terug ben ik daar ook geweest.
years ago am I there also been
'I've been there also years ago.'

A final note may be needed on the expression *het klokje rond*, which refers to a span of time of approximately twelve hours. It seems wrong to interpret the adposition *rond* as a temporal postposition here, since what is implied is that the hour hand of the clock has traversed the path around the clock; therefore we are dealing with a spatial postposition. Note that besides (89a), (89b) is also possible; this may be due to the fact that a year can be measured by means of the zodiac, which is generally represented as a circle.

(89) a. Jan sliep het klokje rond.
Jan slept the clock$_{dim}$ round
'Jan slept for twelve hours.'
b. We zijn weer een jaar rond.
we are again a year round
'Another year has passed.'

1.2.4. Intransitive adpositions

This section discusses intransitive adpositions. Section 1.2.4.1 will show that these adpositions probably do not form a homogeneous group, but must be divided into two groups, viz., locational adpositions and verbal particles. Section 1.2.4.2 will provide a small sample of particle verbs and Section 1.2.4.3 will discuss some syntactic differences between intransitive adpositions and verbal particles. Section 1.2.4.4, finally, is devoted to P + V compounds, which can be easily confused with verbs taking an intransitive adposition or a particle.

1.2.4.1. Intransitive adpositions and particles

Adpositions can sometimes be used without a complement, in which case they are often called INTRANSITIVE ADPOSITIONs or (VERBAL) PARTICLEs. It may be the case that intransitive adpositions and particles do not form a homogeneous group. Consider example (90).

(90) Jan zet zijn hoed op (zijn hoofd).
Jan puts his hat on his head

Example (90) shows that the particle *op* can be used in the same function as the predicative PP *op zijn hoofd*; substituting one for the other does not affect the core meaning of the example, which expresses that the hat is undergoing a change of location. It seems plausible that the fact that *op* can be used as an intransitive adposition is related to the fact that the information conveyed by the complement of the preposition *op* is more or less superfluous; when it is dropped, our knowledge of the world enables us to reconstruct the full event and to determine the new location of the moved entity. Regardless of how one would like to account for this intuition, it is at least clear that there is a close relation between the use of *op* as a preposition and its use as an intransitive adposition. In this respect the intransitive use of *op* resembles the pseudo-intransitive use of transitive verbs like *eten* 'to eat'; when no direct object is present, it is inferred that some canonical object (an entity that is edible) is involved. Intransitive adpositions are generally locational in nature, and are mostly used with verbs denoting activities involving dressing and personal hygiene, as in (91a&b), or refer to pragmatically determinable locations, as in (91c). See Section 1.3.1.5.1 for more discussion.

(91) a. Jan doet zijn sjaal om (zijn nek).
Jan puts his shawl around his neck
b. Jan smeert zonnebrandolie op (zijn lichaam).
Jan smears suntan oil on his body
c. Het postkantoor is dicht bij (mijn huis).
the post office is close to my house

The adposition *af* in (92a) also seems to perform a function similar to the PP *op zijn hoofd* in (90). The main difference is that whereas the intransitive use of *op* in (90) has implications concerning the *new* location of the hat, (92a) identifies the *original* location of the hat. It is, however, less clear whether *af* can indeed be considered an intransitive adposition. If it is one, it must have the lexical property that it can only be used as such, given that it cannot take the noun phrase *zijn hoofd* as its complement. Alternative, one might of course speculate that the particle *af* is somehow related to its use in the circumposition *van* .. *af*; cf. (92b).

(92) a. Jan zet zijn hoed af (*zijn hoofd).
Jan puts his hat off his head
b. Jan zet zijn hoed (?van zijn hoofd) af.
Jan puts his hat from his head off

Often, there is no apparent semantic relation between the use of intransitive adpositions and their prepositional counterparts. In such cases, we will use the notion of (verbal) particle. These particles normally form a more or less fixed semantic unit with their associated main verb and they cannot be replaced by a full PP without affecting the core meaning of the construction. Despite the fact that Dutch orthography requires the particle and the verb to be written as a single word when they are adjacent, the combination probably cannot be considered a morphological compound since the finite form of the verb can be placed in the second position of main clauses while stranding the particle in clause-final position. Illustrations of this split pattern are given in the primed examples in (93).

(93) a. Jan wil wat achterstallig werk *inhalen*.
Jan wants some overdue work prt.-catch
'Jan wants to catch up on some overdue work.'
a′. Jan *haalde* snel wat achterstallig werk *in*.
Jan caught quickly some overdue work prt.
'Jan caught up on some overdue work quickly.'
b. De minister wou cruciale informatie *achterhouden*.
the minister wanted crucial information prt.-keep
'The minister wanted to withhold crucial information.'
b′. De minister *hield* cruciale informatie *achter*.
the minister kept crucial information prt.
'The minister was withholding crucial information.'

The examples above suggest that there is a gradient scale by which intransitive adpositions are related to their prepositional counterparts. In some cases the relation is quite tight, whereas in other cases the relation is looser or perhaps even nonexistent. Although the distinction between intransitive adpositions of the type in (90) and the verbal particles in (93) is often not very clear-cut as a result, we will nevertheless make this distinction. In doing so, we will rely heavily on whether the adposition has retained its original spatial meaning and can appear in the same environment as a predicative PP, or whether it has (partly) lost its meaning and cannot be replaced by a predicative PP (without affecting the core meaning of the construction). Section 1.2.4.3 will discuss a number of syntactic differences between intransitive adpositions and verbal particles, but first we want to discuss the particle verbs in more detail.

1.2.4.2. Particle verbs

Dutch has numerous particle verbs, that is, more or less fixed combinations of verbs and particles. The meanings of these particle verbs are generally not compositionally determined; they are to a certain extent unpredictable and must therefore be listed in the lexicon. This is especially clear from the fact that there are several particle verbs that seem to be derived not from a verb, but from an adjective or noun. Table (94) provides some examples of such cases.

(94) Particle verbs derived from adjectives/nouns

ADJECTIVE/NOUN	VERB	PARTICLE VERB
sterk$_A$ 'strong'	**sterken*	*aan* + *sterken* 'to recuperate'
zwak$_A$ 'weak'	**zwakken*	*af* + *zwakken* 'to tone down'
diep$_A$ 'deep'	**diepen*	*op* + *diepen* 'to bring out'
brief 'letter'	**brieven*	*over* + *brieven* 'to pass on'
dis$_N$ 'meal/dining table'	**dissen*	*op* + *dissen* 'to dish up (a story)'
been$_N$ 'bone'	**benen*	*uit* + *benen* 'to bone'

The fact that the meaning of the particle verbs in (94) must be listed in the lexicon suggests that we are dealing with complex words. Section 1.2.4.4 will show, however, that particle verbs cannot be considered complex words in the normal, morphological sense of the term. For this reason, we will often choose to *not* follow the orthographic rule according to which the particle and the verb are written as a single word (when they are adjacent). Note that the fact that particle verbs are not regular compounds is also recognized by Dutch traditional grammar, which uses the notion of SCHEIDBAAR SAMENGESTELD WERKWOORD "separable compound verb" for these verbs in order to distinguish them from real compounds of the type P + V that do not allow the "split" pattern. A brief discussion of the differences between the particle verbs and these so-called ONSCHEIDBAAR SAMENGESTELDE WERKWOORDEN "inseparable compound verbs" can be found in Section 1.2.4.4 below.

Table 9 provides a small sample of particle verbs that are derived from existing verbs; cf. De Haas & Trommelen (1993: Chapter 2, sub 6) for many more examples. Broadly speaking, the particles can be said to constitute a subset of the spatial prepositions. There are only three exceptions, which are marked with an asterisk in the table. First, the particle *af* has no prepositional counterpart in colloquial Standard Dutch at all (but see the remark above Table 7 in Section 1.2.3). Second, the particle *mee*, which is homophonous to the stranded counterpart of the preposition *met* used in instrumental and comitative phrases, is clearly not spatial. Finally, the particle *na* cannot be used as a spatial preposition (as a preposition it expresses a temporal meaning); perhaps it is an abbreviation of the complex spatial particle *achterna* 'after/behind', which can be used as a postposition, as in *Hij liep de jongen achterna* 'He followed the boy'. The fact that the meanings of the particle verbs are not compositionally determined does not mean that the original spatial meanings of the particles are completely undetectable; many of the particles in Table 9 can still be recognized as–that is, still feel like–spatial adpositions. Consequently, some of the examples in the table come semantically rather close to the examples involving intransitive adpositions discussed in the previous section.

Table 9: Particle-verb combinations

PARTICLE	EXAMPLE	TRANSLATION
aan	*een kaars aan steken* *drie kilo aan komen*	to light a candle to increase three kilo's in weight
achter	*achter blijven* *informatie achter houden*	to stay behind to withhold information
**af*	*af gaan* *een band af spelen* *af studeren*	to fail/lose face to play a tape to graduate
bij	*bij blijven* *de literatuur bij houden* *drie euro bij betalen*	to keep up to date to keep up to date with the literature to pay three Euros as extra charge
binnen	*binnen sijpelen* *een subsidie binnen halen*	to seep inside to obtain a subsidy
boven	*boven komen* *boven liggen*	to come upstairs/on top to lie on top
buiten	*buiten komen* *buiten sluiten*	to come outside to shut out
door	*iets door snijden* *door lopen* *de vakantie ergens door brengen*	to cut something through to continue to walk to spend the vacation somewhere
in	*iets in brengen* *iets in dienen* *iets in schatten*	to insert something to submit something to estimate something
langs	*bij iemand langs gaan* *iets ergens langs brengen*	to briefly visit someone to deliver something somewhere
**mee*	*iets aan iemand mee delen* *aan iets mee doen* *iets meenemen*	to inform someone of something to partake in something to take something along
**na*	*iemand na lopen* *over iets na praten* *iemand na praten*	to run after someone to talk something over to parrot
om	*iets om draaien* *iemand om kopen* *om komen*	to turn something around to bribe someone to die in an accident or a calamity
onder	*iets onder binden* *ergens onder duiken* *iets onder verdelen*	to fasten something (under the feet) go into hiding somewhere to classify something
op	*iets op schrijven* *op houden* *kinderen op voeden*	to put down (on paper) to stop to raise children
over	*over stromen* *over steken* *een tekst over schrijven*	to flood to cross to copy a text

PARTICLE	EXAMPLE	TRANSLATION
rond	*rond rijden* *een nieuwtje rond vertellen* *rond draaien*	to drive around to spread an item of news around to turn/spin (around)
tegen	*iets tegen houden* *iets tegen spreken* *iemand tegen komen*	to stop something to object to/argue with something to meet someone
toe	*toe stromen* *iemand toe dekken* *iets toe geven*	to crowd towards to tuck something in to admit something
tussen	*iets tussen werpen*	to interpolate
uit	*iets uit kotsen* *iets uit sluiten* *iets uit zenden*	to throw up to exclude something to broadcast
voor	*iets voor binden* *iets voordoen*	to put on something to demonstrate
voorbij	*voorbij lopen/rijden/vliegen* *iemand voorbij streven*	to pass to outstrip someone

Besides the particles in Table 9, which clearly have an adpositional counterpart, Dutch has many other elements that are traditionally considered adverbs but that resemble particles in that they may occur in a fixed combination with certain verbs. Moreover, many of them resemble adpositional phrases in that they may express a change of location or direction. A small sample is given in (95); we refer to De Haas & Trommelen (1993:ch.2, sub 6.3.2) for more cases.

(95) a. *heen gaan* 'to die'
b. *weg lopen* 'to walk away'
c. *neer dalen* 'to come down'
d. *terug gaan* 'to go back'
e. *thuis komen* 'to come home'
f. *verder komen* 'to make headway'
g. *verder lopen* 'to continue to walk'
h. *voort lopen* 'to continue to walk'
i. *vooruit komen* 'to make headway'
j. *weer keren* 'to return'
k. Jan komt in de gevangenis terecht.
Jan comes in the prison TERECHT
'Jan will end up in prison.'

In addition, De Haas & Trommelen (1993:ch.2, sub 6.3.3) give a large set of complex particles. Since these complex forms behave just like the simple ones, we will not discuss them here, but confine ourselves to giving a list. The first subset involves particles that are formed with *achter/voor* +P as their first member and that denote a location, direction or time. All forms can also be used as prepositions with the exception of the particles in (96b). Note that the particles *achteraf/vooraf* in (96a) are temporal in nature.

(96) • Complex locational/temporal and directional particles

a. *achteraan/vooraan* 'in the back/front'
achterin/voorin 'in the back/front'
achterom/voorom 'around the back/front'
achterop/voorop 'on the back/front'
achteruit/vooruit 'backwards/forwards'

b. *achteraf/vooraf* 'afterwards/beforehand'
achterna 'after'
omhoog/omlaag 'upwards/downwards'

The second subset in (97) involves particles denoting a state. The particles P + *een* in (97a) alternate with the construction P + *elkaar* 'each other'; cf. *Hij frommelde de papieren in elkaar/ineen* 'He crumpled the papers.'

(97) • Complex particles denoting a state

a. *aaneen* 'on end'
bijeen 'together'
dooreen 'higgledy-piggledy'
opeen 'on each other'
uiteen 'apart'

b. *achterover(liggen)* 'to lie on the back'
voorover (liggen) 'to lie on the front';
onderuit (liggen) 'to lie flat'
omver (duwen) 'to push over'

Although the meanings of the particles are sometimes quite remote from predicatively used adpositional phrases, they share at least one syntactic property with them. First, Section 1.1.3.2.2, sub I, has discussed that the addition of a predicative PP may turn a regular intransitive verb into an °unaccusative verb. As a general rule, the particles in Table 9 have the same effect. Take the case of *af studeren* 'to graduate'. While *studeren* 'to study' in (98a) has all the characteristics of a regular intransitive verb, the particle verb *afstuderen* 'to graduate' in (98a′) has the properties of an unaccusative verb: the (b)-examples show that whereas *studeren* takes the auxiliary *hebben* in the perfect tense, *afstuderen* takes *zijn*; the (c)-examples show that whereas the past/passive participle *gestudeerd* cannot be used as an attributive modifier of a noun that corresponds to the subject of the clause, *af gestudeerd* can; the (d)-examples, finally, show that whereas *studeren* allows impersonal passivization, *afstuderen* does not.

(98) a. Jan studeert vlijtig.
Jan studies diligently

a′. Jan studeert snel af.
Jan graduates quickly prt.

b. Jan heeft/*is vlijtig gestudeerd.
Jan has/is diligently studied

b′. Jan is/*heeft snel afgestudeerd.
Jan is/has quickly prt.-graduated

c. *de vlijtig gestudeerde jongen
the diligently studied boy

c′. de snel afgestudeerde jongen
the quickly prt.-graduated boy

d. Er wordt vlijtig gestudeerd.
there is diligently studied

d′. *?Er wordt snel afgestudeerd.
there is quickly prt.-graduated

In (99) we give similar examples involving *weg* 'away', which is taken from the set of particles in (95): like predicative pre- or postpositional phrases, the particle changes the intransitive verb *lopen* into an unaccusative verb.

(99) a. Jan liep snel.
Jan walked fast
a′. Jan liep snel weg.
Jan walked quickly away
b. Jan heeft/*is snel gelopen.
Jan has/is fast walked
b′. Jan is/*heeft snel weg gelopen.
Jan is/has quickly away walked
c. *de snel gelopen jongen
the fast walked boy
c′. de snel weg gelopen jongen
the quickly away walked boy
d. Er wordt snel gelopen.
there is fast walked
d′. *?Er wordt snel weg gelopen.
there is quickly away walked

Second, the addition of a predicative PP may license as its logical SUBJECT an argument that is not selected by the verb; cf. Section 1.1.3.2.2, sub II. The examples in (100) show that the addition of a particle may have the same effect, and therefore show that the particle is also predicative in nature, despite the fact that it is not always clear what property the particle denotes; see Section 1.3.1.5.2 for a more extensive discussion of the semantics of particles.

(100) a. Jan speelt de band *(af).
Jan plays the tape prt.
'Jan parrots the girl.'
b. Jan praat het meisje *(na).
Jan talks the girl prt.
'Jan Jan parrots the girl.'
c. Jan kots zijn eten *(uit).
Jan throws his food prt.
'Jan throws his food up.'
d. Jan vocht zijn ontslag *(aan).
Jan fought his dismissal prt.
'Jan challenged his dismissal.'

There are other elements that are sometimes considered verbal particles that do not have an adpositional counterpart, like the element *samen* 'together' in (101a). It does not seem to be the case, however, that *samen* acts as a particle in the same sense as the elements discussed above, since it differs not only in meaning but also exhibits a different syntactic behavior. In contrast to the particles in (98) and (99), the addition of *samen* does not change a regular intransitive verb like *werken* 'to work' into an unaccusative one: the verb selects the auxiliary *hebben* in the perfect tense construction in (101b), the past/passive particle in (101c) cannot be used as an attributive modifier of a noun that corresponds to the subject of the clause, and the impersonal passive construction in (101d) is fully acceptable.

(101) a. Marie en Jan werken al jaren samen.
Marie and Jan work already for.years together
'Marie and Jan are already cooperating for years.'
b. Jan en Marie hebben/*zijn al jaren samen gewerkt.
Jan and Marie have/are already for.years together worked
c. *de samengewerkte vrienden
the cooperated friends
d. Er wordt al jaren samen gewerkt.
there is already for.years together worked

The element *samen* further crucially differs from run-of-the-mill verbal particles in that it can readily be separated from the verbs in clause-final position: *dat Jan en Peter samen aan dit project hebben gewerkt* 'that Jan and Peter worked on this project together'. It therefore seems safe to dismiss the claim that *samen* functions as a verbal particle in examples like (101a).

1.2.4.3. Differences between intransitive adpositions and particles

This section discusses several differences between intransitive adpositions and verbal particles.

I. Position with respect to the verbs in clause-final position

The most conspicuous difference between intransitive adpositions and verbal particles is that the former must precede the verbs in clause-final position, whereas the latter may intervene between these verbs. Example (102a), for example, is ambiguous between a reading in which *voor* is used as an intransitive adposition meaning "in front (of something)", and a reading in which *voor* is used as a particle, in which case the combination *voor staan* means "to be leading (in a game)". Example (102b) can only have the latter meaning.

(102) a. dat Jan voor lijkt te staan. [intransitive adposition or particle]
that Jan in.front seems to stand
'Jan seems to be standing in front (of, e.g., the house).'
'Jan seems to be leading in the game.'

b. dat Jan lijkt voor te staan. [particle only]
that Jan seems in.front to stand
'Jan seems to be leading in the game.'

II. PP-over-V

The examples in (103) show that, like adverbially used prepositional phrases, adverbially used intransitive adpositions may undergo PP-over-V, albeit that the result is somewhat marked for some speakers due to "lightness" of the intransitive adposition *achter*; PP-over-V is normally applied to relatively "heavy" constituents.

(103) a. dat Jan graag <achter het huis> speelt <achter het huis>.
that Jan gladly behind the house plays
'that Jan likes to play in the back/behind the house.'

b. dat Jan graag <achter> speelt <%achter>.
that Jan gladly behind plays
'that Jan likes to play in the back/behind (e.g., the house).'

The examples in (104) , on the other hand, show that particles like *voor* behave like predicatively used adpositional phrases like *voor het huis* in that they must precede their verbal associate: this is not really surprising, of course, given that the examples in (98) to (100) have already shown that particles are in fact predicative phrases, which must likewise precede the verb they are selected by.

(104) a. dat Jan <voor het huis> staat <*voor het huis>.
that Jan in.front.of the house stands
'that Jan is standing in front of the house.'
b. dat Jan <voor> staat <*voor>.
that Jan prt. leads
'that Jan is leading the game.'

III. Topicalization

It is easier to topicalize intransitive adpositions than particles, which is probably related to the fact that particles have little semantic content of their own and topicalization is normally used to emphasize some constituent, as in example (105a), in which contrastive accent is indicated by means of small capitals. But even when particles may induce meaning differences, topicalization seems to be disfavored; this is clear from the fact that *voor* and *achter* are preferably interpreted as locational intransitive adpositions in example (105b).

(105) a. VOOR heb ik een woonkamer en ACHTER een werkkamer.
in.front have I a living.room and behind an office
'The living room is in the front and the office in the back (of the ground floor).'
b. #VOOR staat Jan en ACHTER staat Marie.
in.front stands Jan and behind stands Marie
Intended reading: 'Jan is leading the game and Marie is not leading the game.'

Nevertheless, when the locational interpretation is unlikely and the context is sufficiently contrastive, topicalization seems to give rise to a fully acceptable result; cf. Hoeksema (1991a/1991b) and Bennis (1991).

(106) a. OP komt de zon in het oosten; ONDER gaat hij in het westen.
up comes the sun in the east down goes he in the west
'The sun rises in the east and sets in the west.'
b. IN ademen we zuurstof (en UIT kooldioxide).
in breathe we oxygen and out carbon dioxide
'We inhale oxygen and exhale carbon dioxide.'

Note that the acceptability of the topicalization is clearest when the particle verb is finite and the verbal part thus occupies the second position of the clause. When the second position of the clause is filled by an auxiliary, as in (107), °VP-topicalization seems preferred to topicalization of the particle.

(107) a. ??IN hebben we zuurstof geademd (en UIT kooldioxide).
in have we oxygen breathed and out carbon dioxide
b. ?IN geademd hebben we zuurstof (en UIT geademd kooldioxide).
in breathed have we oxygen and out breathed carbon dioxide

IV. Progressive aan het + V *construction*

The examples in (108) show that intransitive prepositions and verbal particle differ in that only the latter can be adjacent to the main verb in the progressive *aan het + V* construction; whereas the verbal particle *voor* in *voorlezen* 'to read aloud' can precede or follow the sequence *aan het*, the intransitive preposition *voor* must precede it.

(108) a. Jan is de kinderen het boek <voor> aan het <voor> lezen.
Jan is the children the book prt. AAN HET read
'Jan is reading the book to the children.'

b. De kinderen zijn <voor> aan het <*voor> spelen.
the children are in.front AAN HET play
'The children are playing in front (of, e.g., the house).'

V. Word formation

Intransitive adpositions and particles differ with respect to word formation. The former are never part of a complex word, whereas the latter can be; the examples in (109) and (110) show that many of the particle verbs in Table 9 can be the input for word formation.

(109) • Nouns derived from particle verbs

a. *aan + steken* 'to light' — a′. *aansteker* 'lighter'
b. *na + praten* 'to parrot' — b′. *naprater* 'parrot'
c. *op + voeden* 'to raise' — c′. *opvoeding* 'education'
d. *over + stromen* 'to flood' — d′. *overstroming* 'flood'

(110) • Adjectives derived from particle verbs

a. *aan + steken* 'to infect' — a′. *aanstekelijk* 'contagious'
b. *om + kopen* 'to bribe' — b′. *onomkoopbaar* 'incorruptible'
c. *op + blazen* 'inflate' — c′. *opblaasbaar* 'inflatable'
d. *op + lossen* 'to solve' — d′. *onoplosbaar* 'unsolvable'
e. *op + merken* 'to note' — e′. *opmerkzaam* 'observant'

VI. Co-occurrence restrictions and coordination

The examples in (111) show that intransitive adpositions can readily co-occur, as in (111a), and be coordinated, as in (111b).

(111) a. Jan speelt *boven* graag *achter*.
Jan plays above gladly behind
'Upstairs, Jan likes to play in the back.'

b. De kinderen spelen zowel *boven* als *achter*.
the children play both above and behind
'The children play both upstairs and in the back.'

The examples in (112) show that juxtaposition and coordination of verbal particles normally lead to severely degraded results and that, as a result, a clause cannot contain more then one single verbal particle. The differences in acceptability are probably due to the fact that the intransitive adpositions in (111) are used as regular locational adverbial phrases, whereas the particles in (112) constitute an inherent part of the meaning of the particle verb; cf. Section 1.2.4.2.

(112) a. *Jan staat *op voor.*
Jan stands up in.front
Intended meaning: 'Jan is standing up and he is leading the game.'
b. *Jan staat zowel *op* als *voor.*
Jan stands both up and in front
Intended meaning: 'Jan is standing up and he is leading the game.'

However, example (113a) seems to show that the ban on coordination is lifted when the particles are antonyms. In principle, two analyses are possible for this example: either we are dealing with coordination of the two particles *in* and *uit*, as in the representation in (113b), or with coordination of the two particle verbs *inademen* 'inhale' and *uitademen* 'exhale' with backward °Conjunction Reduction, as in the representation in (113b′).

(113) a. Je moet rustig in en uit ademen.
you must calmly in and out breathe
'You must breathe in and out calmly.'
b. Je moet rustig [in en out] ademen.
b′. Je moet rustig [[in ~~ademen~~] en [uit ademen]].

It is not easy to decide which of these two analyses is the correct one, and it may in fact be the case that they are both correct. That the analysis in (113b) may be correct is clear from the acceptability of example (114a): whereas the analysis in (114b) is unproblematic, the Conjunction Reduction analysis in (114b′) is untenable given that the infinitive in the first conjunct conjuncts is not licensed by being in the domain of a modal verb.

(114) a. dat je rustig in en uit moet ademen.
that you calmly in and out must breathe
b. dat je rustig [in en uit] moet ademen.
b′. *dat je rustig [[in ~~ademen~~] en [moet uit ademen]].

That the analysis in (113b) may be correct is at least suggested by the acceptability of example (115a). We have added a percentage sign to the analysis in (115b), because Standard Dutch normally does not allow complex phrases to permeate the verbs in a verb cluster. If this restriction is indeed absolute, the analysis must be as given in (115b′). We leave it to future research to investigate whether it is possible to provide more conclusive evidence in favor of the Conjunction Reduction analysis.

(115) a. dat je rustig moet in en uit ademen.
that you calmly must in and out breathe
b. %dat je rustig moet [in en uit] ademen.
b′. dat je rustig moet [[in ~~ademenen~~] en [uit ademen]].

The discussion above has shown that coordination of particles is normally excluded, unless the particle are antonymous and, of course, are associated with the same verbal part. This seems to support the earlier suggestion that the ban on coordination is not syntactic but semantic in nature. For completeness' sake, example (116) shows that intransitive adpositions and particles can readily co-occur.

(116) *Voor* heb ik een plant *neer* gezet.
in.front have I a plant down put
'I have put a plant down in the front.'

VII. Conclusion

We conclude this section with a brief illustration of the first four tests for particle verbs on the basis of the potentially problematic case in (117a), adapted from Hoeksema (1991a). Although the Van Dale dictionary lists *voorstemmen* as a particle verb, the fact that the element *voor* can be replaced by the PP *voor het voorstel* shows that we cannot *a priori* exclude the possibility that we are dealing with an intransitive adposition. Example (117b) suggests, however, that the Van Dale analysis of *voor* as a verbal particle is indeed the correct one: the element *voor* differs markedly from the PP *voor het voorstel* in that it cannot undergo PP-over-V, but must occur to the left of the main verb.

(117) a. Voor (het voorstel) stemde alleen de oppositie.
in.favor.of the proposal voted just the opposition
'Only the opposition voted in favor of the proposal.'

b. dat de oppositie <voor (het voorstel)> stemde <voor *(het voorstel)>.
that the opposition in.favor.of the proposal voted
'that the opposition voted in favor of the proposal.'

Example (117b) thus strongly suggests that *voorstemmen* is indeed a particle verb, and this is further supported by the fact that *voorstemmen* can be the input for agentive ER-nominalization; the noun *voorstemmer* is also listed in the Van Dale dictionary and a Google search on this form resulted in about 24.000 hits.

1.2.4.4. Particle verbs versus P + V compounds

Sections 1.2.4.2 and 1.2.4.3 have shown that particle verbs exhibit several of the properties of compounds. First, the meaning of a particle verb is not compositionally determined; it is normally impossible to fully predict the meaning of a particle verb on the basis of the meaning of the constituent parts, which is also a typical property of compounds. Second, table (94) has shown that there are particle verbs that involve verb forms that are only attested in combination with one specific particle; this seems problematic for an analysis according to which the verb selects the particle in the same way as it would select other adpositional phrases, given that selection generally involves entire classes of entities, not just a single word or phrase. Finally, examples (109) and (110) show that many particle verbs can be the input to morphological processes, which is normal for (complex) words, but much less common for phrases. However, there are also several problems for the claim that particle verbs are complex words. We will make this clear by comparing particle verbs to undisputed P + V compounds like *voorzien* 'to anticipate' and *overzien* 'to calculate'.

I. Verb second

The easiest way to distinguish particle verbs from P + V compounds is by considering main clauses in which the verb in question is finite and thus occupies the second position in the clause. When we are dealing with a particle verb, we get a split pattern, that is, the particle is stranded in clause-final position; when we are dealing with a compound, on the other hand, the split pattern is not possible.

(118) a. Jan <*over>schreef de antwoorden <over>. [particle verb]
Jan prt. wrote the answers
'Jan copied the answers.'
b. Jan <over>zag de consequenties niet meer <*over>. [compound]
Jan over saw the consequences no longer
'Jan could no longer calculate the consequences.'

II. Clause-final verb clusters and te-*infinitives*

When the clause contains a clause-final verb cluster, as in (119a), the particle may either precede the complete cluster or be left-adjacent to the main verb; the P+V compound in (119b), on the other hand, cannot be split by the auxiliary.

(119) a. dat Jan de antwoorden <over> wil <over> schrijven. [particle verb]
that Jan the answers prt. wants write
'that Jan wants to copy the answers.'
b. dat Jan de consequentie niet <*over> kon <over>zien. [compound]
that Jan the consequences not prt. could see
'that Jan couldn't calculate all the consequences.'

In *te*-infinitives like (120), the particle must precede the infinitival marker *te*. This marker cannot, however, permeate the P + V compound; see Section V4.7 for more extensive discussion of word order in verb clusters and *te*-infinitives.

(120) a. Het is verboden [om de antwoorden <over> te <*over> schrijven].
it is forbidden COMP the answers prt. to write
'It is forbidden to copy the answers.'
b. Het is moeilijk [om alle consequenties <*over> te <over>zien].
it is difficult COMP all consequences prt. to see
'It is difficult to calculate all the consequences.'

III. Formation of the past/passive participle

In the case of particle verbs, the past/passive participle is prefixed by *ge-*, and the particle precedes this prefix. This prefix *ge-* does not arise, however, when we are dealing with a P + V compound. In this respect, P + V compounds behave like verbs prefixed with *be-*, *ver-* and *ont-*; cf. for example *verrassen* 'to surprise': *heeft <*ge->ver<*ge->rast* 'has surprised'.

(121) a. Jan heeft de antwoorden over *(ge-)schreven. [particle verb]
Jan has the answers prt. written
'Jan has copied the answers.'
b. Jan heeft niet alle consequenties over(**ge-*)zien. [compound]
Jan has not all consequences overseen
'Jan didn't calculate all the consequences.'

IV. Topicalization

Topicalization of particles is possible with antonym pairs like *inademen* 'to breathe in' and *uitademen* 'to breathe out' in (122a), provided that the particle receives contrastive accent; cf. Section 1.2.4.3, sub III. Topicalization of the P-part of P + V compounds, on the other hand, is never acceptable, and thus also holds for antonym pairs like *onderschatten* 'underestimate' and *overschatten* 'overestimate' in (122b).

(122) a. IN ademen we zuurstof (en UIT kooldioxide). [particle verb]
in breathe we oxygen and out carbon dioxide

b. *ONDER schat Marie zichzelf (en OVER de anderen). [compound]
under estimates Marie herself (and over the others)

V. Stress

Word stress is always on the particle part of a particle verb, whereas in P + V compounds it is always on the verbal part; this is shown in (123), in which we have indicated word stress by means of small capitals.

(123) Stress assignment with participle verbs and P + V compounds

PARTICLE VERBS	P+V COMPOUNDS
DOOR lopen 'to walk on'	doorLOpen 'to attend (a school)'
ONDER duiken 'to go into hiding'	onderNEmen 'to undertake'
OVER schrijven 'to copy'	overZIEN 'to calculate'
VOOR schrijven 'to prescribe'	voorZIEN 'to anticipate'

VI. Conclusion

The data in Subsections I though V show that, despite the fact that particle verbs have certain properties of compounds, the particles and the verbs sometimes also behave like syntactic constituents in their own right. The proper analysis of particle verbs is, however, still the subject of an ongoing debate: the traditional assumption that particles are part of the particle verb has been defended again recently by, e.g., Neeleman (1994b), Neeleman and Weerman (1993/1999); the assumption that the particle is a syntactic constituent in its own right has been defended by, e.g., Bennis (1991), Den Dikken (1995), and Zeller (2001). Koopman (1995) and Den Dikken (2003) reconcile the two views by assuming that the particle syntactically incorporates into the verb. Booij (2010) reconciles the two views within construction grammar by claiming that the phrasal and the compound structure co-exist.

1.2.5. Circumpositions

We conclude our discussion of the formal classification of adpositions by examining circumpositions. We will see that clauses with a predicatively used circumpositional phrase are easy to confuse with clauses with particle verbs that select a PP-complement. Therefore, we will develop some tests that can be used to distinguish the two constructions.

1.2.5.1. General introduction

Circumpositions are complex adpositions that may occur discontinuously, that is, of which some part precedes and some part follows the complement of the adpositional phrase. Some examples are given in (124), in which the two parts of the circumposition are given in italics. The first part of the circumposition is an element that can also be used as a regular adposition. This can but need not be the case for the second part; whereas *door* in (124b) can also be used as an adposition, this is not the case for *heen* in (124a).

(124) • Circumpositions

a. dat Jan *over* het hek *heen* sprong.
that Jan over the gate HEEN jumped
'that Jan jumped over the gate.'

b. dat Marie Peter *tussen* twee lessen *door* belde.
that Marie Peter between two lessons through called
'that Marie called Peter in between two lessons.'

Generally speaking, circumpositions have a spatial meaning, as in (124a), but (124b) shows that there are also temporal instances; cf. Section 1.3.2.3 for more discussion. Below we restrict ourselves to spatial circumpositional phrases, which can be used to indicate both a (change of) location and a direction; see Section 1.1.3.2 for these notions. This is clear from the fact that they can occur as the complement of both locational verbs and verbs of motion, as in (125a&b), and as the complements of verbs of traversing, as in (125c); see Section 1.3.1.4 for further discussion. See Claessen & Zwart (2010) for a detailed discussion of the semantics of circumpositions with *heen*.

(125) a. Het kleed ligt over de tafel heen. [location]
the tablecloth lies over the table HEEN
'The tablecloth is lying over the table.'

b. Jan legt het kleed over de tafel heen. [change of location]
Jan lays the tablecloth over the table HEEN
'Jan is putting the tablecloth over the table.'

c. Jan is over de brug heen gereden. [direction]
Jan is over the bridge HEEN driven
'Jan has driven over the bridge.'

Another special case that we will not discuss here is the phrase *op XP na* in (126) with the specialized meaning "apart from XP", which is only used when some universally quantified or negative noun phrase is present in the clause.

(126) a. Ik heb alles gelezen op de inleiding na.
I have everything read OP the introduction NA
'I have read everything apart from the introduction.'

b. Ik heb op Peter na niemand gezien.
I have OP from NA nobody seen
'Apart from Peter I have seen nobody.'

Table 10 provides a list of elements that are traditionally assumed to be circumpositions, classified by means of their second part, and provides an example of each case. The discussion of circumpositions in this chapter will take this table as its point of departure.

Table 10: Circumpositions classified according to their second member

2ND PART	CIRCUMPOSITION	EXAMPLE
aan	*achter .. aan*	*achter de optocht aan lopen* 'to walk after the parade'
	tegen .. aan	*tegen de deur aan lopen* 'to walk/bump into the door'
af	*van .. af*	*van het dak af springen* 'to jump from the roof'
	op .. af	*op iemand af lopen* 'to walk towards someone'
door	*onder .. door*	*onder de brug door lopen* 'to walk under the bridge'
	tussen .. door	*tussen de bomen door lopen* 'to walk between the trees'
heen	*door .. heen*	*door het stof heen lopen* 'to run through the dust'
	?*langs .. heen*	?*langs de jongen heen lopen* 'to walk past the boy'
	om .. heen	*om het huis heen lopen* 'to walk around the house'
	over .. heen	*over het heen springen* 'to jump over the gate'
in	*tegen .. in*	*tegen de stroom in lopen* 'to walk against the current'
	tussen .. in	*tussen twee meisjes in zitten* 'to sit between two girls'
langs	*achter .. langs*	*achter het huis langs lopen* 'to walk along the back of the house'
	boven .. langs	*boven de brug langs lopen* 'to walk above (along) the bridge'
	onder ..langs	*onder de brug langs lopen* 'to walk down (along) the bridge'
	voor .. langs	*voor het huis langs lopen* 'to walk along the front of the house'
om	*achter .. om*	*achter het huis om lopen* 'to walk around the back of the house'
	buiten .. om	*buiten het huis om lopen* 'to walk around the exterior of the house'
	voor .. om	*voor het huis om lopen* 'to walk around the front of the house'
op	*tegen .. op*	*tegen de muur op klimmen* 'to climb up against the wall'

2ND PART	CIRCUMPOSITION	EXAMPLE
toe	*naar .. toe*	*naar Peter toe lopen* 'to walk towards Peter'
	op .. toe	*op Peter toe lopen* 'to walk towards Peter'
	tot aan .. toe	*tot aan de grens toe lopen* 'to walk up to the border'
uit	*achter .. uit*	*achter de kast uit halen* 'to get out from behind the closet'
	boven .. uit	*boven de bomen uit steken* 'to stick out above the trees'
	onder .. uit	*onder haar jas uit steken* 'to stick out from under her coat'
	tussen .. uit	*tussen de papieren uit steken* 'to stick out from between the papers'
	voor .. uit	*voor de optocht uit lopen* 'to walk in front of the parade'
vandaan	*achter .. vandaan*	*achter de boom vandaan komen* 'to come from behind the trees'
	bij .. vandaan	*bij de buren vandaan komen* 'to come from the neighbors'
	om .. vandaan	*om de hoek vandaan komen* 'to come from around the corner'
	onder .. vandaan	*onder de kast vandaan halen* 'to get from under the closet'
	tussen .. vandaan	*tussen de troep vandaan halen* 'to get out of the middle of the mess'
	uit .. vandaan	*uit de kast vandaan halen* 'to take out of the closet'
	van .. vandaan	*van de kapper vandaan komen* 'to come from the hairdresser'
	voor .. vandaan	*voor de auto vandaan trekken* 'to pull away from in front of the car'

For completeness' sake, example (127) provides the same set, but now classified according to their first part.

(127) • Spatial circumpositions classified according to their first part

a. *achter .. aan/langs/om/uit/vandaan*
b. *bij .. vandaan*
c. *boven .. langs/uit*
d. *buiten .. om*
e. *door .. heen*
f. ?*langs .. heen*
g. *naar .. toe*
h. *om .. heen/vandaan*
i. *onder .. door/langs/uit/vandaan*
j. *op .. af/toe*
k. *over .. heen*
l. *tegen .. aan/in/op*
m. *tot (aan) .. toe*
n. *tussen .. door/in/uit/vandaan*
o. *uit .. vandaan*
p. *van .. af/uit/vandaan*
q. *voor .. langs/om/uit/vandaan*

It is important to note that not all complex adpositions are part of the set of circumpositions: the complex adpositions *tegenover* and *voorbij* in (128a&b) act as prepositions, and the complex adposition *voorbij* in (128b′) acts as a postposition.

(128) a. Jan zat tegen-over de koningin.
Jan sat opposite the queen
'Jan was sitting opposite the queen.'
b. Jan liep voor-bij het huis.
Jan walked past the house
b′. Jan liep het huis voor-bij.
Jan walked the house past
'Jan was walking past the house.'

1.2.5.2. Circumpositions versus PP + particle combinations: five tests

It is sometimes difficult to decide whether we are dealing with a circumposition or with a verbal particle preceded by a prepositional phrase. This is due to the fact that many of the elements in the first column of Table 10 can also be used as verbal particles, which will become clear by comparing this table with Table 9 in Section 1.2.4.2. Therefore, it is useful to design some tests that can be used to establish whether we are dealing with a circumposition or with a construction in which a verbal particle is preceded by some PP. In order to do that, we will compare the syntactic behavior of the two examples in (129). The phrase *achter de optocht aan* in (129a) is a prototypical case of a circumpositional phrase, whereas *neerleggen* 'to put down' is a typical case of a particle verb.

(129) a. dat de kinderen achter de optocht aan renden.
that the children after the parade AAN ran
'that the children ran after the parade.'
b. dat Jan het boek op de tafel neer legde.
that Jan the book on the table down put
'that Jan put the book down on the table.'

I. Omission of the sequence P + NP

The sequence *P + NP* is an inherent part of the circumpositional phrase, and, consequently, omitting this sequence will result in ungrammaticality. This is illustrated in (130a). When we are dealing with a particle verb, on the other hand, there is no *a priori* reason to assume that omission of the PP is impossible, and, as is shown in (130b), dropping the PP indeed gives rise to a grammatical result.

(130) a. *dat de kinderen aan renden.
that the children AAN ran
b. dat Jan het boek neer legde.
that Jan the book down put
'that Jan put the book down.'

II. Pronominalization of the sequence P + NP

The examples in (131) show that locational prepositional phrases can often be replaced by an R-word like *daar* 'there', *hier* 'here', etc.

(131) a. De kinderen spelen in de tuin.
the children play in the garden
'The children are playing in the garden.'
b. De kinderen spelen daar/hier.
the children play there/here

Given that the sequence *P + NP* is an inherent part of the circumpositional phrase, we do not expect pronominalization of this part to be possible. In the case of a particle verb, on the other hand, the sequence *P + NP* is an independent PP, and pronominalization is expected to be possible. The examples in (132) show that these expectations are indeed borne out.

(132) a. *dat de kinderen daar/hier aan renden
that the children there/here AAN ran
b. dat Jan het boek daar/hier neer legde.
that Jan the book there/here down put

For completeness' sake, observe that °R-pronominalization of the *nominal complement* of the circumposition is possible. The same thing holds, of course, for the complement of the preposition. This is shown in (133), where the parts of the discontinuous pronominal PPs are given in italics.

(133) a. de optocht *waar* de kinderen *achter aan* renden
the parade where the children after AAN run
'the parade that the children ran after'
b. de tafel *waar* Jan het boek *op* neer legde
the table where Jan the book on down put
'the table that Jan put the book down on'

III. PP-over-V of the sequence P + NP

The examples in (134) show that the two parts of the circumposition appear in a fixed order. It cannot be changed by °PP-over-V of the sequence *P + NP*. The order of the verbal particle and the PP, on the other hand, can be changed.

(134) a. dat de kinderen <achter de optocht> aan renden <*achter de optocht>.
b. dat Jan het boek < op de tafel> neer legde <op de tafel>.

IV. Topicalization

Since circumpositional phrases are constituents, we expect that they can be topicalized, that is, be placed in clause-initial position, as in (135a). When we are dealing with a particle verb, on the other hand, the PP and the particle do not constitute a constituent and we therefore correctly expect it to be impossible to simultaneously topicalize the PP and the verbal particle; (135b) is marginal at best.

(135) a. ?Achter de optocht aan renden de kinderen.
after the parade AAN ran the children
b. *Op de tafel neer legde Jan het boek.
on the table down put Jan the book

The contrast between the examples in (135a) and (135b) is perhaps not as sharp as one would desire, given that examples like (135a) often sound marked as well; it requires contrastive accent on the topicalized phrase, which suggests that topicalization of circumpositional phrases is only possible in contrastive contexts. The markedness of (135a) may therefore be due to the fact that the circumpositional phrase is not explicitly contrasted with another adpositional phrase. A relatively good example is given in (136).

(136) Over het hek HEEN moet je springen, maar onder het hek DOOR moet je kruipen.
over the gate HEEN must you jump, but under the gate DOOR must you crawl
'You have to jump over the gate, but crawl under it.'

Since the PP is an independent constituent in the case of a particle verb, we correctly expect it to be able to topicalize when the particle remains in clause-final position, as in (137b). It would appear from example (137a) that circumpositional phrases cannot readily be split under topicalization.

(137) a. ??Achter de optocht liepen de kinderen aan.
b. Op de tafel legde Jan het boek neer.

It is probably not the case, however, that the degraded status of (137a) is due to a syntactic constraint on preposing of the sequence *P* + *NP*, given that *wh*-movement of this sequence is fully acceptable. This shows that splitting circumpositional phrases is in principle possible: the markedness of (137a) is therefore somewhat mysterious.

(138) a. Achter welke optocht liepen de kinderen aan?
after which parade walked the children AAN
'After which parade did the children run?'
b. Op welke tafel legde Jan het boek neer?
on which table put Jan the book down
'On which table did Jan put the book?'

V. Adnominal use

Since circumpositional phrases are constituents, they can be used adnominally, just like other adpositional phrases. The PP + particle combinations do not form a constituent, and, as a result, they cannot be used in this way.

(139) a. het geren achter de optocht aan
the running after the parade AAN
'the running after the parade'
b. de plaatsing op de tafel (*neer)
the placement on the table down

VI. Absolute met *construction*

In principle, the distribution of the *P* + *NP* + *P* sequences in absolute *met* constructions like (140a&b) could also be used as a test: the circumpositional phrase can be used as the predicate in this construction, whereas the PP + particle normally cannot.

(140) a. met de kinderen achter de optocht aan
with the children after the parade AAN
b. met de boeken op de tafel (*neer)
with the books on the table down

This test is less reliable, however, due to the fact that some particles, like *aan* in (141a), can also be used as the predicative part of the absolute *met* construction. As a result, we cannot conclude from the acceptability of (141b) that *over zijn kleren aan* is a circumpositional phrase; see Section 1.2.5.3, sub I, for more evidence. For this reason, we will not use the distribution of the *P + NP + P* sequences in absolute *met* constructions as a test to distinguish circumpositional phrases from verbal particles preceded by a prepositional phrase.

(141) a. met zijn toga aan
with his gown on
b. met zijn toga (over zijn kleren) aan
with his gown over his clothes on
'with his gown on over his clothes'

VII. Conclusion

Table 11 summarizes the findings with respect to the five tests we have developed in the previous subsections to distinguish circumpositional phrases from verbal particles preceded by a prepositional phrase. The first row indicates whether the sequence *P + NP* can be omitted, the second row whether this sequence can be replaced by an R-word, and the third row whether it can undergo PP-over-V, that is, whether the word order is fixed or not. The fourth row indicates whether the sequence *P + ... + P* can be topicalized in full and the final row indicates whether it can be used adnominally.

Table 11: Circumpositions vs. PP + Particle combinations

	CIRCUMPOSITION	PP + PARTICLE
OMISSION OF P + NP	—	+
PRONOMINALIZATION OF P +NP	—	+
PP-OVER-V OF P + NP	—	+
TOPICALIZATION OF P + NP + P	+	*?
ADNOMINAL USE OF P + NP + P	+	—

The five tests must be applied with care. More specifically, it is not the case that all PPs preceding a particle verb can be omitted, pronominalized and undergo PP-over-V; there may be independent reasons why these options are blocked. The PP + particle sequence in (142), for example, is fairly well behaved in that it gives a positive result to four of the five tests for assuming that we are dealing with a particle verb; it is only the pronominalization test in (142b) that fails, but this can, of course, be readily explained given that we are dealing not with a locational PP but with a comitative *met*-PP in (142a), which can never be pronominalized by *daar* 'there'. Note in passing that the number sign in (142b) indicates that this example is acceptable when *daar ... mee* is interpreted as an instrumental pronominal PP meaning "with it".

(142) a. dat Jan graag (met Marie) mee reed. [omission of P + NP]
that Jan gladly with Marie MEE drove
'that Jan drove gladly along with Marie.'
b. #dat Jan daar graag mee reed. [pronominalization of P + NP]
c. Met Marie <??mee> reed Jan graag <mee>. [Topicalization]
d. dat Jan graag mee reed met Marie. [PP-over-V]
e. de reis met Marie (*?mee) [adnominal use]
the journey with Marie MEE

The PP + particle sequence in (143) gives a positive result to only three of the five tests for assuming that we are dealing with a particle verb: the omission and pronominalization tests in (143a&b) fail. One might use this as evidence for claiming that we are dealing with a circumpositional phrase, which would imply that positive results for the other tests are not sufficient for arguing against a circumpositional phrase. It seems more plausible, however, to assume that the negative results in (143a&b) are due to the fact that the particle verb *toe zijn* obligatorily selects an *aan*-PP; the failure of the pronominalization test would then be in line with the fact that PP-complements of verbs cannot be pronominalized either. This means that we should take the data in (143c&e) as sufficient evidence for claiming that we are dealing with a particle verb.

(143) a. dat ik wel *(aan een borrel) toe ben. [omission of P + NP]
that I AFF to a drink TOE am
'that I could use a drink.'
b. *dat ik daar wel toe ben. [pronominalization of P + NP]
c. Aan een borrel <??toe> ben ik wel <toe>. [Topicalization]
d. dat ik wel toe ben aan een borrel. [PP-over-V]
e. de behoefte aan een borrel (*toe) [adnominal use]
the need for a drink TOE

The sequence *aan mij voorbij gaan* in (144), finally, satisfies just a single test in favor of assuming that we are dealing with a particle verb. The first two tests give a negative result in the sense that omission or pronominalization of the PP results in the loss of the idiomatic reading, which may again be related to the fact that the PP is selected by the particle verb. The fourth test gives a negative result in that PP-over-V of *aan mij* is highly marked. Since adnominal use is excluded regardless of whether *voorbij* is present or not, we cannot draw any firm conclusion from that either. Therefore, the decision as to whether we are dealing with a circumposition or a particle verb that takes a PP as its complement completely depends on the weight one would like to assign to the topicalization test.

(144) a. dat de lol #(aan mij) voorbij ging. [omission of P + NP]
that the fun to me past went
'that I couldn't see the fun.'
b. #dat de lol daar voorbij ging. [pronominalization of P + NP]
c. Aan mij <*voorbij> ging de lol <voorbij>. [Topicalization]
d. ??dat de lol voorbij ging aan mij. [PP-over-V]
e. *het gaan aan mij (voorbij) [adnominal use]

1.2.5.3. Application of the tests

This section will use the tests discussed in the previous section in order to establish whether the discontinuous sequences in Table 10 are indeed circumpositions. The tests are applied in the order discussed above.

I. P ... aan

The examples in (145) show that the sequence *achter de optocht aan* behaves like a circumpositional phrase: omission and pronominalization of the sequence *achter de optocht* are impossible, topicalization of *achter de optocht aan* is somewhat marked but seems possible, and PP-over-V is excluded. Finally, adnominal use of *achter de optocht aan* is possible.

(145) a. dat de kinderen *(achter de optocht) aan liepen. [omission of P + NP]
that the children after the parade AAN walked
'that the children followed the parade.'
b. *dat de kinderen daar aan liepen. [pronominalization of P + NP]
c. [?]Achter de optocht aan liepen de kinderen. [Topicalization]
d. *dat de kinderen aan liepen achter de optocht. [PP-over-V]
e. het geren achter de optocht aan [adnominal use]
the running after the parade AAN

The sequence *tegen de ladder aan* in (146) behaves essentially the same way, and we are again justified in assuming that we are dealing with a circumposition.

(146) a. dat Jan *(tegen de ladder) aan liep. [omission of P + NP]
that Jan against the ladder AAN walked
'that Jan ran into the ladder.'
b. *dat Jan daar aan liep. [pronominalization of P + NP]
c. [(?)]Tegen de ladder aan liep Jan. [Topicalization]
d. *dat Jan aan liep tegen de ladder. [PP-over-V]
e. de schop tegen de ladder aan [adnominal use]
the kick against the ladder AAN

The primeless examples in (147) show that the sequence *P + NP* cannot readily be topicalized, but the primed examples show that *wh*-movement seems to gives rise to a completely acceptable result.

(147) a. [*?]Achter de optocht liepen de kinderen aan.
a′. Achter welke optocht liepen de kinderen aan?
after which parade walked the children AAN
b. [*?]Tegen de ladder liep Jan aan.
b′. Tegen welke ladder liep Jan aan?
against which ladder walked Jan AAN

This shows again that the ban on topicalization of the *P + NP* sequence is not of a syntactic nature. This conclusion is supported by the examples in (148), which show that the verb of location *staan* 'to stand' and the verb of change of location *zetten* 'to put' do allow topicalization of the *P + NP* sequence. It is not clear what causes the contrasts between the primeless examples in (147) and the examples in (148).

(148) a. Tegen de muur staat een ladder aan.
against the wall stands a ladder AAN
'The ladder is standing against the wall.'
b. Tegen de muur zette Jan een oude ladder aan.
against the wall put Jan an old ladder AAN
'Jan put an old ladder against the wall.'

Not all sequences of the form *P + NP + aan* must be analyzed as circumpositional phrases. Consider the examples in (149a) and (150a), which clearly do not involve circumpositions but the particle verb *aan trekken* 'to put on', which is preceded by the prepositional phrases *over zijn kleren* 'over his clothes' and *onder zijn toga* 'underneath his gown'. There are several indications that support this. First, *aan* can be used as a verbal particle; the (a)-examples show that dropping the sequence *P + NP* does not affect the core meaning of the clause. Second, the sequence *P + NP + aan* cannot be topicalized as a whole, that is, the phrases *over zijn kleren* and *onder zijn toga* cannot be pied piped by topicalization of the element *aan*. Third, the phrases *over zijn kleren* and *onder zijn toga* can be placed in clause-final position as the result of PP-over-V. Finally, the sequence *P + NP + aan* cannot be used in adnominal position.

(149) a. dat hij zijn toga (over zijn kleren) aan trok. [omission of P + NP]
that he his gown over his clothes on put
'He put on his gown over his clothes.'
b. *Over zijn kleren aan trok hij zijn toga. [Topicalization]
b′. Over zijn kleren trok hij zijn toga aan.
c. dat hij zijn toga aan trok over zijn kleren. [PP-over-V]
d. de toga over zijn kleren (*aan) [adnominal use]
the gown over his clothes AAN

(150) a. dat hij een spijkerbroek (onder zijn toga) aan trok. [omission of P + NP]
that he a jean under his gown on put
'He put on jeans under his gown.'
b. *Onder zijn toga aan trok hij een spijkerbroek. [Topicalization]
b′. Onder zijn toga trok hij een spijkerbroek aan.
c. dat hij een spijkerbroek aan trok onder zijn toga. [PP-over-V]
d. de spijkerbroek onder zijn toga (*aan) [adnominal use]
the jean under his gown AAN

Note in passing that Helmantel (2002: appendix) includes examples like (151a&b) as grammatical. For these cases, we cannot assume that *aan* is a particle, because the verb *dragen* 'to wear' cannot be combined with the particle *aan* under the intended reading. According to us, however, the examples in (151a&b) are only acceptable without the particle. For completeness' sake, note that Helmantel also gives example (151c) as acceptable; according to us, it is the circumposition *voor ... uit* that would normally be used in this case.

(151) a. Hij droeg een toga over zijn kleren %(aan).
he wore a gown over his clothes AAN
b. Hij droeg een spijkerbroek onder zijn toga %(aan).
he wore jeans under his gown AAN
c. %Voor de optocht aan liep de fanfare.
in.front.of the parade AAN walked the brass-band

II. P ... af

The only circumpositions with *af* as their second member are *van ... af* and *op ... af*. Example (152) shows that the sequence *van ... af* satisfies all the tests for circumpositionhood, although the result of the pronominalization test is perhaps not as unequivocal as one might hope; (152b) is perhaps slightly marked. The (c)-examples show that topicalization of the *P + NP* sequence is degraded, but that *wh*-movement is allowed.

(152) a. dat Jan *(van het dak) af sprong. [omission of P + NP]
that Jan from the roof AF jumped
b. ?dat Jan daar af sprong. [pronominalization of + NP]
that Jan there AF jumped
c. ?Van het dak af sprong Jan. [Topicalization]
c′. ?Van het dak sprong Jan af.
c″. Van welk dak sprong Jan af? [*Wh*-movement]
from which roof jumped Jan AF
'From which roof did Jan jump?'
d. *dat Jan af sprong van het dak. [PP-over-V]
e. de sprong van het dak af [adnominal use]
the jump from the roof AF

In (153), we give similar examples for the sequence *op ... af*. Example (153b) is acceptable, but not with the intended meaning.

(153) a. dat de tijger *(op het hert) af sprong. [omission of P + NP]
that the tiger towards the deer AF jumped
'that the tiger jumped towards the deer.'
b. #dat de tijger daar af sprong. [pronominalization of P + NP]
that the tiger there AF jumped
c. ?Op het hert af sprong de tijger. [Topicalization]
c′. ?Op het hert sprong de tijger af.
c″. Op welk hert sprong de tijger af? [*Wh*-movement]
towards which deer jumped the tiger AF
'Towards which deer did the tiger jump?'
d. *dat de tijger af sprong op het hert. [PP-over-V]
e. de sprong op het hert af [adnominal use]
the jump towards the deer AF

Again, the results in (152) do not imply that the sequence *van* + NP + *af* is always a circumpositional phrase. In (154), we are clearly dealing with the particle verb *aftrekken* 'to deduct' preceded by an (optional) *van*-PP: the sequence *van het loon af* cannot be placed in clause-initial position, whereas the *van*-PP can be topicalized in isolation without any difficulty and can also be placed after the particle verb by means of PP-over-V.

(154) a. De baas heeft drie euro (van het loon) af getrokken.
the boss has three Euros from the wage prt. deducted
'The boss deducted three Euros from the wages.'
b. *Van het loon af heeft de baas drie euro getrokken.
b′. Van het loon heeft de baas drie euro af getrokken.
c. De baas heeft drie euro afgetrokken van het loon.

III. P ... door

Sequences of the type *P + NP + door* in (155a) and (156a) seem to act as well-behaved circumpositional phrases, although some discussion is needed. The (a)-examples show that the sequence *P + NP* can be dropped, but only at the expense of a change of meaning; the (a)-examples then receive the meaning "to continue to drive". The (b)-examples are also acceptable, but involve R-extraction from a prepositional *door*-phrase, not pronominalization of the *onder*-PP. Topicalization of the full sequence *P + NP + door* is somewhat marked but seems possible. In contrast, topicalization of the sequence *P + NP* is unacceptable (the c′-examples are only marginally possible with the meaning "to continue to drive" and with the topicalized phrase acting as an adverbial PP of place), but *wh*-movement is fully acceptable. As expected, PP-over-V is excluded and the sequence *P + NP + door* can be used adnominally.

(155) a. dat Jan #(onder de brug) door reed. [omission of P + NP]
that Jan under the bridge DOOR drove
'That Jan drove underneath the bridge.'
b. #dat Jan daar door reed. [pronominalization of P + NP]
c. ?Onder de brug door reed Jan. [Topicalization]
c′. *?Onder de brug reed Jan door.
c″. Onder welke brug reed Jan door? [*Wh*-movement]
under which bridge drove Jan DOOR
'Under which bridge did Jan drive?'
d. *dat Jan door reed onder de brug. [PP-over-V]
e. de weg onder de brug door [adnominal use]
the road under the bridge DOOR

(156) a. dat Jan #(tussen de bomen) door reed. [omission of P + NP]
that Jan between the trees DOOR drove
'that Jan drove through the trees.'
b. #dat Jan daar door reed. [pronominalization of P + NP]
c. ?Tussen de bomen door reed Jan. [Topicalization]
c′. *?Tussen de bomen reed Jan door.
c″. Tussen welke bomen reed Jan door? [*Wh*-movement]
between which trees drove Jan DOOR
'Through which trees did Jan drive?'

d. *dat Jan door reed tussen de bomen. [PP-over-V]
e. de weg tussen de bomen door [adnominal use]
the road between the trees DOOR

IV. P ... heen

The sequence *om de boom heen* in (157a) seems to act as a well-behaved circumpositional phrase. The sequence *om de boom* can marginally be dropped, but this changes the meaning of the example: *heen* must then be interpreted as "away" and the marginal status of the resulting sentence is due to the fact that this use of *heen* has an archaic flavor. Example (157b) is acceptable too, but again this has an effect on the meaning: *ergens heen rijden* receives the interpretation "to go somewhere/to someone"; see the discussion in Section 1.3.1.4, sub IV. The (c)-examples show that topicalization of the full sequence *om de boom heen* is marked but acceptable. Topicalization of the sequence *om de boom*, on the other hand, leads to a degraded result, but *wh*-movement is fully acceptable. Examples (157d&e), finally, show that PP-over-V is excluded and that adnominal use of the sequence *om de boom heen* is possible. Other sequences of the form P + NP + *heen* behave in the same way.

(157) a. dat Jan #(om de boom) heen reed. [omission of P + NP]
that Jan around the tree HEEN drove
'that Jan drove around the tree.'
b. #dat Jan daar heen reed. [pronominalization of P + NP]
c. ?Om de boom heen reed Jan. [Topicalization]
c′. *?Om de boom reed Jan heen.
c″. Om welke boom reed Jan heen? [*Wh*-movement]
around which tree drove Jan HEEN
'Around which tree did Jan drive?'
d. *dat Jan heen reed om de boom. [PP-over-V]
e. het paadje om de boom heen [adnominal use]
the path around the tree HEEN

V. P ... in

The sequence *tussen die twee meisjes in* in (158) also behaves like a circumpositional phrase. Example (158a) shows that omission of the *P + NP* sequence is impossible. Example (158b) is grammatical but is clearly derived from a prepositional phrase headed by *in*: Jan is claimed to be inside some object. Topicalization of the sequence *tussen die twee meisjes in* is acceptable, whereas topicalization of *tussen die twee meisjes* is degraded; as always, *wh*-movement of the sequence *P + NP* is fully acceptable. Further, PP-over-V is excluded and adnominal use of the sequence *tussen die meisjes in* is fully acceptable. The sequence *tegen + NP + in* behaves in a similar way.

(158) a. dat Jan *(tussen die twee meisjes) in zit. [omission of P + NP]
that Jan between those two girls IN sits
'that Jan is sitting between those two girls.'
b. #dat Jan daar in zit. [pronominalization of P + NP]

c. [?]Tussen die twee meisjes in zit Jan. [Topicalization]
c′. [*?]Tussen die twee meisjes zit Jan in.
c″. Tussen welke twee meisjes zit Jan in? [*Wh*-movement]
between which two girls sits Jan IN
d. *dat Jan in zit tussen twee meisjes. [PP-over-V]
e. de jongen tussen die twee meisjes in [adnominal use]
the boy between those two girls IN

VI. P ... langs

The sequence *achter het huis langs* in (159a) behaves like a circumpositional phrase. Example (159a) is excluded without the sequence *P* + *NP*. Example (159b) is grammatical, but only when it is derived from a prepositional phrase headed by *langs* as in *dat de muur langs het huis loopt* 'that the wall goes along the side of the house'. The status of the examples in (159c&c′) is as expected, but, surprisingly, the *wh*-construction in (159c″) is degraded as well. As expected, PP-over-V is excluded and adnominal use of the sequence *achter het huis langs* is possible. The other circumpositions with *langs* as their second member behave in a similar way.

(159) a. dat het muurtje *(achter het huis) langs loopt. [omission of P + NP]
that the small wall behind the house LANGS extends
'that a wall extends along the back of the house.'
b. [#]dat het muurtje daar langs loopt. [pronominalization of P + NP]
c. Achter het huis langs loopt het muurtje. [Topicalization]
c′. *Achter het huis loopt het muurtje langs.
c″. [*?]Achter welk huis loopt het muurtje langs? [*Wh*-movement]
behind which house extends a little wall LANGS
d. *dat het muurtje langs loopt achter het huis. [PP-over-V]
e. het muurtje achter het huis langs [adnominal use]
the little wall behind the house LANGS

The examples in (160) show that *langs* can also be used as a verbal particle. Examples like these involve the verbs *komen* 'to come' and *gaan* 'to go', or verbs of traversing like *rijden* 'to drive'. The meaning of the particle verb is approximately "to drop by/to pay a visit". These particle verbs optionally take a *bij*-PP that expresses the goal of the visit. That examples like (160a) do not involve a circumposition, but rather the particle *langs* preceded by a *bij*-PP, is clear from the following facts. Examples (160a&b) show that the *bij*-PP can be omitted and pronominalized without changing the core meaning of the sentence. The (c)-examples in (160) show that topicalization of the sequence *bij* + *NP* must strand *langs*. Example (160d), finally, shows that the *bij*-PP can be placed after the particle *langs* by means of PP-over-V.

(160) a. dat ik morgen toch (bij hem) langs kom/ga. [omission of P + NP]
that I tomorrow anyway with him along come/go
'that I will pay him a visit tomorrow anyway.'
b. dat ik daar morgen toch langs kom/ga. [pronominalization of P + NP]
c. [*?]Bij hem langs kom/ga ik morgen toch. [Topicalization]
c′. Bij hem kom/ga ik morgen toch langs.
d. [(?)]dat ik morgen toch langs kom/ga bij hem. [PP-over-V]

VII. P ... om

The sequence *achter het huis om* in (161a) also behaves like a circumpositional phrase. The string *achter het huis* can be omitted, but this gives rise to a change of meaning into "to make a detour". Example (161b) is perhaps marginally acceptable, but then it is clearly related to a construction involving an adpositional phrase headed by the preposition *om*. The judgments on the examples in (161c) are again as expected, although the *wh*-question in (161c″) is somewhat marked. Examples (161d&e), finally, show that PP-over-V is excluded and that the sequence *achter het huis om* can be used adnominally. The other circumpositions with *om* as their second member behave in a way similar to *achter ... om*.

(161) a. dat Jan #(achter het huis) om liep. [omission of P + NP]
that Jan around the house OM walked
'that Jan walked around the back of the house.'
b. #dat Jan daar om liep. [pronominalization of P + NP]
c. ?Achter het huis om liep Jan. [Topicalization]
c′. *Achter het huis liep Jan om.
c″. ?Achter welk huis liep Jan om? [*Wh*-movement]
behind which house walked Jan OM
'Around the back of which house did Jan walk?'
d. *dat Jan om liep achter het huis. [PP-over-V]
e. het paadje achter het huis om [adnominal use]
the path around the back of the house OM

VIII. Tegen ... op

The sequence *tegen de muur op* in (162) acts as a well-behaved circumpositional phrase. The string *tegen de muur* can be dropped but this gives rise to a different (idiomatic) meaning: "to climbed the corporate ladder". The construction in (162b) is acceptable but is clearly related to a construction involving a prepositional phrase headed by *op*: it is expressed that Jan climbed onto some object. The judgments on the topicalization and *wh*-constructions in (162c) are as usual. PP-over-V is excluded, and adnominal use of the sequence *tegen de muur op* is possible.

(162) a. dat Marie #(tegen de muur) op klom. [omission of P + NP]
that Marie against the wall OP climbed
'that Marie climbed up against the wall.'
b. #dat Marie daar op klom. [pronominalization of P + NP]
c. ?Tegen de muur op klom Marie. [Topicalization]
c′. *?Tegen de muur klom Marie op.
c″. Tegen welke muur klom Marie op? [*Wh*-movement]
against which wall climbed Marie OP
'Against which wall did Marie climb?'
d. *dat Marie op klom tegen de muur. [PP-over-V]
e. de sprong tegen de muur op [adnominal use]
the jump against the wall OP

The results in (162) do not imply that the sequence *tegen* + *NP* + *op* is always a circumpositional phrase. In (163), we are clearly dealing with a particle verb *op zien* that takes a *tegen*-PP as an obligatory complement. The PP *tegen de ontmoeting* cannot be pronominalized, but this is due to the fact that it is not locational. The facts that the particle *op* must be stranded under topicalization and can be followed by the sequence *tegen de ontmoeting op* as a result of PP-over-V clearly show that we are not dealing with a circumposition.

(163) a. dat Marie *(tegen de ontmoeting) op zag. [omission of P + NP]
that Marie against the meeting OP saw
'that Marie didn't like the idea of the meeting.'
b. dat Marie daar *(tegen) op zag. [pronominalization of P + NP]
c. *Tegen de ontmoeting op zag Marie niet. [Topicalization]
c′. Tegen de ontmoeting zag Marie niet op.
d. dat Marie op zag tegen de ontmoeting. [PP-over-V]

IX. P ... toe

The sequence *naar oma toe* in (164) behaves in all respects like a circumpositional phrase. The same thing holds for the sequence *tot (aan) ... toe*, which will not be illustrated here.

(164) a. dat Marie *(naar oma) toe gaat. [omission of P + NP]
that Marie to granny TOE goes
'that Marie goes to granny.'
b. dat Marie daar *(naar) toe gaat. [pronominalization of P + NP]
c. ?Naar oma toe gaat Marie. [Topicalization]
c′. *?Naar oma gaat Marie toe.
c″. Naar wie gaat Marie toe? [*Wh*-movement]
to whom goes Marie TOE
'To whom is Marie going?'
d. *dat Marie toe gaat naar oma. [PP-over-V]
e. de wandeling naar oma toe [adnominal use]
the walk to granny TOE

The examples in (143), however, have already shown that not all sequences of the form *P ... toe* can be considered a circumposition: the string *aan een borrel toe* in *Ik ben aan een borrel toe* 'I need a drink' must be analyzed as a PP followed by a verbal particle.

X. P ... uit

The sequence *onder haar jas uit* in (165a) seems to behave like a circumpositional phrase. First the sequence *onder haar jas* cannot be omitted. Example (165b) without *onder* is acceptable, but is clearly related to a construction with an adpositional phrase headed by the preposition *uit*: it is simply expressed that the border of her skirt sticks out of something. The topicalization and *wh*-examples are all somewhat marked, but exhibit the generally attested contrasts. The impossibility of PP-over-V is expected. The adnominal use of the sequence *onder haar jas uit* is, however, somewhat marked. The other circumpositions with *uit* as their second member behave in a way similar to *onder ... uit*.

(165) a. dat de voering *(onder haar jas) uit hing/stak. [omission of P + NP]
that the lining under her coat UIT hung/stuck
'that the lining was sticking out from under her coat.'
b. #dat de voering daar uit hing/stak. [pronominalization of P + NP]
c. ?Onder haar jas uit hing/stak de voering. [Topicalization]
c′. *Onder haar jas hing/stak de voering uit.
c″. (?)Onder welke jas hing/stak de voering uit? [*Wh*-movement]
under which coat hung/stuck the lining UIT
d. *dat de voering uit hing/stak onder haar rok. [PP-over-V]
e. ??de voering onder haar jas uit [adnominal use]
the lining under her coat UIT

It must be noted that *uit hangen/steken* can also be used as a particle verb. This is illustrated in (166a). This means that (166b) is ambiguous between a reading that involves a particle verb and an adverbially used PP, and a reading involving a predicatively used circumpositional phrase.

(166) a. De vlag hangt/steekt uit.
the flag hangs/sticks out
'The flag is hanging/sticking out.'
b. De vlag hangt/steekt boven de huizen uit.
the flag hangs/sticks above the houses out

XI. P ... vandaan

The examples in (167) show that the sequence *achter de bomen vandaan* seems to behave as a circumpositional phrase in most respects. The only anomalous fact is that pronominalization of the PP seems to be possible. It must be noted, however, that *daar vandaan komen* acts as the antonym of *daar heen gaan*, which is shown to be an idiomatic expression in Section 1.3.1.4, sub IV. Therefore, it seems plausible that *daar vandaan komen* is an idiomatic expression, too.

(167) a. dat Marie achter de bomen vandaan kwam. [omission of P + NP]
that Marie behind the trees VANDAAN came
'that Marie came from behind the trees.'
b. dat Jan daar vandaan kwam. [pronominalization of P + NP]
c. Achter de bomen vandaan kwam Marie. [Topicalization]
c′. *?Achter de bomen kwam Marie vandaan.
c″. Achter welke boom kwam Marie vandaan? [*Wh*-movement]
behind which tree came Marie VANDAAN
'From behind which tree did Marie come?'
d. *dat Marie vandaan kwam achter de bomen. [PP-over-V]
e. de sprong achter de boom vandaan [adnominal use]
the jump behind the tree VANDAAN
'the jump from behind the tree'

XII. Summary

In this section, we have applied the five tests from Section 1.2.5.2 to the formations in Table 10, which are traditionally analyzed as circumpositional phrases. The results are summarized in Table 12 by means of the grammaticality judgments given earlier. The second column shows that in many cases, omission of the *P + NP* sequence is acceptable, although this invariantly results in a shift of meaning; the resulting structure involves a particle verb. The third column shows that replacement of the *P + NP* sequence by an R-word is often possible as well, but again this results in a shift of meaning; the resulting structures are generally derived by R-extraction from a prepositional phrase, and do not involve pronominalization of the *P + NP* sequence; in two cases the resulting structure involves an idiomatic expression. Topicalization of the circumpositional phrase is normally somewhat marked, but this seems to be related to non-syntactic factors; the table does not show that topicalization of the string *P + NP* generally seems to be blocked whereas *wh*-movement of the same string is generally possible. The tests involving PP-over-V and adnominal use of the sequence *P + NP* provide the clearest evidence in favor of the claim that the investigated sequences are circumpositional: PP-over-V of the sequence *P + NP* is excluded in all cases and adnominal use of the circumpositional phrase is virtually always possible.

Table 12: Results of the circumposition tests

2ND MEMBER	OMISSION OF P + NP	PRONOMINALIZATION OF P +NP	TOPICALIZATION OF P + .. + P	PP-OVER-V OF P + NP	ADNOMINAL USE OF P + .. + P
aan	*	*	?	*	+
af	*	?	?	*	+
door	#	#	?	*	+
heen	#	# (idiomatic)	?	*	+
in	*	#	?	*	+
langs	#	#	+	*	+
om	#	#	?	*	+
op	#	#	?	*	+
toe	*	*	?	*	+
uit	*/#	#	?	*	??
vandaan	*	# (idiomatic)	?	*	+

The results therefore show that the traditional view is close to the mark. We must repeat again, however, that even when we have shown that a certain string of the form *Px ... Py* is a circumpositional phrase, this does not imply that all other strings of the form *Px ... Py* involve circumpositional phrases as well; each construction must be investigated in its own right, and we have discussed several cases, in which superficially similar strings of words had to be analyzed differently.

1.2.6. The relation between the four main classes of adpositions

To conclude the discussion of the formal classification of adpositions, we want to discuss the structural relation between the four main classes that we have distinguished. Since this is not a well-studied topic, much of what will be said here is highly speculative and must be seen as no more than a first indication of what the structure of adpositional phrases may look like. Some recent studies attributed to this issue, like Van Riemsdijk (1978/1990), Koopman (1997) and Den Dikken (2003), indicate that the correct analysis may in fact be much more intricate than suggested here.

We start by discussing the relation between pre- and postpositions. One way of describing the difference between the two is by saying that the first take their nominal complement to their right, whereas the latter take their complement to their left. Since we have seen that the postpositions are a proper subset of the prepositions, this can be formalized by assuming the lexical entries in (168): (168a) expresses that adpositions that can be used as prepositions only take their complement to their right, whereas adpositions that can be used either as pre- or as postpositions can take their complement either to their right or to their left.

(168) a. preposition: __ NP
b. postposition: __ NP or NP __

A problem for the proposal in (168) is that the pre- and postpositional phrases differ in meaning: the first typically denote a (change of) location, whereas the latter denote a direction. In German, this difference is not expressed by means of word order but by means of case marking: both locational and directional adpositions are prepositional, but the locational adpositions assign dative, whereas the directional ones assign accusative case. Given that German and Dutch are so closely related, this casts doubt on the lexical entry in (168b). It may be the case that in Dutch also, the directional adpositions take their complement to their right, but that, due to the fact that Dutch has no morphological case, the nominal complement must be moved to the left of the adposition in order to signal the directional meaning of the postposition. This gives rise to the movement analysis in (169b).

(169) a. preposition: __ NP
b. postposition: __ NP
a′. prepositional phrase: [P NP]
b′. postpositional phrase: NP_i [P t_i]

The proposal in (169) can perhaps be supported by the fact that the complement of a preposition cannot be scrambled or topicalized, whereas the complement of a postposition can: this would be surprising if they both occupy the complement position of the adposition but would follow in a natural way if we assume that the base-position of the noun phrase in (169a′) is not accessible to these operations, whereas the derived position in (169b′) is. The relevant data are given in (170).

(170) a. Jan zat daarnet in de boom.
Jan sat just.now in the tree
'Jan sat in the tree just now.'
a′. *Jan zat de boom daarnet in.
a″. *De boom zat Jan daarnet in.

b. Jan klom daarnet de boom in.
Jan climbed just.now the tree into
'Jan climbed into the tree just now.'
b′. Jan klom de boom daarnet in.
b″. De boom klom Jan daarnet in.

If the movement analysis of postpositional phrases in (169b′) is tenable, a similar analysis may be feasible for circumpositional phrases. Instead of assuming that circumpositions are discontinuous heads, as is done in traditional grammar, one may assume that circumpositional phrases actually consist of an adposition which takes a PP as its complement, which (for some reason) must be moved leftwards: see, e.g., Zwart (1993:365ff.) and Claessen & Zwarts (2010}

(171) a. circumposition: __ PP
b. circumpositional phrase: PP_i [P t_i]

The analysis in (171) has several potential advantages. First, it may account for the fact that the PP-part in (171) must have a form that can also be used independently as a prepositional phrase. Second, the analysis in (171) leaves open the possibility that not all prepositions can occur as the second member of circumpositional phrases and that there are certain elements that may occur as the second member (= the P-part in (171b)) of a circumpositional phrase but cannot be used as a preposition. This would follow if we assume that, just as in the case of verbs, complementation of adpositions is lexically constrained; adpositions like *voor*, which can only occur as prepositions, have the categorial frame in (172a), adpositions like *heen* or *vandaan*, which can only occur as the second member of a circumposition, have the categorial frame in (172b), and adpositions like *aan*, which can be used both as a preposition and as the second member of a circumposition, have the categorial frame in (172c).

(172) a. preposition: __ NP
b. circumposition: __ PP
c. preposition or circumposition: __ $\begin{Bmatrix} \text{NP} \\ \text{PP} \end{Bmatrix}$

Third, the movement analysis in (171b) predicts that circumpositional phrases can be split; just like the nominal complement of a postposition, the prepositional complement can be moved further leftwards. This may happen when the prepositional phrase contains a nominal *wh*-phrase, as in (173), which is taken from Section 1.2.5. The question why topicalization of the prepositional complement generally gives rise to a marked result remains unanswered under this analysis.

(173) Achter welke optocht liepen de kinderen aan?
behind which parade walked the children AAN
'After which parade did the children run?'

Finally, the analysis in (171b) may account for the fact that *toe* occurs both as the second member of circumpositional phrases and as the counterpart of *tot* in pronominalized PPs like *er ... toe* in example (174b). All that is needed is to claim that circumpositional phrases and pronominal PPs are both derived by leftward movement of the complements of the adpositions, and that the use of *toe* (instead of *tot*) is a morphological reflex of these movements.

(174) a. dat Jan Marie steeds tot diefstal verleidt.
that Jan Marie all.the.time to theft tempts
'that Jan is tempting Marie to theft all the time.'
b. dat Jan Marie *er* steeds *toe* verleidt.

A potential problem for the assumption that circumpositions are the result of leftward PP-movement is that movement is often assumed to give rise to °Freezing:

the moved phrase becomes an island for extraction. The data concerning R-extraction from circumpositional phrases seem to go against this: the proposal in (171) implies that the PP *bij de koffie* in (175a) occupies its base position, but nevertheless R-extraction is excluded; the PP *over het hek* in (175b), on the other hand, is claimed to have moved leftward, but nevertheless R-extraction is possible from circumpositional phrases like *over het hek heen*; cf. Section 1.2.5 for a more detailed discussion of R-extraction.

(175) a. Die koekjes zijn voor bij de koffie.
Jan bought biscuits for with the coffee
'Those biscuits are intended to be eaten with the coffee.'
a′. *Die koekjes zijn daar voor bij.
b. Jan sprong over het hek heen.
Jan jumped over the fence HEEN
b′. Jan sprong er over heen.

However, it has been suggested that Dutch clauses also have an underlying head-complement order. If that is indeed correct, the preverbal position of a PP-complement is also a derived position, so that in this case also, Freezing is expected. The examples in (176) show, however, that R-extraction is possible from the preverbal position; it is instead R-extraction from postverbal PPs that is impossible.

(176)			
a.	dat Jan wacht op de post. that Jan waits for the post	a′.	*dat Jan er wacht op. that Jan there waits for
b.	dat Jan op de post wacht. that Jan for the post waits	b′.	*dat Jan er op wacht. that Jan there for waits

This means that under the assumption that Dutch has underlying head-complement order, the freezing effect cannot be assumed to arise with all types of movement: PP-movement resulting in the PP-V order or the surface order of circumpositional phrases must be assumed not to give rise to it; the (a)- and (b)-patterns in (177) must then receive a similar analysis. We leave this suggestion for further research.

(177) a. *daar$_i$ ... V [$_{PP}$ P t_i] [cf. (176a′)]
a′. daar$_i$ ... [$_{PP}$ P t_i]$_j$ V t_j [cf. (176b′)]
b. *daar$_i$ ... P [$_{PP}$ P t_i] [cf. (175a′)]
b′. daar$_i$ ... [$_{PP}$ P t_i]$_j$ P t_j [cf. (175b′)]

We conclude with a brief remark about the relation between intransitive adpositions and particles. We have seen that the former probably function as the heads of regular adpositional phrases, and that they are only special in that they do not take a complement, or may leave their complement implicit. This does not hold for particles, however. One difference between particles and all other classes of adpositions is that particles are not able to assign case, as is clear from the fact that their arguments are typically assigned accusative case by the verb or nominative case in the subject position of the clause, just like the logical SUBJECTs of other predicatively used adpositional phrases. There are two analyses that seem compatible with this observation. According to the first analysis, particles are just like intransitive adpositions in that they do not take a complement, which of course raises the question why they exhibit behavior different from intransitive adpositions. According to the second analysis, particles are like °unaccusative verbs in that they do take a complement but are not able to assign case to it, for which reason it must be moved into the case-assigning domain of the verb. Arguments in favor of the second approach can be found in Den Dikken (1995).

1.3. A semantic classification of adpositional phrases

This section provides a semantic classification of the adpositions. We distinguish the three main groups in (178). These three groups will be discussed in the sections indicated between parentheses, where we will divide them further into several subclasses.

(178) a. Spatial adpositions (Section 1.3.1)
 b. Temporal adpositions (Section 1.3.2)
 c. Non-spatial/temporal adpositions (Section 1.3.3)

We will also attempt to give a semantic characterization of the individual adpositions in this section. Due to the fact that detailed studies of the semantics of individual prepositions are lacking, many of the semantic characterizations will be rough and imprecise, and can certainly be refined in the future; what is given here should be seen as no more than a first attempt that can certainly be improved upon.

1.3.1. Spatial adpositions

This section provides a semantic classification of the spatial adpositions; we will confine our discussion mainly to PPs that are used as complementives. Section 1.3.1.1 will start by discussing the relevant notions for the classification and Sections 1.3.1.2 to 1.3.1.5 will subsequently discuss the semantic classification of the spatial pre-, post- and circumpositions and the particles. Section 1.3.1.6, finally, discusses some alternative means of expressing spatial notions. Note that spatial prepositions are sometimes also used as modifiers of noun phrases containing a numeral as in *tegen de duizend boeken* 'nearly a thousand books' and *over de duizend boeken* 'more than a thousand books'. These cases will not be discussed here but in Section N5.1.4.4.2.

1.3.1.1. The semantics of spatial adpositions

This section discusses the semantics of spatial adpositions. We start in Section 1.3.1.1.1 by briefly discussing the central semantic notions of (change of) location and direction. Section 1.3.1.1.2 will show that spatial adpositions can be interpreted in three different ways, which we will refer to as deictic, inherent and absolute. Sections 1.3.1.1.3 and 1.3.1.1.4 will argue that the mathematical notion of a vector is very useful to properly describe the semantics of spatial adpositions. Section 1.3.1.1.5, finally, will go somewhat deeper into the notion of a path that enters the definition of directional PPs.

1.3.1.1.1. (Change of) location and direction

Spatial adpositions like *op* 'on' in (179) can normally be used in two distinct contexts. Example (179a) is ambiguous between two readings: according to the first reading, Jan is situated on the table and he is jumping there; according to the second reading, Jan is performing the action of jumping as the result of which he ends up in a different location, viz., on the table. The ambiguity of (179) is resolved when the clause is put in the perfect tense: when the auxiliary *hebben* is used, as in (179b), only the first reading survives; when the auxiliary *zijn* is used, as in (179c), only the second reading survives.

(179) a. Jan springt op de tafel. [location or change of location]
Jan jumps on(to) the table
b. Jan heeft op de tafel gesprongen. [location]
Jan has on the table jumped
c. Jan is op de tafel gesprongen. [change of location]
Jan has onto the table jumped

It sometimes claimed that these two different readings are due to the adposition *op* itself, that is, that we are dealing with two homonymic adpositions which denote, respectively, a location and a change of location. We will not adopt this position, but instead assume that the specific interpretation of the adposition is due to the verb that is used: when *springen* selects the auxiliary *hebben* it is used as an atelic verb, and hence no change of location is implied; when *springen* selects *zijn* it is used as a °telic verb, and hence a change of location is implied. This would be consistent with the fact, illustrated in (180), that most spatial PPs can be used as complements both of locational verbs like *liggen* 'to lie' and *staan* 'to stand' and of verbs of change of location like *leggen* and *zetten* 'to put'. This shows that adpositions of the sort in (180) are compatible both with a location and with a change of location reading.

(180) a. De lamp staat bij/naast/onder/op de tafel. [location]
the lamp stands near/next.to/under/on the table
'The lamp is standing near/next to/under/on the table.'
a′. De ladder ligt achter/langs/tegen de muur.
the ladder lies behind/along/against the wall
'The ladder is lying behind/along/against the wall.'
b. Jan zet de lamp bij/naast/onder/op de tafel. [change of location]
Jan puts the lamp near/next.to/under/on the table
'Jan is putting the lamp near/next to/under/on the table.'
b′. Jan legt de ladder achter/langs/tegen de muur.
Jan puts the ladder behind/along/against the wall
'Jan is putting the ladder behind/along/against the wall.'

A small number of spatial adpositions are exceptional in that they cannot occur as complements of verbs of (change of) location. These adpositions intrinsically denote a path (cf. Section 1.3.1.1.5), and since we define the notion of direction as "movement along a path", we will refer to such adpositions as DIRECTIONAL adpositions. Directional PPs typically occur as the complement of verbs of traversing (verbs that denote movement along a certain path), such as *rijden* 'to drive'. In (181) an example is given with the preposition *naar* 'to'.

(181) Jan rijdt naar Groningen. [direction]
Jan drives to Groningen
'Jan is driving to Groningen.'

Since the examples in (180) show that the difference between the location and change of location reading of the spatial adpositions is due to the syntactic environment (here: the verb), we may assume that spatial PPs headed by non-directional spatial adpositions simply refer to some point or region in space. We will therefore simply use the notion LOCATIONAL adposition for such non-directional spatial adpositions.

1.3.1.1.2. Deictic, inherent and absolute interpretations

The basic meaning contribution of the locational adpositions is that they establish a spatial relation between two entities. The locational prepositional phrase *in het huis* 'in the house' in (182), for example, situates the subject of the clause *Jan* in space, which we may therefore call the LOCATED OBJECT (other terms found in the literature on spatial relations are *theme*, *figure* and *trajectory*). More precisely, the located object is situated in space with respect to the complement of the preposition *het huis* 'the house', which we may therefore call the REFERENCE OBJECT (other terms found in the literature are *ground* and *landmark*). The precise nature of the spatial relation is determined by the lexical meaning of the locational preposition *in* 'in'; the relation would have been different if we had used *voor* 'in front of' instead of *in*. Therefore, as a first approximation, it seems reasonable to consider the preposition *in* as a two-place predicate, and assign the clause in (182a) the meaning in (182b).

(182) a. Jan is in het huis.
Jan is in the house
b. IN (Jan, het huis)

The meaning assignment to the clause in (182a) seems rather straightforward: Jan is situated inside the house. In some cases, however, things are not that simple. There are actually three different ways in which locational prepositions can be interpreted.

I. The deictic interpretation

Consider example (183a). Assigning this example the semantic representation in (183b) seems to somehow miss the point; see the discussion in Subsection II for an account of this. This representation only establishes a relation between the located and the reference object, whereas a third participant seems to be involved: a speaker who utters (183a) seems to compute the position of Jan in relation to both the tree and himself. Example (183a) refers to the situation in Figure 1B; the situation in Figure 1A seems somehow undefined.

(183) a. Jan staat voor de boom.
Jan stands in.front.of the tree
b. VOOR (Jan, de boom)

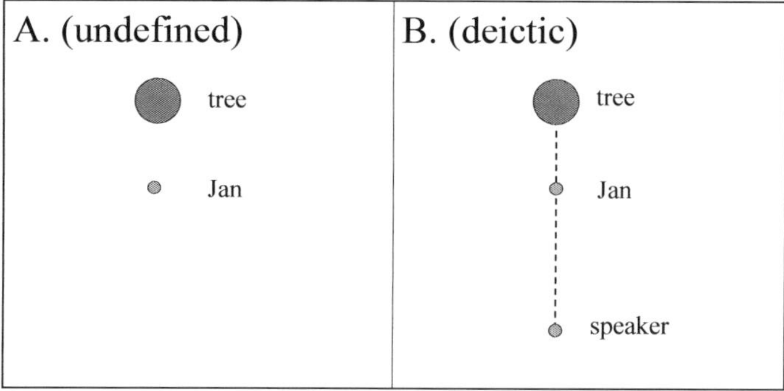

Figure 1: Jan staat voor de boom *'Jan is standing in front of the tree'*

The interpretation in Figure 1B, which is dependent on some additional ANCHORING POINT that also enters into the computation of the location of the located object, is called DEICTIC. When an adpositional phrase is interpreted deictically, we will indicate this in the semantic representation by means of a D in superscript after the adposition: P^{D} (x,y). That we are dealing with the anchoring point z can be indicated as follows: $P^{D,z}$ (x,y). Example (183a), that is, the situation depicted in Figure 1B, can therefore be represented as in (184), where *D,s* indicates that we are dealing with a deictic interpretation of the preposition *voor* with the speaker *s* as its anchoring point.

(184) $\text{VOOR}^{D,s}$ (Jan, de boom)

The examples in (185) show that the anchoring point need not be the speaker. In (185a) the anchoring point is the addressee *a*, and in (185b) it is some other participant in the discourse, viz., *de kerk* 'the church'.

(185) a. Vanuit jou gezien, staat Jan recht voor de boom.
from you seen stands Jan straight in.front.of the tree
'Seen from your position, Jan is standing right in front of the tree.'
a′. $\text{VOOR}^{D,a}$ (Jan, de boom)
b. Vanuit de kerk gezien, staat Jan recht voor de boom.
from the church seen stands Jan straight in.front.of the tree
'Seen from the church, Jan is standing right in front of the tree.'
b′. $\text{VOOR}^{D,\text{de kerk}}$ (Jan, de boom)

II. The inherent interpretation

The anchoring point from which the location of the located object is computed may also be the reference object, that is, the complement of the adposition. This is only possible when the reference object is structured with respect to the relevant dimension(s). Consider example (186a), which can be depicted as in Figure 2A, in which the location of Jan is computed by taking the reference object as the anchoring point; the position of the speaker with respect to Jan and the car is not relevant. The difference between (183a) and (186a) has to do with the dimensional structuring of the reference object; a car can be seen as an object with a back and a front (indicated in Figure 2A by means of an arrow through the object), whereas we normally do not perceive trees in that way. Because of these dimensional properties of cars and trees, we can take the first but not the latter as the anchoring point for the preposition *voor*. The interpretation of locational adpositions in which we take the reference object as the anchoring point will be called INHERENT and henceforth be indicated by means of an I in superscript: P^{I}. On the inherent interpretation, example (186a) can therefore be represented as in (186b). Observe that the deictic interpretation is possible as well; (186a) can also refer to the situation depicted in Figure 2B, which can be assigned the semantic representation in (186c).

(186) a. Jan staat voor de auto.
Jan stands in.front.of the car
'Jan is standing in front of the car.'
b. VOOR^{I} (Jan, de auto)
c. $\text{VOOR}^{D,s}$ (Jan, de auto)

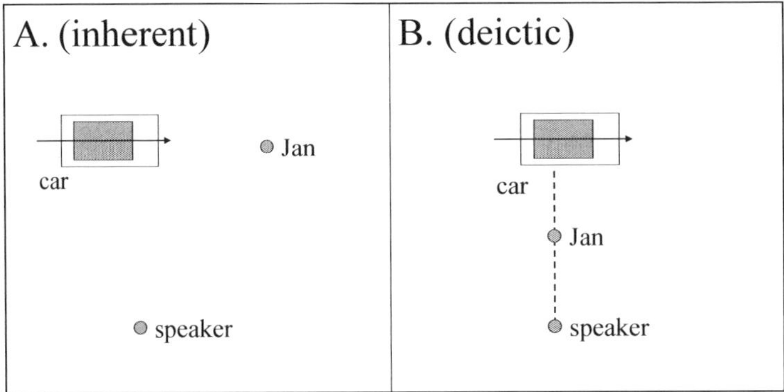

Figure 2: Jan staat voor de auto *'Jan is standing in front of the car'*

The deictic and the inherent interpretations of adpositional phrases differ in their logical properties. This can be illustrated by means of the examples in (187). When we interpret the adpositions deictically, the conclusion in (187c) follows from (187a&b), as can be seen in Figure 3A. However, when we interpret the adpositions inherently, the inference in (187) is no longer valid, as is shown in Figure 3B. The same difference in logical properties holds for other adpositions that can be used both deictically and inherently, like the simple prepositions *achter* 'behind', *naast* 'next to' and the phrasal prepositions *links/rechts van* 'to the left/right of'.

(187) a. De auto staat voor de kerk. AND
'The car is standing in front of the church.'
b. Jan staat voor de *auto*. ⇒
'Jan is standing in front of the car.'
c. Jan staat voor de *kerk*.
'Jan is standing in front of the church.'

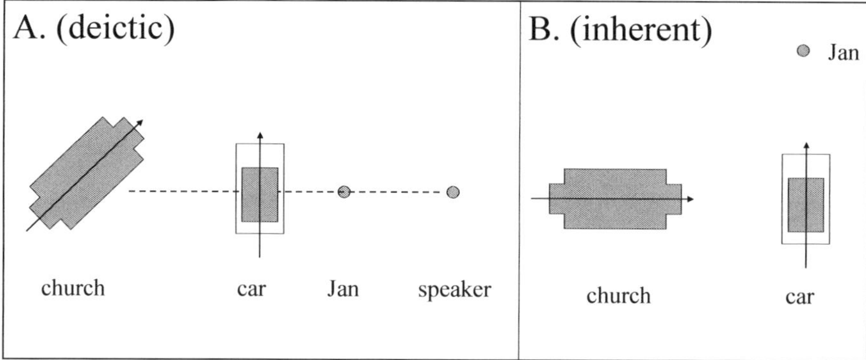

Figure 3: Deictic vs. inherent interpretation of voor *'in front of'*

The inference in (187) is also invalid when we switch from one perspective to another. The preposition *in* in (188a) is inherent, whereas the preposition *voor* in (188b) is interpreted deictically; cf. Figure 1. From these two examples, we cannot conclude that (188c) holds: for example, when Jan is situated in front of the trunk of the tree, and the bird is in the top of the tree, (188c) will clearly be false.

(188) a. De vogel is in de boom. AND
the bird is in the tree
b. Jan staat voor de boom. =/=>
Jan stands in.front.of the tree
c. Jan staat voor de vogel.
Jan stands in.front.of the bird

III. The absolute interpretation

Consider example (189a), which can be depicted as in Figure 4A. The fact that the computation of the location of the painting is independent of the speaker suggests that we are dealing with an inherent interpretation of the prepositional phrase *boven die stoel* 'above that chair': BOVEN^{I} (het schilderij, de stoel). This would be consistent with the fact that a chair can be considered to have a bottom and a top. There is reason to doubt, however, that the dimensions of the chair are really involved in the computation, because (189a) can also be felicitously used to refer to the situation depicted in Figure 4B, where the constellation between the chair and the painting has been changed. Moreover, (189a) cannot be used to refer to the situation in Figure 4C, where the constellation between the chair and the painting is essentially the same as in Figure 4C; note, for completeness' sake that (189a) is also unable to refer to the situation in Figure 4C when we replace the verb *hangen* by *liggen* 'to lie', which may provide a more appropriate description of the positioning of the painting. Interpretations of adpositional phrases that have neither an internal nor an external anchoring point will be called ABSOLUTE (that is, depending only on the natural environment such as the surface of the earth); these interpretations will be indicated without a superscript, as in (189b).

(189) a. Het schilderij hangt boven die stoel.
the painting hangs above that chair
'The painting is hanging above that chair.'

b. BOVEN (het schilderij, de stoel)

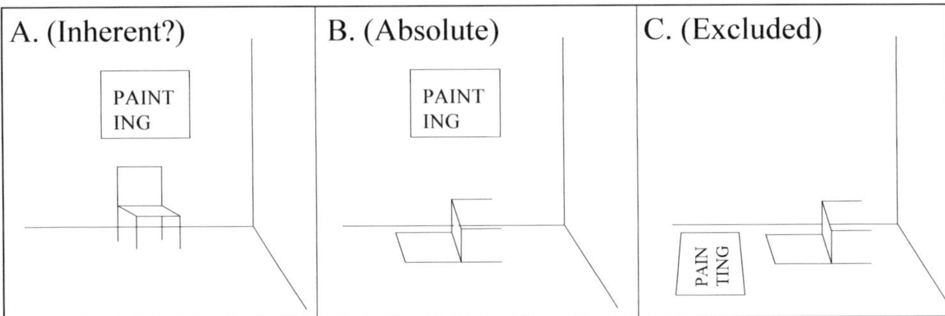

Figure 4: Het schilderij hangt/ligt boven de stoel *'The painting hangs/lies above the chair'*

1.3.1.1.3. Regions and vectors

Locational adpositions locate an object in space with respect to the reference object. It must be noted, however, that the interpretation of locational PPs is often rather vague. Consider the examples in (190). Example (190a) is most naturally interpreted such that the photographer is standing in the position depicted in Figure 5. Example (190b), on the other hand, need not be interpreted such that all the lamps are positioned like lamp 3; they may also occupy the positions of the other lamps as long as they remain in the grey area.

(190) a. De fotograaf staat achter de camera.
the photographer stands behind the camera
'The photographer is standing behind the camera.'

b. De lampen staan achter de camera.
the lamps stand behind the camera
'The lamps are behind the camera.'

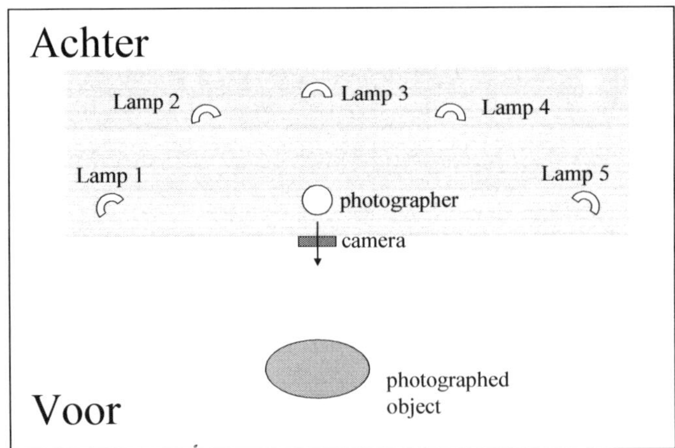

Figure 5: Achter de camera *'behind the camera'*

Figure 5 shows that locational PPs sometimes refer to rather extensive regions. As a result of this the regions denoted by different locational adpositions may overlap. For example, when we specifically want to refer to lamp 1 in Figure 5, we could also say that it stands *naast* 'next to' or *links van* 'to the left of' the camera. We can even express the appropriateness of the chosen adpositions by means of examples like (191), which makes explicit that *achter* 'behind' and *naast* "next to' are both applicable, but that *naast* is the most appropriate preposition to express the intended spatial relation.

(191) Lamp 1 staat meer naast dan achter de camera.
lamp 1 stands more next.to than behind the camera
'Lamp 1 is situated more next to than behind the camera.'

The positions in the region can also be made more specific by modifying the prepositional phrase. When we interpret the preposition *achter* deictically from the point of view of the object photographed, the statements in (192) are true. Note in passing that according to the inherent interpretation of *achter*, which takes the camera as its anchoring point, lamp 2 would be to the *right* of the camera.

(192) a. Lamp 3 staat recht achter de camera.
lamp 3 stands straight behind the camera
'Lamp 3 is positioned straight behind the camera.'
b. Lamp 2 staat links achter de camera.
lamp 2 stands left behind the camera
'Lamp 2 is positioned to the left behind the camera.'

The examples in (192) give an indication of the direction we have to look in order to find the located object in question. As is shown in (193), the distance between the reference and the located object can also be indicated.

(193) a. De fotograaf staat vlak achter de camera.
the photographer stands right behind the camera
'The photographer is standing right behind the camera.'
b. Lamp 3 staat vijf meter achter de camera.
lamp 3 stands five meters behind the camera
'Lamp 3 is positioned five meters behind the camera.'

This means that each point in the region referred to by the locational PP *achter de camera* can be defined by means of a direction and a distance. In other words, the preposition *achter* can be considered to denote a set of vectors that project the position of the reference object onto a potential position of the located object. Consider Figure 6 in which the reference object occupies the (0,0) position. The preposition *achter* denotes those vectors $\begin{pmatrix} x \\ y \end{pmatrix}$ that originate in (0,0), and for which $y > 0$; since the vectors $\begin{pmatrix} -4 \\ 3 \end{pmatrix}$, $\begin{pmatrix} 0 \\ 5 \end{pmatrix}$ and $\begin{pmatrix} 8 \\ 1 \end{pmatrix}$ map the position of the reference object onto the positions of lamps 2, 3 and 5, respectively, the latter are indeed in the region referred to by the PP *achter de camera*.

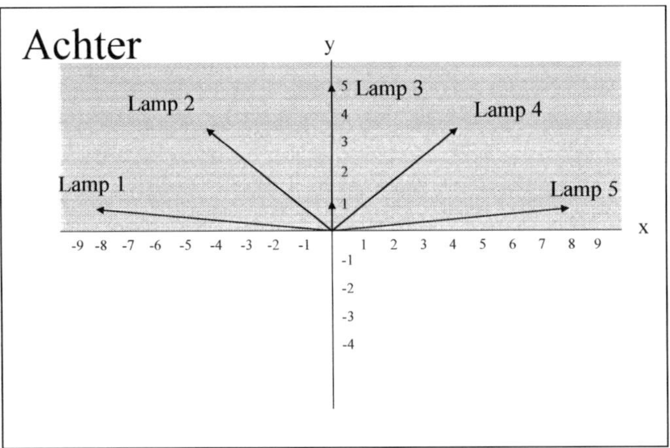

Figure 6: Achter de camera *'behind the camera'*

We can also denote subsets of the set of vectors denoted by the PP *achter de camera* 'behind the camera': the modified PP *recht achter de camera* 'straight behind the camera' denotes the subset of vectors denoted by *achter* in which x = 0, the modified PP *links achter de camera* denotes the subset of vectors in which x < 0, and the modified PP *rechts achter de camera* denotes the subset of vectors in which x > 0. Furthermore, the modified PP *vlak achter de camera* denotes the subset of vectors that are smaller than some contextually determined magnitude (length). These examples show that the assumption that locational prepositions denote a set of vectors will be very useful in the discussion of the modification properties of locational PPs in Section 3.1. For the moment, however, it suffices to observe that locational PPs refer to regions instead of fixed points in space.

1.3.1.1.4. The null vector

Prepositions like *achter* 'behind', and *boven* 'above' seem to express that the magnitude of the vector is larger than zero, that is, that there is some distance between the reference object and the located object. Other prepositions, however, require there to be some physical contact between the two objects: they require that the magnitude of the vector be zero. This difference can be illustrated by means of the prepositions *op* 'on' and *boven* 'above' in (194); example (194a) implies that there is physical contact between the table and the lamp, as in Figure 7A, whereas (194b) suggests the absence of such contact, as in Figure 7B.

(194) a. De lamp staat op de tafel.
the lamp stands on the table
'The lamp is standing on the table.'

b. De lamp hangt boven de tafel.
the lamp hangs above the table
'The lamp is hanging above the table.'

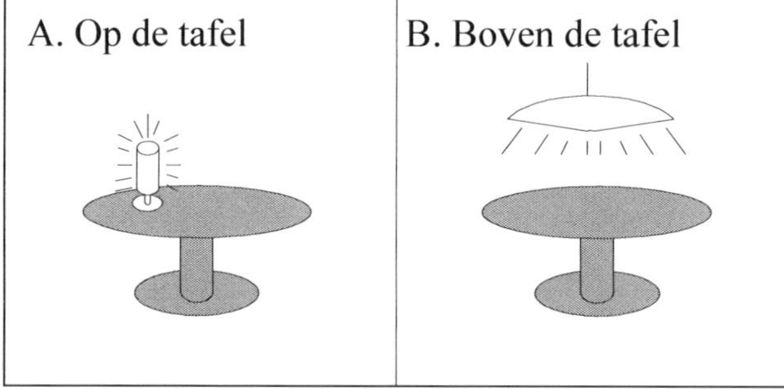

Figure 7: Op *'on' and* boven *'above'*

Note that the choice of verb does not affect the interpretation of the preposition; substituting *hangen* for *staan* in (194b) is possible when we refer to a situation like Figure 7B, in which the lamp is hanging so low that it touches the table. Somewhat more common examples like this are given in (195).

(195) a. De gordijnen hangen op de vensterbank.
the curtains hung on the windowsill
'The curtains are touching the windowsill.'
b. Je rok hangt op the grond.
your skirt hangs on the floor
'The hem of your skirt is touching the floor.'

The fact that the preposition *op* denotes the null vector, whereas *boven* denotes a larger set of vectors with a magnitude greater than 0 accounts for the fact that (on the idealization that the length of the part of the square adjacent to the church does not exceed the length of the side of the church adjacent to the square) the inference in (196) is valid, whereas the one in (197) is not.

(196) a. Jan loopt op het plein. AND
'Jan is walking on the square.'
b. Het plein is voor de kerk. ⇒
'The square is in front of the church.'
c. Jan loopt voor de kerk.
'Jan is walking in front of the church.'

(197) a. De luchtballon zweeft boven het plein. AND
'The hot-air balloon is floating above the square.'
b. Het plein is voor de kerk. =/=>
'The square is in front of the church.'
c. De luchtballon zweeft voor de kerk.
'The hot-air balloon is floating in front of the church.'

There is, however, also a potential problem for the claim that the denotations of prepositions like *achter* and *boven* do not include the null vector. When we assume that the meaning of *achter/boven op* in (198) is compositionally determined, we must conclude that *achter* and *boven* are compatible with the null vector since otherwise a contradiction would arise.

(198) a. De productiedatum staat achter op het blik.
the manufacturing.date stands behind on the can
'The manufacturing date can be found on the back of the can.'

b. De productiedatum staat boven op het blik.
the manufacturing.date stands above on the can
'The manufacturing date can be found on top of the can.'

We will not discuss this problem here, but simply claim that the underlying assumption that the meanings of *achter/boven op* is compositionally determined is false. Section 3.1.3 will show that formations like *achterop* and *bovenop* are compounds, and we therefore expect that the denotation of these formations consists of a subset of the denotation of the second member, the preposition *op*. Given that the reference object *het blik* in (198) is not a point in space but a three-dimensional object, the preposition *op* can be assumed to denote a non-singleton set of null vectors which are situated at different positions on the surface of the reference object, and it is therefore correctly predicted that the compounds *achterop* and *bovenop* denote distinct subsets of this set of null vectors denoted by *op*.

Although the discussion of the examples in (198) clearly shows that this is, strictly speaking, not correct, we will often take the reference object to be a point in space instead of a physical object with three-dimensional extensions in order to simplify the discussion that will follow; this motivates why we will normally refer to "*the* null vector" instead of "*the set of* null vectors". The three-dimensional extensions of the reference object will only be taken into account when this is necessary for the discussion.

1.3.1.1.5. Paths

Directional adpositions differ from locational ones in that they do not situate the located object in a fixed position in space. As a result, the denotation of a directional preposition cannot simply be considered a set of vectors. This does not imply, however, that the notion of vector is irrelevant in the case of directional PPs. Directional PPs express that the located object traverses a certain path. A path can be defined as an ordered set of vectors, each of which is associated with a certain position on the time line. The path denoted by *van A naar B* 'from A to B' can then be represented as in Figure 8, which can be read as a cartoon. In our visual representations below, we will often indicate paths by means of a blocked or dotted arrow.

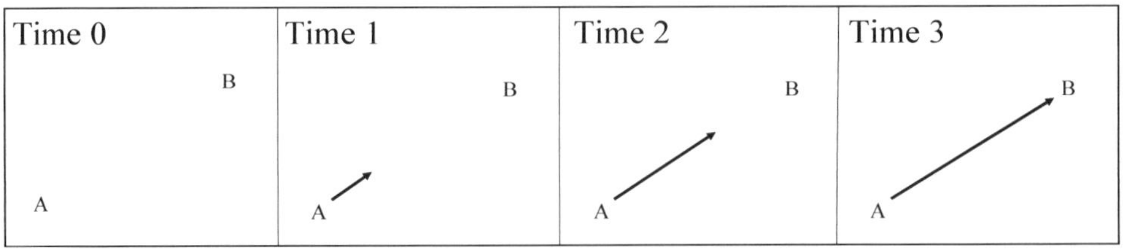

Time 0	Time 1	Time 2	Time 3
B	B	B	B
A	A	A	A

Figure 8: Van A naar B *'from A to B'*

The situation depicted in Figure 8 is an appropriate characterization of the directional phrase in (199a), where the PPs act as complements of the verb of traversing *rijden* 'to drive'. Besides this "core" DIRECTIONAL reading, directional PPs can also have two slightly different readings. The PPs in (199b) do not denote a path that is traversed, but indicate the extent of the located object *deze weg* 'the road'; this example expresses that the road is situated on a path that goes from Utrecht to Groningen. We will refer to this use of the PP in (199b) as the EXTENT reading (note that the verb *lopen* is also used as a verb of traversing meaning "to walk" when the subject is animate). The directional PP in (199c), finally, is used with an ORIENTATION reading.

(199) a. Jan rijdt van Utrecht naar Groningen. [directional reading]
Jan drives from Utrecht to Groningen

b. Deze weg loopt van Utrecht naar Groningen. [extent reading]
this road goes from Utrecht to Groningen

c. De richtingaanwijzer wijst naar Groningen. [orientation reading]
the direction.sign points to Groningen

1.3.1.2. Prepositions

Table 13 gives the subset of simple prepositions from Table 5 in Section 1.2.2 that can be used to express a spatial meaning; we have not included *beneden* because of the limited use of this preposition; cf. the remark below Table 5.

Table 13: Spatial prepositions

aan	on	*naar*	towards	*tot (en met)*	until
achter	behind	*naast*	next to	*tussen*	between
bij	near	*om*	around	*uit*	out
binnen	inside	*onder*	under	*van*	from
boven	above	*op*	on(to)/at	*vanaf*	from
buiten	outside	*over*	across	*vanuit*	from out of
door	through	*rond(om)*	around	*via*	via
in	in(to)	*tegen*	against	*voor*	in front of
langs	along	*tegenover*	across	*voorbij*	past

Spatial prepositions that are mainly used in official language and writing are: *benoorden/beoosten/bewesten/bezuiden* 'to the north/east/west/south of' (in colloquial speech, the phrasal prepositions *ten noorden/oosten/westen/zuiden van* are used), and the related formations *benevens* 'besides' and *bezijden*, the latter of which only occurs in the fixed expression *bezijden de waarheid* 'far from the truth'.

This section will provide a semantic classification of the spatial prepositions in Table 13. We will show that these prepositions can be divided into three main groups: (i) deictic, (ii) absolute, and (iii) inherent prepositions. An even more fine-grained subclassification will be proposed on the basis of vector theory outlined in the previous section. The final classification is summarized in Table 17 at the end of this section.

1.3.1.2.1. Deictic/inherent prepositions

There are only three simple deictic prepositions: *achter* 'behind', *naast* 'next to', and *voor* 'in front of'. In addition to these simple prepositions, there are two phrasal prepositions: *links van* 'to the left of' and *rechts van* 'to the right of'. These prepositions denote vectors with a magnitude greater than 0, that is, it is implied that there is no physical contact between the reference object and the located object.

Table 14: Deictic locational prepositions

PREPOSITION	DEICTIC	INHERENT	ABSOLUTE	NULL VECTOR
achter 'behind'	+	+	—	—
naast 'next to'	+	+	—	—
voor 'in front of'	+	+	—	—
links van 'to the left of'	+	+	—	—
rechts van 'to the right of'	+	+	—	—

The prepositions in Table 14 can all be used inherently as well, so that their use may give rise to ambiguity between the deictic and the inherent reading. This is illustrated in Figure 9 for the prepositions *achter* and *voor* in (200): the A figures represent the deictic use with the speaker as the anchoring point, and the B figures represent the inherent interpretations.

(200) Jan staat achter/voor de auto.
Jan stands behind/in.front.of the car

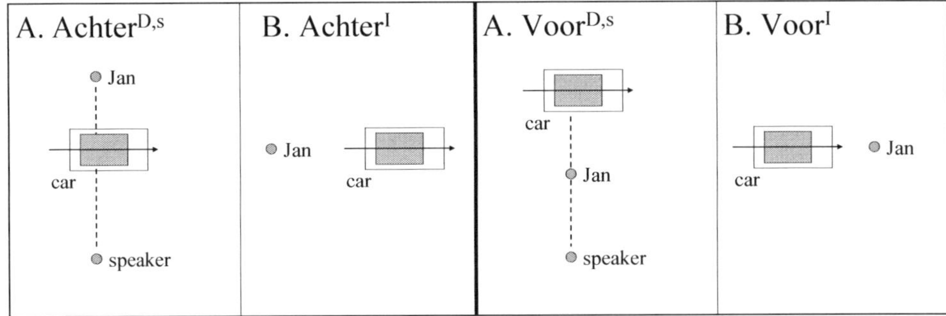

Figure 9: Achter *'behind' and* voor *'in front of'*

The preposition *naast* 'next to' in (201a) is ambiguous in the same way as *achter* and *voor*, but in addition it denotes two separate regions, which are opposite to each other. Due to the ambiguity between the deictic and the inherent reading, (201a) is therefore consistent with Jan being in one of the four positions indicated in Figure 10A&B. As is shown in Figure 11, the phrasal prepositions *links van* and *rechts van* in (201b) only refer to a subset of these positions.

(201) a. Jan staat naast de auto.
Jan stands next.to the car
'Jan is standing next to the car.'

b. Jan staat links/rechts van de auto.
Jan stands left/right of the car
'Jan is standing to the left/right of the car.'

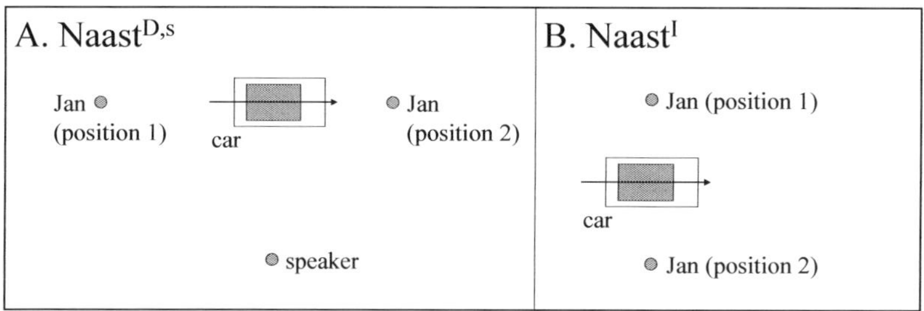

Figure 10: Naast *'next to'*

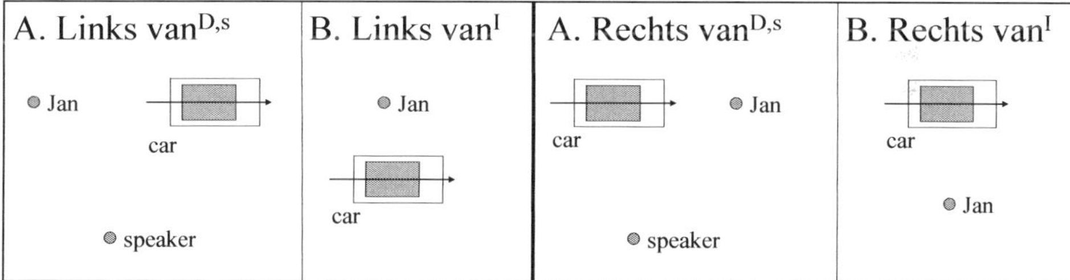

Figure 11 : Links/rechts van *'to the left/right of'*

The deictic interpretation of the prepositions *achter* 'behind' and *voor* 'in front of' becomes impossible as soon as they are combined with prepositions such as *aan* 'on', *in* 'in', or *op* 'on', which can only be used inherently; cf. Section 1.3.1.2.3. This is illustrated in (202) for *achter/voor*, which can only be used to refer to the A situations in Figure 12. Section 3.1.3 will argue that *achterop* and *voorop* are probably compounds. For completeness' sake, note that *aan/op/in* cannot be combined with *naast* 'next to': cf. **naastaan* **naastop*, **naastin*.

(202) Jan zit achter/voor op de auto.
Jan sits behind/in.front.of on the car
'Jan is sitting on the back/front of the car.'

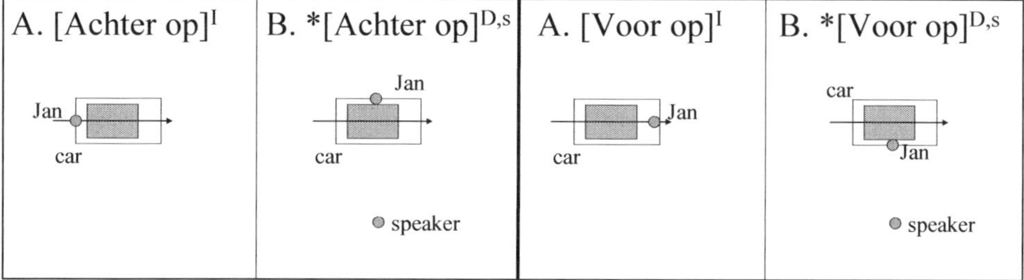

Figure 12: Achter op *'on the back of' and* voor op *'on the front of'*

The examples in (203), finally, show that the PPs headed by the deictic prepositions in Table 14 can be used both to indicate a location, as in (203a), and a change of location, as in (203b).

(203) a. De vuilnisbak staat achter/naast/voor de auto.
the garbage.can stands behind/next.to/in.front.of the car
b. Jan zet de vuilnisbak achter/naast/voor de auto.
Jan puts the garbage.can behind/next.to/in.front.of the car

1.3.1.2.2. Absolute prepositions

Unlike the deictic and the inherent interpretations, the absolute interpretation requires no information about the reference object and/or an external anchoring point; minimal information about the natural environment (such as what the position of the earth or magnetic north is) suffices to properly interpret these prepositions. The absolute prepositions can be divided into two groups, which differ in that the former refers to a (change of) location, whereas the latter is directional.

I. Absolute prepositions that denote a (change of) location

The group of absolute prepositions that denote a (change of) location is given in Table 15. These prepositions denote vectors with a magnitude greater than 0; there is no physical contact between the reference object and the located object. Some examples of PPs headed by these prepositions are given in (204).

Table 15: Absolute locational prepositions

PREPOSITION	DEICTIC	INHERENT	ABSOLUTE	NULL VECTOR	LOCATIONAL	DIRECTIONAL
boven	—	—	+	—	+	—
om	—	—	+	—	+	?
onder	—	—	+	—	+	?
rond	—	—	+	—	+	?
tussen	—	—	+	—	+	?

(204) a. De lamp hangt boven de kast.
the lamp hangs above the cupboard
b. De bal ligt onder de kast.
the ball lies under the cupboard
c. De lamp staat tussen twee vazen.
the lamp stands between two vases
d. De ketting zit om zijn enkel.
the chain sits around his ankle
e. De kaarsen staan rond de kerststal.
the candles stand around the crib

Before we discuss the absolute meaning of the prepositions in Table 15 more extensively, we want to discuss a number of special uses of them. First, the idiomatic expressions with *boven* in (205) seem to have a directional flavor.

(205) a. Dat gaat mij boven de pet.
that goes me above the cap
'That is over my head /I do not understand that.'

b. Hij groeit mij boven het hoofd.
he grows me above the head
'He is outgrowing me/He's leaving me standing.'

The same thing seems to hold for the idiomatic constructions in (206a), in which the adposition *boven* is preceded by the preposition *te*. The examples in (206b&c) show that similar idiomatic constructions are possible with the non-directional inherent prepositions *binnen* 'inside' and *buiten* 'outside', which will be discussed in Section 1.3.1.2.3.

(206) a. Dit gaat mijn verstand te boven.
this goes my understanding TE above
'This goes beyond my power of reasoning.'

b. Dat schoot me net te binnen.
that rushed me just TE inside
'This just came to me/I just remembered this.'

c. Dit gaat alle perken te buiten.
this goes all boundaries TE outside
'This oversteps all bounds.'

The preposition *onder* seems to denote the null vector in the idiomatic construction *zitten* + [$_{PP}$ *onder* ....] in (207a), which expresses that the bird is covered with oil. That we are dealing with an idiom is clear from the fact that the preposition *onder* has no paradigm; it cannot be replaced by any other spatial prepositions. Other constructions in which physical contact seems to be implied are given in the (b)-examples in (207): the (c)-examples show that in these examples *onder* functions as the antonym of the inherent preposition *op*, not of *boven*. This shows that *onder* can be used both as an absolute and as an inherent preposition. This section only discusses the former use.

(207) a. De vogel zit onder de olie.
the bird sits under the oil
Idiomatic: 'The bird has oil all over it.'

b. Jan ligt onder de dekens.
Jan lies under the blankets
'Jan is lying under the blankets.

b′. Jan ligt onder me.
Jan lies under me
'Jan is lying under me.'

c. Jan ligt op/$^{?}$boven de dekens.
Jan lies on/above the blankets
'Jan is lying on the blankets.'

c′. Jan ligt op/*boven me.
Jan lies on/above me
'Jan is lying on top of me.'

The examples in (208), finally, show that, like the deictic prepositions *achter* 'behind' and *voor* 'in front of', the absolute prepositions *boven* and *onder* can be combined with the inherent prepositions *op* 'on' and *in* 'in'. The resulting sequence must be interpreted inherently and denotes the null vector.

(208) a. *bovenop* 'on top of' a′. *bovenin* 'at the top of'
b. *onderop* 'on the bottom of' b′. *onderin* 'at the bottom of'

Let us now turn to the more normal, absolute interpretations of the prepositions *boven* 'above', *om* 'around', *onder* 'beneath', *rond* 'around' and *tussen* 'between' in Table 15. PPs headed by these prepositions can normally be interpreted without taking recourse to the dimensional properties of the reference object (which we therefore represent as a point in Figure 13 below) and/or some external anchoring point. For the interpretation of PPs headed by *boven* and *onder*, however, we do need some information about the natural environment; as is shown in Figure 13A, we have to know where the earth surface is situated. Figure 13B&C shows that minimal information like this is not even needed for the prepositions *om* 'around', *rond* 'around' and *tussen* 'between'.

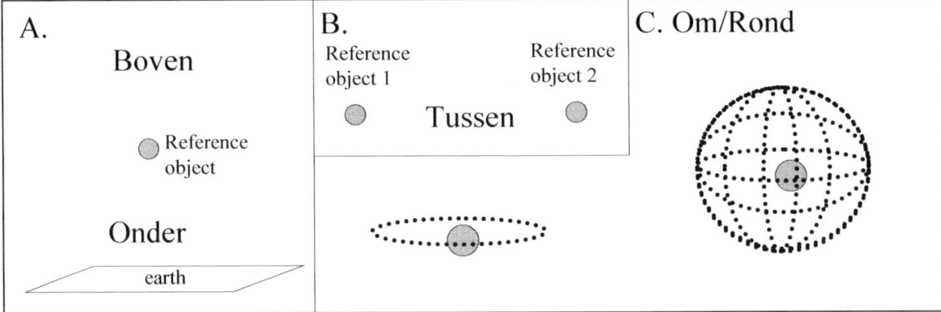

Figure 13: Boven *'above',* onder *'beneath',* tussen *'between' and* om/rond *'around'*

Observe that the preposition *tussen* 'between' is special in that it normally requires a plural complement; the location is computed on the basis of at least two reference objects. This property can also be found with the preposition *halverwege* in (209a), although this preposition can also refer to a certain position on the reference object; in (209b), the position of the located object is computed on the basis of the boundaries (in this case, the bottom and the top) of the reference object.

(209) a. Jan woont halverwege/tussen Groningen en Zuid-Laren.
Jan lives halfway/between Groningen and Zuid-Laren
b. Jan staat halverwege/*tussen de ladder.
Jan stands halfway/between the ladder

There are some exceptions to the general rule that the complement of *tussen* 'between' is plural. In (210), for example, *tussen* takes the singular noun phrase *de deur* 'the door' as its complement. However, what is actually claimed is that Jan's finger got jammed between the door and the door-post.

(210) Jan kreeg zijn vinger tussen de deur.
Jan got his finger between the door

In many cases, the preposition *om* seems to refer to a region in only two dimensions, as in the left figure in Figure 13C, whereas *rond* seems to denote a region in three dimensions, as in the right figure. In other cases, however, the difference between the two is not clear, and both *om* and *rond* seem to be equally well applicable to the two situations in Figure 13C (and the same thing seems to hold for the complex preposition *rondom*). The two examples in (211), for example, seem to be nearly equivalent.

(211) a. De padvinders zitten om het vuur.
the scouts sit around the fire
b. De padvinders zitten rond het vuur.
the scouts sit around the fire

Still, it is not the case that *om* and *rond* are always interchangeable. In examples like (212a), the preposition *om* is possible whereas the preposition *rond* gives rise to a severely degraded result, although it must be noted that Zwarts (2006), who proposes a number of semantic restrictions on the use of *om* and *rond*, assigns a mere question mark to the example with *rond*.

(212) Jan woont om/*rond de hoek.
Jan lives around the corner

The examples in (204) have already shown that PPs headed by the prepositions in Table 15 can be used to indicate a location. The examples in (213) show that these PPs can also be used to indicate a change of location.

(213) a. Jan hangt de lamp boven de kast.
Jan hangs the lamp above the cupboard
b. Jan legt de bal onder de kast.
Jan puts the ball under the cupboard
c. Jan zet de lamp tussen twee vazen.
Jan puts the lamp between two vases
d. Jan wikkelt de ketting om zijn enkel.
Jan winds the chain around his ankle
e. Jan zet kaarsen rond de kerststal.
Jan puts candles around the crib

Although intuitions are again not very sharp, it seems that, with the exception of *boven*, the prepositions under discussion can also be used directionally. One indication for this is that they can at least marginally occur as the complement of a verb of traversing like *rijden* 'to drive' in (214).

(214) a. Jan is ??onder/*boven de brug gereden.
Jan is under/above the bridge driven
b. ??Jan is tussen de bomen gereden.
Jan is between the trees driven
c. Jan is om/?rond het meer gereden.
Jan is around the lake driven

Note that the marginal examples become fully acceptable when *rijden* takes the auxiliary *hebben* in the perfect tense, but *rijden* is then just an activity verb and the PP functions as an adverbial phrase of place. In fact, the same thing holds for *boven*, as will be clear from the following example: *Het zweefvliegtuig heeft/*is boven de hei gevlogen* 'The sailplane has flown over the heath land'.

A clearer indication that these prepositions can be interpreted directionally is that most of them can head PPs with an extent reading. For examples (215a&b), it might be argued that the preposition is an abbreviation of the circumposition *P ... door*, but this is certainly not possible for *om* and *rond* in (215c).

(215) a. De weg loopt onder de brug ?(door).
the road goes under the bridge DOOR
b. De weg loopt tussen de bomen ?(door).
the road goes between the trees DOOR
c. De weg loopt om/rond het meer (*door).
the road goes around the lake DOOR

The more or less formal preposition *te* 'in/at' probably also belongs to the group of absolute prepositions. A PP headed by *te* seems to be preferably interpreted as denoting a location, as in (216a), but the examples in (216b&c) show that such PPs may sometimes also refer to a change of location. Given the formal nature of *te*, it is not surprising that there are several fixed expressions involving a change of location; an example is given in (216d). Note that the examples in (206) above suggest that PPs headed by *te* are sometimes even directional in nature.

(216) a. Jan woont te Amsterdam. [location]
Jan lives in Amsterdam
b. Jan raakte te water. [change of location]
Jan got in water
'Jan got into the water.'
c. Jan vestigt zich te Amsterdam. [(change of) location]
Jan settles REFL in Amsterdam
d. We hebben hem gisteren ter aarde besteld.
we have him yesterday into.the earth delivered
'We buried him yesterday.'

To conclude this discussion of the absolute locational prepositions, we want to note that *boven* and *onder* together with the deictic prepositions discussed in 1.3.1.2.1 give an exhaustive, but not necessarily complementary, division of space. When we take the crossing point of the three axes in the Cartesian-style coordinate system in Figure 14 to represent the position of the reference object, six regions can be distinguished. The regions denoted by *voor* 'in front of' and *achter* 'behind', *boven* 'above' and *onder* 'above' and *links van* 'to the left of' and *rechts van* 'to the right of' do not overlap; they are true antonyms. The other ones, on the other hand, may overlap, which is also clear from the fact that combinations such as *rechts boven* 'right above', *links achter* 'left behind' and ?*voor onder* 'in front under' can be found. Observe that *naast* 'next to' can be used when the left/right distinction is not relevant; similar prepositions do not exist for *voor/achter* or *boven/onder*.

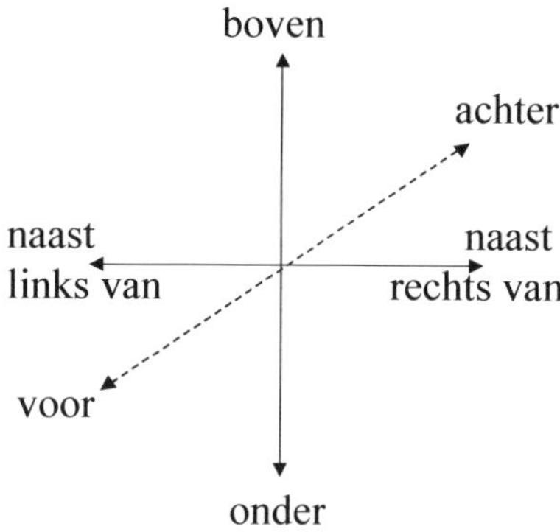

Figure 14: The division of space

As was shown in Figure 13B&C above, in addition to the regions denoted by these six "basic" prepositions, other regions can be denoted by prepositions like *tussen* 'between' and *om/rondom* 'around'. Further, it must be noted that there are also other ways to divide space, for example, by means of the absolute phrasal prepositions *ten noorden/oosten/zuiden/westen van* 'to the north/east/south/west of'.

II. Absolute prepositions that denote a direction

The absolute directional prepositions in Table 16 do not normally refer to a (change of) location, but denote a direction (a movement along a path). Given the fact that the located object is not situated in a fixed location but on a path (an ordered sequence of vectors), they do not involve the null vector by definition.

Table 16: Absolute directional prepositions

PREPOSITION	DEICTIC	INHERENT	ABSOLUTE	NULL VECTOR	LOCATIONAL	DIRECTIONAL
naar	—	—	+	—	—	+
tot (en met)	—	—	+	—	—	+
van	—	—	+	—	—	+
vanaf	—	—	+	—	—	+
vanuit	—	—	+	—	—	+
over (I)	—	—	+	—	—	+
via	—	—	+	—	—	+
voorbij	—	—	+	—	—	+

That the PPs headed by the prepositions in Table 16 do not readily refer to a location is clear from the fact that they cannot head the complements of locational verbs like *liggen* 'to lie' or verbs of change of location like *leggen* 'to put'. In (217), this is illustrated for the prepositions *naar* 'to', *van* 'from' and *via* 'via'.

(217) a. *Het boek ligt naar de boekenkast.
the book lies to the bookshelves
a′. *Jan legt het boek naar de boekenkast.
Jan puts the lamp to the bookshelves
b. *Het boek ligt van de boekenkast.
the book lies from the bookshelves
b′. ?Jan legt het boek van de boekenkast.
Jan puts the book from the bookshelves
c. *Het boek ligt voorbij de boekenkast.
the book lies past the bookshelves
c′. *Jan legt het boek voorbij de boekenkast.
Jan puts the book past the bookshelves

The fact that example (217b′) is relatively good is perhaps due to the fact that *van* can sometimes be used as an abbreviation of the circumposition *van ... af*. Note further that the preposition *voorbij* can be used to indicate a location when the located object is a building or a geographical entity (city, village mountain, etc.); the speaker then has a path in mind stretching from his current position towards the located object; the located object is then situated with respect to the reference object on this path. An example is given in (218a). Another counterexample to the claim that the prepositions in Table 16 are not locational is the possessive dative construction in (218b), which is normally interpreted metaphorically. That we are dealing with a more or less fixed expression is clear from the fact that it does not alternate with the construction in (218b′), where the possessive relation is expressed by a possessive pronoun; see the discussion in V3.3.1.4.

(218) a. Goirle ligt even voorbij Tilburg.
Goirle lies just past Tilburg
b. Het water staat hem tot de lippen.
the water stands him to the lips
'He is in great difficulties.'
b′. *Het water staat tot zijn lippen.
the water stands to his lips

Whereas the prepositions in Table 16 normally do not occur as the complement of verbs of (change of) location, they do typically occur as the complement of verbs of traversing like *rijden* 'to drive', *fietsen* 'cycling', and *lopen* 'to walk'.

(219) a. Jan reed naar Groningen.
Jan drove to Groningen
a′. Jan is naar Groningen gereden.
Jan has to Groningen driven
b. Jan fietst van Utrecht ?(naar Groningen).
Jan cycles from Utrecht to Groningen
b′. Jan is van Utrecht ?(naar Groningen) gefietst.
Jan has from Utrecht to Groningen cycled

c. Jan reed voorbij Groningen.
Jan drove past Groningen

c′. (?)Jan is voorbij Groningen gereden.
Jan has past Groningen driven

The examples in (220) show that these prepositions also occur with °unaccusative verbs like *vertrekken* 'to leave', *komen* 'to come', and *gaan* 'to go'. This need not surprise us, given that the verbs of traversing in (219) also behave like unaccusatives: for example, they must take the auxiliary *zijn* 'to be' in the perfect tense.

(220) a. Jan vertrok/ging naar Groningen.
Jan left/went to Groningen

b. Jan vertrekt/komt van Utrecht.
Jan leaves/comes from Utrecht

c. Jan kwam voorbij Groningen
Jan came past Groningen

Note that when the verbs in (219) take the auxiliary *hebben*, they no longer behave like verbs of traversing but like normal activity verbs; the concomitant result, shown in (221), is that PPs headed by the prepositions in Table 16 become degraded. Note that (221b) is acceptable when the phrase *van Groningen tot Tilburg* is interpreted restrictively in the sense that it is implied that Jan did something else (e.g., driving) during the remainder of the covered path; this adverbial reading is not relevant here.

(221) a. Jan heeft (*naar Groningen) gereden.
Jan has to Groningen driven

b. Jan heeft (#van Utrecht naar Groningen) gefietst.
Jan has from Utrecht to Groningen cycled

c. Jan heeft (*voorbij Groningen) gereden.
Jan has past Groningen driven

The directional prepositions can be divided into three groups. The first group takes the reference object as the endpoint of the implied path. The second group, on the other hand, takes the reference object as the starting point of the path. The prepositions of the third group, finally, denote a path that includes the reference object. This can be represented by means of the two features [±FROM] and [±TO].

(222) a. [-FROM] [-TO]: locational adpositions

b. [-FROM] [+TO]: *naar* 'to'; *tot* 'until'; *in de richting van* 'in the direction of'

c. [+FROM] [-TO]: *van* 'from'; *vanuit* 'from out of'; *vanaf* 'from'

d. [+FROM] [+TO]: *via* 'via'; *over* 'over'; *voorbij* 'past'

The feature constellation in (222a) denotes the set of prepositions that are non-directional, that is, the locational adpositions. The three others divide the directional adpositions into three subclasses depending on whether the adpositions take a reference object denoting the endpoint of a path, a reference object denoting the starting point of a path, or a reference object denoting both the end and the starting point of some subpart of the path. These three subclasses will be discussed below.

A. The reference object as the endpoint of (the relevant subpart of) the path

The complement of the preposition *naar* 'to' refers to the endpoint of a complete path, with the implication that it will be reached. The complement of the preposition *tot (en met)* 'until' denotes an arbitrary point on an implied path, with the implication that this point is the endpoint of a subpart of the complete path. In other words, whereas example (223a) suggests that both Jan and Peter are going to Groningen (see Figure 15A), example (223b) suggests that at least one of the two participants will continue his travel beyond Groningen (in Figure 15B the dotted arrow indicates the remainder of the path that either Jan or Peter is covering). The difference between *tot* and *tot en met* is that in the latter case the relevant subpart of the path includes the position referred to by the reference object, whereas in the first case it can be excluded. Note that the (reduced version of the) phrasal preposition *in de richting* van just indicates the direction of the path, without implying that the reference object is ever reached (see Figure 15C).

(223) a. Jan rijdt met Peter mee naar Groningen.
Jan drives with Peter with to Groningen
'Peter takes Jan with him to Groningen.'

b. Jan rijdt met Peter mee tot Groningen.
Jan drives with Peter with until Groningen
'Peter will drive Jan until Groningen.'

c. Jan rijdt (in de) richting (van) Groningen.
Jan drives into the direction of Groningen

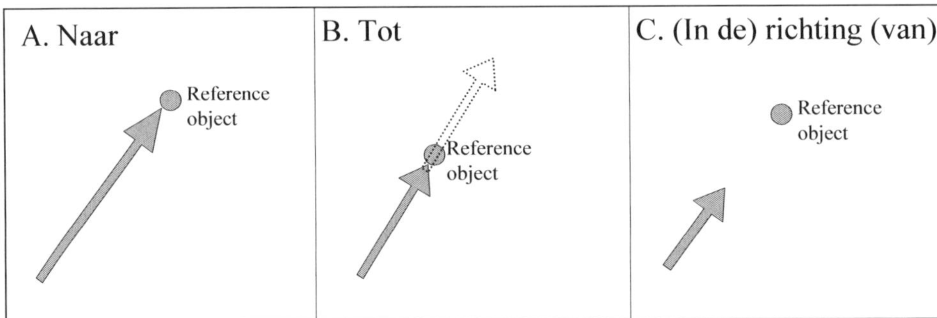

Figure 15: Naar *'to',* tot *'until' and* (in de) richting (van) *'in the direction of'*

PPs headed by the prepositions *naar* 'to' and *in de richting van* 'towards' are special in that they also allow an orientation reading. This is illustrated in (224). The two examples differ in that only in (224a) is the reference object actually pointed at.

(224) a. Jan wijst naar de kerk.
Jan points to the church

b. Jan wijst in de richting van de kerk.
Jan points in the direction of the church

Note that the PPs can be used as attributive modifiers with a similar distinction: according to (225a) the road will lead up to the church, whereas this need not be the case in (225b). Note that PPs headed by *tot* cannot be used as attributive modifiers; we return to this in our discussion of example (230).

(225) a. de weg naar de kerk
the road to the church
b. de weg in de richting van de kerk
de road in the direction of the church

B. The reference object as the starting point of (the relevant subpart of) the path

The prepositions *van*, *vanaf*, and *vanuit* express the starting point of (a subpart of) the implied path; in Figure 16 we indicate this by drawing several arrows from the reference object.

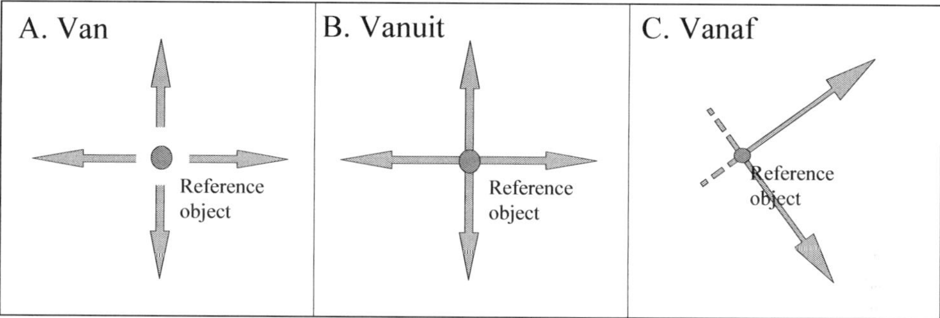

Figure 16: Van/vanaf *'from'*, vanuit *'from out of'*

Van is the most neutral of these three prepositions; it just expresses that there is a path originating from the reference object without necessarily implying that the reference object is included in the path; *vanuit*, on the other hand, expresses that (a region within) the reference object is included; *vanaf* indicates that the path may have started at some other place but that only the part from the reference object onward is considered relevant; in this respect this preposition is similar to *tot (en met)*.

(226) a. dat Jan morgen van Utrecht ?(naar Groningen) rijdt.
that Jan tomorrow from Utrecht to Groningen drives
'that Jan will drive from Utrecht to Groningen tomorrow.'
b. dat Jan morgen vanuit Utrecht (naar Groningen) vertrekt.
that Jan tomorrow from.out.of Utrecht to Groningen departs
'that Jan will head for Groningen from Utrecht tomorrow.'
c. dat Jan morgen vanaf Utrecht met de trein (naar Groningen) gaat.
that Jan tomorrow from Utrecht with the train to Groningen goes
'From Utrecht (on) Jan will go to Groningen by train tomorrow.'

The prepositions *van*, *vanaf*, and *vanuit* leave the endpoint of the path, and therefore also the direction of the path, unspecified; in order to specify the direction we must add a PP that refers to the endpoint of (the relevant part of) the path. Comparison of the examples in (226) and (227) shows that the two PPs are strictly ordered: PPs denoting the starting point must precede PPs denoting the endpoint of the path.

(227) a. *dat Jan morgen naar Groningen van Utrecht rijdt.
b. *dat Jan morgen naar Groningen vanuit Utrecht vertrekt.
c. *dat Jan morgen naar Groningen vanaf Utrecht met de trein gaat.

The examples in (228) show that this holds not only for their relative position in the middle field of the clause, but also for their relative orderings under topicalization (although contrastive focus on the topicalized part may improve the order in the primed examples, especially in generic contexts).

(228) a. Van Utrecht rijdt Jan morgen naar Groningen.
a′. *Naar Groningen rijdt Jan morgen van Utrecht.
b. Vanuit Utrecht vertrekt Jan morgen naar Groningen.
b′. *Naar Groningen vertrekt Jan morgen vanuit Utrecht.
c. Vanaf Utrecht gaat Jan morgen met de trein naar Groningen.
c′. *Naar Groningen gaat Jan morgen vanaf Utrecht met de trein.

In the examples discussed above, the located object actually traverses the path denoted by the spatial PPs. This need not be the case, as is clear from the primeless examples in (229), which involve extent readings of the directional PPs. The same extent readings are found in the primed examples where the PPs function as modifiers of a noun phrase.

(229) a. De weg loopt van Utrecht ??(naar Groningen).
the road walks from Utrecht to Groningen
'The road goes from Utrecht to Groningen.'
a′. de weg van Utrecht ??(naar Groningen)
de road from Utrecht to Groningen
b. De weg loopt vanuit Utrecht (naar Groningen).
the road walks from.out.of Utrecht to Groningen
'The road goes from out of Utrecht to Groningen.'
b′. de weg vanuit Utrecht (naar Groningen)
the road from.out.of Utrecht to Groningen

Example (230a) shows that PPs headed by the directional preposition *vanaf* cannot readily be used as modifiers of the noun phrase. In the previous subsection we noted the same thing for the preposition *tot*; this is illustrated again in (230b). This strongly suggests that PPs that refer to a subpart of some larger implied path cannot be used as modifiers within the noun phrase, although it must immediately be noted that noun phrases modified by *tot*-PPs are common when the reference object is abstract, as in (230b′).

(230) a. *?de weg vanaf Utrecht (naar Groningen)
the road from Utrecht to Groningen
b. *?de weg tot Groningen
the road until Groningen
b′. de weg tot inzicht/de waarheid/God
the road to understanding/the truth/God

C. The reference object is some arbitrary point on the path

Reference objects of the prepositions *over*, *via* and *voorbij* do not act as the starting or the endpoint of the path, but denote just some arbitrary point on the path. In a sense, these prepositions situate the path with respect to the reference object. This could be described by dividing the relevant path in two subparts, the reference object being the endpoint of the first and the starting part of the second subpart. This is shown in Figure 17 for the examples in (231).

(231) a. dat het vliegtuig over de Alpen vliegt.
that the airplane over the Alps flies
b. dat Jan (van Amsterdam) via/over Utrecht (naar Groningen) rijdt.
that Jan from Amsterdam via/over Utrecht to Groningen drives
'that Jan drives from Amsterdam to Groningen via Utrecht.'
b′. *?dat Jan van Amsterdam naar Groningen via/over Utrecht rijdt.
b″. *?dat Jan via/over Utrecht van Amsterdam naar Groningen rijdt.
c. dat Jan voorbij die boom liep.
that Jan past that tree walked
'that Jan walked passed that tree.'

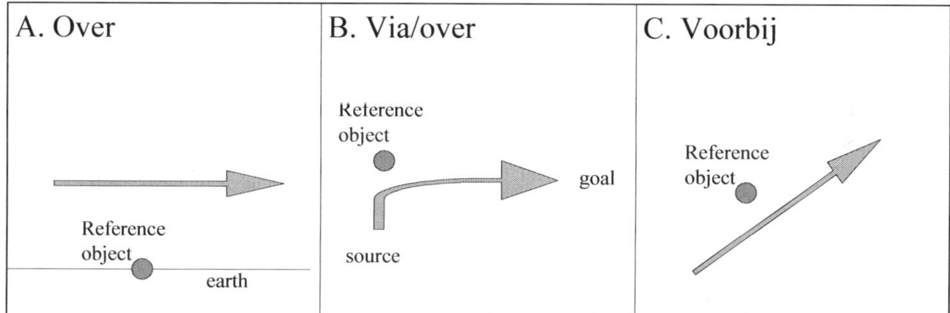

Figure 17: Over *'over',* via *'via',* voorbij *'past'*

For completeness' sake note that example (231b) contains three PPs: a *van*-PP referring to the starting point of the path followed by the *via/over*-PP, which refers to some intermediate point, and a *naar*-PP, which refers to the endpoint. The examples in (232) show that, with a non-contrastive intonation pattern, these PPs must be given in this order; the orders in the primed examples are then severely marked at best; cf. the discussion of (227).

(232) a. dat Jan van Amsterdam via/over Utrecht naar Groningen rijdt.
b. *?dat Jan van Amsterdam naar Groningen via/over Utrecht rijdt.
c. *?dat Jan via/over Utrecht van Amsterdam naar Groningen rijdt.

The examples in (233) show that the located object need not actually traverse the path denoted by the spatial PPs, but that these PPs may also receive an extent reading.

(233) a. De weg loopt via/over Utrecht naar Groningen.
the road walks via/over Utrecht to Groningen
'that the road goes via Utrecht to Groningen.'
b. de weg via Utrecht naar Groningen
the road via Utrecht to Groningen

1.3.1.2.3. Inherent prepositions

Inherent prepositions are interpreted in relation to the dimensional properties of the reference object (the complement of the preposition). The four subsets in (234) can be distinguished; these will be discussed in the Subsections below.

(234) • Inherent prepositions:
  a. Prepositions that denote a set of vectors that situate the located object:
    (i) relative to the dimensions mentally attributed to the reference object: *achter* 'behind', *naast* 'next to', *voor* 'in front of' and *tegenover* 'opposite'
    (ii) relative to the physical dimensions of the reference object: *langs* 'along', *binnen* 'within/inside', *buiten* 'outside', *bij* 'near'
  b. Prepositions that denote the null vector:
    (i) the located object is (partly) in the reference object: *in* 'in', *uit* 'out of', *door* 'through'
    (ii) the located object is in contact with the reference object: *aan* 'on', *op* 'on', *over* (II) 'over', *tegen* 'against'

I. Prepositions that denote a set of vectors

The two sets of prepositions that belong to this group situate the located object with respect to the reference object, without implying that there is physical contact between the two. Two groups can be distinguished: prepositions that situate the located object with respect to the dimensions mentally attributed the reference object and prepositions that situate the located object with respect to the physical dimensions of the reference object.

A. Prepositions that situate the located object with respect to the dimensions mentally attributed the reference object.

Section 1.3.1.2.1 has shown that the prepositions *achter* 'behind', *naast* 'next to' and *voor* 'in front of' can be used both deictically and inherently. The inherent uses of these prepositions are illustrated again in Figure 18.

(235) a. De vuilnisbak staat achter/naast/voor de auto.
  the garbage.can stands behind/next.to/in.front.of the car
 b. Jan zet de vuilnisbak achter/naast/voor de auto.
  Jan puts the garbage.can behind/next.to/in.front.of the car

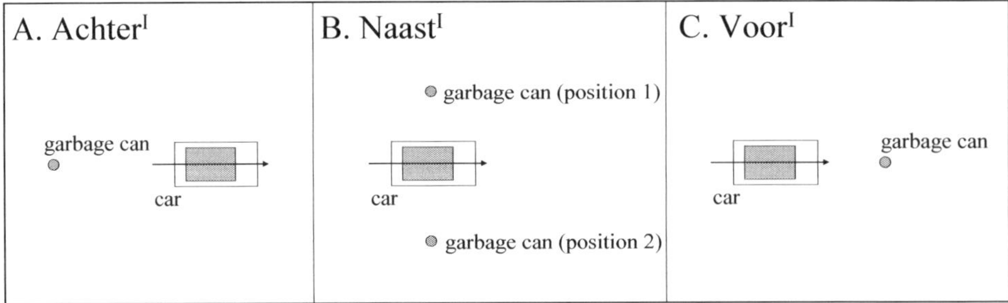

Figure 18: Achter *'behind',* naast *'next to' and* voor *'in front of'*

The computation of the location of the located object depends on what is considered the back or the front of the reference object. It must be noted that this depends largely on convention in the sense that the dimensional properties of the reference object do not play a role. Some examples: the front of a car is determined by the direction the car normally goes, the front of a building is generally determined by its main entrance, and the front of a TV set is determined by the placement of the screen. Other factors may play also a role, as will be clear from comparing the examples in (236).

(236) a. Jan zit voor de televisie.
Jan sits in.front.of the TV.set
'Jan is watching television.'
b. Jan zit achter zijn computer.
Jan sits behind his computer
'Jan is working on his computer.'

Although the examples in (236) imply that Jan is situated in similar positions with respect to the two screens, antonymous prepositions are used. The reason for this is that *achter* is also used to indicate that Jan is operating the reference object. This will be clear from the following examples.

(237) a. Jan zit achter het stuur.
Jan sits behind the steering wheel
'Jan is driving the car.'
b. Jan zit achter de piano.
Jan sits behind the piano
'Jan is playing the piano.'
c. Jan zit achter de knoppen.
Jan sits behind the buttons
'Jan controls everything.'

Another preposition that belongs to this group of inherent prepositions is *tegenover* 'opposite'. It differs from the prepositions *achter*, *naast* and *voor* in that it refers not only to the orientation of the reference object but also that of the located object; it expresses that the located object faces the front of the reference object. This can be made clear by means of example (238a). This example refers to the situation in Figure 19A, in which Jan and Peter are facing each other. Of course this situation can also be described by means of example (238b), but the difference between the two is that the orientation of the located object is not relevant in the case of *voor*; as is shown in Figure 19B, (238b) can be applied to a wider range of situations than (238a).

(238) a. Peter staat tegenover Jan.
Peter stands opposite Jan
'Peter is standing opposite Jan.'
b. Peter staat voor Jan.
Peter stands in.front.of Jan
'Peter is standing in front of Jan.'

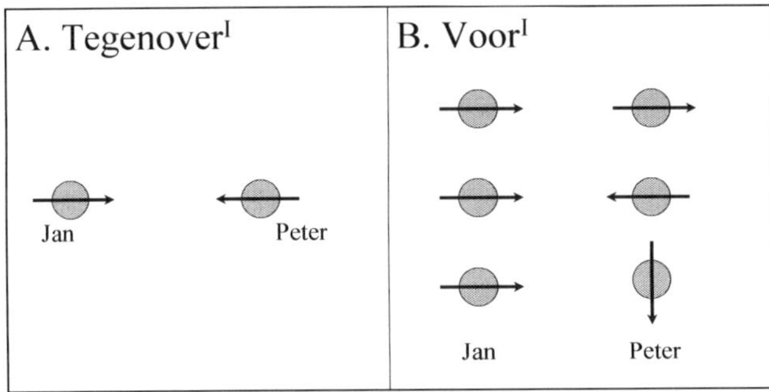

Figure 19: Tegenover *'opposite' versus* voor *'in front of'*

In connection with this difference between *tegenover* and *voor*, it can be noted that the relation expressed by the former is reflexive, whereas this does not hold for the relation expressed by the latter. This is clear from the fact that we may conclude from (239a) that (239a′) holds as well, and vice versa; the difference between the two examples is mainly one of prominence. From (239b), on the other hand, we cannot conclude that (239b′) holds.

(239) a. Peter staat tegenover Jan. ⇔ a′. Jan staat tegenover Peter.
b. Peter staat voor Jan. ⇎ b′. Jan staat voor Peter.

It must be noted, however, that there are cases where the conditions on the use of *tegenover* seem less stringent than in (238a). Example (240a), for example, seems acceptable, although a tree is normally not construed as an object with a front and a back. One may even use (240b) to refer to a situation in which the front of the car is not directed towards the church. Perhaps we must conclude from these examples that only the orientation of the reference object is crucial, and assume that (238a) is a special case. We leave this for future research.

(240) a. De oude kersenboom staat tegenover de kerk.
the old cherry tree stands opposite the church
b. Mijn auto staat tegenover de kerk.
my car stands opposite the church

B. Prepositions that situate the located object with respect to the physical dimensions of the reference object

The discussion above shows that the interpretation of *achter*, *naast* and *voor* is independent of the dimensional properties of the reference object. This does not hold for all prepositions. The preposition *langs* 'along', for instance, is generally interpreted with respect to the length dimension of the reference object (note in this connection that *langs* is probably derived from the adjective *lang* 'long'): in terms of vectors, we could say that *langs* denotes a set of vectors that are more or less parallel, that is, are all perpendicular to the exterior of the reference object. Like *achter*, *naast* and *voor*, the preposition *langs* can be used to denote either a location or a change of location (cf. (241)).

(241) a. De vuilnisbakken staan langs de rivier.
the garbage.cans stand along the river
b. De bewoners zetten hun vuilnisbakken langs de rivier.
the residents put their garbage.cans along the river

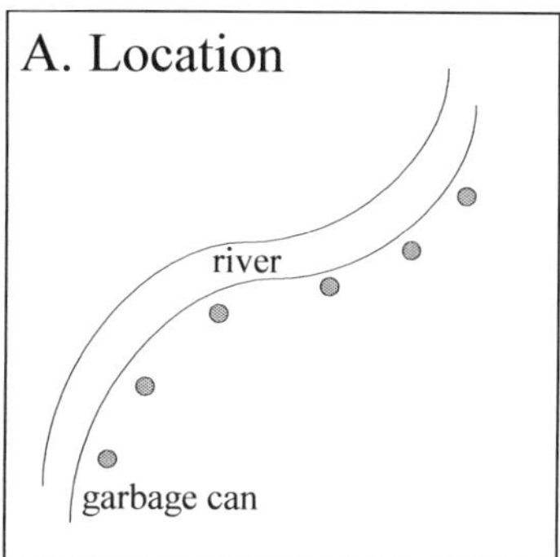

Figure 20: Langs *'along'*

Sometimes the importance of the length dimension of the reference object is weakened. Some examples that illustrate this are given in (242). Further, it must be noted that the preposition *langs* can sometimes also be used directionally; cf. Section 1.3.1.3.2, ex. (282).

(242) a. Jan liep even langs de slager.
Jan walked PRT along the butcher's
'John dropped in at the butcher's.'
b. Jan ging even langs oma.
Jan went PRT along grandma
'Jan paid grandma a visit.'

Other prepositions that depend on the dimensional properties of the reference object are *binnen* 'inside/within', *buiten* 'outside' and *bij* 'near'. They require that the reference object divide space into an interior and an exterior region. A PP headed by *binnen* indicates that the located object has a position in the interior region of the reference object, whereas a PP headed by *buiten* locates it in the exterior region. In this respect, *bij* is the same as *buiten*, but it has the additional requirement that the position be in the vicinity of the reference object (where the meaning of "being in the vicinity" is of course contextually determined). In Figure 21, the PPs in (243) denote a position within the grey area.

(243) a. Het kasteel staat binnen de stadswallen.
the castle stands inside the city walls
'The castle is within the city walls.'
b. Het kasteel staat buiten de stadswallen.
the castle stands outside the city walls
'The castle is outside the city walls.'
c. Het kasteel staat bij de stadswallen.
the castle stands near the city walls

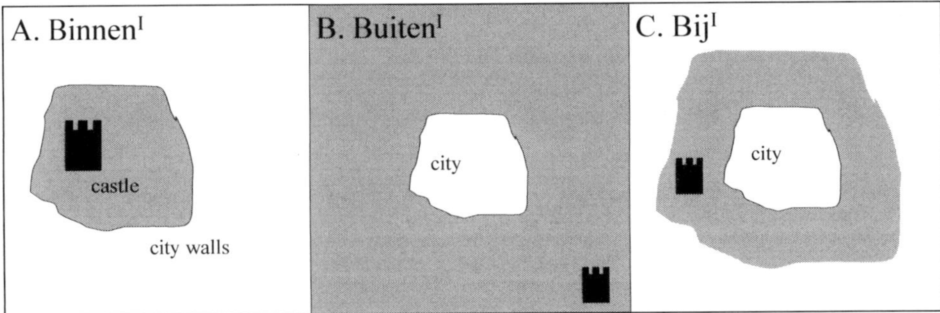

Figure 21: Binnen *'inside/within'*, buiten *'outside'*, bij *'near'*

To conclude the discussion of this group of prepositions, it must be noted that it is not easy to work out the idea that these prepositions denote a set of vectors. In the first place, it is not clear what the starting point of the vectors is. Of course, we could make the idealization that the reference object is a point in space, which the vectors take as their starting point, but this would not help us in the case of *binnen*. Another possibility would be to assume that the positions in the relevant region are defined by means of the shortest vectors from the reference object to the positions in question; cf. Figure 22. This would solve the problem that, despite the fact that the magnitudes of the vectors $\overrightarrow{AB}$ and $\overrightarrow{AC}$ are identical, the location of position B but not position C can be properly described by means of (244a), and (244b) can be used to describe position C but not position B. This is due to the fact that there is a shorter vector $\overrightarrow{DC}$ from the exterior of the reference object, which is not part of the denotation of *ver buiten* but of the denotation of *vlak bij*, so position C can be properly described by means of (244b).

(244) a. B/[#]C ligt ver buiten de stad.
B/C lies far outside the city
'B/C is far from the city.'

b. C ligt vlak bij de stad.
C lies close near the city
'C is close to the city.'

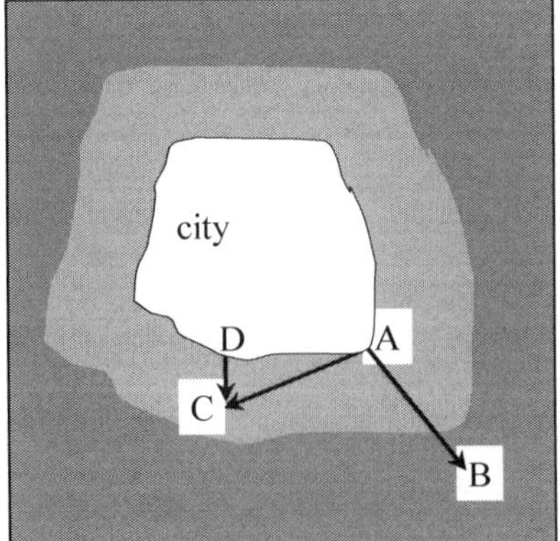

Figure 22: Ver buiten/vlak bij de stad *'far from/close to the city'*

This solution to the problem does not, however, solve the problem that neither the direction nor the magnitude of the vectors denoted by *binnen* 'inside' can be modified. For this reason, it has been assumed that *binnen* actually involves a null vector as well. Since we can offer no account for the facts that led to this assumption, we must leave this problem for future research. See subsection II for the difference between *in/uit* and *binnen/buiten*.

II. Prepositions that denote the null vector

Prepositions that denote the null vector can be divided in two groups: prepositions that express that (part of) the located object is in the reference object, and prepositions that simply imply some contact between the located and reference objects.

A. Prepositions that situate the located object (partly) in the reference object

The prepositions *in* 'in' differs from *binnen* 'inside' in that it requires physical contact between the reference object and the located object, that is, *in* involves a null vector. This can be made clear for the examples in (245) by means of the pictures in Figure 23. The preposition *binnen* in (245a) does not imply any physical contact between Jan and the hedge; Jan must just be somewhere in the grey area in Figure 23A; the preposition *in* in (245b), on the other hand, does require physical contact, so that the situation must be as indicated in Figure 23B.

(245) a. Jan zit binnen de haag.
Jan sits within the hedge

b. Jan zit in de haag.
Jan sits in the hedge

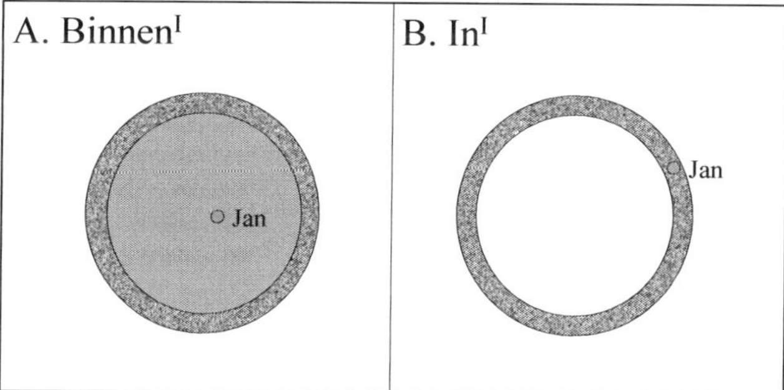

Figure 23: Binnen *'inside' vs.* in *'in'*

A caveat is in order, however. Example (245a) can be represented by making use of only two dimensions. When we are dealing with a three-dimensional object, on the other hand, the situation is slightly different. Given that it is the preposition *in*, and not *binnen*, that is used in the examples in (246), we must conclude that the inside of a three-dimensional object is mentally construed as a part of the reference object rather than as its interior region.

(246) a. De vogel zit in/*binnen de kooi.
the bird sits in/inside the cage
'The bird is in the cage.'

b. Jan is in/*binnen zijn kamer.
Jan is in/inside his room
'Jan is in his room.'

Like *in* but unlike *buiten* 'outside', *uit* 'out of' implies that there is some physical contact with the reference object. For this reason, *buiten* can, but *uit* cannot be used to refer to the situation depicted in Figure 24. Actually, *uit* cannot be used at all in (247b), since, when there is physical contact with the reference object, *in* will take precedence over *uit*; cf. *Jan zit in de haag*.

(247) a. Jan zit buiten de haag.
Jan sits outside the hedge

b. *Jan zit uit de haag.
Jan sits out.of the hedge

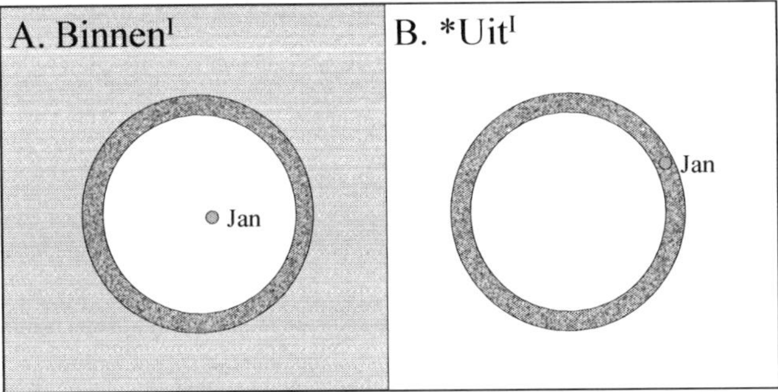

Figure 24: Buiten *'outside' vs.* uit *'out of'*

Buiten also seems to be preferred in the case of three-dimensional objects. Occasionally, however, *uit* can be used as well. It is not clear to us under what conditions *uit* can or cannot be used with three-dimensional objects.

(248) a. De vogel zit buiten/*uit zijn kooi.
the bird sits outside/out.of his cage
'The bird is outside its cage.'

b. De vogel is ?buiten/uit zijn kooi.
the bird is outside/out.of his cage
'The bird is out of its cage.'

c. De pen ligt buiten/uit zijn doos.
the pencil lies outside/out.of his box
'The pencil is out of its box.'

The discussion above shows that the preposition *buiten* is normally preferred to *uit* with stative verbs of location. Example (249b) shows, however, that the preposition *uit* is possible when we use a verb of change of location like *halen* 'to get', whereas *buiten* is not allowed in this context. This is due to the fact that this verb expresses that the contact between the located and reference object is broken.

For completeness' sake, we show in (249a) that the antonym of *halen*, *stoppen* 'to put', licenses *in* only.

(249) a. Jan stopt de vogel in/*binnen de haag.
Jan puts the bird in/inside the hedge
b. Jan haalt de vogel uit/*buiten de haag.
Jan gets the bird out.of/inside the hedge

The prepositions *in* and *uit* imply physical contact between the located and reference object at some point in time. The preposition *in* does not imply, however, that the located object is fully physically enclosed by the reference object; this may only be partially the case. Similarly, the preposition *uit* implies that at least some part of the located object sticks out of the reference object. This can be made clear by means of the examples in (250); the arrows in Figure 25 indicate the points that are relevant for the interpretation of the examples in (250).

(250) a. De naald zit in het speldenkussen.
the needle sits in the pincushion
'The needle sticks in the pincushion.'
b. De naald steekt uit het speldenkussen.
the needle sticks out.of the pincushion
'The needle sticks out of the pincushion.'

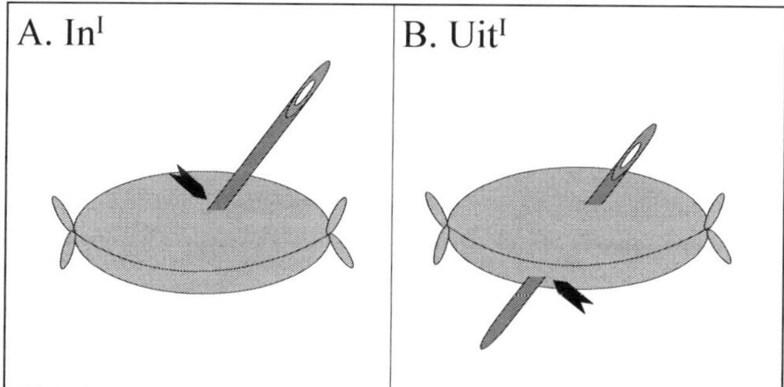

Figure 25: In *'in' and* uit *'out of' (locational)*

In and *uit* differ in that the former is compatible with full encompassment, whereas the latter necessarily implies partial encompassment. This is clear from the fact that the adverbial phrase *helemaal* 'completely' can be used with *in*, but not with *uit* (unless we are dealing with an overstatement). Note that, as expected, substituting *bijna helemaal* 'nearly completely' for *helemaal* in (250b) will give rise to a fully acceptable result. A modifier like *een klein stukje* 'a small piece', which expresses that the encompassment is not complete, is possible with both PPs.

(251) a. De naald zit helemaal/een klein stukje in het speldenkussen.
the needle sits completely/a small piece in the pincushion
'The needle sticks completely/partly in the pincushion.'
b. De naald steekt ??helemaal/een klein stukje uit het speldenkussen.
the needle sticks completely/a small piece out.of the pincushion
'The needle sticks completely/partly out of the pincushion.'

The examples in (249) have already shown that the prepositions *in* and *uit* can also be used to denote a change of location; cf. Figure 26. Some more examples are given in (252): in (252a) the reference object refers to the new position of the located object, and in (252b) it refers to its original one. In this case, the adverbial phrase *helemaal* 'completely' can be readily used with both PPs; *helemaal* in (252b) expresses that the contact between the located and the reference object is completely broken.

(252) a. Jan steekt de naald (helemaal/een klein stukje) in het speldenkussen.
Jan puts the needle completely/a small piece into the pincushion
'Jan puts the needle (completely/partly) into the pincushion.'
b. Jan haalt de naald (helemaal/een klein stukje) uit het speldenkussen.
Jan gets the needle completely/a small piece out.of the pincushion
'Jan gets the needle (completely/partly) out of the pincushion.'

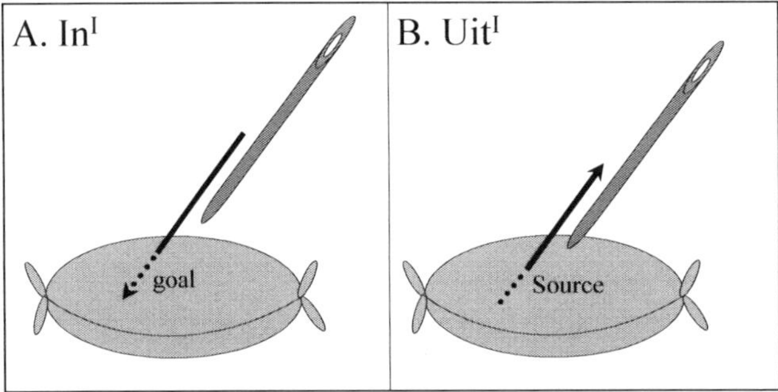

Figure 26: In *'in' and* uit *'out of' (change of location)*

The preposition *door* in a sense combines the meanings of *in* and *uit*. In (253a), the PP *door het speldenkussen* expresses that the located object sticks both in and out of the reference object; in other words both points indicated by means of the arrows in Figure 27A are relevant. In (253b), the PP indicates that the located object ends up in the position in Figure 27A as the result of Jan's action; this is shown in Figure 27B.

(253) a. De naald steekt door het speldenkussen.
the needle sticks through the pincushion
b. Jan steekt de naald door het speldenkussen.
Jan sticks the needle through the pincushion

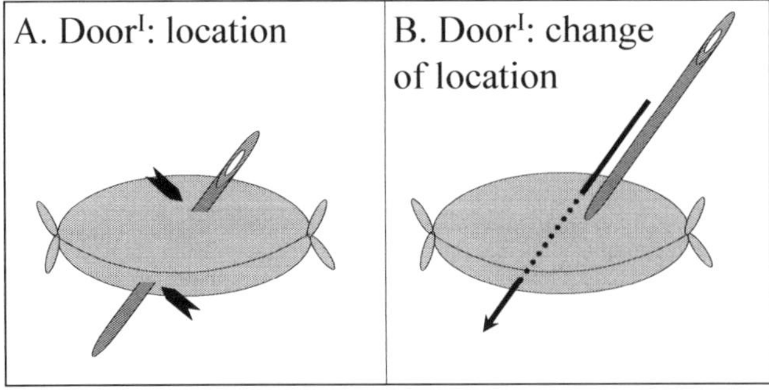

Figure 27: Door *'through'*

The prepositions *in* and *uit*, on the one hand, and *door*, on the other, seem to differ in that the former can only be used in constructions involving (change of) location, whereas the latter can also occur in directional constructions. This is clear from the examples in (238) involving the verb of traversing *rijden* 'to drive'; cf. Section 1.1.3.2. Whereas the examples in (254a) are marginal at best, (254b) is fully acceptable. The primed examples show that the intended directional meanings can (also) be expressed by using the adpositions in question as postpositions.

(254) a. ??De auto is in/uit de autowasserette gereden.
the car is into/out.of the car wash driven
'The car has driven into/out of the car wash.'
a′. De auto is de autowasserette in/uit gereden.
b. De auto is door de autowasserette gereden.
the car is through the car wash driven
'The car has driven through the car wash.'
b′. De auto is de autowasserette door gereden.

There is, however, a slight meaning difference between (254b) and (254b′), although it is hard to pinpoint it. Perhaps another example can clarify it. When Jan is driving on an unfenced path which at a certain point ends at a meadow, and Jan drives right through the meadow to a path on the other side of it, one would use the preposition rather than the postposition *door*, as is shown in the (a)-examples in (255). The contrast becomes even clearer when the reference object is an entity with a relatively small size, like a puddle of rainwater. However, when the unfenced path enters a wood, and Jan drives right through it, one can also use the postposition, as is shown in (255b′). This may suggest that in order to use *door* as a postposition the located object must be completely encompassed by the reference object, whereas this need not be the case when it is used as a preposition. We leave this to future research.

(255) a. Jan is door het weiland/de regenplas gereden.
Jan is through the meadow/puddle driven
'Jan has driven through the meadow/puddle.'
a′. #Jan is het weiland/de regenplas door gereden.
b. Jan is door het bos gereden.
Jan is through the wood driven
'Jan has driven through the woods.'
b′. Jan is het bos door gereden.

B. Prepositions that imply contact between the located and the reference object

Whereas *in*, *uit* and *door* imply that the located object is at least partly located in the reference object, the prepositions *aan*, *op*, *over* and *tegen* in (256) merely require that there be some contact between the two.

(256) a. Er hangt een lamp aan het plafond.
there hangs a painting on the ceiling
b. Er zit een vlek op het plafond.
there is a stain on the ceiling

c. Er ligt een kleed over de tafel.
there lies a cloth over the table

d. Er staat een ladder tegen de muur.
there stands a ladder against the wall

The four prepositions differ with respect to the nature of the contact that is implied. The preposition *aan* is compatible with minimal contact: the lamp in (256a) can be connected to the ceiling by means of its wire only. The preposition *op* suggests more extensive contact between the located and the reference object; the stain in (256b), of course, has maximal contact with the ceiling. The preposition *over* also suggests more extensive contact, but now it is the reference object that must have more extensive contact with the located object.

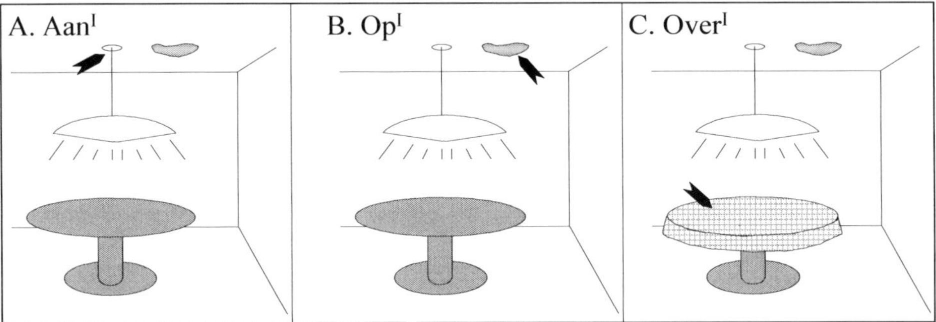

Figure 28: Aan *'on',* op *'on',* over *'over'*

Note that it has also been claimed that the preposition *aan* expresses minimal distance, not minimal contact. Examples that would favor this are given in (257): these examples do not imply physical contact between the ship and the quay, or the house and the lake. If this is the proper characterization then *aan* must be assumed to denote a set of vectors which are smaller than a certain contextually determined magnitude, just like *bij* 'near' shown in (243); *aan* and *bij* differ, however, in that only the former is compatible with physical contact.

(257) a. Het schip ligt aan de kade.
the ship lies on the quay
'The ship is tied up to the quay.'

b. Het huis staat aan het meer.
the house stands on the lake
'The house stands near the lake.'

The examples in (256b&c) perhaps suggest that *op* and *over* imply some notion of full contact. That this is not the case will be clear from the examples in (258); example (258a) suggests that only the bottom of the lamp is in contact with the table (cf. Figure 7A), and (258b) is compatible with a situation in which the chair is only partially covered by the coat.

(258) a. De lamp staat op de tafel.
the lamp stands on the table
b. De jas hangt over de stoel.
the coat hangs over the chair

In (256a-c) the PPs headed by *aan*, *op* and *over* refer to a location. The examples in (259) show that these PPs can also be used to indicate a change of location.

(259) a. Jan hangt een lamp aan het plafond.
Jan hangs a painting on the ceiling
b. Jan zet een lamp op de tafel.
Jan puts a lamp on the table
c. Jan legt een kleed over de tafel.
Jan puts a cloth over the table

Note that *op* in (259b) necessarily means "on top of". This is, however, not the case in the examples in (260). The verb *brengen* 'to bring' in (260a) can be considered a movement verb and the verb *maken* in (260b) functions as a verb of creation.

(260) a. Jan brengt de verf op het doek.
Jan puts the paint on the canvas
b. Jan maakte een vlek op het plafond.
Jan made a stain on the ceiling

The preposition *tegen* 'against' is more difficult to characterize. It is often used in the sense of "touching the side surface of the reference object", as in (256d), but resultative constructions like (261) are possible as well.

(261) a. Jan gooide een pannenkoek tegen het plafond.
Jan threw a pancake against the ceiling
b. Jan sloeg Peter tegen de grond.
Jan hit Peter against the floor

These examples suggest that *tegen* means (or may also mean) something like "touching the reference object while exerting force on it", which would fit in nicely with the non-locational uses of *tegen* in examples like (262).

(262) a. Jan zwom tegen de stroom.
Jan swam against the current
b. Marie protesteerde met kracht tegen dat besluit.
Marie protested with force against that decision
c. Marie vocht hard tegen een ernstige griep.
Marie fought hard against a serious flu

If the notion of exerting force is indeed appropriate in the characterization of the preposition *tegen*, it may be the case that *tegen* and *aan* act as antonyms with respect to the direction of the exerted force (in at least some cases). The examples in (263) may make this clear. The verbs *duwen* 'to push' and *trekken* 'to pull' both express that force is exerted on the complement of the (non-spatial) prepositional complement of the verb: in the first case the force is directed towards it, and only the preposition *tegen* can be used; in the latter case, on the other hand, the direction of the force is reversed, and only the preposition *aan* is possible. This is depicted in Figure 29, in which the arrow indicates the direction of the force exerted by Jan.

(263) a. Jan duwde tegen/*aan het hek.
Jan pushed against/on the gate

b. Jan trok aan/*tegen het hek.
Jan pulled on/against the gate

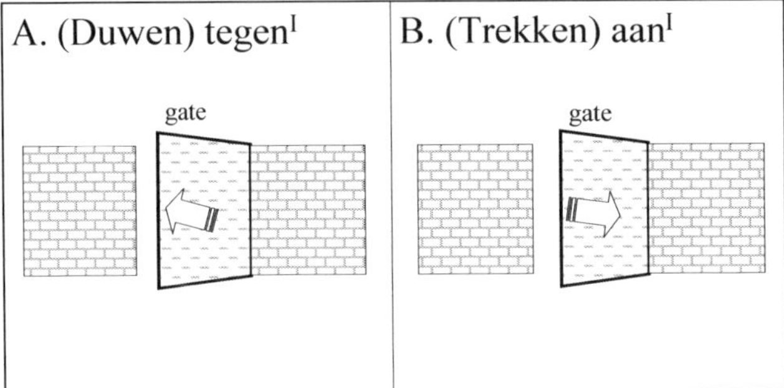

Figure 29: Tegen *'against' and* aan *'on'*

1.3.1.2.4. Summary

This section has discussed three main classes of spatial prepositions: deictic, absolute and inherent prepositions. Our findings are summarized in Table 17 below. The class of deictic prepositions is rather small, and can also be used inherently. The class of absolute prepositions can be divided into two subclasses: the first is locational and possibly also directional in nature, whereas the second is only directional. The inherent prepositions can be divided into two main groups as well; those that denote a set of vectors (type I), and those that denote the null vector (type II). Type I can be further divided into prepositions that resemble the deictic prepositions in that they refer to the dimensions mentally attributed to the reference object (type Ia), and prepositions that make reference to the dimensional properties of the reference object (type Ib). Type II can be further divided into prepositions that require the located object to be in the reference object (type IIa) and prepositions that just assume there to be some contact between the located and the reference object (type IIb). The preposition *te* is special in that it can normally only be used in constructions that refer to a location, whereas all other locational prepositions can be used in constructions that refer to a location or a change of location. Finally, it can be observed that the prepositions can be divided into two main groups on the basis of whether the preposition says something about the orientation/direction of the vectors it denotes, or about their magnitude, that is, the distance between located and reference object. The first group includes all deictic and directional prepositions; for obvious reasons, the latter includes all prepositions that denote the null vector.

Table 17: Spatial prepositions (summary)

TYPE	PREPOSITION	DEICTIC	INHERENT	ABSOLUTE	LOCATIONAL	DIRECTIONAL	VECTOR		
							NULL	ORIENT/DIR	MAGNITUDE
Deictic	*achter* 'behind'	+	+	—	+	—	—	+	—
	naast 'next to'	+	+	—	+	—	—	+	—
	voor 'in front of'	+	+	—	+	—	—	+	—
Absolute Type I	*boven* 'above'	—	—	+	+	—	—	+	—
	om 'around'	—	—	+	+	?	—	+	—
	onder 'under'	—	—	+	+	?	—	+	—
	rond 'around'	—	—	+	+	?	—	+	—
	tussen'between'	—	—	+	+	?	—	+	—
Absolute Type II	*naar* 'to'	—	—	+	—	+	—	+	—
	over (I) 'over/across'	—	—	+	—	+	—	+	—
	tot (en met) 'until'	—	—	+	—	+	—	+	—
	van 'from'	—	—	+	—	+	—	+	—
	vanaf 'from'	—	—	+	—	+	—	+	—
	vanuit 'from out of'	—	—	+	—	+	—	+	—
	via 'via'	—	—	+	—	+	—	+	—
	voorbij 'past'	—	—	+	—	+	—	+	—
Inherent Type Ia	*tegenover* 'opposite'	—	—	+	+	—	—	+	—
	achter, naast, voor	—	—	+	+	—	—	+	—
Inherent Type Ib	*binnen* 'inside'	—	—	+	+	—	?	—	+
	buiten 'outside'	—	—	+	+	—	—	—	+
	bij 'near'	—	—	+	+	—	—	—	+
	langs 'along'	—	—	+	+	?	—	—	+
Inherent Type IIa	*in* 'in'	—	—	+	+	—	+	—	+
	uit 'out of'	—	—	+	+	—	+	—	+
	door 'through'	—	—	+	+	+	+	—	+
Inherent Type IIb	*aan* 'on'	—	—	+	+	—	+	—	+
	op 'on'	—	—	+	+	—	+	—	+
	over (II) 'over'	—	—	+	+	—	+	—	+
	tegen 'against'	—	—	+	+	—	+	—	+
te	*te* 'in/at'	—	+	—	+	—	+	—	+

This section has mainly focused on cases in which the spatial PP is used as a complementive and is hence predicated of some nominal argument of the clause. It must be noted, however, that when the PP is used adverbially the preposition can also be considered a two-place predicate, the only difference being that the located entity is now no longer expressed by a nominal argument but by some projection of the verb. In (264), the preposition *in* establishes a spatial relation between the event of Marie and Jan playing soccer and the garden; the event *e* takes place in the garden, as indicated in (264b).

(264) a. Marie en Jan voetballen in de tuin.
Marie and Jan play.soccer in the garden
'Marie and Jan are playing soccer in the garden.'
b. IN (e, the garden)

Although the complementives and adverbially used PPs behave semantically essentially the same way, it must be noted that directional PPs cannot be used as adverbial phrases. This is consistent with the fact that postpositional phrases, which are always directional, cannot be used adverbially either; cf. Section 1.3.1.3.

1.3.1.3. Postpositions

Section 1.3.1.3.1 will start by recapitulating the discussion of some differences between pre- and postpositions from Section 1.1.3.2. After this, Section 1.3.1.3.2 will provide a classification of the postpositions.

1.3.1.3.1. Differences between pre- and postpositions

Spatial postpositions are always directional: they indicate that the located object is covering a path related to the reference object. In this respect postpositional phrases differ from prepositional phrases, which, with the exception of those headed by the directional prepositions in Table 16, just refer to a (change of) location. This difference accounts for the fact that, whereas prepositional phrases can occur as the complement of both locational verbs like *liggen* 'to lie' and motion verbs like *springen* 'to jump', postpositional phrases are not possible as the complement of locational verbs.

(265) a. Jan ligt/springt in het zwembad.
Jan lies/jumps in(to) the swimming.pool
b. Jan springt/*ligt het zwembad in.
Jan jumps/lies the swimming.pool into

Sometimes it is difficult to distinguish between the change of location reading of prepositional phrases and the directional reading of postpositional phrases: the two examples in (265) with the motion verb *springen* seem nearly synonymous. That only the postpositional phrase involves the notion of a path can be made clear, however, by means of the examples in (266).

(266) a. Jan is op de trap gesprongen (#naar zijn kamer).
Jan is on the stairs jumped to his room
'Jan has jumped onto the stairs (to his room).'
b. Jan is de trap op gesprongen/gerend (naar zijn kamer).
Jan is the stairs onto jumped/run to his room
'Jan has jumped/run up the stairs (into his room).'

In the location constructions in (266a), it is expressed that Jan has been involved in a jumping event as a result of which he has obtained some position on the stairs.

The construction in (266b), on the other hand, does *not* imply that, after finishing the activity, Jan is situated on the stairs; this may or may not be the case, which is clear from the fact that it is possible to add an adverbial phrase like *naar zijn kamer* 'to his room', which refers to the endpoint of the path covered by Jan; with this adverbial phrase added, the perfect tense example in (266b) suggests that Jan is in his room. Adding this adverbial phrase to (266a), on the other hand, give rise to an unacceptable result. Note that the number sign in (266a) indicates that the *naar*-PP can marginally be construed as an attributive modifier of the noun *trap*.

Another difference is that locational prepositional phrases cannot occur as the complement of verbs of traversing (verbs that denote movement along a certain path) like *rijden* 'to drive', *fietsen* 'to cycle', etc. In order to see this, we must consider perfect tense constructions, since a verb like *rijden* is actually ambiguous between a normal activity verb, in which case it takes the auxiliary *hebben*, and a verb of traversing, in which case it takes the auxiliary *zijn*. Thus, in (267a) we are dealing with the activity verb *rijden*, and it is expressed that the event of driving takes place on the mountain. In (267b), on the other hand, we are dealing with a verb of traversing, and it is expressed that Jan is moving along a path up the mountain.

(267) a. Jan heeft/*?is op de berg gereden.
Jan has on the mountain driven
'Jan has driven on the mountain.'
b. Jan is/*heeft de berg op gereden.
Jan has the mountain onto driven
'Jan has driven up the mountain.'

Note in passing that the grammaticality of both (266a) and (266b) suggests that the °unaccusative verb *springen* can be used both as a motion verb and as a verb of traversing. Note further that the intransitive version of *springen*, which takes the auxiliary *hebben*, just acts like an activity verb: *Jan heeft op de trap gesprongen* 'Jan has jumped on the stairs' simply expresses that the activity of jumping takes place on the stairs.

Related to this difference between the two examples in (267) is that example (268a) doesn't imply anything about the position of *Jan* after the activity has finished: it may be the case that he ends his activity at the same place that he started it. This is, however, impossible in the case of (268b): Jan must have traversed the path up the mountain for three kilometers, so that his end position is a position higher on the mountain than his starting position.

(268) a. Jan heeft drie kilometer op de berg gereden.
Jan has three kilometers on the mountain driven
'Jan has driven three kilometers on the mountain.'
b. Jan is drie kilometer de berg op gereden.
Jan has three kilometers the mountain onto driven
'Jan has driven three kilometers onto the mountain.'

1.3.1.3.2. A classification of postpositions

Having recapitulated the main semantic differences between pre- and postpositional phrases, we can now turn to the meaning of the individual spatial postpositions in Table 7, which is repeated here for convenience as Table 18 in a slightly different form. The conclusion to the discussion will be that, generally speaking, there is only one group of postpositions, which corresponds to the inherent prepositions in Table 17: the deictic and absolute prepositions in this table do not have postpositional counterparts.

Table 18: Spatial postpositions (repeated)

POSTPOSITION	EXAMPLE	TRANSLATION
af	*het veld af rennen*	to run from the field
binnen	*het huis binnen gaan*	to go into the house
door	*het hek door lopen*	to walk through the gate
in	*het huis in gaan*	to go into the house
langs	*de beek langs wandelen*	to walk along the brook
om	*de hoek om gaan*	to turn the corner
op	*het veld op rennen*	to run onto the field
over	*het grasveld over rennen*	to run across the lawn
rond	?*het meer rond wandelen*	to walk around the lake
uit	*de auto uit stappen*	to step out of the car
voorbij	*het huis voorbij rijden*	to drive past the house

I. Postpositions that correspond to deictic prepositions

When we compare the list of postpositions in Table 18 with the classification of spatial prepositions in Table 17, we see that there is no deictic preposition with a postpositional counterpart. This is remarkable since the deictic prepositions can also be used inherently and the vast majority of postpositions correspond to the inherent prepositions.

II. Postpositions that correspond to absolute prepositions

Very few absolute prepositions in Table 17 have a postpositional counterpart. For the inherently directional ones like *naar* 'to' this is not surprising given that they already denote a path. The only directional preposition that has a postpositional counterpart is *voorbij* 'past', but this is not surprising either since this preposition can sometimes also be used as a locational preposition; see example (218) in Section 1.3.1.2.2, sub II.

(269) a. Goirle ligt even voorbij Tilburg. [locational reading]
Goirle lies just past Tilburg

b. Jan reed Tilburg voorbij. [directional reading]
Jan drove Tilburg past

Of the non-directional absolute prepositions, only *om* 'around' and *rond* 'around' can be used as postpositions. The use of *om* is very restricted. It can actually only be used in the more or less fixed combinations in (270a&b); examples like (270c) are unacceptable.

(270) a. Jan ging de hoek om.
Jan went the corner around
'Jan turned the corner.'
b. Jan ging een blokje om.
Jan went a BLOKJE around
'Jan took a walk.'
c. *Jan liep de tafel om.
Jan walked the table around

The postposition *rond* is more common. In addition to more or less fixed combinations like (271a), it also occurs in (perhaps slightly marked) examples like (271b).

(271) a. Jan reisde de wereld rond.
Jan traveled the world around
b. (?)Jan wandelde het meer rond.
Jan walked the lake around

Perhaps the limited use of the postpositions *om/rond* is due to the fact, discussed in Section 1.3.1.2.2, that their prepositional counterparts can sometimes at least marginally be used directionally; cf. the discussion of (214c). That they have this ability is also supported by the fact that a prepositional phrase can be used in constructions like (272), where the PP denotes the extent of the road; as we have seen in examples (229) and (233) in Section 1.3.1.2.2, sub II, the extent reading typically involves directional PPs.

(272) De weg loopt rond/om de stad.
the road walks around the city
'The road goes around the city.'

III. Postpositions that correspond to inherent prepositions

The vast majority of postpositions that can be productively used correspond to inherent prepositions. Three groups can be distinguished.

A. In/binnen *'into/inside',* uit *'out of' and* door *'through'*

The first group of postpositions is characterized by the fact that the interior of the reference object is part of the implied path. The postpositional phrases headed by *in* and *binnen* in (273) express that the reference object is the endpoint of the path; the starting point is, however, exterior to the reference object. Note that *binnen* cannot be used when the postpositional phrase has an extent reading or functions as a modifier of a noun phrase.

(273) a. Jan liep de stad in/binnen.
Jan walked the town into
'Jan walked into the town.'
b. de weg loopt de stad in/*binnen
the road walks the town into
'the road leads into town'
c. de weg de stad in/*binnen
the road the town into
'the road into the town'

The postpositional phrase headed by *uit* in (274) expresses that the reference object is the starting point of the path, but the endpoint is exterior to it. Observe that, whereas *binnen* in (273a) can be used as a postposition in predicatively used postpositional phrases, its antonym *buiten* in (274a) cannot.

(274) a. Jan liep de stad uit/*buiten.
Jan walked the town out.of
'Jan walked out of the town.'
b. de weg loopt de stad uit
the road walked the town out.of
'the road leads out of town'
c. de weg de stad uit
the road the town out.of
'the road out of the town'

The postpositional phrase headed by *door* in (275), finally, expresses that the reference object is a subpart of the path: both the starting and the end points of the path are exterior to it. Note in passing that the preposition *door* can also be used in directional constructions; see the discussion of (254) and (255) in Section 1.3.1.2.3 for the difference between the two directional uses of *door*.

(275) a. Jan liep de tunnel door.
Jan walked the tunnel through
'Jan walked through the tunnel.'
b. de weg the tunnel door
the road the tunnel through
'the road through the tunnel'

The claim that *in* and *binnen* take the interior of the reference object as the endpoint of the implied path is supported by the fact that we can infer from (273a) that Jan is in town after completion of the event. The claim that *uit* denotes a path with an endpoint exterior to the reference object is supported by the fact that we can infer from (273b) that Jan is put of town after completion of the event. Note in passing that we cannot substitute *uit* for *buiten* in (276b′), which indicates that after completion of the event there is no longer any contact between the located and the reference object; cf. the discussion of example (247).

(276) a. Jan liep de stad in/binnen. ⇒
a′. Jan bevindt zich in de stad.
Jan is.situated REFL in the town
'Jan is in town.'
b. Jan liep de stad uit. ⇒
b′. Jan bevindt zich buiten de stad.
Jan is.situated REFL outside the town
'Jan is outside (not in) the town.'

The postpositions *in* and *binnen* in (273a) seem to be more or less equivalent. They differ, however, in that the latter requires that the located object end up in a position in the interior of the reference object, whereas the former does not. This is clear from the fact that *binnen* cannot be used in (277a), where it is implied that some subpart of the nail has not entered the wall. Example (277b) shows that the postposition *uit* 'out of' does not require that the located object be (fully) removed from the reference object. This shows that the postpositions behave similarly to the corresponding prepositions in this respect; cf. the discussion of Figure 23 and 25 above.

(277) a. Jan sloeg de spijker (slechts) één cm de muur in/*binnen.
Jan hit the nail only one cm the wall into
b. Jan trok de spijker (slechts) één cm de muur uit/*buiten.
Jan drew the nail only one cm the wall out.of

B. Op *'on',* af *'from' and* over *'over'.*

The second group of postpositions is characterized by the fact that the path goes along the surface of the reference object. The postposition *op* 'onto' indicates that the end but not the starting point of the path is situated on the reference object, while *af* 'from' indicates that the starting but not the endpoint of the path is situated on the reference object. In the case of *over* neither the starting point nor the endpoint of the path is situated on the reference object but some subpart of the path is. The respective paths of the postpositional phrases in (257) are illustrated in Figure 30.

(278) a. De supporter rende het veld op.
the fan ran the field onto
'The fan ran onto the field.'
b. De supporter rende het veld af.
the fan ran the field from
'The fan ran from the field.'
c. De supporter rende het veld over.
the fan ran the field across
'The fan ran across the field.'

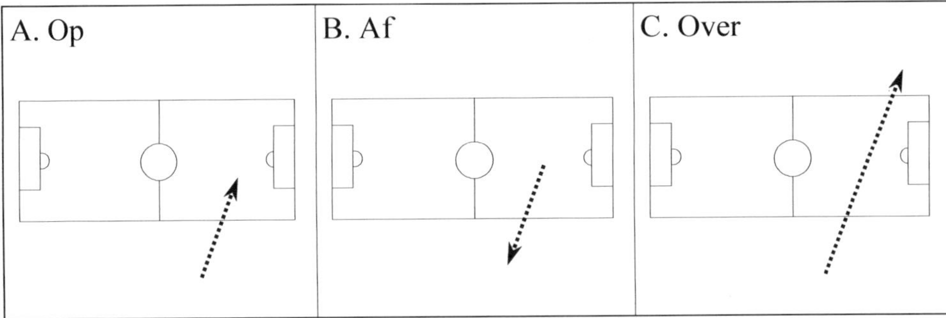

Figure 30: Op *'onto'*, af *'from'*, over *'across'*

The claim that *op* implies that the endpoint of the implied path is situated on the surface of the reference object is supported by the fact that we can infer from (278a) that the fan is on the field after completion of the event. The claim that *af* denotes a path with an endpoint exterior to the reference is supported by the fact that we can infer from (273b) that the fan is not on the field after completion of the event.

(279) a. De supporter rende het veld op. ⇒
a′. De supporter bevindt zich op het veld.
the fan is.situated REFL. on the field
'The fan is on the field.'
b. De supporter rende het veld af. ⇒
b′. De supporter bevindt zich buiten het veld.
the fan is.situated REFL outside the field
'The fan is not on the field.'

The precise interpretation of these postpositions also depends on the properties of the reference object: whereas in the case of a field the proper English translation of *op* and *af* are "onto" and "from", the proper renderings would instead be "up" and "down" when we are dealing with, e.g., a mountain. Although intuitions are not as clear as they were for the examples in (279), the core semantics in Figure 30 also seems present in (280): example (280a) seems preferably interpreted such that only the endpoint of the implied path is situated on the mountain; example (280b) seems preferably interpreted such that only the starting point is situated on the mountain (although this implication is not as strong as in the case of the circumpositional phrase *van de berg af*).

(280) a. Jan reed de berg op.
Jan drove the mountain onto
'Jan drove up the mountain.'
b. Jan reed de berg af.
Jan drove the mountain from
'Jan drove down the mountain.'

C. Langs 'along'

The third group has only one member, the adposition *langs* 'along', and implies that the path is more or less parallel to the length dimension of the reference object. In this respect the pre- and postposition *langs* in (281) behave similarly, as will also be clear from a comparison of Figure 31A below with Figure 20 in Section 1.3.1.2.3.

(281) a. Jan wandelt vaak langs de rivier [preposition]
Jan walks often along the river
b. Jan wandelt vaak de rivier langs. [postposition]
Jan walks often the river along

The difference between the pre- and postposition *langs* is often not very clear, which may be due to the fact that the prepositional phrase in (281a) can also be used directionally. First, the examples in (282) show that the verb *wandelen* 'to walk' can take either the auxiliary *hebben* or *zijn* in the perfect tense. As with other spatial PPs, we expect that in (282a) the PP is locational (the activity of walking takes place along the river), whereas (282b) has a change of location reading. On the latter reading, the implication should be that Jan is situated along the river as the result of the walking event, but this reading is not prominent, to say the least. The more prominent reading of (282b) is a directional one; Jan has to cover a path along the river. Note that this directional reading can also be found in example (282b′), where *langs*-PP functions as an (optional) adverbial phrase that characterizes the course and the predicative *naar*-PP expresses the endpoint of the path.

(282) a. Jan heeft langs de rivier gewandeld.
Jan has along the river walked
b. Jan is langs de rivier gewandeld.
Jan has along the river walked
b′. Jan is (langs de rivier) naar Breda gewandeld.
Jan has along the river to Breda walked

Second, the prepositional phrase can also be used in constructions like (283), where the *langs*-PP denotes the extent of the road: as we have seen in examples (229) and (233) in Section 1.3.1.2.2, sub II, the extent reading typically involves directional PPs.

(283) a. De weg loopt langs de rivier.
the road walks along the river
'The road extends along the river.'
b. de weg langs de rivier
the road along the river

The discussion above strongly suggests that the preposition *langs* can sometimes also be used directionally. The difference between directional pre- and postpositional *langs* may be related to the dimensional properties of the reference object. When the reference object is very long, as in (281) and (282), the path denoted by *langs* may be either smaller or larger than the length of the reference object; when it is relatively short, as in (284), the default interpretation seems to be that the path is longer than the length of the object (see Figure 31B). Given the marked status of (284b), *langs* preferably surfaces as a preposition in the latter case.

(284) a. Jan fietst elke dag langs de kerk.
Jan cycles every day along the church
'Jan cycles everyday past the church.'
b. *?Jan fietst elke dag de kerk langs.

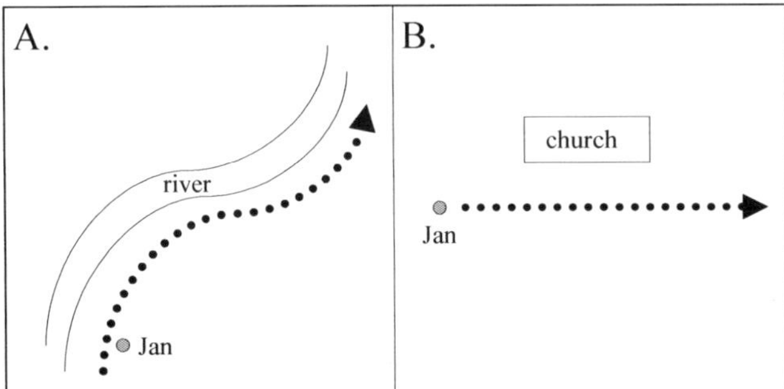

Figure 31: Langs *'along'*

In (284), the paths extend along the horizontal dimension of the reference object. Example (285) shows that the path may also extend in the vertical dimension.

(285) dat Jan langs het touw/de muur geklommen is.
that Jan along the rope/the wall climbed is
'that Jan has climbed along the rope/wall.'

Superficially seen, it seems that the direction of the vertical path can be further specified by means of the elements *omhoog/omlaag* 'upwards/downwards', as in (286a). This is not, however, the proper analysis of this example. The fact, illustrated in (286b), that the PP *langs het touw/de muur* is optional and can undergo PP-over-V shows that we are dealing with a particle verb, *omhoog/omlaag klimmen*, which may be modified by an adverbial locational PP headed by *langs*.

(286) a. dat Jan langs het touw/de muur omhoog/omlaag geklommen is.
that Jan along the rope/the wall upwards/downwards climbed is
'that Jan has climbed upwards/downwards along the rope/wall.'
b. dat Jan omhoog/omlaag geklommen is (langs het touw/de muur).

This shows that example (286a) must be analyzed like example (282b′) above, which also involves an adverbial locational PP headed by *langs*. That this is indeed the case is also clear from (287), which shows that the particle *omhoog/omlaag* can be readily be replaced by the predicative PP *naar boven*.

(287) a. dat Jan (langs het touw/de muur) naar boven geklommen is.
that Jan along the rope/the wall upwards climbed is
'that Jan has climbed upwards along the rope/wall.'
b. dat Jan naar boven geklommen is langs het touw/de muur.

1.3.1.4. Circumpositions

Circumpositional phrases are typically used in directional constructions, but many of these phrases can also be used in locational constructions. There is a conspicuous difference between these two uses: whereas the second part of the circumposition is mostly obligatorily present in the directional construction, it can generally be dropped in the locational construction without affecting the core meaning of the sentence. This casts some doubt on the assumption that we are dealing with constructions of a similar status. This section will discuss the circumpositions from Table 10 and Table 12 from Section 1.2.5 and investigate (i) whether they can be used in the locational and/or the directional construction and (ii) whether the second part can be omitted. Our findings will be summarized in Table 19.

I. P... aan

Examples (288) and (289) illustrate the use of spatial circumpositions with *aan* as their second member, and show that the circumpositional phrase *tegen de muur aan* may indicate a (change of) location or a direction. This does not hold, however, for the circumpositional phrase *achter de optocht aan* in (289b), which can only be used to indicate a direction.

(288) a. Er stond een ladder tegen de muur (aan). [location]
there stood a ladder against the wall AAN
'A ladder stood against the wall.'
b. Jan zette de ladder tegen de muur (aan). [change of location]
Jan put the ladder against the wall AAN
'Jan put a ladder against the wall.'

(289) a. Jan liep tegen de ladder *?(aan). [direction]
Jan walked against the ladder AAN
'Jan ran into the ladder.'
b. Er liepen veel kinderen achter de optocht #(aan). [direction]
there walked many children behind the parade AAN
'Masses of children followed the parade.'

The element *aan* in the locational examples in (288) can be dropped without a notable change in meaning; the presence of *aan* just seems to stress that there is physical contact between the located object and the reference object. In the directional examples in (289), on the other hand, *aan* must be present; without it the construction is either degraded or the directional meaning gets lost. The latter holds for (289b), which can be readily illustrated by considering its perfect tense counterparts in (290): when the verb *lopen* takes the auxiliary *zijn* it is a verb of traversing, which requires a directional complementive, and *aan* is compulsory; when the verb takes *hebben* it is an activity verb, which is compatible with a locational adverbial PP, and *aan* is preferably dropped.

(290) a. Er zijn horden kinderen achter de optocht *(aan) gelopen.
there are masses children behind the parade AAN walked
'Masses of children have followed the parade.'
b. Er hebben horden kinderen achter de optocht (?aan) gelopen.
there have masses children behind the parade AAN walked
'Masses of children have walked behind the parade.'

The locational and directional examples in (288) and (289) seem to differ in another respect as well. The examples in (291) show that the first differ from the latter in allowing the split pattern under a neutral intonation pattern; see also Section 1.2.5.3, sub I.

(291) a. Tegen de muur stond een ladder aan. [location]
a′. Tegen de muur zette Jan de ladder aan. [change of location]
b. *Tegen de ladder liep Jan aan. [direction]
b′. *Achter de optocht zijn horden kinderen aan gelopen. [direction]

This suggests that *achter ... aan* is better not considered a circumposition in the locational construction. Making a distinction between the phrases in the directional and the locational constructions is also supported by the data in (292). In the (change of) locational constructions the element *aan* can occupy a position within the clause-final verb cluster, which is a typical property of particles, whereas this gives rise to a degraded result in the directional construction. We leave it to future research to investigate whether this suggestion is on the right track; see also Section 1.2.5.3, sub I, for relevant information.

(292) a. dat de ladder tegen de muur heeft aan gestaan. [location]
that the ladder against the wall has AAN stood
a′. dat Jan de ladder tegen de muur heeft aan gezet. [change of location]
that Jan the ladder against the wall has AAN put
b. ??dat Jan tegen de ladder is aan gelopen. [direction]
that Jan against the ladder has AAN walked
b′. ??dat er veel kinderen achter de optocht zijn aan gelopen.
that there many children behind the parade are AAN walked

II. Van... af

There are two circumpositions with *af* as their second member: *van ... af* and *op ... af*. The examples in (293) show that the circumpositional phrase *van ... af* may indicate a (change of) location, although it must be noted that (293a) is unnatural. Similar constructions are not possible with *op ... af*. The examples in (294) show that the two circumpositional phrases can both be used directionally.

(293) a. ?Het boek lag van de tafel (af). [location]
the book lay from the table AF
'The book was removed/had fallen from the table.'
b. Jan legde het boek van de tafel (af). [change of location]
Jan put the book from the table AF
'Jan removed the book from the table.'

(294) a. Jan reed van de berg ?(af). [direction]
Jan drove from the mountain AF
'Jan drove down from the mountain.'
b. Jan liep op zijn tegenstander *(af). [direction]
Jan walked towards his opponent AF

In the locational examples in (293), the element *af* can be dropped without a clear change in meaning; the presence of *af* just seems to stress that the physical contact between the located object and the reference object has been broken. At first sight, it appears that *af* can also be dropped in the directional example in (294a), but this may be due to the fact that the preposition *van* can also be used as a directional preposition. In this respect, it is important to note that the absence or presence of *af* affects the meaning of the clause: when *af* is present, as in (295a), the implied path goes downward along the surface of the mountain, as depicted in Figure 32A; when *af* is absent, as in (295b), the clause can also express that Jan is withdrawing from the mountain, as in Figure 32B. In other words, only when *af* is present is it necessarily implied that the starting point of the implied part is situated on the mountain. Since the element *af* cannot be dropped in the case of (294b), it seems safe to conclude that it is actually obligatory in the directional construction, and that the case without *af* involves the directional prepositional phrase *van de berg*.

(295) a. Jan reed van de berg af.
Jan drove from the mountain AF
'Jan drove *down* from the mountain.'

b. Jan reed van de berg ?(naar het meer).
Jan drove from the mountain to the lake
'Jan drove from the mountain to the lake.'

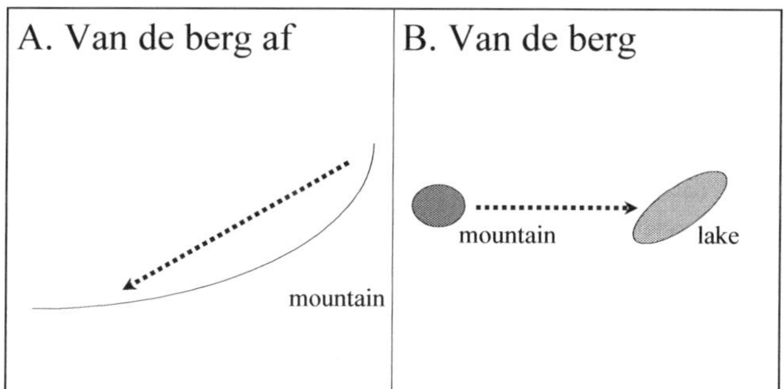

Figure 32: Van de berg (af) *'(down) from the mountain'*

III. P... door

The (a)-examples in (296) show that the circumposition *tussen ... door* cannot be used to indicate a (change of) location. The grammatical use of the circumpositional phrase in (296b) is directional. The same thing holds for *onder ... door*, which we will not illustrate here.

(296) a. Het boek ligt tussen de andere spullen (*door). [location]
the book lies between the other things DOOR

a′. Jan legt het boek tussen de andere spullen (*door). [change of location]
Jan puts the book between the other things DOOR

b. Jan reed tussen de bomen #(door). [direction]
Jan drove between the trees DOOR
'Jan drove along a path that goes through the trees.'

In (296b), *door* must be present; without it the directional meaning is lost. This can be readily illustrated by considering the perfect tense constructions in (297): when the verb *rijden* takes the auxiliary *zijn* it is a verb of traversing, which requires a directional complementive, and *door* is compulsory; when the verb takes *hebben* it is an activity verb, which is compatible with a locational adverbial PP, and *door* is preferably dropped.

(297) a. Jan is tussen de bomen *?(door) gereden.
Jan is between the trees DOOR driven
'Jan has driven through in between the trees.'
b. Jan heeft tussen de bomen (?door) gereden.
Jan has between the trees DOOR driven
'Jan has driven along a path that goes through the trees.'

IV. P... heen

The (a)-examples in (298) show that circumpositions with *heen* as their second member may indicate a (change of) location. The circumpositional phrase in (298b) is directional. In the (a)-examples, *heen* can be dropped without any clear effect on the meaning. This is also the case in (298b), which is not surprising since *over* can also be used as a directional preposition; the same thing holds at least marginally for *langs* 'along' and *om* 'around'.

(298) a. Over zijn schouder (heen) hing een kleurige das. [location]
over his shoulder HEEN hung a colorful scarf
'A colorful scarf was hanging over his shoulder.'
a′. Over zijn schouder (heen) hing Jan een kleurige das. [change of location]
over his shoulder HEEN hung Jan a colorful scarf
'Jan hung a colorful scarf over his shoulder.'
b. Jan reed over de brug (heen). [direction]
Jan drove over the bridge HEEN
'Jan drove over the bridge.'

For completeness' sake we want to note that it is not particularly clear what semantic effect dropping *heen* has on the example in (298b). It has been suggested that *heen* indicates a movement directed away from the speaker (*Woordenboek der Nederlandsche Taal*; entry *heen*[II]) or some other anchoring point, but this certainly cannot be extended to the non-directional cases in (298). Furthermore, it does not seem to provide a correct characterization for directional examples like (299) either.

(299) Jan is drie keer om mij heen gefietst.
Jan is three time around me HEEN cycled
'Jan has traversed the path around me three times on bicycle.'

It must be noted, however, that *heen* can be used as a verbal particle, and in that case it indeed has this implication of movement away from the speaker or some other anchoring point. However, these cases often have an archaic or idiomatic flavor. Some more or less idiomatic examples are given in (300).

(300) a. Jan is heen gegaan.
Jan is away gone
'Jan has departed this life.'

b. Loop heen!
go away
'Go away!' or 'You're kidding.'

c. Ik ga er morgen heen.
I go there tomorrow HEEN
'I will go there tomorrow' or 'I will visit him/her/it/them tomorrow.'

That (300a) is idiomatic is beyond doubt. . Turning to (300b), in addition to its idiomatic meaning "you're kidding!", the more literal meaning "go away!" is special in that in colloquial speech this combination only occurs in the imperative mood: *Jan liep heen* 'Jan walked away' is very formal and perhaps even archaic. That (300c) is more or less idiomatic is perhaps less clear. The main reason for assuming this is that the locational pro-form *er* 'there' cannot be replaced by a full PP; examples like (301a) are completely ungrammatical when *heen* is present (the same thing holds for *iets er heen brengen* 'to bring something to NP'). More idiomatic expressions with *heen* are given in (301b&c).

(301) a. Ik ga morgen naar oma/de bioscoop (*heen).
I go tomorrow to granny/the cinema HEEN
'I will visit granny /go to the movies tomorrow.'

b. achter iets heen gaan
after something HEEN go
'to chase/follow something up'

c. achter iets/iemand heen zitten
after something/someone HEEN sit
'to keep onto something/someone'

V. P... in

The (a)-examples in (302) show that the circumpositional phrase *tussen de meisjes in* may indicate a (change of) location; this is not readily possible, however, with *tegen + NP + in*. Both circumpositional phrases with *in* as their second member can be used directionally. This is illustrated in (302b) for *tegen de stroom in*: this example expresses that the speaker is traversing a path opposite to the direction of the current.

(302) a. Jan zit tussen de twee meisjes (in). [location]
Jan sits between the two girls IN
'Jan is sitting in between the two girls.'

a′. Marie zet Jan tussen de twee meisjes (in). [change of location]
Marie puts Jan between the two girls IN
'Marie is putting Jan in between the two girls.'

b. Tegen de stroom *(in) zwem ik niet graag. [direction]
against the current IN swim I not gladly
'I don't like to swim against the current.'

The element *in* can be dropped without a notable difference in meaning in the non-directional (a)-examples; *in* just seems to function as an emphasizer. In the directional example in (302b), on the other hand, *in* must be present; without it, the directional meaning gets lost.

VI. P... langs

The examples in (303) show that circumpositions with *langs* as their second member are only used as directional adpositions; the non-directional (a)-examples are only acceptable without the element *langs*.

(303) a. De bloemen liggen achter het huis (*langs). [location]
the flowers lie behind the house LANGS
'The flowers are lying behind the house.'
a′. Jan legt de bloemen achter het huis (*langs). [change of location]
Jan puts the flowers behind the house LANGS
'Jan is putting the flowers behind the house.'
b. Jan wandelt achter het huis #(langs). [direction]
Jan walks behind the house LANGS
'Jan is walking along the back of the house.'

In (303b), the element *langs* is obligatory; without it the directional meaning gets lost. This can be readily illustrated by considering the perfect tense constructions in (304): when the verb *wandelen* takes the auxiliary *zijn* it is a verb of traversing, which requires a directional complementive, and *langs* is compulsory; when the verb takes *hebben* it is an activity verb, which is compatible with a locational adverbial PP, and *langs* is preferably dropped.

(304) a. Jan is achter het huis *(langs) gewandeld.
Jan is behind the house LANGS walked
'Jan has walked along the back of the house.'
b. Jan heeft achter het huis (*?langs) gewandeld.
Jan is behind the house LANGS walked
'Jan has walked behind the house.'

VII. P... om

The examples in (305) show that circumpositions with *om* as their second member are only used as directional adpositions; the non-directional (a)-examples are only acceptable without the element *om*. In example (305c), we are dealing with a metaphorical use of the circumpositional phrase *buiten de administratie om*.

(305) a. De bloemen liggen achter het huis (*om). [location]
the flowers lie behind the house OM
'The flowers are lying behind the house.'
a′. Jan legt de bloemen achter het huis (*om). [change of location]
Jan puts the flowers behind the house OM
'Jan is putting the flowers behind the house.'
b. Jan liep achter het huis #(om). [direction]
Jan walked behind the house OM
'Jan walked around the back of the house.'
c. Deze procedure loopt buiten de administratie *(om).
this procedure goes outside the administration OM
'The administration is not involved in this procedure.'

In (305b&c), the element *om* is obligatory; without it the directional meaning of (305b) is lost, and (305c) becomes ungrammatical. The loss of the directional meaning of (305b) can be readily illustrated by considering the perfect tense constructions in (306): when the verb *lopen* takes the auxiliary *zijn* it is a verb of traversing, which requires a directional complementive, and *om* is compulsory; when the verb takes *hebben* it is an activity verb, which is compatible with a locational adverbial PP, and *om* is preferably dropped.

(306) a. Jan is achter het huis *(om) gewandeld.
Jan is behind the house OM walked
'Jan has walked around the back of the house.'
b. Jan heeft achter het huis (*?om) gewandeld.
Jan has behind the house OM walked
'Jan has walked behind the house.'

VIII. Tegen ... op

The examples in (307) show that the circumposition *tegen ... op* can only be used as a directional adposition; the non-directional (a)-examples are only acceptable without the element *op*. In example (307c), we are dealing with an idiomatic construction *tegen de klippen op werken.*

(307) a. De ladder stond tegen de muur (??op). [location]
the ladder stood against the wall OP
'The ladder stood against the wall.'
a′. Marie zette de ladder tegen de muur (??op). [change of location]
Marie put the ladder against the wall OP
'Marie put the ladder against the wall.'
b. Jan klimt tegen de muur #(op). [direction]
Jan climbs against the wall OP
'Jan is climbing up against the wall.'
c. Jan werkt tegen de klippen *(op).
Jan works against the cliffs up
'Jan is working extremely hard.'

The element *op* is obligatory in the directional construction; without it the directional meaning of (307b) gets lost and (307c) becomes ungrammatical. For those people who accept (308b) without *op*, the verb acts as an activity verb, and the PP acts as an adverbial phrase.

(308) a. Jan is tegen de berg *(op) geklommen.
Jan is against the mountain OP climbed
'Jan has climbed up against the wall.'
b. Jan heeft tegen de berg ?(*?op) geklommen.
Jan has against the mountain OP climbed
'Jan has climbed up against the wall.'

IX. P... toe

The examples in (309) show that the circumposition *tot ... toe* cannot readily be used to denote a (change of) location.

(309) a. De stenen liggen tot de heg (*?toe). [location]
the stones lie until the hedge TOE
'The stones are lying up to the hedge.'
b. Jan legt de stenen tot de heg (*?toe). [change of location]
Jan lays the stones until the hedge TOE
'Jan is laying the stones up to the hedge.'

The examples seem to improve slightly when we add a *van*-PP, as in (310). It is, however, doubtful whether the circumpositions refer to a (change of) location in these cases: the *van*-PP is directional (it indicates the starting point of the path) so we expect that the circumpositional phrase is also directional (it indicates the endpoint of the path). Therefore, the examples in (310) are directional, and have an extent reading comparable to *Het pad loopt van hier tot aan de heg (toe)* 'The path extends from here to the hedge'.

(310) a. De stenen liggen van hier tot de heg (?toe).
the stones lie from here until the hedge TOE
b. Jan legt de stenen van hier tot de heg (?toe).
Jan lays the stones from here until the hedge TOE
'Jan is laying the stones from here to the hedge.'

As is shown in (311), the examples in (309) become completely grammatical when the noun phrase *de heg* is preceded by the element *aan*. It has been suggested that *tot aan ... toe* is also a circumposition, albeit of a slightly more complex nature. There are, however, reasons to reject this suggestion: the preposition *tot* is able to take an adpositional complement (see Section 2.2.1, sub III for further discussion), so we may be dealing with the circumposition *tot ... toe*, which takes a PP-complement.

(311) a. De stenen liggen tot aan de heg (toe).
the stones lie until at the hedge TOE
b. Jan legt de stenen tot aan de heg (toe).
Jan lays the stones until at the hedge TOE
'Jan is laying the stones from here to the hedge.'

From the discussion above, we can probably conclude that circumpositions with *toe* are directional only, as in (312). In these examples, *toe* seems to be optional, which is not really surprising given that the prepositions *naar* 'to' and *tot* 'until' are both directional themselves; the meaning contribution of *toe* seems to be mainly a case of adding emphasis. Note that (312b) can also be made more complex by adding the element *aan*; we will return to such examples in Section 2.2.1, sub III.

(312) a. Jan reed naar Peter (toe).
Jan drove to Peter TOE
'Jan drove to Peter.'
b. Jan reed tot <aan> de grens <aan> (toe).
Jan drove until AAN the border TOE
'Jan drove until the border.'

X. P... uit

The circumpositions with *uit* as their second member can be used to refer to a location, as in (313a): the element *uit* must be present in order to obtain the "out from" reading. The corresponding construction involving a change of location in (313b) is infelicitous, which, in this case, may be due to the fact that it seems improbable that Marie would stick out her skirt on purpose.

(313) a. Haar rok hing onder haar jas #(uit). [location]
her skirt hung under her coat UIT
'Her skirt was sticking out from under her coat.'
b. #Marie hing haar rok onder haar jas uit. [change of location]
Marie hung her skirt under her coat UIT

A verb that seems to combine rather easily with the sequence *P + NP + uit* is *steken*, but in this case, too, the change of location reading seems degraded, as is shown in (314a′). Sometimes, however, the change of location construction seems to be possible, as in (314b′), but whether we can conclude something from this is not clear because *uit* can also be used as a verbal particle, which is clear from the fact that the PP *boven de menigte* is optional in this example.

(314) a. Het formulier stak onder zijn papieren uit.
the form stuck under his papers UIT
'The form stuck out from under his papers.'
a′. *Jan stak het formulier onder zijn papieren uit.
Jan stuck the form under his papers UIT
b. Jans hand stak (??boven de menigte) uit.
Jan's hand stuck above the crowd UIT
'Jan's hand was sticking out above the crowd.'
b′. Jan stak zijn hand (boven de menigte) uit.
Jan stuck his hand above the crowd UIT
'Jan stuck out his hand above the crowd.'

Whatever the answer may be to the question whether circumpositions with *uit* can be used in constructions involving a change of location, it is clear that they can be used to refer to directions. One example is given in (315).

(315) De fanfare liep voor de optocht #(uit).
the brass band walked before the parade UIT
'The brass band walked in front of the parade.'

Example (315) shows that the element *uit* is obligatory in the directional construction; when it is absent the directional meaning is lost. This can be readily illustrated by considering the perfect tense constructions in (316): when the verb *lopen* takes the auxiliary *zijn* it is a verb of traversing, which requires a directional complementive, and *uit* is compulsory; when the verb takes *hebben* it is an activity verb, which is compatible with a locational adverbial PP, and *uit* is preferably dropped.

(316) a. De fanfare is voor de optocht *(uit) gelopen.
the brass band is before the parade UIT walked
'The brass band has walked in front of (= led) the parade.'

b. De fanfare heeft voor de optocht (??uit) gelopen.
the brass band has before the parade UIT walked
'The brass band has walked in front of (≠ led) the parade.'

XI. P... vandaan

The examples in (317) show that circumpositions with *vandaan* as their second member are only used as directional adpositions. The non-directional (a)-examples are only acceptable without the element *vandaan*.

(317) a. De bloemen liggen achter het huis (*vandaan). [location]
the flowers lie behind the house VANDAAN
'The flowers are lying behind the house.'

a′. Jan legt de bloemen achter het huis (*vandaan). [change of location]
Jan puts the flowers behind the house VANDAAN
'Jan is putting the flowers behind the house.'

b. Jan reed achter de bomen #(vandaan). [direction]
Jan drove behind the trees VANDAAN
'Jan drove from behind the trees.'

The element *vandaan* is obligatorily present in the directional construction in (317b); without it the directional meaning is lost. This can be readily illustrated by considering the perfect tense constructions in (318): when the verb *rijden* takes the auxiliary *zijn* it is a verb of traversing, which requires a directional complementive, and *vandaan* is compulsory; when the verb takes *hebben* it is an activity verb, which is compatible with a locational adverbial PP, and *vandaan* must be dropped.

(318) a. Jan is achter de bomen *(vandaan) gereden.
Jan is behind the trees VANDAAN driven
'Jan has driven from behind the trees.'

b. Jan heeft achter de bomen (*vandaan) gereden.
Jan has behind the trees VANDAAN driven
'Jan has driven behind the trees.'

Often, circumpositional phrases with *vandaan* can be preceded by the preposition *van*; cf. (319a). This element is not, however, part of the circumposition but a regular preposition, as will be clear from the fact that the circumpositional phrase can be replaced by the adpositional pro-form *daar* 'there'; cf. (319b). We return to this in Section 2.2.1.

(319) a. Jan kwam van achter de bomen vandaan.
Jan came from behind the trees VANDAAN
'Jan can from behind the trees.'

b. Jan kwam van daar.
Jan came from there

Finally, note that the construction in (320) seems to be the antonym of the idiomatic construction *Ik ga er heen* in (300c), and is therefore in all likelihood also an idiomatic expression.

(320) Ik kom er net vandaan.
I come there just from
'I just come from there.' or 'I have just visited him/her/it/them.'

XII. Summary

Table 19 again gives the list of circumpositions and indicates whether they can be used to indicate a (change of) location or a direction. Further, we have indicated whether or not the second part of the circumposition must be present in order for the circumpositional phrase to express the locational/directional meaning.

Table 19: Spatial circumpositions

CIRCUMPOSITION	LOCATIONAL READING		DIRECTIONAL READING	
	AVAILABLE	PARTICLE	AVAILABLE	2ND PART
achter ... aan	—	n.a.	+	obligatory
tegen ... aan	+	optional		
van ... af	+	optional	+	obligatory (but see (294a))
op ... af	—	n.a.		
onder/tussen ... door	—	n.a.	+	obligatory
door/langs/om/ over ... heen	+	optional	+	obligatory
tegen ... in	—	n.a.	+	obligatory
tussen ... in	+	optional		
achter/boven/onder/voor ... langs	—	n.a.	+	obligatory
achter/buiten/voor ... om	—	n.a.	+	obligatory
tegen ... op	—	n.a.	+	obligatory
naar/tot ... toe	—	n.a.	+	optional
achter/boven/onder /tussen/voor ... uit	location: + change of location: —	optional; meaning effect	+	obligatory
achter/bij/om/onder/ tussen/van ... vandaan	—	n.a.	+	obligatory

It will be clear from this table that all circumpositions can have a directional meaning, and that the second part of the circumposition is generally obligatorily present then; it can only be dropped when the first part can also occur as a preposition with a directional meaning.

The table shows further that only a small subset of the circumpositions can be used in a locational construction. Moreover, the second part generally has little impact on the meaning expressed. Perhaps it is therefore even legitimate to ask whether we are really dealing with circumpositions in these cases, or just with prepositional phrases that are somehow emphasized by some sort of particle. We will assume the latter option, although we will leave it to future research to investigate whether this suggestion is indeed on the right track.

To conclude, note that most circumpositional phrases also allow an extent reading. The examples in (321) show that only the circumpositions ending in *aan*, *uit* and *vandaan* seem to resist this use.

(321) De weg loopt ...
a. *?tegen het bos aan
against the wood AAN
b. van de berg af
from the mountain AF
c. tussen de bomen door
between the trees DOOR
d. over de brug heen
over the bridge HEEN
e. ?tussen de bomen in
between the trees IN
f. achter het huis langs
behind the house LANGS
g. voor het huis om
in.front.of the house OM
h. tegen de berg op
against the mountain OP
i. naar het hek toe
towards the gate TOE
j. *achter het bos uit
behind the wood UIT
k. *achter het bos vandaan
behind the wood VANDAAN

1.3.1.5. Intransitive adpositions and verbal particles

Section 1.2.4 has shown that there is a gradient scale by which (the syntactic use or meaning of) intransitive adpositions are related to their corresponding prepositions. In some cases the relation is quite close whereas in other cases the relation is rather loose or, perhaps, even nonexistent. As a result, the distinction between intransitive adpositions and verbal particles is often not clear-cut. Nevertheless, we will discuss the two groups in separate sections. The main purpose of the following sections is to make a distinction between intransitive adpositions, which have retained their original (spatial) meaning and can appear in the same environment as predicative PPs, and verbal particles, which have lost this meaning to at least a certain extent and often cannot be replaced by predicative PPs without affecting the core meaning of the construction.

1.3.1.5.1. Intransitive adpositions

There are at least three cases that are typically eligible for an analysis involving an intransitive adposition, that is, three cases in which the adpositional element has retained its original meaning and behaves both semantically and syntactically like a predicative (locational) PP.

I. Dressing and personal hygiene

Constructions involving dressing typically involve intransitive adpositions. The examples in (322) are self-explanatory in this respect.

(322) a. Jan zet een hoed op (zijn hoofd).
Jan puts a hat on his head
b. Jan doet een das om (zijn nek).
Jan puts a scarf around his neck
c. Jan doet een jas aan (?zijn lijf).
Jan puts a coat on his body

This does not seem to hold, however, for constructions involving undressing. The element *af* in (323a&b) does not occur as a preposition in colloquial speech, so it can at best be related to the circumposition *van* .. *af* in (323a′&b′). This option is not even available in the case of *uit* in (323c), as will be clear from the ungrammaticality of (323c′).

(323) a. Jan zet zijn hoed <af> (*zijn hoofd) <af>.
Jan puts his hat off his head
a′. Jan zet zijn hoed van zijn hoofd af.
b. Jan doet zijn das <af> (*zijn nek) <af>.
Jan puts his scarf off his neck
b′. ?Jan doet zijn das van zijn nek af.
c. Jan doet zijn jas <uit> (*zijn lijf) <uit>.
Jan takes his coat off his body
c′. *Jan doet zijn jas van zijn lijf uit.

That the intransitive prepositions in (322) may have an implicit complement is supported by the fact that examples like these may contain a possessive dative, which refers to the inalienable possessor of the (implicit) complement of the preposition.

(324) a. Jan zet haar een hoed op (het hoofd).
Jan puts her a hat on the head
b. Jan doet haar een das om (de nek).
Jan puts her a scarf around the neck
c. Jan doet haar een jas aan (?het lijf).
Jan puts her a coat on the body

The possessive dative cannot be used with the elements *af* and *uit* in (323). This supports our earlier conclusion that there is no implicit complement and therefore strongly suggests that *af* and *uit* are verbal particles.

(325) a. *Jan zet haar een hoed af.
Jan puts her a hat off
b. *Jan doet haar een das af.
Jan puts her a scarf off
c. *Jan doet haar een jas uit.
Jan takes her a coat off

The adpositional elements in (322) and (323) also differ in that the former can be used in the ABSOLUTE *MET*-CONSTRUCTION, whereas this does not seem readily possible with the latter. This again supports the suggested analysis: intransitive prepositions may function as independent predicates whereas verbal particles only occur in combination with a verb.

(326) a. [Met zijn hoed op/*?af] kwam Jan de kamer binnen.
with his hat on/off came Jan the room inside
'Jan entered the room with his hat on.'

b. [Met zijn das om/*?af] kwam Jan de kamer binnen.
with his scarf around/off came Jan the room inside
'Jan entered the room with his scarf around his neck.'

c. [Met zijn jas aan/??uit] kwam Jan de kamer binnen.
with his coat on/off came Jan the room inside
'Jan entered the room with his coat on.'

Note that the verbs in (322) have very little semantic content. This holds especially for the verb *doen* 'to do', the semantic contribution of which is mainly restricted to the indication that some activity is taking place. The examples in (327a&b) show that the use of a full PP is impossible when we use more contentful verbs like *kleden* 'to dress'. This suggests that the adpositional elements in these examples are probably verbal particles, which would also fit in with the fact that they are in a paradigm with the undisputed particle verb *om kleden* 'to change one's clothes' in (327c). For completeness' sake, note that the object in the primed examples is not a possessive dative but a regular direct object, which is clear from the fact that it is promoted to subject in the passive construction: *Het kind werd aan/uit/om gekleed* 'The child was dressed/undressed/changed clothes.'

(327) a. Jan kleedt zich aan (*zijn lijf).
Jan dresses REFL on his body
'Jan is dressing.'

a′. Jan kleedt het kind aan
Jan dresses the child on
'Jan is dressing the child.'

b. Jan kleedt zich uit (*zijn lijf).
Jan dresses REFL out his body
'Jan is undressing.'

b′. Jan kleedt het kind uit.
Jan dresses the child out
'Jan is undressing the child.'

c. Jan kleedt zich om.
Jan dresses REFL OM.
'Jan is changing his clothes.'

c′. Jan kleedt het kind om.
Jan dresses the child OM
'Jan is changing the child's clothes.'

Other constructions that may contain intransitive adpositions involve verbs of personal hygiene. Two examples are given in (328).

(328) a. Jan smeert zonnebrandolie op (zijn lichaam).
Jan smears suntan oil on his body

b. Jan doet ogenschaduw op (zijn oogleden).
Jan puts eye shadow on his eyelids

Example (329a) is similar to those in (327) in the sense that a full PP is not possible; perhaps it would be justified to speak of a particle verb in this case, especially since (329b) shows that the resulting location of the makeup can be expressed by means of an accusatively marked noun phrase.

(329) a. Jan maakt zich op (*zijn gezicht).
Jan makes REFL on his face
'Jan is making up.'

b. Jan maakt alleen zijn ogen op.
Jan makes only his eyes up
'Jan only makes up his eyes.'

II. Contextually determinable locations

The examples in Subsection I involve body parts that are identifiable from the context. Intransitive adpositions may also arise when a location is involved which can be identified given the context. When (330a) is uttered without the noun phrase *mijn huis* the relevant location is taken to be the speaker's. And the two alternatives in (330b) are synonymous when Jan is participating in a wrestling match.

(330) a. Het postkantoor is dicht bij (mijn huis).
the post office is close to my house
b. Jan ligt onder (zijn tegenstander).
Jan lies under his opponent

The elements *binnen* 'inside', *buiten* 'outside', *beneden* 'downstairs', *boven* 'upstairs' are also used in predicative position. Some examples are given in (331). In the contexts of these examples, these elements do not readily take a nominal complement. This is clearest in the case of *beneden*, where the addition of a noun phrase leads to full ungrammaticality (but see the remark below Table 5 on page 7). When we want to analyze these elements as adpositions, we must conclude that they can only be used intransitively in these constructions.

(331) a. Marie zit binnen (??het huis).
Marie sits inside the house
b. Marie zit buiten (?het huis).
Marie sits outside the house
c. Marie zit beneden (*het huis).
Marie sits downstairs the house
d. Marie zit boven (#het huis).
Marie sits upstairs the house

Note that, in contrast to the other elements discussed in this section, the four adpositions in (331) can also be used as adverbial phrases. This is clear from the fact that the examples in (332) can be paraphrases by means of the adverbial ... *en doet dat PP* '... and does it PP' test. This shows that these adpositions are in fact full PPs; verbal particles are never used adverbially.

(332) a. De hond speelt binnen/buiten/beneden/boven.
the dog plays inside/outside/downstairs/upstairs
b. De hond speelt en hij doet dat binnen/buiten/beneden/boven.
the dog plays and he does that inside/outside/downstairs/upstairs

Something similar to what was found for the elements in (331) holds for the elements in (333). These elements can be used in the same environments as predicative adpositional phrases, but differ from those in (331) in expressing a directional meaning. This is clear from the fact that they can be used as the complement of verbs of traversing. If we want to analyze these elements as adpositions, we must conclude that they can only be used intransitively, since they cannot take a noun phrase as a complement.

(333) a. Het vliegtuig vliegt omhoog/omlaag.
the airplanes flies up/down
b. De auto rijdt vooruit/achteruit.
the car drives forwards/backwards
c. De auto rijdt/slaat linksaf/rechtsaf. [also: *afslaan* 'to turn the corner']
the car drives/goes to the left/right
d. De auto rijdt opzij.
the car drives out.of.the.way

Note in passing that some speakers can also use examples like (334), as is clear from the fact that similar examples occasionally occur on the internet. This means that for those speakers *omhoog* and *omlaag* can also be used as postpositions.

(334) a. %Jan liep de berg omhoog/omlaag.
Jan walked the mountain up/down
'Jan traversed the mountain up/downward.'
b. %De gids trok de auto de berg omhoog.
the guide pulled the car the mountain up
'The guide pulled the car up/down the mountain.'

III. Material composition

Adposition-like elements eligible for an analysis as intransitive adpositions also occur in constructions that involve material composition like (335).

(335) a. Jan naait de knopen aan (zijn shirt).
Jan sews the buttons on his shirt
b. Marie plakt de foto's in (het boek).
Marie pastes the pictures in the book
c. Marie sluit de luidsprekers aan (??de versterker).
Marie connects the speakers to the amplifier

Note, however, that these examples come very close to particle verb constructions. This is clear from the fact that *aan* cannot be used intransitively in examples like (336a); the particle *op* is used in that case instead.

(336) a. Jan hangt het schilderij aan *(de muur).
Jan hangs the painting on the wall
b. Jan hangt het schilderij op (*?de muur).
Jan hangs the painting prt. the wall

1.3.1.5.2. Verbal particles

In contrast to the intransitive adpositions discussed in the previous section, verbal particles need not express a spatial meaning. Often, their meaning is more or less aspectual in nature. The particle *op* 'up' in (337a), for example, transforms the stative verbs *staan* 'to stand' into an activity verb, and *weg* 'away' in (337b) changes the stative verb *drijven* 'to float' into a process verb.

(337) a. staan$_{[+state]}$ ⇒ a′. opstaan$_{[+activity]}$
to stand to stand up
b. drijven$_{[+state]}$ ⇒ b′. wegdrijven$_{[+process]}$
to float to float away

In addition, these verbal particles normally make the event °telic: the particle verb is inherently bounded in time and results in a new location of the located object. That the particle verb is telic is also clear from the fact that it selects the time auxiliary *zijn* 'to be' in the perfect tense, whereas the stative verbs *staan* and *drijven* take the auxiliary *hebben* 'to have'.

(338) a. Jan heeft/*is daar gestaan.
Jan has/is there stood
a′. Jan is/*heeft op gestaan.
Jan is/has up stood
b. De bal/man heeft/*is op het water gedreven.
the ball/man has/is on the water floated
b′. De bal/man is/*heeft weg gedreven.
the ball/man is/has away driven

Exceptions are the particles *door* and *mee* in particle verbs like *doorwerken* 'to continue to work' and *meewerken* 'to cooperate/work along', which are atelic and take the auxiliary *hebben* 'to have' in the perfect tense; cf. Van Hout (1996:96).

The fact that most monadic particle verbs select the auxiliary *zijn* clearly shows that they are °unaccusative verbs; As is illustrated for *weg drijven* in (339), they also satisfy the other criteria for unaccusativity; the past participle can be used attributively (which is excluded in the case of *op staan*, due to a general prohibition involving contraction verbs, which is discussed in Section A9.2.1.1, sub IX), and passivization is excluded.

(339) a. de weg gedreven bal
the away floated ball
b. *Er wordt (door de man) weg gedreven.
there is by the man away floated

Particles of monadic particle verbs are predicative elements that function as a complementive. The examples in (340) illustrate this by showing that, like resultatives, particles have the ability to introduce an additional argument in the clause that is not selected by the verb. This means that the noun phrase *het meisje* 'the girl' in (340b) is semantically licensed by the particle *uit*, which implies that the latter must be a predicate of some sort.

(340) a. Jan lacht (*het meisje).
Jan laughs the girl
b. Jan lacht *(het meisje) uit.
Jan laughs the girl UIT

The hypothesis that particles are complementives is further supported by the fact, illustrated in (341a&b), that both resultatives and particles must be left-adjacent to the verbs in clause-final position. Since a clause can contain at most one complementive, this hypothesis also correctly predicts that examples like (341c), in which a verbal particle co-occurs with a resultative phrase, are ungrammatical.

(341) a. dat Jan de deur <*kapot> gisteren <kapot> trapte <*kapot>.
that Jan the door broken yesterday kicked
'that Jan damaged the door yesterday by kicking it.'
b. dat Jan de deur <*in> gisteren <in> trapte <*in>.
that Jan the door in yesterday kicked
'that Jan kicked in the door yesterday.'
c. *dat Jan de deur gisteren kapot in trapte.
that Jan the door yesterday broken in kicked

There are, however, some apparent counterexamples to the claim that verbal particles and complementives are in complementary distribution. Consider (342). The verb *leggen* 'to put' requires a complementive, and therefore (342b) confirms our hypothesis that the particle *neer* is a complementive, just like the PP *op de tafel* in (342a). However, the PP and the particle can simultaneously appear in constructions like (342c). It must be noted, however, that the PP in (342c) need not precede the clause-final verb, but can also follow it. This strongly suggests that the PP does not function as the complementive of the verb in this example.

(342) a. dat Jan het boek <op de tafel> legde <*op de tafel>.
that Jan the book on the table put
'that Jan put the book on the table.'
b. dat Jan het boek <neer> legde <*neer>.
that Jan the book down put
'that Jan put down the book.'
c. dat Jan het boek <op de tafel> neer legde <op de tafel>.
that Jan the book on the table down put
'that Jan put down the book on the table.'

The precise syntactic function of the PP in (342c) is unclear. Den Dikken (1995), for example, claims that the PP is actually a complement of the particle (cf. Section 4.2.1.2), and that its logical SUBJECT, the noun phrase *het boek*, is raised to the subject position of the particle. In Broekhuis (1992), it is argued that the PP actually has an ambiguous status: it sometimes acts as the complement of the particle, as claimed by Den Dikken, and sometimes as an independent adverbial phrase. The behavior of the PP in (342c) is part of a more general pattern, which will be discussed in Section 4.2.1.2.2, sub III.

Another potential example of this sort, which involves the adjectival complementive *groen* 'green' and the particle *af*, is given in (343). However, given that adjectives never undergo extraposition, it cannot be shown that the adjective does not function as a complementive of the verb in the somewhat marked but passable example in (343c).

(343) a. dat Jan de deur groen verfde.
that Jan the door green painted
'that Jan painted the door green.'
b. dat Jan de deur af verfde.
that Jan the door AF painted
'that Jan finished painting the door.'
c. ?dat Jan de deur groen af verfde.
that Jan the door green AF painted

Particle verbs are often involved in verb alternations. In (344a), we are dealing with a simple predicative construction involving change of location. The constructions in (344b&c) shows that not only the located object *de kleren* but also the reference object *de koffer* may surface as the object of the clause. The primed examples further show that the object is assigned accusative case in both cases. The fact that the reference object from (344a) surfaces as an accusative object in (344c) unmistakably shows that the element *in* in the latter example is not a postposition but a verbal particle.

(344) a. Jan pakte zijn kleren in de koffer.
Jan packed his clothes into his suitcase
b. Jan pakte zijn kleren in.
Jan packed his clothes prt.
b′. Zijn kleren werden (door zijn moeder) ingepakt.
his clothes were by his mother prt.-packed
c. Jan pakte de koffer in.
Jan packed the suitcase prt.
c′. Zijn koffer werd (door zijn moeder) ingepakt.
his suitcase was by his mother prt.-packed

Giving a general description of the meaning contribution of verbal particles seems impossible. It can be aspectual in nature, as in (337), or express a location, as in (344). It may also add a more or less systematic meaning aspect, as in the primed examples in (345), which also allow a periphrastic indirect object with *aan* 'to'; see *Jan gaf het boek aan Marie (door*) and *Jan vertelde het geheim aan Els (door).*

(345) a. Jan gaf Els het boek.
Jan gave Els the book
a′. Jan gaf Els het boek door.
Jan gave Els the book DOOR
'Jan passed Els the book.'
b. Jan vertelde Els het geheim.
Jan told Els the secret
b′. Jan vertelde Els het geheim door.
Jan told Els the secret DOOR
'Jan passed on (betrayed) the secret to Els.'

The meaning of the particle can also be more or less lexicalized, as in (346a&b). Example (346b) is especially telling in this respect, given that the particle verb *overhalen* 'to persuade' subcategorizes for a PP headed by *tot* (which has the form of an anticipatory pronominal PP *er toe* here), which can be selected neither by the verb nor by the particle.

(346) a. De VPRO zendt die documentaire morgen uit.
the VPRO sends that documentary tomorrow prt.
'The VPRO broadcasts this documentary tomorrow.'
b. Jan haalde Peter er toe over om te vertrekken.
Jan fetched Peter there TOE prt. to to leave
'Jan persuaded Peter to leave.'

The examples in (347) show that particles also occur in completely idiomatic constructions.

(347) a. Dat is bij het zwarte af.
that is with the black AF
'That is nearly black.'
b. Dat is bij de beesten af.
that is with the beast AF
'That is beastly.'

This all suggests that the best place to account for the meaning contribution of particles is the lexicon, and hence that it is best to describe the meaning of particle verbs not in a grammar but in a dictionary. We will therefore not try to provide any more details here.

1.3.1.6. Appendix: alternative means of expressing spatial relations

The expression of spatial relations typically involves the use of adpositional phrases or prepositional pro-forms like *daar* 'there'. It must be noted, however, that there are alternative ways of expressing such notions: Section 1.3.1.6.1 will discuss alternative ways of expressing a change of location, and Section 1.3.1.6.2 alternative ways of expressing a direction.

1.3.1.6.1. Change of location

The examples in (348) involve a change of location: in (348a) the located object *planten* 'plants' is located in the reference object *de tuin* 'the garden', in (348b) the located object *boter* 'butter' is located on the reference object *het brood* 'the bread', and in (348c) the located object *de posters* is located on the reference object *de muur* 'the wall'. The subsections below will show that there are several alternative ways of expressing similar relations. Most cases involve verbs derived by means of the prefixes *be-*, *ver-* and *ont-*, which will be discussed more extensively in Section V3.

(348) a. Jan zet planten in de tuin.
Jan puts plants in the garden
b. Jan smeert boter op het brood.
Jan smears butter on the bread
c. Jan plakt de posters op de muur.
Jan pastes the posters on the wall

I. Denominal verbs prefixed with be-

The primeless examples in (349) are alternative ways of expressing the same contentions as in (348a&b). In a sense, the located object has become an inherent part of the verb, and the function of the preposition has been taken over by the prefix *be-*. The reference object from (348) now acts as the direct object of the verb, which is clear from the fact that it becomes the subject of the clause in the passive construction in the primed examples.

(349) a. Jan *be*-plant de tuin (met rozen).
Jan BE-plants his garden with roses
a′. De tuin wordt beplant (met rozen).
the garden is planted with roses
b. Jan *be*-botert het brood (met margarine).
Jan BE-butters the bread with margarine
b′. Het brood wordt beboterd (met margarine).
the bread is buttered with margarine

Although the constructions in (348a&b) and (349) are more or less synonymous, there is a conspicuous difference between them: whereas the contentions in the primeless examples in (349) can be made more specific by adding a *met*-PP, the addition of such a PP leads to ungrammaticality in the constructions in (348a&b), as is shown in the primeless examples in (350). In order to express the more specific contentions, we must substitute the noun phrase *rozen/margarine* for the direct object *planten/boter*, as in the primed examples of (350).

(350) a. Jan zet planten in zijn tuin (*met rozen).
Jan puts plants in his garden with roses
a′. Jan zet rozen in zijn tuin.
b. Jan smeert boter op zijn brood (*met margarine).
Jan smears butter on his bread with margarine
b′. Jan smeert margarine op zijn brood.

The examples in (351) show that the formation of BE-verbs is not fully productive. The nouns in the primeless examples cannot act as the stem of BE-verbs, which suggests that the attested denominal BE-verbs are listed in the lexicon.

(351) a. Jan zet rozen in zijn tuin.
Jan puts roses in his garden
a′. *Jan beroost zijn tuin.
b. Jan smeert jam op zijn brood.
Jan smears jam on his bread
b′. *Jan bejamt zijn brood.

A small sample of BE-verbs of the type in (349) is given in Table 20. The first column provides the stem of the verb and its English translation, the second column gives the derived verb, and the third column gives a translation or paraphrase in English.

Table 20: Denominal verbs prefixed with be- *expressing a location*

STEM	VERB	TRANSLATION
bos 'wood'	*bebossen*	to afforest
dijk 'dike'	*bedijken*	to put dikes around/next to
mest 'manure'	*bemesten*	to manure
modder 'mud'	*bemodderen*	to put mud on
schaduw 'shadow'	*beschaduwen*	to cast shadow on
vracht 'load'	*bevrachten*	to put a load on
water 'water'	*bewateren*	to water

II. Deverbal verbs prefixed with be-

Another way to express a similar contention to those in (348b&c) is given in the primeless examples in (352): the verb is prefixed with *be-*, the preposition *op* 'on' is dropped, and the passive constructions in the primed examples show that the reference object has become the direct object of the construction. The located object can but need not be overtly expressed by means of a *met*-PP. When the located object is not overtly realized, it is semantically implied in the sense that, without the PP, the examples in (352) imply a located object that is, respectively, "smearable" and "pastable".

(352) a. Jan *be*-smeert het brood (met boter).
Jan BE-smears the bread with butter
'Jan butters the bread.'
a′. Het brood wordt *be*-smeerd (met boter).
the bread is BE-smeared with butter
b. Jan *be*-plakt de muur (met posters).
Jan BE-pastes the wall with posters
b′. De muur wordt *be*-plakt (met posters).
the wall is BE-pasted with posters

There is, however, a meaning difference between the examples in (348b&c) and (352): whereas the former are compatible with a reading in which the located object covers only part of the reference object, the latter imply that the reference object is fully (or at least to a very large extent) covered by the located object. This can be made clear relatively easily by comparing the singular counterparts of (348c) and (352b) in (353). Replacement of this plural noun phrase *de posters* 'the posters' by a singular one is readily possible in the former case but not in the latter.

(353) a. Jan plakt de poster op de muur.
Jan pastes the poster on the wall
'Jan is pasting the poster on the wall.'
b. #Jan *be*-plakt de muur met de poster.
Jan BE-pastes the wall with the poster

Example (353b) is only possible in (the improbable) case that the poster completely covers the wall. In other words, the deverbal BE-verb has a sense of "completiveness" or "even distribution"; the wall must end up fully covered with posters, or with posters more or less evenly distributed on it. That this is the case is perhaps also supported by the fact that whereas the examples in (348) alternate with the primeless constructions in (354) in which the notion of "total affectedness" is expressed by means of the adjective *vol* 'full', this adjective is not compatible with the deverbal BE-verbs. This could be accounted for by claiming that the primed examples are tautologous: *vol* and the prefix *-be* in a sense perform the same semantic function.

(354) a. Jan plant de tuin vol (met rozen).
Jan plants the garden full with roses
a′. *Jan *be*-plant de tuin vol (met rozen).
b. Jan smeert het brood vol (met boter).
Jan smears the bread full with butter
b′. *Jan *be*-smeert het brood vol (met boter).
c. Jan plakt de muur vol (met posters).
Jan pastes the wall full with posters
c′. *Jan *be*-plakt de muur vol (met posters).

Table 21 provides a small sample of verbs of the type in (353). Observe that it is sometimes not clear whether we are dealing with a denominal or a deverbal verb. *Beplanten*, for example may be denominal (cf. *Jan zet planten in de tuin* in (348a)) or deverbal (cf. *Jan plant rozen in de tuin* 'Jan plants roses in the garden').

Table 21: Deverbal verbs prefixed with be- *expressing a change of location*

STEM	VERB	TRANSLATION
hangen 'to hang'	*behangen met*	to paper with
planten 'to plant'	*beplanten met*	to plant with
sproeien 'to spray'	*besproeien met*	to spray with
strooien 'to strew'	*bestrooien met*	to strew with

III. Denominal verbs prefixed with ont-

Denominal verbs prefixed with *ont-*, such as *ontharen* 'to depilate' and *ontkurken* 'to uncork' in (355), are in a sense the opposite of the denominal verbs prefixed with *be-*. Whereas the latter are related to change of location constructions where the reference object is the new position of the located object, the former is related to change of location constructions like (356) where the reference object is the original position. As in the case of the denominal BE-verbs, the reference object acts as the direct object of the verb prefixed by *ont-*, which is clear from the fact that it becomes the subject of the clause in the passive construction. In Table 22, some more examples of denominal verbs prefixed by *ont-* are given.

(355) a. Jan *ont*-haart zijn benen.
Jan ONT-hair-s his legs
'Jan depilates his legs.'
a′. Zijn benen worden *ont*-haard.
his legs are ONT-hair-ed
b. Marie *ont*-kurkt de fles.
Marie ONT-cork-s the bottle
'Jan uncorks the bottle.'
b′. De fles wordt *ont*-kurkt.
the bottle is ONT-cork-ed

(356) a. Jan haalt de haren van zijn benen.
Jan removes the hairs from his legs
b. Jan haalt de kurk uit de fles.
Jan removes the cork out.of the bottle

Table 22: Denominal verbs prefixed with ont- *expressing a location*

STEM	VERB	TRANSLATION
bos 'forest'	*ontbossen*	to deforest
grond 'soil/basis'	*ontgronden*	to take away the soil/basis
hoofd 'head'	*onthoofden*	to decapitate
kalk 'lime'	*ontkalken*	to decalcify
volk 'people'	*ontvolken*	depopulate

Sometimes denominal BE- and ONT-verbs are in true opposition, as in *bebossen* and *ontbossen*, but in many other cases there are no antonym pairs. This shows again that the formation of BE- and ONT-verbs is not a productive process and that the attested cases must therefore be part of the lexicon.

IV. Simple verbs

In a very limited number of cases, a simple verb can also express a change of location. The clearest example is *zadelen* 'to saddle' in example (357b), which can be paraphrased by means of the construction in (357a). In Dutch, this process is certainly not as productive as in English: verbs like *to shelve*, *to box* or *to file* cannot be translated by means of simple verbs in Dutch.

(357) a. Jan legt het zadel op zijn paard.
Jan puts the saddle on his horse
b. Jan zadelt zijn paard.
Jan saddles his horse

1.3.1.6.2. Direction (path)

The examples in (358) involve a path: in (358a), the referent of the noun phrase *Jan* covers a path that has its endpoint within the reference object "the hall", and in (358b) the referent of the noun phrase *Jan* covers a path that goes to the top of the mountain. The subsections below will show that there are alternative ways of expressing similar relations.

(358) a. Jan treedt de zaal binnen.
Jan steps the hall inside
'Jan steps into the hall.'
b. Jan klimt de berg op.
Jan climbs the mountain onto
'Jan climbs onto the mountain.'

I. Deverbal BE-verbs

The examples in (359) are alternative ways to express the same contentions as in (358). The verb is prefixed with *be-*, and the postposition is dropped. The stem of these directional BE-verbs typically belongs to the class of °unaccusative verbs. Some other examples are given in Table 23.

(359) a. Jan *be*-treedt de zaal.
Jan BE-steps the hall
'Jan enters the hall.'
b. Jan *be*-klimt de berg
Jan BE-climbs the mountain
'Jan climbs onto the mountain.'

Table 23: Deverbal directional verbs prefixed with be-

STEM	VERB	TRANSLATION
naderen 'approach'	*benaderen*	to approach (something)
springen 'to jump'	*bespringen*	to jump on
stijgen 'to rise'	*bestijgen*	to mount/ascent

The examples in (360) illustrate the inability of "transitive" verbs (verbs with a complementive that is predicated of the accusative argument) to act as the stem of a directional BE-verb.

(360) a. Jan duwt de auto's de berg op.
Jan pushes the cars the mountain onto
'Jan pushes the cars onto the mountain.'
a′. *Jan *be*-duwt de berg (met de auto's).
b. De politie slaat de demonstranten het ziekenhuis in.
the police hits the demonstrators the hospital into
'The police are hitting the demonstrators into the hospital.'
b′. *De politie *be*-slaat het ziekenhuis (met demonstranten).

The directional BE-verbs differ in this respect from the BE-verbs denoting a change of location, as will be clear from the difference between the (b)-examples in (360) and the examples in (361). In fact, the stems of the deverbal BE-verbs discussed in Section 1.3.1.6.1 are typically "transitive".

(361) a. Jan slaat de platen op de muur.
Jan hits the slabs onto the wall
b. Jan *be*-slaat de muur met platen.

II. Denominal VER-verbs

Section 1.3.3.1 has discussed that the notion of path is also applicable to non-spatial/temporal semantic fields. The examples in (362), for instance, denote a metaphorical "path" from one state of affairs into another. The referent of the noun phrase *Krakas* (a character from a Dutch series of children's books) changes from a state in which it has the form of an unappetizing looking bird into a state in which it looks like a tasty duck that can be used as an ingredient for soup.

(362) a. De heks verandert Krakras in een smakelijke soepeend.
the witch changes Krakras into a tasty soup.duck
b. Krakras verandert in een smakelijke soepeend.
Krakras changes into a tasty soup-duck

Constructions like (362) often alternate with constructions involving denominal VER-verbs. Some examples are given in (363); transitive examples, like (363a′), are sometimes a bit cumbersome.

(363) a. De hitte veranderde het water in damp.
the heat changed the water into vapor
a′. ?De hitte verdampte het water.
the heat evaporated the water
b. Het water veranderde in damp.
the water changed into vapor
b′. Het water verdampte.
the water evaporated

More examples are given in Table 24. Sometimes the meaning of the VER-verb has narrowed to the paraphrase given after the sign "⇒".

Table 24: Denominal change of state verbs prefixed with ver-

STEM	VERB	TRANSLATION
film 'movie'	*verfilmen*	change into a movie ⇒ adapt (a story) for the screen
gas 'gas'	*vergassen*	change into gas
gras 'grass'	*vergrassen*	change into grassland
kool 'coal'	*verkolen*	carbonize
snoep 'sweets'	*versnoepen*	change into sweets ⇒ spend money on sweets
water 'water'	*verwateren*	change into water ⇒ dilute

Note in passing that the deadjectival verbs prefixed by *ver-* in (364) express a meaning aspect similar to those in Table 24, but are related to inchoative copular or resultative constructions.

(364) a. De lakens worden geel.
the sheets become yellow
a′. De lakens vergelen.
the sheets get.yellow
b. Deze zeep maakt de was zachter.
this soap makes the laundry softer
b′. Deze zeep verzacht de was.
this soap softens the laundry

III. Simple verbs

Occasionally, simple verbs inherently express the notion of a path. This is clear from the fact that the primeless and primed examples in (365) are virtually synonymous; the only difference between the two sets of examples is that in the primeless examples the manner of motion is made explicit.

(365) a. Jan loopt voorbij de winkel.
Jan walks past the shop
a′. Jan passeert de winkel.
Jan passes the shop
b. Jan loopt de zaal uit.
Jan walks the hall out-of
b′. Jan verlaat de zaal.
Jan leaves the hall

1.3.1.6.3. Summary

This section has shown that various types of spatial relations can be expressed without an adpositional phrase by means of verbs prefixed with *be-*, *ver-* and *ont-*, and a small set of simplex verbs. Note that such derived verbs are not only used to express spatial notions, but can be used for other purposes as well. For a more comprehensive discussion of these verbs, we refer the reader to De Haas & Trommelen (1993: chapter 2, sub 4,2).

1.3.2. Temporal adpositions

The vast majority of temporal adpositional phrases are prepositional in nature, although post- and circumpositions can sometimes also be used; verbal particles are not used to express temporal relations. The sections below will discuss the three types of adpositional phrases that do occur.

1.3.2.1. Prepositions

This section discusses the semantics of temporal prepositions. After a more general discussion, we will consider the individual prepositions in more detail.

I. General discussion

Table 25 gives the subset of prepositions that can be productively used temporally: they are characterized by the fact that they can take any complement, provided that the latter refers to an entity that occupies a fixed position/interval on the time line.

Table 25: Temporal prepositions

PREPOSITION	EXAMPLE	TRANSLATION
gedurende	*gedurende de voorstelling*	during the performance
na	*na de les*	after the lesson
sinds	*sinds de laatste vergadering*	since the last meeting
tijdens	*tijdens de les*	during the lesson
tot (en met)	*tot (en met) mijn vakantie*	until my holiday
tussen	*tussen kerst en Nieuwjaar*	between Christmas and New Year
vanaf	*vanaf mijn vakantie*	from my holiday
voor	*voor mijn vakantie* (also: *tien voor vijf*)	before my holiday ten (minutes) to five (4.50 h)

The preposition *sinds* 'since' has the more formal counterpart *sedert*. The preposition *vanaf* can be replaced by the Latinate preposition *per* when followed by a date: *vanaf/per 23 februari* 'from February 23'.

The prepositions in Table 26 differ from those in Table 25 in that they impose selection restrictions on their complement; they require a complement referring to a certain time, date or well-defined period of time (such as a certain part of the day, holidays such as Easter and Christmas, and so on). Although the list of possible complements in the fourth column of Table 26 is not exhaustive, it will probably give some feeling for the restrictions imposed on the complement. The prepositional phrases preceded by a number sign are possible but cannot be used with a temporal meaning, for which reason we refrain from providing a translation of the prepositions involved.

Table 26: Temporal prepositions imposing selection restrictions on their complement

	EXAMPLE	TRANSLATION	POSSIBLE COMPLEMENTS
in	*in de ochtend*	during the morning	parts of the day, months, seasons, years
	#*in de voorstelling*	— the performance	
met	*met kerstmis*	during Christmas	holidays, seasons (except *lente* 'spring')
	#*met de les*	— the lesson	
om	*om tien over drie*	at ten past three	times of the day
	#*om de vakantie*	— the holiday	
omstreeks	*omstreeks kerstmis*	around Christmas	holidays, dates, months, seasons, years
	**omstreeks de les*	— the lesson	
op	*op kerstavond*	at Christmas eve	parts of holidays, dates
	#*op de vergadering*	— the meeting	
rond	*rond kerstmis*	around Christmas	holidays, dates
	#*rond de voorstelling*	— the performance	
tegen	*tegen kerstmis*	towards Christmas	holidays, times, dates, months, seasons
	#*tegen de les*	— the lesson	
van	*van de week*	some moment during last/next week	seasons, *week* 'week', *weekend* 'weekend'
	#*van de les*	— the lesson	

Note in passing that, as an alternative to (366a), it is possible to use example (366b). In this use, the complement of the preposition *bij* must be a numeral followed by the affix *-en*. The preposition *naar* in (366c) is similar to *bij* in this respect. The examples in (366) all express that it is nearly 9 o′clock.

(366) a. Het loopt al tegen negen uur.
it walks already towards nine o′clock
'We are approaching the time of nine o′clock.'

b. Het is al bij negenen.
it runs/is already close.to nine o′clock
'It is almost nine o′clock.'

c. Het loopt al naar negenen.
it walks already towards nine o′clock
'We are gradually approaching the time of nine o′clock.'

This "approximation" meaning of *tegen* is even more salient in (367), where it is used as a kind of adverbial modifier: the phrase *tegen de twee uur* seems to be more or less synonymous with *ongeveer twee uur*. More discussion of the approximative use of prepositions can be found in Section N5.1.4.3.

(367) a. Het examen duurt tegen de twee uur.

b. Het examen duurt ongeveer twee uur.
the exam lasts approximately two hours

Another special case that needs mention is given in (368a). The PP *met de dag* does not refer to a specific time on the time line but rather functions like a frequency adverb like *elke dag* 'every day'. It differs from the regular frequency adverbs, however, in that it only occurs in accumulative constructions like (368a).

(368) a. Het wordt met de dag/elke dag warmer.
it becomes with the day/every day hotter
'It is getting hotter every day.'
b. Jan komt hier elke dag/*met de dag.
Jan comes here every day/with the day

From a semantic point of view temporal prepositions are two-place predicates that establish a temporal relation between their two arguments: the referents of these arguments are situated on the time line in positions relative to each other. In (369a), for example, the temporal PP *voor de vakantie* 'before the holiday' situates the subject of the clause *de vergadering* 'the meeting' on a position on the time line preceding the position of the complement of *voor*, *de vakantie* 'the holiday'; this can be represented by means of the graph in (369b) or the logical formula in (369c).

(369) a. De vergadering is nog voor de vakantie.
the meeting is PRT before the holiday
b.
—— de vergadering ——— de vakantie ———→
time
c. VOOR (de vergadering, de vakantie)

When we consider the time line as a representation of "temporal space", we can call *de vergadering* the LOCATED OBJECT, and *de vakantie* the REFERENCE OBJECT, just as in the case of spatial prepositions. However, since the interpretation of the temporal prepositions in Table 25 is largely determined by the properties of the one-dimensional time line, it does not seem useful to make a distinction between inherent and absolute interpretations, as this distinction can only be made by appealing to at least two dimensions. This leaves us with the question whether there are temporal PPs with a deictic interpretation. Some potential cases of such deictic PPs are given in Table 27. We will show, however, that there are reasons to assume that these PPs are not temporal in nature.

Table 27: Temporal prepositions?

PREPOSITION	EXAMPLE	TRANSLATION
binnen	*binnen tien minuten*	within an hour
in	*in tien minuten*	(with)in ten minutes
over	*over tien minuten* (also: *tien over vijf*)	in ten minutes ten (minutes) past five (5.10 h)
om	*om de week* (lit.: around the week)	once every second week

In the examples in (370), the PPs denote a span of time of ten minutes calculated from the speech time. This means that the complement of the preposition does not act as the reference point from which the position of the located object is calculated.

In fact, the complements of the prepositions do not occupy a place on the time line at all, and are therefore not even suitable to act as the reference point.

(370) a. Ik ben binnen tien minuten bij je.
I am within ten minutes with you
'I'll be with you within ten minutes (from now).

b. Ik ben in tien minuten bij je.
I am in ten minutes with you
'I'll be with you (with)in ten minutes (from now).'

c. Ik ben over tien minuten bij je.
I am in ten minutes with you
'I'll be with you in ten minutes (from now).'

The fact that the complement of the preposition does not seem to play a role in the computation of the temporal location of the located object casts serious doubt on any claim that we are dealing with temporal prepositional phrases. Instead, the PPs in (370) seem to play a similar role as the manner adverb *snel* 'soon' or the adverbial element *zo* in (371).

(371) a. Ik ben snel/zo bij je.
I am soon/in.a.moment with you

Perhaps we can think of PPs like (370) as modifiers of the (implicit) reference time. For the PP *binnen tien minuten*, for example, it can be demonstrated that it can act as a modifier of a temporal adpositional phrase; in (372a), this PP has a function similar to that of the adjectival modifier *kort* 'shortly' in (372b).

(372) a. Het slachtoffer overleed binnen tien minuten na het ongeluk.
the victim died within ten minutes after the accident

b. Het slachtoffer overleed kort na het ongeluk.
the victim died shortly after the accident

The PP headed by *om* in (373a) does not seem to act as a truly temporal PP either. Instead, it seems to act as an adverbial phrase of frequency comparable to adjectives like *regelmatig* 'regularly' or *wekelijks* 'weekly' in (373b). This use is discussed more extensively in Section N5.1.4.3, sub IB.

(373) a. Jan komt hier om de week.
Jan comes here OM the week
'Jan comes here every second week.'

b. Jan komt hier regelmatig/wekelijks.
Jan comes here regularly/weekly
'Jan comes here regularly/weekly.'

The discussion above therefore leads to the conclusion that the prepositions in Table 27 are not temporal in nature.

II. The semantics of temporal prepositions

The discussion of (369) has shown that the semantics of temporal and spatial adpositional phrases is similar in the sense that they can both be considered two-place predicates. The temporal relations that can be expressed are simpler than the spatial relations, however, due to the fact that space is three-dimensional, whereas the time line is only one-dimensional. An exhaustive description of the spatial relations at least requires notions like IN FRONT OF, AT, BEHIND, NEXT TO, ABOVE and BELOW (see Figure 14), whereas the temporal relations can be exhaustively described by means of the three relations BEFORE, SIMULTANEOUS, and AFTER, as in (374); cf. Comrie (1985)

(374) • Time line

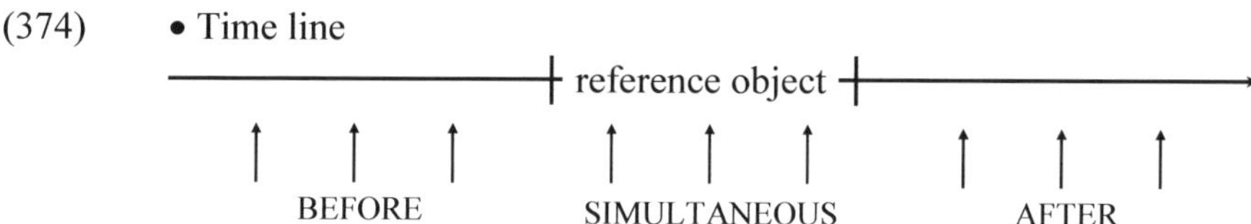

Although spatial and the temporal prepositions can be described in similar ways, there is a conspicuous difference between the two. Spatial PPs are common both as complementive and adverbial phrases, whereas temporal PPs are mainly used as adverbial phrases; although the complementive use of temporal PPs does not seem impossible (example (369a) might be a case in hand), this use is certainly rare. This difference in use is probably related to the nature of the entities involved. Whereas spatial adpositional phrases locate *objects* or *events* in space, temporal adpositional phrases locate *events* on the time line. Since objects are typically denoted by noun phrases and events by verbal projections, spatial adpositional phrases can be predicated both of noun phrases and verbal projections, whereas temporal adpositional phrases are typically predicated of verbal projections. This being said, we can continue discussing the temporal relations depicted in (374) in more detail.

A. BEFORE

The anteriority relation BEFORE can be expressed by means of the prepositions *voor* 'before' and *tot (en met)* 'until' from Table 25. The two differ in that the former refers to some specific point(s) on the time line preceding the position of the reference object, whereas the latter refers to an interval that starts at some point preceding the position of the reference object and extends until the position of the reference point is reached. The difference between *tot* and *tot en met* is that the interval denoted by the former does not include the position of the reference object, whereas the one denoted by the latter does.

(375) • Time line: *voor* 'before' and *tot (en met)* 'until'

a.

b.

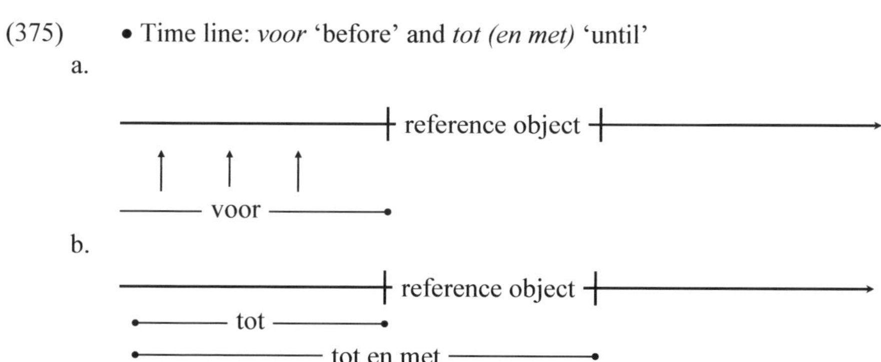

The preposition *tegen* 'towards' from Table 26 denotes a point or an interval preceding the reference object, but in addition it expresses some notion of proximity: the located object must be situated closely to the reference object.

(376) • Time line: *tegen* 'towards'

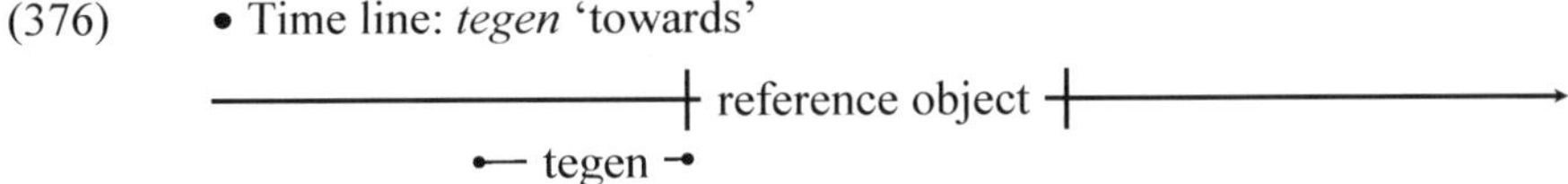

B. SIMULTANEOUSNESS

The notion SIMULTANEOUSNESS can be expressed by means of the prepositions *tijdens* 'during' and *gedurende* 'during' from Table 25. Although intuitions are not as clear as in the case of *voor* and *tot (en met)*, the two prepositions seem to differ in the same way: *tijdens* preferably refers to some specific point(s) on the time line occupied by the reference object, whereas *gedurende* refers to an interval included in the interval occupied by the reference object.

(377) • Time line: *tijdens* 'during' and *gedurende* 'during'

gedurende

reference object

tijdens

The prepositions *in*, *met*, and *op* from Table 26 also denote a point or an interval included in the interval occupied by the reference object. The preposition *om* is special in that it does not refer to some point(s) or an interval, but to one specific position; this is probably due to the fact that the reference object refers to a specific time, as in *om tien over drie* 'at ten past three'.

The prepositions *omstreeks* 'around' and *rond* 'around' from Table 26 differ from the prepositions discussed above in that the located object need not be placed within the time interval that is covered by the reference object; however, as in the case of *tegen* 'towards', a notion of proximity is involved: the located object must at least be situated closely to the reference object, which itself may but need not be included.

(378) Time line: *omstreeks* 'around' and *rond* 'around'

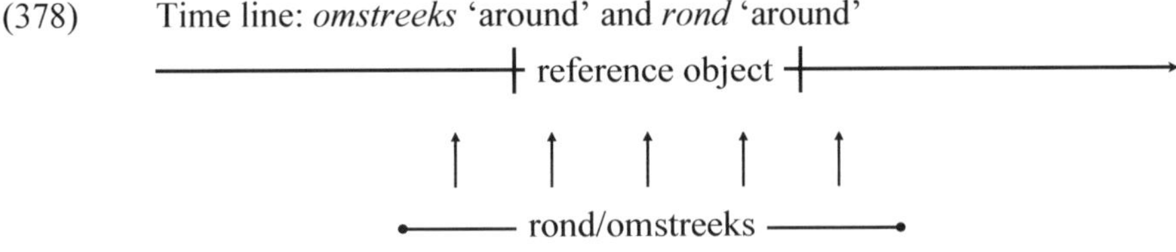

C. AFTER

The posteriority relation AFTER can be expressed by means of the prepositions *na* 'after', *sinds* 'since' and *vanaf* '(starting) from' in Table 25. The prepositions differ in the same way as *voor* and *tot (en met)*: *na* refers to some specific point(s) on the time line following the position of the reference object; *sinds* and *vanaf* refer to an interval on the time line starting at or immediately after the position of the reference object.

(379) • Time line: *na* 'after', *sinds* 'since' and *vanaf* 'from'

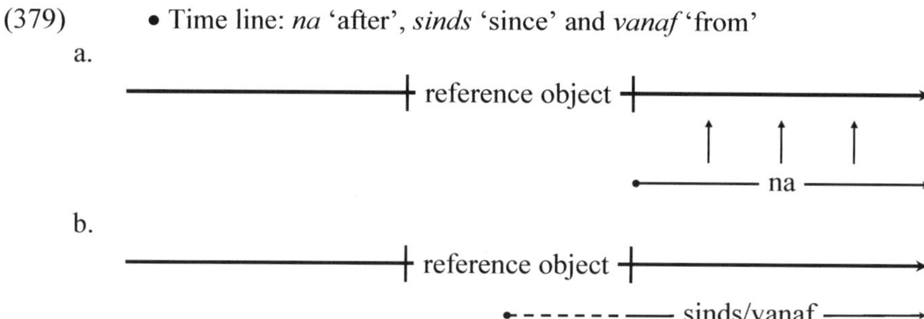

The difference between *sinds* and *vanaf* seems to be related to the position of the speech time. In the case of *sinds*, the position of the reference object must precede the speech time, as in (380a), whereas in the case of *vanaf* the position of the reference object preferably follows the speech time, as in (380b).

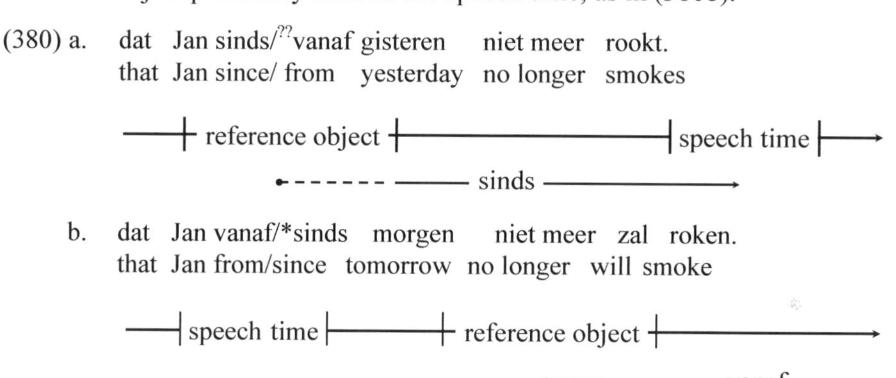

(380) a. dat Jan sinds/??vanaf gisteren niet meer rookt.
that Jan since/ from yesterday no longer smokes

b. dat Jan vanaf/*sinds morgen niet meer zal roken.
that Jan from/since tomorrow no longer will smoke

Occasionally, however, *vanaf* can also be used to refer to the situation depicted in (381b), but this requires a special syntactic context, such as the perfect tense in (381a), or an adverb like *al* 'already' in (381a′).

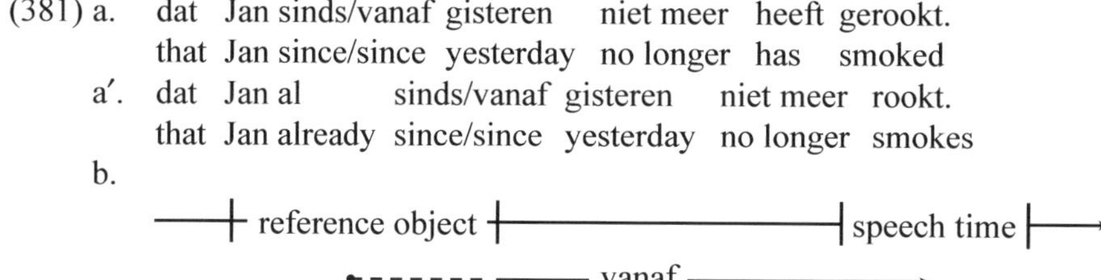

(381) a. dat Jan sinds/vanaf gisteren niet meer heeft gerookt.
that Jan since/since yesterday no longer has smoked
a′. dat Jan al sinds/vanaf gisteren niet meer rookt.
that Jan already since/since yesterday no longer smokes
b.

D. The preposition tussen *'between'*

Like its spatial counterpart, the temporal preposition *tussen* normally requires a plural complement (often in a coordinated structure). The location of the located object on the time line is computed on the basis of two reference objects, as in (382).

(382) tussen Kerstmis *(en Nieuwjaar)
between Christmas and New Year

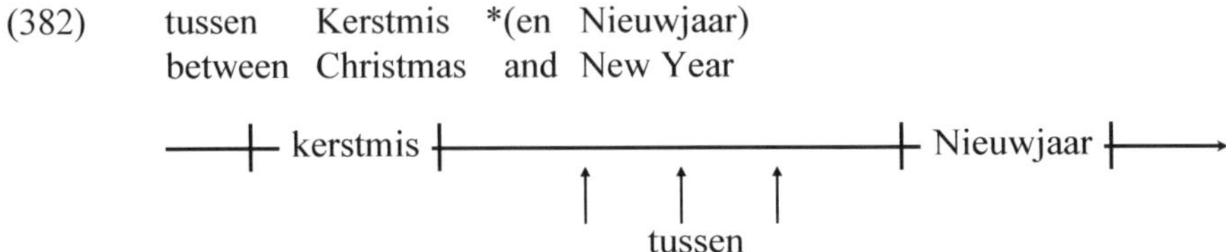

1.3.2.2. Postpositions

The set of temporal postpositions is even smaller than the set of spatial postpositions: it is restricted to *in* 'into', *uit* 'out of' and *door* 'throughout'. The use of these postpositions is also rather restricted. The temporal postposition *in* indicates that the endpoint of the implied (temporal) path is situated within the interval on the time line occupied by the reference object. The reference object generally refers to a conventional time unit such as *week* 'week', *maand* 'month', *jaar* 'year', etc., preceded by the attributive adjective *nieuw* 'new', as in (383a). The temporal postposition *uit* probably indicates that the starting point is situated within the interval on the time line occupied by the reference object, but this is hard to tell as it is only used in the more or less fixed expression .... *in* .... *uit*, where the dots indicate a noun phrase like *dag* 'day', *week*, *maand* 'month', *jaar* 'year', etc.

(383) a. We gaan volgende week het nieuwe jaar in.
we go next week the new year into
'Next week, the new year will begin.'
b. Jan doet dag in dag uit hetzelfde werk.
Jan does day into day out.of the.same work
'Jan is doing the same sort of work, day after day.'

The postposition *door* does not impose similar restrictions on its complement: any noun phrase that refers to an entity that occupies an interval on the time line is possible. It seems, however, that the quantifier *heel* is obligatory.

(384) a. Jan was zijn hele vakantie door ziek.
Jan was his complete holiday through ill
'Throughout his holiday, Jan was ill.'
b. Jan zeurde de hele vergadering door over zijn baas.
Jan nagged the complete meeting through about his boss
'Throughout the meeting, Jan was nagging about his boss.'

1.3.2.3. Circumpositions

Table 28 provides a list of temporal circumpositions classified according to their second part. Comparing this table to Table 19 will reveal that the number of temporal circumpositions is much smaller than the number of spatial ones.

Table 28: Temporal circumpositions

2ND PART	CIRCUMPOSITION	EXAMPLE	TRANSLATION
aan	*tegen ... aan*	?*tegen de avond aan*	towards the evening
af	*van ... af*	*van dat moment af*	since that moment
door	*tussen ... door*	*tussen de lessen door*	in between the lessons
heen	*door ... heen*	*door de jaren heen*	throughout the years
in	*tussen ... in*	*tussen kerst en Nieuwjaar in*	between Christmas and New Year
toe	*naar ... toe*	*naar kerstmis toe*	towards Christmas
	tot ... (aan) toe	*tot de ochtend (aan) toe*	until the morning

As in the case of the temporal postpositions the complement of these temporal circumpositions is more or less restricted to noun phrases denoting a conventional time unit. The only exception seems to be *tussen ... door/in*. In (385), we give some examples of each case.

(385) a. Tegen de avond (?aan) kom ik naar huis.
towards the evening AAN come I to home
'Towards the evening I will come home.'

b. Van dat moment *(af) wilde hij schilder worden.
from that moment AF wanted he painter become
'Since that moment he wanted to become a painter.'

c. Jan rookt tussen de lessen (door).
Jan smokes between the lessons DOOR
'Jan smokes in between the lessons.'

d. Door de jaren (heen) is het dorp steeds groter geworden.
through the years HEEN is the village continuously bigger become
'Throughout the years the village has become bigger and bigger.'

e. Tussen die twee lessen ?(in) werd Jan gearresteerd.
between those two lessons IN was Jan arrested
'Jan was arrested in between those two lessons.'

f. Het loopt al naar de dageraad *(toe).
it walks already towards the dawn TOE
'It is nearly dawning.'

The examples in (385) show that the second part of the circumposition can be dropped in many cases without a clear effect on the meaning of the examples; this may indicate that we are actually not dealing with circumpositions but with prepositional phrases that are somehow emphasized by some sort of particle; cf. 1.3.1.4, sub XII, where we suggested the same thing for apparent circumpositional phrases with a locational interpretation.

Example (386) shows that the circumposition *van ... af* in (385b) alternates with the complex preposition *vanaf*, again without a clear effect on the meaning of the example.

(386) Vanaf dat moment wilde hij schilder worden.
from that moment wanted he painter become
'Since that moment he wanted to become a painter.'

Example (387) is also noteworthy, since the complement seems to involve a noun (*kind* 'child') or adjective (*jong* 'young') suffixed with *-s*; these circumpositional phrases are idiomatic in nature.

(387) Van kinds/jongs *(af) wilde hij schilder worden.
from childhood AF wanted he painter become
'Ever since he was a child he wanted to become a painter.'

Note, finally, that example (388) probably does not involve a circumpositional phrase *tot (aan) ... toe*, but the preposition *tot* 'until' followed by an adpositional complement. This is at least suggested by the fact that the latter can be replaced by the pro-form *dan* 'then'; cf. Section 2.2.1.

(388) a. Het feest duurt tot (aan) de ochtend toe.
the party lasts until AAN the morning TOE
'The party will last until the morning.'
b. Het feest duurt tot dan.
the party lasts until then

1.3.3. Non-spatial/temporal prepositions

This section discusses non-spatial/temporal adpositional phrases. Section 1.3.3.1 will start by discussing predicative adpositional phrases, and Section 1.3.3.2 will discuss adpositional phrases with other functions.

1.3.3.1. Prepositions that take a "reference object"

Many of the spatial/temporal prepositions can also be used to denote a non-spatial/temporal relation. Such prepositional phrases often involve a metaphorical spatial relation in the sense that they express that the "located object" is in the state denoted by the "reference object"; example (389a), for instance, expresses that the house is in the state of being afire. If (389a) is indeed comparable to the locational construction, the (b)-examples are comparable to the change of location construction; these examples express that a change of state takes place.

(389) a. Het huis staat in brand. [state]
the house stands on fire
'The house is on fire.'
b. Het huis raakt in brand. [change of state]
the house gets on fire
'The house bursts into flames.'
b′. Jan zet/steekt het huis in brand. [change of state]
Jan puts the house on fire
'Jan sets the house on fire.'

More examples of the same sort are given in (390). Example (390a) expresses that Jan is in the state of being in trouble, whereas the (b)-examples express that a change of state is taking place.

(390) a. Jan zit in de problemen. [state]
Jan sits in the problems
'Jan is in problems/trouble.'
b. Jan raakt in de problemen. [change of state]
Jan gets into the problems
'Jan gets into problems/trouble.'
b′. Peter brengt Jan in de problemen. [change of state]
Peter brings Jan into the problems
'Peter gets Jan into problems/trouble.'

There are numerous prepositional predicates of this type that denote mental states, and are therefore predicated of human SUBJECTs only. Most of these predicates, a small sample of which are given in (391), have an idiomatic flavor. This is clear from the fact that attributive modification of the nominal complement of the preposition is normally excluded; an exception is *op zijn (dooie) gemak* 'at his ease', in which *dooie* 'dead' functions as an amplifier and cannot be replaced by any other adjective. The PPs in (391) are normally used predicatively, although *op zijn (dooie) gemak* again constitutes an exception in that it can also be used as an adverbial phrase of manner: *Jan werkte op zijn dooie gemak* 'Jan worked at his ease'. For the possible origin/meaning of the unglossed words in small caps, we refer to the *Woordenboek der Nederlandsche Taal*.

(391) a. Jan is (zeer) op zijn gemak.
Jan is very at his ease
'Jan is at his ease.'
b. Jan is (helemaal) in z'n knollentuin/nopjes/sas/schik.
Jan is completely in his vegetable garden/NOPJES/SAS/SCHIK
'Jan is (very) pleased'
c. Jan was/raakte (erg) uit zijn humeur.
Jan was/got very out his mood
'Jan was/got in a bad mood.'
d. Jan is niet (helemaal goed) bij zijn verstand.
Jan is not totally well with his senses
'Jan is not in possession of his senses.'
e. Jan is (goed) op zijn hoede.
Jan is very on his guard
'Jan is on the alert.'
f. Jan is (flink) bij de pinken.
Jan is quite with the PINKEN
'Jan is (very) smart.'
g. Jan is (erg) in de contramine.
Jan is very in the CONTRAMINE
'Jan is (very) uncooperative.'

h. Jan is/komt helemaal op gang/dreef.
Jan is/comes completely on going/DREEF
'Jan has/gets the hang of it.'

i. Jan was/raakte (zeer) van streek.
Jan was/got very of STREEK
'Jan was/got upset.'

Section 3.3, sub I, will show that PPs of this sort behave like adjectives in several respects; for the moment it suffices to note that their modification possibilities are more typical for adjectival than for prepositional phrases; the amplifier *zeer* 'very' in (391a&i), for example, can normally be used for modification of adjectives only. See Section A3 for a comprehensive discussion of modification of APs.

The examples in (389) to (391) all involve a (change of) state. The examples in (392), on the other hand, are perhaps more appropriately described as involving a path. They express a (gradual) change from one state into another; cf. (362).

(392) a. Jan veranderde (van een verlegen jongen) in een oproerkraaier.
Jan changed from a shy boy into an agitator

a′. State 1: Jan is a shy boy
State ...: Jan is in some intermediate stage
State n: Jan is an agitator

b. Het water wordt nu omgezet in waterstof en zuurstof.
the water is now converted into hydrogen and oxygen

1.3.3.2. Prepositions that do not take a "reference object"

Besides the spatial and temporal prepositions, there is a set of prepositions with different meanings. Some of them are used to express certain specific semantic roles in the clause. For example, the preposition *aan* 'to' can be used to introduce a goal and *voor* 'for' can be used to introduce the beneficiary argument of the verb. Prepositions of this kind, which we will conveniently call ROLE prepositions, will be discussed in 1.3.3.2.1. A second group of prepositions consists of prepositions that are selected by the verb, like English *for* in *to wait for*. Prepositions of this kind, which we will call FUNCTIONAL prepositions, will be discussed in 1.3.3.2.2. Finally, Section 1.3.3.2.3 will discuss prepositions heading non-spatial/temporal adverbial phrases.

1.3.3.2.1. Prepositions introducing specific semantic roles

This section discusses various role prepositions, that is, prepositions that are used to introduce noun phrases with specific semantic roles in the clause.

I. Door *'by'*

The role preposition *door* 'by' has three functions. The first function involves the introduction of an agent in a passive clause, as in (393a). Its second function is the introduction of a cause in (active or passive) clauses, as in (393b). Example (393c), finally, shows that *door*-phrases can also express a means, provided that its complement is an infinitival clause.

(393) a. Jan werd ontslagen door zijn baas.
Jan was sacked by his boss
b. Jan raakte gewond door een omvallende boom.
Jan got hurt by a falling tree
c. Door hard te werken werd Jan topmanager van het bedrijf.
by hard to work became Jan top manager of the company
'By working hard Jan became a top manager of the company.'

Since agentive and causal *door*-PPs can both occur in a passive construction, they can be easily confused. This is illustrated in the primeless examples in (394). They differ, however, in that °R-extraction is only fully acceptable from passive *door*-phrases; R-extraction from a *door*-PP introducing a cause gives rise to a marked result. This is illustrated in the primed examples by means of R-extraction in relative clauses.

(394) a. Het ongeluk werd door Jan veroorzaakt.
the accident was by Jan caused
'The accident was caused by Jan.'
a′. de jongen *waar* het ongeluk *door* veroorzaakt werd
the boy where the accident by caused was
'The boy by whom the accident was caused.'
b. Het ongeluk werd door nalatigheid veroorzaakt.
the accident was by negligence caused
'The accident was caused by a falling tree.'
b′. ??de nalatigheid *waar* het ongeluk *door* veroorzaakt werd
the negligence where the accident by caused was

Agentive *door*-phrases are not restricted to passive constructions. In (395), it is shown that they can also occur in nominalizations, especially when the noun is derived from a transitive verb; when the noun is derived from an intransitive verb (or when the direct object is not expressed) the preposition *van* is normally preferred; see N2.2.3.2 for extensive discussion.

(395) a. het lachen van/?door Urgje
the laughing of/by Urgje
b. het lezen van boeken door/*?van Jan
the reading of books by/of Jan

Example (396b) further shows that agentive *door*-phrases can also be used to express the agent of a transitive verb embedded under the causative verb *laten* 'to make'; cf. V3.2.1, sub V.

(396) a. Marie liet de studenten het boek bestuderen.
Marie made the students the book study
'Mary made the students study the book.'
b. Marie liet het boek door de studenten bestuderen.
Marie made the book by the students study

II. Aan *'to' and* voor *'for'*

The role preposition *aan* introduces a goal. In the general case, the construction with *aan* alternates with the double object construction (although not all double object constructions alternate with constructions with an *aan*-PP; See V3.3.1.1).

(397) a. Marie gaf het boek aan Peter.
Marie gave the book to Peter
b. Marie gaf Peter het boek.
Marie gave Peter the book

The role preposition *voor* introduces a beneficiary. Unlike the goal-construction with *aan*, the construction with the *voor*-PP normally does not alternate with a double object construction in Standard Dutch. The construction is common in many other varieties of Dutch, though, for which reason we marked (398b) with a percentage sign.

(398) a. Marie kocht een cadeautje voor Jan.
Marie bought a present for Jan
b. %Marie kocht Jan een cadeautje.
Marie bought Jan a present

The examples in (399) show that the alternation can also be found in Standard Dutch in a number of more or less fixed expressions; these two examples differ in that (399b) expresses that the drink is intended for Marie, whereas (399a) simply expresses that Jan is performing the action on behalf of Marie, that is, the drink may but need not be for her. We refer the reader to V3.3.1.5 for more discussion.

(399) a. Jan schonk een borrel voor Marie in.
Jan poured a drink for Marie prt.
b. Jan schonk Marie een borrel in.
Jan poured Marie a drink prt.

Voor-PPs can also be used to refer to the benefit of the action, as in (400a&b). An example like (400c) is ambiguous between the beneficiary and benefit reading: on the former reading, the example means that Marie does anything for someone who has a pretty face, on the latter that she is doing anything in order to get a pretty face.

(400) a. Jan werkt daar alleen maar voor de centen.
Jan works there only for the cents
'Jan is working there only for the money.'
b. Jan beledigde haar alleen maar voor de lol.
Jan insulted her only for fun
'Jan insulted her just for the fun of it.'
c. Marie zou alles doen voor een leuk gezichtje.
Marie would everything do for a pretty face
'Marie would do anything for a pretty face.'

Finally, *voor*-PPs may refer to media of exchange with verbs like *kopen* 'to buy' and *verkopen* 'to sell', and *betalen* 'to pay', as in (401a&b). An example like (401c) is ambiguous between the beneficiary and the countertransfer reading; on the former reading Jan is given 50 euro that he can spend in order to purchase a CD-player, whereas on the second reading he is receiving 50 euro in exchange for his CD-player.

(401) a. Jan (ver)kocht het boek voor 15 euro.
Jan bought/sold the book for 15 euro
'Jan bought/sold the book for 15 euros.'
b. Jan betaalde 15 euro voor het boek.
Jan paid 15 euro for the book
'Jan paid 15 euros for the book.'
c. Jan kreeg 50 euro voor zijn cd-speler.
Jan received 50 euro for his CD-player
'Jan received 50 euros for his CD-player.'

III. Met *'with'*

The role preposition *met* can perform three functions. It can introduce an instrument, a co-agent, or a located object. In (402), we give several examples with an instrumental *met*-PP.

(402) a. Jan opende de kist met een breekijzer.
Jan opened the box with a crowbar
b. Marie bekeek het lijk met een zaklamp.
Marie looked.at the body with a flashlight

The primeless examples in (403) involve comitative *met*-PPs, that is, PPs in which *met* introduces a co-agent. A typical property of such examples is that they alternate with constructions in which the agent and the co-agent are coordinated in subject position; cf. the primed examples. The main semantic difference between the primeless and primed examples is related to prominence; in the primeless examples the referent denoted by the noun phrase in subject position is considered a more prominent participant in the event than the referent in the *met*-PP, whereas in the primed example the two coordinated noun phrases in subject position are presented as equally important.

(403) a. Jan wandelde met Peter naar het park.
Jan walked with Peter to the park
a′. Jan en Peter wandelen naar het park.
Jan and Peter walk to the park
b. Marie is gisteren met Peter getrouwd.
Marie has yesterday with Peter married
b′. Marie en Peter zijn gisteren getrouwd.
Marie and Peter have yesterday married

A remarkable fact is that the presence of a comitative *met*-PP triggers plural agreement on a predicatively used noun phrase in (404c). First consider the examples in (404a&b), which show that the singular noun phrase *Jan* triggers singular agreement on the predicative noun phrase *een vriendje van Marie* 'a friend of Marie', and that the plural noun phrase *Jan en Peter* triggers plural agreement: *vriendjes van Marie* 'friends of Marie'. The plural agreement on the predicative noun phrase in (404c) has led to the hypothesis that, underlyingly, the phrase headed by *met* is a coordinate structure (*Jan met Peter*). This plural coordinated structure acts as the °logical SUBJECT of the predicatively used noun phrase and thus triggers plural agreement; the surface structure is derived by placing the first conjunct into the subject position of the clause, where it triggers singular agreement on the verb. See Kayne (1994) for more discussion.

(404) a. Jan is een vriendje van Marie.
Jan is a friend of Marie's
b. Jan en Peter zijn vriendjes van Marie.
Jan and Peter are friends of Marie's
c. Jan is vriendjes/*een vriendje met Peter.
Jan is friends/*a friend with Peter

At first sight, it seems that comitative *met*-PPs are not only construed with subjects, but also with direct objects, as in (405a). It is not so clear, however, whether the *met*-PP acts as an independent constituent in this example. Given that it is pied piped with the direct object under topicalization, it seems more plausible that it acts as a modifier of the noun *doperwten* 'peas' or, perhaps, as the second conjunct of a coordinate structure.

(405) a. Jan eet graag doperwten met biefstuk.
Jan eats gladly peas with beefsteak
'Jan likes to eat peas with beefsteak.'
b. Doperwten met biefstuk eet Jan graag.

The third and final function of the role preposition *met* is to introduce a located object; cf. Mulder (1992). Consider the examples in (406). Example (406a) is a simple change of location construction, in which it is expressed that the located object *het hooi* is given a location on the reference object *de wagen*. The construction in (406b) expresses essentially the same situation (the difference being that in this case the wagon must end up completely filled with hay, or, at least, that the hay is evenly distributed on the wagon). However, the located object no longer acts as the direct object of the construction (the reference object does that) but is expressed as the complement of the *met*-PP.

(406) a. Jan laadde het hooi op de wagen.
Jan loaded the hay on the wagon
b. Jan belaadde de wagen met hooi.
Jan loaded the wagon with hay

This use of the *met*-PP is very common with verbs that are prefixed with *be*- or *ver*- and compound verbs with a preposition/particle as their first member, as in (407). Note that, at least synchronically seen, these verbs are not derivationally related to the verbs *dekken* 'cover', *trekken* 'to draw' or *singelen* 'to gird', which accounts for the fact that they do not alternate with constructions in which the located object surfaces as the direct object and the reference object is expressed by a PP. This is especially clear in the case of *omsingelen* given that *singelen* does not belong to the present-day vernacular.

(407) a. Jan *be*-dekte de tafel met een kleed.
Jan BE-covered the table with a cloth
b. Jan *over*-trok de stoel met katoen.
Jan OVER-covered the chair with cotton
c. De vijand *om*-singelde de stad met kanonnen.
the enemy OM-surrounded the city with cannons

This use of the *met*-PP is quite rare with simplex verbs and verbs without particles: one example is the verb *vullen* 'to fill' in (408a). Example (408b) gives the corresponding example in which the located object acts as a direct object and the reference object is expressed by a PP.

(408) a. Jan vulde de tank met water.
Jan filled the tank with water
b. Jan stopte water in de tank.
Jan put water into the tank

For completeness' sake, it must be noted that *met* can also be used in phrases of accessory or concomitant circumstance. In this function *met* is probably not a role preposition but probably related to the preposition in the so-called absolute *met*-construction, discussed in Section 2.5.1. An example is given in (409a). This suggestion seems supported by the fact that such *met*-PPs differ from the ones discussed earlier in that they do not allow R-extraction, as will be clear by comparing example (409a′) to those in (409b′-d′).

(409) a. Jan speelt altijd met veel lawaai. [concomitant circumstance]
Jan plays always with much noise
'Jan always plays with a lot of noise.'
a′. *het lawaai waar Jan altijd mee speelt
the noise that Jan always with plays
b. Jan opende de kist met een breekijzer. [instrumental]
Jan opened the box with a crowbar
b′. het breekijzer waar Jan de kist mee opende
the crowbar that Jan the box with opened
c. Jan speelde met zijn vriendje. [comitative]
Jan played with his friend
c′. het vriendje waar Jan mee speelde
the friend that Jan with played
d. Jan laadt de wagen met hooi. [located object]
Jan loads the wagon with hay
d′. het hooi waar Jan de wagen mee laadt
the hay that Jan the wagon with loads

IV. Bij *'with'*

The preposition *bij* in (410a) is used to express inalienable possession; *Marie* is construed as the inalienable possessor of the body part *nek* 'neck'; cf. Corver (1992). That the *bij*-PP is dependent on the presence of the possessed entity is clear from the fact that it cannot be used when the PP *in de nek* is dropped. Note that the possessive *bij*-phrase alternates with the prenominal genitival possessor in (410b) and the possessive dative in (410c).

(410) a. Jan bijt bij Marie *(in de nek).
Jan bites with Marie in the neck
'Jan is biting in Marie's neck.'
b. Jan bijt in Maries/?de nek.
Jan bites in Marie's/the neck
c. Jan bijt Marie in de nek.
Jan bites Marie in the neck

The inalienable possessive construction in (410a), which in Standard Dutch can only occur when the possessed entity is the complement of predicative locational PP, is more extensively discussed in Section V3.3.1.4.

V. Van *'of' (in noun phrase)*

The role preposition *van* is typically used in noun phrases. The examples in (411a-c) show that it can introduce a possessor, an agent or a theme. The contrast between (411b) and (411d) shows that agentive *van*-PPs are mainly used in nominalizations of monadic verbs; when the noun is derived from a dyadic verb, an agentive *door*-phrase is used instead. See Section N2.2.3.2 for more detailed discussion.

(411) a. het boek van Jan
the book of Jan's
b. het dansen van de kinderen
the dancing of the children
c. het opeten van de taart
the prt.-eating of the cake
d. het eten van de pinda's door/*?van de kinderen
the eating of the peanuts by/of the children

The examples in (412) show that *van*-PPs can sometimes also be used to express causes.

(412) a. Hij rilt van de kou
he trembles of the cold
'He shivers'

b. Ik sterf van de honger
I am dying of the hunger
'I am starving.'

1.3.3.2.2. Functional prepositions: prepositions heading PP-complements

Classifying prepositions heading PP-complements on semantic grounds does not seem to be useful. The actual choice of the prepositions in (413) is fully determined by the selectional properties of the governing verb, noun or adjective, and does not seem to be necessarily related to the meaning of the preposition itself. This of course does not imply that it is never possible to relate the functional preposition to its spatial meaning: *volgen uit* 'to follow from' or *zondigen tegen* 'to sin against', for example, are cases where this is possible; in this respect, it is worthwhile to note that many functional prepositions are homophonous with locational prepositions.

(413) a. Jan zoekt naar een mooi boek.
Jan looks "to" a nice book
'Jan is looking for a nice book.'
b. de lengte van het pad
the length of the pad
c. trots op zijn kinderen
proud "on" his children
'proud of his children'

Table 29 provides a list of adpositions that can be used as functional prepositions; note that the prepositional complements of nouns are mainly "inherited" arguments of a verb or an adjective under nominalization.

Table 29: Functional Prepositions

VERB	NOUN	ADJECTIVE
lijden aan 'to suffer from'	*de behoefte aan* 'the want of'	*gehoorzaam aan* 'obedient to'
passen bij 'to fit with'	*bijlage bij* 'appendix to'	*betrokken bij* 'involved with'
geloven in 'to believe in'	*het geloof in* 'the faith/belief in'	*bedreven in* 'skilful in'
dwepen met 'to idolize'	*de tevredenheid met* 'the contentment with'	*tevreden met* 'satisfied with'
verlangen naar 'to desire'	*het verlangen naar* 'the desire for'	*nieuwsgierig naar* 'curious about'
vechten om 'to fight for'	*het gevecht om* 'the fight for'	*beroemd om* 'famous for'
bezwijken onder 'give way under'	*het bezwijken onder* 'the giving way under'	*kalm (blijven) onder* '(to remain) calm under'
wachten op 'to wait for'	*de jacht op* 'the hunt for'	*boos op* 'angry with'
klagen over 'to complain about'	*een artikel over* 'an article on'	*verontwaardigd over* 'indignant about'
zondigen tegen 'to sin against'	*de zonde tegen* 'the sin against'	*gekant tegen* 'opposed to'
bijdragen tot 'to contribute to'	*een bijdrage tot* 'a contribution to'	*bereid tot* 'willing to'
kiezen tussen 'to choose between'	*de keuze tussen* 'the choice between'	—
volgen uit 'to follow from'	*een selectie uit* 'a selection from'	—
houden van 'to love/like'	*een tekening van* 'a drawing of'	*(on)zeker van* '(not) convinced of'
zwichten voor 'to knuckle under'	*de angst voor* 'the angst for'	*bang voor* 'afraid of'

1.3.3.2.3. Prepositions heading non-spatial/temporal adverbial phrases

Some common examples of prepositions heading adverbial phrases with a specialized meaning are given in Table 30; it must be kept in mind, however, that many of the prepositions in Table 13 and Table 25 can also express non-spatial and non-temporal meanings. PPs headed by the prepositions in Table 30 can only be used adverbially. It does not seem useful to classify these prepositions any further on semantic grounds, because their meaning seems to be purely a lexical matter.

Table 30: Prepositions with a specialized meaning (normal speech)

PREPOSITION	EXAMPLE	TRANSLATION
dankzij	*dankzij zijn hulp*	thanks to his help
gezien	*gezien deze problemen*	in view of these problems
namens	*namens zijn broer*	in name of his brother
ondanks	*ondanks zijn tegenwerking*	despite his opposition
ongeacht	*ongeacht de kosten*	regardless of the costs
per	*per post/auto/kilo*	by mail/car/the kilo
vanwege	*vanwege de kosten*	because of the costs
volgens	*volgens Peter*	according to Peter
wegens	*wegens de kou*	because of the cold
zonder	*zonder zijn broer*	without his brother

1.4. Borderline cases

This section is concerned with certain elements that resemble adpositions, but also differ from them in several ways. We just report the differences here.

I. Als/dan *'as/than'*

Just like adpositions, *als* and *dan* may take a noun phrase as their complement. They differ from adpositions since, in at least some cases, they do not assign case; in a sense they are "case-transparent". This is clearest in comparison constructions. The noun phrase complement of *als/dan* in (414) has the same case as the noun phrase in the main clause to which it is compared: when it is compared with the subject of the clause, as in (414a), it is assigned nominative case; when it is compared to the object of the clause, as in (414b), it is assigned accusative case.

(414) a. Marie is even intelligent als hij/$^{\%}$hem.
Marie is as intelligent as he/him
a′. Marie is intelligenter dan hij/$^{\%}$hem.
Marie is more intelligent than he/him
b. Ik vind Marie even intelligent als hem/*hij.
I consider Marie as intelligent as him/he
b′. Ik vind Marie intelligenter dan hem/*hij.
I consider Marie more intelligent than him/he

The percentage sign in the (a)-examples indicate that non-nominative pronouns are frequently found in speech, but generally considered substandard. The fact that such examples are common indicates that for many speakers of Dutch the element *als* may also act as a regular preposition.

Als can also be used in other constructions. In (415a) and (415b), for example, it is used as, respectively, a °complementive and a °supplementive. In these cases, we cannot check whether these elements assign case since the nominal complements cannot be replaced by a pronoun. That we are not dealing with adpositions, however, is suggested by the fact that the nominal complement in (415a) can be replaced by an adjective, which is certainly not common in adpositional phrases.

(415) a. Ik beschouw hem als held/intelligent.
I consider him as hero/intelligent
b. Als student woonde hij in Amsterdam.
as student lived he in Amsterdam

II. Behalve/uitgezonderd *'except'*

Like *als* and *dan* discussed in the previous subsection, *behalve* is "case-transparent": when the phrase headed by *behalve* excludes entities from the set denoted by the subject of the clause, its complement is assigned nominative case; when it excludes entities from the set denoted by the object, its complement is assigned accusative.

(416) a. Alle studenten zijn aanwezig behalve hij/*hem.
all students are present except he/him
b. Ik heb alle studenten gezien behalve hem/*hij.
I have all students seen except him/he

The same thing holds for he somewhat formal form *uitgezonderd*; just as in (416a), the pronoun in (417a) is assigned nominative case. Note that the more colloquial phrasal adposition *met uitzondering van* in the primed examples does assign objective case.

(417) a. Alle studenten zijn aanwezig uitgezonderd hij/*hem.
all students are present except he/him
a′. Alle studenten zijn aanwezig met uitzondering van hem/*hij.
all students are present with the exception of him/he
b. Ik heb alle studenten gezien uitgezonderd hem/*hij.
I have all students seen except him/he
b′. Ik heb alle studenten gezien met uitzondering van hem/*hij.
I have all students seen with the exception him/he

III. Van die + *NP*

The phrase *van die + NP* can be used in regular nominal positions; it is used as a direct object in (418a) and as a subject in (418b). In the latter case, the verb agrees with the noun in number, which clearly shows that *van* is a spurious preposition in these examples. Note that the expletive *er* is used in (418b), which shows that the phrase *van die + NP* functions as an indefinite noun phrase.

(418) a. Ze verkopen hier van die lekkere broodjes.
they sell here VAN those nice buns
'They sell these nice buns here.'

b. Er $worden_{pl}$ hier van die lekkere $broodjes_{pl}$ verkocht.
there are here VAN those nice buns sold
'These nice buns are sold here.'

Generally, the noun phrase is plural in this construction. The only exception is when the noun phrase is headed by a substance noun. The examples in (419) show that the determiner *die*/*dat* 'that' agrees in gender with the mass noun then, just as in the case of regular demonstratives.

(419) a. Ze hebben daar van *die* lekkere $limonade_{[-neuter]}$.
they have there VAN that tasty lemonade
'They have that tasty lemonade there.'

b. Ze hebben daar van *dat* lekkere $bier_{[+neuter]}$.
they have there VAN that tasty beer
'They have that tasty beer there.'

IV. Wat voor + NP *'what kind of NP'*

As in the case of the *van die + NP* construction, number agreement on the verb is triggered by the nominal complement of *wat voor*. Again, this suggests that *voor* does not act as a regular adposition; see Section N4.2.2 for a more extensive discussion of this construction.

(420) a. Wat voor $boek_{sg}$ is_{sg} dat?
what VOOR book is that
'What kind of book is that?'

b. Wat voor $boeken_{pl}$ $zijn_{pl}$ dat?
what VOOR books are that
'What kind of books are that?'

1.5. Bibliographical notes

The notions of deictic, inherent, absolute adposition are taken from Grabowski & Weiß (1995) and Levelt (1996). The vector analysis of the spatial adpositions has been adopted from a series of papers by Zwarts (1994/1994/1996/1997), Zwarts and Winter (1997), and Helmantel (1998/2002). Jackendoff's work (1983/1990) has been a source of inspiration in many respects. A more technical but good overview of a number of recent semantic approaches to adpositions can be found in Gehrke (2008: Section 2.2).

Chapter 2
Projection of adpositional phrases: Complementation

Introduction

This section discusses the complementation of adpositional phrases. Sections 2.1-2.3 will show that, in the core case, the complement of an adposition is a noun phrase: adpositional phrases are not common as complements of adpositions, although there is a small set of prepositions that may occur with them; adjectival phrases acting as the complement of an adposition are extremely rare, if possible at all. Section 2.4 will show that complementation by finite and infinitival clauses is readily possible, but normally involves an anticipatory pronominal PP (that is, a PP with an °R-pronoun as its complement); this section will pay special attention to formations like *voordat* 'before', which is analyzed in traditional grammar as a complex subordinator, but which may involve the preposition *voor* 'before' followed by a finite clause introduced by *dat* 'that'. Although adpositional and adjectival phrases are not common as complements of adpositional phrases, they do occur as the predicative part of the so-called absolute *met*-construction, which will be discussed in Section 2.5.

2.1. Nominal complements

Complements of adpositions are normally noun phrases. A distinction must be made between noun phrases with a determiner and (singular) bare noun phrases, that is, noun phrases without a determiner. As is to be expected, the first are normally referential in nature; the noun phrase *het kantoor* 'the office' in (1a) just refers to a building, and it is claimed that Jan is working there. The bare noun phrase *kantoor* in (1a′), on the other hand, does not refer to a specific building, and the PP does not refer to a specific location; instead, it is claimed that Jan has an occupation that in some way is related to the noun: he may be an office or administrative worker. Similarly, (1b) expresses that Jan is located at the office, while (1b′) simply expresses that Jan is at work.

(1) a. Jan werkt op het kantoor.
Jan works at the office
'Jan is employed at the office.'
a′. Jan werkt op kantoor.
Jan works at office
'Jan is an office employee.'
b. Jan zit op dit moment op het kantoor.
Jan sits at this moment at the office
'Jan is at the office at this moment.'
b′. Jan zit op dit moment op kantoor.
Jan sits at this moment at office
'Jan is at work at this moment.'

Example (2) shows that the difference in referentiality is also reflected in the modification possibilities of the noun phrase complements: whereas referential noun phrases can be modified by, e.g., an attributive adjective like *nieuwe* 'new', this is normally excluded in the case of bare noun phrases.

(2) a. Jan werkt op het nieuwe kantoor.
a′. *Jan werkt op nieuwe kantoor.
b. Jan zit op dit moment op het nieuwe kantoor.
b′. *Jan zit op dit moment op nieuwe kantoor.

Exceptions to the general rule that bare noun phrases cannot be modified are fixed collocations denoting mental states like *in verwarring* or *in verlegenheid*; the examples in (3) show that such collocations do allow for a limited set af attributive modifiers with an amplifying function.

(3) a. Zij brengt hem in (totale) verwarring.
she brings him in complete confusion
'She totally confuses him.'
b. Zij bracht hem in (grote) verlegenheid.
she brought him in big embarrassment
'She greatly embarrassed him.'

I. Referential noun phrases

The examples throughout this study amply illustrate that the core case of complementation of an adpositional phrase involves a noun phrase. The only restriction on nominal complements seems to be of a semantic nature. For example, when we use the spatial preposition *binnen* 'inside' or *buiten* 'outside', the nominal complement must have dimensional properties that are compatible with these prepositions. Example (4a) is acceptable because a city can be conceived of as an entity with an interior and an exterior. Example (4b) is semantically anomalous because *een dak* 'a roof' is normally not used to divide space in this way; we really have to force an exceptional interpretation on this example in order to make it acceptable. An example like (4c), finally, is completely unacceptable because space is not involved at all. It seems that, as long as the semantic restrictions imposed by the adpositions are met, any noun phrase can be used as a complement.

(4) a. Jan woont binnen/buiten de stad.
Jan lives within/outside the city
b. $Jan zit binnen/buiten het dak.
Jan sits within/outside the roof
c. *Jan is binnen/buiten de vreugde.
Jan is within/outside the joy

II. Bare singular noun phrases

The set of prepositions that may take a bare singular noun phrase as their complement is rather limited. Some examples are given in (5): the (a)-examples involve the locational prepositions *in* 'in' and *op* 'at', and the (b)-examples the directional prepositions *naar* 'to' and *van* 'from'; examples (5c&d) show that the reduced phrasal directional prepositions *richting* 'in the direction of' and the temporal prepositions *voor* 'before' and *na* 'after' can also take a bare noun phrase.

(5) a. Jan ligt in bed.
Jan lies in bed
a′. Jan is op school.
Jan is at school
b. Jan gaat vroeg naar huis.
Jan goes early to home
'Jan goes home early.'
b′. Jan komt vroeg terug van school.
Jan comes early back from school
c. Deze tram rijdt richting centrum.
this tram drives direction center
'This tram goes in the direction of the center.'

d. Jan komt voor/na school even langs.
Jan comes before/after school a.moment past
'Jan drops by before/after school.'

The interpretation of such PPs is often rather special. The PPs *op school* and *op kantoor* in (6), for example, are not spatial in nature, but express that Jan has a certain occupation; note that the location in these examples is expressed by the deictic locational pro-form *hier* 'here'. These readings are virtually lost when a determiner is used; the noun phrases then preferably refer to the actual objects, and the PP is interpreted spatially.

(6) a. Jan zit hier op school.
Jan sits here on school
'Jan is enrolled as a student here (= at this school).'
a′. Jan zit op deze school.
Jan sits at this school
'Jan is enrolled/employed/... at this school.'
b. Jan zit hier al jaren op kantoor.
Jan sit here for.years on office
'Jan has been employed here (= at this office) as a clerk for years.'
b′. Jan zit al jaren op dit kantoor.
Jan sits for.years on this office
'Jan has worked (not necessarily as a clerk) at this office for years.'

Not only is the number of prepositions that can enter this construction limited, there are also a number of badly understood restrictions on the nominal complement. For example, given the acceptability of the examples in (6), one might expect that (7a) would also be acceptable with the meaning "Jan is enrolled as a student here (= at this university)". This example is, however, severely degraded; the only way to express the intended meaning is by using the definite determiner *de* preceding the noun, as in (7b).

(7) a. *Jan zit (hier) op universiteit.
Jan sits here at university
b. Jan zit (hier) op de universiteit.
Jan sits here at the university
'Jan is enrolled as a student (at this university).'

In the examples above, the bare singular nominal complements give rise to interpretations involving occupations, but they may also give rise to event interpretations, which may or may not be idiomatic in nature. Apart from the fact that the use of a definite determiner is excluded, the meaning of (8a) seems fully compositional. Example (8b), on the other hand, has the more specialized interpretation that Jan has gone to bed in order to get some sleep (which will be lost when the article *het* 'the' is added). Note that in cases like (8c), the presence or absence of the definite determiner does not seem to make much difference for the interpretation.

(8) a. Jan zit op (*de) schoot.
Jan sits on the lap
'Jan is sitting on (someone's) lap.'
b. Jan ligt al in bed.
Jan lies already in bed
'Jan already went to bed/is already sleeping.'
c. De sleutels liggen op (de) tafel.
the keys lie on the table
'The keys are on the table.'

The contrasts between the Dutch and English examples in (9) suggest that bare singular nominal complements are not as common in Dutch as in English; see for more English data Quirk et al. (1985: 277-9), from which we have also taken the primed examples. These contrasts strongly suggest that the collocations consisting of a preposition and a bare noun phrase are listed in the mental lexicon.

(9)				
	a.	Jan ligt in bed.	a′.	Jan is in bed.
	b.	Marie zit op school.	b′.	Marie is in/at school.
	c.	Het boek ligt op (*de*) tafel	c′.	the book is on *(*the*) table.
	d.	Jan zit op (*zijn*) schoot.	d′.	Jan is sitting on *(*his*) lap.
	c.	Jan ligt in *het* ziekenhuis.	c′.	Jan is in hospital.
	d.	Marie zit in *de* gevangenis.	d′.	Marie is in jail.
	e.	Jan reist met *de* trein.	e′.	Jan travels by train.
	f.	met *de* dageraad	f′.	at dawn
	g.	na *de* lunch	g′.	after lunch
	h.	in *de* herfst	h′.	in (*the*) autumn/in *the* fall

Finally, note that the Latinate preposition *per* in (10) is characterized by the fact that it can only take bare noun phrases.

(10) a. per (*de) trein/(*de) bus/(*de) auto
by the train/the bus/the car
b. per (*de) minuut/(*het) uur/(*de) dag
per the minute/the hour/the day

The preposition *in* in (11) often occurs with the verbs *zijn* 'to be' or *brengen* 'to bring' in more or less fixed collocations, many of which denote mental states.

(11)			
	a.	*in aantocht zijn*	'to be on the way'
	b.	*in aanbouw zijn*	'to be under construction'
	c.	*in ontroering brengen*	'to move/touch'
	d.	*in verwachting zijn*	'to be pregnant'
	e.	*in verlegenheid brengen*	'to embarrass'
	e.	*in verleiding brengen*	'to tempt'
	f.	*in verwarring brengen*	'to confuse'

2.2. Adpositional complements

Adpositions normally do not take adpositional complements. This section discusses two sets of exceptions: the directional prepositions *van* 'from' and *tot* 'until' in 2.2.1, and the preposition *voor* 'for', which expresses an intended goal, in 2.2.2.

2.2.1. Directional van/tot + *PP*

The first exception to the general rule that adpositions do not take adpositional complements involves the directional prepositions *van* 'from' and *tot* 'until', which refer to, respectively, the starting and the endpoint of an implied path; the exceptional behavior holds both for the spatial and the temporal uses of these prepositions.

I. Spatial van-*PPs*

The preposition *van* 'from' is a directional preposition that denotes the starting point of the implied path. It is therefore not surprising that its complement refers to a location: in (12a) the city Utrecht is the starting point of the path that ultimately leads to Groningen (the complement of the directional preposition *naar* 'to'), and in (12b) the location of the cupboard is the starting point of the path that ultimately leads to the door.

(12) a. Jan reed van Utrecht naar Groningen.
Jan drove from Utrecht to Groningen
b. Marie liep van de kast naar de deur.
Marie walked from the cupboard to the door

Since locations are typically expressed by means of locational adpositional phrases, it is not really surprising that we also find prepositional or circumpositional phrases as complements of *van*. Some examples are given in (13).

(13) a. van boven/onder de kast (vandaan)
from above/under the cupboard VANDAAN
b. van voor/achter het huis (vandaan)
from in.front.of/behind the house VANDAAN
c. van naast het huis (vandaan)
from next.to the house VANDAAN
d. van links/rechts van het huis (vandaan)
from left/right of the house VANDAAN

That we are really dealing with *van*-PPs with a PP-complement, and not with morphologically complex prepositions like *vanboven*, can be motivated on basis of the facts given in Subsections A-C. Subsection D will discuss a number of cases that can readily be confused with *van*-PPs with a PP-complement.

A. Pronominalization of the PP

The PP-complement can be replaced by the locational pro-form *daar/hier* 'there/here', just like other locational preposition phrases: example (14), for instance, provides the demonstrative variants of the examples in (13).

(14) van daar/hier
from there/here

B. Placement of the R-word in cases of R-extraction

The examples in (15) show that, like all locational PPs, the PPs in (13) allow R-extraction. The fact that the R-word *daar* intervenes between *van* 'from' and the second preposition unambiguously shows that we are not dealing with compounds.

(15) a. De muis kwam van boven/onder de kast (vandaan).
the mouse came from above/under the cupboard VANDAAN
b. De muis kwam van daar boven/onder (vandaan).
the mouse came from there above/under VANDAAN

The fact, illustrated in the examples in (16), that the R-word must follow and cannot precede *van* also supports the claim that we are not dealing with compounds, given that the examples in (17) show that the R-word must precede the first member of undisputed compounds like *tegenover* 'opposite'; cf. 1.2.1, sub II.

(16) a. daar boven/onder (vandaan).
there above/under VANDAAN
'from under/above it'
a′. *daar van boven/onder (vandaan)
b. van daar voor/achter/naast
from there in.front.of/behind/next.to
'from in front of/behind/next to it'
b′. *daar van voor/achter/naast
c. van links/rechts daar van
from left/right there of
'from the left/right of it'
c′. *daar van links/rechts van

(17) a. tegenover het huis
opposite the house
b. daar tegenover
there opposite
c. *tegen daar over

C. Modification of the PP

Like other locational prepositional phrases, the complement of *van* can be modified by means of adverbs of orientation and distance. The primed examples in (18) show that the modifier must intervene between *van* and the PP-complement. This shows that we cannot be dealing with compounds, given that the modifier must precede the first member of compounds like *tegenover* 'opposite' in (19).

(18) a. Er klonk een stem van diep onder het puin (vandaan).
there sounded a voice from deep under the wreckage VANDAAN
'A voice came from deep under the wreckage.'
a′. *?Er klonk een stem diep van onder het puin.
b. De auto naderde van schuin/ver achter het huis (vandaan).
the car approached from diagonally/far behind the house VANDAAN
b′. *De auto naderde schuin/ver van achter het huis.

(19) a. Het café staat schuin tegenover de kerk.
the bar stands diagonally opposite the church
'The bar is situated diagonally across from the church.'
b. *Het café staat tegen schuin over de kerk.

D. Apparent cases of van *with a PP-complement*

Although the discussion above has shown that *van* 'from' may take a PP-complement, not all sequences of *van* and a preposition-like element must be analyzed as involving complementation. We start with the form *vanaf* 'from' in (20a), which is probably a complex preposition. One potential argument in favor of this analysis is that R-pronouns cannot intervene between *van* and *af* in (20b), but this may not be sufficient given that R-extraction doesn't seem to be possible at all; example (20c) is also unacceptable. However, the fact that *af Groningen* cannot be used as a locational PP in isolation, and cannot be replaced by the locational pro-form *daar* 'there' (cf. (20d)) strongly suggests that we are indeed dealing with a compound.

(20) a. Jan zeurt al vanaf Groningen om een ijsje.
Jan nags already from Groningen for an ice.cream
'Jan has been pestering for an ice cream since Groningen.'
b. ??Jan zeurt al van daar af om een ijsje.
c. *Jan zeurt al daar vanaf om een ijsje.
d. Jan zeurt al van??(af) daar om een ijsje.

In passing we note that the claim that *vanaf* in (20a) is a compound does not imply that the sequence *daar van af* never occurs. It does, but it has a different source, namely the circumpositional phrase *van ... af* in (21a). This circumpositional phrase does allow R-extraction and thus gives rise to the sequence in question; cf. (21b).

(21) a. Jan sprong van het dak af.
Jan jumped from the roof AF
'Jan jumped down from the roof.'
b. Jan sprong daar van af.
Jan jumped there from AF
'Jan jumped down from there.'

Given the data in (21), the relative acceptability of (20c) can also readily be accounted for: it has more or less the same marginal status as ??*Jan zeurt al van Groningen af om een ijsje*.

Confusion may also arise between example (22a) and the somewhat marked example with the circumpositional phrase *van deze positie uit* in (22b).

(22) a. Van uit deze positie kan je de optocht goed zien.
from out.of this position can you the parade well observe
'You can observe the parade well from this position.'
b. ?Van deze positie uit kan je de optocht goed zien.

In fact, it is not quite clear how the construction in (22a) should be analyzed. At first sight, example (23a) seems to suggest that we are dealing with a PP headed by *van* and a PP complement *uit deze positie*. However, since *hier* cannot be replaced by the typical R-pronoun *er*, it is not evident that *hier* must be analyzed as an R-pronoun or as a locational pro-form. In the latter case (23a) should be analyzed as a circumpositional phrase, so we can no longer use this example to exclude the compound analysis for *vanuit* in (22a). The fact that (22b) is marginal at best, on the other hand, seems to go against the idea that *vanuit* in (22a) is a compound.

(23) a. Van hier uit kan je de optocht goed zien.
from here out.of can you the parade well observe
'You can observe the parade well from here.'
b. ??Hier van uit kan je de optocht goed zien.

We will not try to solve this puzzle here, but simply leave it to future research to decide what the correct analysis is for example (22a).

To conclude note that the sequence *er van uit* in (24b) is fine, but that this example involves neither the complex preposition *vanuit* nor the circumposition *van ... uit*. This example involves the particle verb *uit gaan* 'to assume', which takes an obligatory PP-complement headed by *van*; this is clear from the fact that in (24a) the *van*-PP can either precede or follow the particle *uit*.

(24) a. Jan ging <uit> van de volgende vooronderstellingen <uit>.
Jan went prt. from the following assumptions
'Jan adopted the following assumptions.'
b. Jan ging er van uit dat ....
Jan went there from prt. that
'Jan assumed that ...'

II. Temporal van-*PPs*

The preposition *van* 'from' takes not only locational PPs as its complement, but can also take temporal PPs. Two examples are given in (25a) and (26a). As with locational PPs, there are again several facts that suggest that we are not dealing with the complex prepositions *vanvoor* and *vanna*. First, the (b)-examples show that the temporal PPs can be combined with a modifier of "distance", which intervenes between *van* and the temporal prepositions. Second, the (c)-examples show that temporal PPs allow R-extraction and that the R-words intervene between *van* and the temporal prepositions; the R-words cannot precede *van*, which would be expected if we were dealing with a compound. Finally, the (d)-examples show that the temporal PPs can be replaced by the pro-form *toen* 'then'.

(25) a. van voor de oorlog
from before the war
b. van vlak voor de oorlog
from just before the war
c. <*daar> van <daar> voor
there from before
'from before it'
d. van toen
from then

(26) a. van na de oorlog
from after the war
b. van vlak na de oorlog
from just after the war
c. <*er> van vlak <er> na
there from just after
'from just after it'
d. van toen
from then

In passing, observe that *van* can also take a temporal clause as its complement, as in the primeless examples in (27). The temporal clause must be finite; infinitival clauses, as in the primed examples, lead to ungrammaticality.

(27) a. Dit model dateert van voordat ik geboren was.
this model dates from before I born was
'This model dates from before I was born.'
a′. *Hij herinnert zich dat van voor te zijn geboren.
he remembers REFL that from before to be born
b. van nadat hij ontslagen was
from after he fired was
b′. *van na ontslagen te zijn
from after fired to be

The formation *vanaf* 'from' does not seem to involve complementation on its temporal reading either, but instead acts like a complex preposition. Example (28b) shows that an R-pronoun cannot intervene between *van* and *af*, which is again not sufficient to claim that we are dealing with a compound, since R-extraction doesn't seem to be possible at all; example (28c) is also unacceptable. However, the fact that *af zijn verjaardag* cannot be used as a locational/temporal PP in isolation and cannot be replaced by the temporal pro-form *toen* 'then' strongly suggests that we are indeed dealing with a compound.

(28) a. Jan is al vanaf zijn verjaardag ziek.
b. *Jan is al van daar af ziek.
c. *Jan is al daar vanaf ziek.
d. *Jan is al van toen ziek.

Note that the existence of the temporal circumposition *van .. af* does not complicate matters in this case, given that it never allows R-extraction: *daar van af* has only a spatial meaning.

III. Spatial tot*-PPs*

The preposition *tot* 'until' is also a directional preposition, but in contrast to *van* 'from' it expresses what the endpoint of the implied path is. As in the case of *van*, the complement of *tot* refers to a location; in (29) the city Groningen is the endpoint of the path.

(29) Jan rijdt tot Groningen.
Jan drives until Groningen

Example (30a) shows that the preposition *tot* can also take a locational prepositional phrase. That we are dealing with a PP-complement is clear from the following facts. First, (30a) shows that the locational PP can be combined with a modifier like *vlak* 'just', which must intervene between *tot* and the locational preposition. Second, the (b)-examples show that the locational PP allows R-extraction and the R-word intervenes between *tot* and the locational preposition; the R-word cannot precede the preposition *tot* or its stranded allomorph *toe*, which would be expected if we were dealing with a compound. Example (30c), finally, shows that the PP can be replaced by the locational pro-forms *daar/hier* 'there/here'.

(30) a. Jan reed de auto <*vlak> tot <vlak> voor de garage.
Jan drove the car just until in.front.of the garage
b. Jan reed de auto tot er voor.
Jan drove the car until there in.front.of
b′. *Jan reed de auto er tot/toe voor.
Jan drove the car there until in.front.of
c. Jan reed de auto tot daar/hier.
Jan drove the car until there/here

For completeness' sake, note that the constructions in (30) can be extended by means of the elements *aan* and *toe*, as in (31). These elements can also be used in constructions like (32), in which case *aan* can even occupy two different positions with respect to the reference object *het station* 'the station'. It is not clear to us what the function of the elements *aan* and *toe* is.

(31) a. Jan reed de auto tot (vlak) voor de garage aan toe.
Jan drove the care until just in.front.of the garage AAN TOE
b. Jan reed de auto tot er voor aan toe.
c. Jan reed de auto tot daar/hier aan toe.

(32) tot <aan> het station <aan> toe
until AAN the station TOE

IV Temporal tot*-PPs*

The (a)-examples in (33) and (34) show that the preposition *tot* 'until' takes not only locational PPs as its complement, but can also take temporal PPs. As in the case with locational PPs, we are not dealing here with the complex prepositions *totvoor* and *totna*, which is clear from the following facts. First, the (b)-examples show that the temporal PPs can be combined with a modifier of "distance", which intervenes between *tot* and the temporal prepositions. Second, the (c)-examples show that the temporal PPs allow R-pronominalization and that the R-word intervenes between *tot* and the temporal preposition; the R-word cannot precede *tot* (or its stranded alternate *toe*), which would be expected if we were dealing with a compound. Finally, the (d)-examples show that the temporal PP can be replaced by the pro-form *dan* 'then'. Note that this phrase *tot dan!* is also used as a fixed collocation meaning "see you later!".

(33) a. tot voor de oorlog
until before the war
b. tot vlak voor de oorlog
until just before the war
b. <*daar> tot <daar> voor
there until before
d. ?tot dan
until then

(34) a. tot na de oorlog
until after the war
b. tot lang na de oorlog
until long after the war
c. <*daar> tot <daar> na
there until after
d. ?tot dan
until then

The examples in (35) show that, like *van, tot* can also take a finite, but not an infinitival, temporal clause as its complement.

(35) a. Wacht tot nadat we gegeten hebben!
wait until after we eaten have
b. *Wacht tot na gegeten te hebben!
wait until after eaten to have

The (d)-examples in (33) and (34) are perhaps somewhat marked, but they improve considerably when we add the elements *(aan) toe*, as in (36a). This possibility is undoubtedly related to the fact, illustrated in the (b)-examples in (36), that these elements can also be added to the (b)-examples in (33) and (34). Note that, as in (32), the element *aan* can either precede or follow the reference object *de morgen* 'the morning' in (37). In these cases, the function of the elements *aan* and *toe* is again not clear to us.

(36) a. tot dan (aan) toe
b. tot vlak voor de oorlog (aan) toe
until just before the war AAN TOE
b′. tot lang na de oorlog (aan) toe
until long after the war AAN TOE

(37) tot <aan> de morgen <aan> toe
until AAN the morning TOE

V. Other directional adpositions

The previous subsections has shown that the directional prepositions *van* 'from' and *tot* 'until' may take a PP-complement. This may lead to the expectation that other directional prepositions behave similarly. This is not the case, however, which is demonstrated by means of the directional preposition *naar* 'to' in (38). This suggests that the fact that *van* and *tot* refer to, respectively, the starting and endpoint of the path is crucial for allowing a PP as a complement.

(38) a. *naar boven/onder de kast
to above/under the cupboard
b. *naar voor/achter het huis
to in.front.of/behind the house
c. *naar naast het huis
to next.to the house
d. *naar links/rechts van het huis
to left/right of the house

Nevertheless it must be noted that *naar* can be followed by intransitive prepositions when it is in construction with *van* 'from'; see the examples with the sequence *van ... naar ...* in (39). The unacceptability of *?*van voor naar boven* 'from the front to the top' shows that the intransitive adpositions must be antonyms, which suggests that we are actually dealing with lexicalized expressions.

(39) a. Hij liep van voor naar achter.
he walked from the.front to the.back
b. Hij bekeek het voorwerp van onder tot boven.
he looked.at the object from the.bottom to the.top
c. Hij schoof het boek van links naar rechts.
he slid the book from the.left to the.right

2.2.2. Voor *+ PP expressing a goal*

Another exception to the general rule that adpositions do not take adpositional complements is the preposition *voor* 'for' in its function of expressing an intended goal. First consider the examples in (40), in which the complement of *voor* is the person for which the biscuits are intended.

(40) a. De koekjes zijn voor jou.
the biscuits are for you
b. de koekjes voor jou
the biscuits for you

The examples in (41) show that the intended goal need not be an animate entity but can also refer to a certain occasion.

(41) a. De koekjes zijn voor mijn verjaardag.
the biscuits are for my birthday
'The biscuits are intended for my birthday.'
b. de koekjes voor mijn verjaardag
'the biscuits intended for my birthday'

The examples in (42) show that the occasion in question need not be referred to directly, but can also be referred to indirectly by means of an element that denotes a time, as in the (a)-examples, or a location, as in the (b)-examples.

(42) a. De koekjes zijn voor morgen.
the biscuits are for tomorrow
'The biscuits are intended for an occasion that will take place tomorrow.'
a′. de koekjes voor morgen
'the biscuits intended for an occasion that will take place tomorrow'
b. De koekjes zijn voor daar.
the biscuits are for there
'The biscuits are intended for an occasion that will take place there.'
b′. de koekjes voor daar
'the biscuits intended for an occasion that will take place there'

Given the fact that times and locations are typically expressed by means of a prepositional phrase, it does not really come as a surprise that the occasion in question can also be referred to by means of a PP. In (43a), an example is given that involves the temporal PP *na het eten* 'after dinner'. That we are really dealing with a PP-complement, and not with a compound *voorna*, is clear from the fact illustrated in (43b) that, after R-extraction, the R-pronoun intervenes between *voor* and the temporal preposition *na*, and cannot precede the preposition *voor*; cf. Section 1.2.1, sub II.

(43) a. De koekjes zijn voor na het eten.
the biscuits are for after dinner
b. De koekjes zijn <*er> voor <er> na.
the biscuits are there for after

In (44), we give comparable examples involving the locational PP *in de duinen* 'in the dunes'. Unfortunately, however, R-pronominalization is completely blocked in this case. The main argument for claiming that we are not dealing with the complex preposition *voorin* is that the PP can be replaced by a locational pro-form; this was shown earlier in the (b)-examples in (42).

(44) a. De koekjes zijn voor in de duinen.
the biscuits are for in the dunes
b. *De koekjes zijn <er> voor <er> in.
the biscuits are there for in

Example (45a), finally, is an example, in which the goal is an object that is in the process of being manufactured; it expresses that the eggs are ingredients intended for the pancakes. The example in (45b) shows, again, that the PP must be considered a complement of *voor*, that is, that *voorin* is not a complex preposition in (45).

(45) a. De eieren zijn voor in de pannenkoeken.
the eggs are for in the pancakes
'The eggs are intended for the pancakes.'
b. De eieren zijn <*er/*daar> voor <er/daar> in.
the eggs are there for in

2.3. Adjectival complements

Adjectives acting as the complement of an adpositional phrase are rare. This possibility seems to be restricted to temporal constructions like (46).

(46) a. sinds lang/kort
since long/recently
b. voor hoe lang
for how long

All other cases involve lexicalized constructions. Example (47a), for instance, typically arises with antonymous adjectives and expresses universal quantification; (46a) is more or less synonymous with the universal pronoun *iedereen* 'everyone'. The examples in (46b&c) show that the construction is also possible with numerals and antonymous adpositions.

(47) a. van groot tot klein
from big to small
'everyone'

b. van 1 tot 80
from 1 to 80
'everyone'

c. van onder tot boven
from upstairs to downstairs
'everywhere (e.g., in the house)'

Another case that can be mentioned is the idiomatic expression *van jongs af* 'from early childhood', in which the adjective is adorned with an *-s* ending. Probably this is an abbreviated relic from an older expression *van jongs been af* 'from young-s leg on'; cf. *Woordenboek der Nederlandsche Taal*, lemma *kindsbeen*.

2.4. Clausal complements

This section discusses prepositions with a clausal complement. Section 2.4.1 and Section 2.4.2 will be devoted to, respectively, finite clauses and infinitival clauses with the infinitival marker *te*.

2.4.1. Finite clauses

It is generally taken for granted that adpositions do not take clausal complements. The main reason for this is that PP-complements of verbs or adjectives normally do not contain a clause as their complement; see the primeless examples in (48). Instead, they normally form an anticipatory pronominal PP with the R-word *er* 'there', which introduces (or refers to) a clause that is placed in clause-final position; see the primed examples in (48). Note that the pronominal PP is sometimes optional; an example like (48a′) can also surface as *dat Jan verlangt dat Peter komt*.

(48) a. *dat Jan naar dat Peter komt verlangt.
that Jan for that Peter comes longs

a′. dat Jan *er* *naar* verlangt dat Peter komt.
that Jan there for longs that Peter comes
'that Jan is longing for Peter to come.'

b. *dat Jan trots op dat hij goed zingen kan is.
that Jan proud of that he well sing can is

b′. dat Jan *er* trots *op* is dat hij goed zingen kan.
that Jan there proud of is that he well sing can
'that Jan is proud of it that he can sing well.'

Section 2.4.1.1 will show, however, that it is not completely true that PP-complements cannot have a clause as their complement. The generalization that emerges is that adpositions can at least marginally take a clause as their complement whenever they occupy a position in which R-extraction is not allowed. This conclusion is important, since it bears on the question whether elements like *voordat* 'before', *nadat* 'after', and *doordat* 'because' must be analyzed as complex subordinating conjunctions (complementizers), as is normally claimed in traditional grammar, or whether we are actually dealing with regular prepositions that take a finite clause as their complement. This issue is discussed in Section 2.4.1.2. The discussion will further show that, insofar as complementation by a clause is possible, this always involves declarative clauses.

2.4.1.1. Clausal complements of object-PPs

As a general rule, adpositions do not take clausal complements. This is quite clear from the fact, illustrated in (49a&b), that the noun phrase *het vuurwerk* in the PP-complement of the verb *wachten* 'to wait' cannot be replaced by a clause. In order to express the intended contention in (49b), we must make use of the anticipatory pronominal PP *er ... op* 'on it' and place the clause in clause-final, postverbal position, as in (49c).

(49) a. dat Jan op het vuurwerk wacht.
that Jan for the firework waits
'that Jan is waiting for the fireworks.'
b. *dat Jan op dat het vuurwerk afgestoken wordt wacht.
that Jan for that the firework prt.-lit is waits
c. dat Jan *er* niet langer *op* wacht dat het vuurwerk wordt afgestoken.
that Jan there no longer for waits that the firework is prt.-lit
'that Jan won't wait any longer for the moment that the fireworks are lit.'

However, it seems too strong to assume a general prohibition on clausal complements of prepositions, since PP-constructions like (49b) appear to improve considerably when the PP is moved into some other position; cf. Haslinger (2007:ch.3). In (50), we give examples involving topicalization, scrambling and PP-over-V; although many speakers still consider these examples marked, most agree that they are considerably better than example (49b).

(50) a. ?Op dat het vuurwerk afgestoken wordt, wacht ik niet.
for that the firework prt.-lit is wait I not
'I won't wait for the moment that the fireworks are lit.'
b. ?dat ik op dat het vuurwerk afgestoken wordt niet langer wacht.
that I for that the firework prt.-lit is no longer wait
'that I won't wait any longer for the moment that the fireworks are lit.'
c. ?dat Jan niet langer wacht op dat het vuurwerk afgestoken wordt.
that Jan no longer wait for that the firework prt.-lit is
'that Jan won't wait any longer for the moment that the fireworks are lit.'

Given the fact that PP-over-V gives rise to a reasonably acceptable result, it does not come as a surprise that in clauses without a verb in clause-final position the R-word *er* is apparently optional; this follows if we assume that the version of (51) with *er* corresponds with the embedded clause in (49c), and the one without *er* with the embedded clause in (50c).

(51) Jan wacht ?(er) niet langer op dat het vuurwerk afgestoken wordt.
Jan waits there no longer for that the firework prt.-lit is
'Jan won't wait any longer for the moment that the fireworks are lit.'

Provided that the contrast between (49b) and the examples in (50) is real, the answer to the question what accounts for this contrast that presents itself is that the

PP in the former case is occupying a position in which R-extraction is normally possible, whereas the PPs in the latter cases are occupying positions in which R-extraction is blocked. Given that (52) shows that the anticipatory pronominal PP cannot be placed as a whole in the relevant positions either, there is no other alternative than using the constructions in (50).

(52) a. **Er op* wacht ik niet dat het vuurwerk wordt afgestoken.
b. *dat ik *er op* niet langer wacht dat het vuurwerk wordt afgestoken.
c. *dat ik niet langer wacht *er op* dat het vuurwerk wordt afgestoken.

For completeness' sake, note that the examples in (52) become more or less acceptable when the demonstrative pronominal PP *daarop* substitutes for *erop*, and the clause *dat het vuurwerk wordt afgestoken* is preceded by a comma intonation. The construction involving the anticipatory pronominal PP *er .. op* does not require such an intonation break, so we can put the cases with *daarop*, which probably involve Right Dislocation, aside in the present discussion.

2.4.1.2. Adverbial clauses

Although the data in (50) are perhaps not as robust as one would like them to be, they cast serious doubt on the assumption that there is a general ban on clausal complements of prepositions. This is important since it may bear on the issue of whether the adverbial phrase in (53a) must be analyzed as involving the complex subordinating conjunction (complementizer) *voordat*, as in (53b), or as the preposition *voor* which takes a clausal complement, as in (53c); cf. Hoekstra (1984b).

(53) a. Jan kuste zijn vader voordat hij vertrok.
Jan kissed his father before he left
b. [$_{\text{CLAUSE}}$ [$_{\text{COMPLEMENTIZER}}$ voordat] hij vertrok]
c. [$_{\text{PP}}$ [$_{\text{PREPOSITION}}$ voor] [$_{\text{CLAUSE}}$ dat hij vertrok]]

A third analysis would involve the postulation of an empty noun phrase, as in (54a). In other words, (53a) would then receive an analysis similar to that of the (slightly awkward) relative construction in (54b). Under the analysis in (54a), the *dat*-clause acts as a relative clause that takes the empty noun phrase as its antecedent.

(54) a. voor [$_{\text{NP}}$ ∅ [$_{\text{RELATIVE CLAUSE}}$ dat hij vertrok]]
b. voor [$_{\text{NP}}$ het moment [$_{\text{RELATIVE CLAUSE}}$ dat hij vertrok]]
before the moment that he left

This section investigates whether one of the three analyses in (53) and (54) is to be preferred. Our conclusion will be that at this moment the available potential arguments are not conclusive. In this connection, it must be mentioned that in the literature generally not much effort is devoted to defending the position that is taken, so that much of what follows can be considered an elaboration of arguments that seem to be implicitly assumed in the literature. We will first discuss cases involving temporal phrases in Section 2.4.1.2.1, which will be followed by a briefer discussion of non-temporal cases in Section 2.4.1.2.2.

2.4.1.2.1. Temporal phrases

Before we can discuss the question of which analysis in (53) and (54) is to be preferred we have to discuss the main facts. Example (55) provides some finite adverbial temporal clauses that illustrate the anteriority relation BEFORE: the event expressed by the main clause precedes the event expressed by the adverbial clause. Examples (55a) and (55b) differ in that the event time of the main clause is preferably construed as a specific point on the time line in the former and as an interval in the latter case. Example (55c) has an "irrealis/future tense" flavor, which may account for the fact that the verb cannot readily be in the past tense. The primed examples show that the complementizer-like element *dat* can be dropped in (55a&b), but not in (55c).

(55) • BEFORE

a. voordat hij vertrekt/vertrok
before.that he leaves/left
'before he leaves/left'

a′. voor hij vertrekt/vertrok

b. totdat hij vertrekt/vertrok
until.that he he leaves/left
'until he leaves/left'

b′. tot hij vertrekt/vertrok

c. tegen dat hij vertrekt/?vertrok
close.to that he left/leaves
'close to the moment that he leaves'

c′. *tegen hij vertrekt/vertrok

The examples in (56) illustrate the SIMULTANEOUSNESS relation. The contrast between the primeless and primed examples shows that in this case the complementizer-like element *dat* cannot be realized. Examples (56a) and (56b) again seem to differ in that the event time of the main clause is preferably construed as a specific point on the time line in the former and as an interval in the latter case. The unacceptability of (56a′) with the verb in the present tense is due to the fact that *toen* can only refer to a position on the time line preceding the speech time. Example (56c) clearly has an "irrealis/future tense" interpretation, which straightforwardly accounts for the fact that the verb cannot be in the past tense.

(56) • SIMULTANEOUS

a. *toen dat hij vertrok/vertrekt
when that he left/leaves

a′. toen hij vertrok/*vertrekt
when he left/leaves

b. ??terwijl dat hij vertrekt/vertrok
while that he leaves/left

b′. terwijl hij vertrekt/vertrok
while he leaves/left

c. *als dat hij vertrekt/vertrok
when that he leaves/left

c′. als hij vertrekt/*vertrok
when he leaves/left

The examples in (57) illustrate the posteriority relation AFTER: the event expressed by the main clause follows the event expressed by the adverbial clause. Examples (57a) and (57b) differ again in that the event time of the main clause is preferably construed as a specific point on the time line in the former and as an interval in the latter case. The ungrammaticality of (57b) with the verb in the present tense is due to the fact that *sinds* requires the starting point of the interval to precede the speech time; cf. Section 1.3.2.1, sub II. Although (57c) can have an "irrealis/future tense" interpretation, this example is also acceptable with a past tense, which is due to the fact that, under certain conditions, *vanaf* can be used in a similar way as *sinds*; cf. Section 1.3.2.1, sub II. The primed examples show that the complementizer-like element *dat* cannot be dropped in these examples.

(57) • AFTER

a.	nadat hij vertrekt/vertrok after.that he leaves/left	a′. *na hij vertrekt/vertrok
b.	sinds dat hij vertrok/*vertrekt since that he left/leaves	b′. sinds hij vertrok/*vertrekt
c.	vanaf dat hij vertrekt/vertrok from that he leaves/left	c′. *vanaf hij vertrok/vertrekt

Now that we have reviewed the relevant data, we may start to consider the question of which of the analyses in (53) and (54) is best able to account for the data.

I. Arguments in favor of the complex complementizer analysis

We will start with two arguments in favor of the complex complementizer analysis.

A. The paradigm with dat *is not complete*

The first argument in favor of a complex complementizer analysis for *voordat*, etc. is that the paradigm is not complete. When temporal adpositions are able to take a clause as their complement, there is no obvious reason why we use morphologically simple words like *toen* and *terwijl* instead of the clumsy sounding sequences *tijdens dat* 'during that' and *gedurende dat* 'during that'. When formations like *voordat* are listed in the lexicon as complex complementizers, the clumsiness of *tijdens dat* and *gedurende dat* could just be considered accidental morphological gaps.

B. The distribution of dat

The distribution of the element *dat* seems largely unpredictable: in (55a&b) and (57b) the presence of *dat* seems optional, in (55c) and (57a&c) *dat* is obligatory, and in the examples in (56) *dat* can never be realized. Since in embedded declarative complement clauses the complementizer *dat* is normally present, the fact that *dat* sometimes can or must be omitted is a problem for the analysis in (53c), according to which the clause is a complement of the preposition and supports the analysis in (53b), which would be compatible with the claim that we are dealing with complex complementizers that are listed in the lexicon, some of which have shorter allomorphs.

II. Arguments in favor of the complementation and relative clause analysis

Although the arguments in the previous subsection provide strong support in favor of the complex complementizer analysis, there are also arguments in favor of the competing analysis in (53c).

A. The adverbial clause has the appearance of a regular PP

An obvious argument in favor of the analysis according to which we are dealing with a preposition that takes a clause as its complement is that the adverbial clause has the appearance of a regular PP, where the nominal complement is replaced by the clause. Also the semantics seems to be completely regular. An example like (53a), repeated here as (58a), expresses that the "kissing" event denoted by the main clause precedes the "leaving" event denoted by the adverbial clause. In this respect, there is no difference with example (58b). This also holds for the other sequences *P+dat* ... in (55).

(58) a. Jan kuste zijn vader voordat hij vertrok.
Jan kissed his father before he left
b. Jan kuste zijn vader voor zijn vertrek.
Jan kissed his father before his departure

The counterargument given above that not all temporal prepositions take a clause as their complement can be countered by claiming that, despite their clumsiness, sequences like *tijdens/gedurende dat* are in fact grammatical. Further, the proponents of the regular PP analysis could point out that, whereas *voordat*, *nadat*, and *totdat* are explicitly treated as subordinators in the traditional grammars and dictionaries, this is not the case with *tegen dat*, *sinds dat*, and *vanaf dat*. This might support the claim that, in general, temporal prepositions are able to take clauses as their complement. The clumsiness of *tijdens/gedurende dat* might just be due to lexical blocking, that is, to the fact that the lexicon contains the complementizers *toen* and *terwijl*.

B. The distribution of dat

Even though the proponents of the complementation analysis in (53c) might acknowledge the problem of the distribution of *dat*, they may point out that it should make us suspicious that the presumed "complex complementizers" with *dat* can only occur with prepositional elements. This could be used as an argument in favor of the idea that in (55) and (57) we are actually dealing with prepositions taking a finite clause as their complement.

C. Similarities in modification of temporal PPs and temporal clauses

That we are dealing with a regular preposition is also suggested by the fact that there are some correspondences between the prepositions and the presumed complex complementizers with respect to modification. As is shown in (59) the temporal prepositions *voor* and *na* can be modified by the same elements as the sequences *voor dat* and *na dat*. This supports the hypothesis that we are actually dealing with regular PPs in the primed examples.

(59) a. kort/een tijdje voor de oorlog
shortly/a while before the war
a′. kort/een tijdje voor dat de oorlog uitbrak
shortly/a while before the war started

b. vlak/drie jaar na het begin van de oorlog
just/three years after the start of the war

b′. vlak/drie jaar na dat de oorlog uitbrak
just/three years after the war started

III. Argument in favor of the relative clause analysis

A conclusive argument in favor of a complementation analysis would be an example in which an element intervenes between the preposition and the finite clause, that is, constructions of the type *tot* ***vlak*** *voor de deur* 'until just in front of the door' or *voor* ***daar*** *bij* 'for with it' discussed in Section 2.2. Unfortunately, however, such examples cannot be constructed because clauses allow neither modification nor R-extraction. Still there are semantic facts that suggest that certain phonetically empty elements can be place in between the preposition and the complementizer but these seem to support the relative clause analysis rather than complex complementizer analysis.

Consider example (60a), which is ambiguous between two readings, cf. Larson (1990) and Haslinger (2007). Under the first reading, the temporal expression *na* 'after' takes scope over the complete string that it precedes (*dat hij beweerde dat hij vertrokken was*): this gives rise to the paraphrase in (60b). Under the second reading the scope of the temporal expression is restricted to the more deeply embedded clause (*dat hij vertrokken was*): this gives rise to paraphrase in (60c), which aims at expressing that the killer has committed perjury.

(60) a. De dader was op het feest gezien nadat hij beweerde dat hij vertrokken was.
the culprit was at the party seen after he claimed that he left was
'The culprit was seen at the party after he claimed that he had left.'

b. The culprit was seen at the party after he made a claim, viz., that he had left.

c. The culprit was seen at the party after the time he claimed that he had left (it).

The crucial fact is that the slightly awkward construction in (61a) has the same scope properties as example (60a).

(61) a. De dader was op het feest gezien na het moment dat hij beweerde
the culprit was at the party seen after the moment that he claimed
dat hij vertrokken was.
that he left was
'The culprit was seen at the party after the moment he claimed that he had left.'

b. Jan was seen at the party after the moment he made the claim that he had left.

c. Jan was seen at the party after the moment he claimed that he had left (it).

This suggests that we may account for the ambiguity of (60a) by assuming that the temporal expression is related to its scope position by means of a phonetically empty relative element REL with the function of an adverbial phrase of time. This empty element is moved into the position preceding the complementizer *dat* and takes an empty noun as its antecedent, that is, into the position that is occupied by overt relative pronouns. This would mean that the reading in (60b) corresponds to the structure in (62a), in which REL originates in the matrix clause, and the reading in (60c) to that in (62b), where REL originates in the embedded clause. For completeness' sake, the structures related to the two readings of (61a) are given in the primed examples.

(62) De moordenaar was op het feest gezien ...
- a. na [$_{NP}$ ∅ [$_{REL.CLAUSE}$ REL$_i$ dat hij beweerde t_i [dat hij vertrokken was]]]
- a′. na [$_{NP}$ het moment [$_{REL.CLAUSE}$ REL$_i$ dat hij beweerde t_i [dat hij vertrokken was]]]
- b. na [$_{NP}$ ∅ [$_{REL.CLAUSE}$ REL$_i$ dat hij beweerde [dat hij vertrokken was t_i]]]
- b′. na [$_{NP}$ het moment [$_{REL.CLAUSE}$ REL$_i$ dat hij beweerde [dat hij vertrokken was t_i]]]

IV. Conclusion

The discussion above makes clear that it is hard to give explicit criteria that could definitely settle the issue concerning the proper analysis of the sequences P + *dat* on the basis of the currently available evidence.

2.4.1.2.2. Non-temporal phrases

Many sequences of the form *P+dat* ... can also be found in the non-temporal domain, and the same analyses as discussed in 2.4.1.2.2 present themselves. Example (63) provides a short list.

(63)
- a. *doordat* 'because'
- b. *in plaats (van) dat* 'instead of'
- c. *niettegenstaande dat* 'in spite of'
- d. *omdat* 'because'
- e. *ondanks dat* 'despite'
- f. *opdat* 'so that'
- g. *zonder dat* 'without'

The formations in (63) pose a potential problem for the complementation analysis, because the meaning of the formation is not always fully compositional. For example, the (somewhat archaic) sequence *opdat* introduces an adverbial clause which expresses a goal, whereas a PP headed by *op* normally does not express a goal (a possible exception is the standard formula *Op je gezondheid!* 'Your health!'). The proponents of the complex complementizer analysis should be willing to accept that some of the complementizers in the lexicon are phrasal in nature; examples (63b&c) are cases for which this is generally assumed.

2.4.2. Infinitival clauses with te

This section continues the discussion of clausal complements of adpositions with infinitival complement clauses.

2.4.2.1. Complement clauses preceded by om

Dutch has three types of infinitival complement clauses, which are illustrated in (64). The first type is the bare infinitival *accusativus cum infinitivo* construction which occurs as the complement of perception verbs like *zien* 'to see' and the causative/permissive verb *laten* 'to make/let'. In the second type, the infinitival marker *te* 'to' must be present. The third type can often be found in the same position as the second type, but is preceded by the preposition-like element *om* (often translated by English *for* but different from it by lacking the ability to assign case to the subject of the infinitival clause). Since bare infinitives like (64a) never occur as the complement of a preposition, we will focus below on the *te*-infinitives in (64b&c), in which °PRO stands for the implied subject of the infinitival clause.

(64) a. Jan zag [Peter vertrekken].
Jan saw Peter leave
b. Hij beloofde Marie [PRO op tijd te vertrekken].
he promised Marie on time to leave
c. Hij beloofde Marie [om PRO op tijd te vertrekken].
he promised Marie OM on time to leave

The status of *om* in (64c) is unclear; some regard it as an infinitival complementizer, whereas others consider it a regular preposition. The former position seems the most plausible one. A first argument in favor of this position is that, like the complementizer *dat* 'that', *om* seems to have no clear semantic content; both are just used to introduce embedded clauses. Another argument in favor of this position is that it is not the case that the verb *beloven* 'to promise' in (64c) selects a PP headed by *om*; cf. *Jan beloofde Marie (*om) dat boek* 'he promised Marie the book'. Finally, the examples in (65) show that, like *dat*, *om* may also appear when an anticipatory pronominal PP is present.

(65) a. dat Marie er naar verlangt [(om) PRO op vakantie te gaan].
that Marie there for longs COMP on holiday to go
b. dat Marie er tegenop ziet [(om) te moeten verhuizen].
that Marie there against sees COMP to must move
'that Marie doesn't like the idea of having to move.'

For these reasons we will assume that *om* is a complementizer. If it turns out that, despite the three arguments given above, the element *om* is a preposition, one must conclude that it is certainly not a preposition selected by the verb *beloven* in (64c) or the prepositions *naar* and *tegen* in (65).

2.4.2.2. Adverbial infinitival clauses

This section will discuss whether *te*-infinitives may occur as the complement of temporal or non-temporal adverbial PPs.

I. Temporal clauses

There are only two types of temporal infinitival clauses. The first type expresses the anteriority relation BEFORE, as in (66a), and the second the posteriority relation AFTER, as in (66b); temporal infinitival clauses expressing the relation of SIMULTANEOUSNESS do not exist.

(66) a. Alvorens (*om) PRO te vertrekken, kuste Jan zijn vader.
before COMP to leave kissed Jan his father
'Jan kissed his father before departing.'
b. Na (*om) zijn vader gekust te hebben, vertrok Jan.
after COMP his father kissed to have left Jan
'After having kissed his father, Jan left.'

When we adopt the assumption that *om* is a complementizer, the ungrammaticality of (66a) with *om* present can be accounted for by assuming that *alvorens* is also a complementizer. From this it would follow that the two elements are competing for the same position, so that only one can be realized (viz. the one with semantic content). In order to obtain the same result for (66b), it must be assumed that *na* is also a complementizer.

For the proponents of the complementation analysis of *nadat* 'after', the same result could be obtained by claiming that infinitival clauses do not have (an overtly realized) complementizer, and that *om*, *alvorens* and *na* are all prepositions. But this would leave us with the problems indicated in Section 2.4.2.1.

II. Non-temporal clauses

Some of the sequences of the form *P + dat* in (63) have counterparts that consist only of *P*. Those who adhere to the complex complementizer analysis of *doordat* are likely to also analyze the elements *door*, *in plaats van* and *zonder* as complementizers. For the proponents of the alternative analysis, these cases involve regular prepositions taking an infinitival clause (without an overtly realized complementizer) as their complement.

(67) a. [Door PRO hard te werken] werd Marie een belangrijk wetenschapper.
by hard to work became Marie an important scientist
'Marie became an important scientist by working hard.'
b. [In plaats van PRO te werken] zit Jan te luieren.
instead of to work sits Jan to loaf
'Jan is being idle instead of working.'
c. [Zonder PRO iets te vragen] pakte Marie een koekje.
without something to ask took Marie a biscuit
'Marie took a biscuit without asking.'

2.4.3. Conclusion

This section has addressed the question of whether clauses can be complements of prepositions. At this moment, no definite answer can be given. Much depends on whether one is willing to abandon the traditional idea that sequences of the type *P + dat* are complex complementizers in favor of the idea that we are dealing with prepositions that take a finite clause or a free relative construction. As far as we can see, conclusive arguments in favor of one of these analyses are not available at present.

2.5. Absolute PPs

This section is concerned with absolute prepositional phrases, that is, constructions in which the complement of the preposition consists of two parts that stand in a predication relation: in (68), for instance, the locational PP *in het doel* 'in the goal' is predicated of the located object *een goede keeper*. The difference between *met* and *zonder* in (68a&b) is that the first makes a positive statement about the predicative relation, whereas the latter makes a negative statement.

(68) a. Met een goede keeper in het doel kunnen we niet verliezen.
with a good goalkeeper in the goal can we not lose
'With a good goalkeeper in the goal we cannot lose.'

b. Zonder een goede keeper in het doel kunnen we niet winnen.
without a good goalkeeper in the goal can we not win
'Without a good goalkeeper in the goal we cannot win.'

A note on the used terminology may be in order. The constructions in (68) are called absolute because they seem to behave like the modern Indo-European counterparts of the old Indo-European absolute constructions which made use of absolute case forms: Dutch still has some fossilized relics of absolute case, such as *blootshoofds* 'with his head bare' with an old genitive.

2.5.1. Absolute met-*construction*

This section is concerned with the absolute *met*-construction. Section 2.5.1.1 starts by showing that the construction constitutes a phrase. Sections 2.5.1.2 to 2.5.1.4 continue by discussing, respectively, the properties of the predicative part of the construction, the syntactic uses of the construction, and the properties of the noun phrase of which the predicative part of the construction is predicated. Section 2.5.1.5 concludes by discussing some syntactic properties of the construction as a whole.

2.5.1.1. Constituency

That the phrase *met Jan in het doel* in (69a) forms a constituent is clear from the fact illustrated in (69b&c) that it can be placed in clause-initial or extraposed position; cf. the °constituency test. Furthermore, the primed examples show that the construction cannot be split; this is illustrated in the (b)-examples for topicalization and in the (c)-examples for °PP-over-V.

(69) a. We kunnen [met Jan in het doel] niet verliezen.
we can with Jan in the goal not lose
'We cannot lose with Jan in the goal.'

b. [Met Jan in het doel] kunnen we niet verliezen.

b′. *Met Jan kunnen we in het doel niet verliezen.

b″. *In het doel kunnen we met Jan niet verliezen.

c. We kunnen niet verliezen [met Jan in het doel].

c′. *We kunnen met Jan niet verliezen in het doel.

c″. *We kunnen in het doel niet verliezen met Jan.

2.5.1.2. The predicative part

The subsections below will show that the predicative part of the absolute *met*-construction can be of several categories.

I. Adpositional predicates

Adpositional predicates are probably the most common in the absolute *met*-construction. When the adposition is prepositional, as in (70), the PP may express either a location or a direction.

(70) a. [Met Jan in het doel] kunnen we niet verliezen.
with Jan in the goal can we not lose
'With Jan in the goal we cannot lose.'
b. [Met de baby naar de crèche] kan Jan weer gaan werken.
with the baby to the crèche can Jan again go work
'With the baby to the crèche Jan can work again.'

Given that the directional reading is possible, it will not come as a surprise that postpositional and circumpositional phrases are also possible; cf. (71).

(71) a. [Met Marie het huis uit] kan Jan een eigen kamer krijgen.
with Marie the house out can Jan an own room get
'With Marie out of the house Jan can get a room of his own.'
b. [Met de draad door de naald heen] kan ik eindelijk mijn broek repareren.
with the thread through the needle HEEN can I finally my trousers repair
'With the thread through the needle I can finally repair my trousers.'

Example (72a) shows that intransitive prepositions can also be used. Verbal particles like *op* in (72b) are marginally possible when they occur with the main verb *hebben* 'to have' (like *Hij heeft zijn borrel op* 'He has finished his drink') or when they can be used in a copular construction (cf. *De drank is op* 'The booze is finished'), and are excluded in all other cases.

(72) a. [Met een nette das om] ging hij de club binnen.
with a neat tie around went he the club inside
'He went inside the club with a neat tie around (his neck).'
b. ?[Met de drank op] vertrok iedereen snel.
with the booze OP left everyone quickly
'With the booze finished everyone left quickly.'

II. Adjectival predicates

The examples in (73) show that the predicative part of an absolute *met*-construction may also be an adjectival phrase. In order to be able to occur in this construction, the adjective must denote a transitory property: typical stage-level adjectives like *ziek* 'ill' and *dronken* 'drunk' generally give rise to a felicitous result, whereas typical individual-level predicates like *intelligent* 'intelligent' or *klein van stuk* 'small of posture' are excluded in this construction.

(73) • Stage-level adjectives
a. [Met Jan ziek] kan de vergadering niet doorgaan.
with Jan ill can the meeting not take.place
'With Jan ill the meeting cannot take place.'
b. [Met de helft van de ploeg dronken] verliezen we zeker.
with the half of the team drunk lose we certainly
'With half of the team drunk, we will certainly lose.'

(74) • Individual-level adjectives
a. *[Met Jan intelligent] lossen we alles op.
with Jan intelligent solve we everything prt.
b. *[Met Peter en Jan klein van stuk]
with Peter and Jan small of posture
kunnen ze gemakkelijk in één bed slapen.
can they easily in one bed sleep

III. Nominal predicates

Nominal predicates cannot readily be used in the absolute *met*-construction. Instead, the nominal predicate appears preceded by the element *als* 'as', which also appears in the supplementive and complementive constructions in (76).

(75) a. ??[Met Jan voorzitter] zal de vergaderen snel verlopen.
with Jan chairman will the meeting quickly proceed
b. [Met Jan als voorzitter] zal de vergaderen snel verlopen.
with Jan as chairman will the meeting quickly proceed
'With Jan as chairman, the meeting will proceed quickly.'

(76) a. Als voorzitter is Jan verantwoordelijk voor de procedure.
as chairman is Jan responsible for the procedure
'As chairman, Jan is responsible for the procedure.'
b. Ik beschouw Jan als onze voorzitter.
I consider Jan as our chairman

IV. Past/Present participles and modal infinitives

It seems that participles and infinitives can at best marginally act as predicates in absolute *met*-constructions. Example (77a) is a potentially acceptable example that involves a passive participle. The judgments on this example seem to vary from "perfect" to "marginal"; that we are dealing here with a (verbal) passive participle is supported by the fact that a passive *door*-phrase is present. However, including the perfect participle *gedronken* 'drunk' in example (77b) leads to an ungrammatical result; the particle *op* must stand alone. In order to be able to fully appreciate the importance of (77b), it must be noted that many apparent cases of past/passive participles may actually involve deverbal adjectives. Example (77c) illustrates this; that we are dealing with an adjective in this example is clear from the fact that *gesloten* 'closed' expresses a stative property.

(77) a. %[Met Jan achtervolgd door de politie] moeten we nu voorzichtig zijn.
with Jan chased by the police must we now careful be
'With Jan chased by the police, we must be careful.'
b. [Met een borrel op (*gedronken)] mag je geen auto besturen.
with a drink up drank may you no car steer
'One is not allowed to drive a car after drinking.'
c. [Met het museum gesloten] is hier niets te doen.
with the museum closed is here nothing to do
'With the museum closed, there is nothing to do here.'

The use of present participles, as in (78a), is generally judged as marginal. However, when the present participle is suffixed with an *-e* ending, as in (78b), the result is well-formed, which is of course related to the fact that such forms can also be used in copular constructions like (78b′); cf. Section A9.3.1.2.

(78) a. [Met Jan naast mij (??lopend)] voel ik me niet op mijn gemak.
with Jan next.to me walking feel I REFL not at my ease
'With John (walking) beside me, I don't feel at my ease.'
b. [Met Jan stervende/??stervend] kunnen we niet op vakantie gaan.
with Jan dying can we not on holiday go
'With Jan dying we cannot go on holiday.'
b′. Jan bleek stervende/*stervend.
Jan turned.out dying

Modal infinitives can also be used in this construction, which is not surprising since they can also appear as predicates of copular constructions. The fact that the *te* + infinitive sequences precede the finite verbs in the primed examples shows that they are not dependent clauses, since clausal *te*-infinitives never precede the finite verb in clause-final position; cf. Section V4.7.

(79) a. [Met nog drie wedstrijden te spelen] ...
with yet three games to play
a′. dat er nog drie wedstrijden te spelen zijn.
that there yet three games to play are
'that there are still three games to play.'
b. [Met nog drie kilometer te gaan] ...
with yet three kilometer to go
b′. dat er nog drie kilometer te gaan is.
that there yet three kilometer to go is
'that there are still three kilometers to go.'

Example (80a) shows that the use of regular, non-modal (*te*-)infinitives is excluded in Standard Dutch. It can be noted, however, that this use does occur in certain dialects spoken in Flanders and Brabant. The grammatical example in (80b) is from the Flemish dialect spoken in Wambeek, the properties of this construction are discussed in Haslinger (2007: Chapter 3).

(80) a. *[Met Marie (te) werken] moet hij de hele dag thuis blijven.
with Marie to work must he the whole day home stay
b. [Mè zaai te werken] moest-n-ai de gieln dag toisj blaaiven
with she to work must-he the whole day home stay
'With her working, he had to stay home all day.'

2.5.1.3. Syntactic uses

The absolute *met*-construction can perform various syntactic functions, which will be discussed in this section. We will also compare the absolute constructions with constructions involving the main verb *hebben* 'to have' and the copular verb *zijn* 'to be', since this comparison has played an important role in the discussion about the internal structure of the absolute *met*-construction; see Subsection IV for a brief summary of this discussion.

I. Attributive use

In (81a&b), the absolute *met*-construction is used attributively, as is clear from the fact that the sequence consisting of the noun phrase and the absolute construction is placed in clause-initial position. When the absolute construction is used attributively, there are several additional restrictions on the predicative part of the absolute construction, as is clear from the unacceptability of the examples in (81c&d).

(81) a. [$_{NP}$ Die man [$_{PP}$ met een revolver in zijn hand]] is gevaarlijk.
that man with a revolver in his hand is dangerous
b. [$_{NP}$ Die vrouw [$_{PP}$ met dat boek voor zich]] is de nieuwe hoogleraar.
that woman with that book in.front.of REFL is the new professor
'That woman with that book in front of her is the new professor.'
c. *[$_{NP}$ Die man [$_{PP}$ met zijn vrouw ziek]] is ongelukkig.
that man with his wife ill is unhappy
d. *[$_{NP}$ Die vrouw [$_{PP}$ met haar benen verlamd]] is de nieuw hoogleraar.
that woman with her legs paralyzed is the new professor

The data in (81) suggest that adjectives are not possible in attributively used absolute *met*-constructions. It has been argued, however, that the difference between the two cases is related to the fact that the constructions in (81a&b) can be paraphrased by means of a relative clause containing the verb *hebben*, whereas the examples in (81c&d) cannot.

(82) a. Die man die een revolver in zijn hand heeft ...
that man who a revolver in his hand has
b. Die vrouw die een boek voor zich heeft ...
that woman who a book in.front.of REFL has
c. *?Die man die zijn vrouw ziek heeft ...
that man who his wife ill has
d. *?Die vrouw die haar benen verlamd heeft ...
that woman who her legs paralyzed has

It must be noted, however, that the correspondence between the absolute *met*-construction and the relative construction with *hebben* does not work in reverse: whereas the construction with a relative clause in (83b) is fully acceptable, the absolute construction in (83a) is ungrammatical.

(83) a. *[De man [met zijn schoenen nu eindelijk schoon]] is mijn broer.
the man with his shoes now finally clean is my brother
b. [De man [die zijn schoenen nu eindelijk schoon heeft]] is mijn broer.
the man who his shoes now finally clean has is my brother
'The man who has his shoes finally clean is my brother.'

II. Adverbial use

Adverbially used absolute *met*-constructions express an accessory circumstance with respect to the event expressed by the clause: they may express a cause, as in (84a), specify a condition under which the event in the main clause takes place, as in (84b), describe a state or an event that simultaneously takes place, as in (84c), etc.

(84) a. We schaatsen altijd [met zoveel sneeuw op straat].
we skate always with so.much snow in the.street
'With so much snow in the streets, we're always skating.'
b. Jan spijbelt altijd [met zo'n voetbalwedstrijd op TV].
Jan plays.truant always with such.a soccer.game on TV
'Jan always plays truant with such a soccer game on TV.'
c. Jan slaapt altijd [met het raam open].
Jan sleeps always with the window open
'Jan always sleeps with his window open.'

In this respect the absolute *met*-constructions in (84) do not differ from the PPs in (85), the complements of which do not involve predication.

(85) a. We schaatsen altijd met zulk mooi weer.
we skate always with such beautiful weather
'With such beautiful weather we're always skating.'
b. Jan spijbelt altijd met zo'n voetbalwedstrijd.
Jan plays.truant always with such.a soccer.game
'Jan always plays truant with such a soccer game.'
c. Jan slaapt altijd met een open raam.
Jan sleeps always with an open window
'Jan always sleeps with an open window.'

The examples in (86) and (87) show that the constructions in (84) and (85) are not only semantically, but also syntactically similar: they do not allow R-extraction, in contrast to what is normally the case with other types of *met*-PPs; cf. the discussion of example (409) in Section 1.3.3.2.1.

(86) a. *De sneeuw *waar* we [*mee* op straat] schaatsen.
the snow that we with in the.street skate
b. *De voetbalwedstrijd *waar* Jan altijd [*mee* op TV] spijbelt.
the soccer.game that Jan always with on TV plays.truant
c. *Het raam *waar* Jan altijd [*mee* open] slaapt.
the window that Jan always with open sleeps

(87) a. *Het mooie weer *waar* we altijd *mee* schaatsen.
the beautiful weather that we always with skate
b. *De voetbalwedstrijd *waar* Jan altijd *mee* spijbelt.
the soccer.game that Jan always with plays.truant
c. *Het open raam *waar* Jan altijd *mee* slaapt.
the open window that Jan always with sleeps

This similarity in meaning and syntactic behavior seems to justify the assumption that the two constructions are essentially the same, the only difference being that in (84) the preposition *met* takes a complex phrase expressing a predicative relation as its complement, whereas in (85) the preposition simply takes a nominal complement. We refer the reader to Beukema & Hoekstra (1984) for an alternative account for the ungrammaticality of the examples in (86) and to Section 2.5.1.2, sub III, for some apparent counterexamples to the claim that R-extraction from absolute *met*-constructions is excluded.

For completeness' sake, we want to note that the absolute constructions in the examples in (84) can be paraphrased by means of copular constructions.

(88) a. We schaatsen altijd als er zoveel sneeuw op straat is.
we skate always when there so.much snow in the.street is
'When there is so much snow in the street, we're always skating.'

b. Jan spijbelt altijd als er zo'n voetbalwedstrijd op TV is.
Jan plays.truant always when there such.a soccer.game on TV is
'Jan always plays truant when there is such a soccer game on TV.'

c. Jan slaapt altijd terwijl het raam open is.
Jan sleeps always while the window open is
'Jan always sleeps while the window is open.'

III. Supplementive use

The examples in the previous subsection involve cases in which the absolute PP is used adverbially and refers to some accessory circumstance under which the event denoted by the verb takes place. The absolute PP can, however, also be used as a supplementive and thus convey additional information about one of the arguments of the verb. This is illustrated in (89).

(89) a. Marie zag *de rover* [met een revolver in *zijn* hand] wegrennen.
Marie saw the robber with a revolver in his hand away ran
'Marie saw the robber run away with a revolver in his hand.'

b. *Marie* liep [met een revolver in *haar* hand] naar de rover toe
Marie walked with a revolver in her hand to the robber TOE
'Marie walked to the robber with a revolver in her hand.'

c. *De auto reed [met een revolver in haar/de hand] weg.
the car drove with a revolver in her/the hand away

In (89a) the absolute PP modifies the direct object of the clause: it expresses that the robber, who is running away, has a revolver in his hand, which is clear from the fact (indicated by means of italics) that the possessive pronoun *zijn* 'his' must be construed as coreferential with the noun phrase *de rover* 'the robber'. Like supplementive APs, supplementive absolute PPs can also modify the subject of the clause; in (89b), the absolute PP expresses that Marie, who is approaching the robber, has a revolver in her hand, which is clear from the fact that the possessive pronoun *haar* 'her' must be construed as coreferential with the noun phrase *Marie*. Supplementive absolute PPs must modify some argument of the verb: in (89c) no suitable antecedent is available and the sentence is ungrammatical.

Like attributively used absolute PPs, the supplementive absolute PPs in (89) can be paraphrased by means of a construction involving *hebben*; cf. (90).

(90) a. Marie zag de rover wegrennen terwijl hij een revolver in zijn hand had.
Marie saw the robber away.run while he a revolver in his hand had
b. Marie liep naar de rover toe terwijl zij een revolver in haar hand had.
Marie went to the robber prt. while she a revolver in her hand had

The examples in (91) show that when the *hebben*-construction is excluded, the supplementive use of the absolute *met*-PP is not possible either.

(91) a. *Jan vertrok [met zijn vrouw ziek].
Jan left with his wife ill
b. *Jan vertrok terwijl hij zijn vrouw ziek had.
Jan left while he his wife ill had

IV. Concluding remarks

The preceding subsections have shown that, in terms of paraphrases, there is a difference between the adverbial use of the absolute construction, on the one hand, and its attributive and supplementive use, on the other. The fact that the latter must allow a paraphrase with *hebben* 'to have' has led to the hypothesis in (92a), according to which the complement of *met* has a clause-like structure with an empty abstract verb $[_V$ *e*] meaning "to have" and a PRO-subject that corresponds to the subject of the paraphrase with *hebben*; cf. Klein (1983). This hypothesis has been refuted by pointing to adverbially used absolute constructions, which certainly do not involve the postulated empty verb or a PRO-subject, in favor of the "Small Clause" structure in (92b); cf. Beukema & Hoekstra (1983), and also Van Riemsdijk (1978) for additional arguments against structures like (92a). However, a problem with the proposal in (92b), which was also defended within a non-generative framework by Duinhoven (1985), is that it does not account for the clause-like properties of the complement of *met*: Section 2.5.1.5 will show that the complement of *met* may contain all kinds of phrases that we would expect within a clause rather than within a Small Clause; these include adverbial phrases, supplementives, (moved) R-words, etc. An attempt to reconcile the two approaches can be found in Smits & Vat (1985), who assume that the complement of *met* is a verbal projection which is smaller than a full clause and therefore does not contain a PRO-subject, as in (92c). To our knowledge, the discussion on the internal structure of the absolute *met*-construction has not been continued since.

(92) a. $[_{PP}$ met/zonder $[_S$ PRO ... NP PRED $[_V$ e]]]
b. $[_{PP}$ met/zonder $[_{SC}$ NP PRED]]
c. $[_{PP}$ met/zonder $[_{VP}$ ... NP PRED ..$[_V$ *e*]]]

2.5.1.4. The noun phrase part

The examples in (84) and (85) above have shown that the predicative part of the absolute *met*-construction is (in a sense) optional. This does not hold for the noun phrase that the predicative part of the construction is predicated of. Dropping it results in ungrammaticality, as is illustrated in (93) on the basis of the examples in (84).

(93) a. We schaatsen altijd met *(zoveel sneeuw) op straat.
we skate always with so much snow in the.street
b. Jan spijbelt altijd met *(zo'n voetbalwedstrijd) op TV.
Jan plays.truant always with such a soccer.game on TV
c. Jan slaapt altijd met *(het raam) open.
Jan sleeps always with the window open

The noun phrase is assigned case by the preposition. It cannot be demonstrated whether dative or accusative case is involved since Dutch has no morphological case marking, but the German examples in (94) suggest that dative case is involved: the noun phrase is assigned dative case by *mit* 'with', just like a simple nominal complement of *mit* would be. This strongly suggests that case-assignment in the absolute *met*-construction is of the exceptional type in the sense that the noun phrase is assigned case by *met* across the boundary of the complement of the preposition. That is, the absolute construction behaves like English constructions such as *I consider [him to be nice]*, where the verb *consider* assigns case to the subject of the embedded infinitival clause.

(94) a. [Mit dem Gepäck$_{dat}$ im Flugzeug] kann die Reise jetzt anfangen.
with the luggage in.the airplane can the journey now start
b. [Mit dem Fenster$_{dat}$ offen] schläft man besser.
with the window open sleeps one better

Note in passing that Beukema & Hoekstra (1983) point out that assuming this form of exceptional case marking is problematic for structure (92a). First, we would expect the empty verb to assign accusative case to the noun phrase, and, second, PRO should be excluded since it only occurs in positions in which case cannot be assigned. Smits & Vat (1985) try to solve this problem for (92c) by assuming that there is no PRO argument and that the empty position is not a real verb but an empty position licensed by the preposition; as a result, the preposition can be held indirectly responsible for case-assignment to the noun phrase.

There are virtually no restrictions on the noun phrase in the absolute *met*-construction. The examples in (95a-f) show that all regular NP types are possible in this construction, with the exception of weak pronouns. The lack of restrictions is important to note, since Section 2.5.2 will show that the absolute *zonder*-construction does impose restrictions on the noun phrase. Note further that the use of a bare singular noun phrase, as in (95g), leads to ungrammaticality; the absolute *zonder*-construction will be shown to behave differently in this respect as well.

(95) a. [Met Jan in het doel] kunnen we niet verliezen. [proper noun]
with Jan in the goal can we not lose
'With Jan in the goal we cannot lose.'
b. [Met hem/*'m in het doel] ... [strong/weak pronoun]
with him/him in the goal
c. [Met de juiste man in het doel] ... [definite NP]
with the right person in the goal

d. [Met die keeper in het doel] ... [demonstrative NP]
with that goalkeeper in the goal

e. [Met een goede keeper in het doel] ... [existentially quantified NP]
with a good goalkeeper in the goal

e′. [Met alle spelers in het doel] ... [universally quantified NP]
with all players in the goal

f. [Met wie in het doel] ...? [interrogative phrase]
with whom in the goal

g. *[Met goede keeper in het doel] ... [bare singular NP]
with good goalkeeper in the goal

The prohibition on weak pronouns in the absolute *met*-construction is due to the fact that the absolute *met*-construction has a characteristic accentuation pattern; the examples in (96) show that both the noun phrase and the predicate must receive accent, which is indicated by means of small capitals.

(96) a. met JAN in het DOEL
with Jan in the goal

b. met SNEEUW op STRAAT
with snow in the.street

c. met het RAAM open
with the window open

Since only strong pronouns can be assigned stress, this causes the unacceptability of the weak pronouns in the examples in (97). Note in passing that Standard Dutch has no weak forms for the first and second person plural pronouns in (97d&e).

(97) a. met MIJ/*me in het DOEL
with me in the goal

b. met JOU/*je in het DOEL
with you in the goal

c. met HEM/*'m in het DOEL
with him in the goal

c′. met HAAR/*'r in het DOEL
with her in the goal

d. met ONS in het DOEL
with us in the goal

e. met JULlie in het DOEL
with you$_{pl}$ in the goal

f. met HUN/*ze in het DOEL
with them in the goal

The fact that weak pronouns cannot occur in the absolute *met*-construction may help us to distinguish examples that involve the sequence of a *met*-PP and some other PP from the absolute *met*-construction. The examples in (98), for instance, involve a comitative *met*-PP followed by a complementive PP.

(98) a. Jan stond met me voor de deur.
Jan stood with me in.front.of the door

b. Jan liep met je naar school toe.
Jan walked with you to school

c. Jan stond met 'm/'r/ze voor de deur.
Jan stood with hem/her/them in.front.of the door

In (97), we did not include examples with the neuter pronoun *het*. The examples in (99) show that this pronoun can never be used in the absolute *met*-construction, neither in its weak nor in its strong form. This is due to the fact that *het* normally resists assignment of accent; cf. N5.2.1.

(99) a. met het RAAM open
with the window open
b. *met HET/het/'t open
with it open

If this explanation of the ungrammaticality of (99b) is indeed correct, the impossibility of this example need not be stated in terms of the general rule that the neuter pronoun *het* cannot occur as the complement of a preposition; see Section 5.1 for discussion. This may be important for analyses of the type in (92) that do not consider the noun phrase to be the complement of the preposition but part of a larger phrase.

2.5.1.5. Some syntactic properties

This section discusses a number of syntactic properties of (the constituting parts of) absolute *met*-constructions. We will start our discussion with the °binding properties of the noun phrases that may occur within the absolute *met*-construction.

I. Binding

The examples in (100) show that the noun phrases *Jan* and *Marie en Jan* may act as the antecedent of an anaphor in the complement of the predicative adjectival phrases headed by *geïnteresseerd* 'interested' and *verliefd* 'in love' (coreference is indicated by means of identity of indices). This supports the idea that the nominal part of the absolute construction acts as the °logical SUBJECT of the predicative part; when the anaphors *zichzelf* and *elkaar* are complements of the adjectival head, they can only be bound by the SUBJECT of the predicative AP; see Section N5.2.1.5, sub III, for extensive discussion.

(100) a. met Jan_i alleen geïnteresseerd in $zichzelf_i$
with Jan just interested in himself
b. met [Marie en $Jan]_i$ verliefd op $elkaar_i$
with Marie and Jan in.love with each other

Example (101a) shows that when the predicative part of the absolute *met*-construction is a locational PP the (long-distance) simple reflexive pronoun *zich* cannot be bound by the nominal part of the absolute *met*-construction, but must be bound by an argument of the main clause. This again supports the idea that the noun phrase acts as the SUBJECT of the predicative part of the absolute construction, given that the SUBJECT of a predicative PP can never act as the binder of simplex reflexive *zich*; cf. Section N5.2.1.5, sub III. Example (101b) shows that when the absolute *met*-construction is used attributively, *zich* can also be coreferential with the head of the modified noun phrase.

(101) a. Marie$_i$ liep naar buiten [met een knappe man$_j$ naast zich$_{i/*j}$].
Marie walked outside with a handsome man next.to REFL
'Marie came outside with a handsome man next to her.'
b. Ik zag [$_{NP}$ een man$_i$ [met een hond$_j$ naast zich$_{i/*j}$]].
I saw a man with a dog next.to REFL
'I saw a man who had a dog next to (with) him.'

Examples (102a&b) show that the nominal part of the construction may also appear in a reflexive form. A remarkable restriction is that the predicate must be adpositional or appear as an *als*-phrase; when the predicate is adjectival, as in (102c), the construction is excluded. This may be a pragmatic matter, given that the supplementive *ziek* in (102c′) is able to express the intended meaning more economically than the absolute construction *met zichzelf ziek*; see Smits & Vat (1985) for an alternative proposal.

(102) a. [Met zichzelf$_i$ in de hoofdrol] wou Jan$_i$ de film wel financieren.
with himself in the leading part wanted Jan the movie PRT finance
'With himself playing the leading.part, Jan was willing to finance the movie.'
b. [Met zichzelf$_i$ als voorzitter] kon Jan$_i$ het voorstel goedgekeurd krijgen.
with himself as chairman could Jan the proposal prt.-approved get
'With himself as chairman, Jan was able to get the proposal approved.'
c. *[Met zichzelf$_i$ ziek] kon Jan$_i$ niet vertrekken.
with himself ill could Jan not leave
c′. Ziek kon Jan niet vertrekken.
ill could Jan not leave
'Being ill, Jan couldn't leave.'

Since personal and reflexive pronouns are normally in complementary distribution, it does not come as a surprise that *zichzelf* cannot be replaced by *hem* without changing the coreferentiality relation: the examples in (103a&b) are only possible when *hem* refers to some person other than Jan. The fact that the pronoun *hem* in (103c) cannot be bound by *Jan* either supports our earlier suggestion that (102c) is blocked by the more economical expression in (102c′) and is thus not due to the binding conditions on *zichzelf*; if *zichzelf* were excluded by the binding conditions, we would expect binding of *hem* to be possible in (103c).

(103) a. [Met hem$_{j/*i}$ in de hoofdrol] wou Jan$_i$ de film wel financieren.
b. [Met hem$_{j/*i}$ als voorzitter] kon Jan$_i$ het voorstel goedgekeurd krijgen.
c. [Met hem$_{j/*i}$ ziek] kon Jan$_i$ niet vertrekken.

Note that some speakers allow replacement of *zichzelf* in (102a&b) by the anaphoric-like form *'mzelf*, as in (104a&b); cf. Section N2.2.5.2. Observe that substituting *'mzelf* for *zichzelf* in (102c) does not improve this example, which again supports the claim that the contrast between (102a&b) and (102c) is not due to some binding restriction on *zichzelf*.

(104) a. [Met 'mzelf$_i$ in de hoofdrol] wou Jan$_i$ de film wel financieren.
b. [Met 'mzelf$_i$ als voorzitter] kon Jan$_i$ het voorstel goedgekeurd krijgen.
c. *[Met 'mzelf$_{j/*i}$ ziek] kon Jan$_i$ vertrekken.

The simplex reflexive *zich* cannot be substituted for any of the occurrences of *zichzelf* in the examples in (102). It is not *a priori* clear whether this is due to the binding restrictions on the reflexive form: since *zich* is phonetically weak, the fact that we are unable to substitute *zich* for *zichzelf* may also follow from the fact that the pronoun must be strong; cf. example (97).

(105) a. *[Met zich$_{i/j}$ in de hoofdrol] wou Jan$_i$ de film wel financieren.
b. *[Met zich$_{i/j}$ als voorzitter] kon Jan$_i$ het voorstel goedgekeurd krijgen.
c. *[Met zich$_{i/j}$ ziek] kon Jan$_i$ niet vertrekken.

II. Modification

The complement of the preposition *met* can be modified by temporal, locational and other adverbial phrases. In (106), we give some examples with the temporal phrases *nog altijd/steeds* 'still' and *voortdurend* 'continuously'.

(106) a. met Jan nog altijd boos over die opmerking
with Jan still always angry about that remark
'with Jan still angry about that remark'
b. met nog steeds dezelfde soort bloemen voor het raam
with still always the.same kind [of] flowers in.front.of the window
'with still the same kind of flowers in the window'
c. met zijn vader voortdurend dronken
with his father continuously drunk

The temporal phrases in (106) are quantified and are normally used as clause adverbs. The addition of temporal VP adverbs that refer to a fixed point on the time line, on the other hand, gives rise to an infelicitous result. This is shown in (107).

(107) a. *?met Jan gisteren boos over die opmerking
with Jan yesterday angry about that remark
b. *?met morgen dezelfde soort bloemen voor het raam
with tomorrow the.same kind of flowers in.front.of the window
c. *?met zijn vader vroeg dronken
with his father early drunk

In (108) we give examples with locational phrases. Note that the use of locational phrases may lead to ambiguity; the primed (b)-examples show that it is not clear whether we must consider the *als*-phrase or the locational phrase *voorop* as the predicate in (108b). The examples in (109) involve modal adverbial phrases.

(108) a. een veld met hier en daar wat bloemen in het gras
a field with here and there some flowers in the grass
b. een optocht met Jan <als aanvoerder> voorop <als aanvoerder>
a parade with Jan as leader in front
b′. een optocht met Jan als aanvoerder
b″. een optocht met Jan voorop

(109) a. een jurk met helaas wat vlekken op de zoom
a dress with unfortunately some stains on the border
b. een jurk met natuurlijk een rits op de rug
a dress with of course a zipper on the back

Besides adverbial phrases, the absolute PP may also contain supplementive phrases. In (110a), the adjective *verfrommeld* preceding the locational PP functions as a supplementive predicated of the noun phrase *zijn hoed* and in (110a) the adjectival participle phrase *vastgebonden* is predicated of the noun phrase *zijn handen*.

(110) a. met zijn hoed verfrommeld op zijn hoofd
with his hat crumpled on his head
b. met zijn handen vastgebonden achter zijn rug
with his hands tied behind his back

Example (111) further shows that the predicative PP can be modified by a modifier of distance or direction; cf. Section 3.1.4.1 for a discussion of these modifiers.

(111) [Met de tafel [vlak/schuin voor de kast]] lijkt de kamer kleiner.
with the table close/diagonally in.front.of the closet seems the room smaller

Example (112), finally, shows that the absolute *met*-construction itself can also be modified; this is restricted to the addition of focus particles like *alleen* 'only', *zelfs* 'even', etc.

(112) [Alleen/Zelfs met Jan in het doel] kunnen we winnen.
only/even with Jan in the goal can we win

III. R-extraction and R-words

The (b)-examples in (113) show that the predicative PP *voor de kast* may undergo R-extraction. The fact that the R-word must follow the preposition *met* but precede the modifier *vlak* shows that the landing site is internal to the absolute *met*-phrase but external to the predicative PP.

(113) a. met de tafel vlak voor de kast
with the table close in.front.of the cupboard
b. met de tafel er vlak voor
with the table there close in.front.of
b′. *... er ... mee/met de tafel vlak voor
there with the table close in.front.of

It has been claimed that locational *er* 'there' can also be used in the absolute *met*-construction. We do not agree with this; according to us the use of the strong form *daar* is much preferred, which may be related to the stress properties of the construction; cf. the discussion of (96) to (99). Expletive *er* is never possible; insofar as the use of *er* is acceptable in (114), it must be construed as an adverbial phrase of place.

(114) met daar/%er zoveel mensen op de stoep
with there so many people on the doorstep

Example (115b) shows that absolute *met*-PPs may contain °quantitative *er*. Further, example (115d) shows that *er* can even simultaneously perform the quantitative and prepositional function of *er*; this conflation of functions, which also occurs in the clausal domain, is more extensively discussed in Section 5.5.3. The somewhat marked status of the examples in (115c-d) may again be due to the stress properties of the construction.

(115) a. met nog drie snoepjes in zijn zak
with still three candies in his pocket
b. (?)met er nog drie [*e*] in zijn zak [quantitative *er*]
with there still three in his pocket
c. (?)met *er* nog drie snoepjes *in* [prepositional *er*]
with there still three candies in
'with still three candies in it'
d. (?)met *er* nog drie [*e*] *in* [quantitative + prepositional *er*]
with there still three in
'with still three in it'

Example (116) illustrates that the nominal part of the absolute *met*-construction cannot undergo R-extraction. There are, however, some apparent counterexamples, which will be the topic of the remainder of this subsection.

(116) a. met het boek in de kast
with the book/it in the bookcase
b. *... er ... mee/met in de kast
there with in the bookcase

Consider the examples in (117). The singly-primed examples illustrate that the sequences *met* + NP + PP can be placed in clause-initial position, which shows that these sequences form a constituent and can therefore be analyzed as absolute *met*-PPs. Nevertheless, the doubly-primed examples show that R-extraction is possible.

(117) a. Jan zit daar met een baby op zijn arm.
Jan sits there with a baby on his arm
'Jan is sitting there with a baby on his arm.'
a′. Met een baby op zijn arm zit Jan daar.
a″. de baby *waar* Jan *mee* op zijn arm zit
the baby where Jan with on his arm sits
b. Jan loopt daar met zijn hond aan de lijn.
Jan walks there with his dog on the leash
b′. Met zijn hond aan de lijn loopt Jan daar.
b″. de hond *waar* Jan *mee* aan de lijn loopt
the dog where Jan with on the leash walks

The fact that these sequences can be construed as absolute *met*-PPs need not imply, of course, that they *must* be so construed. Actually, there are various reasons to assume that the structures in (117a&b) are ambiguous between a reading with an absolute *met*-PP and a reading with a *met*-PP and an independent locational PP. First, the (a)-examples in (118) and (119) demonstrate that the *met* + NP + PP sequences can be split, which is never possible with the absolute *met*-construction; cf. 2.5.1.1. Second, the (b)-examples show that the noun phrase following *met* can be a weak pronoun; Section 2.5.1.4 has shown that this is not possible in the absolute *met*-construction either.

(118) a. de baby waarmee Jan op zijn arm zit
the baby where.with Jan on his arm sits
a′. Met wiens baby zit Jan op zijn arm?
with whose baby sits Jan on his arm
a″. Jan zit met die baby altijd op zijn arm.
Jan sits with that baby always on his arm
b. Jan zit met 'r op zijn arm.
Jan sits with her on his arm

(119) a. de hond waarmee Jan aan de lijn loopt
the dog where.with Jan on the leash walks
a′. Met wiens hond loopt Jan aan de lijn?
with whose dogs walks Jan on the leash
a″. Jan loopt met zijn hond altijd aan de lijn.
Jan walks with his dog always on the leash
b. Jan loopt met 'm aan de lijn.
Jan walks with him on the leash

The examples in (118) and (119) strongly suggest that the doubly-primed examples in (117) can be analyzed as cases of R-extraction, not from an absolute *met*-construction, but from a regular *met*-PP, which happens to be followed by some independent locational PP. We therefore conclude that R-extraction from absolute *met*-constructions is indeed blocked.

IV. Extraposition

Example (120b) shows that adverbial phrases contained in absolute *met*-constructions can be placed after the predicative PP, that is, we find a process similar to °PP-over-V in clauses. The adverbial PP must, however, remain within the absolute phrase; movement of this PP across the verb(s) in clause-final position leads to ungrammaticality, as is shown in (120c).

(120) a. dat Jan [met een warme sjaal tegen de kou om zijn nek] vertrok.
that Jan with a warm scarf against the cold around his neck left
'that Jan left with a warm scarf around his neck against the cold.'
b. dat Jan [met een warme sjaal om zijn nek tegen de kou] vertrok.
c. *dat Jan [met een warme sjaal om zijn nek] vertrok tegen de kou.

The examples in (121) and (122) show that the same thing holds for, respectively, relative clauses and attributive PPs. The (b)-examples show that extraposition is possible from the nominal part of the construction; the resulting structures are perhaps somewhat marked, but this is probably due to their complexity. The (c)-

examples show that the moved clause/PP must occupy a position in the right periphery of the absolute construction; placing it in a position to the right of a verb in clause-final position is not possible.

(121) a. dat Jan [met die das die hij van zijn Els gekregen had om zijn nek] vertrok.
that Jan with that tie that he from Els got had around his neck left
'that Jan left with that tie that was given to him by his sister around his neck.'
b. ?dat Jan [met die das om zijn nek die hij van zijn zusje gekregen had] vertrok.
c. *dat Jan [met die das om zijn nek] vertrok die hij van zijn zusje gekregen had.

(122) a. dat Jan [met die das van zijn oudste broer om zijn nek] vertrok.
that Jan with that tie of his eldest brother around his neck left
b. ?dat Jan [met die das om zijn nek van zijn oudste broer] vertrok.
c. *dat Jan [met die das om zijn nek] vertrok van zijn oudste broer.

V. Coordination

The complement of *met* can be a coordinated phrase. The predicates of the two conjuncts can but need not be of the same category: in (123a), the two predicates are both of the category PP, whereas in (123b) we are dealing with a predicative PP in the first conjunct and a predicative AP in the second.

(123) a. met [[zijn moeder in het ziekenhuis] en [zijn vader naar zijn werk]]
with his mother in the hospital and his father to his work
b. met [[zijn moeder in het ziekenhuis] en [zijn vader voortdurend dronken]]
with his mother in the hospital and his father continuously drunk

VI. Inversion

When the noun phrase is heavy, e.g., a modified noun phrase, the absolute *met*-construction allows inversion of the noun phrase and the predicate, provided that the predicate is adpositional or an *als*-phrase, as in (124).

(124) a. met de beste keeper aller tijden/Jan in het doel
with the best keeper of all times/Jan in the goal
a′. met in het doel de beste keeper van alle tijden/*Jan
b. met de directeur van Philips/Jan als voorzitter
with the director of Philips/Jan as chairman
b′. met als voorzitter de directeur van Philips/*Jan

The examples in (125) show that inversion is not possible when the predicate is an intransitive adposition, a particle, or an adjectival phrase.

(125) a. met een mooie lange sjaal om (zijn nek)
with a beautiful long scarf around his neck
a′. met om *(zijn nek) een mooie lange sjaal
b. met een stevige borrel op
with a stiff drink up
b′. *met op een stevige borrel
c. met de directeur van Philips ziek
with the director of Philips ill
c′. *met ziek de directeur van Philips

Inversion of the noun phrase and a predicative PP is also allowed in contrastive contexts like (126a), in which contrastive accent is indicated by means of small capitals, and in constructions in which both the noun phrase and the nominal complement of the predicative PP are quantified, as in (126b); compare this example to example (23) in Section 4.2.1.1.2.

(126) a. een huis met aan de LINkerkant een boom en aan de RECHterkant een hek
a house with on the left side a tree and on the right side a fence
'a house with a tree on the left and a lamppost on the right side'
b. met in elke vaas twee rozen
with in each vase two roses
'with two roses in each vase'

VII. Conclusion

Let us conclude by considering again the structures proposed for the absolute *met*-construction by Beukema & Hoekstra (1983) and Smits & Vat (1985), which were given earlier as (92b&c) and are repeated here as (127).

(127) a. [$_{PP}$ met/zonder [$_{SC}$ NP PRED]]
b. [$_{PP}$ met/zonder [$_{VP}$ ... NP PRED ..[$_{V}$ *e*]]]

The subsections above have discussed several syntactic properties of absolute *met*-constructions that seem to favor the more complex structure in (127b). First, absolute *met*-constructions allow modification by adverbial phrases that may also occur as clause adverbs. Second, absolute *met*-phrases exhibit several word order phenomena that can also be found in clauses and which suggest a fair amount of movement within these phrases: R-extraction seems to target some position external to the predicative PP but internal to the absolute *met*-construction; extraposition is possible to the right periphery of the phrase; the construction also allows inversion of the predicate and its SUBJECT. This, of course, does not unequivocally show that the absolute *met*-construction contains some empty verb, as in (127b), but at least strongly suggests that it must have a more articulate structure than the one given in (127a). Establishing what this more articulate structure looks like is, of course, a matter for future research.

2.5.2. Absolute zonder*-construction*

The absolute *zonder*-construction seems more restricted than the absolute *met*-construction: it appears to be felicitous only with locational adpositional phrases and intransitive prepositions.

(128) a. Zonder bril op zijn neus ziet hij er jonger uit.
without glasses on his nose looks he there younger UIT
'Without glasses on his nose, he looks much younger.'
b. Zonder laken over de tafel heen is het ongezellig.
without cloth over the table HEEN is it not.cozy
'It is not cozy without a cloth over the table.'
c. Zonder das om mag je de club niet in.
without tie around may you the club not into
'One is not allowed to enter the club without a tie around (the neck).'

Directional adpositional phrases like (129a), and predicates of other categories do not seem to be possible. Given examples like *without the chairman present we cannot start the meeting*, English is more permissive in this respect.

(129) a. ??Zonder kind het huis uit hebben we hier te weinig ruimte.
without child the house out have we here too little space
Intended reading: 'With all the children still living home, we don't have enough space.'

b. ??Zonder iemand ziek zullen we zeker winnen.
without someone ill will we certainly win

c. ??Zonder iemand als voorzitter kunnen we niet beginnen.
without someone as chairman can we not start
'Without someone as chairman, we cannot start.'

d. ??Zonder iemand achtervolgd door de politie kan ons niets gebeuren.
without someone chased by the police can us nothing happen
'Without someone chased by the police, nothing can happen to us.'

A potential problem for the claim that predicative *als*-phrases like *als voorzitter* in (129c) cannot be used as the predicative part of the absolute *zonder*-construction is that Haeseryn (1997: 929) gives example (130a) as grammatical. It is not entirely clear, however, whether this is indeed an absolute *zonder*-construction, because example (131a) below will show that proper nouns do not give rise to fully acceptable results in this construction. Perhaps, the *als*-phrase must be seen as a modifier of the proper noun. That this is an option is illustrated in (130b). Since we have no further insights to offer, we leave the analysis of this example to future research.

(130) a. Zonder Hannelore als raadsvrouwe is zij nergens.
without Hannelore as counselor is she nowhere
'Without Hannelore as counselor, she is lost.'

b. Een advocate als raadsvrouwe is zeer nuttig.
a lawyer as counselor is very useful

Not only is there a restriction on the type of predicate, there also seems to be a restriction on the nominal part of the construction. Proper nouns, pronouns and definite noun phrases and interrogative phrases all give rise to a degraded result, and, to a lesser degree, the same thing seems to hold for quantified noun phrases. Demonstrative and indefinite noun phrases, on the other hand, are fully acceptable. Surprisingly, absolute *zonder*-constructions differ from absolute *met*-constructions in that they allow and, in fact, typically occur with a bare singular noun as their nominal part; compare (131g) with (95g).

(131) a. ??Zonder Jan in het doel kunnen we niet winnen. [proper noun]
without Jan in the goal can we not win
'Without Jan in the goal we cannot win.'

b. ??Zonder hem in het doel ... [definite pronoun]
without him in the goal

c. ??Zonder de keeper in het doel ... [definite NP]
without the goalkeeper in the goal

d. Zonder die keeper in het doel ... [demonstrative NP]
without that goalkeeper in the goal

e. Zonder een goede keeper/[?]iemand in het doel ... [existentially quantified NP]
without a good goalkeeper/someone in the goal

e′. [?][Zonder alle spelers in het doel] ... [universally quantified NP]
without all players in the goal

f. [??]Zonder wie in het doel ...? [interrogative phrase]
without whom in the goal

g. Zonder goede keeper in het doel ... [bare NP]
without good goalkeeper in the goal

Finally, it can be noted that *zonder* licenses negative polarity items like *ook maar (iets)* 'any(thing)' or *een cent* 'a single penny'. This is illustrated in (132).

(132) a. Zonder ook maar één bloemetje in huis vierde hij zijn jubileum.
without OOK MAAR one bouquet in house celebrated he his jubilee
'He celebrated his jubilee without having a single bouquet in his house.'

b. Zonder een cent op zak trok hij de wijde wereld in.
without a cent on pocket traveled he the wide world into
'Without a single penny in his pocket he went out into the world.'

2.6. Bibliographical notes

In the literature, relatively little attention has been paid to complementation of adpositional phrases. The generally accepted claim that clauses and PPs cannot appear as complements of adpositional phrases was formalized as Stowell's (1981) Case Resistance Principle, but we have seen in this chapter that there are a number of exceptions to this claim; see Hoekstra (1984a/1984b). The absolute *met*-construction has received ample attention and we refer the reader to Paardekooper (1977/1986), Reuland (1978), Van Riemsdijk (1978), Klein (1983), Everaert (1986), Beukema & Hoekstra (1983/1984), Hoekstra (1984a), Van der Lubbe (1985) and Smits & Vat (1985) for more detailed discussions.

Chapter 3
Projection of adpositional phrases: Modification

Introduction

Generally speaking, adpositional phrases resist modification with the exception of the spatial and temporal ones. So, whereas the non-spatial/temporal adpositional phrase in (1a) cannot be modified, the spatial and temporal adpositional phrases in (1b&c) can.

(1) a. Vanwege de vakantie is de bibliotheek gesloten.
because.of the vacation is the library closed
'The library is closed because of the vacation.'
b. (Vlak) voor de deur stond een grote lamp.
just in.front.of the door stood a big lamp
'A big lamp stood just in front of the table.'
c. (Vlak) voor zijn vakantie moest hij plotseling naar het ziekenhuis.
just before his vacation had he suddenly to the hospital
'Just before his vacation he suddenly had to go to the hospital.'

Note, however, that this does not hold for focus particles like *alleen* 'only' and *juist* 'especially' in (2a&b), nor for *pas* 'only' in (2c), which can also be used to modify non-temporal/spatial PPs. We will not discuss this in the present chapter because these particles can be construed with all lexical categories (see Barbiers 1995:ch.3), and thus deserve a discussion in their own right.

(2) a. Alleen vanwege de sneeuw blijf ik niet thuis.
only because.of the snow stay I not home
'I won't stay at home just because of the snow.'
b. Juist vanwege de sneeuw wil ik wandelen.
especially because.of the snow want I walk
'It is precisely because of the snow, that I want to make a stroll.'
c. Pas na de vakantie heb ik weer tijd.
only after the vacation have I again time
'I only have time after the holiday.'

Section 3.1 discusses modification of spatial adpositional phrases and will show that the hypothesis that spatial adpositions denote a set of vectors is very helpful in describing the modification possibilities. Section 3.2 will show that the description of the modification possibilities of the spatial adpositional phrases can be straightforwardly extended to the temporal ones. Section 3.3 concludes by discussing the rare cases of non-spatial/temporal adpositional phrases that may undergo modification.

3.1. Spatial adpositional phrases

This section is concerned with modification of spatial adpositional phrases. It will be shown that the hypothesis that spatial adpositions denote sets of vectors is very helpful in describing the modification possibilities. For an extensive discussion of the vector hypothesis, we refer the reader to Section 1.3.1.1.

3.1.1. General introduction

Section 1.3.1.1 has shown that a locational adposition situates the located object in space relative to the reference object. However, instead of placing the located object in a specific position, the adposition locates it in a region. The PP *achter de camera* in (3a) denotes the complete grey area in Figure 1. This is clear from the fact that the located object need not occupy a specific point in space, as in (3a), but can also be more dispersed, as in (3b); cf. the more extensive discussion of this figure in Section 1.3.1.1.3.

(3) a. De fotograaf staat achter de camera.
the photographer stands behind the camera

b. De lampen staan achter de camera.
the lamps stand behind the camera

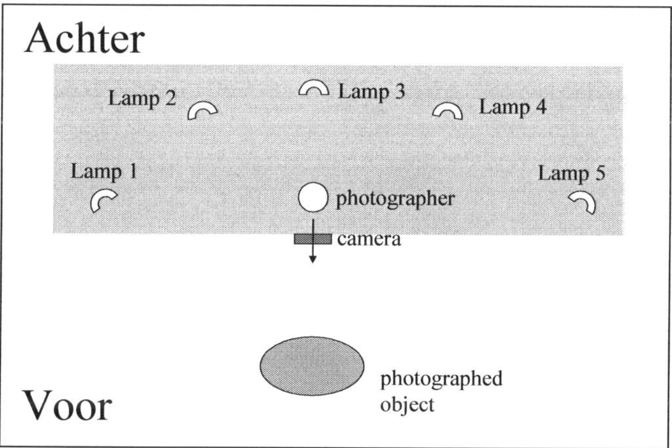

Figure 1: achter de camera *'behind the camera' (repeated)*

The region denoted by the adpositional phrase can be restricted by making use of modifiers. The use of a modifier like *recht* 'straight' in (4a), for example, restricts the region such that only the noun phrases *de fotograaf* and *lamp 3* can be substituted for "NP". The use of a modifier like *vlak* 'right' in (4b) restricts the region such that, under the right pragmatic conditions, only the noun phrase *de fotograaf* can be substituted for "NP".

(4) a. NP staat recht achter de camera.
NP stands straight behind the camera
'NP is straight behind the camera.'

b. NP staat vlak achter de camera.
NP stands right behind the camera
'NP is right behind the camera.'

The difference between modifiers like *recht* 'straight' and *vlak* 'right' is that the former specifies the spatial relation between the located and the reference object with respect to the ORIENTATION, whereas the latter specifies the DISTANCE between the two. That these two kinds of modifications are possible is not a coincidence;

Section 1.3.1.1 suggested that, instead of referring to a region, locational PPs can be considered to denote sets of vectors that take the reference object as their starting point, as in the more abstract representation of the situation in Figure 1 given in Figure 2, which is also taken from Section 1.3.1.1.3.

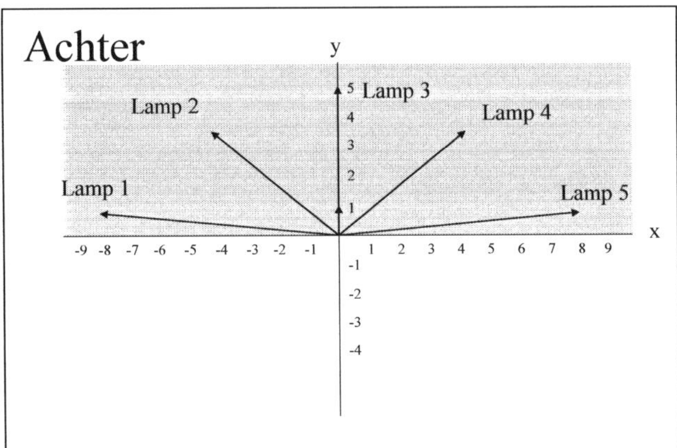

Figure 2: Achter de camera *'behind the camera' (repeated)*

The PP *achter de camera* denotes the set of vectors $\binom{x}{y}$ that originate in (0,0) (= the position of the camera), and have their endpoint somewhere in the grey area, that is, for which y > 0. Modifiers are used to restrict this set. The modifiers of orientation select a subset on the basis of the direction of the vectors: the modifier *recht* 'straight' in (4a) selects the subset of vectors for which x = 0, whereas the modifier *schuin* 'diagonally' would select the vectors for which x ≠ 0. The modifiers of distance select a subset on the basis of the magnitude (length) of the vector: the modifier *vlak* 'right' in (4b) restricts the set of vectors to those that are smaller than a certain contextually given magnitude m, whereas the modifier *ver* 'far' restricts the set to those vectors that are longer than a certain contextually given magnitude m′, where m < m′.

In the examples above, the reference object is represented as a point in space. The vector approach to prepositions becomes slightly more complicated when the reference object is represented as a three-dimensional object. Consider the examples in (5). Example (5a) can refer to the situation in Figure 3A when the nominal modifier is *twee kilometer* but not when it is *vier kilometer*. Similarly, (5b) can refer to Figure 3B when the adjectival modifier is *recht*, but not when it is *schuin*. The contrasts found in (5) would of course be unexpected if the vectors $\overrightarrow{AC}$ and $\overrightarrow{BC}$ were both part of the vector set denoted by the adpositional phrases. This suggests that some minimality requirement is involved: only the shortest vectors that go from the reference object to the located object are part of the set denoted by the adpositional phrase.

(5) a. Het kasteel staat twee/#vier kilometer buiten de stad.
the castle stands two/four kilometers outside the city
b. De lamp hangt recht/#schuin boven de tafel.
the lamp hangs straight/diagonally above the table

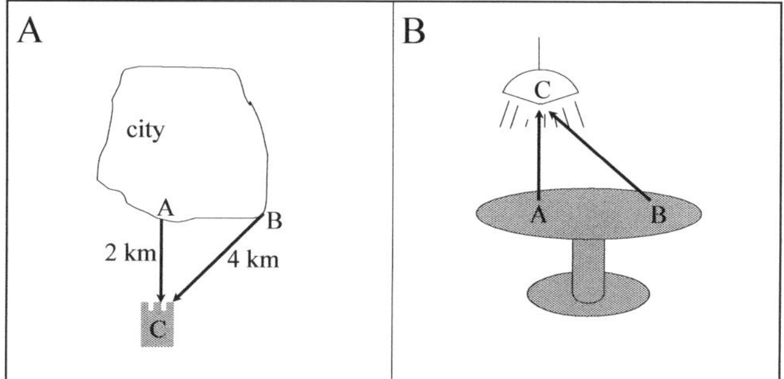

Figure 3: Minimality of vectors

Note in passing that the modifier *recht* in (5b) can also be used to express that the lamp is situated right above the center of the table. This may follow if we assume that, under that reading, the table is in fact mentally represented as a point in space, but we will not dwell on this.

Now that we have recapitulated the basic aspects of vector theory, we can discuss modification of spatial adpositional phrases. We will show in Section 3.1.2 that vector theory provides us with a proper understanding of the modification possibilities: PPs headed by prepositions that denote sets of vectors can be modified for orientation and distance, which is clearly connected to the fact that vectors have an orientation and a magnitude. Given the fact that the null vector lacks these properties (the magnitude of the null vector is zero, and the vector therefore does not have an orientation either), it is to be expected that locational PPs that denote the null vector cannot be modified by modifiers of orientation or distance. Section 3.1.3 will show that, despite seeming counterexamples, this prediction is indeed borne out. Section 3.1.4, finally, discusses modification of directional adpositional phrases. It will be shown that in this case the possibilities are restricted to modifiers that express to what extent the implied path has actually been covered.

3.1.2. Locational PPs that denote a set of vectors

This section is concerned with adpositions like *voor* 'in front of' and *achter* 'behind', which denote a set of vectors. It will be shown that the denoted set can be delimited by making use of modifiers that restrict the orientation or the magnitude of the vectors.

3.1.2.1. Modifiers of orientation

Modifiers that indicate the orientation of the located object with respect to the reference object are limited in number. The modifier *recht* in (6a) and the modifiers *schuin*/*links*/*rechts* in (6b) are in a sense complementary: whereas the former restricts the set of vectors to those in which x = 0, the latter exclude these. Note that we have topicalized the modified PPs in these examples to unambiguously show that the modifier and the PP form a constituent; cf. the °constituency test.

(6) a. Recht voor/achter Jan zit Marie.
straight in.front.of/behind Jan sits Marie
b. Schuin/Links/Rechts voor/achter Jan zit Marie.
diagonally/left/right in.front.of/behind Jan sits Marie

The modifiers in the primed examples could be called approximative modifiers given that they all express that the y-value of the vectors is smaller than some contextually determined norm *n*, that is, that the vectors in the denotation set stay close to the y-axis. The modifiers *precies/exact* stress that there is no deviation (the y-value is precisely 0), whereas the modifiers *ongeveer/zowat* express that the deviation is small (y < n).

(7) a. Precies/Exact voor/achter Jan zit Marie.
precisely/exactly in.front.of/behind Jan sits Marie
b. Ongeveer/Zowat voor/achter Jan zit Marie.
approximately/more or less in.front.of/behind Jan sits Marie

The primeless examples in (8) show that modifiers of orientation cannot be extracted from the adpositional phrase by means of *wh*-movement, and we will see in Section 3.1.2.2 that they differ in this respect from modifiers of distance.

(8) a. #Hoe recht zit Marie voor/achter Jan?
how straight sits Marie in.front.of/behind Jan
b. #Hoe schuin zit Marie voor/achter Jan?
how diagonally sits Marie in.front.of/behind Jan

It seems likely that this ban on extraction is related to the fact that, in contrast to modifiers of distance, modifiers of orientation are not gradable; cf. the primeless examples in (9). It is therefore not the extraction but the modification by the interrogative degree modifier *hoe* that is excluded, as will also be clear from the primed examples in (9), in which the PPs are pied piped by *wh*-movement of the modifiers.

(9) a. #Marie zit erg recht voor/achter Jan.
Marie sits very straight in.front.of/behind Jan
a′. #Hoe recht voor/achter Jan zit Marie?
b′. #Marie zit erg schuin voor/achter Jan.
Marie sits very diagonally in.front.of/behind Jan
b. #Hoe schuin zit Marie voor/achter Jan?

The number signs in (8) and (9) indicate that the examples are acceptable when *recht/schuin* refers to the posture of Marie; under this reading it acts as an adjectival supplementive modifying *Marie*; cf. the discussion of the examples in (14) and (15) below. In this connection it can also be noted that it is not surprising that the adjectives *recht* and *schuin* are used as modifiers of orientation, since they also denote orientations when they are used attributively or predicatively. Consider the examples in (10a&b): when we use *recht* 'upright', the orientation of the tower is parallel to the vertical axis in the three-dimensional space diagram in Figure 4 below, whereas the orientation diverges from it when we use *schuin* 'leaning'. Something similar holds for the adjectives *links* and *rechts* in (10c), although in these cases a reference object is always implied, which can be made explicit by adding a modifying *van*-PP.

(10) a. De toren staat recht/schuin.
the tower stands upright/leaning
b. een rechte/schuine toren
a(n) upright/leaning tower
c. Jan staat links/rechts (van de auto).
Jan stands left/right of the car
'Jan is standing to the left/right of the car.'

Not all locational PPs that denote a set of vectors can be combined with the three types of modifiers illustrated in the examples in (6). Table 1 provides a list of the relevant prepositions and indicates whether modification by these modifiers is possible or not; the percentage sign expresses that modification is blocked due to pragmatic factors and the number sign that modification is possible but does not give rise to the intended reading.

Table 1: Modifiers of orientation

PREPOSITION	TRANSLATION	*recht* 'straight'	*ongeveer* 'approximately'	*schuin* 'diagonally'
achter *voor*	behind in front of	+	+	+
boven *onder*	above under	+	+	+
naast *links/rechts van*	next to to the left/right of	%	%	%
buiten *bij*	outside near	—	—	—
om *rond*	around around	—	—	—
tegenover	opposite	+	+	+
langs	along	—	+	—
tussen	between	—	#	—

When we assume the Cartesian-style coordinate system in Figure 4 (cf. Section 1.3.1.2.2), we may conclude that at least the modifiers of orientation *recht* and *schuin* can only modify prepositions that are related to one single axis, that is, to one single dimension in space. We will discuss this below.

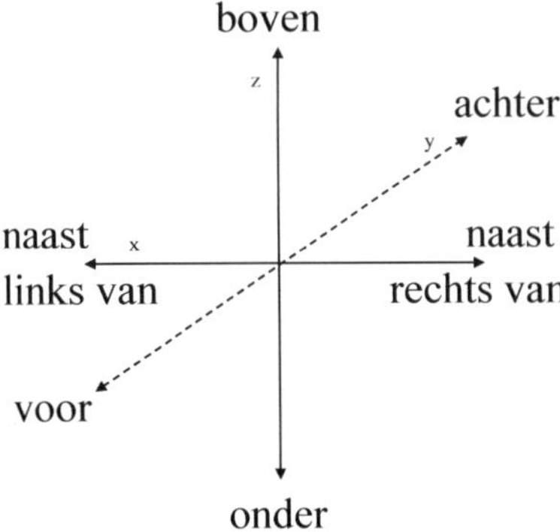

Figure 4: The division of space (repeated)

The proposed constraint on the use of modifiers of orientation immediately accounts for the fact that *voor/achter* and *onder/boven* are eligible for modification, since they are related to only a single axis (the z- and the y-axis, respectively). We would also expect modification of *naast* to be possible, but the judgments on such examples are less clear. The primed examples in (11) have been given as grammatical in the literature, but according to us they are certainly not as felicitous as the primeless examples involving *voor/achter* and *onder/boven*: (11a′) seems to be unacceptable, (11b′) is at least marked, and the same thing holds for (11c′).

(11) a. Jan zit recht voor/achter Marie.
Jan sits straight in.front.of/behind Marie

a′. %Jan zit recht naast Marie.
Jan sits straight next.to Marie

b. Jan zit schuin voor/achter Marie.
Jan sits diagonally in.front.of/behind Marie

b′. %Jan zit schuin naast Marie.
Jan zits diagonally next.to Marie

c. Jan zit links/rechts voor/achter Marie.
Jan sits left/right in.front.of/behind Marie

c′. %Jan zit links/rechts naast Marie.
Jan sits left/right next.to Marie

We have assigned the primed examples a percentage sign given that their infelicitousness may be due to pragmatic rather than to syntactic factors. This holds especially for the examples in (11b′&c′); the intended meaning of these examples can in principle also be expressed by means of the corresponding primeless examples. Given that the latter are more precise in the sense that they denote a smaller set of vectors, we may be dealing with a pragmatic blocking effect; in accordance with Grice's Maxim of Quantity, the more precise and therefore more informative contention is preferred over the less informative one.

The proposed constraint on the distribution of modifiers of orientation straightforwardly accounts for the fact indicated in Table 1 that modification of *buiten* and *bij* is excluded given that they involve two axes (dimensions), viz. the x- and the y-axis; cf. Figure 21 in Section 1.3. Similarly, modification of *om* and *rond* is excluded since they also involve at least two axes; cf. the discussion of Figure 13C&D in Section 1.3.1.2.2, sub I. Modification of *tegenover* is possible since it refers to a subset of situations in which *voor* is applicable, and hence involves just a single axis; see the discussion of Figure 19 in Section 1.3.

(12) Het café staat recht/schuin tegenover de kerk.
the bar stands straight/diagonally opposite the church

The preposition *langs* 'along' is special in that the vectors it denotes do not have the same starting point (which actually also holds for the prepositions *buiten* and *bij* but in a less conspicuous way). Instead, the vectors are more or less parallel; see the discussion of Figure 20 in Section 1.3. Therefore, *langs* also involves more than one dimension, and modification by *recht* and *schuin* is correctly predicted to be excluded in (13a). Nevertheless, the use of the modifiers *precies* and *ongeveer* is possible (13b); the two modifiers differ in that the former expresses that the garbage cans are placed in a neat line, whereas the latter expresses that their arrangement is a bit sloppier.

(13) a. *De vuilnisbakken staan recht/schuin langs de rand van de stoep.
the garbage.cans stand straight/diagonally along the edge of the sidewalk
b. De vuilnisbakken staan precies/?ongeveer langs de rand van de stoep.
the garbage.cans stand exactly/approximately along the edge of the sidewalk

The preposition *tussen* deserves special discussion. As can be seen in (14a), the PP seemingly can be modified by the modifier *recht*. However, the meaning of *recht* seems to differ from the intended meaning. It does not modify the position of the located object *Jan* with respect to the reference objects *de twee agenten*, but refers to Jan's posture: the example expresses that Jan is standing between the two agents, and that his posture is straight. In other words, *recht* seems to be predicated of Jan rather than modifying the PP; it is equivalent to the supplementive *rechtop* 'upright', which can never be used as a modifier. That we are really dealing with a supplementive, not a modifier, is also clear from the fact that the AP can appear when the PP is not present, and from the fact illustrated in (14b) that the adjective can be topicalized in isolation.

(14) a. Jan staat recht/rechtop (tussen de agenten).
Jan stands upright between the cops
b. Recht/Rechtop staat Jan tussen de agenten.

The same arguments can be repeated for the adjective *schuin* in (15), which performs a similar function as the supplementive *gebogen* 'stooped'. Therefore, we may conclude that the modifiers *recht* and *schuin* cannot be used to modify a PP headed by *tussen*.

(15) a. Jan staat schuin/gebogen (tussen de agenten).
Jan stands diagonally/stooped between the cops
b. Schuin/Gebogen staat Jan tussen de agenten.

Modification of *tussen* by means of *precies* ‘exactly’ is possible, but then the modifier expresses that the distances from the located object and the relevant reference objects are all equal. Example (16a) expresses that the distance between the painting and candlestick 1 is equal to the distance between the painting and candlestick 2. Note that it is not necessarily the case that the painting is located on the straight line between the two candlesticks; the painting may be hanging in the region above the candlesticks. The same thing holds for *ongeveer* ‘approximately’; example (16b) only expresses that the distance between the painting and candlestick 1 is approximately the same as the distance between the painting and candlestick 2. We therefore conclude that PPs headed by *tussen* cannot be modified by modifiers of orientation; *precies* and *ongeveer* must have some other function.

(16) a. Het schilderij hing precies tussen de twee kandelaars.
the painting hung exactly between the two candlesticks
b. Het schilderij hing ongeveer tussen de twee kandelaars.
the painting hung approximately between the two candlesticks

Example (17b) shows that the modifiers discussed in this section do not modify the preposition itself, but the full PP. This is clear from the fact that in case of R-pronominalization, the R-word *er* can intervene between the modifier and the preposition. Note that the R-word can also precede the modifier, but this is not relevant as this simply shows that the R-word can undergo R-extraction, that is, be moved further to the left.

(17) a. Recht/Schuin/Precies achter die zuil staat een klein beeldje.
straight/diagonally/exactly behind that pillar stands a small statue
b. [Recht/Schuin/Precies [$_{PP}$ er achter]] staat een klein beeldje.
straight/diagonally/exactly there behind stands a small statue

Finally, it can be observed that the degree of appropriateness of the use of two prepositions can be compared; example (18a) expresses that, as far as the orientation of the vector is concerned, both *boven* ‘above’ and *naast* ‘next to’ seem to be applicable, but that *boven* is the more accurate term. Note that the set of vectors denoted by the adpositions must partly overlap; (18b) shows that antonymous adpositions, which do not satisfy this condition, cannot be used in this construction. Note that the number sign indicates that (18b) is acceptable when *meer* is interpreted as a frequency adverb meaning “more often”.

(18) a. De kogel zit meer boven dan naast het hart.
the bullet sits more above than next.to the heart
b. #Jan zit meer voor dan achter Marie.
Jan sits more in.front.of than behind Marie

3.1.2.2. Modifiers of distance

Whereas modifiers of orientation are always adjectival in nature, modifiers of distance (the modifiers of the magnitude of the vectors in the denoted set) can be either adjectival or nominal. This is shown in (19), where we have topicalized the modified PP in order to unambiguously show that the modifier and the PP form a constituent; cf. the °constituency test. We will discuss the adjectival and nominal modifiers in separate subsections.

(19) a. Hoog boven de deur hangt een schilderij. [adjectival distance phrase]
high above the door hangs a painting
b. Twee meter boven de deur hangt een schilderij. [nominal measure phrase]
two meter above the door hangs a painting

I. Adjectival modifiers and adverbs

Adjectival modifiers are sensitive to the meaning of the modified PP. The adjectival modifier *hoog* 'high' in (19a), for example, can only modify PPs headed by *boven* 'above'. Since, to our knowledge, the modification possibilities of locational PPs have not been investigated thoroughly, we restrict ourselves to the discussion of a limited set of modifiers: the pair *diep/hoog* 'deep/high', which may amplify the antonymous adpositions *boven and onder*, the more or less antonymous pair *dicht-ver* 'close-far', which may amplify the adpositions *bij* 'near' and *buiten* 'outside', and the adverbial modifiers *vlak/pal* 'close'. Table 2 gives an overview of the modification possibilities, which will be discussed in more detail in the following subsections.

Table 2: Adjectival modifiers of distance

PREPOSITION		*diep* 'deep'	*hoog* 'high'	*dicht* 'close'	*ver* 'far'	*vlak* 'close'	*pal* 'close'
achter *voor*	behind in front of	—	?	—	+	+	+
boven *onder*	above under	— +	+ —	—	%	+	+
naast *links van* *rechts van*	next to to the left of to the right of	—	—	— — —	% — —	+ —	+ —
buiten *bij*	outside near	—	—	— +	+ —	— +	+ —
om *rond*	around around	—	—	—	—	—	—
tegenover	opposite	—	—	—	—	—	— cf. (27)
langs	along	—	—	—	—	+	+
tussen	between	—	—	—	—	—	—

A. Adjectival modifiers

The examples in (20) provide some concrete examples of locational PPs modified by the adjectives *diep/hoog* and *dicht/ver*.

(20) a. Jan zat ver voor/achter/*naast de anderen.
Jan sat far in.front.of/mext.to the others
b. De ballon hing hoog/?ver boven het huis.
the balloon hung high/far above the house
b′. Amsterdam ligt diep/?ver onder de zeespiegel.
Amsterdam lies deep/far under the sea level
c. Jan woont ver/*dicht buiten de stad.
Jan lives far/close outside the city
c′. Jan woont dicht/*ver bij de stad.
Jan lives close/far near the city

The first percentage sign in the column headed by *ver* in Table 2 indicates that, although the (b)-examples are marked with the modifier *ver*, this modifier can sometimes readily be used in metaphorically used locational *boven*-PPs like *dat gaat ver boven mijn macht* 'that is far beyond my power'. The examples in (21) illustrate the same point.

(21) a. Haar prestatie steekt ver/??hoog boven die van Jan uit.
her performance sticks far/high above that of Jan out
'Her performance is much better than Jan′s.'
b. De wolkenkrabber steekt hoog/?ver boven de andere huizen uit.
the skyscraper sticks high/far above the other houses out
'The skyscraper towers over the other houses.'

The second percentage sign indicates that although (20a) shows that *ver* normally cannot be used to modify locational PPs headed by *naast*, there are a number of more or less idiomatic constructions in which this is possible. One of the most common cases is the change of location construction in (22a) from sports jargon, in which *naast* can also be used as an intransitive adposition; note that the antonym *dicht* cannot replace the modifier *ver* in this construction. Example (22a′) shows that *ver* cannot be used as a modifier of locational PPs headed by the phrasal adpositions *links/rechts van*. Example (22b) provides another more or idiomatic construction; note that the literal meaning "Jan sat next to it" is not available.

(22) a. Jan schoot de bal ver/*dicht naast (het doel).
Jan shot the ball far/close next.to the goal
a′. *Jan schoot de bal ver/dicht links/rechts van het doel.
Jan shot the ball far/close left/right of the goal
b. Jan zat er ver/*dicht naast.
Jan sat there far/close next.to
'Jan was completely wrong.'

Ver can also modify *naast*-PPs when it is preceded by *niet*, as in (23a). Example (23a′) shows that locational PPs headed by the phrasal adpositions *links/rechts van* do not have this modification possibility, however; (23b) shows that the idiomatic expression in (22b) can also be modified by *niet ver*.

(23) a. Niet ver/*dicht naast de deur zat the brievenbus.
not far/close next.to the door sat the mailbox
'The mailbox was close to the door.'
a′. *Niet ver/dicht links/recht van de deur zat the brievenbus.
not far/close left/right of the door sat the mailbox
b. Jan zat er niet ver/*dicht naast.
Jan sat there not far/close next.to
'Jan was nearly right.'

The fact that the adjectival modifiers in (20) are all used as amplifiers is consistent with the fact that adjectival downtoners are rare; cf. Section A3.1.2.2, sub II. The only seeming exception is the modifier *dicht* 'close' in (20c′), but this is due to the fact that *bij* 'near' itself already indicates that the distance is small, and it is the smallness of the distance that is emphasized by the modifier *dicht*. The other modifiers in (20) indicate that the distance between the located and the reference object is large; there are no antonyms that indicate that the distances are small.

B. Adverbs

The fact that all the adjectival modifiers in (20) can be seen as amplifiers does not imply, however, that downtoning is not possible. There is a small set of °adverbs that can perform this function. Some examples are given in (24).

(24) a. vlak/pal achter de deur
close behind the door
b. net buiten de stad
just outside the city
c. direct boven de deur
directly above the door

Below, we will focus our discussion on the adverbs *vlak* and *pal*. As is shown in (25), these adverbial modifiers can be used in virtually all examples in (20). The percentage sign in the (c)-examples indicate that, although we judge these examples as considerably marked, many cases of this sort can be found on the internet.

(25) a. Jan zat vlak/pal voor/achter/naast de anderen.
Jan sat close in.front.of/behind/next.to the others
b. De ballon hing vlak/pal boven het huis.
the balloon hung close above the house
b′. Leiden ligt vlak/pal onder de zeespiegel.
Leiden lies close under the surface of the sea
c. Jan woont pal/%vlak buiten de stad.
Jan lives close outside the city
c′. Jan woont vlak/%pal bij de stad.
Jan lives close near the city

For those speakers who reject the forms marked by the percentage sign, lexical restrictions seem to play a role: *buiten* in (25c) can only be modified by *pal*, whereas *bij* can only be modified by *vlak*. An alternative approach to these restrictions may be to argue that the markedness of *vlak buiten de stad* is due to a blocking effect, since the intended meaning of *vlak buiten* can also be expressed by means of *(vlak) bij*. Such a blocking account may imply that the markedness of *pal bij de stad* in (25c′) is due to the availability of *dicht bij de stad*, which is perhaps less plausible.

Table 2 shows that the adverbs *vlak* and *pal* can also modify locational PPs headed by *langs*, which cannot be amplified by means of adjectival amplifiers. An example is given in (26a). When we want to express that the distance between the waterside and the houses is large, we have to take recourse to the adjectival construction in (26b).

(26) a. De huizen staan vlak/pal langs de waterkant.
the houses stand close along the waterside
b. De huizen staan ver van de waterkant.
the houses stand far from the waterside

It is not immediately clear whether *tegenover* 'opposite' can be modified by means of the adverbs under discussion. As is shown in (27a), *vlak* gives rise to a severely degraded result, whereas *pal* seems to be more or less equivalent to the modifier of orientation *recht* 'straight' in (12), an interpretation which is also possible in the case of *voor*. We therefore conclude that PPs headed by *tegenover* do not allow modification with respect to distance. The remaining prepositions *om/rond* and *tussen* are not eligible for modification by *pal* and *vlak* either.

(27) a. Het café staat #pal/*vlak tegenover de kerk.
the bar stands frontally/close opposite the church
b. Het café staat pal voor de kerk.
the bar stands frontally in.front.of the church

C. Two additional remarks

A difference between the adjectival modifiers *diep/hoog* and *dicht/ver* and the adverbs *vlak* and *pal* is that the first are gradable (that is, eligible for modification and comparative/superlative formation), whereas the latter are not. This is shown for *dicht bij* and *vlak bij* in (28).

(28) a. Jan woont heel dicht/*vlak bij de stad.
Jan lives very close near the city
b. Jan woont dichter/*vlakker bij de stad (dan Marie).
Jan lives closer near the city than Marie
c. Jan woont het dichtst/*vlakst bij de stad.
Jan lives the closest near the city

Like all gradable adjectives, *dicht* can also be questioned. As is illustrated in (29a), the modifier can then be extracted from the PP and be put in clause-initial position. Being non-gradable, questioning of the adverbs *vlak* and *pal* is impossible. This is shown in (29b) for *vlak*.

(29) a. Hoe dicht$_i$ woont Jan t_i bij de stad?
how close lives Jan near the city
b. *Hoe vlak$_i$ woont Jan t_i bij de stad?
how close lives Jan near the city

Finally, it can be noted that the modifiers in (28a) do not modify the preposition itself but the full PP. This is clear from the fact that in case of R-pronominalization, the R-word *er* can intervene between the modifier and the preposition. In passing, note that this also shows that *vlak bij* cannot be considered a compound, contrary to what the orthographic convention of writing *vlakbij* as a single word suggests.

(30) a. Dicht/Vlak bij het huis stond een boom.
close near the house stood a tree
'A tree stood close to the house.'
b. [Dicht/Vlak [$_{PP}$ er bij]] stond een boom.
close there near stood a tree

II. Nominal measure phrases

Any nominal phrase that can be used to measure distance can be used as a modifier to express the precise magnitude of the vectors involved. Some examples with the nominal measure phrase *twee (kilo)meter* 'two (kilo)meters' are given in Table 3, which shows that the locational prepositions can be divided into two groups on the basis of whether they can or cannot be modified by such phrases.

Table 3: Nominal modifiers of distance

PREPOSITION	EXAMPLE	TRANSLATION
achter *voor*	twee meter achter het doel twee meter voor het doel	two meters behind the goal two meters in front of the goal
boven *onder*	twee meter boven de deur twee meter onder de grond	two meters above the door two meters under the ground
naast *links van* *rechts van*	twee meter naast de paal ?twee meter links van de deur ?twee meter rechts van de deur	two meters next to the pole two meters to the left of the door two meters to the right of the door
buiten *bij*	twee kilometer buiten de stad *twee kilometer bij de stad	two kilometers outside of the town *two kilometers near the town
om *rond*	—	
tegenover	—	
langs	—	
tussen	—	

It must be noted that the primeless examples in (31) are acceptable, but in such examples the nominal phrase does not modify the magnitude of the vectors involved, which is clear from the fact that the locational PP can be dropped without changing the core meaning of the sentence. The noun phrase instead functions as the complement of the motion verb and refers to the distance that has been covered by the subject of the clause. That the noun phrase does not modify the PP but is selected by the motion verb is also clear from the fact that the primed examples involving a locational verb are not acceptable.

(31) a. Jan liep twee kilometer (rond de stad).
Jan walked two kilometer around the city
a′. De huizen stonden *(twee kilometer) rond de stad.
the houses stood two kilometers around the city
b. Jan liep twee kilometer (langs het kanaal).
Jan walked two kilometers along waterway
b′. Het huis stond *(twee kilometer) langs het kanaal.
the house stood two kilometer along the waterway

The examples in (32) show that, like adjectival modifiers, nominal measure phrases can be extracted from the PP and be put in clause-initial position in interrogative clauses; cf. Corver (1990).

(32) a. Hoeveel kilometer$_i$ ligt jouw huis [$_{PP}$ t_i buiten de stad]?
how.many kilometers lies your house outside the city
b. Hoeveel meter$_i$ ligt Amsterdam [$_{PP}$ t_i onder de zeespiegel]?
how.many meters lies Amsterdam under the surface of the sea

Further, the examples in (33) show that the measure phrases do not modify the preposition itself but the full PP. This is clear from the fact that in case of R-pronominalization, the R-word *er* can intervene between the modifier and the preposition.

(33) a. [Twee centimeter [$_{PP}$ er naast]] lag een klein doosje.
two centimeter there next.to lay a small box
b. [Drie meter [$_{PP}$ er voor]] viel hij op de grond.
three meter there in.front.of fell he on the ground

3.1.2.3. Summary

This section has discussed the modification possibilities of locational PPs headed by prepositions that denote vector sets and has shown that such PPs can be divided in three groups. The first group consists of PPs headed by prepositions that are related to one single axis of the coordinate system in Figure 4; the PPs in this group can readily be modified both by modifiers of orientation and by modifiers of distance. The second group consists of PPs headed by the prepositions *buiten* and *bij*, which can be modified by modifiers of distance (with a possible lexical restriction on the choice of the adverbs *vlak* and *pal*; cf. (25c&c′)), but not by modifiers of orientation. The remaining locational PPs form the third group, which can be modified neither for orientation nor for distance; exceptions are PPs headed by *tegenover*, which can be modified by modifiers of orientation like *recht* ‘straight’ and *schuin* ‘diagonally’, and PPs headed by *langs*, which can be modified by adverbial modifiers of distance like *vlak* and *pal*. These findings are summarized in Table 4.

Table 4: Modifiers of locational PPs

PREPOSITION	TRANSLATION	ORIENTATION	DISTANCE		
		adjectival modification	adjectival modification	*vlak/pal* 'close'	nominal modification
achter *voor*	behind in front of	+	+	+	+
boven *onder*	above under	+	+	+	+
naast *links van* *rechts van*	next to to the left of to the right of	%	—	+ — —	+
buiten/bij	outside/near	—	+	+	+
om/rond	around	—	—	—	—
tegenover	opposite	+	—	—	—
langs	along	—	—	+	—
tussen	between	—	—	—	—

3.1.3. Locational PPs that refer to the null vector

It is to be expected that locational PPs that refer to the null vector cannot be modified by modifiers of orientation or distance; the magnitude of the null vector is zero, and, as a result, it does not have an orientation either. As is illustrated in (34) by means of the preposition *binnen*, this expectation is normally borne out.

(34) a. *Het huis staat recht/schuin binnen de stadsmuur.
the house stands straight/diagonally within the city walls
b. *Het huis staat twee kilometer binnen de stadsmuur.
the house stands two kilometer within the city wall

Section 3.1.3.1 will show, however, that there are a number of potential counterexamples to the claim that PPs referring to the null vector cannot be modified by modifiers of orientation and distance. Section 3.1.3.2 discusses some other types of modification of these PPs.

3.1.3.1. Modifiers of orientation and distance

This section discusses several examples that at first sight seem to involve modification for orientation or distance. We will show, however, that these examples do not involve true counterexamples to the claim that PPs referring to the null vector cannot be modified by modifiers of orientation or distance.

I. Recht/schuin *'straight/diagonal'*

Example (35a) is fully acceptable, but the meaning of *recht/schuin* seems to differ from the intended modification meaning (viz. orientation); *recht/schuin* do not modify the position of the located object *het schilderij* with respect to the reference object *de muur*, but seem to refer to the way the painting is hanging on the wall, as in Figure 5. In other words, the adjectives *recht/schuin* are predicated of the noun phrase *het schilderij* 'the painting' and must therefore be analyzed as supplementives, just like the adjectives in (35b). That *recht* and *schuin* do not act as a modifier of the PP is supported by the fact that they can also appear when the locational PP is dropped.

(35) a. Het schilderij hangt recht/schuin (aan de muur).
the painting hangs straight/diagonal on the wall
b. Het schilderij hangt netjes/scheef/slordig (aan de muur).
the painting hangs properly/diagonal/untidy on the wall

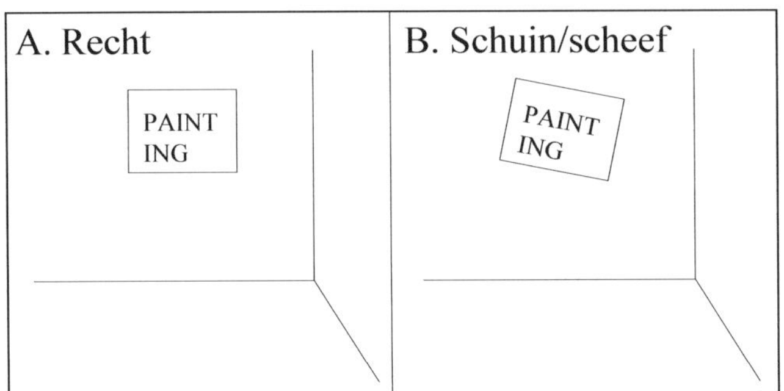

Figure 5: Supplementives recht *and* schuin/scheef

II. Rechts/links *'right/left',* midden *'middle',* voor *'in front of',* achter *'behind', etc.*

Rechts 'right' and *links* 'left' in (36a) also seem to lack the intended modification meaning: these prepositions just indicate the place of attachment of the flashing blue light, and do not modify the orientation of the (null) vector denoted by the preposition *op* 'on'. In this respect, they resemble elements like *midden* 'middle' and *voor/achter* 'in front of/behind' in (36b).

(36) a. Het zwaailicht zit rechts/links op de auto.
the blue light sits right/left on the car
'The flashing blue light is attached to the left/right side of the car.'
b. Het zwaailicht zit midden/voor/achter op de auto.
the blue light sits middle/in.front.of/behind on the car
'The flashing blue light is attached to the center/front/back of the car.'

Other elements that can be used in a way similar to *links/rechts*, *midden* and *achter/voor* in (36) are *boven/onder* 'above/under' which are in a paradigm with *midden*. Some examples are given in (37).

(37) a. Jan zit midden op de ladder.
Jan sits middle on the stepladder.
'Jan is sitting in the middle of the stepladder.'
b. Jan zit boven/onder op de ladder.
Jan sits above/under on the stepladder
'Jan is sitting on top/ at the bottom of the stepladder.'

The examples in (36) and (37) do, of course, involve some kind of modification of the locational PP *op de ladder*, which expresses the core meaning of the clause *Jan zit op de ladder* 'Jan is sitting on the stepladder'. This is clearest in the cases of *midden* and *onder*, since the relevant examples in (37) become ungrammatical when the PP is dropped, as is shown in (38a). In the other cases, this is less clear because the resulting structures are acceptable; the meaning of the clauses, however, changes considerably. This is illustrated in (38b) for *boven* in (37b), which now receives the meaning "upstairs".

(38) a. *Jan zit midden/onder.
b. Jan zit boven.
'Jan is sitting upstairs.'

Note in passing that, in accordance with this, example (37b) with *boven* is actually ambiguous: it can be translated not only as "Jan is sitting on top of the stepladder" but also as "Jan is sitting upstairs on the stepladder". In the latter case, it does not act as the antonym of *onder*, but as the antonym of *beneden* 'downstairs'; see Section 3.5 for discussion.

The question we want to address now is whether the examples in (36) and (37) involve adverbial modification of the locational PP or modification of some other sort. Although it is difficult to give a definite answer to this question, the following subsections will show that there are several reasons to assume that we are not dealing with adverbial modification, but with compounding.

A. R-pronominalization

The examples in (30), repeated here as (39), have shown that it is not the preposition itself that is modified by an adverbial phrase but the full PP. This is clear from the fact that in case of R-pronominalization, the R-word *er* can intervene between the modifier and the preposition.

(39) a. Dicht/Vlak bij het huis stond een boom.
close near the house stood a tree
'A tree stood close to the house.'
b. [Dicht/Vlak [$_{PP}$ er bij]] stond een boom.
close there near stood a tree

When we consider examples involving the elements *links/rechts*, *midden*, *achter/voor* and *boven/onder*, however, it turns out that the R-pronoun cannot intervene between most of these elements and the PP. This is shown in the primed examples in (40).

(40) a. Links/Rechts op de auto zit een zwaailicht.
left/right on the car sits a blue light
a′. *Link/Rechts er op zit een zwaailicht.
b. Voor/Achter/Midden in de kerk staat een groot orgel.
in.front.of/behind/middle in the church stands a big organ
'A big organ stands in the front/back/middle of the church.'
b′. *Voor/Achter/Midden er in staat een groot orgel.
c. Boven/Onder op het blikje staat de productiedatum.
above/under on the can stands the manufacturing.date
'The manufacturing date can be found on top/the bottom of the can.'
c′. *Boven/Onder er op staat de productiedatum.

It is not entirely clear how conclusive the primed examples in (40a&b) are, given that (41a&b) show that the order in which the R-pronoun precedes the "modifier" is also bad/marked. In (41c), however, this order gives rise to a fully acceptable result.

(41) a. *Er links/recht op zit een zwaailicht.
b. ?Er voor/achter/midden in staat een groot orgel.
c. Er boven/onder op staat de productiedatum.

The acceptability of (41c) thus shows that the cause of the unacceptability of the primed examples in (40) is not that R-pronominalization itself is impossible, and suggests that the sequence of the modifier and the preposition is impenetrable, which would be consistent with a compound analysis; cf. 1.2.1, sub II.

B. Intransitive use

There are cases in which the complex forms can be used as intransitive adpositions, whereas the simple forms cannot. If *achter* acts as a modifier of the preposition *op* in (42a), the ungrammaticality of (42a′) with an intransitive adposition would, of course, be highly surprising. In (42b), we give similar examples with *bovenin.*

(42) a. Jan zit achterop (de fiets).
Jan sits on.the.back.of the bike
'Jan is sitting on the back of the bike.'
a′. Jan zit op *(de fiets).
b. Het geld ligt bovenin (de kast).
the money lies in.the.upper.part.of the closet
b′. Het geld ligt in *(de kast).

When we are dealing with compounds, on the other hand, the difference in acceptability between the primeless and primed examples could simply be accounted for by claiming that the syntactic valence of the simple and complex prepositions differ.

C. Permeation of the clause-final verb cluster

Section 3.1.6 has shown that modified intransitive adpositions cannot permeate the clause-final verb cluster. The complex forms under discussion, on the other hand, can, as is shown in (43). This again favors a compound analysis of the complex forms.

(43) a. dat Marie de hele tijd voorop heeft gelopen.
that Marie the whole time in.front has walked
'that Marie walked in front all the time.'
b. dat Marie de hele tijd heeft voorop gelopen.

D. Concluding remarks

The discussion above suggests that elements like *links/rechts*, *midden*, *voor/achter* and *boven/onder* in (36) and (37) are not adverbial modifiers but the first members of a compound. Table 5 gives the possible combinations of these elements with prepositions that denote the null vector. The fact that there are so many question marks in this table indicates that more research is needed.

Table 5: Links/rechts, midden, achter/voor *and* boven/onder

preposition	*links/rechts*	*midden*	*achter/voor*	*boven/onder*
in 'in/into'	+	+	+	+
uit 'out/out of'	?	?	+	+
door 'through'	—	?	—	—
aan 'on'	?	?	+	+
op 'on'	+	+	+	+
over 'over'	?	?	—	—
tegen 'against'	+	+	—	—
binnen 'inside'	—	—	—	—

Note that a "—" mark does not necessarily imply that the pertinent sequence cannot be found, but that the modification relation is not present. The examples in (44) are acceptable, but they do not involve modification of the PP by the elements *achter/voor*. This will be clear from the paraphrases; note also that in these cases *voor* and *achter* can be topicalized in isolation, which shows that they are independent constituents, comparable to the more common element *boven* with the meaning "upstairs"; cf. Section 3.5.

(44) a. De ladder stood achter tegen de muur.
the ladder stood back against the wall
'At the back of the house, the ladder stood against the wall.'
a′. Achter stond de ladder tegen de muur.
b. Jan liep voor door de deur.
Jan walked front through the door
'Jan walked through the front door.'
b′. Voor liep Jan door de deur.

3.1.3.2. Other kinds of modification

So far we have not encountered any clear cases of adverbial modification of locational PPs headed by a preposition denoting the null vector, so perhaps we must conclude that such modification is not possible. There are, however, several cases that may involve modification, which we will investigate in this section.

I. Precies *'exactly' and* bijna *'nearly'*

The elements *precies* 'exactly' and *bijna* 'nearly' seem common as modifiers of PPs headed by the prepositions *in* 'in' and *op* 'on'. Some examples are given in (45). We are not dealing with modifiers of orientation or distance in these examples, but with modification of the location of the located object: the use of *precies* emphasizes that the located object has actually reached the reference object, whereas *bijna* implies that this nearly was the case.

(45) a. Hij schoot de pijl precies/bijna in de roos.
he shot the arrow exactly/nearly into the bull's-eye
b. Zij gooide de bal precies/bijna op Peters neus.
she threw the ball exactly/nearly on Peter's nose

That *precies* acts as a modifier of the PP is clear from the fact illustrated in the (a)-examples in (46) that the phrase *precies in de roos* must be topicalized as a whole. It is not so clear, however, whether *bijna* acts as a modifier of the PP: the (b)-examples show that topicalization of the phrase *bijna in de roos* gives rise to a degraded result, the option of moving *bijna* in isolation being much preferred.

(46) a. Precies in de roos schoot hij de pijl.
a′. *Precies schoot hij de pijl in de roos.
b. ??Bijna in de roos schoot hij de pijl.
b′. Bijna schoot hij de pijl in de roos.

Although this suggests that *bijna* does not act as a modifier of the PP but of the clause, drawing such a conclusion may be premature since topicalization of *bijna* sometimes results in a change of meaning. This is perhaps not so clear in the case of the (b)-examples in (46), but the shift of meaning can be made more conspicuous by means of the examples in (47).

(47) a. Jan viel bijna in het water.
Jan fell nearly into the water
b. Bijna viel Jan in het water.
nearly fell Jan into the water

Example (47a) has two readings. The first reading involves modification of the event; it expresses that Jan was about to fall into the water, but succeeded in avoiding it. The second reading involves modification of the location: it is claimed that Jan actually fell, and that he ended up in a position close to the water as a result. Now, when we consider the topicalization construction in (47b), it turns out that only the first reading survives. This suggests that on its second reading, *bijna* does not act a modifier of the clause but of the PP. If this is indeed the case, the infelicitousness of topicalization constructions like (46b) remains mysterious.

II. Modification of in *'in/into' and* uit *'out of'?*

As the examples in (48) show, PPs headed by *in* and *uit* appear to constitute counterexamples to the claim that PPs referring to the null vector cannot be modified by modifiers of distance and orientation. At first sight, the adjectival and nominal phrases in the primeless examples seem to act as modifiers of distance, and the adjectives in the primed examples as modifiers of orientation. We will show in the following subsections, however, that it is not so clear whether we are really dealing with modifiers of the PP.

(48) a. De spijker zit diep/drie cm in de muur.
the nail sits deep/three cm in the wall
a′. De spijker zit schuin in de muur.
the nail sits diagonally in the wall
b. De spijker steekt drie cm uit de muur.
the nail sticks three cm out.of the wall
b′. De spijker steekt schuin uit de muur.
the nail sticks diagonally out.of the wall

A. Meaning

The meaning expressed by the presumed modifiers in (48) is of a completely different nature than in the case of PPs denoting a set of vectors. This is clearest in the case of the alleged modifiers of distance. With PPs denoting a set of vectors, these modifiers indicate what the distance between the reference object and the located object is. In the case of *in/uit*, on the other hand, the modifier indicates to what extent the located object penetrates/protrudes from the wall; cf. Figure 6A&B. Similarly, *schuin* in the primed examples indicates in what way the nail penetrates or protrudes from the wall (cf. Figure 6A′&B′).

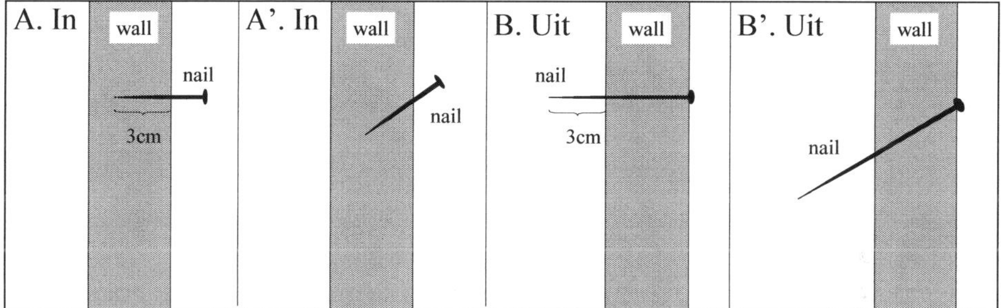

Figure 6: Modification of in *'into' and* uit *'out of'?*

It has been suggested that PPs headed by *in* and *uit* do involve vectors, but that they are different from the vectors discussed earlier in that they are not necessarily outward oriented with respect to the reference object, but can also be inward oriented. Note, however, that the nominal measure phrases in (48a&b) are in a paradigm with *gedeeltelijk* 'partly', *helemaal* 'entirely', and *voor de helft* 'half' (lit: for the half), which seem to modify or to be predicated of the located object rather than modifying the PP, so that it is not *a priori* clear whether we are really dealing with PP modification.

(49) a. De spijker zit gedeeltelijk/helemaal/voor de helft in de muur.
the nail sits partly/entirely/half in the wall
b. De spijker steekt gedeeltelijk/helemaal/voor de helft uit de muur.
the nail sticks partly/entirely/half out.of the wall

The elements discussed above can be used not only in the locational constructions in (48), but also in constructions involving a change of location, as in (50). Observe further that *uit* differs from *in* in that it (marginally) takes the adjectival *ver* 'far' as a modifier of distance, not *diep* 'deep'.

(50) a. Jan sloeg de spijker drie cm/diep/helemaal in de muur.
Jan hit the nail three cm/deep/entirely into the wall
b. Jan trok de spijker drie cm/?ver/helemaal uit de muur.
Jan pulled the nail three cm/far/entirely out.of the wall

The ungrammaticality of the examples in (51) shows that these modifiers can only occur with PPs denoting the null vector when some physical contact between the reference and located object is implied. This is consistent with the suggestion above that the modifiers in question actually do not modify a(n inwardly oriented) vector but the located object itself; when there is no physical contact, the located object cannot penetrate/protrude from the reference object, and hence modification is excluded. If so, the notion of “inwardly oriented vector” can be dismissed, and we must conclude that modification of adpositional phrases denoting the null vector is not possible; example (51b) is given a number sign given that it (marginally) allows a reading in which *schuin/recht* refer to Jan’s posture.

(51) a. *Jan stond 3 meter/diep/ver binnen de muur.
Jan stood 3 meters/deep/far within the wall
b. #Jan stond schuin/recht binnen de muur.
Jan stood diagonally/straight within the wall

Still, it must be noted that examples like (52), in which the distance from the outer boundary of the reference object is measured, are acceptable. Perhaps this is due to the fact that these examples do not involve three-dimensional space. If the budget is one million Euros, example (52a) expresses that the estimate is less. If the time limit is two hours, (52b) expresses that it took the athlete less time to finish. And if the broadcasting station has a range of 100 km, (52c) expresses that Jan lives less than 100 km from it; so it is actually the distance between Jan’s house and the broadcasting station that is relevant in this example.

(52) a. De begroting bleef ruim/net binnen de grenzen van het budget.
the estimate remained amply/just within the boundaries of the budget
b. De atleet kwam ruim/net binnen de gestelde tijd binnen.
the athlete came amply/just within the settled time inside
‘The athlete remained amply/just within the time limit.’
c. Jan woont ruim/net binnen het bereik van de zender.
Jan lives amply/just within the range of the broadcasting station

B. Topicalization

A second reason to doubt that the examples in (48) involve modification of the PPs is that topicalization of the alleged modified PPs gives rise to a marked result. This is clearest with examples involving the preposition *uit* in the (b)-examples in (48): the examples in (53) seem unacceptable. This is suspect since in cases where we are unambiguously dealing with modification, topicalization of the full modified PP is readily possible: *Een meter boven de deur hangt een schilderij* ‘A painting is hanging one meter above the door’.

(53) a. *Drie cm uit de muur steekt de spijker.
three cm out.of the wall sticks the nail
b. *Schuin uit de muur steekt de spijker.
diagonally out.of the wall sticks the nail

Leftward movement of the noun/adjective phrase in isolation gives rise to significantly better results: topicalization, as in the primeless examples in (54), is perhaps still somewhat marked but *wh*-movement, as in the primed examples, is perfectly acceptable. Unfortunately, however, this does not tell us much, since we have seen that extracting nominal and adjectival modifiers from the PP is possible as well.

(54) a. [?]Drie cm steekt de spijker uit de muur.
three cm sticks the nail out.of the wall
a′. Hoeveel cm steekt de spijker uit de muur?
how.many cm sticks the nail out.of the wall
b. [??]Schuin steekt de spijker uit de muur.
diagonally sticks the nail out.of the wall
b′. [?]Hoe steekt de spijker uit de muur?
how sticks the nail out.of the wall

Example (55a) seems somewhat better than (53a). The interpretation of this example differs, however, from that of example (48a); it can no longer express the situation in Figure 6A, but suggests that the nail has completely entered the wall and is now situated on a distance of three centimeters from the surface of the wall. The other examples in (55) do not, however, receive such a divergent interpretation and the judgments are more or less similar to those in (53) and (54).

(55) a. [??]Drie cm in de muur zit de spijker.
three cm in the wall sits the nail
a′. [?]Drie cm zit de spijker in de muur.
three cm sits the nail in the wall
a″. Hoeveel cm zit de spijker in de muur?
how.many cm sits the nail in the wall
b. *Schuin in de muur zit de spijker.
diagonally in the wall sits the nail
b′. [?]Schuin zit de spijker in de muur.
diagonally sits the nail in the wall
b″. Hoe zit de spijker in de muur?
how sits the nail in the wall

The topicalization data discussed in this section at least suggest that example (48) does not involve modification of the PP. We will return to this issue when we discuss modification of directional adpositional phrases; cf. the discussion in Section 3.1.4.3.

III. Conclusion

The previous subsections have shown that the modification possibilities of PPs referring to the null vector are very limited, possibly restricted to modifiers of the type *precies* 'exactly' and *bijna* 'nearly' discussed in Subsection I. In all likelihood, nominal measure phrases like *drie cm* 'three cm' and the adjectives *rechts/schuin* 'straight/diagonally' in the examples discussed in Subsection II do not function as modifiers of the PP.

3.1.4. Directional adpositional phrases

Directional PPs express that the located object traverses a certain path. A path can be defined as an ordered set of vectors, each of which is associated with a certain position on the time line. The path denoted by *van A naar B* 'from A to B' can then be represented as in Figure 7, taken from Section 1.3.1.1.5, which can be read as a cartoon.

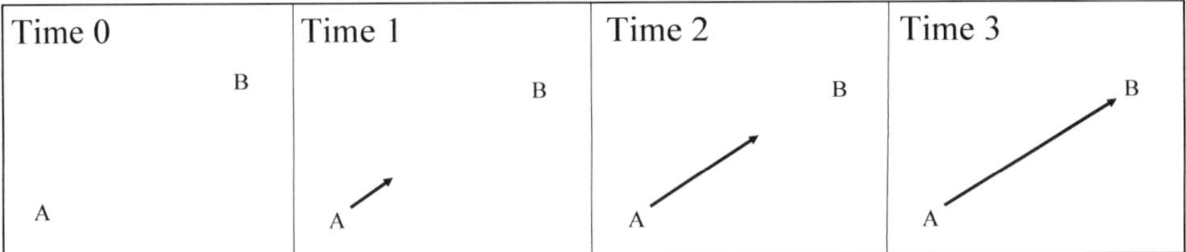

Figure 7: Van A naar B 'from a to B' (repeated)

The following sections will discuss some potential cases of modification of directional PPs. It will be shown that the modification possibilities are restricted to modifiers that express to what extent the implied path has been covered.

3.1.4.1. Modifiers of orientation and distance

The fact that the directional PPs also involve vectors may give rise to the expectation that directional PPs can also be modified by means of adverbial phrases of orientation and distance. This, however, does not seem to be borne out. Consider the examples in (56).

(56) a. #Jan liep recht/schuin naar de barkruk.
    Jan walked straight/diagonally to the bar stool
  b. *Jan liep ver/vlak/pal naar de barkruk.
    Jan walked far/close to the bar stool

The examples in (56a) are acceptable but not on the intended reading in which *recht* 'straight' and *schuin* 'diagonally' modify the path that Jan is traversing; these examples are only acceptable when *recht* and *schuin* are interpreted as supplementives predicated of *Jan* that express something about Jan's posture. This shows that *recht* and *schuin* are comparable to elements like *rechtop* 'upright', which can never be used as a modifier of a PP. The examples in (56b) are clearly unacceptable.

The discussion above does not automatically entail that directional PPs cannot be modified. Perhaps the PP *via een omweg* 'via a detour', which is in a paradigm with the adjective *rechtstreeks* 'directly', can be considered such a modifier. However, the fact that these examples can be paraphrased by means of the *... en doet dat + AP/PP* '... and does that AP/PP' strongly suggests that we are dealing with VP adverbs; cf. °adverb tests.

(57) a. Jan rijdt rechtstreeks/via een omweg naar Groningen.
    Jan drives directly/via a detour to Groningen
  b. Jan rijdt naar Groningen en hij doet dat rechtstreeks/via een omweg.
    Jan drives to Groningen and he does that directly/via a detour

The elements *midden*, *achter*, *voor*, *boven* and *onder*, discussed in the previous section, cannot readily be used in combination with a directional adpositional phrase either. The examples in (58) are all unacceptable under the intended reading, where the located object is situated with respect to the reference object. The number sign indicates that (58b) is acceptable when *boven* is interpreted as "upstairs"; this reading, on which *boven* functions as an adverbial phrase that refers to the place where the event of throwing the picture into the cupboard took place, is irrelevant here.

(58) a. Jan sprong (*midden) de plas in.
Jan jumped middle the puddle into
b. Jan gooide de foto (#boven/*onder) de kast in.
Jan threw the picture above/under the cupboard into
'Jan threw the picture in the top/lower drawer of the cupboard.'
c. Jan sprong (*achter/*voor) de auto op.
Jan jumped behind/in.front.of the car onto

3.1.4.2. Modifiers of the implied path

Modification of directional adpositional phrases seems possible with modifiers that express to which extent the implied path is covered. Modifiers of this type come in two kinds: nominal measure phrases and adjectives. The adjectives *helemaal* 'completely' and *gedeeltelijk* 'partly' deserve some special attention.

I. Nominal measure phrases and adjectival modifiers

Clear cases of modification of directional adpositional phrases are given in (59); note that the reference object can either precede or follow the modifier. Given that the reference object can also be placed in front of VP adverbs like *snel* 'quickly' (*Jan wandelde de berg snel op* 'Jan ascended the mountain quickly'), it seems plausible that the order in which the object precedes the modifier is derived by means of leftward movement of the noun phrase.

(59) a. Jan wandelde <het bos> 3 km <het bos> in.
Jan walked the wood 3 km into
'Jan walked three kilometers into the woods.'
b. Jan wandelde <de berg> 3 km <de berg> op.
Jan walked the mountain 3 km onto
'Jan walked three kilometers up the mountain.'

In (60), we give similar examples involving an adjectival modifier; the choice of the modifier again depends on the nature of the reference object.

(60) a. Jan wandelde <het bos> diep <het bos> in.
Jan walked the wood deep into
'Jan walked into deep into the woods.'
b. Jan klom hoog de boom in.
Jan climbed high the tree into
'Jan climbed high up into the tree.'

The modifications in (59) and (60) do not involve the orientation or the magnitude of the vectors involved, but the implied path: it is expressed that a subpart of the implied path has been covered. The examples in (59), for example, presuppose a trajectory that goes into the wood/up the mountain and it is claimed that the located object has covered 3 kilometers of this trajectory. The difference between the directional constructions in (59) and the non-directional constructions in (61) is that in the latter Jan may return to his starting position after he has finished walking 3 kilometers, whereas in the former Jan must be located in the woods/up the mountain.

(61) a. Jan wandelde 3 km in het bos.
Jan walked 3 km in the wood
'Jan walked three kilometers in the woods.'
b. Jan wandelde 3 km op de berg.
Jan walked 3 km on the mountain
'Jan walked three kilometers on the mountain.'

The adjectives in the non-directional constructions in (62) differ from the directional ones in (60) in that they just specify the place where the event is taking place: (62a) expresses that the activity of walking took place deep in the woods, and (62b) that the activity of climbing took place high in the tree.

(62) a. Jan wandelde diep in het bos.
Jan walked deep in the wood
'Jan was walking in the depth of the woods.'
b. Jan klom hoog in de boom.
Jan climbed high in the tree
'Jan was climbing high in the tree.'

Modification of the type in (59) and (60) is only possible when the path is not intrinsically bounded, that is, when the starting and the endpoint of the path are not fixed. In (59a), this condition is met; even though the path must be situated somewhere in the woods, it is left implicit where the starting and endpoint of the path are situated; any position external to the woods is an appropriate starting point and any position internal to the woods is an appropriate endpoint of the implied path. Something similar holds for the path denoted by the postpositional phrase in (59b). That the boundedness of the paths is relevant can also be demonstrated by means of the contrast between the use of the directional PPs headed by the prepositions *van* 'from', *naar* 'to' and *tot* 'until' in (63a), and the use of the directional PPs headed by the phrasal preposition *in de richting van* 'towards' in (63b). The intuition is that the length of the path in (63a) is determined by some implied anchoring point, for instance, the position of the speaker. This means that the length of the implied path is contextually fixed, and therefore cannot be modified. In (63b), on the other hand, the starting and endpoint of the implied path are not given (neither explicitly nor implicitly), so that the length of the implied path is not contextually determined and modification is possible.

(63) a. *Jan reed twee kilometer van/naar/tot Groningen.
Jan drove two kilometer from/to/until Groningen
b. Jan reed twee kilometer in de richting van Groningen.
Jan drove two kilometers towards Groningen

Other cases of directional phrases denoting paths that are inherently bounded and that therefore cannot be modified, are given in (64). In (64a-c), for example, the length of the implied paths is largely determined by the dimensions of the reference object; the starting and endpoint of the implied paths are bounded by two positions adjacent to and at opposite sides of the field/tunnel/house. Note that it is not clear whether the degraded example in (64d) can be accounted for in a similar way.

(64) a. *Jan liep twintig meter het veld over.
Jan walked twenty meters the field across
b. *Jan liep twee kilometer de tunnel door.
Jan walked two kilometers the tunnel through
c. ??Jan liep twee meter het huis voorbij.
Jan walked two meter the house past
d. ??Jan liep drie kilometer het kanaal langs.
Jan walked three kilometers the canal along

Finally, it can be noted that both the nominal and the adjectival modifiers can be extracted from the adpositional phrase by means of *wh*-movement. This is demonstrated in (65) by means of the interrogative counterparts of the examples in (59) and (60).

(65) a. Hoeveel kilometer wandelde Jan het bos in?
how.many kilometers walked Jan the wood into
a′. Hoeveel kilometer wandelde Jan de berg op?
how.many kilometers walked Jan the mountain onto
b. Hoe diep wandelde Jan het bos in?
how deep walked Jan the woods into
b′. Hoe hoog klom Jan de boom in?
how high climbed Jan the tree into

II. Helemaal *'completely' and* gedeeltelijk *'partly'*

The boundedness of the implied path is also relevant in the case of modification by *helemaal/gedeeltelijk* 'completely/partly', which indicates whether the implied path is fully or partly covered. When the path is not inherently bounded, as in (66a), the use of these modifiers does not make sense and therefore results in unacceptability. Given the discussion of (59b) above, the grammaticality of (66b) may come as a surprise, but the difference in acceptability of (59b) and (66b) goes hand in hand with a difference in interpretation: in (59b) the endpoint of the implied path is left implicit in the sense that it can be situated anywhere on the mountain, whereas in (66b) the endpoint must be *the top of* the mountain. In other words, in the former case *op* is interpreted as "onto", whereas in the latter case it is interpreted as "on top of". When the "on top of" reading is not possible, as in (66b′), the judgments are as expected. Note that, in contrast to what is the case in (59b), the modifier in (66b) must follow the reference object (under neutral intonation of the sentence).

(66) a. *Jan wandelde <het bos> helemaal/gedeeltelijk <het bos> in.
Jan walked the wood completely/partly into
b. Jan wandelde <de berg> helemaal/gedeeltelijk <*de berg> op.
Jan walked the mountain completely/partly onto
b′. *De supporter rende <het veld> helemaal/gedeeltelijk <het veld> op.
the fan ran the field completely/partly onto

The pattern we find in (67) is more or less what we expect: the PPs in (67a) denote bounded paths and modification by *helemaal* is correctly predicted to be possible, although it is surprising that the use of *gedeeltelijk* gives rise to a somewhat marked result; the PPs in (67b) denote unbounded paths, and modification by *helemaal/gedeeltelijk* is correctly predicted to be impossible.

(67) a. Jan reed helemaal/$^{?}$gedeeltelijk van/naar/tot Groningen.
Jan drove completely/partly from/to/until Groningen
b. *Jan reed helemaal/gedeeltelijk in de richting van Groningen.
Jan drove completely/partly towards Groningen

The examples in (68) all involve inherently bounded paths, and the use of *helemaal/gedeeltelijk* is possible, as predicted. Note that in these cases, the modifier also follows the reference object (under neutral intonation of the sentence).

(68) a. Jan liep <het veld> helemaal/gedeeltelijk <*het veld> over.
Jan walked the field completely/partly across
b. Jan liep <de tunnel> helemaal/gedeeltelijk <*de tunnel> door.
Jan walked the tunnel completely/partly through
c. Jan liep <het huis> helemaal/gedeeltelijk <*het huis> voorbij.
Jan walked the house completely/partly past
d. Jan liep <het kanaal> helemaal/gedeeltelijk <*het kanaal> langs.
Jan walked the canal completely/partly along

For completeness' sake, it can be noted that the modification possibilities in (66) and (68) correlate nicely with the (im)possibility to use the adjective *heel* 'whole' in (69) as an attributive modifier or predeterminer of the noun phrase expressing the reference object. There seems, however, to be a subtle difference in meaning between the two sets of constructions: whereas the examples in (66) and (68) suggest that the path proceeds along a more or less straight line, the examples in (69) suggest that the path proceeds in a more disordered fashion. This perhaps also accounts for the contrast between (69c&d) and (69e&f); while it is certainly possible to cross a field or proceed through a tunnel in a disorderly fashion, it seems less likely to pass a house of follow a canal in this way.

(69) a. *Jan liep <heel> het <hele> bos in.
Jan walked whole the whole wood into
b. Jan liep <*heel> de <$^{?}$hele> berg op.
Jan walked whole the whole mountain onto
c. Jan liep <heel> het <hele> veld over.
Jan walked whole the whole field across
d. Jan liep <heel> de <hele> tunnel door.
Jan walked whole the whole tunnel through
e. $^{?}$Jan liep <heel> het <hele> huis voorbij.
Jan walked whole the whole house past
f. $^{?}$Jan liep <heel> het <hele> kanaal langs.
Jan walked whole the whole canal along

The intuition that the implied paths in (69) are of a more disordered nature may be related to the fact that *heel* 'whole' forces a distributive reading when used as an attributive modifier of the head of a reference object in a locational construction. Consider the examples in (70).

(70) a. Er wonen mensen in het kasteel.
a′. Er wonen mensen in het hele kasteel.
there live people in the whole castle
'The (whole) castle is inhabited by people.'
b. Er liggen palen langs de weg.
b′. Er liggen palen langs de hele weg.
there lie poles along the whole road
'Poles are lying (all) along the road.'

Whereas (70a) is compatible with one family living in the castle (or with only a part of the castle being inhibited), example (70a′) implies that the castle is divided into separate housing units; people are more or less evenly distributed in the castle. Similarly, (70b) could be used to express that one pile of poles is lying at the side of the road, whereas (70b′) implies that the poles are placed along the road at certain intervals. In the same vein, it may be the case that the examples in (69) express that the implied path is more or less "evenly distributed" on the reference object; see Section N7.2 for more extensive discussion of the attributive modifier *heel*.

3.1.4.3. A seeming case of modification

At first sight, the type of modification in (59a&b) seems of a similar sort to that found in the examples involving locational PPs in (48). This impression is getting even stronger when we consider the directional counterparts of the examples in (48) in (71).

(71) a. Jan sloeg de spijker 3 cm de muur in.
Jan hit the nail 3 cm the wall into
'Jan hit the nail 3 cm into the wall.'
a′. Jan sloeg de spijker recht/schuin de muur in.
Jan hit the nail straight/diagonally the wall into
'Jan hit the nail straight/diagonally into the wall.'
b. Jan trok de spijker 3 cm de muur uit.
Jan pulled the nail 3 cm the wall out.of
'Jan pulled the nail 3 cm out of the wall.'
b′. Jan trok de spijker recht/schuin de muur uit.
Jan pulled the nail straight/diagonally the wall out.of
'Jan pulled the nail straight/diagonally out of the wall.'

As in the case of the prepositional phrases headed by *in/uit*, the nominal measure phrases of the postpositional phrases in the primeless examples of (71a&b) indicate to what extent the located object penetrates/protrudes from the wall; cf. Figure 6A&B. Similarly, the modifiers *recht* and *schuin* in the primed examples indicate in what way the nail penetrates/protrudes from the wall; cf. the discussion of Figure

6A′&B′. So, if we are dealing with *modification* involving distance and orientation, the adpositional phrases headed by *in* and *uit* must denote inward oriented vectors.

It is, however, doubtful that we are really dealing in (71) with adpositional phrases denoting inwardly oriented vectors. Consider the examples in (72). Section 3.1.4.2, sub II, has shown that the modifiers in (72a) indeed seem to specify the part of the path denoted by the directional adpositional phrase covered by *Jan*, which is also clear from the fact that they cannot be used in the construction in (72b), where the PP acts as a locational (adverbial) phrase.

(72) a. Jan wandelde de berg gedeeltelijk/helemaal/voor de helft op.
Jan walked the mountain partly/entirely/halfway onto
'Jan walked partly/completely/halfway to the top of the maintain.'
b. *Jan wandelde gedeeltelijk/helemaal/voor de helft op de berg.
Jan walked partly/entirely/halfway on the mountain

In (73a), on the other hand, the modifiers do not require the presence of a directional phrase; when we replace the directional postpositional phrase by a locational prepositional one, as in (73b), the result is still fully acceptable. This is due to the fact that the examples in (73) do not involve modification of the path covered, but modification of the part of the located object that has penetrated the reference object; in other words, we are not dealing with modification of the adpositional phrase but with modification or predication of the located object.

(73) a. Jan sloeg de spijker gedeeltelijk/helemaal/voor de helft de muur in.
Jan hit the nail partly/entirely/halfway the wall into
b. Jan sloeg de spijker gedeeltelijk/helemaal/voor de helft in de muur.
Jan hit the nail partly/entirely/halfway in the wall

A weaker argument against assuming that (73a) involves modification of the implied path is that it does not alternate with example (74), in which the adjective *heel* 'whole' is used as a predeterminer or an attributive modifier of the noun phrase referring to the reference object; example (69) has shown that this is often possible when *heel* functions as a modifier of the implied path.

(74) *Jan sloeg de spijker <heel> de <hele> muur in.
Jan hit the nail whole the whole wall into

3.1.5. Circumpositional phrases

Generally speaking, all circumpositional phrases can be used directionally, just like postpositional phrases. It is therefore not surprising that circumpositional phrases have the same modification possibilities as the postpositional ones. When the denoted path is not inherently bounded, as in (75a), the circumpositional phrase can be modified by a nominal measure phrase. When the path is bounded, as in (75b), the modifiers *helemaal* and *gedeeltelijk* can be used.

(75) a. Jan zwom drie kilometer tegen de stroom in.
Jan swam three kilometers against the current IN
b. Jan rende gedeeltelijk/helemaal naar Groningen toe.
Jan ran partly/completely to Groningen TOE

3.1.6. Intransitive adpositions and particles

Intransitive adpositions allow modification for orientation and distance, as is shown in (76a) and (76b&c), respectively. The modifiers of distance can be amplifiers like *ver* 'far', downtoning adverbs like *vlak* and *pal*, or nominal measure phrases like *twee meter* 'two meters'.

(76) a. dat hij de bal recht/schuin over schoot.
that he the ball straight/diagonally over shot
'that he shot the ball straight/diagonally over the goal.'
b. dat hij de bal ver/pal/vlak over schoot.
that he the ball far/close over shot
'that he shot the ball far/right over the goal.'
c. dat hij de bal twee meter naast schoot.
that he the ball two meter next.to shot
'that he shot the ball two meters next to the goal.'

The particle of a particle verb can sometimes also be modified, as is illustrated in (77) for the particle verb *voor/achter staan* 'to be ahead/down'; in (77a), we are dealing with an adjectival modifier, and in (77b) with a nominal measure phrase. Section 1.2.4.3 has shown that particles can normally permeate a clause-final verb cluster, but this is no longer possible when the particle is modified; the singly-primed examples show this for cases in which the modifier is pied piped and the doubly-primed examples for cases in which the modifier is stranded.

(77) a. dat hij bij winst ruim voor zal staan.
that he with gain amply ahead will stand
'that he will be amply ahead, when he wins.'
a′. dat hij bij winst zal (*ruim) voor staan.
a″. dat hij bij winst (??ruim) zal voor staan.
b. dat hij bij verlies twee punten achter zal staan.
that he with loss two points behind will stand
'that he will be two points behind, when he loses.'
a′. dat hij bij winst zal (*twee punten) achter staan.
a″. dat hij bij winst (??twee punten) zal achter staan.

As usual, the nominal measure phrase can be extracted from the adpositional phrase by means of *wh*-movement. In (78a), this is shown for the intransitive adposition *naast* and in (78b) for the particles *voor* and *achter*.

(78) a. Hoeveel meter schoot hij de bal naast?
how.many meters shot he the ball next.to
'How many meters did he shoot the ball besides to the goal?'
b. Hoeveel punten staat hij voor/achter?
how.many points stands he ahead/behind
'How many points is he ahead/behind?'

3.1.7. Summary

This section has discussed modification of spatial adpositional phrases. It has been shown that modification of locational phrases denoting a set of vectors is possible for orientation and distance. Modification of locational phrases denoting the null vector seems impossible, despite some seeming counterexamples. Directional phrases, finally, can occur with modifiers that indicate what part of the path denoted by the phrase is actually covered.

3.2. Temporal adpositional phrases

Section 1.3.2.1, sub II, has shown that the vector approach to spatial adpositional phrases can be straightforwardly applied to temporal adpositional phrases. Due to the fact that the time line is only one-dimensional, an exhaustive description of the temporal relation requires only the three relations BEFORE, SIMULTANEOUS, AFTER, as in (79).

(79) • Time line

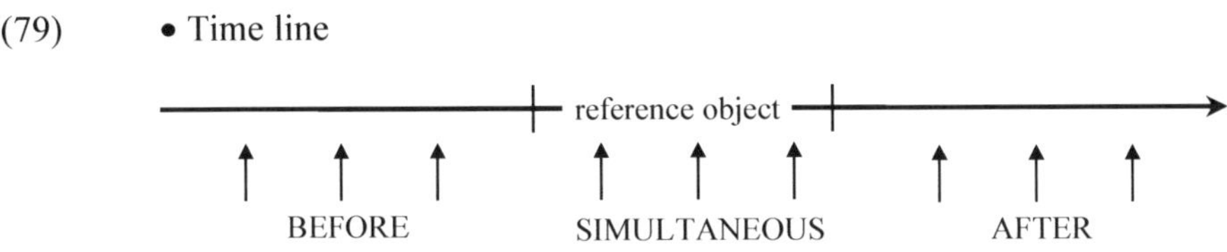

The relations BEFORE and AFTER involve vectors with opposite orientations; SIMULTANEOUS can be assumed to denote the null vector. Given the conclusions in Section 3.1.7, we therefore expect that modification is possible in the case of BEFORE and AFTER (which of course only involve the magnitude of the vector and not the orientation, due to the one-dimensional nature of the time line), but not in the case of SIMULTANEOUS. The examples in (80) show that this expectation is indeed borne out.

(80) a. Dat gebeurde lang/vlak voor de tweede wereldoorlog.
that happened long/just before World War II
b. *Dat gebeurde lang/vlak tijdens de tweede wereldoorlog.
that happened long/just during World War II
c. Dat gebeurde lang/vlak na de tweede wereldoorlog.
that happened long/just after World War II

Subsection I starts by discussing modification of temporal PPs that take a noun phrase as their complement, and Subsection II continues with temporal PPs that take a clause as their complement.

I. Temporal prepositions with a noun phrase as their complement

PPs headed by *voor* 'before' and *na* 'after' are the only temporal PPs that can be modified. As is illustrated in (81) and (82), the modifier can be an adjectival phrase or an adverb, a nominal phrase, and, in the case of *na*, a prepositional phrase headed by *binnen* 'within'. These modifiers all indicate the "distance" on the time line between the position of the reference object and the position of the event expressed by the remainder of the clause.

(81) a. Jan vertrok lang/kort/vlak voor de voorstelling.
Jan left long/shortly/shortly before the performance
b. Jan vertrok twee dagen voor de voorstelling.
Jan left two days before the performance
c. *Jan vertrok binnen tien minuten voor de voorstelling.
Jan left within ten minutes before the performance

(82) a. Het slachtoffer overleed lang/kort/vlak na het ongeluk.
the victim died long/shortly/shortly after the accident
b. Het slachtoffer overleed twee dagen na het ongeluk.
the victim died two days after the accident
c. Het slachtoffer overleed binnen tien minuten na het ongeluk.
the victim died within ten minutes after the accident

The following subsections will discuss these three types of modifiers in more detail.

A. Adjectival Modifiers and adverbs

The adjectival modifiers are mainly *lang* 'long' and *kort* 'shortly', although one may also finds the adjectives *snel* 'quickly' or the adverb *spoedig* 'soon' as modifiers of *na*-PPs. The adverbs are the same that are used for modification of spatial adpositional phrases: *vlak*/*pal* 'shortly'.

(83) a. Jan vertrok (zeer) lang/kort voor de voorstelling.
Jan left very shortly/long before the performance
b. Jan vertrok (*zeer) vlak voor de voorstelling.
Jan left very shortly before the performance

It is important to note that *lang* and *kort* are antonymous expressions, which is rather special given that antonymous expressions cannot be used to modify spatial *voor*-PPs. The fact that *lang* and *kort* are antonyms accounts for the contrast found in (84a); these examples show that adjectival modifiers are gradable and can be extracted by *wh*-movement, but that, as always in the case of antonymous APs, the neutral form *hoe lang* 'how long' is preferred over *hoe kort* 'how shortly'; cf. Section A1.3.2.2.1, sub IV. Example (84b) is ungrammatical due to the earlier established fact that adverbs are not gradable.

(84) a. Hoe lang/?kort voor de voorstelling vertrok Jan?
how long/shortly before the performance left Jan
'How long before the performance did Jan leave?'
b. *Hoe vlak voor de voorstelling vertrok Jan?
how shortly before the performance left Jan

Note that, as in the case of spatial PPs, the modifier does not modify the preposition but the full PP. This is clear from the fact that an R-pronoun can intervene between the modifier and the preposition, as is shown in (85).

(85) a. Kort daar voor/na vertrok hij.
shortly there before/after left he
b. *Daar kort voor/na vertrok hij.
there shortly before/after left he

B. Nominal measure phrases

All nominal expressions that can be used to denote a stretch of time can be used as modifiers: *twee dagen* 'two days', *een jaar* 'one year', *een tijdje* 'a while', etc. The nominal modifier can also be questioned.

(86) a. Jan vertrok twee dagen voor de voorstelling.
Jan left two days before the performance
b. Hoeveel dagen voor de voorstelling vertrok Jan?
how.many days before the exhibition left Jan

Like the adjectival modifiers, the nominal measure phrases modify the full PP, which is again clear from the fact that an R-pronoun can intervene between the modifier and the preposition, as is shown in (87).

(87) a. Twee dagen daar voor/na vertrok hij.
two days there before/after left he
c. *Daar twee dagen voor/na vertrok hij.
there two days before/after left he

C. Adpositional phrases

The use of adpositional phrases as modifiers of temporal PPs is extremely restricted, the only possibility being PPs headed by *binnen* 'within', which furthermore seems compatible only with temporal adpositional phrases headed by *na* 'after'; cf. the unacceptability of (81c). Note that the modifier can also be questioned in this case.

(88) a. Het slachtoffer overleed binnen tien minuten na het ongeluk.
the victim died within ten minutes after the accident
b. Binnen hoeveel minuten na het ongeluk overleed het slachtoffer?
within how many minutes after the accident died the victim

In light of the examples in (85) and (87) it is remarkable that the presence of a PP modifier seems to block R-pronominalization of the temporal PP; whereas *daar na overleed het slachtoffer* 'after that the victim died' is fully acceptable, the examples in (89) are both degraded. It is not clear to us what brings about this effect.

(89) a. *Binnen tien minuten daar na overleed het slachtoffer.
within ten minutes there after died the victim
b. *Daar binnen tien minuten na overleed het slachtoffer.
there within ten minutes after died the victim

II. Temporal prepositions with a clause as their complement

As is discussed in Section 2.4.1.2.1, adverbial clauses preceded by sequences like *voordat* 'before' or *nadat* 'after' can be analyzed either as involving a complex subordinator or as PPs headed by the preposition *voor/na*, which takes a finite clause as its complement. Whatever the right analysis may be, the examples in (90) and (91) show that such temporal adverbial clauses can be modified in the same way as PPs that take a noun phrase as their complement; cf. (81) and (82). Since the modifiers behave the same way with respect to questioning, we will not illustrate this here.

(90) a. Jan vertrok lang/kort/vlak voor dat de voorstelling begon.
Jan left long/shortly/shortly before that the performance begun

b. Jan vertrok twee dagen voor dat de voorstelling begon.
Jan left two days before that the performance begun

c. *Jan vertrok binnen tien minuten voor dat de voorstelling begon.
Jan left within ten minutes before that the performance begun

(91) a. Het slachtoffer overleed lang/kort/vlak na dat hij aangereden was.
the victim died long/shortly/shortly after that he over.run was
'The victim died long/shortly/just after he was run over.'

b. Het slachtoffer overleed twee dagen na dat hij aangereden was.
the victim died two days after that he over.run was

c. Het slachtoffer overleed binnen tien minuten na dat hij aangereden was.
the victim died within ten minutes after that he over.run was

The examples in (92) show, however, that in contrast to finite clauses, infinitival temporal clauses do not allow modification. Note that we cannot illustrate this for *voor* 'before', given that it cannot be used to introduce infinitival clauses; the corresponding infinitival complementizer is *alvorens*; cf. Section 2.4.2.2.

(92) a. *Het slachtoffer overleed vlak na overreden te zijn.
the victim died just after over.run to be
Intended reading: 'The victim died just after being overrun.'

b. *Vlak alvorens te gaan eten, dronken we een glas sherry.
just before to go eat, drank we a glass sherry
Intended reading: 'Just before eating, we drank a glass of sherry.'

3.3. Non-spatial/temporal adpositional phrases

Generally speaking, modification is restricted to spatial and temporal adpositional phrases. There are, however, at least two exceptions to this general rule, which are discussed in the following subsections.

I. Predicative PP idioms

Section 1.3.3.1 has discussed idiomatic PPs like *in z'n knollentuin* 'very happy' (lit.: in his vegetable garden) in copular constructions like (93a). Such PPs do not express locational meaning, but generally refer to a mental state of the entity they are predicated of. In this respect, they behave like the adjective *tevreden* 'satisfied' in (93b) and this similarity goes beyond this superficial semantic correlation; such PPs also behave syntactically more like adjectives than like "regular" PPs. For example, like *tevreden* in (93b), the idiomatic PPs in (93a) may take a PP-complement, which is certainly not a common feature of regular PPs.

(93) a. Jan is in z'n knollentuin/nopjes/sas/schik met dit boek.
Jan is IN Z'N KNOLLENTUIN/NOPJES/SAS/SCHIK with this book
'Jan is very happy with this book.'

b. Jan is tevreden met dit boek.
Jan is satisfied with this book

The idiomatic PPs in (93a) also behave more or less like adjectives with respect to modification; see the examples (391) in Section 1.3.3.1 for a larger sample of modification possibilities. Example (94a), for instance, shows that amplification by means of *zeer/erg* 'very' gives rise to a perfect result. They differ from adjectives, however, in that downtoners like *vrij* in (94b) are not possible, which is perhaps due to the fact that these idiomatic PPs inherently express a relatively high degree.

(94) a. Jan is erg/zeer in z'n knollentuin/... met dit boek.
Jan is very IN Z'N KNOLLENTUIN/... with this book
'Jan is extremely happy with this book.'
b. *?Jan is vrij in z'n knollentuin/... met dit boek.
Jan is rather IN Z'N KNOLLENTUIN/... with this book

The examples in (95) show that the idiomatic PPs in (93a) also behave like adjectives in that they allow (periphrastic) comparative/superlative formation. Not all °degrees of comparison give rise to an equally felicitous result, however; the majorative and maximative degree in (95a) are clearly better than the equative in (95b), and the minorative and minimative degree in (95c). Possibly this is due to the same reason why downtoners give rise to a marked result: insofar as the minorative degree is acceptable it feels like an understatement meaning "Jan is *not* happy with this book".

(95) a. Jan is meer/het meest in z'n knollentuin/... met dit boek.
Jan is more/the most IN Z'N KNOLLENTUIN/... with this book
'Jan is happier/happiest with this book.'
b. *Jan is even in z'n knollentuin/... met dit boek.
Jan is as IN Z'N KNOLLENTUIN/... with this book
Intended reading: 'Jan is just as happy with this book.'
c. Jan is ?minder/??het minst in z'n knollentuin/... met dit boek.
Jan is less/the least IN Z'N KNOLLENTUIN/... with this book
'Jan is less/the least happy with this book.'

Observe that the modifiers modify the complete PP, which is clear from the fact, illustrated in (96a), that the PP-complement can (at least marginally) occupy the position between the modifier and the idiomatic PP. It is even more clearly shown by the fact that stranded prepositions of PP-complements may intervene between the modifier and the idiomatic PP, as is shown in (96b). In this respect these idiomatic PPs resemble the pseudo-participles discussed in Section A2.3.1.3.

(96) a. ?dat Jan erg/zeer met dit boek in z'n knollentuin is.
that Jan very with this book IN Z'N KNOLLENTUIN is
b. dat Jan er erg/zeer <mee> in z'n knollentuin <mee> is.
that Jan there very with IN Z'N KNOLLENTUIN is

II. The "negative" preposition zonder *'without'*

The prepositions *met* 'with' and *zonder* 'without' function as antonyms. The first can be characterized as existential in the sense that it implies the existence of its complement, whereas the latter can be characterized as its "negative" counterpart in the sense that it denies the existence of its complement. This means that, in a sense, *met* and *zonder* differ in the same way as the indefinite articles *een* 'a' and ∅ and their negative counterpart *geen* 'no'. Given that the preposition *met* is existential, its nominal complement is compatible with a numeral: (97a) expresses that there are (two) exceptions. Being the negative counterpart of existential *met*, the preposition *zonder* is not compatible with a numeral on its nominal complement: (97b) can express that there are no exceptions, but not that two exceptions do not exist.

(97) a. met (twee) uitzonderingen
with two exceptions
b. zonder (*twee) uitzonderingen
without two exceptions

The examples in (98) show that the "negative" preposition *zonder* and the "negative" indefinite article *geen* are also similar in that they can both be modified by means of approximative modifiers like *vrijwel* 'virtually' and absolute modifiers like *helemaal* 'completely', which indicate whether or not the implied negation is absolute.

(98) a. vrijwel/helemaal geen uitzonderingen
virtually/completely no exceptions
b. vrijwel/helemaal zonder uitzondering
virtually/completely without exception

3.4. Comparative/superlative formation

With the exception of the predicative PP idioms discussed in Section 3.3, sub I, adpositional phrases cannot undergo comparative/superlative formation. It must be noted, however, that formations like *voorste* 'front' and *achterste* 'back' do occur. They retain their spatial meaning and do have a kind of superlative meaning, but they no longer act as adpositions; the fact that they may occur in prenominal attributive position, as in (99), show that they instead behave like true adjectives. Observe that these adjective are in a paradigm with *middelste* 'middle', which is not derived from a preposition.

(99) a. de bovenste/onderste plank
the top/bottom shelf
b. de achterste/voorste rij
the final/first row
c. de middelste plank
the middle shelf

3.5. Some ambiguous constructions

Section 3.1.3, sub II, has discussed examples like (100a) and argued that *achterop* is a compound. The main reason for this is that under R-pronominalization the R-word cannot intervene between *achter* and *op*, as shown in (100b), which would be possible if we were dealing with a construction in which *achter* acts as a premodifier of *op*, or with a construction in which *op de auto* is a complement of the preposition *achter*; cf. the discussion in Section 1.2.1, sub II.

(100) a. Achterop de auto zit een zwaailicht.
back.on the car sits a blue light
'A flashing blue light is attached on the back of the car.'
b. <Er> achter <*er> op zit een zwaailicht.
there back on sits a blue light

What we did not discuss there, however, is that there are seemingly similar constructions that behave slightly differently. This will become clear by considering the examples in (101). Although at first sight the clause structures of (100a) and (101a) seem completely parallel, R-pronominalization is excluded in the latter case. The number sign is added to (101b) with *er* preceding *achterop*, given that this order is acceptable on the reading "on the back of it", but on this reading it is clearly not related to (101a).

(101) a. Achter op de plaats staat een vuilnisbak.
back on the yard stands a garbage.can
'There is a garbage can in the back yard.'
b. <#Er> achter <*er> op staat een vuilnisbak.
there back on stands a garbage.can

In order to fully appreciate the difference between (100a) and (101a), one must know that adpositions like *achter*, *voor*, *boven* and *beneden* can also be used as referring expressions: in a domestic situation, for instance, *achter* may refer to the rooms in the back of the house, the back yard, etc.; *voor* may refer to some room in the front of the house; and *boven* and *beneden* can be translated as "upstairs" and "downstairs", respectively. The semantics of the construction in (101) seems to be that *achter* refers to a certain subpart of the house and that the PP *op de plaats* further specifies the intended place, that is, that the PP functions as a postmodifier of the referring expression *achter*.

The difference between the two constructions can be made clearer by means of the ambiguous example in (102). On the compound reading of *bovenop*, the sentence expresses that a new shirt is lying on top of the wardrobe. On the postmodification reading, the sentence expresses that the shirt is lying on the wardrobe upstairs. As would be expected on the basis of the data in (100) and (101), R-pronominalization is only compatible with the compound reading: (102b) can only mean that the shirt is lying on one of the top shelves of the wardrobe. Another difference between the two readings is that the phrase *boven op de kast* can be split on the modification reading, but that this is impossible (for obvious reasons) on the compound reading: (102c) is therefore only compatible with the modification reading. For completeness' sake, we want to note the intriguing fact that, on the modification reading, it seems possible to reverse the order of *boven* and the PP, as in (102c′).

(102) a. Boven op de kast ligt een nieuw overhemd. [ambiguous]
above on the wardrobe lies a new shirt
'A new shirt is lying on top of the wardrobe/on the wardrobe upstairs.'
b. Er bovenop ligt een nieuw overhemd. [compound reading]
there on.top.of lies a new shirt
'A new shirt is lying on top of it.'

c. Boven ligt een nieuw shirt op de kast. [modification reading]
upstairs lies a new shirt on the wardrobe
'Upstairs, a new shirt is lying on the wardrobe.'
c′. Op de kast boven ligt een nieuw shirt. [modification reading]

Note that the ambiguity that arises with *boven* is due to the fact that it can be used both as the first member of the compound *bovenop* and as a referring expression meaning "upstairs". A similar ambiguity does not arise with *onder*, simply because the "downstairs" reading is lacking; the (c)-examples in (103) are uninterpretable as a result.

(103) a. Onderin de kast ligt een nieuw overhemd.
on.the.bottom.of the wardrobe lies a new shirt
'A new shirt is lying on one of the lower shelves of the wardrobe.'
b. Er onderin ligt een nieuw overhemd.
there on.the.bottom.of lies a new shirt
c. *Onder ligt een nieuw overhemd in de kast.
c′. *In de kast onder ligt een nieuw overhemd.

For the "downstairs" reading, it is the preposition *beneden* in (104a) that is used. Since a compound reading is not available for **benedenin*, it does not come as a surprise that the judgments on the (b)- and (c)-examples in (104) are the mirror image of the corresponding examples in (103).

(104) a. Beneden in de kast ligt een nieuw overhemd.
downstairs in the wardrobe lies a new shirt
b. *Er benedenin ligt een nieuw overhemd.
c. Beneden ligt een nieuw overhemd in de kast.
c′. In de kast beneden ligt een nieuw overhemd.

We conclude by briefly addressing another potential case of ambiguity, which can be found in (105a). On one reading, this example seems to express that the plane is flying high, with the PP *boven de wolken* functioning as a postmodifier of the adjective *hoog* 'high', specifying more precisely the position of the plane. On the alternative reading, it is expressed that the plane is flying above the clouds, with the adjective *hoog* acting as a premodifier specifying the distance between the plane and the clouds. The first reading seems similar to the modification reading that we discussed for *boven* 'upstairs' and *beneden* 'downstairs' above, and the second reading is similar to that of constructions like *10 km boven de wolken* '10 km above the clouds', where a nominal measure phrase is used as a premodifier of the PP. The fact illustrated in (105b&c) that both *hoog* and *boven de wolken* can be used as the predicative part of the construction is consistent with this account of the observed ambiguity.

(105) a. Het vliegtuig vloog hoog boven de wolken.
the plane flew high above the clouds
b. Het vliegtuig vloog hoog.
b′. Het vliegtuig vloog boven de wolken.

The facts in (106b&c) suggest that (106a) is ambiguous in a way similar to (105a), although it does not seem readily possible in this case to pinpoint a corresponding semantic difference.

(106) a. Het vliegtuig vloog laag over de stad.
the plane flew low over the city
b. Het vliegtuig vloog laag.
c. Het vliegtuig vloog over de stad.

3.6. Bibliographical note

Since the discussion on modification in this section is mainly based on the vector theory of spatial adpositions, we can again refer the reader again to the series of papers by Zwarts (1994/1994/1996/1997), Zwarts and Winter (1997), and Helmantel (1998/2002), which were mentioned in connection with Chapter 1.

Chapter 4
Syntactic uses of the adpositional phrase

Introduction

This section is concerned with the syntactic uses of adpositional phrases shown in Table 1. For all these syntactic uses we will investigate at least the following four syntactic properties: the possibility of °topicalization, °scrambling, °PP-over-V, and °R-extraction.

Table 1: The syntactic use of the adpositional phrase

argument				§ 4.1
predicative	complementive	spatial	locational	§ 4.2.1.1.2
			directional	§ 4.2.1.1.3
		non-spatial		§ 4.2.1.2
	supplementive			§ 4.2.2
attributive				§ 4.3
adverbial				§ 4.4

4.1. Adpositional phrases used as arguments

The use of adpositional phrases in positions that are normally occupied by a nominative or an accusative noun phrase is restricted to constructions in which the adpositional phrase acts as the °logical SUBJECT of a complementive: the two examples in (1) illustrate, respectively, a copular and a *vinden*-construction, in which the locational prepositional phrase *onder het bed* 'under the bed' functions as the SUBJECT of the nominal predicate *een leuke plek* 'a nice spot'.

(1) a. Waarschijnlijk is onder het bed een leuke plek.
probably is under the bed a nice spot
b. Ik vind onder het bed een leuke plek.
I consider under the bed a nice spot

Example (2) provides similar examples in which the directional postpositional phrase *de berg op* functions as the SUBJECT of the adjectival predicate *gemakkelijker* 'easier'.

(2) a. De berg op is gemakkelijker dan de berg af.
the mountain up is easier than the mountain down
'It is easier to ascend the mountain than to descend it.'
b. Ik vind de berg op gemakkelijker dan de berg af.
I consider the mountain up easier than the mountain down
'I consider ascending the mountain easier than descending it.'

It has been argued that in examples like *Het is warm in de kamer* 'It is warm in the room', the PP *in de kamer* 'in the room' also functions as a SUBJECT of the adjectival predicate *warm* 'warm', albeit that the pronoun *het* 'it' is used as an anticipatory pronoun introducing the SUBJECT-PP. Constructions like these are not be discussed here but in Section A6.6.3.

Examples in which an adpositional phrase acts as the SUBJECT of a main verb cannot readily be constructed and generally sound quite forced. Adpositional phrases can, however, readily be used as complements of lexical heads; they frequently occur as complements of verbs, adjectives and nouns, as illustrated in (3). It is, however, quite uncommon for adpositional phrases to occur as the complement of an adposition; see Section 2.2 for a few such exceptional cases.

(3) a. Marie kijkt graag naar mooie jongens. [complement of V]
Marie looks gladly at beautiful boys
'Marie likes to look at beautiful boys.'
b. Jan is erg trots op zijn mooie lange haar. [complement of A]
Jan is very proud of his beautiful long hair
c. Jan verafschuwt de jacht op wilde zwijnen. [complement of N]
Jan loathes the hunt on wild boars

That it is the lexical head of the construction that selects the PP is clear from the fact that the actual choice of the adposition fully depends on the selectional properties of the head; replacement of the prepositions in (3) by any other preposition results in ungrammaticality. Since the prepositions seem to be mainly present for syntactic reasons and do not seem to contribute in a compositional way to the meaning of the sentences, we will call them FUNCTIONAL PREPOSITIONs. We refer the reader to Table 29 in Section 1.3.3 for a list of these functional prepositions and more examples, and continue here with an investigation of four syntactic properties of argument PPs: topicalization, scrambling, PP-over-V and R-extraction.

I. Topicalization

PPs acting as the subject/object of the clause can be topicalized. This is shown in (4) for the examples in (1): (1a) illustrates the case in which the subject PP occupies the regular subject position of the clause, which is right adjacent to the finite verb, and (4a) provides the counterpart of this example with topicalization of the subject-PP *onder het bed*; example (4b) is the topicalization counterpart of (1b).

(4) a. Onder het bed is waarschijnlijk een leuke plek.
under the bed is probably a nice spot
b. Onder het bed vind ik een leuke plek.
under the bed consider I a nice spot

The examples in (5) are the topicalization counterparts of the examples in (3). Examples (5a&b) show that PP-complements of verbs and predicatively used adjectives can readily be topicalized. Topicalization of the PP-complement of the definite noun phrase in (3c), on the other hand, seems impossible; we refer the reader to Subsection V for a discussion of the topicalization behavior of PP-complements of indefinite noun phrases.

(5) a. Naar mooie jongens kijkt Marie graag.
at beautiful boys looks Marie gladly
b. Op zijn mooie lange haar is Jan erg trots.
of his beautiful long hair is Jan very proud
c. *?Op wilde zwijnen verafschuwt Jan de jacht.
on wild boars loathes Jan the hunt

II. Scrambling

Example (6) shows that PPs that act as the object of a *vinden*-construction can undergo °scrambling, and are thus able to either precede or follow the adverbs. As with nominal objects, the two forms differ with respect to the information structure of the clause: when the PP precedes the clause adverb, it is construed as belonging to the presupposition of the clause, whereas it is construed as part of the °focus ("new" information) when it follows the clause adverb.

(6) dat Jan <onder het bed> misschien <onder het bed> een leuke plek vindt.
that Jan under the bed possibly a nice spot considers

The examples in (7a&b) show that prepositional complements of verbs and adjectives can also undergo scrambling. In these examples the difference does not involve the distinction between presupposition and focus but, rather, the distinction between emphatic and contrastive focus; when it is scrambled, the PP is emphasized. Example (7c) shows that, like topicalization in (5c), scrambling of the PP-complement of a noun gives rise to a degraded result.

(7) a. dat Marie <naar mooie jongens> graag <naar mooie jongens> kijkt.
that Marie at beautiful boys gladly looks
b. dat Jan <op zijn mooie lange haar> erg trots <op zijn mooie lange haar> is.
that Jan of his beautiful long hair very proud is
c. dat Jan <*?op wilde zwijnen> de jacht <op wilde zwijnen> verafschuwt.
that Jan on wild boars the hunt loathes

III. PP-over-V

The primed examples in (8) show that PP-over-V of the subject/object PPs in the examples in (1) is excluded; they behave like nominal subjects/objects in this respect. The number sign # indicates that (8b′) is acceptable when *vinden* acts as a transitive verb meaning "to find", in which case the PP functions as a locational adverbial phrase, which is clear from the fact that it is optional; this interpretation of the PP is, of course, also available in (4b) and (8b).

(8) a. dat onder het bed een leuke plek is.
that under the bed a nice spot is
a′. *dat een leuke plek is onder het bed.
b. dat ik onder het bed een leuke plek vind.
that I under the bed a nice spot consider
b′. #dat ik een leuke plek vind (onder het bed).

The examples in (9a&b) show that PP-over-V of PP complements of verbs and adjectives is possible. PP-over-V seems be blocked, however, with PP complements of definite noun phrases; we refer the reader to Subsection V for a discussion of the extraposition behavior of PP-complements of indefinite noun phrases.

(9) a. dat Marie graag kijkt naar mooie jongens.
that Marie gladly looks at beautiful boys
b. dat Jan erg trots is op zijn mooie lange haar.
that Jan very proud is of his beautiful long hair
c. *?dat Jan waarschijnlijk de jacht verafschuwt op wilde zwijnen.
that Jan probably the hunt loathes on wild boars

IV. R-extraction

All argument PPs discussed above allow °R-pronominalization. The examples differ, however, with respect to the question of whether the R-word *er* must be adjacent to the preposition, or whether the two can be separated by some other element as a result of R-extraction. The examples in (10) show that pronominal PPs that act as the subject or the object of the clause cannot be split.

(10) a. Om te spelen is waarschijnlijk *daar onder* een leuke plek.
for to play is probably there under a nice spot
'Under there will probably be a nice place for playing.'
a′. *Om te spelen is *daar* waarschijnlijk *onder* een leuke plek.
b. Ik vind waarschijnlijk *daar onder* een leuke plek.
I consider probably there under a nice spot
'I think that under there will probably be a nice spot for playing.'
b. *Ik vind *daar* waarschijnlijk *onder* een leuke plek.

The examples in (11a&b) show that the split pattern is possible when the pronominal PP is the complement of a verb or an adjective. When the PP is a complement of a definite noun phrase, however, the split pattern seems to be excluded; we again refer the reader to Subsection V for a discussion of the behavior of PP-complements of indefinite noun phrases in this respect.

(11) a. dat Marie <*daar*> graag <*daar*> *naar* kijkt.
that Marie there gladly at looks
'that Marie gladly looks at that.'
b. dat Jan <*daar*> waarschijnlijk erg trots <*daar*> *op* is.
that Jan there probably very proud of is
'that Jan is of course very proud of that.'
c. dat Jan <*?*daar*> de jacht <*daar*> *op* verafschuwt.
that Jan there the hunt on loathes
'that Jan loathes the hunt on it.'

V. Conclusion

Table 2 summarizes the results from Subsections I to IV. The second column refers to PPs that are used in positions where we would normally have a nominative or an accusative noun phrase. The third column gives the cases in which a PP is used as a complement of V, A or N.

Table 2: Adpositions used as arguments

	SUBJECT OF COMPLEMENTIVE		COMPLEMENT OF		
	SUBJECT	OBJECT	V	A	N
TOPICALIZATION	+	+	+	+	—
SCRAMBLING	n.a.	+	+	+	—
PP-OVER-V	—	—	+	+	—
R-EXTRACTION	—	—	+	+	—

The data in Subsections I to IV suggest that PP-complements of verbs and adjectives differ from PP-complements of nouns in that only the former can undergo topicalization, scrambling, PP-over-V and R-extraction. It is not clear, however, whether it is really the case that PP-complements of nouns categorically resist these processes; when we are dealing with indefinite noun phrases, the results appear to be totally different. In (12a), for example, the PP *over ruimtevaart* 'about space travel' is often claimed to be a complement of the noun *boek* 'book', and the examples in (12b-e) show that topicalization, scrambling, PP-over-V, and R-extraction are all nevertheless possible when the noun phrase is indefinite.

(12) a. Marie heeft een/het boek over ruimtevaart gelezen.
Marie has a/the book on space travel read
b. Over ruimtevaart heeft Marie een/??het boek gelezen. [Topicalization]
c. Marie heeft over ruimtevaart een/??het boek gelezen. [Scrambling]
d. Marie heeft een/??het boek gelezen over ruimtevaart. [PP-over-V]
e. Marie heeft er een/??het boek over gelezen. [R-extraction]
Marie has there a/the book on read
'Marie read a book on it.'

The claim that we are dealing with a PP complement in (12) is not uncontroversial, however: it is sometimes claimed that, at least in (12b-e), the PP is not a complement of the noun but a restrictive adverbial phrase. We will not discuss this issue here, but refer the reader to Section N2.2.1 and subsequent sections for an extensive discussion of this and many other intricate questions concerning adpositional complements of nouns.

4.2. Predicative use of adpositional phrases

This section is devoted to predicatively used adpositional phrases. Section 4.2.1 starts with a discussion of complementive adpositional phrases and 4.2.2 continues with supplementive adpositional phrases. We conclude in Section 4.2.3 with a brief discussion of absolute *met*-constructions.

4.2.1. Complementives

Adpositional °complementives are generally spatial in nature, as in example (13a), where the locational adpositional phrase *in het zwembad* 'in the swimming pool' is predicated of the noun phrase *Jan*. Section 1.3.1.1.2 has argued that the adposition can be considered a two-place predicate that denotes a spatial relation between its complement (the reference object) and the argument the full adpositional phrase is predicated of (the located object). This means that the semantic interpretation of example (13a) is as given in (13b).

(13) a. Jan is in het zwembad.
Jan is in the swimming.pool
b. IN (Jan, het zwembad)

However, there are also adpositional complementives that are non-spatial in nature. In the idiomatic examples in (14a), for instance, the PP denotes a mental state of the subject of the clause and therefore typically takes a [+HUMAN] SUBJECT; these PPs are mostly fixed expressions, which is clear from the fact that the noun *sas* is possible in this construction only. Although they seem less numerous, there are also more or less fixed expressions like (14b), which are predicated of [-HUMAN] entities.

(14) a. Hij is in de wolken/z'n sas.
he is in the clouds/his SAS
'He is on cloud nine.'
b. Die regeling is al drie jaar van kracht.
that regulation is already three years in force
'That regulation has already been in effect for three years.'

Spatial and non-spatial complementives will be discussed more extensively in, respectively, Section 4.2.1.1 and Section 4.2.1.2.

4.2.1.1. Spatial constructions

Although we do not intend to extensively repeat the discussion of spatial adpositions that was given in Section 1.1.3.2, we will nevertheless start in Section 4.2.1.1.1 by giving a brief indication of the main difference between locational and directional adpositional phrases, which will be the topics of, respectively, Section 4.2.1.1.2 and Section 4.2.1.1.3.

4.2.1.1.1. General introduction

Spatial adpositional complementives can either denote a location or a direction. The actual interpretation of clauses with a locational complementive depends on the main verb: when the verb is stative, as in (15a), the clause just expresses that the SUBJECT of the adpositional phrase occupies a certain location, but when the verb denotes an activity or a process, as in (15b), the clause expresses that the SUBJECT is undergoing a change of location. Since directional complementives always imply a change of location, they require that the main verb denote an activity or a process, as is shown in (15c).

(15) a. Jan ligt in het zwembad. [location]
Jan lies in the swimming.pool
b. Jan valt in het zwembad. [change of location]
Jan falls into the swimming.pool
c. Jan valt/*ligt het zwembad in. [directional]
Jan falls the swimming.pool into

Locational adpositional phrases are normally headed by prepositions (although occasionally a circumposition can be used as well). Directional phrases, on the other hand, can either be headed by a directional preposition like *naar* 'to' or a post- or circumposition; cf. Section 1.3.

The semantic difference between constructions like (15b) and (15c) is often not immediately clear. The main difference between locational and directional adpositional phrases is that the latter implies the notion of a path, whereas the former does not and simply indicate the (new) position of the located object. The fact that the two types of adpositional phrases differ can be made clear by means of the *XP met die NP!* construction. For most speakers, the XP must be a directional phrase; when the XP is a locational phrase, the construction gives rise to a marked result. This accounts for the difference between (16a′) and (16b′).

(16) a. We gooien die jongen in het zwembad. [change of location]
we throw that boy into the swimming.pool

a′. %In het zwembad met die jongen!
into the swimming.pool with that boy

b. We gooien die jongen het zwembad in. [directional]
we throw that boy the swimming.pool into

b′. Het zwembad in met die jongen!
the swimming.pool into with that boy

Verbs with spatial complementives may differ with respect to the selectional restrictions they impose on spatial PPs: the (stative) locational verbs in (17a) are only compatible with adpositional phrases that denote a location; the verbs of change of location in (17b) force a change of location reading on the adpositional phrase, and can be seen as the causative counterparts of the verbs in (17a); the verbs of traversing in (17c), finally, seem compatible only with adpositional phrases that denote a direction (= change of location along a path).

(17) a. Verbs of location (monadic): *hangen* 'to hang', *liggen* 'to lie', *staan* 'to stand', *zitten* 'to sit'

b. Verbs of change of location (dyadic): *hangen* 'to hang', *leggen* 'to lay', *zetten* 'to put'

c. Verbs of traversing: *fietsen* 'to cycle', *rijden* 'to drive', *wandelen* 'to walk', etc.

An illustration of the restrictions imposed by these verbs on an adpositional predicate is given in (18). In (18a), the locational verb *staan* 'to stand' indicates that the car is situated on the hill. Example (18b) also expresses that the car is situated on the hill, but in addition it is claimed that this position of the car is the result of an action by Jan, that is, that a change of location is involved. That the verb *zetten* 'to put' is not compatible with a directional adpositional phrase is clear from the fact illustrated in (18b′) that the prepositional phrase cannot be replaced by the postpositional one *de heuvel op* 'onto the hill'. Example (18c) also indicates a change of location, but in addition it is expressed that the car is covering some path. That *rijden* 'to drive' preferably takes a directional adpositional phrase is clear from the fact that it is at best marginally compatible with the prepositional phrase *op de heuvel* 'on the hill'; see Section 1.1.3.2.1 for exceptions and more discussion.

(18) a. De auto staat op de heuvel.
the car stands on the hill
'The car is standing on the hill.'
b. Jan zet de auto op de heuvel.
Jan puts the car onto the hill
'Jan is putting the car onto the hill.'
b′. *?Jan zet de auto de heuvel op.
c. Jan rijdt de auto de heuvel op.
Jan drives the car the hill onto
'Jan is driving the car onto the hill.'
c′. ??Jan rijdt de auto op de heuvel.

Now that we have repeated some of the basic distinctions between the various types of spatial adpositional phrases, we can continue by discussing their behavior with respect to topicalization, scrambling, PP-over-V, and R-extraction: Section 4.2.1.1.2 will start by discussing spatial complementives denoting a (change) of location, which is followed by a discussion of the directional complementives in 4.2.1.1.3.

4.2.1.1.2. Locational constructions

This section investigates four syntactic properties of the predicative constructions in (19), which express a (change of) location of the referent of the noun phrase *het boek* 'the book'. Subsequently, we will discuss topicalization, scrambling, and PP-over-V of, and R-extraction from the adpositional complementives.

(19) a. Het boek lag gisteren op de tafel.
the book lay yesterday on the table
b. Jan legde het boek net op de tafel.
Jan put the book just on the table
:Jan put the book on the table just now.

I. Topicalization

The examples in (20) show that topicalization of a predicative adpositional phrase denoting (change of) location is readily possible.

(20) a. Op de tafel lag gisteren een boek.
on the table lay yesterday a book
b. Op de tafel legde Jan net een boek.
on the table put Jan just a book

II. Scrambling

Generally speaking, scrambling of locational complementives gives rise to degraded results. As is shown in (21), the locational PP normally immediately precedes, that is, is left-adjacent to the verb(s) in clause-final position.

(21) a. dat het boek <*op de tafel> gisteren <op de tafel> lag.
that the book on the table yesterday lay
b. dat Jan <*op de tafel> het boek <*op de tafel> net <op de tafel> legde.
that Jan on the table the book just put
'that Jan put the book on the table just now.'

There are, however, at least two exceptions to this general rule. First, when the locational complementive is assigned emphatic focus (indicated by italics) or when it is preceded by a focus particle like *zelfs* 'even', scrambling is possible. So, whereas scrambling is excluded in the neutrally pronounced (22a), it is possible in (22b&c).

(22) a. dat Jan <*in de vaas> rozen <in de vaas> zet.
that Jan in the vase roses puts
'that Jan probably puts the roses in the vase.'
b. dat Jan <in *deze* vaas> rozen <in *deze* vaas> zet.
that Jan in this vase roses puts
c. dat Jan zelfs <in *deze* vaas> rozen <in *deze* vaas> zet.
that Jan even in this vase roses puts
'that Jan even puts roses in this vase.'

Second, example (23b) shows that scrambling is also licensed when the located and reference object are quantified. At first sight, the two variants in (23a&b) seem to have the same meaning in (23c): for every vase (in the domain of discourse), there is a rose such that Jan puts that rose in it. The main difference seems to be that the order in which the noun phrase *een roos* precedes the PP requires emphatic focus on the noun phrase.

(23) a. ?dat Jan een roos in elke vaas stopte.
that Jan a rose in every vase put
b. dat Jan in elke vaas een roos stopte.
that Jan in every vase a rose put
c. ∀x (vase (x) → ∃y (rose (y) ∧ Jan put y in x))

The claim that the two orders in (23a&b) express the same meaning is wrong, however, given that the two orders in (24a&b) do express different meanings. The most prominent reading of (24a) is that one of Jan's fingers is put in all bowls (e.g., Jan is tasting the content of each bowl by using the forefinger of his right hand), whereas (24b) is most readily interpreted as involving more fingers, with each finger put in another bowl. If these intuitions are correct, we may conclude that the two orders differ in the relative scope of the two quantified nouns, as is formally expressed in (24a′&b′).

(24) a. dat Jan een vinger in elk schaaltje stopt.
that Jan a finger in every bowl puts
'that Jan puts a finger in every bowl.'
a′ ∃x (finger (x) ∧ ∀y (bowl (y) → Jan puts x in y))
b. dat Jan in elk schaaltje een vinger stopt.
that Jan in every bowl a finger puts
'that Jan puts a finger in every bowl.'
b′. ∀x (bowl (x) → ∃y (finger (y) ∧ Jan puts y in x))

The conclusion that the order of the noun phrase and the PP (24a&b) reflects the relative scope of the two phrases also accounts for the fact that placing the PP left-adjacent to the verb gives rise to a somewhat marked result in (23a) when the sentence is pronounced without emphatic focus on the noun phrase: the resulting interpretation that there is only one rose, which is put in every vase, does not refer to a plausible situation.

The discussion above strongly suggests that scrambling of locational PPs is excluded unless they are assigned emphatic focus or the relative scope of the located and the reference objects is indicated.

III. PP-over-V

Although the precise judgments on status of the primed examples in (25) seem to differ somewhat among speakers, the general consensus seems to be that PP-over-V of complementive adpositional phrases denoting a (change of) location gives rise to a degraded result.

(25) a. dat het boek op de tafel lag.
that the book on the table lay
'that the book lay on the table.'
a′. *?dat het boek lag op de tafel.
b. dat Jan het boek op de tafel legde.
that Jan the book on the table put
'that Jan put the book on the table.'
b′. *?dat Jan het boek legde op de tafel.

It must be noted, however, that the ban on PP-over-V is lifted when we are dealing with particle verbs or certain prefixed verbs. Example (26) illustrates this for the particle verb *neerleggen* 'to put down'; we will return to this fact in Sections 4.2.1.2.2 and 4.2.1.2.3.

(26) a. dat Jan het boek op de tafel neer legde.
that Jan the book on the table down put
'that Jan put the book down on the table.'
b. dat Jan het boek neer legde op de tafel.

IV. R-extraction

R-extraction from predicative adpositional phrases denoting a (change of) location is possible. The examples in (27) illustrate this by means of a relative clause, in which the relative R-pronoun corresponds to the complement of the locational adposition.

(27) a. de tafel *waar* het boek *op* lag
the table where the book on lay
'the table that the book lay on'
b. de tafel *waar* Jan het boek *op* legde
the table where Jan the book on put
'the table that Jan put the book on'

V. Conclusion

The previous subsections have shown that whereas locational complementives do allow topicalization, they cannot be scrambled or extraposed. Furthermore, we have seen that these complementive readily allow R-extraction. The next section will show that directional complementives exhibit more or less the same behavior.

4.2.1.1.3. Directional constructions

Locational adpositional phrase are generally prepositional, whereas the examples in (28) show that directional ones can be pre-, post- or circumpositional. Below we will see that these three types of adpositional phrases exhibit different behavior with respect to the four syntactic processes under discussion.

(28) a. Jan reed naar zijn buitenhuis. [prepositional]
Jan drove to his country.house
b. Jan reed de berg op. [postpositional]
Jan drove the mountain onto
'Jan drove onto the mountain.'
c. Jan sprong van de tafel af. [circumpositional]
Jan jumped from the table AF
'Jan jumped from the table.'

I. Topicalization

Topicalization of directional complementives requires that contrastive accent be assigned to some specific part of the adpositional phrase; the part that must be accented depends on whether we are dealing with a pre-, post- or circum-positional phrase. Example (29a) shows that topicalization of a prepositional phrase requires that the nominal complement of the PP be assigned contrastive accent (indicated by small caps). Topicalization of a postpositional phrase, as in (29b), requires that the postposition be assigned contrastive accent; when the accent is on the complement of the postposition, the complement may be topicalized but the postposition must be stranded in its original position. Topicalization of a circumpositional phrase requires that contrastive accent be assigned to the second part of the adposition, as in (29c).

(29) a. Naar zijn BUItenhuis reed Jan.
to his country.house drove Jan
b. De berg OP reed Jan (niet AF).
the mountain onto drove Jan not down
b′. De BERG <*op> reed Jan <op> (niet de BRUG).
the mountain onto drove Jan not the bridge
c. Van de tafel AF sprong Jan.
from the table AF jumped Jan

II. Scrambling

The examples in (30) show that, just as in the case of the predicatively used locational PPs, scrambling is generally excluded with directional PPs. Example (30a′) is excluded and cannot even be saved by giving emphatic accent to the PP. The same thing holds for (30b′), although it may be worthwhile to note that scrambling of the nominal complement of the postposition, as in (30b″), does lead to an acceptable result. The (c)-examples show that Scrambling of circumpositional phrases is again excluded.

(30) a. dat Jan met zijn dienstauto naar zijn buitenhuis reed.
that Jan with his company.car to his country.house drove
a′. *dat Jan naar zijn buitenhuis met zijn dienstauto reed.
b. dat Jan snel de berg op reed.
that Jan quickly the mountain up drove
b′. *dat Jan de berg op snel reed.
b″. dat Jan de berg snel op reed.
c. dat Jan snel van de tafel af sprong.
that Jan quickly from the table AF jumped
c′. *dat Jan van de tafel af snel sprong.

III. PP-over-V

The examples in (31) show that, just as in the case of the predicatively used locational PPs, PP-over-V of directional adpositional phrases leads to a degraded result.

(31) a. dat Jan naar zijn buitenhuis reed.
that Jan to his country.house drove
a′. *?dat Jan reed naar zijn buitenhuis.
b. dat Jan de berg op reed.
that Jan the mountain onto drove
b′. *dat Jan reed de berg op.
c. dat Jan van de tafel af sprong.
that Jan from the table AF jumped
c′. *dat Jan sprong van de tafel af.

IV. R-extraction

R-extraction from directional prepositional phrases gives rise to a degraded result. This is illustrated in (32a) by means of a relative clause, in which the relative pronoun corresponds to the complement of the directional preposition *naar*; see Section 5.2.1.1, sub II for a more detailed discussion. R-extraction from postpositional phrases is excluded as well; example (32b) is allowed but strongly favors a locational reading of the adposition *op*, which shows that we are dealing with the pre-, not the postposition *op*. Example (32c) shows that R-extraction from circumpositional phrases, on the other hand, is readily possible.

(32) a. *het buitenhuis *waar* Jan *naar* reed
the country.house where Jan to drove
b. #de berg *waar* Jan *op* reed
the mountain where Jan onto drove
c. de tafel *waar* Jan *van* *af* sprong
the table where Jan from AF jumped

Example (33b) shows that (32a) becomes grammatical when the element *toe* is added, but that is not surprising in the light of the acceptability of (32c) given that we are probably dealing then with the circumposition *naar ... toe* from (33a). It is not clear whether the unacceptability of (32a) should be attributed to some (unknown) syntactic constraint or whether the acceptable example in (33b) is preferred for some reason and thus blocks realization of (32a).

(33) a. Jan reed naar het buitenhuis toe.
Jan drove to the country.house TOE
b. het buitenhuis *waar* Jan *naar* *(*toe*) reed
the country.house where Jan to TOE drove

In order to obtain a directional reading in (32b), *waar* must be replaced by the relative pronoun *die* 'that' as in (34b). This is remarkable given the fact that the relative pronoun *die* gives rise to an ungrammatical result in prepositional and circumpositional constructions like (34a&c).

(34) a. *het buitenhuis die Jan *naar* (*toe*) reed
the country.house that Jan to TOE drove
b. de berg die Jan *op* reed
the mountain that Jan onto drove
c. *de tafel die Jan *van* af sprong
the table that Jan from AF jumped

Note in passing that the judgments on the (b)-examples in (32) and (34) are somewhat idealized and actually vary somewhat among speakers. Further, there are some postpositional constructions in which the R-pronoun can also be used. Since discussing these data in detail would lead to a laborious digression, we postpone this issue to Section 5.2.2.

The acceptability of (34b) is probably related to the fact that the postposition and its nominal complement need not be adjacent: the nominal complement can be topicalized, as in (29b′) repeated below as (35a); it can be scrambled, as in (35b), and in the southern varieties of Dutch it can be separated from the postposition by incorporation of the latter into the verb cluster, as in (35c).

(35) a. De BERG reed Jan op (niet de BRUG).
the mountain drove Jan onto not the bridge
b. Jan reed de berg snel op.
Jan drove the mountain quickly onto
c. %dat Jan de berg wou op rijden.
that Jan the mountain wanted onto drive
'that Jan wanted to drive onto the mountain.'

Although the complement of the postposition seems to behave in this respect as an independent constituent, it is important to note that it is assigned case not by the verb but by the postposition. This is clear from the fact that examples like (36a) cannot be passivized; actually, the fact that verbs of traversing are °unaccusative *a priori* militates against assuming that the noun phrase *de berg* is assigned accusative case by the verb *rijden* 'to drive' in (36a).

(36) a. dat Jan de berg snel op reed.
that Jan the mountain quickly onto drove
b. *dat de berg snel werd op gereden.
that the mountain quickly was onto driven

The claim that it is the postposition *op* that assigns case to the noun phrase *de berg* is also supported by the fact that it is the located object *de auto's* 'the cars' that is assigned accusative case by the verb in the resultative construction in (37b); as expected, passivization results in promotion of the located object to subject, and not of the reference object *de berg* 'the mountain', as can be readily verified from (the lack of) number agreement between the noun phrases and the finite verb in (37b).

(37) a. dat Jan de auto's de berg op reed.
that Jan the car the mountain onto drove
'that Jan drove the car onto the maintain.'

b. dat de auto's$_{pl}$ de berg$_{sg}$ werden$_{pl}$ op gereden.
that the cars the mountain were onto driven
'that the cars were driven onto the mountain.'

4.2.1.1.4. Summary

Table 3 summarizes the discussion of the syntactic behavior of predicatively used spatial adpositional phrases in the previous subsections. Recall that the ban on scrambling of the locational PPs is lifted when the PP is contrastively focused or when the located and reference object are quantified; see the discussion of the examples in (22) and (23). R-extraction is possible from directional circumpositional phrases, but not from pre- and postpositional ones. This means that there is also a contrast between locational and directional prepositional phrases in this respect, but it is not clear whether this difference is syntactically motivated or whether some other constraint is involved; see the discussion of (32a) and (33).

Table 3: Predicatively used spatial adpositional phrases

	LOCATIONAL	DIRECTIONAL
TOPICALIZATION	+	+
SCRAMBLING	—	—
PP-OVER-V	—	—
R-EXTRACTION	+	— (pre- and postpositions) + (circumpositions)

4.2.1.2. Non-spatial constructions

Although adpositional complementive phrases are normally spatial in nature, they can sometimes also receive a non-spatial interpretation. This section will discuss a number of cases that involve (idiomatic) copular constructions in 4.2.1.2.1, the resultative construction in 4.2.1.2.2, and the *vinden*-constructions in 4.2.1.2.3.

4.2.1.2.1. The copular construction (idioms)

Non-spatial adpositional complementives are rare. The largest group by far consists of predicative prepositional phrases that denote a mental state, and therefore typically take a [+HUMAN] SUBJECT. Some examples are given in (38); see Section 1.3.3.1 and A8.4.3 for more examples. These PPs are mostly fixed, idiomatic expressions.

(38) a. Marie is in de wolken/'r sas/'r knollentuin.
Marie is in the clouds/her SAS/her vegetable.garden
'Marie is on cloud nine.'
b. Jan is van streek/over z'n toeren.
Jan is VAN STREEK/OVER his TOEREN
'Jan is distressed.'

Although they seem less numerous, there are also more or less fixed expressions that are predicated of [-HUMAN] entities. Two examples are given in (39a&b). Perhaps we can also consider the possessive *van*-PP in (39c) as a complementive.

(39) a. Die regeling is al drie jaar van kracht.
that regulation is already three years in force
'That regulation has been in effect for three years already.'
b. De voorzieningen zijn nog niet op peil.
the facilities are yet not on standard
'The facilities are still not up to the required standard.'
c. Dit boek is van Jan.
this book is of Jan
'This book belongs to Jan.'

Below, we will investigate how these non-spatial complementives behave with respect to topicalization, scrambling, PP-over-V and R-extraction.

I. Topicalization

The complementives in (38) and (39) can be topicalized, provided that the PP is assigned contrastive accent, as in (40).

(40) a. In z'n SAS is Jan.
b. Van KRACHT is die regeling al drie jaar.
c. Van JAN is dat boek.

II. Scrambling

The examples in (41) show that scrambling of the complementives in (38) and (39) is prohibited. The primed examples do not improve when the moved PP is assigned contrastive stress.

(41) a. dat Jan al de hele dag in z'n sas is.
that Jan already the whole day in his SAS is
a′. *dat Jan in z'n sas al de hele dag is.
b. dat de regeling al drie jaar van kracht is.
that the regulation already three years in force is
b′. *dat de regeling van kracht al drie jaar is.
c. dat dit boek waarschijnlijk van Jan is.
that this book probably of Jan is
c′. *dat dit boek van Jan waarschijnlijk is.

III. PP-over-V

PP-over-V of the complementives in (38) and (39) gives rise to a degraded result, just as in the case of the spatial complementives.

(42) a. dat Jan in z'n sas is.
that Jan is in his SAS
a′. *dat Jan is in z'n sas.
b. dat die regeling al drie jaar van kracht is.
that that regulation already three years in force is
b′. *dat die regeling al drie jaar is van kracht.
c. dat dit boek van Jan is.
that this book of Jan is
c′. *dat dit boek is van Jan.

IV. R-extraction

Non-spatial complementives generally do not allow R-extraction, which may be due to the idiomatic nature of these constructions, that is, to the fact that the complements of the prepositions normally do not refer to an entities in the domain of discourse. If this suggestion is on the right track, example (43a) is unacceptable because the complement of the PP, *sas*, has no denotation at all and example (43a′) is only acceptable when the complement of the PP is interpreted literally, that is, when *knollentuin* refers to some kind of garden. Something similar holds for example (43b), since the noun *kracht* has no denotation in the domain of discourse. The possessive construction in (43c) is possible due to the fact that the noun *jongen* does have a denotation.

(43) a. *de sas *waar* Jan *in* is
the SAS where Jan in is
a′. #de knollentuin *waar* Jan *in* is
the vegetable.garden where Jan in is
b. *de kracht *waar* de regeling *van* is
the force where the regulation in is
c. de jongen *waar* dit boek *van* is
the boy where this book of is
'the boy to whom this book belongs'

4.2.1.2.2. The resultative construction

This section is concerned with non-spatial adpositional resultative constructions like those given in (44). Such constructions generally involve a prepositional phrase headed by the preposition *tot* (literally "until") followed by a bare (possibly modified) noun phrase and express that, as the result of some action of the subject of the clause, the referent of the accusative argument in the clause obtains the state of having the property denoted by the nominal complement of the preposition, that is, that it obtains the state of being a knight, a chairman, or a teacher, respectively.

(44) a. De koningin slaat Els morgen tot ridder in de orde van Oranje-Nassau.
the queen hits Els tomorrow TOT knight in the order of Orange-Nassau
'The queen will knight Els tomorrow.'
b. We benoemen Marie morgen tot voorzitter van het AVT-bestuur.
we appoint Marie tomorrow TOT chairman of the AVT-board
'Tomorrow, we appoint Marie chairman of the AVT-board.'
c. We leiden onze studenten binnen een jaar tot leraar op.
we train our students within a year TOT teacher prt.
'We train our students as teachers within a year.'

In (45a), we give some more examples that involve the preposition *tot*. The resultative construction is not restricted to PPs headed by *tot*: in (45b&c), we give other potential examples involving *als*, and *in*/*te*. The discussion below will focus on the examples in (45a).

(45) a. *tot ridder slaan* 'to knight', *tot vijand maken* 'to make into an enemy', *aanstellen tot (penningmeester)* 'to appoint (treasurer)', *bekeren tot (christen)* 'to convert to Christianity', *benoemen tot (secretaris)* 'to appoint to (secretary)', *bevorderen tot (generaal)* 'promote to general', *promoveren tot doctor* 'to take the doctor degree', *tot moes stampen* 'to hit to pulp', *tot schuim kloppen* 'to whip to foam'
b. *aanstellen als* 'to appoint as', *benoemen als* 'to appoint as', *kiezen als* 'to elect as', *erkennen als* 'to recognize as'
c. *in scherven/te pletter vallen* 'to smash to smithereens', *in mootjes hakken* 'to cut into pieces'

I. Topicalization

As in the case of the spatial complementives, topicalization gives rise to a fully acceptable result, provided that the complement of the PP is assigned emphatic accent.

(46) a. Tot RIDder slaat de koningin Els morgen.
TOT knight hits the queen Els tomorrow
b. Tot VOORzitter benoemen we Marie morgen.
TOT chairman appoint we Marie tomorrow
c. Tot LEraar leiden we onze studenten binnen een jaar op.
TOT teacher train we our students within a year prt.

II. Scrambling

Scrambling is categorically blocked and, again, the non-spatial resultatives behave like the spatial ones in this respect.

(47) a. dat de koningin Els morgen tot ridder slaat.
that the queen Els tomorrow TOT knight hits
a′. *dat de koningin Els tot ridder morgen slaat.
b. dat we Marie morgen tot voorzitter benoemen.
that we Marie tomorrow TOT chairman appoint
b′. *dat we Marie tot voorzitter morgen benoemen.

c. dat we onze studenten binnen een jaar tot leraar opleiden.
   that we our students within a year TOT teacher prt.-train

c′. *dat we onze studenten tot leraar binnen een jaar opleiden.

III. PP-over-V

The question of whether non-spatial adpositional resultatives allow PP-over-V is complex. The (a)-examples in (48) suggest that PP-over-V is prohibited, but the (b)- and (c)-examples show that in the majority of cases PP-over-V is allowed.

(48) a. dat de koningin Els morgen tot ridder slaat.
   that the queen Els tomorrow TOT knight hits

a′. *dat de koningin Els morgen slaat tot ridder.

b. dat we Marie morgen tot voorzitter benoemen.
   that we Marie tomorrow TOT chairman appoint

b′. dat we Marie morgen benoemen tot voorzitter.

c. dat we onze studenten binnen een jaar tot leraar opleiden.
   that we our students within a year TOT teacher prt.-train

c′. dat we onze studenten binnen een jaar opleiden tot leraar.

This difference in acceptability of PP-over-V seems to be related to the fact that the verb in the (a)-examples is simple, whereas it is prefixed or combined with a verbal particle in the (b)- and (c)-examples. The examples in (49), which were given earlier in (25) and (26), show that in the case of locational constructions also, the addition of a particle like *neer* 'down' lifts the prohibition on PP-over-V of the PP; (49b) is only acceptable when the particle *neer* is present, and thus suggests that the difference between (48a′) and (48c′) can also be accounted for by the fact that only the latter involves a verbal particle. The acceptability of (48b′) shows that a prefixed verb like *benoemen* essentially behaves like a particle verb in this respect. For completeness' sake, (49c) shows that the locational PP resembles the PPs in (48) in that it resists scrambling.

(49) a. dat Jan het boek gisteren op de tafel (neer) legde.
   that Jan the book yesterday on the table down put
   'that Jan put the book (down) on the table yesterday.'

b. dat Jan het boek gisteren *?(neer) legde op de tafel.

c. dat Jan het boek op de tafel gisteren *?(neer) legde.

Interestingly, the verb need not be complex from a synchronic point of view given that *benoemen* in (48b) is not productively related to the verb *noemen* 'to mention/call'; the mere fact that *be-* is still recognizable as a prefix is apparently sufficient to license PP-over-V. Examples (50) and (51) give two more resultative verbs that allow PP-over-V but are (synchronically speaking) not derived by means of prefixation. For *veranderen* 'to change', this is quite clear since the verb *anderen* is not part of the present-day vocabulary (according to the *Woordenboek der Nederlandsche Taal*), it used to occur with the same meaning as non-causative *veranderen* in syntactic frames like (50a)). The doubly-primed examples show that, like the other PPs above, the PP *in een schildpad* 'into a turtle' in (50) cannot undergo scrambling.

(50) a. dat de heks gisteren in een schildpad veranderde.
that the witch yesterday into a turtle changed
a′. dat de heks gisteren veranderde in een schildpad.
a″. *dat de heks in een schildpad gisteren veranderde.
b. dat de heks de kabouter gisteren in een schildpad veranderde.
that the witch the goblin yesterday into a turtle changed
'that the witch turned the goblin into a turtle.'
b′. dat de heks de kabouter gisteren veranderde in een schildpad.
b″. *dat de heks de kabouter in een schildpad gisteren veranderde.

Semantically, the verb *herleiden (tot)* 'to reduce (to)' is only remotely related to *leiden* 'to direct' and it is therefore doubtful whether present-day speakers are still able to relate the two verbs. Scrambling of the PP is again excluded.

(51) a. dat ze het probleem gelukkig tot een misverstand konden herleiden.
that they the problem fortunately to a misconception could reduce
'that they could fortunately reduce the problem to a misconception.'
b. dat ze het probleem gelukkig konden herleiden tot een misverstand.
c. *dat ze het probleem tot een misverstand gelukkig konden herleiden.

IV. R-extraction

The examples in (52) show that R-extraction leads to a degraded or at least marked result. This may be due to the fact that the nouns denote properties and do not refer to specific entities in the domain of discourse.

(52) a. *dat de koningin hem *er* *toe* sloeg.
that the queen him there TOE hit
a′. *de waardigheid *waar* de koningin hem *toe* sloeg
the dignity where the queen him TOE hit
b. *?dat we Marie *er* *toe* benoemen.
that we Marie there TOE appoint
b′. ?de functie *waar* we Marie *toe* benoemen
the function where we Marie TOE appoint
c. *?dat we onze studenten *er* *toe* opleiden.
that we our students there TOE prt.-train
c′. ?het beroep *waar* we onze studenten *toe* opleiden
the profession where we our students TOE prt.-train

That we are dealing with a semantic and not with a syntactic constraint on R-extraction can be supported by the fact illustrated in (53) that the syntactically similar locational resultative construction with a particle verb in (49) does allow it.

(53) a. dat Jan het boek *er* gisteren *op* neer legde.
that Jan the book there yesterday on down put
'that Jan put the book down on it yesterday.'
b. de tafel *waar* Jan het boek gisteren *op* neer legde
the table where Jan the book yesterday on down put
'the table on which Jan put the book down yesterday'

Examples like (51), in which the complement of the preposition is preceded by an article and hence more likely to refer to some entity, also seems to give rise to a better result, at least in the relative clause construction in (54b).

(54) a. ?dat ze het probleem *er* gelukkig *toe* konden herleiden.
that they the problem there fortunately TOE could reduce
'that they fortunately were able to reduce the problem to it.'
b. het misverstand *waar* ze het probleem *toe* konden herleiden
the misconception where they the problem TOE could reduce
'The misconception that they were fortunately able to reduce the problem to.'

4.2.1.2.3. The vinden-*construction*

The name *vinden*-construction is, in fact, a misnomer for the constructions discussed in this section, because they do not involve the verb *vinden* 'to consider', but the verbs in (55). However, like true *vinden*-constructions like *Ik vind Marie aardig* 'I consider Marie nice', constructions headed by the verbs in (55) express a subjective evaluation by the referent of the subject of the clause. The verbs in the (a)-examples are followed by a phrase headed by *als* and those in the (b)-examples by a phrase headed by *voor*.

(55) a. *behandelen als* 'to treat as', *beschouwen als* 'to consider'
b. *aanzien voor* 'to mistake for', *houden voor* 'to look upon as', *uitmaken voor* 'to call (names)', *verslijten voor* 'to take for'

The phrases headed by *als* and *voor* take a (possibly modified) adjective, a bare noun or a noun preceded by the indefinite determiner *een* 'a' as their complement. The complement is used to denote some property attributed to the referent of the accusative argument of the clause by the referent of the subject of the clause. The number of verbs that can be used in this construction is quite limited. Some full-fledged examples are given in (56).

(56) a. Ik beschouwde hem als heel knap/(een) held.
I considered him ALS very bright/a hero
'I considered him very bright/a hero.'
b. Ze versleten Peter voor dom.
they took Peter VOOR stupid
'They took Peter for stupid.'
c. Ze zien Peter voor gek aan.
they see Peter VOOR foolish prt.
'They see Peter as foolish.'
c′. Ze zien Peter voor iemand anders/een dief aan.
they see Peter VOOR someone else/a thief prt.
'They mistake Peter for someone else/a thief.'
d. Ze maakten Marie voor leugenaar uit.
they made Marie VOOR liar prt.
'They called Marie a liar.'

It is important to note that there are various unsolved problems with the constructions in (56). First, it is not clear whether *als* should be seen as a preposition; cf. Section 1.4, sub I. Neither is it clear what determines whether the noun can or cannot be preceded by the indefinite article *een* 'a': the article optionally precedes the noun *held* in (56a), it must precede the noun *dief* in (56c′), and it cannot precede the noun *leugenaar* in (56d). The verb *verslijten* in (56b) seems to require that the property denoted by the complement of *voor* be negatively valued: **Ze versleten Peter voor slim* (intended reading: "They took Peter for a smart person"). We will ignore all these questions and leave them for future research.

Just as in the case of the non-spatial resultative constructions, the "*vinden*"-constructions are headed by prefixed verbs, as in (56a&b), or particle verbs, as in (56c&d). Note that from a synchronic point of view the prefixed verbs are not derived by means of a productive process: *beschouwen* is not perceived as being derived from *schouwen* 'to look (at)', which is archaic anyway, and neither is *verslijten* perceived as being derived from *slijten* 'to wear (out)'; the productively derived form *verslijten* means "to wear out". The following subsections will discuss the behavior of the "*vinden*"-constructions in (56) with respect to topicalization, scrambling, PP-over-V and R-extraction.

I. Topicalization

The examples in (57) show that, when the adpositional phrase is assigned emphatic accent, topicalization generally gives rise to a reasonably acceptable result in the "*vinden*"-construction.

(57) a. ?Als heel KNAP/HELD beschouwde ik hem.
b. Voor DOM versleten ze Peter.
c. Voor GEK zagen ze Peter aan.
c′. Voor iemand ANders zagen ze Peter aan.
d. Voor LEUgenaar maakten ze Marie uit.

II. Scrambling

Scrambling leads to an unacceptable result in the "*vinden*"-construction.

(58) a. Ik beschouwde hem altijd al als heel knap/held.
I considered him always already ALS very bright/hero
a′. *Ik beschouwde hem als heel knap/held altijd al.
b. Ze versleten Peter vaak voor dom.
they took Peter often VOOR stupid
b′. *Ze versleten Peter voor dom vaak.
c. Ze zagen Peter natuurlijk voor gek/iemand anders aan.
they saw Peter of.course VOOR foolish/someone else prt.
c′. *Ze zagen Peter voor gek/iemand anders natuurlijk aan.
d. Ze maakten Marie gisteren voor leugenaar uit.
they made Marie yesterday VOOR liar prt.
d. *Ze maakten Marie voor leugenaar gisteren uit.

III. PP-over-V

Since we are dealing with prefixed verbs and particle verbs, our discussion of PP-over-V in resultative constructions in Section 4.2.1.2.2 would lead us to expect that PP-over-V is acceptable. This expectation is only partly borne out; the examples in (59) show that PP-over-V is marked in the "*vinden*"-construction when the complement of the preposition is adjectival in nature.

(59) a. dat ik hem altijd al als held/heel knap beschouwde.
that I him always already ALS hero/very bright considered
a′. dat ik hem altijd al beschouwde als held/[?]heel knap.
b. dat ze Peter altijd al voor dom versleten.
that they Peter always already VOOR stupid took
b′. [??]dat ze Peter altijd al versleten voor dom.
c. dat ze Peter voor iemand anders/gek aanzagen.
that they Peter VOOR someone else/foolish prt.-saw
c′. dat ze Peter aanzagen voor iemand anders/[??]gek.
d. dat ze Marie voor leugenaar uitmaakten.
they Marie VOOR liar prt.-made
d′. dat ze Marie uitmaakten voor leugenaar.

IV. R-extraction

R-extraction seems to be excluded in the "*vinden*"-construction. In the case of *als* this is not surprising, given that it never allows stranding. In the case of *voor*, the degraded result of R-extraction may be due to the fact that its complement is not referential in nature but denotes a property. The relevant examples are given in (60); note that the examples in (60b&d) improve somewhat when *er* is replaced by the interrogative R-word *waar*.

(60) a. *Ik beschouwde hem *er* *als*.
I considered him there ALS
b. *Ze versleten Peter *er* *voor*.
they took Peter there VOOR
b′. [?]Waar versleten ze Peter voor?
where took they Peter VOOR
c. [#]Ze zagen Peter *er* *voor* aan.
they saw Peter there VOOR prt.
d. *Ze maakten Marie *er* *voor* uit.
they made Marie there VOOR prt.
d′. [?]Waar maakten ze Peter voor uit?
Where made they Peter VOOR prt.

The number sign in (60c) is used to indicate that this example is acceptable as an idiomatic construction meaning approximately "They considered Peter capable of doing such a (bad) thing". This construction also occurs in the interrogative form *Waar zie je mij voor aan?* meaning "What do you take me for?"

4.2.1.2.4. Summary

Table 4 summarizes our discussion of the predicative use of non-spatial adpositional phrases in copular, resultative and "*vinden*"-constructions. Topicalization is possible across the board, provided that the topicalized PP is assigned contrastive accent. Scrambling, on the other hand, is categorically blocked. PP-over-V is blocked with simple verbs, but allowed when the verb is prefixed or selects a verbal particle. R-extraction is normally blocked, which does not seem to be the result of some syntactic constraint but of the non-referential nature of the nominal or adjectival complements of these adpositional complementives.

Table 4: Predicatively used non-spatial adpositional phrases

	COPULAR CONSTRUCTION	RESULTATIVE CONSTRUCTION	"*VINDEN*"-CONSTRUCTION
TOPICALIZATION	+	+	+
SCRAMBLING	—	—	—
PP-OVER-V	—	— (simple verb) + (prefixed/particle verb)	— (simple verb) + (prefixed/particle verb)
R-EXTRACTION	—/+	—	—

4.2.2. Supplementives

The °supplementive use of adpositional phrases is very restricted. In traditional grammar, it is assumed that only *als*-phrases and absolute *met*-constructions are used in this function. Some examples are given in (61); the primeless examples illustrate the relation of "simultaneousness" and the primed ones the relation of "material implication".

(61) a. Als student was hij lid van de studentenvereniging.
as a student was he member of the students'.union
'When he was a student, he was a member of the students' union.'

a′. Als student kan je daar goedkoper eten.
as a student can one there cheaper eat
'If one is a student, one gets dinner cheaper there.'

b. Met krulspelden in zijn haar kwam Jan de kamer binnen.
with curlers in his hair came Jan the room into
'Jan entered the room while he had curlers in his hair.'

b′. Met krulspelden in zijn haar voelt Jan zich wat verlegen.
with curlers in his hair feels Jan REFL. somewhat embarrassed
'When Jan has curlers in his hair, he feels somewhat embarrassed.'

We may add to this that predicative PP idioms like *in de war* 'confused' and *over zijn toeren* 'upset' can also be used as supplementives, which need not surprise us given that such PP idioms behave like adjectives in many respects; cf. Section 3.3, sub I.

(62) a. Jan stond volkomen in de war op het station.
Jan stood completely confused at the station
'Totally confused, Jan stood at the station.'
b. Jan vertrok volkomen over zijn toeren.
Jan left completely OVER his TOEREN
'Jan left totally cracked up.'

Although traditional grammar analyzes the spatial adpositional phrases in (63) as adverbial phrases, it seems likely that they, too, can be used as supplementives. Example (63) is at least threefold ambiguous: it may be the case that Jan was in the garden while observing the moles, or that the moles were in the garden while being observed, or that the event of observing took place in the garden. Since the characteristic of the supplementive is that it is predicated of the subject or the direct object of the clause, we must be dealing with the supplementive use of the adpositional phrase under the first two readings of (63); only under the third reading are we dealing with an adverbially used PP.

(63) dat Jan de mollen gisteren in de tuin observeerde.
that Jan the moles yesterday in the garden observed
'that Jan observed the moles in the garden yesterday.'

The suggestion that spatial adpositional phrases may also be used as supplementives is supported by the fact that these phrases may express a relation of "material implication"; example (64) can be paraphrased as "when Jan is in school, he is always very obedient". Since, to the best of our knowledge, the contrast between the supplementive and adverbial reading of spatial adpositional phrases is not described in the literature, we will not discuss it any further.

(64) Op school is Jan altijd zeer gehoorzaam.
at school is Jan always very obedient
'When Jan is at school, he is always very obedient.'

What is extensively described in the literature is the distinction between the supplementive and the adverbial use of the *als*-phrases; cf. Haeseryn (1997). Consider the examples in (65). In (65a) we are dealing with a supplementive *als*-phrase: the example expresses that Jan's being a student and Jan's living in lodgings took place simultaneously. In (65b), on the other hand, the *als*-phrase is used as an adverbial phrase expressing a comparison: Jan is living in lodgings *as if* he were a student. The two *als*-phrases differ in that the complement of the supplementive phrase is the bare noun phrase *student*, whereas the complement of the adverbial phrase contains an indefinite article: *een student*. Furthermore, modification by the attributive adjective *echt* is only possible in the adverbial construction.

(65) a. Als (*echte) student woonde hij op kamers. [supplementive]
as true student lived he in rooms
'When he was a student, he was in lodgings.'
b. Als een (echte) student woonde hij op kamers. [adverbial]
like a true student lived he in rooms
'He lived in lodgings like a (true) student.'

Another difference between the two uses of *als*-phrases is that the complement of the supplementive phrase does not agree in number with the noun phrase it is predicated of. In order to obtain the supplementive reading in (66a), the complement of *als* must be singular, despite the fact that the noun phrase the *als*-phrase is predicated of (the subject of the clause) is plural. The complement of the adverbial phrase in (66b), on the other hand, must be plural as well.

(66) a. Als student/#studenten woonden zij op kamers. [supplementive]
as student/students lived they in rooms
'When they were students, they were in lodgings.'
b. Als studenten/*een student woonden zij op kamers. [adverbial]
like students/a student lived they in rooms
'They lived in lodgings like students.'

When the complement of the adverbial phrase denotes a collective, like *stel* 'couple' in (65), number agreement is not needed for the adverbial reading to arise. The difference between the supplementive and adverbial use of the *als*-phrase can then again be detected by the absence or presence of the indefinite article *een* 'a'.

(67) a. Als getrouwd stel leefden zij samen. [supplementive]
as married couple lived they together
'When they were a married couple they lived together.'
b. Als een getrouwd stel leefden zij samen. [adverbial]
like a married couple lived they together
'They lived together as if they were a married couple.'

The following subsections will discuss the behavior of the supplementive adpositional phrases with respect to topicalization, scrambling, PP-over-V and R-extraction.

I. Topicalization and scrambling

The primeless examples in (61) and the (a)-examples in (65) to (67) have amply illustrated that topicalization of the supplementive is possible. It is, however, difficult to decide whether scrambling of supplementives is possible, since it is not clear what the base position of the supplementive is. The only thing we know is that it is generated in some position in the middle field of the clause, which is clear from the fact that when the supplementive is not topicalized, it must follow the argument it is predicated of. In (68a), the supplementive follows both the subject and the object of the clause and it may be predicated of either of the two; the reading in which the supplementive is predicated of the object *Jan* may be the most salient one for some speakers, but example (68a′) clearly shows that an intervening object does not block the predication relation between the supplementive and the subject. In (68b), on the other hand, the supplementive precedes the object, so that it can only be predicated of the subject.

(68) a. dat ik Jan als student erg aardig vond.
that I Jan as student very nice considered
'When Jan was a student, I considered him to be very nice.'
'When I was a student, I considered Jan to be very nice.'
a′. dat ik dat boek als student erg mooi vond.
that I that book as student very beautiful considered
'When I was a student, I considered that book to be very beautiful.'
b. dat ik als student Jan erg aardig vond.
that I as student Jan very nice considered
'When I was a student, I considered Jan to be very nice.'

Since it is likely that the meaning difference between the primeless examples in (68) is related to differences in the underlying position of the supplementive phrase, it will be clear that it would be hard to establish that such phrases can be scrambled. Note that whatever the base position of the supplementive may be, it is clear that it must precede the complementive; cf. **dat ik Jan erg aardig als student vond.*

II. PP-over-V

The examples in (69) show that PP-over-V of the supplementive seems possible. Like (68c), example (69a) seems to be ambiguous between a reading in which the supplementive is predicated of the object and a reading in which it is predicated of the subject of the clause. The reading in which the supplementive is predicated of the object may again be the most salient one for some speakers, but (69b) clearly shows that an intervening object does not block the predication relation between the supplementive and the subject.

(69) a. dat ik Jan erg aardig vond als student.
that I Jan very nice considered as student
'When Jan was a student, I considered Jan to be very nice.'
'When I was a student, I considered Jan to be very nice.'
b. dat ik dat boek erg mooi vond als student.
that I that book very beautiful considered as student
'When I was a student, I considered that book to be very beautiful.'

III. R-extraction

R-extraction is excluded, but that need not surprise us given that *als* never allows it.

(70) a. dat ik Jan als student erg aardig vond.
that I Jan as student very nice considered
b. *dat ik *er* Jan *als* erg aardig vond.
that I there Jan as very nice considered

4.2.3. Absolute met*-construction*

Since the absolute *met*-construction is extensively discussed in Section 2.5.1, this section will confine itself to noting that the predicative part of the absolute *met*-construction can be a spatial PP, a PP denoting the mental state of the noun phrase in the construction, or an *als*-phrase.

(71) a. Met Jan in het doel zullen we zeker winnen.
with Jan in the goal will we certainly win
'With Jan in the goal, we will certainly win.'

b. Met Jan in zo'n goede stemming wordt het feest zeker een succes.
with Jan in such a good mood becomes the party certainly a success
'With Jan in such a good mood, the party will certainly become a success.'

c. Met Paul van Nevel als dirigent is het koor op zijn best.
with Paul van Nevel as director is the choir at its best
'With Paul van Nevel as its director, the choir is at its best.'

4.3. Attributive use of adpositional phrases

Adpositional phrases can be used attributively. This is illustrated in (72) by means of spatial adpositions. As usual the prepositional phrase *in het bos* denotes a location, and the post- and circumpositional phrases denote a direction.

(72) a. de weg in het bos [locational only]
the road in the wood
'the road in the woods'

b. de weg het bos in [directional only]
the road the wood into
'the road into the woods'

c. de weg onder de brug door
the road under the bridge DOOR
'the road that goes underneath the bridge'

Intransitive adpositions and particles do not occur, unless one cares to consider the attributively used elements in (73) as such. Note that the formations in (73b) are generally considered compounds and, in accordance with that, written as a single word: *stroomafwaarts*/*stroomopwaarts*.

(73) a. de weg omhoog/omlaag
the road upwards/downwards
'up/down the road'

b. stroom afwaarts/opwaarts
stream downwards/upwards
'down/upstream'

Attributively used adpositional phrases normally do not seem to be able to undergo topicalization, scrambling, PP-over-V or R-extraction. We will illustrate this by means of the examples in (74) with the attributively used PP *in het bos* 'in the woods'. Example (74b) is acceptable, but only when the PP is construed as an adverbial phrase: "In the woods Jan followed the road". The same thing holds for the examples in (74c&d). Example (74e) shows that R-extraction is excluded.

(74) a. dat Jan het pad in het bos volgde.
that Jan the path in the wood followed
'Jan traversed the road in the woods.'
b. #In het bos volgde Jan het pad.
in the wood followed Jan the path
c. #dat Jan in het bos het pad volgde.
d. #dat Jan het pad volgde in het bos.
e. *dat Jan *er* het pad *in* volgde.

The same thing is illustrated in (75) for a non-spatial PP. Example (75a) is ambiguous between an attributive reading (shown in the paraphrase), which expresses that the man observed by Jan has binoculars, and an adverbial reading, which expresses that Jan is using binoculars to look at the man. The attributive reading is lost in the examples in (75b-e).

(75) a. Jan zag de man met de verrekijker.
Jan saw the man with the binoculars
'Jan saw the man who carried the binoculars.'
b. #Met de verrekijker zag Jan de man.
with the binoculars saw Jan the man
c. #dat Jan met de verrekijker de man zag.
d. #dat Jan de man zag met de verrekijker.
e. #dat Jan *er* de man *mee* zag.
that Jan there the man with saw

More can be said about attributively used adpositional phrases, but for this we refer the reader to Section N3.3.1.

4.4. Adverbial use of adpositional phrases

This section is concerned with adverbially used adpositional phrases. Sections 4.4.1 and 4.4.2 provide a discussion of, respectively, spatial and temporal PPs. Section 4.4.3 concludes with a discussion of non-spatial/temporal adpositional phrases.

4.4.1. Spatial PPs

Adverbially used spatial adpositional phrases are generally prepositional. Sometimes it is not easy to determine whether a spatial PP is used adverbially or not. Example (76), for instance, is ambiguous between a reading in which the PP is used as a complementive and a reading in which it is used as an adverbial phrase.

(76) Jan springt in de sloot.
Jan jumps in/into the ditch
Complementive reading: 'Jan jumps into the ditch.'
Adverbial reading: 'Jan is jumping in the ditch.'

The two readings of (76) can be distinguished by putting the clause in the perfect tense, as in (77): when the PP acts as a complementive, the verb is unaccusative and the auxiliary *zijn* is used; when the PP is an adverbial phrase, the verb is intransitive and the auxiliary *hebben* is used. Taking the two examples in (77) as our point of departure, we can investigate the differences between the two uses of the PP.

(77) a. Jan is in de sloot gesprongen.
Jan is into the ditch jumped
Complementive reading only: 'Jan jumped into the ditch.'
b. Jan heeft in de sloot gesprongen.
Jan has in the ditch jumped
Adverbial reading only: 'Jan has jumped in the ditch.'

I. Topicalization

The two uses of the spatial PPs do not seem to differ with respect to topicalization; both (78a) and (78b) are acceptable. The examples perhaps differ in that the complementive requires contrastive accent, while this is not necessary in the case of the adverbial phrase.

(78) a. In de SLOOT is Jan gesprongen. [complementive]
into the ditch is Jan jumped
b. In de sloot heeft Jan gesprongen. [adverbial]
in the ditch has Jan jumped

II. Word order in the middle field

The examples in (79) show that a complementive PP must be left-adjacent to the verb(s) in clause-final position, whereas the adverbially used PP can occur in several positions in the middle field.

(79) • Placement with respect to the clause-final verbs
a. dat Jan vaak in de sloot sprong.
that Jan often in/into the ditch jumped
Complementive reading: 'that Jan often jumped into the ditch.'
Adverbial reading: 'that Jan often jumped in the ditch.'
b. dat Jan in de sloot vaak sprong.
that Jan in the ditch often jumped
Adverbial reading only: 'that Jan often jumped in the ditch.'

From the fact that the verb *springen* takes the auxiliary *zijn* when the PP is a complementive and the fact that complementives must be left-adjacent to the verbs in clause-final position, it correctly follows that (80a′) is excluded: the auxiliary *zijn* forces a complementive reading, so that the PP must be left-adjacent to the clause-final verbs. Since adverbial PPs can occur in other positions in the middle field, (80b′) is of course predicted to be possible.

(80) a. dat Jan vaak in de sloot is gesprongen. [complementive]
that Jan often into the ditch is jumperd
a′. *dat Jan in de sloot vaak is gesprongen.
b. dat Jan vaak in de sloot heeft gesprongen. [adverbial]
that Jan often in the ditch has jumperd
b′. dat Jan in de sloot vaak heeft gesprongen.

Note that we have avoided the use of the notion of scrambling above. The reason for this is that scrambling is generally taken to be movement across the adverbs in the clause; it is not clear whether we are dealing with movement here or whether the adverbial phrases are simply base-generated in different positions. The latter possibility is supported by the fact that there can be more than one spatial adverbial phrase in a single clause. Observe that the adverbial phrases in (81) are strictly ordered: the more general one (*in Amsterdam/de tuin*) must precede the more specific one (*bij Peter/onder de boom*).

(81) a. dat Jan in Amsterdam vaak bij Peter logeert.
that Jan in Amsterdam often with Peter stays
'that Jan often stays with Peter in Amsterdam.'
a′. *dat Jan bij Peter vaak in Amsterdam logeert.
b. dat Jan in de tuin vaak onder de boom speelt.
that Jan in the garden often under the tree plays
'that, in the garden, Jan often plays under the tree.'
b′. *dat Jan onder de boom vaak in de tuin speelt

Note that example (82a) does not refute the claim that the more general spatial phrase must precede the more specific one: example (82b) shows that these two PPs may be part of a larger constituent, in which the PP *in de tuin* functions as an attributive modifier of the noun *boom*: [$_{PP}$ *onder* [$_{NP}$ *de boom* [$_{PP}$ *in de tuin*]]].

(82) a. dat Jan onder de boom in de tuin graag speelt.
that Jan under the tree in the garden gladly plays
'that Jan likes to play under the tree in the garden.'
b. Onder de boom in de tuin speelt Jan graag.

III. PP-over-V

PP-over-V can be also used to disambiguate the two constructions in (76): when PP-over-V does not apply, as in (83a), both readings are available; when PP-over-V does apply, as in (83b), only the adverbial reading survives.

(83) a. dat Jan in de sloot sprong.
that Jan in/into the ditch jumped
Complementive reading: 'that Jan jumped into the ditch.'
Adverbial reading: 'that Jan was jumping in the ditch.'
b. dat Jan sprong in de sloot.
that Jan jumped in the ditch
Adverbial reading only: 'that Jan was jumping in the ditch.'

From the fact that the verb *springen* takes the auxiliary *zijn* when the PP is a complementive and the fact that complementives cannot be extraposed, it correctly follows that (84a′) is excluded: the auxiliary *zijn* forces a complementive reading, so that the PP must precede the clause-final verbs. Since adverbial PPs can be extraposed (84b′) is correctly predicted to be possible. This fact was noted earlier in (80), but the examples are repeated her for convenience.

(84) a. dat Jan vaak in de sloot is gesprongen. [complementive]
a′. *dat Jan in de sloot vaak is gesprongen.
b. dat Jan vaak in de sloot heeft gesprongen. [adverbial]
b′. dat Jan in de sloot vaak heeft gesprongen.

When the clause contains more than one (spatial) PP, PP-over-V reverses the order these PPs have in the middle field of the clause; cf. Koster (1974). This becomes clear by comparing the examples in (85) with those in (81). Note that example (85b) also allows an analysis in which *in de tuin* 'in the garden' is an attributive modifier of the noun *boom* 'tree'. Note further that the primed examples in (85) become acceptable when the PPs *in Amsterdam*/*onder de boom* are presented as an afterthought, in which case they must be preceded by an intonation break.

(85) a. dat Jan vaak logeert bij Peter in Amsterdam.
that Jan often stays with Peter in Amsterdam
'that Jan often stays with Peter in Amsterdam.'
a′. *dat Jan vaak logeert in Amsterdam bij Peter.
b. dat Jan vaak speelt onder de boom in de tuin.
that Jan often plays under the tree in the garden
b′. *dat Jan vaak speelt in de tuin onder de boom.

IV. R-extraction

It seems that R-extraction is not readily possible with spatial adverbial phrases. Whereas extraction of a relative R-pronoun is perfectly acceptable from the complementive PP in (86a), it leads to a marked status when applied to the spatial adverbial PP in (86b); see Section 5.3 for more discussion.

(86) a. de sloot *waar* Jan *in* is gesprongen [complementive]
the ditch where Jan into is jumped
'the ditch into which Jan jumped'
b. ??de sloot *waar* Jan *in* heeft gesprongen [adverbial]
the ditch where Jan in has jumped
'the ditch in which Jan jumped'

There are, however, many unclear cases and speakers' judgments seem to differ considerably on R-extraction from spatial adverbial clauses, especially when we are dealing with relative clauses. Some speakers find examples like (87a) quite acceptable, whereas others require pied piping of the preposition, as in (87b). Some speakers even object to both (87a) and (87b) and prefer the option of simply using the relative adverbial pro-form *waar* 'where' in (87c).

(87) a. %de tuin *waar* we een feest *in* zullen geven
the garden where we a party in will give
b. de tuin waarin we een feest zullen geven
the garden where.in we a party will give
'the garden in which we will give a party'
c. de tuin waar we een feest zullen geven
the garden where we a party will give
'the garden where we will give a party'

V. Conclusion

The previous subsections have shown that adverbially used PPs differ in various respects from complementive adpositional phrases. The differences have been summarized in Table 5. Recall from the discussion of (63) in Section 4.2.2 that spatial adpositional phrases can possibly also be used as supplementives. It seems, however, that the distinction between supplementive and adverbial adpositional phrases can only be made on the basis of their semantic relation to (the arguments of) the clause.

Table 5: Complementive versus adverbial spatial adpositional phrases

	COMPLEMENTIVES	ADVERBIAL PHRASES
TOPICALIZATION	+	+
ADJACENCY TO CLAUSE-FINAL VERBS	obligatory	not necessary
PP-OVER-V	—	+
R-EXTRACTION	+	—/?

4.4.2. Temporal PPs

Temporal adpositional phrases are generally prepositional, but there are also a limited number of temporal postpositional phrases. In (88), we give one example of each. Below we will show that these temporal adpositional phrases behave just like the adverbially used spatial PPs.

(88) a. Jan heeft Marie in de oorlog ontmoet.
Jan has Marie in the war met
'Jan met Marie during the war.'
b. Het heeft de hele dag door geregend.
it has the whole day through rained
'It has rained all day.'

I. Topicalization

The examples in (89) show that topicalization of temporal PPs is possible.

(89) a. In de oorlog heeft Jan Marie ontmoet.
in the war has Jan Marie met
b. De hele dag door heeft het geregend.
the whole day through has it rained

II. Word order in the middle field

As in the case of adverbially used spatial PPs, the notion of scrambling should be avoided because it might be the case that temporal phrases can be base-generated in different positions. This is supported by example (90a), which shows that, as in the case of the spatial PPs, the clause may contain more than one temporal PP. These temporal PPs are strictly ordered: the more general phrase *op vrijdag* 'on Friday' must precede the more specific phrase *om drie uur* 'at three o'clock'.

(90) a. dat ik op vrijdag waarschijnlijk om drie uur langs kom.
that I on Friday probably at three o'clock along come
'On Friday I will probably drop by at three o'clock.'
b. *dat ik om drie uur waarschijnlijk op vrijdag langs kom.

III. PP-over-V

PP-over-V of temporal prepositional phrases is perfectly acceptable. PP-over-V of postpositional phrases, on the other hand, seems marked. It is not clear what causes this difference.

(91) a. dat Jan Marie heeft ontmoet in de oorlog.
that Jan Marie has met in the war
b. ??dat het heeft geregend de hele dag door.
that it has rained the whole day through

When the clause contains more than one (temporal) PP, PP-over-V reverses the order the PPs have in the middle field of the clause. This becomes clear by comparing example (90) with (92). It is difficult to show that the order must be reversed, given that (92b) is also acceptable, but it seems plausible that the acceptability of this example is due to the fact that the PP *om drie uur* 'at three o'clock' can be used as an attributive modifier of the noun *vrijdag* 'Friday': cf. *Vrijdag om drie uur vertrek ik* 'I leave Friday at three o'clock'.

(92) a. dat ik waarschijnlijk langs kom om drie uur op vrijdag.
that I probably along come at three o'clock on Friday
'On Friday I will probably drop by at three o'clock.'
b. #dat ik waarschijnlijk langs kom op vrijdag om drie uur.

IV. R-extraction

R-extraction from a temporal prepositional phrase is excluded, which is not surprising given that temporal adpositions normally do not even allow the process of R-pronominalization; see Section 5.3.2.3, sub II, for some exceptions.

(93) a. dat Jan Marie in de oorlog heeft ontmoet.
that Jan Marie in the war has met
b. *dat Jan Marie *daar in* heeft ontmoet.
that Jan Marie there in has met

4.4.3. Non-spatial/temporal PPs

Non-spatial/temporal adverbial PPs like those given in (94) behave like spatial and temporal adverbial PPs: they can be topicalized and undergo PP-over-V, but they do not allow R-extraction.

(94) a. dat Jan dankzij haar hulp zijn werk kan afmaken.
that Jan thanks.to her help his work can finish
'that Jan could finish his work thanks to her help.'
b. dat de reis vanwege de kou wordt afgelast.
that the trip because.of the cold is canceled
'that the trip is canceled because of the cold.'

I. Topicalization

The examples in (95) show that topicalization of a non-spatial/temporal adverbial phrase is possible.

(95) a. Dankzij haar hulp kan Jan zijn werk afmaken.
thanks.to her help can Jan his work finish
b. Vanwege de kou wordt de reis afgelast.
because of the cold is the trip canceled

II. Word order in the middle field

As with spatial and temporal adverbial phrases, the notion of scrambling does not apply in the case of the non-spatial/temporal adverbial phrases. We can simply assume that such adverbial phrases occupy their base-position in the middle field. The word order between the adverbial phrases does, however, have an impact on the semantics of the clause. This is especially clear when a modal clause adverb like *waarschijnlijk* is involved. Consider the examples in (96).

(96) a. Jan kan waarschijnlijk dankzij haar hulp zijn werk afmaken.
Jan can probably thanks.to her help his work finish
'Jan can probably finish his work thanks to her help.'
a′. Jan kan dankzij haar hulp waarschijnlijk zijn werk afmaken.
Jan can thanks.to her help probably his work finish
'Thanks to her help Jan can probably finish his work.'
b. De reis wordt waarschijnlijk vanwege de kou afgelast.
the trip is probably because.of the cold canceled
'The trip is probably canceled because of the cold.'
b′. De reis wordt vanwege de kou waarschijnlijk afgelast.
the trip is because.of the cold probably canceled
'Because of the cold the trip is probably canceled.'

Semantically, the primeless and primed examples differ in the relative scope of the modal adverb and the adverbial PPs; the adverbial PPs are in the scope of the clause adverb in the primeless but not in primed examples. This results in the following meaning differences: (96a) expresses that Jan will finish his work and that this is probably possible thanks to her help, whereas (96a′) expresses that thanks to her help Jan will probably finish his work; (96b) expresses that the trip is canceled and that this is probably because of the cold, whereas (96b′) expresses that because of the cold the trip is likely to be canceled.

III. PP-over-V

The examples in (97) show that PP-over-V of the non-spatial/temporal PPs is possible.

(97) a. dat Jan zijn werk kan afmaken dankzij haar hulp.
that Jan his work can finish thanks.to her help
'that Jan can finish his work thanks to her help.'
b. dat de reis wordt afgelast vanwege de kou.
that the trip is canceled because.of the cold
'that the trip is canceled because of the cold.'

When two (non-spatial/temporal) PPs are strictly ordered in the middle field of the clause, the order is reversed under PP-over-V. This is illustrated in (98).

(98) a. Jan heeft wegens ziekte van de voorzitter namens de commissie gesproken.
Jan has because.of illness of the chairman in.name.of the committee spoken
'Because of the illness of the chairman Jan spoke on behalf of the committee.'
a′. *Jan heeft namens de commissie wegens ziekte van de voorzitter gesproken.
b. Jan heeft gesproken namens de commissie wegens ziekte van de voorzitter.
b′. *Jan heeft gesproken wegens ziekte van de voorzitter namens de commissie.

IV. R-extraction

R-extraction from non-spatial/temporal PPs is generally excluded, which is not surprising given that such adverbial PPs normally do not even allow the process of R-pronominalization. This is illustrated in (99).

(99) a. dat Jan dankzij haar hulp zijn werk kan afmaken.
that Jan thanks.to her help his work can finish
a′. *dat Jan *daar dankzij* zijn werk kan afmaken.
that Jan there thanks.to his work can finish
b. dat de reis vanwege de kou wordt afgelast.
that the trip because.of the cold is canceled
b′. *dat de reis *daar vanwege* wordt afgelast.
that the trip there because is canceled

There are, however, a number of PPs that are traditionally assumed to be adverbial in nature that nevertheless do allow R-extraction. An example is the instrumental *met*-PP in (100). We will return to cases like these in Section 5.2.1.3.

(100) a. Jan opende het blik met een schroevendraaier.
Jan opened the can with a screw driver
b. Jan opende *er* het blik *mee*.
Jan opened there the can with
'Jan opened the can with it.'

4.4.4. Summary

This section has discussed the syntactic properties of adverbially used adpositional phrases. It has been shown that all semantic types allow topicalization and PP-over-V, and resist R-extraction. Although the notion of "scrambling" is not relevant (or defined) for adverbial phrases, we did discuss some issues in relation to their relative order.

4.5. Bibliographical notes

There is an extensive Dutch literature on PP-complements and some articles that should be mentioned in this connection are: Van den Toorn (1971/1981), Zwaan (1972), Paardekooper (1986), Schermer-Vermeer (1988/1990), Haeseryn et al. (1997), Duinhoven (1989). Neeleman & Weerman (1999), Klooster (2001), Helmantel (2002), Loonen (2003), Broekhuis (2004/2007) and Schermer-Vermeer

(2006/2007). The complementive use of adpositional positional phrases received a lot of attention during the advent of Stowell's (1981) small clause theory: important studies are Hoekstra (1984a), Hoekstra et al. (1987), Mulder & Wehsmann (1989) and Hoekstra and Mulder (1990), and also Teun Hoekstra's paper *Small Clauses everywhere*, which was published posthumously in Hoekstra (2004).

Chapter 5
R-pronominalization and R-words

Introduction

This section is devoted to R-PRONOMINALIZATION and R-EXTRACTION. The first notion refers to pronominalization of the nominal complement of a preposition by means of a so-called R-word, which must precede the preposition. In (3) we give two examples with the R-word *er*, which will be glossed as *there* for reasons that will become clear when we discuss the examples in (6).

(1)	a.	Jan kijkt naar de film. Jan looks at the movie 'Jan is watching the movie.'	a′.	Jan kijkt ernaar. the movie there.at 'Jan is watching it.'
	b.	Jan wacht op de bus. Jan waits for the bus 'Jan is waiting for the bus.'	b′.	Jan wacht erop. Jan waits there.on 'Jan is waiting for it.'

Pronominal R-words like *er* will normally be referred to as R-PRONOUNS, although we will also use the notation [+R] pronouns when they are discussed in contrast to [-R] pronouns like *hij/hem* 'he/him'. The combination of an R-pronoun and its associate adposition will be referred to as a PRONOMINAL PP.

Table 1, which is based on the classification of the pronouns developed in Section N5.2, shows that all third person, non-anaphoric [-R] pronouns that can be used independently as arguments have a [+R] counterpart. The fact that these [+R] pronouns all contain an /r/ is responsible for their name.

Table 1: Types of R-pronouns

SUBGROUP A		[–NEUTER]	[+NEUTER]	R-PRONOUN
REFERENTIAL		*hij/zij* 'he/she'	*het* 'it'	*er* 'there'
DEMON-STRATIVE	PROXIMATE	*deze* 'that'	*dit* 'this'	*hier* 'here'
	DISTAL	*die* 'this'	*dat* 'that'	*daar* 'there'
RELATIVE		*die* 'who'	*dat* 'which'	*waar* 'where'
SUBGROUP B		[+HUMAN]	[–HUMAN]	R-PRONOUN
INTERROGATIVE		*wie* 'who'	*wat* 'what'	*waar* 'where'
QUANTIFI-CATIONAL	EXISTENTIAL (POSITIVE AND NEGATIVE)	*iemand* 'someone'	*iets* 'something'	*ergens* 'somewhere'
		niemand 'no one'	*niets* 'nothing'	*nergens* 'nowhere'
	UNIVERSAL	*iedereen* 'everyone'	*alles* 'everything'	*overal* 'everywhere'

Table 1 shows that the [-R] pronouns can be divided into four main groups by means of the features [±NEUTER] and [±HUMAN]. For the referential, demonstrative and relative pronouns (group A), the gender distinction is the most prominent one, although it must be noted that most nouns that refer to [+HUMAN] entities are [-NEUTER] as well; nouns with the feature constellation [+NEUTER] and [+HUMAN] are typically diminutives (exceptions are the noun *meisje* 'girl', which has the formal characteristics of a diminutive, the noun *kind* 'child', and a number of nouns with a negative connotation like *wijf* 'bitch of a woman' and *mens* 'person'). For the interrogative and quantificational pronouns (group B), only the distinction between [+HUMAN] and [-HUMAN] is relevant. As illustrated in (2), and to be discussed more extensively in Section 5.1, [+R] pronouns are typically, but not exclusively, used as alternative realizations of [-HUMAN] pronouns; see Table 2 in Section 5.1.7 for an overview.

(2) a. We kijken naar hem/??er naar.
we look at him/there at
'We are looking at him.'
b. We kijken er naar/*naar het.
we look there at/at it
'We are looking at it.'

In contrast to English, preposition stranding in Dutch cannot arise by extracting a full noun phrase or a regular pronoun from a prepositional phrase. This means that English constructions like (3a&b) are not possible in Dutch, as shown by the unacceptability of the primed examples in (3).

(3) a. Which book$_i$ are you looking [$_{PP}$ at t_i]?
a′. *Welk boek$_i$ kijk je [$_{PP}$ naar t_i]?
which book look you at
b. What$_i$ are you looking [$_{PP}$ at t_i]?
b′. *Wat$_i$ kijk je [$_{PP}$ naar t_i]?
what look you at

Dutch does not have so-called pseudo-passives either, which is clear from the fact that English (4a) cannot be translated in Dutch by means of (4b), but must be rendered by means of the impersonal passive construction in (4b).

(4) a. These topics$_i$ have been talked [$_{PP}$ about t_i] a lot.
b. *Deze onderwerpen$_i$ zijn veel [$_{PP}$ over t_i] gesproken.
these topics have.been a.lot about talked
b′. Er is veel over deze onderwerpen gesproken.
there has.been a.lot about these topics talked

Preposition stranding is often possible, however, when we are dealing with pronominal PPs. We will refer to this type of preposition stranding, which is illustrated in the primed examples in (5) by means of *wh*-movement of the R-word, as R-EXTRACTION. In order to indicate that the R-word and the stranded preposition form a semantic unit, we will often mark the discontinuous pronominal PP by means of italics.

(5) a. Jan kijkt naar de film.
Jan looks at the movie
'Jan is watching the movie.'
a′. *Waar* kijkt Jan *naar*?
where looks Jan at
'What is Jan looking at?'
b. Jan wacht op de bus.
Jan waits for the bus
'Jan is waiting for the bus.'
b′. *Waar* wacht Jan *op*?
where waits Jan for
'What is Jan waiting for?'

Example (6) illustrates R-extraction for all R-pronouns in Table 1. We will follow the custom in the linguistic literature to gloss the R-pronouns by means of an English spatial pro-form. This custom is due to the fact, illustrated in the primed examples, that all R-words can also be used as spatial pro-forms.

(6)

	• R-pronouns		• Spatial pro-forms
a.	Jan keer *er* zojuist *naar*. Jan looked there just now at 'Jan looked at it just now.'	a′.	Jan was er. Jan was there 'Jan was there.'
b.	Jan keek *hier/daar* goed *naar*. Jan looked here/there well at 'Jan looked at this/that well.'	b′.	Jan zat hier/daar. Jan sat here/there 'Jan was sitting here/there.'
c.	het boek *waar* ik *naar* keek the book where I at looked 'the book that I looked at'	c′.	de stad waar Jan woont the city where Jan lives 'the city where Jan is living'
d.	*Waar* keek je *naar*? what looked you at 'What did you look at?'	d′.	Waar woont Jan? where lives Jan 'Where does Jan live?'
e.	Jan keek *ergens* goed *naar*. Jan looked something well at 'Jan looked at something carefully.'	e′.	Dat boek is ergens. that book is somewhere 'That book is somewhere.'
f.	Jan keek *nergens* goed *naar*. Jan looked nothing well at 'Jan looked at nothing carefully.'	f′.	Dat boek is nergens. that book is nowhere 'That book is nowhere.'
g.	Jan keek *overal* goed *naar*. Jan looked everywhere well at 'Jan looked at everything carefully.'	g′.	de boeken liggen overal. the books lie everywhere 'The books are lying everywhere.'

To conclude this brief introduction to R-extraction, we want to discuss a potential problem for our earlier conclusion, which was based on the examples in (3) to (5), that preposition stranding is only possible with R-pronouns, viz., the observation that examples like (7a) are more or less acceptable for many speakers. In principle, there are two possible analyses for this construction. The first analysis is given in (7b) and assumes that we are dealing with preposition stranding of the English type in the sense that it is the noun phrase that has been extracted from the PP. This analysis faces the problem that it forces us to develop some independent account for the ungrammaticality of the Dutch examples in (3) and (4b). Furthermore, it is rather surprising under this analysis that the noun phrase *bananen* cannot be moved into some position in the middle field of the clause: **Ik ben bananen dol op*. The second analysis is given in (7c) and assumes that the movement involves an R-pronoun which is subsequently deleted; in essence, we are dealing with a °left dislocation construction with a deleted resumptive pronoun.

(7) a. $^{\%}$Bananen ben ik dol op.
bananas am I fond of
'Bananas I am fond of.'

b. Bananen$_i$ ben ik dol [$_{PP}$ op t_i].

c. Bananen, ~~daar~~$_i$ ben ik dol [$_{PP}$ op t_i].

The analysis in (7c) has at least four advantages. First, it is in accordance with our conclusion on the basis of the examples in (3) and (4b) that preposition stranding is only possible with R-pronouns. Second, it receives some support from the fact that the resumptive pronoun can also be overt: *Bananen, daar ben ik dol op*. Third, the (b)-examples in (8) shows that the preposition *met* must surface in its stranded form *mee*, both in the construction with and without *daar*; cf. Klooster (2001:324).

(8) a. Ik ben blij met dat cadeau.
I am happy with that present
b. Dat cadeau, daar ben ik blij mee/*met.
that present, there am I happy with/with
b′. Dat cadeau ben ik blij %mee/*met.
that present, am I happy with/with

Fourth, the analysis in (7c) does not predict the acceptability of constructions like**Ik ben bananen dol op*. And, finally, it correctly predicts that PPs that do not allow R-extraction cannot undergo the form of preposition stranding shown in (7a) either; cf. Klooster (2001:324).

(9) a. *Die dagen (*daar*) werk ik nooit *op*.
those days there work I never on
b. *Amsterdam (*daar*) woon ik niet *in*.
Amsterdam there live I not in
c. *Die manier (*daar*) doet hij het niet *op*.
that way there does he it not in

For these reasons, we will adopt the analysis in (7c) and assume that the markedness of (7a) is due to the fact that, for many speakers of Dutch, deletion of the R-pronoun is apparently not a favored option. For more discussion, see Klooster (1989), Van der Horst & Van der Horst (1999), and Van der Horst (2008).

Before we start our more comprehensive discussion of R-pronominalization and R-extraction, we want to point out that, besides its use as a spatial pro-form, the R-word *er* can also function as an expletive in impersonal passives and existential/presentational sentences like (10a&b), and as the licenser of the nominal gap *[e]* in so-called °quantitative *er* constructions like (10c).

(10) a. Er werd gedanst. [expletive]
there was danced
b. Er waren drie studenten in de tuin. [expletive]
there were three students in the garden
c. Jan heeft er [$_{NP}$ drie [*e*]] gekocht. [quantitative]
Jan has there three bought
'Jan has bought three [e.g., books].'

Realizing that *er* can perform more than one function is important because one occurrence of *er* can occasionally express more than one of these functions at the same time. In (11b), for example, *er* simultaneously performs the function of expletive, licenser of the nominal gap in the noun phrase remnant that corresponds to *drie sigaren* in (11a), and the complement of the stranded preposition *in*. We will discuss examples like these more extensively in Section 5.5.3.

(11) a. Gisteren zaten er nog drie sigaren in de doos.
yesterday sat there still three cigars in the box
'Yesterday, there were still three cigars in the box.'

b. Gisteren zaten *er* nog [$_{NP}$ drie [*e*]] *in*.
yesterday sat there still three in
'Yesterday, there were still three in it.'

This chapter is organized as follows. Sections 5.1 through 5.3 will discuss the restrictions on R-pronominalization and R-extraction: Section 5.1 starts by discussing the semantic restriction that, in the general case, the R-pronoun refers to a [-HUMAN] entity; Section 5.2 continues with the lexical restrictions on the adpositions, e.g., that locational but not temporal prepositions can readily be part of a pronominal PP; Section 5.3 concludes with the discussion of a number of syntactic conditions on R-extraction. Section 5.4 provides some examples of idiomatic constructions containing pronominal PPs, and Section 5.5 finally, explores a domain that goes slightly beyond the discussion of R-pronominalization and R-extraction by discussing the co-occurrence restrictions on the R-words in (6) and (10) as well as *er*'s ability, illustrated in (11b), to simultaneously perform more than one function.

5.1. [-HUMAN] restriction on the formation of pronominal PPs

Dutch pronominal PPs have the same semantic value as prepositions followed by a pronoun in English. For example, English P + *it* would typically be translated by means of *er* + P in Dutch. This does not mean that all English P + pronoun combinations can or must be translated by means of a pronominal PP in Dutch. The discussion below will show that the formation of a pronominal PP is often blocked when the antecedent of the pronoun is [+HUMAN] (and the same may hold for pronouns referring to pets). A typical case is given in (12): whereas the pronoun *hem* in (12a) may refer to the [+HUMAN] antecedent, the R-pronoun in (12b) typically refers to a [-HUMAN] antecedent, that is, the music by Bach. Since the various functional/semantic types of pronouns differ with respect to the [-HUMAN] restriction, we will discuss them in separate sections.

(12) a. Bach, ik ben dol op hem.
Bach I am fond of him
'Bach, I am fond of him.'

b. Bach, ik ben er dol op.
Bach I am there fond of
'Bach, I am fond of it.'

5.1.1. Referential (personal) R-pronouns

Whether a pronominal PP can arise often depends on whether the complement of the preposition is [+HUMAN] or [-HUMAN]. This is especially clear in the case of referential personal pronouns. Resumptive pronoun constructions of the type in (13) make it possible to test the restrictions on the co-occurrence of certain types of antecedents and the R-pronoun.

(13) a. *NP*, ik ben dol op *pronoun*.
NP I am fond of pronoun
'NP, I am fond of *pronoun*.'
b. *NP*, ik ben *er* dol *op*.
NP I am there fond of
'NP, I am fond of *pronoun*.'

For completeness' sake, note that the resumptive pronoun *er* must appear in its phonetically strong form *daar* when it is placed in clause-initial position, as in (14).

(14) *NP*, *daar*/**er* ben ik dol *op*.
NP there am I fond of

This may be due to the fact that (with the exception of subject pronouns and the expletive *er*) phonetically weak elements cannot be placed in clause-initial position; the difference between (13b) and (14) is therefore similar in nature to the difference between the two examples in (15). We refer the reader to Section N5.2.1.1.5, sub II, for more detailed discussion.

(15) a. Jan, ik heb 'm niet gezien.
Jan I have him not seen
'Jan, I haven't seen him.'
b. Jan, die/hem/*'m heb ik niet gezien.
Jan him have I not seen

We will discuss the behavior of [-HUMAN] and [+HUMAN] referential pronouns with respect to the resumptive pronoun test in separate subsections.

I. [-HUMAN] pronouns

This subsection discusses the [-HUMAN] personal pronouns. The singular and plural forms are discussed in separate subsections. Note that we use the weak forms of the personal pronouns in the examples below, because strong pronouns normally can only be used to refer to [+HUMAN] antecedents; cf. Section N5.2.1.1,5 sub III.

A. Singular [-HUMAN] pronouns

When a singular [-HUMAN] pronoun occurs as the complement of a preposition, the PP is obligatorily realized as a pronominal PP; this is indicated in (16a) by placing an asterisk in front of the P + pronoun sequence. The (b)- and (c)-examples show that a pronominal PP must appear in the resumptive pronoun constructions, regardless of the gender of the pronoun's antecedent.

(16) • Singular [±NEUTER][-HUMAN] pronouns
a. *P + 't/'m/'r ⇒ er +P
P + it there + P
b. *Dat boek, ik ben dol op 't.
that book$_{[+neuter]}$ I am fond of it
b′. Dat boek, ik ben *er* dol *op*.
that book$_{[+neuter]}$ I am there fond of
'That book, I am fond of it.'

c. *Die soep, ik ben dol op 'r.
that soup$_{\text{[-neuter]}}$ I am fond of her
c′. Die soep, ik ben *er* dol *op*.
that soup$_{\text{[-neuter]}}$ I am there fond of
'That soup, I am fond of it.'

B. Plural [-HUMAN] pronouns

The plural [-HUMAN] pronoun *ze* 'them' cannot occur as the complement of a preposition either, regardless of the gender of the pronoun's antecedent. We illustrate this in the (b)- and (c)-examples in (17) by means of the [+NEUTER] noun *boeken* 'books' and the [-NEUTER] noun *chocoladerepen* 'chocolate bars'.

(17) • Plural [–HUMAN] pronouns
a. *P + ze ⇒ er + op
P + them there + on
b. *?Die boeken, ik ben dol op ze.
those books$_{\text{[+neuter]}}$ I am fond of them
b′. Die boeken, ik ben *er* dol *op*.
those books$_{\text{[+neuter]}}$ I am there fond of
'Those books, I am fond of them.'
c. *?Die chocoladerepen, ik ben dol op ze.
those chocolate bars$_{\text{[-neuter]}}$ I am fond of them
c′. Die chocoladerepen, ik ben *er* dol *op*.
those chocolate bars$_{\text{[-neuter]}}$ I am there fond of
'Those chocolate bars, I am fond of them.'

Section 5.2 will show that some prepositions do not allow R-pronominalization. Since the [-HUMAN] restriction also holds for such prepositions, [-HUMAN] noun phrases can never be pronominalized in PPs headed by such prepositions. Example (18) illustrates this for the preposition *volgens*.

(18) a. Volgens Jan/het weerbericht gaat het vandaag regenen.
according.to Jan/the weather.forecast goes it today rain
b. Volgens hem/*'t gaat het vandaag regenen.
according.to him/it goes it today rain
c. *Er volgens gaat het vandaag regenen.
there according.to him/it goes it today rain

II. [+HUMAN] pronouns

This section discusses the [+HUMAN] personal pronouns. The singular and plural forms are again discussed in separate subsections.

A. Singular [+HUMAN] pronouns

A [+HUMAN] pronoun like *hem* 'him' or *haar* 'her' is perfectly acceptable as the complement of a preposition. The alternative realization as a pronominal PP is possible but slightly marked. This is due to a general preference to interpret the pronominal PP *er op* as involving a [-HUMAN] entity; only when the antecedent is explicitly mentioned in the discourse is a [+HUMAN] interpretation of the R-pronoun available.

(19) • Singular [-NEUTER][+HUMAN] pronouns
a. P + hem/haar⇒ ^(?^er + P
P + him/her there + P
b. Mijn echtgenoot, ik ben dol op hem.
my husband I am fond of him
'My husband, I am fond of him.'
b′. ^(?)^Mijn echtgenoot, ik ben *er* dol *op*.
my husband I am there fond of

Although judgments are subtle, it might be the case that a kind of scale is involved: for at least some people, the pronominal PP *er op* is close to perfect in examples like (19b′), where the antecedent has some intrinsic relation to the speaker, but marked when it involves some other [+HUMAN] entity, as in (20a). The pronominal PP *er op* seems to be excluded when the antecedent of the R-pronoun is referred to by means of a proper noun, as in (20b).

(20) a. Die jongen, ik ben dol op hem.
that boy I am fond of him
'That boy, I am fond of him.'
a′. ^?^Die jongen, ik ben *er* dol *op*.
that boy I am there fond of
'That boy, I am fond of him.'
b. Jan, ik ben dol op hem.
Jan I am fond of him
'Jan, I am fond of him.'
b′. *Jan, ik ben *er* dol *op*.
Jan I am there fond of
'Jan, I am fond of him.'

In contrast to the non-neuter pronouns in (19), the neuter pronoun *het* in (21) must also be replaced by an R-pronoun when it refers to a [+HUMAN] entity, which suggests that it is not the feature [±HUMAN] that is relevant here, but gender: prepositions simply cannot be followed by the pronoun *het*.

(21) • Singular [+NEUTER][+HUMAN] pronoun
a. *P + het ⇒ er + P
P + it there + P
b. *Dat kind, ik ben dol op het.
that child$_{[+neuter]}$ I am fond of it
b′. Dat kind, ik ben *er* dol *op*.
that child$_{[+neuter]}$ I am there fond of
'That child, I am fond of it.'

Note that in examples like these, grammatical gender can be overruled by sex. This will be clear from example (22a), in which the [+NEUTER] noun *meisje* 'girl' refers to a young female person and the [-R] pronoun used is not the neuter form *het* 'it' but the feminine form *haar* 'her'.

(22) a. Dat meisje, ik ben dol op haar/*het.
that $\text{girl}_{[+\text{neuter}]}$ I am fond of her/it
b. Dat meisje, ik ben *er* dol *op*.
that $\text{girl}_{[+\text{neuter}]}$ I am there fond of
'That girl, I am fond of her.'

B. Plural [+HUMAN] pronouns

The phonetically weak and strong plural third person [+HUMAN] pronouns, *ze* 'them' and *hen* 'them' can both appear as the complement of a preposition, and the use of a pronominal PP is somewhat marked.

(23) • Plural [+HUMAN] pronouns
a. P + hen/ze ⇒ $^{(?)}$er + P
P + them there + P
b. Mijn dochters, ik ben dol op ze/hen.
my daughters I am fond of them
'My daughters, I am fond of them.'
b′. $^{(?)}$Mijn dochters, ik ben *er* dol *op*.
my daughters I am there fond of

As in the case of the singular [+HUMAN] pronouns, some scale may be involved: for at least some speakers, the pronominal PP *er op* is close to perfect in examples like (23b′), where the antecedent has some intrinsic relation to the speaker, but marked when it involves some other [+HUMAN] entity, as in (24a). The pronominal PP *er op* is excluded when the antecedent of the R-pronoun is referred to by means of a proper noun, as in (24b).

(24) a. Die jongens, ik ben dol op ze.
those boys I am fond of them
'Those boys, I am fond of them.'
a′. $^{?}$Die jongens, ik ben *er* dol *op*.
those boys I am there fond of
b. Jan en Marie, ik ben dol op ze/hen.
Jan and Marie I am fond of them
b′. *Jan en Marie, ik ben *er* dol *op*.
Jan and Marie I am there fond of

The examples in (25), which should be compared to the (a)-examples in (24), show, however, that pronominal PPs are fully acceptable in generic constructions with bare plurals. Example (25b) in fact sounds more natural than example (25a).

(25) a. $^{?}$Jongens, ik ben dol op ze.
$\text{boys}_{[-\text{neuter}]}$ I am fond of them
b. Jongens, ik ben *er* dol *op*.
$\text{boys}_{[-\text{neuter}]}$ I am there fond of
'Boys, I am fond of them.'

Although (16) and (21) have shown that the neuter pronoun *het* can never appear as the complement of a preposition, the primeless examples in (26) show that its plural counterpart *ze* can. From this we must conclude that it is only the singular [+NEUTER] pronoun *het* 'it' that is excluded as a complement of a preposition, not its plural counterpart *ze* 'them'. This is not so surprising given that the feature [±NEUTER] normally does not play a role in the plural and the pronoun *ze* can therefore be said to simply lack this feature.

(26) • Plural [+HUMAN] pronouns
a. Die kinderen, ik ben dol op ze.
that children$_{[+neuter]}$ I am fond of them
'Those children, I am fond of them.'
a′. (?)Die kinderen, ik ben *er* dol *op*.
that children$_{[+neuter]}$ I am there fond of
b. Die meisjes, ik ben dol op ze.
those girls$_{[+neuter]}$ I am fond of them
'Those girls, I am fond of them.'
b′. (?)Die meisjes, ik ben *er* dol *op*.
those girls$_{[+neuter]}$ I am there fond of

5.1.2. Demonstrative R-pronouns

The demonstrative R-pronouns *daar* 'there' and *hier* 'here' from Table 1 are also preferably interpreted as referring to [-HUMAN] antecedents. Examples like (27a) are perfectly natural when the speaker refers to some object, but distinctly odd when used to refer to a certain person. Example (27b) shows again that pronominal PPs are acceptable in generic constructions with [+HUMAN] bare plural antecedents.

(27) a. Die snoepjes/?die jongens, ik ben *daar* dol *op*.
those sweets/those boys I am there fond of
'I am fond of that.'
b. Snoepjes/Jongens, ik ben *daar* dol *op*.
sweets/boys I am there fond of

Although this is perfectly possible in subject or object position, demonstrative pronouns are at least marked when used as an independent argument (= without an accompanying noun) in the complement position of a preposition.

(28) a. Ik ben dol op deze/die ??(plaat/jongen).
I am fond of that/this record/boy
b. Ik ben dol op dit/dat *?(boek/meisje).
I am fond of that/this book/girl

5.1.3. Relative R-pronouns

The examples in (29) show that relative pronouns with a [+HUMAN] antecedent can be realized both as regular relative personal pronouns and as relative R-pronouns. Despite the fact that normative grammars are generally opposed to (29b), it is this form that is normally found in colloquial speech. Observe that the preposition must be pied piped by the [-R] pronoun, whereas preposition stranding is possible and even slightly better in the case of an [+R] pronoun. This confirms again that preposition stranding is possible with R-pronouns only; cf. example (3).

(29) a. de jongen op wie ik wacht
the boy for whom I wait
'the boy I am waiting for'
a′. *de jongen wie ik op wacht
b. (?)de jongen waarop ik wacht
the boy where.for I wait
'the boy I am waiting for'
b′. de jongen *waar* ik *op* wacht

The examples in (30) show that the formation of a pronominal PP is obligatory when the antecedent of the relative pronoun is [-HUMAN]. This shows that the relative pronouns *die*/*dat* cannot occur as the complement of a preposition.

(30) a. *de brief$_{[\text{-neuter}]}$ op die ik wacht
the letter for which I wait
a′. de brief *waar* ik *op* wacht
the letter where I for wait
'the letter I am waiting for'
b. *het boek$_{[\text{+neuter}]}$ op dat ik wacht
the book for which I wait
b′. de boek *waar* ik *op* wacht
the book where I for wait
'the book I am waiting for'

5.1.4. Interrogative R-pronouns

Interrogative pronominal PPs can only be used when the preposition has a [-HUMAN] complement. A speaker who knows that Jan is waiting for a person will not use the construction in (31b); this construction can only be used when the speaker expects that the answer will involve a [-HUMAN] entity, or when he has no expectation at all. The primed examples show that preposition stranding is excluded with the [-R] pronoun *wie* but fully acceptable, and even preferred, with the corresponding [+R] pronoun. From this we may again conclude that preposition stranding is possible with R-pronouns only.

(31) a. Op wie wacht je?
for who wait you
'For whom are you waiting?'
a′. #Wie wacht je op?
b. ?Waarop wacht je?
where.for wait you
'What are you waiting for?'
b′. *Waar* wacht je *op*?

The examples in (32) show that the formation of a pronominal PP is strongly preferred when the speaker expects that the answer will involve a [-HUMAN] entity; examples like (32a) are only acceptable as echo-questions.

(32) a. #Op wat wacht je?
for what wait you
b. *Waar* wacht je *op*?
where wait you for
'What are you waiting for?'

5.1.5. *Existentially quantified R-pronouns*

Existentially quantified R-pronouns also refer strictly to [-HUMAN] entities. A speaker who uses (33b) expresses that the thing he is waiting for is not a [+HUMAN] entity. Something similar holds for the negative counterpart of this R-pronoun in (33b′).

(33) a. Ik wacht op iemand.
I wait for someone
'I am waiting for someone.'
a′. Ik wacht op niemand.
I wait for no.one
'I am waiting for no one.'
b. Ik wacht *ergens* *op*.
I wait somewhere for
'I am waiting for something.'
b′. Ik wacht *nergens* *op*.
I wait nowhere for
'I am not waiting for anything.'

It seems that, when the existentially quantified pronoun refers to a [-HUMAN] entity, the formation of the pronominal PP is more or less optional. This is shown in (34).

(34) a. Ik wacht op iets.
I wait for something
'I am waiting for something.'
a′. Ik wacht *ergens* *op*.
I wait somewhere for
'I am waiting for something.'
b. Ik wacht op niets.
I wait for nothing
'I am not waiting for anything.'
b′. Ik wacht *nergens* *op*.
I wait nowhere/somewhere for
'I am not waiting for anything.'

When the complement of the preposition expresses sentence negation, it must be moved to a certain position in the °middle field of the clause. This is clear from the fact that the PP-complement of the adjective in (35a) cannot occupy its regular postadjectival position but must precede the adjective; cf. Section A2.3.1.2, sub IIB. The contrast between (35a′) and (35b′) shows that preposition stranding is possible (or, rather, obligatory) with the R-pronoun only. This again confirms our earlier claim that preposition stranding is restricted to R-pronouns.

(35) a. dat Jan [op niemand]$_i$ erg dol t_i is.
that Jan of no.one very fond is
'that Jan isn't very fond of anyone.'
a′. *dat Jan niemand$_i$ erg dol [op t_i] is.
b. *dat Jan [nergens op]$_i$ erg dol t_i is.
b′. dat Jan *nergens*$_i$ erg dol [*op* t_i] is.
that Jan nowhere very fond of is
'that Jan isn't very fond of anythin g.'

5.1.6. Universally quantified R-pronouns

In the case of universally quantified pronouns, pronominal PPs also refer strictly to [-HUMAN] entities. A speaker who uses (36b) expresses that the things the doctor is going to look at are not [+HUMAN] entities. So, (36a) can be used to express that the doctor will examine all patients, whereas (36b) expresses that the doctor will examine the patient(s) thoroughly.

(36) a. De dokter zal naar iedereen kijken.
the doctor will at everyone look
'The doctor will examine everyone.'
b. De dokter zal *overal* *naar* kijken.
the doctor will everywhere at look
'The doctor will examine everything.'

The examples in (37) show that, as in the case of the existentially quantified pronouns, the formation of the pronominal PP is more or less optional when the universally quantified pronoun refers to a [-HUMAN] entity.

(37) a. De dokter kijkt naar alles.
the doctor looks at everything
'The doctor examines everything.'
b. De dokter kijkt *overal* *naar*.
the doctor looks everywhere at
'The doctor examines everything.'

5.1.7. Summary

This section has shown that [+HUMAN] pronouns normally do not readily allow R-pronominalization, although two exceptions are attested. First, although non-neuter referential personal pronouns only marginally allow it, R-pronominalization of neuter pronouns is readily possible and even obligatory when the neuter pronoun is singular. Second, R-pronominalization of [+HUMAN] relative pronouns seems to be the preferred option in colloquial speech. R-pronominalization of [-HUMAN] pronouns, on the other hand, is normally obligatory; only the (existentially and universally) quantified pronouns behave differently in this respect. The discussion from the previous sections is summarized in Table 2, in which P stands for the preposition in question.

Table 2: Regular and pronominal PPs and the feature [±HUMAN]

			+HUMAN		-HUMAN	
			P + PRONOUN	PRONOMINAL PP	P + PRONOUN	PRONOMINAL PP
REFERENTIAL	SINGULAR	NON-NEUTER	✓P hem/haar ‘P him/her’	?er P	*P hem/haar ‘P it’	✓er P
		NEUTER	*P het ‘P it’	✓er P	*P het ‘P it’	✓er P
	PLURAL	NON-NEUTER	✓P ze/hen ‘P them’	?er P	*P ze ‘P them’	✓er P
		NEUTER	✓P ze/hen ‘P them’	✓er P	*P ze ‘P them’	✓er P
DEMON-STRATIVE	PROXI-MATE		??P deze/dit ‘P this’	*hier P	*P deze/dit ‘P this’	✓hier P
	DISTAL		??P die/dat ‘P that’	*daar P	*P die/dat ‘P that’	✓daar P
RELATIVE			✓P wie ‘P whom’	✓waar P	*P wat ‘P which’	✓waar P
INTERROGATIVE			✓P wie ‘P whom’	*waar P	*P wat ‘P what’	✓waar P
EXIS-TENTIAL	POSITIVE		✓P iemand ‘P someone’	*ergens P	✓P iets ‘P something’	✓ergens P
	NEGATIVE		✓P niemand ‘P no one’	*nergens P	✓P niets ‘P nothing’	✓nergens P
UNIVERSAL			✓P iedereen ‘P everyone’	*overal P	✓P alles ‘P everything’	✓overal P

5.2. Lexical restrictions on the formation of pronominal PPs

Apart from the [-HUMAN] restriction on the R-pronominalization, there are several additional restrictions that are related to the lexical properties of the adpositions heading the PPs. In order to license the formation of a pronominal adpositional phrase, the adposition must be able to take a nominal complement. This means that only pre-, post- and circumpositions are eligible for it: intransitive prepositions and particles do not take a complement. This does not mean, however, that all adpositions taking a complement can undergo R-pronominalization. The following sections will discuss the restrictions that hold for pre-, post- and circumpositions, respectively.

5.2.1. Prepositions

This section discusses the restrictions on R-pronominalization of prepositional phrases. We start with a discussion of spatial PPs in Section 5.2.1.1, which is followed by a discussion of temporal PPs in Section 5.2.1.2. We conclude with a discussion of non-spatial/temporal PPs in Section 5.2.1.3.

5.2.1.1. Spatial prepositions

Subsections I and II will discuss R-pronominalization of, respectively, locational and directional prepositional phrases. We will show that R-pronominalization is a fairly productive process for locational PPs; virtually all locational PPs have a pronominal counterpart. Directional PPs, on the other hand, generally seem unable to undergo this pronominalization process.

I. Locational prepositional phrases

Chapter 1 has shown that locational PPs typically occur in the complement of the verbs of location in (38a) and the verbs of change of location in (38b). We can therefore test whether locational PPs can be replaced by a pronominal PP by placing the pronominal form in the frames *NP Vloc PP* and *NP Vloc NP PP*.

(38) a. Verbs of location (monadic: NP V_{loc} PP):
hangen 'to hang', *liggen* 'to lie', *staan* 'to stand', *zitten* 'to sit'
b. Verbs of change of location (dyadic: NP V_{loc} NP PP):
hangen 'to hang', *leggen* 'to lay', *zetten* 'to put'

A. Deictic and inherent prepositions

A PP headed by a deictic or an inherent preposition can always be replaced by a pronominal PP. In (39), we give an example for all deictic/inherent prepositions from Table 17 in Section 1.3.1.2.4. Note that for many speakers the pronominal form *er tegen* in (39g′) seems less preferred than the form *er tegen aan* which is formed on the basis of the circumpositional phrase *tegen de muur aan*.

(39) a. De auto staat voor/achter/naast/tegenover de kerk.
the car stands in.front.of/behind/next.to/opposite the church
a′. De auto staat er voor/achter/naast/tegenover.
b. Het huis staat net binnen/buiten de stadsgrens.
the house stands just within/outside the city border
b′. Het huis staat er net binnen/buiten.
c. De huizen staan vlak bij/langs de rivier.
the houses stand just near/along the river
c′. De huizen staan er vlak bij/langs.
d. De naald steekt in/uit/door het speldenkussen.
the needle sticks in/out.of/through the pincushion
d′. De naald steekt er in/uit/door.
e. Het amulet hangt aan een kettinkje.
the amulet hangs on a necklace
e′. Het amulet hangt er aan.
f. Het kleed ligt op/over de tafel.
the cloth lies on/over the table
f′. Het kleed ligt er op/over.
g. De ladder staat tegen de muur (aan).
the ladder stands against the wall AAN
g′. De ladder staat er tegen ??(aan).

The examples in (39) all involve locational verbs, but the results with verbs denoting a change of location are exactly the same. This is shown in the examples in (40), which provide the change of location counterparts of the primed examples in (39).

(40) a. Jan zet de auto er voor/achter/naast/tegenover.
Jan puts the car there in.front.of/behind/next.to/opposite
b. De architect zet het huis er net binnen/buiten.
the architect puts the house there just within/outside
c. De architect zet de huizen er vlak bij/langs.
the architect puts the houses there just near/along
d. Jan steekt de naald er in/uit/door.
Jan sticks the needle there in/out.of/through
e. Jan hangt het amulet er aan.
Jan hangs the amulet there on
f. Jan legt het kleed er op/over.
Jan puts the cloth there on/over
g. Jan zet de ladder er tegen ??(aan).
Jan puts the ladder there against AAN

B. Absolute prepositions

The absolute prepositions from Table 17 in Section 1.3.1.2.4 show mixed behavior. The prepositions *boven* 'above', *onder* 'under' and *tussen* 'between' can readily be part of a pronominal PP.

(41) a. De lamp hangt boven de tafel.
the lamp hangs above the table
a′. De lamp hangt er boven.
b. De brief ligt onder/tussen die papieren.
the letter lies under/between those papers
b′. De brief ligt er onder/tussen.

However, R-pronominalization seems more problematic in the case of *om/rond* 'around'; the pronominal form *er om heen*, which is based on the circumposition *om ... heen* 'around', is much preferred over the form *er om*; judgments on the acceptability of *er rond* seem to vary, but to us this form seems degraded. With the compound *rondom* 'around', on the other hand, the result of R-pronominalization seems a bit formal but acceptable.

(42) a. De meisjes staan om het kampvuur (heen).
the girls stand around the campfire HEEN
a′. De meisjes staan er om ??(heen).
b. De meisjes staan rond het kampvuur.
the girls stand around the campfire
b′. %De meisjes staan er rond.
c. De meisjes staan rondom het kampvuur.
the girls stand around the campfire
c′. De meisjes staan er rondom.

The examples in (41) and (42) all involve locational verbs but the results with verbs denoting a change of location are exactly the same. This is shown in (43) and (44), which give the change of location counterparts of the primed examples in (41) and (42).

(43) a. Jan hangt de lamp er boven.
Jan hangs the lamp there above

b. Jan legt de brief er onder/tussen.
Jan puts the letter there under/between

(44) a. Marie zet de meisjes er om ??(heen).
Marie puts the girls there around HEEN

b. %Marie zet de meisjes er rond.
Marie puts the girls there around

c. Marie zet de meisjes er rondom.
Marie puts the girls there around

II. Directional prepositional phrases

Directional PPs typically occur in the complement of verbs of traversing, as in (45a). These verbs differ from the corresponding activity verbs by not taking the auxiliary *hebben* 'to have' in the perfect tense, but the auxiliary *zijn* 'to be'. We can therefore test whether a directional PP can be replaced by a pronominal PP by placing the pronominal form in the PP-position in frame (45b).

(45) a. Verbs of traversing: *rijden* 'to drive', *fietsen* 'to cycle', *wandelen* 'to walk', etc.

b. Marie is PP gereden/gefietst/gewandeld.
Marie is PP driven/cycled/walked

It seems that most directional PPs from Table 17 in Section 1.3.1.2.4 cannot be part of a pronominal PP. This is illustrated for the directional preposition *naar* 'to' in the (a)-examples in (46); the (b)-examples show that a pronominal PP based on the directional circumposition *naar ... toe* is much preferred.

(46) a. Marie is helemaal naar Groningen gewandeld.
Marie is completely to Groningen walked

a′. *Marie is *er* helemaal *naar* gewandeld.
Marie is there completely to walked

b. Marie is helemaal naar Groningen toe gewandeld.
Marie is completely to Groningen TOE walked

b′. Marie is *er* helemaal *naar toe* gewandeld.
Marie is there completely to TOE walked

A similar contrast, with perhaps slightly less absolute judgments, can be observed in (47) with the directional preposition *over* 'across' and the directional circumposition *over ...heen* 'across'.

(47) a. Marie is over de brug gefietst.
Marie is over the bridge cycled
a′. ??Marie is *er* *over* gefietst.
Marie is there over cycled
b. Marie is over de brug heen gefietst.
Marie is over the bridge HEEN cycled
b′. Marie is *er* *over heen* gefietst.
Marie is there over HEEN cycled

Note in passing that the directional prepositions *naar* and *over* differ sharply in this respect from the functional prepositions *naar* and *over* in (48), which can readily occur as part of pronominal PPs.

(48) a. Marie keek naar de schilderijen.
Marie looked at the paintings
a′. Marie keek *er* *naar*.
Marie looked there at
b. Zij hebben urenlang over dat probleem gedebatteerd.
they have for.hours about that problem debated
b′. Zij hebben *er* urenlang *over* gedebatteerd.
they have there for.hours about debated

Like *naar* and *over*, the directional prepositions *van* 'from' and *via* 'via' do not allow the formation of a pronominal PP, and in this case no circumpositional variant is possible either.

(49) a. Marie is van/via Utrecht (naar Groningen) gereden.
Marie is from/via Utrecht to Groningen driven
b. *Marie is *er* *van/via* (naar Groningen) gereden.
Marie is there from/via to Groningen driven

At first sight, the directional preposition *voorbij* 'past' in (50) does seem to be able to occur in a pronominal PP, but we probably have to put this example aside as irrelevant; the fact that the R-pronoun *hier* 'here' can be dropped indicates that it does not act as the complement of the preposition *voorbij* but as an independent adverbial phrase, so that *voorbij* is actually an intransitive preposition or a verbal particle in this example.

(50) Marie is (hier) een momentje geleden voorbij gereden.
Marie is there a moment ago past driven

The prepositions *langs* 'along' and *door* 'through', which can be used both as locational PPs and as directional PPs, seem to allow R-pronominalization not only in the locational constructions in (39c&d), but also in the directional constructions in (51). Note that the use of the pronominal PP *er door* in (51b′) has more or less the same degree of acceptability as the use of the pronominal circumpositional phrase *er door heen*.

(51) a. Marie is gisteren langs het kanaal gereden.
Marie is yesterday along the canal driven
a′. Marie is er gisteren langs gereden.
Marie is there yesterday along driven
b. Marie is twee keer door de tunnel (heen) gefietst.
Marie is two times through the tunnel HEEN cycled
b′. Marie is er twee keer door (heen) gefietst.
Marie is there two times through HEEN cycled

5.2.1.2. Temporal prepositions

The formation of pronominal PPs with the temporal prepositions from Table 25 in Section 1.3.2.1, sub I, is very restricted. Only the prepositions *voor* 'before' and *na* 'after' seem to allow it. This is illustrated in (52).

(52) a. Jan moest voor/na de vergadering telefoneren.
Jan must before/after the meeting phone
'Jan had to make a phone call before/after the meeting.'
b. Jan moest er voor/na telefoneren.
Jan must there before/after phone
'Jan had to make a phone call before/after it.'

The other temporal prepositions in (53) categorically resist the formation of pronominal PPs. For completeness' sake, note that the pronominal PP *er tussen* in (53e) is acceptable when it is interpreted locationally, and that *er ... vanaf* in (53f) is possible as a locational pronominal circumpositional phrase. The last column of the table shows that the restriction that the complement of a preposition cannot be a [-HUMAN] pronoun also holds. This means that pronominalization of the complement of these temporal prepositions is completely impossible.

(53) Pronominalization of/in temporal PPs

	EXAMPLE	PRONOMINAL PP	PRONOUN
a.	*tijdens de boottocht* during the boat trip	**er tijdens* there during	**tijdens 'm* during $it_{[-human]}$
b.	*gedurende de vergadering* during the meeting	**er gedurende* here during	**gedurende 'r* during $it_{[-human]}$
c.	*sinds het einde van de vakantie* since the end of the holiday	**er sinds* there since	**sinds 't* during $it_{[-human]}$
d.	*tot het einde van de vakantie* until the end of the holiday	**er tot/toe* there until	**tot 't* during $it_{[-human]}$
e.	*tussen de lessen* between the lessons	#*er tussen* here between	**tussen ze* between $them_{[-human]}$
f.	*vanaf het begin* since the beginning	#*er vanaf* there since	**vanaf 't* during $it_{[-human]}$

5.2.1.3. Non-spatial/temporal prepositions

Section 1.3.3.2 has made a distinction between three types of non-spatial/temporal prepositions: (i) prepositions introducing a specific semantic role, (ii) prepositions heading PP-complements, and (iii) prepositions heading non-spatial/temporal adverbial phrases. Below, we will see that only the first two groups can be involved in the formation of pronominal PPs.

I. Prepositions introducing a specific semantic role

Section 1.3.3.2 has discussed several prepositional phrases that are not selected by the verb (or the head of some other phrase they are part of) but introduce a referent that plays a certain semantic role in the clause (or other relevant phrase). Such PPs generally allow the formation of a pronominal PP. This will be illustrated below for the individual prepositions that may head such phrases.

A. Door *'by'*

The first preposition is *door* 'by', which introduces an agent in a passive clause or a cause in an active clause. The primed examples in (54) illustrate that R-pronominalization is possible by means of relative pronominal PPs.

(54) • Passive/causal *door*-phrase

a. Jan is door deze automobilist aangereden.
Jan has.been by this car.driver over.run
'Jan was run over by this car driver.'

a′. de automobilist *waar* Jan *door* aangereden is
the car.driver that Jan by over.run has.been

b. Het raam brak door de explosie.
the window broke by the explosion
'The explosion caused the window to break.'

b′. de explosie *waar* het raam *door* brak
the explosion that the window by broke

B. Aan *'to' and* voor *'for'*

The prepositions *aan* 'to' and *voor* 'for' introduce, respectively, a recipient and a beneficiary. The primed examples in (55) show that PPs headed by these prepositions allow R-pronominalization.

(55) • Recipient *aan*- and beneficiary *voor*-phrases

a. Ik heb het boek aan de jongen gegeven.
I have the book to the boy given
'I gave the book to the boy.'

a′. de jongen *waar* ik het boek *aan* gegeven heb
the boy where I the book to given have

b. Ik heb een trui voor mijn kleindochter gebreid.
I have a sweater for my granddaughter knitted
'I knitted a sweater for my granddaughter.'

b′. mijn kleindochter *waar* ik een trui *voor* gebreid heb
my granddaughter where I a sweater for knitted have

The preposition *voor* can also head a purpose clause and in this case, too, the formation of a pronominal PP is possible. It is not clear whether this use of *voor* is similar to the use of *voor* in the beneficiary PP.

(56) • Purpose *voor*-phrase
  a. Jan doet het voor het geld.
     Jan does it because.of the money
  b. Het geld, *daar* doet Jan het *voor*.
     the money there does Jan it because.of
     'The money, that is what Jan is doing it for.'

C. Met *'with' and* zonder *'without'*

The complement of the preposition *met* 'with' can denote an instrument (57a), a co-agent (57b), or a located object (57c), and R-pronominalization is possible in all these cases.

(57) • *Met*-phrases
  a. Jan opende de kist met een breekijzer. [instrumental]
     Jan opened the box with a crowbar
  a′. het breekijzer *waar* Jan de kist *mee* opende
     the crowbar where Jan the box with opened
  b. Marie speelde met Jan. [comitative]
     Marie played with Jan
  b′. de jongen *waar* Marie *mee* speelde
     the boy where Marie with played
  c. Jan belaadde de wagen met hooi. [located object]
     Jan loaded the wagon with hay
  c′. het hooi *waar* Jan de wagen *mee* belaadde
     the hay where Jan the wagon with loaded

This does not hold for all *met*-PPs, however. When the *met*-PP expresses an accessory circumstance, as in (58), R-pronominalization is excluded, and the same thing holds when *met* is the head of an absolute *met*-construction; cf. Section 2.5.1.

(58) a. Jan slaapt met het raam open. [accessory circumstance]
     Jan sleeps with the window open
  b. *het raam *waar* Jan *mee* open slaapt
     the window where Jan with open sleeps

Judgments on the preposition *zonder* 'without' sometimes seem to vary; although the interrogative counterpart of (59a) is ungrammatical for most speakers, some of our informants do accept it and we also found a number of at least marginally acceptable examples on the internet in which the string *[er zonder]* clearly functions as a pronominal PP, e.g., *Water heeft de eigenschap dat je er zonder niet kunt leven* 'Water has the property that one cannot live without it'. In most cases, however, R-pronominalization of a *zonder*-PP leads to a severely degraded result. This is shown in (59b′), which can be compared with example (57a′).

(59) a. Jan zit zonder geld.
Jan sits without money
'Jan has no money.'
a′. %*Waar* zit je *zonder*?
b. Jan opende de kist zonder het breekijzer.
Jan opened the box without the crowbar
b′. *het breekijzer *waar* Jan de kist *zonder* opende
the crowbar where Jan the box without opened

D. Bij *'with'*

Example (60) shows that possessive *bij*-phrases in locational constructions can also be pronominalized.

(60) • The possessive *bij*-phrase
a. Marie zit graag bij hem op schoot.
Marie sits with pleasure with him on lap
'Marie is sitting on his lap with pleasure.'
b. de jongen *waar* Marie graag *bij* op schoot zit
the boy where Marie with pleasure with on lap sits

E. Van *'of'*

Van-PPs may express a possessor, an agent, or a theme in a nominal construction. The primed examples in (61) show that possessive and agentive *van*-PPs cannot undergo R-pronominalization.

(61) • Possessive or agentive *van*-phrases
a. het boek van de bibliotheek [possessive]
the book of the library
a′. *?het boek ervan
b. het dansen van de kinderen [agentive]
the $\text{dance}_{\text{inf}}$ of the children
b′. *?het dansen ervan

Van-PPs expressing a theme, on the other hand, may be pronominalized. The two examples in (62) differ in that the nominal infinitives *lezen* and *vallen* are derived from, respectively, a transitive and an °unaccusative verb.

(62) • *Van*-phrases expressing a theme
a. het lezen van het boek [theme of transitive verb]
the read_{inf} of the book
c′. het lezen ervan
d. het vallen van de bladeren [theme of unaccusative verb]
the fall_{inf} of the leaves
d′. het vallen ervan

II. Functional prepositions (PP-complements)

PP-complements of verbs, adjectives, nouns and adpositions all allow R-pronominalization. Since we discuss this more extensively in Section 5.3.2.1, we will only give an example of each case here.

(63) a. Jan verlangt erg naar vakantie.
Jan longs much for holiday
a′. Jan verlangt *er* erg *naar*.
Jan longs there much for
b. Jan is nieuwsgierig naar je werk
Jan is curious to your work
b′. Jan is *er* nieuwsgierig *naar*.
Jan is there curious to
c. de jacht op ganzen
the hunt on geese
c′. de jacht *er op*
the hunt there on
d. voor bij de maaltijd
for with the meal
d′. voor *er bij*
for there with

III. Prepositions heading non-spatial/temporal adverbial phrases

Adverbial phrases headed by a non-spatial/temporal preposition cannot undergo R-pronominalization, that is, the prepositions in Table 30 in Section 1.3.3.2.3 cannot head a pronominal PP. The last column of Table (64) shows that these prepositions cannot be followed by a weak pronoun either, irrespective of whether the pronoun is [-HUMAN] or [+HUMAN]. The examples with *dankzij*, *namens*, *ondanks*, *vanwege*, *volgens* and *zonder* become acceptable when the weak pronoun is replaced by a phonetically strong [-NEUTER] one, which is always used to denote a [+HUMAN] entity.

(64) Pronominalization of/in non-spatial/temporal PPs

	EXAMPLE	PRONOMINAL PP	PRONOUN
a.	*dankzij de computer* thanks.to the computer	**er dankzij* there thanks.to	**dankzij ’m* thanks.to it
b.	*gezien deze problemen* in.view.of these problems	**er gezien* there in.view.of	**gezien ze* in.view.of them
c.	*namens de firma* in.name.of the firm	**er namens* there in.name.of	**namens ’r* in.name.of it
d.	*ondanks zijn tegenzin* despite his reluctance	**er ondanks* there despite	**ondanks ’m* despite it
e.	*ongeacht de kosten* irrespective.of the costs	**er ongeacht* there irrespective.of	**ongeacht ze* irrespective.of them
f.	*per post/auto/kilo* by mail/car/the.kilo	**er per* there by	**per ’r/’m/’t* by it
g.	*vanwege de kosten* because.of the costs	**er vanwege* there because.of	**vanwege ze* because.of them
h.	*volgens het nieuws* according.to the news	**er volgens* there according.to	**volgens ’t* according.to it
i.	*wegens het slechte weer* because.of the bad weather	**er wegens* there because.of	**wegens ’t* because.of it
j.	*zonder het geld* without the money	**er zonder* there without	**zonder ’t* without it

Apparent counterexamples to the claim that non-spatial/temporal PPs do not allow R-pronominalization are *daaromtrent* 'as to that' and *hieromtrent* 'hereabout'. These formations are, however, better considered fossilized lexical items, because they are in a severely limited paradigm. The formation *eromtrent*, for example, is not possible. Note in this connection that the morpheme *daar* also occurs in formations like *daarentegen* 'on the other hand' and *daarenboven* 'moreover', which are based on the medieval prepositions *entegen* and *enboven* (*Woordenboek der Nederlandsche Taal*).

5.2.2. Postpositions

This section discusses the question of whether postpositional phrases may undergo R-pronominalization, and it will show that it is not easy to answer this question. In view of the fact, illustrated in (65b), that nominal complements of postpositions can be pronominalized by means of a [-R] pronoun, one might expect R-pronominalization to be blocked. However, constructions like (65b) often occur alongside constructions like (65c), which involve R-pronominalization.

(65) a. dat hij die boom in is geklommen.
that he that tree into is climbed
'that he has climbed into that tree.'
b. de boom die hij in is geklommen
the tree that he into is climbed
c. de boom waar hij in is geklommen
the tree where he into is climbed

Of course, this may be accidental given that *waar ... in* in (65c) may be the pronominalized counterpart of the prepositional phrase *in de boom* in the change of location construction *dat hij in die boom is geklommen*, but speakers' intuitions concerning the semantic difference between the two examples in (65b&c) are generally not sharp enough to be conclusive.

One test that may help to determine whether the pronominal PP in examples like (65c) can be postpositional in nature or not is based on the observation that, like verbal particles, postpositions can permeate clause-final verb clusters, whereas (stranded) prepositions are not able to do this. This is illustrated in (66).

(66) a. dat Jan op het bericht heeft gewacht.
that Jan for the message has waited
'that Jan has waited for the message.'
a′. dat Jan *er* lang <*op*> heeft <**op*> gewacht. [stranded preposition]
that Jan there long for has waited
b. dat Jan de berg <op> is <op> gelopen. [postposition]
that Jan the mountain onto is walked
c. dat Jan Marie <op> heeft <op> gebeld. [verbal particle]
that Jan Marie prt. has called
'that Jan called Marie up.'

However, using permeation of the clause-final verb cluster as a test is problematic for various reasons. First, permeation of the verb cluster by a stranded preposition is perfectly acceptable in certain southern varieties of Dutch: see Section V4.3 and V4.5. The test will therefore only provide reliable results when we restrict ourselves to speakers of the northern part of the Netherlands.

A second problem is that even those speakers who give the judgments in (66a′) are often not very sure about their judgments on the relevant relative constructions, which may furthermore vary from case to case. Consider the examples in (67). Most northern speakers we consulted strongly prefer the use of a regular relative pronoun in (67a&b); the use of the relative R-pronoun *waar* in the corresponding primed examples is generally considered marked. The two alternatives in (67c&c′), on the other hand, are generally judged equally well and some speakers even prefer the use of the relative R-pronoun *waar*.

(67) a. de weg die hij is in gewandeld
the road that he is into walked
'the road he walked into'
a′ *?de weg waar hij is in gewandeld
the road where he is into walked
b. de berg die hij is op geklommen
the mountain that he is onto climbed
'the mountain he climbed onto'
b′. ?de berg waar hij is op geklommen
the mountain where he is onto climbed
c. de boom die hij is in geklommen
the tree that he is into climbed
'the tree he climbed into'
c′. de boom waar hij is in geklommen
the tree where he is into climbed

If the proposed test is reliable, we should conclude that the adpositions *in* and *op* in (67) are postpositional; they all permeate the verb cluster consisting of the auxiliary *is* and the past participle. This shows that we cannot account for the acceptability judgments in the (a)- and (b)-examples by assuming that some lexical restriction on the postposition itself is involved; R-pronominalization gives rise to a severely degraded result with the postposition *in* in (67a′), but to a fully grammatical result with the same postposition in (67c′).

A third problem is that there is evidence that goes against the claim that we are dealing with pronominalized postpositional phrases in the primed examples in (67). The examples in (68) show that the judgments on the use of the relative R-pronoun *waar* in the primed examples in (67) are more or less identical to those on the use of prepositional phrases in the primed examples in (68). This strongly suggests that the primed examples in (67) involve pronominalized prepositional phrases after all, which would imply in turn that postpositional phrases cannot undergo R-pronominalization.

(68) a. dat hij die weg in is gewandeld.
that he that road into is walked
a′. *dat hij in die weg is gewandeld.
b. dat hij die berg op is geklommen.
that he that mountain onto is climbed
b′. [?]dat hij op die berg is geklommen.
c. dat hij die boom in is geklommen.
that he that tree into is climbed
c′. dat hij in die boom is geklommen.

This conclusion is also supported by the minimal pairs in (69) with the complex postposition *achterna* 'after' and circumposition *achter ... aan* 'after'. The primed examples show that the nominal complement of the postposition *achterna* can only be pronominalized by a [-R] pronoun, whereas it must be pronominalized by means of a [+R] pronoun in the case of the circumposition *achter ... aan*.

(69) • Circumpositions vs. postpositions
a. Jan rent de kat achterna.
Jan runs the cat after
'Jan is chasing the cat.'
a′. Jan rent hem/*er achterna.
Jan runs it/there after
'Jan is chasing it.'
b. Jan rent achter de kat aan.
Jan runs after the cat AAN
'Jan is chasing the cat.'
b′. Jan rent er/*hem achter aan.
Jan runs there/him after AAN
'Jan is chasing it.'

The discussion above seems to show that the permeation test is not fully reliable and that, despite the fact that the stranded adpositions permeate the clause-final verb cluster, we are dealing with pronominalized prepositional phrases in the primed examples of (67). There is, however, also a problem with the claim that postpositional phrases do not allow R-pronominalization. Consider the resultative construction in (70), in which the postpositional phrase *de haven in* cannot be replaced by the prepositional phrase *in de haven*. Although pronominalization of the nominal complement of the postposition does not seem readily possible, the judgments on the relative construction in (70b) show that the relative pronoun must be an R-word: whereas the use of *waar* gives rise to a marked but reasonably acceptable result, the use of the regular pronoun *die* is (surprisingly) rejected by most speakers.

(70) a. dat de kapitein het schip de haven in gevaren heeft.
that the captain the ship the harbor into navigated has
'that the captain steered the ship into the harbor.'
a′. [??]dat de kapitein het schip in de haven gevaren heeft.
that the captain the ship into the harbor navigated has
b. De haven [?]waar/*die de kapitein het schip in gevaren heeft.
the harbor that the captain the ship into navigated has

A second potential problem is constituted by example (71b). Since the adposition *af* cannot be used as a preposition, this example may involve a pronominalized postpositional phrase. In this case, however, there is also an alternative analysis, according to which the R-word does not act as a pronoun corresponding to the noun phrase *de berg* in (71a) but as a pro-form of the adpositional phrase *van de berg*.

(71) a. Ik ben (van) de berg af geskied.
I am from the mountain AF skied
'I have skied from the mountain.'
b. de berg waar/die ik ben af geskied
the mountain where/that I am AF skied

It will be clear from the discussion above that we are not yet able to provide an unambiguous answer to the question whether postpositional phrases can undergo R-pronominalization or not. If there really is a general ban on stranded prepositions within the verb cluster, we must conclude that R-pronominalization of postpositional phrases is possible (which will leaves us without an account for the relative grammaticality judgments in (67)). If it turns out that stranded prepositions can sometimes permeate the verb cluster, the answer depends on whether one is willing to declare (70b) grammatical with the R-word *waar*. If so, we may have to conclude that R-pronominalization of postpositional phrases is possible; if not, we can maintain that R-pronominalization of postpositional phrases is impossible (and thus account for the grammaticality judgments on the examples in (67) by referring to the similar judgments on the examples in (68)). Since we are not able to shed more light on this issue at this point, we must leave this topic to future research, and simply conclude, despite the problematic cases discussed above, that postpositional phrases normally do not allow R-pronominalization.

5.2.3. Circumpositions

Circumpositional phrases are generally spatial in nature, and R-pronominalization is quite productive. Below, we will group the examples according to the second member of the circumposition. As is shown in (72), circumpositional phrases with *aan* as their second member can readily be pronominalized.

(72) • P ... *aan*
a. De kinderen liepen achter de optocht aan.
the children walked behind the parade AAN
'The children followed the parade.'
a′. De kinderen liepen *er achter aan*.
b. Jan liep tegen de ladder aan.
Jan walked against the ladder AAN
'Jan ran into the ladder.'
b′. Jan liep *er tegen aan*.

Adpositional phrases headed by *van* ... *af* 'from' also allow pronominalization; it must however be noted that the *van* + NP part of the construction can also be replaced by an R-word, as in the perhaps slightly marginal example (73c).

(73) • *Van ... af*
a. Jan sprong van het dak af.
Jan jumped from the roof AF
'Jan jumped from the roof.'
b. Jan sprong *er van af.*
b′. (?)Jan sprong *er af.*

The examples in (74) show that R-pronominalization of circumpositional phrases with *door* as their second member give rise to fully acceptable results.

(74) • P … *door*
a. Jan reed onder de brug door.
Jan drove under the bridge DOOR
'Jan drove underneath the bridge.'
a′. Jan reed *er onder door.*
b. Jan reed tussen de bomen door.
Jan drove between the trees DOOR
'Jan drove through the trees.'
b′. Jan reed *er tussen door.*

Circumpositional phrases with *heen* as their second member, on the other hand, show mixed behavior: normally R-pronominalization is fine, but in the case of *langs ... heen* 'along', which is somewhat marked anyway, the result is severely degraded. Recall that the circumposition *om ... heen* 'around' differs from the preposition *om* 'around' in that the latter cannot undergo R-pronominalization; cf. example (42).

(75) • P … *heen*
a. Jan liep door/om/?langs het huis heen.
Jan walked through/around/along the house HEEN
'Jan walked through/around/along the house.'
a′. Jan liep *er door/om/*?langs heen.*
b. Jan sprong over het hek heen
Jan jumped over the gate HEEN
'Jan jumped over the gate.'
b′. Jan sprong *er over heen.*

The examples in (76) show that circumpositional phrases with *in* as their second member are again fully compatible with R-pronominalization.

(76) • P … *in*
a. Jan zwom tegen de stroom in.
Jan swam against the current IN
'Jan swam against the current.'
a′. Jan zwom *er tegen in.*
b. Jan zit tussen twee meisjes in.
Jan sits between two girls IN
'Jan is sitting between two girls.'
b′. Jan zit *er tussen in.*

The same thing seems to hold for circumpositional phrases with *langs* as their second member, although the resulting structures in (77b′) feel perhaps somewhat uncomfortable; this may be due to the fact that the circumpositions *boven/onder ... langs* are not very commonly used.

(77) • P ... *langs*

a. Jan liep achter/voor het huis langs.
Jan walked behind/in.front.of the house LANGS
'Jan walked along the back/front of the house.'

a′. Jan liep *er achter/voor langs*.

b. Jan liep boven/onder de brug langs.
Jan walked above/under the bridge LANGS
'Jan walked above/down along the bridge.'

b′. (?)Jan liep *er boven/onder langs*.

Circumpositional phrases with *om* as their second member seem exceptional in not readily allowing R-pronominalization; the primed examples in (78) are marginally acceptable at best. In passing, note that these examples become fully acceptable when *er* is omitted, which shows that *achterom*, *voorom* and *buitenom* can be used as intransitive adpositions; it is not clear to us whether this is related to the degraded status of the primed examples.

(78) • P ... *om*

a. Jan liep achter/voor het huis om.
Jan walked behind/in.front.of the house OM
'that Jan walked around the back/front of the house.'

a′. *?Jan liep *er achter/voor om*.

b. De waterleiding loopt buiten het huis om.
the waterworks go outside the house OM
'The waterworks go around the exterior of the house.'

b′. *?De waterleiding loopt *er buiten om*.

Circumpositional phrases with *tegen ... op* 'against' are again fully compatible with R-pronominalization.

(79) • *Tegen ... op*

a. Marie klom tegen de muur op.
Marie climbed against the wall OP
'Marie climbed up against the wall.'

a′. Marie klom *er tegen op*.

Circumpositional phrases with *toe* as their second member in (80) behave ambiguously. Whereas R-pronominalization of circumpositional phrases headed by *naar ... toe* 'to' is perfectly acceptable, it is not possible when *tot (aan) ... toe* 'up to' is the head. Recall that directional PPs headed by the preposition *naar* 'to' do not allow R-pronominalization; cf. example (46).

(80) • P ... *toe*

a. Marie gaat naar die film toe.
Marie goes to that movie TOE
'Marie goes to that movie.'

a′. Marie gaat *er naar toe*.

b. De stenen liggen tot de heg toe.
the stones lie until the hedge TOE
'The stones are lying until the hedge.'

b′. *De stenen liggen *er toe toe*.

For completeness' sake, note that Section 2.2.1, sub III, has argued that example (81a) does not involve a circumposition *tot aan ... toe*; instead, we are dealing with the preposition *tot*, which takes as its complement a circumpositional positional phrase headed by the circumposition *aan... toe*. Example (81b) shows that this circumpositional phrase does allow R-pronominalization, albeit that the strong form *daar* in (81b) cannot be replaced by the phonetically weak form *er*. However, extraction of the R-word from the *tot*-phrase, as a result of which *tot* would get the stranded form *toe*, leads to an unacceptable result. This is shown in (81b′).

(81) a. De stenen liggen tot aan de heg toe.
the stones lie until to the hedge TOE

b. De stenen liggen tot daar aan toe.

b′. *De stenen liggen daar toe aan toe.

R-pronominalization is fully productive for circumpositional phrases with *uit* as their second member. We give some examples in (82); R-pronominalization of PPs headed by *achter/tussen/voor ... uit* (lit.: behind/between/in.front.of ... OUT) leads to equally acceptable results.

(82) • P ... *uit*

a. De vlag stak boven de huizen uit.
the flag stuck above the houses out
'The flag stuck out above the houses.'

a′. De vlag stak *er boven uit*.

b. De jurk stak onder de jas uit.
the dress stuck under the coat out
'The dress protruded from under (was slightly longer than) the coat.'

b′. De jurk stak *er onder uit*.

The (a)- and (b)-examples in (83) show that circumpositional phrases with *vandaan* as their second member are normally compatible with R-pronominalization. The circumposition *om ... vandaan* is perhaps an exception, which may be due to the fact that this formation is restricted to the (somewhat marginal) phrase *om de hoek vandaan*.

(83) • P ... *vandaan*

a. De muis kwam achter/voor/onder de kast vandaan.
the mouse came behind/in.front.of/under the cupboard VANDAAN
'The mouse came from behind/in front of/under the cupboard.'

a′. De muis kwam *er achter/voor/onder vandaan.*

b. Marie haalde het geheime document tussen de rommel vandaan.
Marie got the secret document between the trash VANDAAN
'Marie got the secret document from between the trash.'

b′. Marie haalde het geheime document *er tussen vandaan.*

c. ?Jan kwam om de hoek vandaan.
Jan came around the corner VANDAAN
'Jan came around the corner.'

c. *?Jan kwam *er om vandaan.*

For completeness' sake note that Section 2.2.1, sub I, has argued that example (84a) does not involve a circumposition *van achter ... vandaan*; instead, we are dealing with the preposition *van*, which takes as its complement a circumpositional positional phrase headed by the circumposition *achter ... vandaan*. The (b)-examples show that this circumpositional phrase does allow R-pronominalization, but that the R-word must remain within the PP headed by *van*.

(84) a. De muis kwam van achter de kast vandaan.
the mouse came from behind the cupboard VANDAAN
'The mouse came from behind the cupboard.'

b. De muis kwam van er/daar achter vandaan.

b′. ??De muis kwam er/daar van achter vandaan.

5.3. Syntactic restrictions on R-extraction

Section 5.2 has discussed the lexical restrictions on the formation of pronominal PPs. The ability to form a pronominal PP is not sufficient, however, to allow R-extraction; additional syntactic conditions must be met in order to license preposition stranding. These conditions will be discussed in this section.

5.3.1. General introduction

The examples in (85) show that R-extraction is possible when the adpositional phrase acts as a PP-complement or as a °complementive. Example (85a) shows that R-extraction from the complement of the verb *wachten* 'to wait' is possible; witness the fact that the adverbial phrase *de hele dag* 'the whole day' can intervene between the R-pronoun and the preposition *op*. Example (85b) shows that R-extraction is also possible from PPs that act as complementives, as is clear from the fact that the accusative object *het boek* 'the book' can intervene between the R-pronoun and the preposition *in*.

(85) a. Jan heeft de hele dag op een bericht gewacht. [PP-complement]
Jan has the whole day for a message waited
'Jan waited for a message the whole day.'
a′. Jan heeft *er* de hele dag *op* gewacht.
b. Jan zette het boek in de kast. [complementive]
Jan put the book in the bookcase
b′. Jan zette *er* het boek *in*.

Adverbially used adpositional phrases, on the other hand, generally do not allow R-extraction, which is illustrated by the examples in (86); the (b)-examples show that, despite the fact that R-pronominalization of the temporal *voor*-PP is fully acceptable, R-extraction gives rise to an unacceptable result.

(86) a. Jan komt waarschijnlijk voor zijn vakantie nog even langs. [adjunct]
Jan comes probably before his holiday PRT. briefly along
'Jan will probably visit (us) briefly before his holiday.'
b. Jan komt waarschijnlijk ervoor nog even langs.
b′. *Jan komt *er* waarschijnlijk *voor* nog even langs.

The examples in (85) and (86) suggest that R-extraction is only possible with PP-complements and complementives. This would be in line with a generalization from the generative literature (which was formulated as part of Huang's (1982) Condition on Extraction Domains) according to which adjuncts are islands for extraction. There is, however, a group of adpositional phrases that are traditionally analyzed as adverbial clauses that do nevertheless allow R-extraction. This is illustrated in (87), for an instrumental PP headed by *met* 'with'; see Section 5.2.1.3, sub I, for more PPs of this sort.

(87) a. Jan opende de kist met een breekijzer.
Jan opened the box with a crowbar
b. Jan opende *er* de kist *mee*.

This may give rise to two possible conclusions: either we assume the generalization that only PP-complements and complementives can undergo R-extraction is wrong, or we have to assume that instrumental PPs actually function as a kind of complement of the verb, albeit that they differ from PP-arguments like *op een bericht* in (85a) or predicative complements like *in de kast* in (85b) in not being obligatorily. Here we will leave the question of which alternative is correct open.

Besides the requirement that the adpositional phrase must be a complement, a complementive, or involve a specific semantic role (like instrumental *met*), it must also occupy a certain position in the clause in order to license R-extraction: the stranded preposition must be left-adjacent to the verb(s) in clause-final position (with some qualifications that will follow below). This is illustrated in (88) by means of the pronominalized form of the instrumental PP *met een breekijzer* from (87); R-extraction is possible when the pronominalized PP *daarmee* is left-adjacent to the clause-final verbs but not when it precedes the negative adverb *niet* or when it is placed in a position following the clause-final verbs.

(88) a. dat je de kist niet daarmee mag openen.
that you the box not with.that be.allowed open
'that you are not allowed to open the box with it.'
a′. dat je *daar* de kist niet *mee* mag openen.
b. dat je de kist daarmee niet mag openen.
that you the box with.that not be.allowed open
'that you are not allowed to open the box with it.'
b′. *dat je *daa*r de kist *mee* niet mag openen.
c. dat je de kist niet mag openen daarmee.
that you the box not be.allowed open with.that
'that you are not allowed to open the box with it.'
c′. *dat je *daa*r de kist niet mag openen *mee*.

5.3.2. The syntactic function of the adpositional phrase

This section successively discusses R-extraction from adpositional phrases functioning as complements, as complementives, and as adverbial phrases.

5.3.2.1. PP-complements

Adpositional phrases that act as a complement generally allow the formation of a pronominal PP. Whether R-extraction (the split pattern) is also allowed depends on the category of the head selecting the PP: complements of verbs and adjectives normally do allow the split pattern, whereas complements of nouns generally do not. R-extraction is categorically excluded in the rare cases in which the selecting head is a preposition itself.

I. Complements of verbs

Prepositional complements of verbs are always headed by a functional preposition, that is, a preposition that has relatively little semantic content and is selected by the verb; see Table 29 in Section 1.3.3.2.3 for a representative set of examples. All prepositional complements of verbs allow R-extraction. We illustrate this in (89) for some of the examples in Table 29.

(89) a. Jan lijdt al jaren aan slapeloosheid.
Jan suffers already years from insomnia
a′. Jan lijdt *er* al jaren *aan*.
Jan suffers there already years from
b. Die schoenen passen heel goed bij die jurk.
those shoes fit very well with that dress
b′. Die schoenen passen *er* heel goed *bij*.
those shoes fit there very well with
c. Jan verlangt erg naar vakantie.
Jan longs very for holiday
c′. Jan verlangt *er* erg *naar*.
Jan longs there very for

d. Jan klaagt voortdurend over de kou.
Jan complains continuously about the cold
d′. Jan klaagt *er* voortdurend *over*.
Jan complains there continuously about
e. Jan zwicht natuurlijk voor dat aanbod.
Jan knuckles of course under that offer
e′. Jan zwicht *er* natuurlijk *voor*.
Jan knuckles there of course under

II. Complements of adjectives

The set of functional prepositions heading prepositional complements of adjectives seems slightly smaller than the set of functional prepositions heading prepositional complements of verbs; cf. Table 29 in Section 1.3.3.2.3. All prepositional complements of adjectives allow R-extraction. In (90), we illustrate this for some of the examples in Table 29.

(90) a. Jan is erg bedreven in voetballen.
Jan is very skilled in soccer
a′. Jan is *er* erg bedreven *in*.
Jan is there very skilled in
b. Jan is erg nieuwsgierig naar je vorderingen.
Jan is very curious to your progress
b′. Jan is *er* erg nieuwsgierig *naar*.
Jan is there very curious to
c. Jan is erg verontwaardigd over dat aanbod.
Jan is very indignant about that offer
c′. Jan is *er* erg verontwaardigd *over*.
Jan is there very indignant about

III. Complements of nouns

The set of functional prepositions heading prepositional complements of nouns also seems slightly smaller than the set of functional prepositions heading prepositional complements of verbs (cf. Table 29 in Section 1.3.3.2.3). Although the adpositional complements do allow the formation of a pronominal PP, the possibilities for R-extraction (the split pattern) are limited: movement of *er* preferably targets some position within the noun phrase; movement to a position external to the noun phrase normally gives rise to a marked result. We illustrate this In (91) for some of the examples in Table 29.

(91) a. Jan uitte zijn behoefte aan genegenheid.
Jan expressed his need of affection
a′. Jan uitte <??er> zijn behoefte <er> aan.
Jan expressed there his need of
b. Jan verloor zijn geloof in de mensheid.
Jan lost his belief in mankind
b′. Jan verloor <??er> zijn geloof <er> in.
Jan lost there his belief in

c. De minister verbood de jacht op ganzen.
the minister prohibited the hunt on geese

c′. De minister verbood <$^{??}$er> de jacht <er> op.
the minister prohibited there the hunt on

The only cases in which R-extraction seems to be fully acceptable involve indefinite/demonstrative noun phrases taking an adpositional complement headed by the prepositions *over* and *van*. Some examples are given in (92).

(92) a. Ik heb een/dat/het boek over ruimtevaart gelezen.
I have a/that/the book on space.travel read

a′. Ik heb een/dat/het boek *er over* gelezen.
I have a/that/the book there on read

a″. Ik heb *er* een/dat/$^{*?}$het boek *over* gelezen.

b. Ik heb een/die/de foto van de berg gezien.
I have a/that/the picture of the mountain seen

b′. Ik heb een/die/de foto *er van* gezien.
I have a/that/the picture there of seen

b″. Ik heb *er* een/die/$^{??}$de foto *van* gezien.

Further, there are poorly understood restrictions governing the possibility of R-extraction in examples like (92). For example, when the main verbs are replaced by a verb like *verbranden* 'to burn', the split pattern gives rise to a degraded result. It is therefore not obvious whether the split pronominal PPs in (92) indeed function as complements of the nouns, or whether they are functioning as, e.g., restrictive adverbial phrases. For an extensive discussion of this issue we refer the reader to Section N2.2.1 and subsequent discussions.

IV. Complements of adpositions

Section 2.2 has shown that only a few prepositions take adpositional complements. The list is exhausted by *van* 'from', *tot* 'until' and *voor* 'for' in (93). The singly primed examples in (93) show that the adpositional complements of these prepositions may be replaced by pronominal PPs. The doubly-primed examples show, however, that these pronominal PPs cannot readily be split; leftward movement of the R-word is impossible, irrespective of whether the landing site is internal or external to the PP.

(93) a. van vlak achter de kast
from just behind the cupboard

a′. van vlak <er> achter
from just there behind

a″. <*er> van <*er> vlak achter

b. tot vlak voor de deur
until just in.front.of the door

b′. tot vlak <er> voor
until just there in.front.of

b″. <*er> tot <$^{??}$er> vlak voor

c. voor direct na de maaltijd
for immediately after the meal

c′. voor direct <er> na
for immediately there after

c″. <*er> voor <$^{??}$er> direct na

5.3.2.2. Complementives

The (a)-examples in (94) illustrate that locational predicative PPs readily allow R-extraction. Since the (b)-examples show that directional predicative PPs categorically reject R-pronominalization, they, of course, do not allow R-extraction either; see Section 5.2.1.1 for discussion and more examples.

(94) a. Jan zet de bloemen in de vaas.
Jan puts the flowers into the vase
a′. Jan zet *er* de bloemen *in*.
Jan puts there the flowers into
b. Marie is naar de bibliotheek gewandeld.
Marie is to the library walked
'Marie has walked to the library.'
b′. *Marie is *er* *naar* gewandeld.
Marie is there to walked

The question of whether predicatively used postpositional phrases can undergo R-pronominalization and R-extraction has already been discussed in Section 5.2.2, where it is shown that the answer depends on certain assumptions that are not relevant here. We therefore refer the reader again to this section for discussion.

Predicatively used circumpositional phrases do allow R-pronominalization and R-extraction, regardless of whether they are locational or directional. One example of each type is given in (95); see Section 5.2.3 for more examples and discussion.

(95) a. De ladder staat al tegen de muur aan.
the ladder stands already against the wall AAN
'The ladder is already standing against the wall.'
a′. De ladder staat *er* al *tegen* *aan*.
the ladder stands there already against AAN
b. Marie is gisteren naar de bibliotheek toe gewandeld.
Marie is yesterday to the library TOE walked
'Marie has walked to the library yesterday.'
b′. Marie is *er* gisteren *naar* *toe* gewandeld.
Marie is there yesterday to TOE walked

5.3.2.3. Adverbial adpositional phrases

Although R-pronominalization is occasionally possible with adverbially used adpositional phrases, they do not allow R-extraction. Before we can illustrate this, it must be noted that prepositional phrases introducing specific semantic roles, such as instrumental *met*-PPs or passive *door*-phrases, which are often also counted as adverbial phrases, do allow R-extraction. We will not discuss PPs of this sort here, but refer the reader to Sections 5.2.1.3, sub I, and 5.3.1 for further discussion.

I. Adverbially vs. predicatively used locational phrases

When an adverbially used locational phrase is pronominalized, it is generally replaced by a locational pro-form like *daar* 'there', as in (96b). R-pronominalization and R-extraction, on the other hand, normally lead to ungrammaticality, although it must be noted that speakers tend to have varying judgments in the case of relative constructions: *de zolder waar Jan vaak (%op) speelt.*

(96) a. Jan speelt vaak op zolder.
Jan plays often in the attic
'Jan is playing in the attic often.'
b. Jan speelt daar vaak.
Jan plays there often
'Jan is playing there often.'
c. *Jan speelt *<er>* vaak *<er>* *op*.
Jan plays there often on

The examples in (97) show that although predicatively used adpositional phrases can sometimes also be replaced by the pro-form *daar*, R-pronominalization is generally possible as well.

(97) a. Het boek ligt op de keukentafel.
the book lies on the kitchen table
a′. Het boek ligt daar (op).
the book lies there on
b. Jan legt het boek op de keukentafel.
Jan puts the book on the kitchen table
b′. Jan legt het boek daar (op).
Jan puts the book there on

In some cases, R-pronominalization is even the only available option for predicatively used PPs. Consider the examples in (98). As we have already argued several times, (98a) is ambiguous between an activity reading, in which case the PP is interpreted as an adverbial phrase, and a change of location reading, in which case the PP is interpreted as a predicative phrase. The examples in (98b&c) show that the choice between the pro-form *daar* and the pronominal PP *daar in* disambiguates the sentence; in (98b) the verb can only be interpreted as an activity verb, and in (98c) it can only be interpreted as a change of location verb.

(98) a. Jan springt in de sloot.
Jan jumps in/into the ditch
b. Jan springt daar. [unacceptable with a change of location reading]
Jan jumps there
c. Jan springt daar in. [only acceptable with a change of location reading]
Jan jumps there into

This finding is confirmed by the examples in (99). In the perfect tense, the activity verb *springen* takes the auxiliary *hebben*, and (99a′) shows that the perfect tense construction with *hebben* is only compatible with the pro-form *daar*. The change of location verb, on the other hand, takes the auxiliary *zijn*, and (99b′) shows that the perfect tense construction with *zijn* is only compatible with the pronominal PP *daar in*.

(99) a. Jan heeft in de sloot gesprongen.
Jan has in the ditch jumped
a′. Jan heeft daar (*in) gesprongen.
Jan has there in jumped
b. Jan is in de sloot gesprongen.
Jan is into the ditch jumped
b′. Jan is daar *(in) gesprongen.
Jan is there into jumped

II. Temporal prepositions

Section 5.2.1.2 has shown that only the temporal prepositions *voor* 'before' and *na* 'after' allow the formation of a pronominal PP, which is illustrated again by means of the contrast between (100b&c) and (100d). This does not imply, however, that R-extraction is also allowed with these prepositions. The examples in (100b′&c′) show that it is not; the R-pronoun must be adjacent to (the modifier of) the preposition, and the split pattern leads to ungrammaticality.

(100) a. Hij heeft het boek (vlak) voor/na/tijdens de vakantie gelezen.
he has the book just before/after/during the holiday read
'He has read the book (just) before/after/during the holiday.'
b. Hij heeft het boek *er* (vlak) *voor* gelezen.
b′. *Hij heeft *er* het boek (vlak) *voor* gelezen.
c. Hij heeft het boek *er na* gelezen.
c′. *Hij heeft *er* het boek *na* gelezen.
d. *Hij heeft het boek *er tijdens* gelezen.
d′. *Hij heeft *er* het boek *tijdens* gelezen.

The impossibility of R-extraction is probably due to the fact that temporal PPs normally have an adverbial function, and thus falls under the general prohibition on extraction from adverbial phrases.

III. Other cases

Section 5.2.1.3, sub III, has shown that adverbial PPs headed by non-spatial/temporal prepositions do not allow R-pronominalization. For obvious reasons they therefore they do not allow R-extraction either.

5.3.3. Cases of obligatory R-extraction

The previous sections have investigated the syntactic contexts that allow R-extraction. This does not mean that R-extraction *must* be applied in those cases. The examples in (101) show that the preposition can also be pied piped by movement of the R-pronoun; in the primeless examples in (101), the preposition is stranded by the moved R-word, whereas in the primed examples the preposition is pied piped.

(101) a. Jan heeft *daar/hier* de hele dag *naar* gezocht.
Jan has there/here the whole day for looked
a′. Jan heeft daar/hier naar de hele dag gezocht.
b. *Daar/Hier* heeft Jan de hele dag *naar* gezocht.
b′. Daarnaar/Hiernaar heeft Jan de hele dag gezocht.

This option of pied piping seems to be most common with demonstrative R-pronouns. As is shown in (102a), scrambling of the referential R-pronoun *er* must strand the preposition. The topicalization examples in (102b) are of course inconclusive, since topicalization of the unstressed R-pronoun *er* is excluded anyway.

(102) a. Jan heeft *er* de hele dag *naar* gezocht.
Jan has there the whole day for looked
a′. *Jan heeft ernaar de hele dag gezocht.
b. **Er* heeft Jan de hele dag *naar* gezocht.
b′. *Ernaar heeft Jan de hele dag gezocht.

The examples in (103) show that the interrogative and relative R-pronouns preferably strand the preposition; the primed, pied piping examples are acceptable, but marked with respect to the primeless, stranding examples.

(103) a. *Waar* heeft Jan de hele dag *naar* gezocht?
where has Jan the whole day for looked
'What did Jan look for all day long?'
a′. (?)Waarnaar heeft Jan de hele dag gezocht?
b. het pakje *waar* Jan de hele dag *naar* gezocht heeft
the parcel where Jan the whole day for looked has
'The parcel that Jan was looking for all day long.'
b″. (?)het pakje waarnaar Jan de hele dag gezocht heeft

The examples in (104) and (105) show that scrambling and topicalization of quantified R-pronouns require, or at least strongly prefer, preposition stranding.

(104) a. Jan heeft *overal* al *naar* gezocht.
Jan has everywhere already for looked
'Jan has already looked for everything.'
a′. *Jan heeft overal naar al gezocht.
b. *Overal* heeft Jan al *naar* gezocht.
b′. *Overal naar heeft Jan al gezocht.

(105) a. Jan heeft *ergens/nergens* lang *naar* gezocht.
Jan has somewhere/nowhere long for looked
'Jan has looked for something a long time.'
a′. *Jan heeft ergens/nergens naar lang gezocht.
b. *Ergens/Nergens* heeft Jan lang *naar* gezocht.
b′. *Ergens/??Nergens naar heeft Jan lang gezocht.

We therefore may conclude that, with the exception of the demonstrative R-pronouns *daar* and *hier*, movement of R-pronouns at least preferably strand the preposition; in some cases, pied piping of the preposition even leads to unacceptable results.

5.3.4. The position of stranded prepositions

Example (106b) shows that stranded prepositions are normally left-adjacent to the verb(s) in clause-final position; when, for example, an adverbial phrase intervenes between the stranded preposition and the verb(s), the result is unacceptable. The same thing holds when the stranded preposition occurs in post-verbal position.

(106) a. Jan heeft <op de brief> lang <op de brief> moeten wachten <op de brief>.
Jan has for the letter long have.to wait
'Jan had to wait for the letter a long time.'
b. Jan heeft er <*op> lang <op> moeten wachten <*op>.
Jan has there for long have.to wait
'Jan had to wait for it a long time.'

An example like (107b) is only an apparent exception to this general rule, since it does not involve R-extraction but movement of a complete pronominal PP. This is clear from the fact illustrated in (107c) that *daar over* cannot be split by, e.g., an adverbial phrase; this example contrasts sharply with the example in (107d) that does involve R-extraction.

(107) a. Jan heeft met Peter over dat probleem gesproken.
Jan has with Peter about that problem talked
'Jan talked with Peter about that problem.'
b. Jan heeft [$_{PP}$ daar over] met Peter gesproken.
Jan has there about with Peter talked
c. *Jan heeft daar$_i$ gisteren [$_{PP}$ t_i over] met Peter gesproken.
Jan has there yesterday about with Peter talked
d. Jan heeft daar$_i$ gisteren met Peter [$_{PP}$ t_i over] gesproken.
Jan has there yesterday with Peter about talked

There are, however, two true exceptions to the general rule that stranded prepositions are left-adjacent to the verb(s) in clause-final position: first, a predicatively used AP or PP may intervene between the stranded preposition and the verb(s); second, when more than one stranded preposition is present at least one of them cannot be adjacent to the verb(s).

I. Predicative complements

Predicative complements, which must generally also be left-adjacent to the verb(s) in clause-final position, can intervene between the stranded preposition and the verb. As is shown in (108), generally two orders are possible; either the predicate or the stranded preposition may be adjacent to the verb. Various factors may influence the grammaticality judgments; we refer the reader to Section A6.2.4.3 for a discussion of some of the factors that force an adjectival predicate to precede the stranded preposition.

(108) a. dat Jan het zakje met zijn zakmes open maakte.
that Jan the bag with his pocketknife open made
'that Jan opened the bag with his pocketknife.'
a′. dat Jan *er* het zakje <*mee*> open <*mee*> maakte.
b. dat Jan de spijker met een hamer in de muur sloeg.
that Jan the nail with a hammer into the wall hit
b′. dat Jan *er* de spijker <*mee*> in de muur <*mee*> sloeg.

Section 1.3.1.5.2 has argued that verbal particles also act as a kind of predicate. This correctly predicts that they can also intervene between the stranded preposition and the verbs in clause-final position. Unlike the predicative phrases in (108), however, the particle cannot precede the stranded preposition.

(109) a. dat Jan Marie steeds tot diefstal aanzet.
that Jan Marie all.the.time to theft prt.-puts
'that Jan is putting Marie up to theft all the time.'
a′. dat Jan Marie *er* steeds <*toe*> aan <**toe*> zet.
b. dat zij graag voor zijn kundigheid instaat.
that she gladly for his competence prt.-vouches
'that she gladly vouches for his competence.'
b′. dat zij *er* graag <*voor*> in <**voor*> staat.

II. Multiple stranded prepositions

When more than one stranded preposition is present, the two compete for the position left-adjacent to the verb(s) in clause-final position. The order that is well-formed generally reflects the unmarked order of the two full prepositional phrases. This is easiest to see when one of the stranded prepositions heads a predicatively used PP, as in (110a); since the predicative phrase must be adjacent to the verb in clause-final position, the stranded preposition must also be adjacent to it. Observe that the R-word *er* in (110b) is interpreted as the pronominal R-word associated to both *mee* and *in*. This conflation of syntactic functions is more extensively discussed in Section 5.5.3.

(110) a. dat Jan de schroef met een schroevendraaier in de muur draaide.
that Jan the screw with a screwdriver into the wall turned
'that Jan put the screw into the wall with a screwdriver.'
a′. *dat Jan de schroef in de muur met een schroevendraaier draaide.
b. dat Jan *er* de schroef *mee in* draaide.
that Jan there the screw with into turned
b′. *dat Jan *er* de schroef *in mee* draaide.

5.4. Idiomatic pronominal PPs

In some cases, pronominal PPs with *er* are part of an idiomatic construction. The examples in (111) show that replacement of *er* by one of the other R-pronouns normally leads to ungrammaticality; for a more extensive discussion of the construction in (111a), we refer the reader to Section A10.1.3.

(111) a. Ze ziet er/*daar goed uit.
she looks there nice UIT
'She is looking well/good.'

b. Marie is er/*daar gloeiend bij.
Marie is there glowing BIJ
'Marie has been caught in the act.'

c. Hij is er/*daar met mijn spullen van door.
he is there with my things VAN DOOR
'He made off with my things.'

d. We trokken er/*daar op uit.
we went there OP UIT
'We went on a trip.'

e. Hij kreeg er/*daar van langs
he got there VAN LANGS
'Somebody severely hit him.'

In the examples in (112) replacement of *er* by one of the other R-pronouns results in the loss of the idiomatic reading, as is clear from the fact that the primed examples can only be interpreted literally; *hier* in (112a) must be construed as a place adverb and in (112b&c) the pronominal PPs *daar .. op* and *hier ..in* must be construed referentially.

(112) a. De trein komt er aan.
the train comes there AAN
'The train is arriving (soon).'

a′. De trein komt hier aan.
the train comes here at
'The train arrives here.'

b. Hij sloeg er meteen op.
he hit there immediately OP
'He was immediately violent.'

b′. Hij sloeg er/daar meteen op.
he hit there immediately on
'He hit on it/that immediately.'

c. Marie trapte er niet in.
Marie kicked there not IN
'Marie wasn't fooled by that.'

c′. Marie trapte er/daar niet in.
Marie stepped there not into
'Marie didn't step into it/that.'

5.5. Appendix: The syntax of R-words

This section concludes the discussion on R-pronominalization and R-extraction by delving more deeply into the behavior of R-words, which, strictly speaking, goes beyond the limited domain of R-pronouns. The examples in (113) start by showing that R-pronouns can also be used as locational pro-forms.

(113) • R-pronouns

a. Jan keer *er* zojuist *naar*.
Jan looked there just now at
'Jan looked at it just now.'

b. Jan keek *hier/daar* goed *naar*.
Jan looked here/there well at
'Jan looked at this/that well.'

c. het boek *waar* ik *naar* keek
the book where I at looked
'the book that I looked at'

d. *Waar* keek je *naar*?
what looked you at
'What did you look at?'

• Locational pro-forms

a′. Jan was er.
Jan was there
'Jan was there.'

b′. Jan zat hier/daar.
Jan sat here/there
'Jan was sitting here/there.'

c′. de stad waar Jan woont
the city where Jan lives
'the city where Jan is living'

d′. Waar woont Jan?
where lives Jan
'Where does Jan live?'

e.	Jan keek *ergens* goed *naar*. Jan looked something well at 'Jan looked at something carefully.'	e′.	Dat boek is ergens. that book is somewhere 'That book is somewhere.'
f.	Jan keek *nergens* goed *naar*. Jan looked nothing well at 'Jan looked at nothing carefully.'	f′.	Dat boek is nergens. that book is nowhere 'That book is nowhere.'
g.	Jan keek *overal* goed *naar*. Jan looked everywhere well at 'Jan looked at everything carefully.'	g′.	de boeken liggen overal. the books lie everywhere 'The books are lying everywhere.'

In addition, it is shown there that the R-word *er* is also used as an expletive in impersonal passive and existential/presentational constructions, and as the indicator of a nominal gap in quantitative *er* constructions. This is shown again in (114).

(114) a. Er werd gedanst. [expletive *er* in impersonal passive]
there was danced

b. Er waren drie studenten in de tuin. [expletive *er* in presentational constr.]
there were three students in the garden

c. Jan heeft er [$_{NP}$ drie [*e*]] gekocht. [quantitative *er*]
Jan has there three bought
'Jan has bought three [e.g., books].'

The distribution of the types of R-words in (113) and (114) interacts in various intricate ways. This interaction will be the topic of this section. Section 5.5.1 starts by discussing the difference between *er* and the other R-words. Section 5.5.2 continues with a discussion of the co-occurrence restrictions on the different types of R-words. Section 5.5.3 concludes this appendix by discussing the typical property of *er* that it can perform more than one function at the same time.

5.5.1. Weak and strong R-words

The R-word *er* behaves like a phonetically weak pronoun, whereas the other R-words behave like strong pronouns. This is illustrated in (115): spatial *er* behaves like the weak personal subject and object pronouns *ze* 'she' and *'m* 'him' in that it cannot be used in coordinated structures; the other spatial R-words, on the other hand, can be used in this context, just like the strong personal pronouns *zij* 'she' and *hem* 'him'.

(115) a. zij/*ze en Jan
she and Jan

b. Marie en hem/*'m
Marie and him

c. hier en daar/*er
here and there

The assumption that *er* is a weak pro-form also accounts for the fact that, as a general rule, it cannot be placed in sentence-initial position; the (a)-examples in (116) show that the normal position of weak object pronouns is right-adjacent to the finite verb in second or the subject in non-topicalized position, and the (b)-, (c)- and (d)-examples show that the same thing holds for the locational pro-form *er* as well as prepositional and quantitative *er*.

(116) a. Jan heeft 'm gisteren bezocht. [weak object pronoun]
Jan has him yesterday visited
'Jan visited him yesterday.'
a′. Gisteren heeft Jan 'm bezocht.
a″ Hem/*'M heeft Jan gisteren bezocht.
b. Jan heeft er jaren gewerkt. [locational pro-form]
Jan has there for.years worked
'Jan has worked there for years.'
b′. Jaren heeft Jan er gewerkt.
b″. Daar/*er heeft Jan jaren gewerkt.
c. Jan heeft *er* gisteren *op* gewacht. [prepositional *er*]
Jan has there yesterday for waited
'Jan waited for it yesterday.'
c′. Gisteren heeft Jan *er op* gewacht.
c″. *Daar/*Er* heeft Jan gisteren *op* gewacht.
d. Jan had er gisteren [$_{NP}$ drie [*e*]]. [quantitative *er*]
Jan had there yesterday three
'Jan had three (e.g., books) yesterday.'
d′. Gisteren had Jan er [$_{NP}$ drie [*e*]].
d″. *Er had Jan gisteren [$_{NP}$ drie [*e*]].

Weak subject pronouns (with the exception of the weak third person masculine pronoun *-ie* 'he') behave markedly differently in this respect and, as is shown in (117a), they may either occur in sentence-initial position or follow the finite verb in second position. Since it is generally assumed that expletive *er* acts as a place-holder of the subject position, it is not really surprising that it exhibits the same behavior as the weak subject pronouns.

(117) a. Gisteren heeft zij/ze het boek gelezen. [subject pronoun]
yesterday has she the book read
a′. Zij/Ze heeft gisteren het boek gelezen.
b. Gisteren heeft er iemand tegen mij gelogen. [expletive *er*]
yesterday has there someone to me lied
'Yesterday, someone lied to me.'
b′. Er heeft gisteren iemand tegen mij gelogen.

Note in passing that the generalization that non-expletive *er* cannot occur in sentence-initial position does not hold when it is part of a larger constituent occupying the sentence-initial position. This is especially the case when the first constituent is a (nominalized) infinitival clause; in (118), we give examples involving the locational pro-form *er* as well as prepositional and quantitative *er*.

(118) a. [Er drie maanden per jaar wonen] zou ik wel willen. [locational]
there three months a year live would I PRT want
'I would like to live there for three months a year.'

b. [*Er* alleen *over* klagen] helpt niet. [prepositional]
there only about complain helps not
'It doesn't help to just complain about it.'

c. [Er [$_{NP}$ zes *e*] achter elkaar opeten] is wat overdreven. [quantitative]
there six after each.other prt.-eat is a.bit excessive
'To eat six [e.g., buns] one after the other is a little excessive.'

Example (119a) shows that weak object pronouns are obligatorily moved into a position preceding clause adverbs like *waarschijnlijk* 'probably'. Example (119b) shows that the same thing holds for the prepositional *er* (unless one of the syntactic restrictions discussed in Section 5.3 prohibits movement of *er*), and (119c) provides a similar example with quantitative *er*. We do not give an example with locational *er* given that place adverbs can be base-generated in a position preceding the clause adverbs.

(119) a. Jan heeft <hem/'m> waarschijnlijk <hem/*'m> bezocht. [object pronoun]
Jan has him probably visited
'Jan probably visited him.'

b. Jan heeft <daar/er> waarschijnlijk <daar/*er> op gewacht. [prepositional]
Jan has there probably for waited
'Jan probably has waited for it.'

c. Jan heeft <er> waarschijnlijk <*er> [$_{NP}$ drie [*e*]]. [quantitative]
Jan has there probably three
'Jan has probably three [e.g., books].'

Note that the strong form *daar* in (119b) may occupy a position within PP since the complete sequence *daar op* can be scrambled or be placed in sentence-initial position, as is shown in the primed (a)-examples in (120). The primed (b)-examples show that scrambling or topicalization is not possible with *er op*; this follows from the property of *er* illustrated in (119b) that it must be moved into some position external to the PP in the middle field of the clause.

(120) a. Jan heeft waarschijnlijk [daar op] gewacht.
a′. Jan heeft [daar op] waarschijnlijk gewacht.
a″. [Daar op] heeft Jan waarschijnlijk gewacht.
b. *Jan heeft waarschijnlijk [er op] gewacht.
b′. *Jan heeft [er op] waarschijnlijk gewacht.
b″. *[Er op] heeft Jan waarschijnlijk gewacht.

The discussion above has shown that the R-word *er* behaves like a weak pro-form that must be moved into the position indicated by means of [+R] in (121); the only exception is expletive *er*, which, like weak subject pronouns, may also occupy the first position in the sentence, indicated by XP. The other R-words are more like strong pronouns in that they need not move into [+R], that is, they may remain in their original position, and they may also occupy the sentence-initial position XP.

(121) XP V_{+fin} (Subject) [+R] ... ADV_{clause} ... V_{-fin}

There are two further remarks that can be made with respect to the position of the R-words. First, it must be noted that what holds for the "pure" expletive form *er* in (122a) also holds for the occurrence of *er* in (122b), which functions simultaneously as expletive and as prepositional *er*. This shows that prepositional *er* is possible in clause-initial position, as long as it also performs the function of expletive. Note that example (122c) shows that quantitative *er* behaves differently in this respect: it can never precede the finite verb in second position. We will return to these cases in Section 5.5.3.

(122) a. Er_{expl} zitten vier sigaren in de sigarenkist.
there are four cigars in the cigar box
b. *Er*$_{expl+prep}$ zitten vier sigaren *in*.
there are four cigars in
b′. *Er_{expl} zitten *er*$_{prep}$ vier sigaren *in*.
c. Er_{expl} zitten er_{quant} [$_{NP}$ vier *e*] in de sigarenkist.
there are there four in the cigar box
c′. *$Er_{expl+quant}$ zitten [$_{NP}$ vier *e*] in de sigarenkist.

Second, it can be observed from the (b)- and (c)-examples in (123) that movement of weak R-words is clause-bounded, that is, the landing site must be in the same clause as its original position. The (a)-examples show that R-words again behave similarly to weak pronouns in this respect.

(123) a. Jan zegt [dat Peter 'm$_i$ waarschijnlijk t_i zal bezoeken]. [pronoun]
Jan says that Peter him probably will visit
'Jan says that Peter will probably visit him.'
a′. *Jan zegt 'm$_i$ [dat Peter waarschijnlijk t_i zal bezoeken].
b. Jan zegt [dat hij er$_i$ zeker [t_i op] zal wachten]. [prepositional]
Jan says that he there certainly for will wait
'Jan says that he will certainly wait for it.'
b′. *Jan zegt er$_i$ [dat hij zeker [t_i op] zal wachten].
c. Els zegt [dat Jan er waarschijnlijk [$_{NP}$ drie [*e*]] heeft]. [quantitative]
Els says that Jan there probably three has
'Els says that Jan has probably three [e.g., books].'
c′. Els zegt er [dat Jan waarschijnlijk [$_{NP}$ drie [*e*]] heeft]

5.5.2. Co-occurrence of R-words

It is possible to have more than one R-word in a single clause, but there are several restrictions on their co-occurrence. Sections 5.5.2.1 and 5.5.2.2 show that, in the general case, a clause can never contain more than one weak or more than one strong R-word, whereas Section 5.5.2.3 will show that a weak and a strong form can co-occur. Before we start a caveat is in order. The data in this section are very complex, and it is hard sometimes for native speakers to give their judgments on the examples discussed; it is not surprising, therefore, that conflicting judgments can be found in the literature. Moreover, many additional factors seem to play a role in the acceptability of certain sentences, some of which have scarcely been investigated. It is therefore virtually impossible to give an exhaustive review of this topic. We therefore recommend that the reader also consult the existing literature (e.g., Bech 1952, Van Riemsdijk 1978, Bennis 1980/1986, Huybregts 1991, Odijk 1993 and the references cited therein) if one wants to investigate this topic more thoroughly.

5.5.2.1. Co-occurrence of multiple weak R-words

In the general case, a clause can contain at most one weak R-word, which will be demonstrated below by means of examples of clauses with two weak R-words with distinct functions. We start with a discussion of the distribution of weak R-words in embedded clauses, which is followed by a discussion of their distribution in main clauses.

I. Embedded clauses

Consider the examples in (124). Since the (a)- and the (b)-example are impersonal passives, the first occurrence must be expletive *er*; and the same thing holds for the (c)-example since the associate noun phrase *[twee [e]]* of quantitative *er* is an indefinite noun phrase. As is shown in these three examples, expletive *er* cannot co-occur with the other uses of *er*. The function of the occurrences of *er* are indicated by the following abbreviations: expl = expletive, loc = locational, quant = quantitative, and pron = pronominal.

(124) a. *dat er er gedanst wordt. [.. expl .. loc ..]
that there there danced is
Intended reading: 'People are dancing there.'

b. *dat er er over gesproken wordt. [.. expl .. pron ..]
that there there about spoken is
Intended reading: 'People are talking about it.'

c. *dat er er [$_{NP}$ twee [*e*]] gestolen zijn. [.. expl .. quant ..]
that there there two stolen have.been
Intended reading: 'Two [e.g., computers] have been stolen.'

The pattern in (124) has given rise to the idea that *er* must be placed into a unique, designated [+R]-position in the middle field of the clause, that is, the [+R]-position in (121). The postulation that this position is unique accounts for the fact that only one occurrence of *er* is allowed; [+R] can be occupied by one R-word only, so that the other occurrence(s) would violate Axiom I.

(125) Axiom I: *Er* must be moved into a unique [+R]-position in the middle field of the clause.

Axiom I also gives the correct predictions for the examples in (126): the examples in (126a&b) show that an R-pronoun cannot be combined with a locational pro-form or quantitative, and (126c) shows that the co-occurrence of quantitative *er* and a locational pro-form is also correctly excluded. Since the grammaticality judgments on the examples in (126) remain the same when we reverse the interpretations (e.g., when we interpret the first occurrence of *er* in (126c) as locational and the second as quantitative), we have discussed all possible combinations.

(126) a. *dat Jan *er* er *over* praatte. [.. pron .. loc ..]
that Jan there there about talked
'that Jan talked about it there.'

b. *dat Jan *er* er drie *in* stopte. [.. pron .. quant ..]
that Jan there there three into put
'that Jan put three [e.g., cigars] in it.'

c. *dat Jan er er [$_{NP}$ twee [*e*]] gezien heeft. [.. quant .. loc ..]
that Jan there there two seen has
'that Jan saw two [e.g., rats] there.'

Note that axiom I is overruled for occurrences of *er* that must be adjacent to the preposition, like *er* in the temporal phrase *er voor/na* 'before/after it'; cf. (127). This exception to Axiom I follows from the fact, discussed in Section 5.3.1, that these temporal PPs do not allow R-extraction; since *er* remains PP-internal, it is correctly predicted that the clause may contain two occurrences of *er* in such cases.

(127) a. dat Jan *er* misschien [er voor] iets *over* zal zeggen.
that Jan there maybe there before something about will say
'that maybe Jan will say something about it before it.'

b. dat er waarschijnlijk [er na] nog iets werd gedronken.
that there probably there after prt. something was drunk
'that people probably drank something afterwards.'

II. Main clauses

The pattern of grammaticality judgments is slightly different when we are dealing with main clauses. When expletive *er* occupies the regular subject position after the finite verb, as in (128), the pattern we find is identical to the one in (124).

(128) a. *Morgen wordt er er gedanst. [.. expl .. loc ..]
tomorrow is there there danced

b. *Morgen wordt er *er* *over* gesproken. [.. expl .. pron ..]
tomorrow is there there about spoken

c. *Gisteren zijn er er [$_{NP}$ twee [*e*]] gestolen. [.. expl .. quant ..]
yesterday have.been there there two stolen

However, when expletive *er* occupies the clause-initial position, as in (129), it can co-occur with quantitative *er* (but not with pronominal or locational *er*). Whereas the pattern in (128) follows directly from axiom I, the pattern in (129) is somewhat mysterious; we will not provide an explanation here for this deviant pattern.

(129) a. *Er wordt er morgen gedanst. [.. expl .. loc ..]
there is there tomorrow danced

b. *Er wordt *er* morgen *over* gesproken. [.. expl .. pron ..]
there is there tomorrow about spoken

c. Er zijn er gisteren [$_{NP}$ twee [*e*]] gestolen. [.. expl .. quant ..]
there have.been there yesterday two stolen

Similar problems do not arise with the other types of *er* given that these never occur in sentence-initial position; they therefore invariably exhibit the pattern in (126) in main clauses as well.

III. Conclusion

We conclude from the discussion in the previous subsections that Axiom I provides an apt description of the attested facts; the only problem is the grammaticality judgment on example (129c). In order not to confuse the reader at a later stage in the discussion, we want to note here that the ungrammaticality of the examples in (124), (126), (128), and (129a&b) does not necessarily mean that the intended meanings cannot be expressed. Some of them can, due to the fact that *er* is able to perform more than one function at the same time. Discussion of this is postponed to Section 5.5.3.

5.5.2.2. Co-occurrence of multiple strong R-words

This section discusses the co-occurrence restrictions on strong R-forms like *hier* and *daar*. In what follows we can ignore the expletive or quantitative uses of R-words, given that these uses always involve the weak form *er*, which leaves us with the locational and pronominal R-words. The examples in (130) show that strong demonstrative pronominal and locational R-forms cannot co-occur. Example (130a) is the reference sentence. The examples in (130b) and (130c) illustrate, respectively, that it is possible to replace the adverbial phrase *op dit congres* by the locational pro-form *daar* and to pronominalize the prepositional complement of the verb *over de oorlog*. The (d)-examples in (130) show, however, that it is impossible for a clause to simultaneously contain a locational pro-form and a pronominalized PP; this holds regardless of the order of the R-words.

(130) a. Zij heeft op dit congres vaak over de oorlog gesproken.
she has at this conference often about the war spoken
'She spoke often about the war at this conference.'
b. Zij heeft daar vaak over de oorlog gesproken. [.. loc ..]
c. Zij heeft *hier* op dit congres vaak *over* gesproken. [.. pron ..]
d. *Zij heeft *hier* daar vaak *over* gesproken. [.. pron .. loc ..]
d′. *Zij heeft daar *hier* vaak *over* gesproken. [.. loc .. pron ..]

The pattern in (124) has given rise to the idea that the strong demonstrative R-words can also be placed into a unique, designated [+R]-position in the middle field of the clause. The postulation that the position is unique again accounts for the fact that only one occurrence of a strong demonstrative R-word is allowed.

(131) Axiom II: A strong demonstrative R-word may be moved into a unique [+R]-position in the middle field of the clause.

Axiom II is phrased slightly more weakly than Axiom I in (125) in that it does not require that a strong demonstrative R-word be moved into the [+R]-position. This is needed to account for examples like (132). Given the fact that the pronominal R-word follows the (optional) clause adverb *vaak*, we may claim that it occupies its base-position within PP (an option independently argued for in Section 5.5.1), so that we correctly predict this example to be grammatical: the unique [+R]-position is occupied by the locational R-word *daar* only, while the pronominal R-word *hier* is still PP-internal.

(132) Zij heeft daar (vaak) [PP hier over] gesproken. [.. loc .. pron ..]
she has there often here about spoken
'She often spoke about this there.'

It must be noted, however, that example (133), provided by Hans Bennis (p.c.), is a potential problem for axiom II; presumably, the locational pro-form *hier* occupies the [+R]-position, but even so the pronominal R-word *daar* can be moved out of its PP. Our informants provide somewhat diverging judgments on this example, which seems best when the pronominal R-word is assigned contrastive accent; theories that postulate a designated focus position in the clause may perhaps account for the relative acceptability of (133) by claiming that the pronominal R-word occupies this focus position.

(133) %Jan heeft hier met mij *daar* vaak *over* gesproken. [.. loc .. pron ..]
Jan has here with me there often about spoken
'Jan often talked with me about that here.'

Note that Axiom II is restricted to demonstrative R-words and is not concerned with quantified R-words. Examples that contain both a demonstrative and a quantified R-word are ambiguous: the demonstrative pronoun *daar* in (134a-c) can either be interpreted as a locational pro-form or as a pronominal R-word (with perhaps a slight preference for the latter). This suggests that quantified R-words need not move into the [+R]-position, which is confirmed by the fact that an adverbial phrase may occur between the two R-words.

(134) a. Jan heeft daar (gisteren) ergens over gesproken.
Jan has there yesterday somewhere about spoken
'Jan spoke there about something yesterday.'
'Jan spoke about that somewhere yesterday.'

b. Jan heeft daar (gisteren) nergens over gesproken.
Jan has there yesterday nowhere about spoken
'Jan spoke there about nothing yesterday.'
'Jan spoke nowhere about that yesterday.'

c. Jan heeft daar (gisteren) overal over gesproken.
Jan has there yesterday everywhere about spoken
'Jan spoke there about everything yesterday.'
'Jan spoke about that everywhere yesterday.'

5.5.2.3. Co-occurrence of weak and strong R-words

Axioms I and II give rise to the expectation that weak and strong R-words cannot co-occur either. This expectation is not borne out, however, as can be seen in the examples in (135), which correspond to the examples in (124a&b).

(135) a. dat er hier gedanst wordt. [.. expl .. loc ..]
that there here danced is
Intended reading: 'People are dancing here.'

b. dat er *hier* vaak *over* gesproken wordt. [.. expl .. pron ..]
that there here often about spoken is
Intended reading: 'People are talking about this.'

The examples in (136) show that strong R-words can also co-occur with quantitative *er*.

(136) a. dat Jan er hier [$_{NP}$ twee [*e*]] gezien heeft. [.. quant .. loc ..]
that Jan there here two seen has
'that Jan saw two [e.g., rats] here.'

b. dat Jan er *hier* [$_{NP}$ drie [*e*]] *in* stopte. [.. quant .. pron ..]
that Jan there here three into put
'that Jan put three [e.g., cigars] in this.'

Example (137a) shows that a weak pronominal R-word can also be combined with a strong locational R-word. A strong pronominal R-word, on the other hand, cannot be combined with a weak locational R-word, as is shown in (137b).

(137) a. dat Jan *er* hier vaak *over* praatte. [.. pron .. loc ..]
that Jan there here often about talked
'that Jan often talked about it here.'

b. *dat Jan er *hier* vaak *over* praatte. [.. loc .. pron ..]

Note that the examples in (135b) and (136b) are actually ambiguous and also allow a reading in which *hier* acts as a locational pro-form. In (135b) *er* then simultaneously performs the functions of expletive and pronominal R-word, and in (136b) it functions then both as licenser of the nominal gap *[e]* and as part of the pronominal PP; cf. Section 5.5.3.1.

In view of the data in (135) to (137) it seems clear that we cannot maintain the idea that the designated [+R]-positions in Axiom I and II can be identified, but that we need two distinct [+R]-positions. Given the fact that the weak R-pronoun always precedes the strong one, we postulate that the weak [+R]-position precedes the strong one. This gives rise to the clause structure in (138). Axioms I and II are now rephrased as in (138a&b).

(138) XP V_{+fin} (Subject) $[+R]_{weak}$ ... $[+R]_{strong}$ ... CLAUSE ADVERB ... V_{-fin}

a. Axiom I: *Er* must be moved into the unique weak [+R]-position.

b. Axiom II: A strong demonstrative R-word may be moved into the unique strong [+R]-position.

The axioms in (138) still leave the ungrammaticality of (137b) unexplained. The fact that the locational phrase is always the second (strong) R-word in the examples above has given rise to the idea that the second [+R]-position in (138) must *always* be used as a landing site for a demonstrative locational R-word, if there is one. From this two predictions follow. First, it is correctly predicted that only weak R-pronouns can be used in the presence of a locational R-word (but see example (133) for a potential problem); the strong R-position is occupied by the locational R-word and hence inaccessible to other strong R-words. Second, it is predicted that the locational R-word must be strong in the presence of another R-word; if the locational R-word were weak, it would have to move to the weak [+R]-position *via* the strong [+R]-position so that all landing sites for R-pronouns are occupied, the weak one by the phonetically realized locational R-word and the strong one by a

°trace of it. This gives an exhaustive account of the data discussed so far with the exception of (129c), which we have put aside.

5.5.2.4. Wh-*movement and topicalization in multiple R-word constructions*

This section will discuss *wh*-movement and topicalization in multiple R-word constructions and show that there is a restriction on the co-occurrence of demonstrative and interrogative/topicalized R-words. Subsection I will show that *wh*-movement and topicalization seem to be blocked by the presence of certain demonstrative R-words; we will account for this in terms of the two [+R]-positions in (138). Subsection II will discuss an example in which *wh*-movement and topicalization of a [-R] word seems to be blocked by the presence of an R-word.

I. Wh-*movement and topicalization in double R-word constructions*

In some cases, *wh*-movement of an R-word is blocked by the presence of another R-word. Consider examples (139a), which is ungrammatical under the interpretation that *waar* is part of the pronominal PP. This has been accounted for by assuming that the *wh*-word *waar* cannot be moved into clause-initial position in one fell swoop, but must first be placed into one of the [+R]-positions in (138). However, since we have seen that the locational R-word *er* is moved via the strong [+R]-position into the weak one, these positions are no longer available for the *wh*-word, so that movement of *waar* into the clause-initial position is blocked. When the locational R-word is strong, as in (139b), it does not move into the weak [+R]-position. Hence, this weak position is accessible to the *wh*-phrase and *wh*-movement is predicted to be possible.

(139) a. **Waar* heeft Jan er vaak *over* gepraat? [.. $pron_{wh}$ .. loc ..]
where has Jan there often about talked
a′. .... V_{+fin} ... $[_{+R}$ $er_i]$ ... $[_{+R}$ $t_i]$ t_i vaak [waar over] ...
b. *Waar* heeft Jan hier vaak *over* gepraat? [.. $pron_{wh}$ .. loc ..]
where has Jan here often about talked
'What did Jan talk often about here?'
b. $waar_j$ V_{+fin} ... $[_{+R}$ $t_j]$ ... $[_{+R}$ $hier_i]$ t_i vaak $[t_j$ over] ...

The examples in (140) show that the same contrast can be found in the case of topicalization of demonstrative R-words.

(140) a. **Daar* heeft Jan er vaak *over* gepraat. [.. $pron_{demonstr}$ .. loc ..]
there has Jan there often about talked
b. *Daar* heeft Jan hier vaak *over* gepraat. [.. $pron_{demonstr}$ .. loc ..]
there has Jan here often about talked
'Jan talked often about that here.'

The judgments on the examples in (139) change under the reverse interpretation, that is, with the preposed interrogative R-word as locational and the second R-word as pronominal. In (141a), pronominal *er* can be placed in the weak [+R]-position, and the locational phrase can be moved via the strong [+R]-position into the clause-initial position. In (141b), however, the locational R-word has been moved via the strong R-position into clause-initial-position, so there is no landing position for the demonstrative R-word *hier* (the empty weak [+R]-position is of course not accessible to *hier* since it is not a weak R-word).

(141) a. Waar heeft Jan *er* vaak *over* gepraat? [.. loc_{wh} .. pron ..]
where has Jan there often about talked
'Where did Jan talk about it often?'
a′. $waar_i$ V_{+fin} ... $[_{+R}$ $er_j]$ ... $[_{+R}$ $t_i]$ t_i vaak $[t_j$ over] ...
b. ??Waar heeft Jan *hier* vaak *over* gepraat? [.. loc_{wh} .. pron ..]
where has Jan here often about talked
b′. $waar_i$ V_{+fin} ... $[_{+R}$ ..] ... $[_{+R}$ $t_i]$ t_i vaak [hier over] ...

The examples in (142) show that the same thing seems to hold for demonstrative pronominal R-words.

(142) a. Daar heeft Jan *er* vaak *over* gepraat. [.. $loc_{demonstr}$ .. pron ..]
there has Jan there often about talked
'Jan talked about it often there.'
b. ??Daar heeft Jan *hier* vaak *over* gepraat. [.. $loc_{demonstr\cdot}$ .. pron ..]
there has Jan here often about talked

The judgments on the examples in (141b) and (142b), which are the ones given in Huybregts (1991), are disputed by Bennis (p.c), who considers (141b) and (142b) fully acceptable and suggests that the relevant reading can be forced in relative clauses like (143). Although a locational interpretation of the relative pro-form *waar* seems more or less acceptable to us, the pronominal reading of *waar* remains the more prominent one, which would be in line with Huybregts' judgments on (141b) and (142b).

(143) de universiteit waar Jan hier vaak over gesproken heeft
the university where Jan here often about spoken has
preferred reading: 'the university that John spoke often about here'
possible reading: 'the university where John spoke a lot about this'

The suggested analysis correctly predicts that expletive and quantitative *er* never block *wh*-movement of a locational or pronominal R-word: the latter can be moved via the strong [+R]-position into the clause-initial position. The examples in (144) and (145), which are the *wh*-movement counterparts of (135) and (136), show that this prediction is indeed borne out. Note in passing that, like (135b) and (136b), (144b) and (145b) also allow a reading in which *waar* 'where' acts as a locational pro-form; the weak R-word *er* then simultaneously performs the functions of expletive and pronominal R-word; cf. Section 5.5.3.1.

(144) a. Waar wordt er gedanst? [.. loc_{wh} .. expl ..)]
where is there danced
'Where do people dance?'
b. *Waar* wordt er vaak *over* gesproken? [.. $pron_{wh}$ .. expl ..]
where is there often about talked
'What are people often talking about?'

(145) a. Waar heeft Jan er twee gezien? [.. loc_{wh} .. quant ..]
where has Jan there two seen
'Where did Jan see two [e.g., rats]?'
b. Waar stopte Jan *er* drie *in*? [.. $pron_{wh}$ .. quant ..]
where put Jan there three into
'Where did Jan put three [e.g., cigars] into?'

It has been reported, however, that topicalization differs from *wh*-movement; examples like (146) with topicalized demonstrative *daar* differ sharply from the examples in (144), which involve interrogative *waar*.

(146) a. *Daar wordt er gedanst. [.. $loc_{demonstr}$ .. expl ..)]
there is there danced
'People are dancing there.'
b. **Daar* wordt er vaak *over* gesproken. [.. $pron_{demonstr}$ .. expl ..]
there is there often about talked
'People are talking about that?'

The unacceptability of the examples in (146) is probably not due to the fact that the expletive blocks movement of the topicalized R-word, but to the fact that the presence of expletive *er* depends not only on whether a (definite) subject is present but also on whether the clause contains material that belongs to the presupposition of the clause; see Section N8.1.4 and Bennis (1986) for more discussion on this restriction on expletive *er*. For instance, example (147a), in which both the subject and the direct object are (nonspecific) indefinite, must contain the expletive, whereas (147b), which contains a definite direct object, is marginal at best when expletive *er* is present; when the direct object is a pronoun, as in (147c), *er* must definitely be absent. The contrast between (144) and (146) can therefore be traced back to the fact that interrogative elements like *waar* are indefinite by definition, whereas demonstrative elements like *daar* are definite.

(147) a. dat *(er) iemand gisteren iets vertelde.
that there someone yesterday something told
'that someone told a story yesterday.'
b. dat (??er) iemand het verhaal gisteren vertelde.
that there someone the story yesterday told
c. dat (*er) iemand het gisteren vertelde.
that there someone it yesterday told

The examples in (148) show that replacement of *waar* by *daar* does not affect the grammaticality judgments when we are dealing with quantitative *er*; the judgments on the examples in (148) are similar to those in (145).

(148) a. Daar heeft Jan er twee gezien? [.. $loc_{demonstr}$ .. quant ..]
there has Jan there two seen
'Jan saw two [e.g., rats] there?'
b. *Daar* stopte Jan er drie *in*? [.. $pron_{demonstr}$ .. quant ..]
there put Jan there three into
'Jan put three [e.g., cigars] into that ?'

That the judgments on (145) and (148) are similar is consistent with the fact, illustrated in (149), that quantitative *er* must be realized irrespective of the presence of presuppositional material.

(149) a. Jan heeft er [$_{NP}$ twee *e*] een verhaal verteld.
Jan has there two a story told
'Jan told a story to two [e.g., children].'

b. Jan heeft er [$_{NP}$ twee *e*] het verhaal verteld.
Jan has there two the story told

c. Jan heeft het er [$_{NP}$ twee *e*] verteld.
Jan has it there two told

A problem for the hypothesis developed above are multiple *wh*-questions like (150), in which the first [+WH] R-word must be interpreted as locational and the second one as pronominal. When the locational *wh*-phrase must be *wh*-moved via the strong R-position, the landing site of the pronominal *wh*-phrase should be occupied by a trace, so that we wrongly predict (150a) to be ungrammatical. Example (150b), on the other hand, is predicted to be possible, since the pronominal R-word can in principle be moved via the weak R-position. We leave these data for future research.

(150) a. Waar$_i$ heeft zij waar$_j$ t_i vaak [$_{PP}$ t$_j$ over] gepraat? [.. loc$_{wh}$ .. pron ..]
where has she where often about talked
'Where did she talk often about what?'

b. *Waar$_j$ heeft zij waar$_i$ t_i vaak [$_{PP}$ t$_j$ over] gepraat? [.. pron$_{wh}$ .. loc ..]
where has she where often about talked
'Where did she talk often about what?'

Note that is (150b) much improved when emphatic accent is assigned to the second occurrence of *waar*. This suggests that focused locational pro-forms need not be moved into the strong [+R]-position when they are contrastively focused. Section 5.5.2.6 will provide more evidence in favor of this conclusion.

II. Wh-*movement and topicalization of [-R] phrases across R-words*

R-words can sometimes also block *wh*-movement and topicalization of [-R] phrases. We will illustrate this by means of *wh*-movement and topicalization of predicative locational phrases. Subsection A will show that the blocking effect arises especially when the R-word is a pronominal R-word, and Subsection B will argue that it cannot be established whether locational R-words have a similar blocking effect. Subsection C will show that expletive and quantitative *er* do not have this blocking effect. Subsection D, finally, shows that non-predicative phrases can freely cross R-words.

A. Wh-*movement and topicalization across a pronominal R-word*

Consider the reference sentences in (151a&a′). Although the examples in (151b&c) are perhaps slightly marked, *wh*-movement and topicalization of the predicatively used locational phrase seems to be possible. In the corresponding primed examples, on the other hand, *wh*-movement and topicalization are completely blocked.

Apparently, the pronominal R-word *daar/er* blocks the movements in question; these examples are also marked when the R-word is adjacent to the preposition.

(151) a. Jan sloeg de spijker met een hamer in de muur.
Jan hit the nail with a hammer into the wall
'Jan hit the nail into the wall with a hammer.'
a′. Jan sloeg er/daar de spijker mee in de muur.
Jan hit there the nail with into the wall
'Jan hit the nail into the wall with it/that.'
b. (?)In welke muur sloeg Jan de spijker met een hamer?
into which wall hit Jan the nail with a hammer
b′. *In welke muur sloeg Jan daar/er de spijker mee?
into which wall hit Jan there the nail with
c. (?)In de muur sloeg Jan de spijker met een hamer.
into the wall hit Jan the nail with a hammer
c′. *In de muur sloeg Jan daar/er de spijker mee.
into the wall hit Jan there the nail with

B. Wh-*movement and topicalization across a locational R-word*

When the clause contains an adverbial locational phrase, as in (152), movement of the predicative locational PP is also blocked; since this blocking effect occurs regardless of whether the adverbial phrase is a full PP or an R-word, the examples in (152) do not shed any further light on the issue of whether R-words may block *wh*-movement and topicalization of [-R] phrases.

(152) a. Jan sloeg in de huiskamer/daar de spijker in de muur.
Jan hit in the living room/there the nail into the wall
'In the living room/There Jan hit the nail into the wall.'
b. *In welke muur sloeg Jan in de huiskamer/daar de spijker?
into which wall hit Jan in the living room/there the nail
c. *In de muur sloeg Jan in de huiskamer/daar de spijker.
into the wall hit Jan in the living room/there the nail

C. Wh-*movement and topicalization across expletive and quantitative* er

The examples in (153) show that movement across expletive *er* is possible. Note that when *wh*-movement or topicalization applies the expletive can be optionally dropped; in (153c), the presence of expletive *er* is even somewhat marked.

(153) a. Er stonden twee grammatica's in de kast.
there stood two grammars in the bookcase
'There were two grammars in the bookcase.'
b. In welke kast stonden (er) twee grammatica's?
in which bookcase stood there two grammars
c. In die kast stonden (?er) twee grammatica's.
in that bookcase stood there two grammars

Quantitative *er* does not have a blocking effect either; the examples in (154b&c) show that *wh*-movement and topicalization are possible across quantitative *er*.

(154) a. Jan zette er [$_{NP}$ twee *e*] in de kast.
Jan put there two into the bookcase
'Jan put two [e.g., grammars] into the bookcase.'

b. In welke kast zette Jan er twee?
into which bookcase put Jan there two
'Into which bookcase did Jan put two [e.g., grammars]?'

c. In de kast zette Jan er twee.
into the bookcase put Jan there two
'Into the bookcase Jan put two [e.g., grammars].'

D. Wh-*movement and topicalization of non-predicative PPs*

Subsection A has shown that a pronominal R-word may block *wh*-movement and topicalization of a [-R] phrase. This does not imply, however, that it always blocks such movements. The examples in (155), for instance, show that movement of the adverbial phrase *met wie/Peter* may cross the pronominal R-word *daar*.

(155) a. Jan heeft *daar* gisteren met Peter *over* gepraat.
Jan has there yesterday with Peter about talked
'Jan talked about it with Peter yesterday.'

b. Met wie heeft Jan *daar* gisteren *over* gepraat?
with whom has Jan there yesterday about talked
'With whom did Jan talk about it yesterday?'

c. Met Peter heeft Jan *daar* gisteren *over* gepraat.
with Peter has Jan there yesterday about talked

The data in (151) and (155) therefore suggest that the pronominal R-word only blocks movement of predicative locational phrases, which may give rise to the hypothesis that the strong [+R]-position is also relevant for movement of such locational phrases. The question of whether this suggestion can be upheld, we leave as a topic for future research.

5.5.2.5. Co-occurrence of multiple pronominal PPs

So far, we have only discussed the co-occurrence of two R-words with different functions. It is, however, also possible to have more than one pronominal PP. Consider the examples in (156), in which (156a) is the reference sentence. In (156b&c) it is shown that both the PP *voor dat boek* and the circumpositional phrase *naar de bibliotheek toe* allow pronominalization. Example (156d) shows that it is not possible to have two occurrences of *er*, which follows from the claim expressed by axiom I in (138a) that there is only one weak [+R]-position available. However, when the second occurrence of *er* is replaced by a strong demonstrative form, as in (156d′), the result is fully acceptable; this would follow from Axiom II in (131), according to which demonstrative R-words can be placed in the strong [+R]-position.

(156) a. Jan is gisteren voor dat boek naar de bibliotheek toe gegaan.
Jan is yesterday for that book to the library TOE went
'Jan went to the library for that book yesterday.'

b. Jan is *er* gisteren *voor* naar de bibliotheek toe gegaan.
Jan is there yesterday for to the library TOE went
'Jan went to the library for it yesterday.'

c. Jan is *er* gisteren voor dat boek *naar toe* gegaan.
Jan is there yesterday for that book to TOE went
'Jan went there (to it) for that book yesterday.'

d. *Jan is er er gisteren voor naar toe gegaan.
Jan is there there yesterday for to TOE went
'Jan went there (to it) for it yesterday.'

d′. Jan is er hier gisteren voor naar toe gegaan.
Jan is there there yesterday for to TOE went
'Jan went to it for this yesterday.' or 'Jan went to this (place) for it yesterday.'

In fact, (156d′) seems to be ambiguous: the pronoun *er* can either be construed as the complement of the preposition *voor* or as the complement or the circumposition *naar ... toe*; judgments are subtle, though, and it might be the case that speakers of Dutch prefer one of the two readings, possibly also depending on the intonation pattern of the example.

Given the assumptions so far, we predict that *wh*-movement is possible when we are dealing with two pronominal PPs, and that the resulting example will be ambiguous. Although giving judgments on the data is somewhat tricky, we have the impression that this prediction is indeed correct.

(157) a. Waar is Jan er gisteren voor naar toe gegaan?
where is Jan there yesterday for to TOE went

b. Waar$_i$ is Jan [$_{+R}$ er$_j$] ...[$_{+R}$ t_i] gisteren [$_{PP}$ t_j voor] [$_{PP}$ t_i naar toe] gegaan?
'Where (to what place) did Jan go to for it yesterday?'

b′. Waar$_j$ is Jan [$_{+R}$ er$_i$] ...[$_{+R}$ t_j] gisteren [$_{PP}$ t_j voor] [$_{PP}$ t_i naar toe] gegaan?
'What did Jan go there (to it) for yesterday?'

The ambiguity of example (157a) is also supported by the fact that, despite their complexity, the two relative constructions in (158) are reasonably acceptable.

(158) a. het boek waar Jan *er* gisteren voor *naar toe* is gegaan
the book where Jan there yesterday for to TOE is gone
'the book for which Jan went to it yesterday'

b. de bibliotheek waar Jan *er* gisteren *voor* naar toe is gegaan
the library where Jan there yesterday for to TOE is gone
'the library to which Jan went for it'

The judgments on (157a) do not seem to change when we replace *er* by a strong form, as in (159a). The derivation then takes place as indicated in the (b)-examples.

(159) a. Waar is Jan daar gisteren voor naar toe gegaan?
where is Jan there yesterday for to TOE gone/come
b. Waar$_i$ is Jan [$_{+R}$ t_i]... [$_{+R}$ daar$_j$] gisteren [$_{PP}$ t_j voor] [$_{PP}$ t_i naar toe] gegaan?
'Where did Jan go for that yesterday?'
b′. Waar$_j$ is Jan [$_{+R}$ t_j]... [$_{+R}$ daar$_i$] gisteren [$_{PP}$ t_j voor] [$_{PP}$ t_i naar toe] gegaan?
'What did Jan go there for yesterday?'

Note that the reading in (160b′), with the strong R-word *hier* 'here', is not readily available with the verb *gaan* 'to go' but requires *komen* 'come'. This is due to the fact that the verb *komen* 'to come' can, but the verb *gaan* 'to go' cannot be readily combined with the locational pronominal PP *hier ... naar toe*: *Jan komt/??gaat hier naar toe* 'Jan comes/goes to this place'. The fact that the choice of verb tends to disambiguate example (160a) provides additional evidence for the claim that the ambiguity reported for (157a) and (159a) is real.

(160) a. Waar is Jan hier gisteren voor naar toe gegaan/gekomen?
where is Jan here yesterday for to TOE gone/come
b. Waar$_i$ is Jan [$_{+R}$ t_i]... [$_{+R}$ hier$_j$] gisteren [$_{PP}$ t_j voor] [$_{PP}$ t_i naar toe] gegaan?
'Where did Jan go for this yesterday?'
b′. Waar$_j$ is Jan [$_{+R}$ t_j]... [$_{+R}$ hier$_i$] gisteren [$_{PP}$ t_j voor] [$_{PP}$ t_i naar toe] gekomen?
'What did Jan come here for yesterday?'

5.5.2.6. Co-occurrence of multiple locational pro-forms

Example (161a) shows that clauses may contain two locational phrases, and (161b) shows that both locational phrases can be replaced by a locational pro-form. Since the two pro-forms in (161b) seem to require emphatic accent, it is not surprising that the pro-forms must both be strong; (161c) shows that using a weak pro-form gives rise to a severely degraded result.

(161) a. Jan slaapt thuis altijd op de zolderkamer.
Jan sleeps at.home always in the attic
'At home Jan is always sleeping in the attic.'
b. Jan slaapt hier altijd daar.
Jan sleeps here always there
c. *Jan slaapt er altijd daar/hier.
Jan sleeps there always there/here

The unacceptability of (161c) is as expected, given our earlier conclusion that the weak locational pro-form *er* is moved into the weak [+R]-position via the strong [+R]-position, so that the latter is no longer accessible to the demonstrative locational pro-form. The acceptability of (161b) is surprising, however, since we have seen that only one strong [+R]-position is available. Perhaps this shows that emphatic focus exempts the strong locational pro-form from moving to the strong [+R]-position, which would be consistent with the fact that placement of the second strong R-word in front of the adverb *altijd* gives rise to a marked result: ??*Jan slaapt hier daar altijd*. See also the discussion of (150b) in Section 5.5.2.4, sub I.

Given the ungrammaticality of (161c) it is not surprising that (162a) is unacceptable as well: *wh*-movement must proceed through the [+R]-positions, but these are occupied by the weak locational pro-form *er* and its trace. Example (161b) seems marked, which would follow if *hier* occupies the strong [+R]-position; note that this example is hard to pronounce with emphatic accent on the locational pro-form *hier*.

(162) a. *Waar slaapt Jan er altijd?
where sleeps Jan there always
b. ??Waar slaapt Jan hier altijd?
where sleeps Jan here always

5.5.2.7. Summary

This section has discussed various restrictions on the co-occurrence of R-words. First, it is impossible to combine two weak or two strong R-words in the middle field of the clause. This has been accounted for by assuming that there are two unique [+R]-positions, one for weak and one for strong R-words. Under the assumption that the weak [+R]-position precedes the strong one, we correctly predict that only (163c) is possible.

(163) a. *... er ... er ...
b. *... R_{strong} ... R_{strong}
c. ... er ... R_{strong}

From (163), it also follows that the expletive and the quantitative R-word cannot co-occur in the middle field of the clause, since they only appear in the weak form *er*; when an expletive or a quantitative R-word is present, it always occurs in the first [+R]-position, so that the second occurrence of the R-word is either locational or pronominal. The weak locational and pronominal R-words differ in that only the latter can be combined with a second strong R-word. This has been accounted for by assuming that all locational forms must be placed in the strong [+R]-position even when they do not occupy it in the surface structure of the clause; when we are dealing with a weak locational R-word both positions are filled—the weak one by the morphologically realized R-word, the strong one by a °trace left by movement of the R-word. In Table 3 we give the predicted judgments, and a reference to the relevant examples.

Table 3: Co-occurrence of weak and strong R-words

WEAK [+R]-POSITION	STRONG [+R]-POSITION	JUDGMENT	EXAMPLE
expletive	locational	✓	(135a)
	pronominal	✓	(135b)
quantitative	locational	✓	(136a)
	pronominal	✓	(136b)
locational	locational	*	(161c)
	pronominal	*	(137b)
pronominal	locational	✓	(137a)
	pronominal	✓	(156d′)

In cases of *wh*-movement, the interrogative R-word must be moved via one of the two R-positions into the clause-initial *wh*-position. The intermediate landing site is indicated by "t_{+wh}" in Table 4. Examples (139a) and (162b) are excluded for the same reason (137b) in Table 3 is; the strong [+R]-position is occupied by a trace of the locational R-word, so that the interrogative R-word cannot use it as an intermediate landing site. Examples (162b) and (141b) are excluded because the non-interrogative R-words occupy the strong [+R]-position so that, by assumption, the interrogative locational R-word must be moved through on its way to the sentence-initial position. Table 4 can be reduplicated for topicalization.

Table 4: Wh-*movement in double R-word constructions*

WH-WORD	WEAK [+R]-POSITION	STRONG [+R]-POSITION	JUDGMENT	EXAMPLE
locational	expletive	t_{+wh}	✓	(144a)
pronominal		t_{+wh}	✓	(144b)
locational	quantitative	t_{+wh}	✓	(145a)
pronominal		t_{+wh}	✓	(145b)
pronominal	locational	t_{-wh} (trace of R_{loc})	*	(139a)
	t_{+wh}	locational	✓	(139b)
locational	locational	t_{+wh}	*	(162a)
		locational	??	(162b)
locational	pronominal	t_{+wh}	✓	(141a)
		pronominal	??	(141b)
pronominal	pronominal	t_{+wh}	✓	(157)
	t_{+wh}	pronominal	✓	(159)

5.5.3. Conflation of functions of er

One occurrence of *er* can simultaneously perform more than one function. However, not all functions of *er* can be conflated. It is generally accepted that *er* cannot simultaneously perform the functions of locational and pronominal *er*, and according to us (but not others), the functions of locational and quantitative *er* cannot be conflated either. If this is indeed true, than only the seven meaning combinations given in Table 5 in Section 5.5.3.2.3 can be simultaneously expressed by *er*. Section 5.5.3.1 starts by discussing cases in which *er* expresses more than one function. Section 5.5.3.2 continues with a discussion of cases in which *er* expresses the same functions more than once.

5.5.3.1. Conflation of two or more different functions of er

This section discusses the conflation of two or more different functions of *er*. Since embedded and main clauses differ somewhat in this respect, we devote separate sections to these two syntactic environments. We start, however, with a general discussion of the question of which functions of *er* can be conflated.

I. Which functions of er *can be conflated?*

The R-word *er* can perform four different functions. It can be used as an expletive in, e.g., an existential construction (164a), as the pronominal R-part of a pronominal

PP (164b), as a locational pro-form (164c), and as the indicator of the nominal gap in quantitative constructions (164d).

(164) a. Er loopt een man op straat. [.. expl ..]
there walks a man in the.street
b. Jan wacht *er* al tijden *op*. [.. pron ..]
Jan waits there for ages for
c. Jan staat er al. [.. loc ..]
Jan stands there already
d. Jan heeft er [$_{NP}$ drie [*e*]] [.. quant ..]
Jan has there three

Sometimes the element *er* can be used to express more than one of these functions at the same time. In (165d), for example, *er* performs the function of both the noun phrase *de sigarenkist* 'the cigar box' and the noun *sigaren* 'cigars' in (165a). This can be proved very easily: in (165b), *er* must be part of the pronominal PP *er ... in*, and since it cannot be dropped, we conclude that it is obligatorily present; in (165d), we are dealing with quantitative *er*, and since it cannot be dropped, we again conclude that it is obligatorily present; since both pronominal and quantitative *er* are obligatorily present, *er* must perform both functions in (165d).

(165) a. Marie stopte drie sigaren in de sigarenkist.
Marie put three cigars into the cigar.box
b. Marie stopte *(er) drie sigaren in. [.. pron ..]
Marie put there three cigars into
c. Marie stopte *(er) [$_{NP}$ drie [*e*]] in de sigarenkist. [.. quant ..]
Marie put there three into the cigar.box
d. Marie stopte er [$_{NP}$ drie [*e*]] in. [.. quant+pron ..]
Marie put there three into

It seems not to be the case, however, that all functions can be conflated. First, example (166b) shows that locational *er* cannot be conflated with pronominal *er* given that *er* can only be interpreted as part of the pronominal PP *er ... op*; pronominalization of the locational PP *op het bal* in (166a) requires that a strong locational R-word like *daar* 'there' be used.

(166) • Pronominal and locational *er* cannot be conflated:
a. Zij vertelde Jan gisteren op het bal over haar jeugd.
she told Jan yesterday at the ball about her youth
'Yesterday she told Jan about her youth at the ball.'
b. Zij vertelde *er* (daar) Jan gisteren *over*. [.. pron ..)]
she told there there Jan yesterday about
'Yesterday, she told Jan about it.'

Second, example (167b) shows that the same thing holds for quantitative and locational *er*. According to us, *er* can only be interpreted as the licenser of the nominal gap *[e]*; pronominalization of the locational PP *in Amsterdam* in (167a) requires that a strong locational R-word like *daar* 'there' or *hier* 'here' be used.

(167) • Locational and quantitative *er* cannot be conflated:
a. Zij bezit drie huizen in Amsterdam.
she owns three houses in Amsterdam
b. Zij bezit er (daar/hier) [$_{NP}$ drie [*e*]]. [.. quant ..]
she owns there there/here three
'She owns three (here).'

By claiming that the functions of locational and quantitative *er* cannot be conflated, we go against a long-standing tradition starting with Bech (1952) that claims otherwise. Examples that are given in support of the assumption that these two functions can be conflated generally take the form in (168), where the context, provided in (168a), restricts the contention of (168b) to students that are in the class. The question we have to ask, however, is whether the fact that the students referred to in (168b) are situated in the class is expressed by the element *er* or is simply an inference made from the context. In order to answer that question, we have to look at example (168c), where *er* can only be taken to be the locational pro-form: according to us, this example sounds pretty forced with *er* present (due to its redundancy). This suggests that *er* does *not* express the locational meaning in (168b) and that we are simply dealing with an inference made from the context.

(168) a. Gewoonlijk heb ik twintig leerlingen in de klas, ...
usually have I twenty students in the class
b. ... maar vandaag heb ik er maar vijf.
but today have I there only five
c. ... maar vandaag heb ik (??er) maar vijf studenten.
but today have I there only five students

Our claim that quantitative and locational *er* cannot be conflated also contradicts the claim in Bennis (1986: 180) that the primeless examples in (169) are acceptable: since *wonen* 'to live' and *doorbrengen* 'to spend time' require the presence of a locational phrase, these examples would provide evidence in favor of the assumption that the quantitative and locational functions of *er* can be conflated. However, we believe that in these cases the presence of a strong locational R-word, as in the primed examples, is much preferred; the primeless examples are marginal at best.

(169) a. %dat er maar [$_{NP}$ twee *e*] wonen.
that there only two live
a′. dat er hier maar [$_{NP}$ twee *e*] wonen.
that there here only two live
'that only two [e.g., students] live here.'
b. %Hij bracht er [$_{NP}$ twee *e*] door.
he spent there two prt.
b′. Hij bracht er hier [$_{NP}$ twee *e*] door.
he spent there here two prt.
'He spent two [e.g., vacation days] here.'

We leave it to the reader to decide whether our arguments against the traditional view are conclusive, but in the following we will assume they are. Therefore, when we put aside for the moment the possibility that *er* performs the same function more than once (see Section 5.5.3.2 for cases in which *er* is part of two pronominal PPs or quantitative noun phrases at the same time), we predict the following conflations of functions to be possible: all other combinations are excluded by the two observational generalizations in (166) and (167).

(170) a. Single function: expletive; locational; pronominal; quantitative
b. Dual function: expletive + pronominal ; expletive + quantitative; quantitative + pronominal ; expletive + locational
c. Triple function: expletive + pronominal + quantitative

The possibilities in (170a) are of course trivial: no conflation has taken place, as in the examples in (164). In the following sections, we will therefore focus on the options in (170b&c) and show that these combinations do indeed occur.

II. Embedded clauses

This section will show that the predicted conflations of functions in (170b&c) do indeed arise. The dual functions expletive + pronominal and expletive + quantitative are illustrated in (171b&c), and in (171d) the only possibility of combining three functions is illustrated.

(171) a. dat er gisteren drie potloden op tafel lagen. [.. expl ..]
that there yesterday three pencils on the.table lay
'that there were three pencils lying on the table yesterday.'
b. dat er gisteren drie potloden op lagen. [.. expl+pron ..]
that there yesterday three pencils on lay
'that there were three pencils lying on it yesterday.'
c. dat er gisteren drie op tafel lagen. [.. expl+quant ..]
that there yesterday three on the table lay
'that there were three lying on the table yesterday.'
d. dat er gisteren drie op lagen. [.. expl+pron+quant ..]
that there yesterday three on lay
'that there were three lying on it yesterday.'

The dual function quantitative + pronominal has already been demonstrated in (165), and we simply repeat the examples here.

(172) a. Marie stopte drie sigaren in de sigarenkist.
Marie put three cigars into the cigar.box
b. Marie stopte *(er) drie sigaren in. [.. pron ..]
Marie put there three cigars into
c. Marie stopte *(er) [$_{NP}$ drie [*e*]] in de sigarenkist. [.. quant ..]
Marie put there three into the cigar.box
d. Marie stopte er [$_{NP}$ drie [*e*]] in. [.. quant+pron ..]
Marie put there three into

Example (173c) demonstrates the final option in (170b). That we are dealing here with a conflation of the expletive and locational functions of *er* is clear from the examples in (173a&b): (173a) shows that (in the absence of some other locational phrase or qualifying adjectival phrase) locational *er* is obligatorily present in this construction, and (173b) shows that an indefinite noun phrase requires the presence of expletive *er*. As a consequence, we must conclude that *er* performs both functions in (173c).

(173) a. dat Jan *(er) woont. [.. loc ..]
that Jan there lives
'that Jan lives there.'
b. dat *(er) veel mensen wonen in Amsterdam. [.. expl ..]
that there many people live in Amsterdam
'that many people walk.'
c. dat er veel mensen wonen. [.. expl+loc ..]
that there many people live
'that many people live there.'

III. Main clauses

Section 5.5.1 has shown that the behavior of the weak R-word *er* resembles that of weak object pronouns in that it is normally not able to occupy the clause-initial position in main clauses. The only exception to this generalization is expletive *er*, which behaves like weak subject pronouns in that it may occur in first position. This exceptional status of expletive *er* raises the question whether the placement of expletive *er* affects the conflation of the functions of *er*. In order to establish this, we will investigate the main clauses corresponding to (171) and (173).

The examples in (174) show that when expletive *er* occupies the regular subject position after the finite verb in second position, the judgments are just the same as in the embedded clauses in (171).

(174) a. Gisteren lagen er drie potloden op tafel. [.. expl ..]
yesterday lay there three pencils on the table
'Yesterday there were lying three pencils on the table.'
b. Gisteren lagen er drie potloden op. [.. expl+pron ..]
yesterday lay there three pencils on
c. Gisteren lagen er drie op tafel. [.. expl+quant ..]
yesterday lay there three on the table
d. Gisteren lagen er drie op. [.. expl+pron+quant ..]
yesterday lay there three on

Example (175a) just illustrates that expletive *er* can also occupy the first position in the clause. The two examples in (175b) show that conflation of the expletive and pronominal functions of *er* is not affected by the sentence-initial placement of the expletive; expressing the pronominal function by means of a separate occurrence of *er*, as in (175b′), leads to ungrammaticality.

(175) a. Er lagen gisteren drie potloden op tafel. [.. expl ..]
b. Er lagen gisteren drie potloden op. [.. expl+pron ..]
b′. *Er lagen er gisteren drie potloden op. [.. expl .. pron ..]

Things are different, however, in the case of expletive and quantitative *er*. The (b)-examples in (176) shows that conflation of the two functions is not possible; the quantitative function must be expressed by means of a separate occurrence of *er* in the regular position of non-expletive *er*, as in (176c′).

(176) a. Er lagen gisteren drie potloden op tafel. [.. expl ..]
b. *Er lagen gisteren drie op tafel. [.. expl+quant ..]
b′. Er lagen er gisteren drie op tafel. [.. expl .. quant ..]

When we are dealing with three functions, as in (177), one additional occurrence of *er* is again required. In view of the data in (175) and (176), it seems we are justified in assuming that the first occurrence of *er* expresses the expletive and the pronominal functions, whereas the second one only expresses the quantitative function, but it must be noted that we do not have independent evidence bearing on this claim.

(177) Er lagen er gisteren drie op. [.. expl+pron .. quant ..]

The examples in (178), finally, provide the main clause counterpart of (173c) and show that the locational pro-form behaves like pronominal *er* in that conflation with the expletive is also required when *er* occupies the sentence-initial position.

(178) a. Toen woonden er nog veel mensen. [.. expl+loc ..]
then lived there still many people
'Many people lived there then.'
b. Er wonen veel mensen. [.. expl+loc ..]
there live many people
'There live many people there.'
b′. *Er wonen er veel mensen. [.. expl .. loc ..]
there live there many people

5.5.3.2. Conflation of two similar functions of er

Section 5.5.3.1 has discussed the conflation of two or more *different* functions of *er*. It is, however, also possible that two *similar* functions of *er* are conflated. This is not possible with expletive *er* for the obvious reason that a clause contains at most one expletive. It does not occur with locational *er* either, but it is possible with pronominal and quantitative *er*.

5.5.3.2.1. Conflation of two pronominal R-words

Example (179a) contains two PPs that both allow R-extraction; cf. (179b&c). The (d)-examples show that two stranded prepositions must occur with just a single occurrence of pronominal *er*, which shows that two occurrences of pronominal *er* are obligatorily conflated. Similar examples are given in (180).

(179) a. Jan is speciaal voor dat boek naar de bibliotheek toe gegaan.
Jan is especially for that book to the library went
'Jan went to the library for that book especially.'
b. Jan is *er* speciaal *voor* naar de bibliotheek toe gegaan.
c. Jan is *er* speciaal voor dat boek *naar toe* gegaan.
d. Jan is er speciaal voor naar toe gegaan.
d′. *Jan is er er speciaal voor naar toe gegaan.

(180) a. Jan heeft de sleutel met een tang uit het slot gehaald
Jan has the key with a pair of tongs out.of the lock taken
'Jan took the key out of the lock with pliers.'
b. Jan heeft *er* de sleutel *mee* uit het slot gehaald.
c. Jan heeft *er* de sleutel met een tang *uit* gehaald.
d. Jan heeft er de sleutel mee uit gehaald.
d′. *Jan heeft er er de sleutel mee uit gehaald.

However, constructions in which *er* is construed with two stranded adpositions are not always available. Examples like (181d) and (182d), for example seem ungrammatical, despite the fact that the (b)- and (c)-examples show that the two PPs both allow R-extraction on their own.

(181) a. Jan heeft net met de lepel in de soep geroerd.
Jan has just.now with the spoon in the soup stirred
'Jan has stirred the soup with that spoon.'
b. Jan heeft *er* net met de lepel *in* geroerd.
c. Jan heeft *er* net *mee* in de soep geroerd.
d. *?Jan heeft er net mee in geroerd.
d′. *Jan heeft er er net mee in geroerd.

(182) a. Jan keek net met zijn verrekijker naar een bootje.
Jan looked just. now with his binoculars to a small boat
'Jan looked at a small boat with his binoculars.'
b. Jan keek *er* net met zijn verrekijker *naar*.
c. Jan keek *er* net *mee* naar een bootje.
d. *Jan keek er net mee naar.
d′. *Jan keek er er net mee naar.

The difference between (179) and (180), on the one hand, and (181) and (182), on the other, has not been discussed in the literature and therefore we can only speculate about what causes the difference in judgments on the two sets of examples. The most conspicuous difference is that the former set involves complementive locational/directional PPs (*naar de bibliotheek toe* and *uit het slot*, respectively), whereas the latter two examples do not. Our conjecture is therefore that this type of conflation is possible only when one of the two pronominal PPs is a complementive, that is, acts a predicatively used locational or directional phrase. Future research must show whether this conjecture is on the right track.

Given that R-words other than *er* may also strand prepositions, the question arises whether the possibility of conflation is a typical property of *er* or a more general property of R-words. The data in (183) suggest that the former is the case; note that we are not able to give examples with relative pronouns since their reference is determined by their (unique) antecedent.

(183) a. *Jan heeft *hier/daar* de sleutel *mee* *uit* gehaald.
Jan has here/there the key with out.of taken
Intended reading: 'Jan took the key out of this/that with this/that.'

b. *Jan heeft *ergens* de sleutel *mee* *uit* gehaald.
Jan has somewhere the key with out.of taken
Intended reading: 'Jan took the key out of something with something.'

c. *Jan heeft *overal* de sleutel *mee* *uit* gehaald.
Jan has everywhere the key with out.of taken
Intended reading: 'Jan took the key out of everything with everything.'

d. **Waar* heeft Jan de sleutel *mee* *uit* gehaald?
where has Jan the key with out.of taken
Intended reading: 'With what did Jan take the key out of what?'

In order to have two stranded prepositions, in general two R-words must be present as in (184). The examples are somewhat hard to process but it seems that the first R-word in each of the examples in (184) must be interpreted as the pronominal object of the locational preposition *uit* 'out of'; the reading in which the first R-word is construed as the pronominal object of the stranded preposition *mee* 'with' seems to be excluded. This also holds for the interrogative R-word in (184d), where *waar* is construed as the pronominal object of *uit*. These examples therefore all have a similar structure involving a nested dependency: .. R-word$_i$ ... R-word$_j$ .. P$_j$ .. P$_i$, where the indices indicate which R-word is construed with which adposition.

(184) a. Jan heeft er hier/daar de sleutel mee uit gehaald.
Jan has there here/there the key with out.of taken
Intended reading: 'Jan took the key out of it with this/that.'

b. ?Jan heeft er ergens de sleutel mee uit gehaald.
Jan has there somewhere the key with out.of taken
Intended reading: 'Jan took the key out of it with something.'

c. ?Jan heeft er overal de sleutel mee uit gehaald.
Jan has there everywhere the key with out.of taken
Intended reading: 'Jan took the key out of it with everything.'

d. Waar heeft Jan er de sleutel mee uit gehaald?
where has Jan there the key with out.of taken
Intended reading: 'What did Jan take the key out of with it?'

To conclude this section, we want to discuss one more example, taken from Haeseryn (1997:488). As in (179) and (180), the example in (185) involves one complementive PP, viz. *in de krant*, so that this example falls under the earlier hypothesis that one of the two PPs involved must be a complementive. What is special about this example, however, is that the *over*-PP seems to function as the modifier of a subject noun phrase. Since the subject noun phrase is indefinite, *er* in (185a) is an expletive. In (185b&c), *er* simultaneously functions as an expletive and as a pronominal R-word. In (185d), *er* is construed with two stranded prepositions. We have added (185e) just to illustrate how complex constructions like these can become: in addition to the three functions it already has in (185d), *er* also functions as quantitative *er* in this example.

(185) a. Vandaag staan er twee artikelen over zure regen in de krant.
today stand there two articles about acid rain in the newspaper
'Today, there are two articles about acid rain in the paper.'

b. Vandaag staan *er* twee artikelen *over* in de krant.
today stand there two articles about in the newspaper

c. Vandaag staan *er* twee artikelen over zure regen *in*.
today stand there two articles about acid rain in

d. Vandaag staan *er* twee artikelen *over* in.
today stand there two articles about in

e. Vandaag staan er [$_{NP}$ twee [*e*] over] in.
today stand there two about in

5.5.3.2.2. Conflation of two occurrences of quantitative er

Example (186a) shows that it is also possible to conflate two instances of quantitative *er*. That we are dealing with conflation here is clear from the examples in (186b&c): when the direct object is a full noun phrase, as in (186b), *er* is obligatorily present to indicate the nominal gap in the subject; when the subject is a full noun phrase, *er* is present to indicate the nominal gap in the direct object: consequently, *er* in (186a) must simultaneously perform both functions. Note that a subject with a nominal gap may precede quantitative *er*; see Section N6.3 for further discussion.

(186) Iedere student heeft een onvoldoende gekregen ...
every student has an unsatisfactory mark gotten
'Every student got an unsatisfactory mark ...'

a. ... en [$_{NP}$ drie *e*] hebben er zelfs [$_{NP}$ twee *e*].
and three have there even two
'... and three even got two.'

b. ... en [$_{NP}$ drie *e*] hebben *(er) zelfs twee onvoldoendes.
and three have there even two unsatisfactory marks
'... and three even got two unsatisfactory marks.'

c. ... en drie studenten hebben *(er) zelfs [$_{NP}$ twee *e*].
and three students have there even two
'... and three students even got two.'

5.5.3.2.3. Summary

This section has discussed the conflation of functions of *er*. We have shown that all functions of *er* can be conflated with the exception of (i) the locational and the pronominal function and (ii) the locational and the quantitative function; cf. (166) and (167). Consequently, *er* can simultaneously express up to three different functions; cf. (170). A single occurrence of *er* can also be construed with more than one pronominal PP or quantitative noun phrase. Table 5 gives an overview of the possibilities, with references to the examples in question that illustrate them. Recall that main clauses with expletive *er* in first position exhibit a slightly deviant pattern; cf. (176).

Table 5: Conflation of functions of er

FUNCTION			EXAMPLE
expletive	pronominal		(171b)
	quantitative		(171c)
	locational		(173c)
	pronominal	quantitative	(171d)
quantitative	pronominal		(165d)
	quantitative		(186a)
pronominal	pronominal		(179d)/(180d)

More complex examples can be constructed by combining conflation of different and similar functions. We conclude this section by giving one such example. In (187a), *er* only has an expletive function. In (187b), there are two quantitative noun phrases, so *er* simultaneously performs the expletive function once and the quantitative function twice. In (187c), R-pronominalization has been applied to the PP *uit de boekenkast*, so that *er* performs the pronominal function on top of the other functions in (187b).

(187) a. dat er twee studenten drie boeken uit de boekenkast gehaald hebben.
that there two students three books out.of the bookcase fetched have
'that two students fetched three books out of the bookcase.'

b. dat er [$_{NP}$ twee *e*] [$_{NP}$ drie *e*] uit de boekenkast gehaald hebben.

c. dat er [$_{NP}$ twee *e*] [$_{NP}$ drie *e*] uit gehaald hebben.

5.6. Bibliographical notes

The discussion of R-pronominalization and R-extraction in this section is mainly based on the seminal PhD theses by Van Riemsdijk (1978), Bennis (1986) as well as a lesser known (Dutch) paper on the distribution of *er* by Huybregts (1991). Other important works that contain relevant discussions are Bech (1952), Coppen (1991), Geerts (1984), Beeken (1993), Odijk (1993), Zwart (1993), Barbiers (1995), and Haeseryn (1997). Quantitative and expletive *er* are more extensively discussed in Section N6.3 and N8.1.4.

Glossary

Adverb:
The notion of adverb does not refer to entities with a certain categorial status, as do the notions verb, noun, adjective and preposition, but to lexical elements that can perform a certain syntactic function in the clause, more specifically that of an adverbial phrase. Our use of this notion should therefore be seen as shorthand for “adverbially used adjective” given that many adverbs exhibit adjectival properties: they may be used attributively or predicatively in other contexts, or exhibit typical syntactic or morphological properties like the ones given in (i).

(i) a. Modification by *erg/heel/zeer* ‘very’
b. Comparative and superlative formation
c. *On-* prefixation
d. Having an adjectivizing suffix

Despite the fact that we do not acknowledge the existence of a lexical category “adverb”, it cannot be denied that there are certain adverbs, like the intensifiers *zeer* ‘very’ and *heel* ‘very’ mentioned in (ia), for which there is no direct syntactic or morphological evidence that they are adjectival in nature. However, the fact that they cannot be inflected for tense and agreement shows that they are not verbs, and the fact that they can neither be preceded by a determiner nor appear in an argument position strongly suggests that they are not nouns either. Therefore, we provisionally conclude that they must be adjectives, which is supported by the fact that they share the semantic property of being able to modify an adjective.

Adverb tests:
In cases of modification of a verbal projection, at least two types of adverbial phrases must be distinguished. The first type involves modification of the proposition expressed by the clause, which is therefore referred to as a clause adjunct. Clauses that contain this type of adverbial phrase can be paraphrased as in (ia); a concrete example is given in (ia′&a″). The second type involves modification of the verb (phrase) only, and is referred to as a VP adjunct. Clauses that contain this type of adverbial phrase can be paraphrased as in (ib), in which the pronoun must be construed as identical to the subject of the clause; a concrete example is given in (ib′&b″). See Section A8.2 for further discussion.

(i) a. Clause adjunct: Het is ADVERB zo dat CLAUSE
a′. Jan werkt natuurlijk.
Jan works of.course
a″. Het is natuurlijk zo dat Jan werkt.
it is of.course the.case that Jan works
b. VP adjunct: [$_{CLAUSE}$ subject$_i$ ...] en pronoun$_i$ doet dat ADVERB
b′. Jan lacht hard.
Jan laughs loudly
b″. Jan$_i$ lacht en hij$_i$ doet dat hard.
Jan laughs and he does that loudly

Binding:
A noun phrase (typically a pronoun) is said to be bound when it is coreferential with a °c-commanding antecedent. Noun phrases differ with respect to the syntactic domain within which they must or can be bound. This is clear from the fact illustrated by the examples in (ia&b) that reflexive and referential personal pronouns like *zichzelf* and *hem* are in complementary distribution. Referential expressions like *de jongen* in (ic) normally remain free (= not bound) within their sentence.

(i) a. Ik denk dat Jan$_i$ zichzelf$_i$/*hem$_i$ bewondert.
I think that Jan himself/him admires
'I think that Jan admires himself.'
b. Jan$_i$ denkt dat ik hem$_i$/*zichzelf$_i$ bewonder.
Jan thinks that I him/himself admire
'Jan thinks that I admire him.'
c. *Jan$_i$ denkt dat ik de jongen$_i$ bewonder.
Jan thinks that I the boy admire

Data like (i) have given rise to the formulation of the three binding conditions in (ii), in which the notion of local domain has not been defined. For the examples in (i), we may provisionally assume that it refers to the minimal clause containing the relevant noun phrase, but there are data that complicate matters; cf. Section N5.2.1.5, sub III. for a more detailed discussion.

(ii) • Binding conditions
a. Anaphors like *zichzelf* 'himself' must be bound within their local domain.
b. Pronouns like *hem* 'him' must be free (= not bound) within their local domain.
c. Referential expressions like *Jan* or *de jongen* 'the boy' must be free.

C-command:
C-command refers to an asymmetric relation between the constituents in a phrase, which is generally defined in structural terms of a tree diagram: α c-commands β if (i) α ≠ β, (ii) α does not dominate β, and (iii) the node that immediately dominates α also dominates β. When we restrict ourselves to clauses and ignore the verbs, this relation can also be expressed by the functional hierarchy in (i), where A > B indicates that A c-commands B and everything that is embedded in B. This means, for example, that the subject c-commands the nominal objects, the periphrastic indirect object, the PP-complement(s) and all the adjuncts of its clause, including everything that may be embedded within these constituents.

(i) C-command hierarchy: subject > indirect object-NP > direct object > indirect object-PP > PP-complement > adjunct

Comparison:
See °degrees of comparison.

Complementive:
This notion refers to the predicative complement of the verb in copular, resultative or *vinden*-constructions. In (i) some examples are given with adjectival predicates.

A complementive may also be a nominal or a (spatial) adpositional phrase, e.g., *Jan is leraar* 'Jan is a teacher' and *Jan heeft het boek in de kast gelegd* 'Jan has put the book on the shelves'. In neutral sentences complementives are left-adjacent to the clause-final verb. This is especially clear with PP-complementives as these differ from other PPs in that they cannot undergo °PP-over-V: **Jan heeft het boek gelegd in de kast.*

(i) a. Jan is *erg aardig.*
Jan is very nice
b. Jan slaat de hond *dood.*
Jan hits the dog dead
c. Ik vind Jan *erg aardig.*
I consider Jan very nice

Conjunction Reduction:
Within a coordinated structure, deletion of a phrase within a conjunct under identity with a phrase within the other conjunct. If the deleted phrase belongs to the first conjunct, the deletion operation is referred to as BACKWARD Conjunction Reduction; if the deleted phrase belongs to the second conjunct, the operation is referred to as FORWARD Conjunction Reduction.

(i) a. [Jan kocht een blauwe __] en [Peter kocht een groene auto].
Jan bought a blue and Peter bought a green car
b. [Jan kocht een boek] en [__ leende een plaat].
Jan bought a book and borrowed a record

Backward Conjunction Reduction is also known as Right Node Raising because early transformational grammar derived examples like (ia) by rightward movement of the apparently deleted element simultaneously from the left and the right conjunct. This movement analysis is controversial given that it forces us to assume movements that are not independently motivated: in (i), for example, the movement analysis has to assume that the head noun *auto* can be extracted from the complex noun phrase *een blauwe/groene auto*, which is not attested in more uncontroversial cases of leftward movement. The existence of Forward Conjunction Reduction is also controversial; examples like (ib) can readily be derived by assuming that some lower verbal projections are coordinated: *Jan [[kocht een boek] en [leende een plaat]].*

Constituency test:
Test involving movement of a string of words into the sentence-initial position, that is, the position immediately preceding the finite verb in main clauses. Any string of words that can occupy this position in Dutch is considered a constituent. Satisfying this test is sufficient for assuming constituency, but not necessary given that constituents can be embedded within larger constituents that do not allow extraction. The test provides pretty reliable results when it comes to the determination of the clausal constituents (the arguments and the adjuncts of the clause). Other tests that are occasionally used are coordination and clefting.

Degrees of comparison:
The degrees of comparison are given in (i). Instead of laborious terms like *comparative in relation to a higher degree*, we will use the shorter terms like *majorative degree*. In (i), these terms are given in small caps. See A4 for more discussion.

(i) a. POSITIVE degree — *groot* 'big'
b. Comparison in relation to a higher degree:
(i) comparative: MAJORATIVE degree — *groter* 'bigger'
(ii) superlative: MAXIMATIVE degree — *grootst* 'biggest'
c. Comparison in relation to the same degree:
EQUATIVE degree — *even groot* 'as big'
d. Comparison in relation to a lower degree:
(i) comparative: MINORATIVE degree — *minder groot* 'less big'
(ii) superlative: MINIMATIVE degree — *minst groot* 'least big'

DO-subject:
The subject of a passive or an °unaccusative verb. This notion is used to express that the subjects of unaccusative and passive verbs have various properties in common with the direct objects of transitive verbs. Other notions that can be found in the literature referring to the same notion are DERIVED SUBJECT and LOGICAL OBJECT.

Extraposition:
A movement operation that is assumed to place a clause to the right of the verbs in clause-final position. Under the traditional OV-analysis of Dutch, complement clauses are base-generated to the left of the main verb, as in (ib), and obligatorily moved to the right of the verb. Extraposition of PPs is called °PP-over-V. Extraposition of noun phrases and APs is not possible in Dutch.

(i) a. dat Jan [dat hij ziek is] denkt ⇒
that Jan that he ill is thinks
b. dat Jan t_i denkt [dat hij ziek is]$_i$

Since Kayne (1994), there is a still-ongoing debate concerning whether (ib) is derived from (ia) by means of Extraposition or whether the complement is base-generated to the right of V; cf. Baltin (2006) and Broekhuis (2008:ch.2) for a review of a number of the currently available proposals. In this work, we will use the notion of Extraposition as a purely descriptive term in order to refer to the placement of the clause to the right of the verb.

Focus:
The notion of focus is used in several different ways that should be kept strictly apart; see De Swart and De Hoop (2000) for a more extensive discussion of this notion.

I. When we are concerned with the information structure of the clause, the notion focus refers to the "new" information of the clause. As such it is opposed to the notion of presupposition, which refers to the "old" information in the clause.

II. The notion of focus is also used for certain elements in the clause that are phonetically emphasized by means of accent. Often, a distinction is made between emphatic, contrastive and restrictive focus. EMPHATIC focus simply highlights one of the constituents in the clause, as in (ia). CONTRASTIVE focus is normally used when one or more specific referents are part of the domain of discourse to which the proposition does not apply, and can also be used to deny a certain presupposition on the part of the hearer, as in (ib). RESTRICTIVE focus implies that the proposition in question is not true of any other referents: a specific, restricted set is selected and a proposition is said to hold for this set only. It is often used for restrictive adverbial phrases like *van Jan* in (ic): assigning focus to this phrase suggests that the other relevant persons in the discourse did not yet hand in the assignment.

(i) a. Ik heb hem een BOEK gegeven.
I have him a book given
'I have given him a BOOK.'
b. Nee, ik heb hem een BOEK gegeven (en geen PLAAT).
no, I have him a book given and not.a record
'No, I gave him a BOOK (not a RECORD).'
c. Van JAN heb ik de opdracht al ontvangen.
from Jan have I the assignment already received
'From JAN, I have already received the assignment.'

Freezing:
The phenomenon that extraction from certain moved constituents is not possible. For example, if a prepositional complement occupies its "unmarked" position immediately to the left of the clause-final verb(s), °R-extraction is possible, as shown by (ia'). However, if it occupies a position more to the left, R-extraction is excluded, as is shown by (ib′). In the primed examples the stranded preposition and its moved complement are given in italics.

(i) a. dat Jan al tijden op dat boek wacht.
that Jan already ages for that book waits
'that Jan has already been waiting for that book for ages.'
a′. het boek *waar* Jan al tijden *op* wacht
the book where Jan already ages for waits
'the book that Jan has already been waiting for for ages'
b. dat Jan op dat boek al tijden wacht.
b′. *het boek *waar* Jan *op* al tijden wacht

Left dislocation:
A construction akin to topicalization that does not involve movement of the dislocated element. The dislocated element is probably external to the clause, which is clear from the fact that it is associated with a resumptive element that is moved into the sentence-initial position immediately preceding the finite verb in second position. In (ia), the noun phrase *dat boek* is the left-dislocated element, and the resumptive element is the demonstrative pronoun *dat*. If the left-dislocated element is logically the object of a preposition, the resumptive element is an °R-pronoun or a complete PP, as in (ib) and (ic), respectively.

(i) a. Dat boek, dat heb ik gisteren gelezen.
that book that have I yesterday read
b. Die jongen, *daar* heb ik gisteren *over* gesproken.
that boy there have I yesterday about spoken
c. Die jongen, over hem heb ik gisteren gesproken.
that boy about him have I yesterday spoken

Logical SUBJECT (vs. subject):
The constituent of which some other constituent is predicated. The notion coincides with the notion of external argument in generative grammar. This notion of logical SUBJECT, which is based on the thematic relation within the clause, differs from the traditional notion of subject that is used to refer to the nominative argument in the clause.

Middle field:
The middle field of the clause is defined as that part of the clause bounded to the right by the verbs in clause-final position (if present), and to the left by the complementizer in an embedded clause or the finite verb in second position of a main clause. The middle field of the examples in (i) is given in italics.

(i) a. Gisteren heeft *Jan met plezier dat boek* gelezen.
yesterday has Jan with pleasure that book read
b. Ik denk [dat *Jan met plezier dat boek* gelezen heeft].
I think that Jan with pleasure that book read has

It is important to realize that the middle field of a clause is not a constituent, but simply refers to a set of positions within the clause. This set of positions includes the base positions of the nominal arguments of the verb within VP (but not the verb itself), as well as a variety of positions external to VP such as the positions of the adverbial phrases and positions that can act as a landing site for °scrambling.

PP-over-V:
Many adpositional phrases can occur both in a position preceding and in a position following the verb(s) in clause-final position. Some examples are given in (i). In traditional generative grammar, it is assumed that the order in (ia) is the base order and that the other orders are derived by °extraposition of the PPs: (ib) is derived by PP-over-V of the adverbial adjunct of place *op het station* 'at the station', example (ic) by PP-over-V of the PP-complement of the main verb, *op zijn vader* 'for his father', and example (id) by PP-over-V of both PPs. Observe that the PPs occur in inverted order in (ia) and (id), that is, PP-over-V of more than one PP results in a mirroring of the original order; cf. Koster (1974).

(i) a. Jan heeft op het station op zijn vader gewacht.
Jan has at the station for his father waited
'Jan has waited for his father at the station.'
b. Jan heeft op zijn vader gewacht op het station.
c. Jan heeft op het station gewacht op zijn vader.
d. Jan heeft gewacht op zijn vader op het station.

PP-over-V seems to be related to the information structure of the clause. In Dutch the presence of expletive *er* signals that the clause does not contain a constituent expressing a presupposition. Given the fact that the expletive is optional in (iia), we must conclude that the PP *in het stadion* can be interpreted either as part of the focus of the clause or as a presupposition. However, the obligatory presence of the expletive in (iib) indicates that the postverbal PP must be part of the focus of the clause; see also Koster (1978), Guéron (1980), Scherpenisse (1985), and Bennis (1986).

(ii) a. dat (er) in het stadion gevoetbald wordt.
that there in the stadium played.soccer is
'People are playing soccer in the stadium.'
b. dat *(er) gevoetbald wordt in het stadion.

The traditional assumption that PP-over-V involves extraposition of the PP (Koster 1973/1974) has recently been challenged, and many alternative proposals are available at this moment; see, e.g., Kayne (1994), Kaan (1992), Barbiers (1995), Bianchi (1999), Koster (2000), De Vries (2002), and Broekhuis (2008) for relevant discussion. Since it is descriptively simpler, we adopt the traditional view in the main text, but it must be kept in mind that this is not the generally accepted view at the present moment.

Preposition stranding:
See °R-extraction.

Presupposition:
See °focus.

PRO:
A phonetically unrealized pronominal noun phrase that may act as the subject of, e.g., an infinitival clause. PRO may be controlled by (= construed as coreferential with) some noun phrase in the matrix clause, as in (ia), or be interpreted as having arbitrary reference, as in (ib).

(i) a. $John_i$ tries [PRO_i to fix the sink].
b. It is nice [PRO to visit Mary].

Projection:
Each lexical head L is assumed to form a projection (= a larger structure) LP by combining with its arguments and (optional) modifiers. Generally, it is assumed that a projection is hierarchically structured: first, L combines with its complement(s) and after that it combines with its subject and modifiers. Evidence for this comes, e.g., from °binding: a subject can bind an object but not vice versa.

In current generative grammar it is commonly assumed that functional heads (like complementizers, numerals or determiners) project a so-called functional projection FP by combining with some lexical projection LP or some other functional projection. For example, the noun phrase *de drie kleine kinderen* 'the three little children' is assumed to have the structure in (i): first, the lexical N *kinderen* 'children' combines with its attributive modifier *kleine* to form the lexical projection NP; after that, the numeral *drie* 'three' forms the functional projection NumP by combining with the NP; finally, the determiner *de* 'the' combines with the NumP, and forms the functional projection DP.

(i) $[_{DP}$ de $[_{NumP}$ drie $[_{NP}$ kleine kinderen]]]
the three little children

Quantitative *er*:
Indefinite (but not definite) noun phrases containing a cardinal numeral or a weak quantifier may co-occur with so-called quantitative *er*; cf. (ia&b). A noun phrase associated with quantitative *er* is characterized as containing an interpretative gap [*e*]. The descriptive content of this gap must be recoverable from the discourse or the extra-linguistic context. Example (ic) shows that the empty noun must be [+COUNT]; when it is [-COUNT], quantitative *er* cannot be used. Quantitative *er* is discussed in more detail in Section N6.3.

(i) a. Jan heeft twee (mooie) boeken en Piet heeft er [drie [*e*]]. [indefinite]
Jan has two beautiful books and Piet has ER three
a′. *Jan heeft de twee boeken en Piet heeft er [de drie [*e*]]. [definite]
Jan has the two books and Piet has ER the three
b. Jan heeft weinig boeken maar Marie heeft er [veel [*e*]].
Jan has few books but Marie has ER many
c. *Jan heeft veel wijn maar Piet heeft er [weinig [*e*]].
Jan has much wine but Piet has ER little

R-extraction:
In Dutch, °preposition stranding is not possible through movement of an NP-complement of the adposition, but only through extraction of an °R-pronoun (*er*/*waar*) from pronominal PPs like *er onder* 'under it' or *waar onder* 'under what'. Stranding of the preposition may be the result of, e.g., scrambling of the R-pronoun, as in (ia), or *wh*-movement or relativization, as in (ib&b′). Generally, we use italics to indicate the parts of the discontinuous PP. A comprehensive discussion of R-extraction is given in Chapter 5.

(i) a. Jan heeft *er* gisteren *naar* gevraagd.
Jan has there yesterday for asked
'Jan asked for it yesterday.'
b. *Waar* heeft Jan *naar* gevraagd?
where has Jan for asked
'What did Jan ask for?'
b′. het boek *waar* Jan *naar* gevraagd heeft
the book where Jan for asked has
'the book that Jan has asked for'

R-pronominalization:
The process of creating a pronominal PP, that is, a PP consisting of a preposition and an °R-pronoun; see Chapter 5.

R-pronoun:
In Dutch, prepositions cannot be followed by third person, neuter pronouns like *het* 'it' or *iets* 'something'. So, whereas (ia) is fully acceptable, (ib) is excluded: the neuter pronoun is obligatorily replaced by a so-called R-pronoun *er/daar/ergens/...*, as in (ib′). Occasionally, the replacement by an R-pronoun is optional, e.g., in the case of the quantificational pronouns *iets* 'something' or *niets* 'nothing' in (ic).

(i) a. naar hem/haar 'to him/her'
b. *naar het — b′. er naar 'to it'
c. naar (n)iets 'to something/nothing' — c′. (n)ergens naar 'to something/nothing'

Scrambling:
The word order of Dutch in the °middle field of the clause is relatively free. Generally this is accounted for by assuming that Dutch has a set of "short" leftward movements that target clause-internal positions. In this way constituents may be moved across adverbial phrases, thus giving rise to word order variation. This is illustrated in (i).

(i) a. Jan zal waarschijnlijk morgen dat boek kopen.
Jan will probably tomorrow that book buy
'Jan will probably buy that book tomorrow.'
b. Jan zal waarschijnlijk dat boek morgen kopen.
c. Jan zal dat boek waarschijnlijk morgen kopen.

Scrambling is not a unitary phenomenon but actually functions as a cover term for several types of movement. In the prototypical case, scrambling is related to the information structure of the clause. In an example like (ia), in which the noun phrase *het boek* is not scrambled, the noun phrase typically belongs to the °focus ("new" information) of the clause. In (ic), where it is scrambled, it belongs to the PRESUPPOSITION ("old" information) of the clause; in this example it is rather the adverb *morgen* that constitutes the focus of the clause. Scrambling can, however, also apply for other reasons. In (iia′), for example, the scrambled AP *zo aardig* is assigned emphatic focus, and in (iib′), scrambling of the PP *voor niemand* is forced due to the presence of negation on the nominal complement of the preposition.

(ii) a. dat Jan nog nooit zo aardig geweest is.
that Jan yet never that nice been is
'that Jan has never been that kind before.'
a′. dat Jan ZO aardig nog nooit geweest is.
b. *?dat Jan aardig voor niemand is.
that Jan nice for nobody is
'that Jan isn't kind for anybody.'
b′. dat Jan voor niemand aardig is.

There are many controversies concerning the nature of scrambling, including the question of whether movement is involved, and, if so, whether this movement has properties normally associated with A-movement (like the movement that places the subject into the regular subject position), or with A′-movement (like *wh-*

movement or topicalization), or with both. There is a vast literature on scrambling; here we mention only some important more recent contributions: Verhagen (1986), Vanden Wyngaerd (1988/1989), Grewendorf & Sternefeld (1990), De Hoop (1992), Corver & Van Riemsdijk (1994), Neeleman (1994b), and Broekhuis (2000/2008).

SUBJECT (vs. subject):
See °logical SUBJECT.

Supplementive:
The supplementive is a constituent of the clause that denotes a property of the subject or the direct object. This is illustrated in (ia&b) by means of supplementive adjectives. In (ia), the adjective *dronken* 'drunk' denotes a property of the subject *Jan*, and in (ib) the adjective *leeg* 'empty' denotes a property of the direct object *de fles* 'the bottle'.

(i) a. *Jan* ging *dronken* naar huis.
Jan went drunk to home
'Jan went home drunk.'
b. Marie zet *de fles* *leeg* in de kast.
Marie puts the bottle empty into the cupboard
'Marie is putting the bottle into the cupboard empty.'

The relation between the supplementive and the clause is one of "simultaneousness" or "material implication". The property expressed by the supplementives in (i) holds at the same time as the action expressed by the clause. Example (ib), for instance, can be paraphrased as "Marie puts the bottle in the cupboard *while* it is empty". In (ii), we give an example in which the relation is a material implication: "that you will iron your shirt smoother *when* it is wet". The supplementive is extensively discussed in A6.3.

(ii) dat je je overhemd nat gladder strijkt.
that you your shirt wet smoother iron
'that you will iron your shirt smoother wet.'

Telic verb:
The notion of telic verb is used for verbs like *vallen* 'to fall' that denote events with a natural end point, whereas the notion of atelic verb is used for verbs like *huilen* 'to cry' that lack such a natural end point. Some researchers object to the notions of (a)telic verb given that telicity need not be a property of the verb, but of the larger structure that the verb occurs in. For example, the verb *wandelen* 'to walk' in a sentence like *Jan wandelt* 'Jan is walking' refers to an atelic event, but the addition of a (predicative) locational phrase may introduce a terminal point and thus make the construction as a whole telic: *Jan wandelt naar huis* 'Jan is walking home'. The shift in telicity often goes hand in hand with a shift in the syntactic status of the verb: *wandelen* behaves like an intransitive verb in *Jan wandelt* but as an °unaccusative verb in *Jan wandelt naar huis*.

Topicalization:
Topicalization is a movement operation that places some constituent into the clause-initial position of a main clause, that is, into the position in front of the finite verb. In (i), the italicized phrases are topicalized, although it has been suggested that the subject NP in (ia) has not been topicalized but occupies the regular subject position; cf. V6.1.2 and Zwart (2011:ch.10) for relevant discussion.

(i) a. *Marie* heeft dat boek gisteren op de markt gekocht.
Marie has that book yesterday at the market bought
'Marie bought that book at the market yesterday.'
b. *Dat boek* heeft Marie gisteren op de markt gekocht.
c. *Gisteren* heeft Marie dat boek op de markt gekocht.
d. *Op de markt* heeft Marie gisteren dat boek gekocht.

Pragmatically seen, a topicalized phrase can have several functions. It may be the topic of discourse: in (ia), for example, the discussion is about Marie, in (ib) about the book, etc. The topicalized phrase may also be used contrastively, for instance to contradict some (implicitly or explicitly made) supposition in the discourse, as in (ii). In these cases, the topicalized phrase receives contrastive accent.

(ii) a. MARIE heeft het boek gekocht (niet JAN).
Marie has the book bought not Jan
b. BOEKEN heeft ze gekocht (geen PLATEN).
books has she bought not records

Trace (*t*):
A formal means of marking the place a constituent once held before it was moved to another position. The trace and the moved constituent are coindexed.

Unaccusative verb:
Unaccusative verbs never take an accusative object. The subject of these verbs stands in a similar semantic relation with the unaccusative verb as the direct objects with a transitive verb. This is quite clear in the pair in (i); the nominative noun phrase *het glas* 'the glass' in the unaccusative construction (ib) stands in the same relation to the verb as the accusative noun phrase *het glas* in the transitive construction in (ia).

(i) a. Jan breekt het glas.
Jan breaks the glass
b. Het glas breekt.
the glass breaks

It is assumed that the subject in (ib) originates in regular direct object position but is not assigned accusative case by the verb, so it must be moved into subject position, where it can be assigned nominative case. For this reason, we call the subject of an unaccusative verb a °DO-subject. The fact that (ib) has a transitive alternate is an incidental property of the verb *breken* 'to break'. Some verbs, such as *arriveren* 'to arrive', only occur in an unaccusative frame.

It is often assumed that regular intransitive verbs and unaccusative verbs have three distinguishing properties: (a) intransitives take the perfect auxiliary *hebben* 'to have', whereas unaccusatives take the auxiliary *zijn* 'to be'; (b) the past/passive participle of unaccusatives can be used attributively to modify a head noun that corresponds to the subject of the verbal construction, whereas this is not possible with intransitive verbs; (c) the impersonal passive is possible with intransitive verbs only. These properties are illustrated in (ii) by means of the intransitive verb *lachen* 'to laugh' and the unaccusative *arriveren* 'to arrive', cf. Hoekstra (1984a). See Section V2.1.2 for a comprehensive discussion.

(ii)	• Intransitive		• Unaccusative
a.	Jan heeft/*is gelachen. Jan has/is laughed	a′.	Jan is/*heeft gearriveerd. Jan is/has arrived
b.	*de gelachen jongen the laughed boy	b′.	de gearriveerde jongen the arrived boy
c.	Er werd gelachen. there was laughed	c′.	*Er werd gearriveerd. there was arrived

There are, however, cases that show only part of the prototypical behavior of unaccusative verbs. Locational verbs like *hangen*, for example, enter an alternation similar to the verb *breken* in (i), but nevertheless the verb *hangen* in (iiib) does not exhibit the behavior of the verb *arriveren* in (ii). It has been suggested that this might be due to the fact that there is an aspectual difference between the verbs *arriveren* and *hangen*: the former is telic whereas the latter is not.

(iii) a. Jan hangt de jas in kast.
   Jan hangs the coat into the wardrobe
 b. De jas hangt in de kast.
   the coat hangs in the wardrobe

VP-topicalization:
Topicalization of a projection of the main verb. This construction is possible only when an auxiliary verb or the semantically empty verb *doen* 'to do' is present. Some examples are given in (ia).

(i) a. [$_{VP}$ die boeken lezen]$_i$ wil ik niet t_i
   those books read want I not
   'I don't want to read those books.'
 b. [$_{VP}$ dat boek gelezen]$_i$ heb ik niet t_i
   that book read have I not
   'I didn't read that book.'
 c. [$_{VP}$ dat boek lezen]$_i$ doe ik niet t_i
   that book read do I not
   'I don't read that book.'

Occasionally, topicalization of the verb strands the direct object. Still, it can be maintained that in that case a projection of the verb has also been moved into sentence-initial position. The only reason that the examples in (ii) appear to involve movement of the verb in isolation is that the direct object has been scrambled out of the VP, so that what is moved into sentence-initial position is a VP containing the trace of the direct object.

(i) a. $[_{VP}\ t_j$ lezen$]_i$ wil ik die boeken$_j$ niet t_i
b. $[_{VP}\ t_j$ gelezen$]_i$ heb ik dat boek$_j$ niet t_i
c. $[_{VP}\ t_j$ lezen$]_i$ doe ik dat boek$_j$ niet t_i

Subject Index

A

D

N

O

P

R

S

T

U

V

W

References

Adger, David & Graeme Trousdale. 2007. Variation in English syntax: theoretical implications. *English Language and Linguistics* 11:261-278.

Baltin, Mark. 2006. Extraposition. In *The Blackwell companion to syntax*, eds. Martin Everaert & Henk van Riemsdijk, 237-271. Malden, MA/Oxford: Blackwell Publishing.

Barbiers, Sjef. 1995. The syntax of interpretation, University of Leiden/HIL: PhD thesis.

Barbiers, Sjef, Hans Bennis, Gunther De Vogelaer, Magda Devos & Margreet Van de Ham. 2005. *Syntactic Atlas of the Dutch Dialects, Volume I*. Amsterdam: Amsterdam University Press.

Bech, Gunnar. 1952. Über das niederländische Adverbialpronomen *er*. *Traveaux du Cercle Linguistique de Copenhague VIII, Copenhague/Amsterdam*. Also published in J.Hoogteijling (ed.), *Taalkunde in artikelen*, Wolters-Noordhoff 1968, and in S.Barbiers et al. (eds.), *De Nederlandse taalkunde in honderd artikelen*, www.dbnl.org/tekst/tekstsynt.php.

Beeken, J. 1993. *Spiegelstructuur en variabiliteit: pre- en postposities in het Nederlands*. Leuven: Peeters.

Bennis, Hans. 1980. *Er*-deletion in a modular grammar. In *Linguistics in the Netherlands 1980*, eds. Saskia Daalder & M. Gerritsen. Amsterdam/Oxford/New York: North-Holland.

Bennis, Hans. 1986. *Gaps and dummies*. Dordrecht: Foris.

Bennis, Hans. 1991. Theoretische aspekten van partikelvoorpplaatsing II. *Tabu* 21:89-95.

Beukema, Frits & Teun Hoekstra. 1983. *Met* met PRO of *met* zonder PRO. *De Nieuwe Taalgids* 76:532-548.

Beukema, Frits & Teun Hoekstra. 1984. Extractions from *with*-constructions. *Linguistic Inquiry* 15:689-698.

Bianchi, Valentina. 1999. *Consequences of antisymmetry. Headed relative clauses*. Berlin/New York: Mouton de Gruyter.

Booij, Geert. 2010. *Construction Morphology*. Oxford/New York: Oxford University Press.

Broekhuis, Hans. 1992. Chain-government: issues in Dutch syntax, University of Amsterdam/HIL: PhD thesis.

Broekhuis, Hans. 2000. Against feature strength: the case of Scandinavian object shift. *Natural Language and Linguistic Theory* 18:673-721.

Broekhuis, Hans. 2004. Het voorzetselvoorwerp. *Nederlandse Taalkunde* 9:97-131.

Broekhuis, Hans. 2007. Worstelen met het voorzetselvoorwerp: opmerkingen bij Ina Schermer-Vermeers artikel. *Nederlandse Taalkunde* 12:351-358.

Broekhuis, Hans. 2008. *Derivations and evaluations: object shift in the Germanic languages*. Berlin/New York: Mouton de Gruyter.

Broekhuis, Hans. 2013. *Syntax of Dutch. Adjectives and adjective phrases*. Amsterdam: Amsterdam University Press.

Broekhuis, Hans & Norbert Corver. in prep. *Syntax of Dutch. Verbs and verb phrases*. Amsterdam: Amsterdam University Press.

Broekhuis, Hans & Marcel Den Dikken. 2012. *Syntax of Dutch, nouns and noun phrases, volume 2*. Amsterdam: Amsterdam University Press.

Broekhuis, Hans & Evelien Keizer. 2012. *Syntax of Dutch, nouns and noun phrases, volume 1*. Amsterdam: Amsterdam University Press.

Claessen, Charlie & Joost Zwarts. 2010. On the directional particle *heen*. In *Linguistics in the Netherlands 2010*, eds. Jacqueline Van Kamper & Rick Nouwen. Amsterdam/Philadelphia: John Benjamins.

Comrie, Bernard. 1985. *Tense*. Cambridge: Cambridge University Press.

Coppen, Peter-Arno. 1991. *Specifying the noun phrase*. Amsterdam: Thesis Publishers.

Cornips, Leonie. 1994. Syntactische variatie in het Algemeen Nederlands van Heerlen, University of Amsterdam: PhD thesis.

Corver, Norbert. 1990. The syntax of left branch extraction, University of Tilburg: PhD thesis.

Corver, Norbert. 1992. "Bij Marie in de nek": interne structuur en extractiegedrag. *Gramma/TTT*:21-40.

Corver, Norbert & Henk van Riemsdijk. 1994. *Studies on scrambling: movement and non-movement approaches to free word-order phenomena*. Berlin/New York: Mouton de Gruyter.

De Haas, Wim & Mieke Trommelen. 1993. *Morfologisch handboek van het Nederlands: een overzicht van de woordvorming*. 's-Gravenhage: SDU Uitgeverij.

De Hoop, Helen. 1992. Case configuration and noun phrase interpretation, University of Groningen: PhD thesis.

De Sutter, Gert. 2005. Rood, groen, corpus! Eeen taalgebruikersgebaseerde analyse van woordvolgordevariatie in tweeledige werkwoordelijke eindgroepen, University of Leuven: PhD thesis.

De Sutter, Gert. 2007. Naar een corpusgebaseerde, cognitief-functionele verklaring van de woordvolgordevariatie in tweeledige werkwoordelijke eindgroepen. *Nederlandse Taalkunde* 12:302-330.

De Vries, Mark. 2002. The syntax of relativization, University of Amsterdam: PhD thesis.

Den Dikken, Marcel. 1995. *Particles: on the syntax of verb-particle, triadic, and causative constructions*. New York/Oxford: Oxford University Press.

Den Dikken, Marcel. 2003. On the syntax of locative and directional adpositional phrases. Ms., *Unpublished manuscript CUNY*, www.gc.cuny.edu/Page-Elements/Academics-Research-Centers-Initiatives/Doctoral-Programs/Linguistics/Faculty-Bios/Marcel-den-Dikken.

Den Dikken, Marcel. 2003. When particle don't part. Ms. Graduate Center of the City University of New York.

Duinhoven, A.M. 1985. De deelwoorden vroeger en nu. *Voortgang* 6:97-138.

Duinhoven, A.M. 1989. Het voorzetselvoorwerp. Een zinspatroon in wording. *Nederlandse Taalgids* 82:40-45.

Everaert, Martin. 1986. *The syntax of reflexivization*. Dordrecht/Riverton: Foris.

Geerts, Guido. 1984. *Algemene Nederlandse spraakkunst* Groningen: Wolters-Noordhoff.

Gehrke, Berit. 2008. Ps in motion. On the semantics and syntax of P elements and motion events, University of Utrecht: PhD thesis.

Grabowski, J. & P. Weiß. 1995. The prepositional inventory of languages: a factor that affects comprehension of spatial prepositions. *Arbeiten der Forschungsgruppe Sprache und Kognition (Universität Mannheim)* 57.

Grewendorf, Günther & Wolfgang Sternefeld (eds.) 1990. *Scrambling and barriers*. Amsterdam: Benjamins.

Grimshaw, Jane. 1991. Extended projections. Ms. Brandeis University, Walthamm, MA.

Guéron, Jacqueline. 1980. On the syntax and semantics of PP extraposition. *Linguistic Inquiry* 11:637-678.

Haegeman, Liliane. 1992. *Theory and description in generative syntax: a case study in West Flemish*. Cambridge: Cambridge University Press.

Haeseryn, Walter, Kirsten Romijn, Guido Geerts, Jaap De Rooij & Maarten C. Van den Toorn. 1997. *Algemene Nederlandse spraakkunst*. Groningen: Nijhoff.

Haslinger, Irene. 2007. The syntactic location of events. Aspects of verbal complementation in Dutch, University of Tilburg: PhD thesis.

Helmantel, Marjon. 1998. Simplex adpositions and vectors. *The Linguistic Review* 15:361-388.

Helmantel, Marjon. 2002. Interactions in the Dutch adpositional domain, LOT Dissertation Series 66, University of Leiden: PhD thesis.

Hoeksema, Jack. 1991a. Theoretische aspekten van partikelvooropplaatsing. *TABU* 21:18-26.

Hoeksema, Jack. 1991b. Nogmaals Partikelvoorpplaatsing. *Tabu* 21:141-144.

Hoekstra, Eric & Caroline Smit (eds.) 1997. *Vervoegde voegwoorden.Cahiers van het P.J. Meertens-instituut 9*. Amsterdam: P.J. Meertens-instituut.

Hoekstra, Teun. 1984a. *Transitivity. Grammatical relations in government-binding theory*. Dordrecht/Cinnaminson: Foris Publications.

Hoekstra, Teun. 1984b. Government and the distribution of sentential complementation in Dutch. In *Sentential complementation*, eds. W. De Geest & Y. Putseys, 105-116. Dordrecht/Cinnaminson: Foris Publications.

Hoekstra, Teun. 2004. *Arguments and structure. Studies on the architecture of the sentence*. Berlin/New York: Mouton de Gruyter.

Hoekstra, Teun, Monic Lansu & Marion Westerduin. 1987. Complexe verba. *Glot* 10:61-77. [[A translation of this paper by Frits Beukema appeared in Teun Hoekstra: *Arguments and structure*. Studies on the architecture of the Sentence: Berlin/New York: Mouton de Gruyter]].

Hoekstra, Teun & René Mulder. 1990. Unergatives as copular verbs: locational and existential predication. *The Linguistic Review* 7:1-79.

Huang, Cheng-Teh James. 1982. Logical relations in Chinese and the theory of Grammar, MIT: PhD thesis.

Huybregts, Riny. 1991. Clitics. In *Grammatische analyse*, ed. Jan Model. Dordrecht: ICG Printing.

Jackendoff, Ray. 1983. *Semantics and cognition*. Cambridge, MA/London: MIT Press.

Jackendoff, Ray. 1990. *Semantic structures*. Cambridge, MA: MIT Press.

Kaan, Edith. 1992. A minimal approach to extraposition, University of Groningen: MA thesis.

Kayne, Richard S. 1994. *The antisymmetry of syntax*. Cambridge, MA: MIT Press.

Klein, M. 1983. Over de zgn. absolute *met*-constructie. *De Nieuwe Taalgids* 76:151-164.

Klooster, Wim. 1989. "Bananenzinnen". In *Liber amicorium Kåre Langvik-Johanessen*, eds. Karel Porteman & Kurt Erich Schöndorf, 35-43. Leuven.

Klooster, Wim. 2001. *Grammatica van het hedendaags Nederlands. Een volledig overzicht*. Den Haag: SDU Uitgeverij.

Koopman, Hilda. 1995. On verbs that fail to undergo V-second. *Linguistic Inquiry* 26:137-163.

Koopman, Hilda. 1997. Prepositions, postpositions, circumpositions and particles: the structure of Dutch PPs. Ms. UCLA.

Koster, Jan. 1973. PP over V en de theorie van J. Emonds. *Spektator* 2:294-309.

Koster, Jan. 1974. Het werkwoord als spiegelcentrum. *Spektator* 3:601-618.

Koster, Jan. 1978. *Locality principles in syntax*. Dordrecht: Foris.

Koster, Jan. 2000. Extraposition as parallel construal. Ms. University of Groningen, odur.let.rug.nl/~koster/papers/parallel.pdf.

Larson, Richard K. 1990. Extraction and multiple selection in PP. *The Linguistic Review* 7:169-182.

Levelt, Willem. 1996. Perspective taking and ellipsis in spatial descriptions. In *Language and space*, ed. Paul Bloom, 77-107. Cambridge, MA: MIT Press.

Loonen, Nard. 2003. Stante pede gaande van dichtbij langs AF bestemming @, University of Utrecht: PhD thesis.

Mulder, René. 1992. The aspectual nature of syntactic complementation, HIL Dissertations, University of Leiden: PhD thesis.

Mulder, René & Pim Wehrmann. 1989. Locational verbs as unaccusatives. In *Linguistics in the Netherlands1989*, eds. Hans Bennis & Ans Van Kemenade, 111-122. Dordrecht: Foris.

Neeleman, Ad. 1994b. Complex predicates, University of Utrecht: PhD thesis.

Neeleman, Ad & Fred Weerman. 1993. The balance between syntax and morphology: Dutch particles and resultatives. *Natural Language and Linguistic Theory* 11:433-475.

Neeleman, Ad & Fred Weerman. 1999. *Flexible syntax. A theory of case and arguments*. Dordrecht/Boston/London: Kluwer.

Odijk, J. 1993. Compositionality and syntactic generalizations, Tilburg University: PhD thesis.

Paardekooper, P.C. 1977. Met jouw tanden in m'n nek als bw. bep. *De Nieuwe Taalgids* 70:387-406.

Paardekooper, P.C. 1986. *Beknopte ABN-syntaksis*. Eindhoven: P.C. Paardekooper.

Pauwels, A. 1950. *De plaats van hulpwerkwoord, verleden deelwoord en infinitief in de Nederlandse bijzin*. Leuven: Symons.

Quirk, Randolph, Sidney Greenbaum, Geoffrey Leech & Jan Svartvik. 1985. *A comprehensive grammar of the English language*. London/New York: Longman.

Reuland , Eric. 1978. Principles of subordination and construal, University of Groningen: PhD thesis.
Schermer-Vermeer, E.C. 1988. De grammatische status van het zogenaamde voorzetselvoorwerp. *Glot* 11:11-26.
Schermer-Vermeer, E.C. 1990. Het voorzetselvoorwerp en het begrip "vorm". *De nieuwe taalgids* 83:238-247.
Schermer-Vermeer, Ina. 2006. Worstelen met het voorzetselvoorwerp. *Nederlandse Taalkunde* 11:146-167.
Schermer-Vermeer, Ina. 2007. Worstelen rond het voorzetselvoorwerp: een reactie op de opmerkingen van Hans Broekhuis. *Nederlandse Taalkunde* 12:358-365.
Scherpenisse, Wim. 1985. Scrambling in German. *Groninger Arbeiten zur Germanistischen Linguistik* 26:61-78.
Smits, R.J.C. & J. Vat. 1985. Met jouw tanden in mijn bek, een onderzoek naar *met*-constructies. *Spektator* 14:445-470.
Stowell, Tim. 1981. Origins of phrase structure, MIT: PhD thesis.
Van den Toorn, M.C. 1971. Het voorzetselvoorwerp als nominale constituent. *Studia Neerlandica* 6:114-130.
Van den Toorn, M.C. 1981. *Nederlandse grammatica*. Groningen: Wolters-Noordhoff: 7th, revised edition.
Van der Horst, Joop. 2008. *Geschiedenis van de Nederlandse Syntaxis, Vol 1 & 2*. Leuven: Universitaire Pers Leuven.
Van der Horst, Joop & Kees Van der Horst. 1999. *Geschiedenis van het Nederlands in de twintigste eeuw*. Den Haag/Antwerpen: Sdu Uitgevers & Standaard Uitgeverij.
Van der Lubbe, H.F.A. 1985. De structuur van de absolute *met*-constructie. *De Nieuwe Taalgids* 78:6-17.
Van Haeringen, C.B. 1939. Congruerende voegwoorden. *Tijdschrift voor Nederlandse taal en Letterkunde* 58:161-176. www.dbnl.org/titels/titel.php?id–haer001cong01.
Van Hout, Angeliek. 1996. Event semantics of verb frame slternations: a case study of Dutch and its acquisition, Tilburg University: PhD thesis.
Van Riemsdijk, Henk. 1978. *A case study in syntactic markedness: the binding nature of prepositional phrases*. Lisse: Peter de Ridder Press.
Van Riemsdijk, Henk. 1990. Functional prepositions. In *Unity in diversity. Papers presented to Simon C. Dik on his 60th birthday.*, eds. Harm Pinkster & Inge Genee, 229-241. Dordrecht: Foris.
Vanden Wyngaerd, Guido. 1988. Raising-to-object in English and Dutch. *Dutch Working Papers in English Language and Linguistics* 14.
Vanden Wyngaerd, Guido. 1989. Object shift as an A-movement rule. In *MIT Working Papers in Linguistics*, 256-271. Cambridge, MA: MIT.
Verhagen, Arie. 1986. *Linguistic theory and the function of word order in Dutch. A study on interpretive aspects of the order of adverbials and noun phrases*. Dordrecht: Foris.
Zeller, Jochen. 2001. *Particle verbs and local domains*. Amsterdam: John Benjamins.
Zwaan, F.L. 1972. Het voorzetselvoorwerp. *Levende Talen*:347-350.

Zwart, Jan-Wouter. 1993. Dutch syntax. A minimalist approach, University of Groningen: PhD thesis.

Zwart, Jan-Wouter. 1997. *Morphosyntax of verb movement. A minimalist approach to the syntax of Dutch*. Dordrecht: Kluwer Academic Publishers.

Zwart, Jan-Wouter. 2011. *The syntax of Dutch*. Cambridge: Cambridge University Press.

Zwarts, Joost. 1994. Een algabraïsche semantiek voor lokatieve PP's. *Tabu* 24:127-140.

Zwarts, Joost. 1994. A vector-based semantics for locative PPs. Ms. University of Utrecht.

Zwarts, Joost. 1996. Rekenen met richting. *Nederlandse Taalkunde* 1:177-190.

Zwarts, Joost. 1997. Vectors as relative positions: a compositional semantics of modified PPs. *Journal of Semantics* 14:57-86.

Zwarts, Joost. 2006. *Om* and *rond*: een semantische vergelijking. *Nederlandse Taalkunde* 11:101-123.

Zwarts, Joost & Yoad Winter. 1997. A semantic characterization of locative PPs. In *Proceedings of Semantics and Linguistic Theory 7*.

Syntax of Dutch will include the following volumes:

Nouns and Noun Phrases (volume 1): Hans Broekhuis & Evelien Keizer	[appeared in 2012]
Nouns and Noun Phrases (volume 2): Hans Broekhuis & Marcel den Dikken	[appeared in 2012]
Adjectives and Adjective Phrase Hans Broekhuis	[appeared in 2013]
Adpositions and Adpositional Phrases Hans Broekhuis	[this volume]
Verbs and Verb Phrases (volume 1) Hans Broekhuis & Norbert Corver	[to appear in 2014]
Verbs and Verb Phrases (volume 2) Hans Broekhuis & Norbert Corver	[to appear in 2014/5]
Verbs and Verb Phrases (volume 3) Hans Broekhuis & Norbert Corver	[to appear in 2015]

Comprehensive Grammar Resources – the series

With the rapid development of linguistic theory, the art of grammar writing has changed. Modern research on grammatical structures has tended to uncover many constructions, many in depth properties, many insights that are generally not found in the type of grammar books that are used in schools and in fields related to linguistics. The new factual and analytical body of knowledge that is being built up for many languages is, unfortunately, often buried in articles and books that concentrate on theoretical issues and are, therefore, not available in a systematized way. The *Comprehensive Grammar Resources* (CGR) series intends to make up for this lacuna by publishing extensive grammars that are solidly based on recent theoretical and empirical advances. They intend to present the facts as completely as possible and in a way that will "speak" to modern linguists but will also and increasingly become a new type of grammatical resource for the semi- and non-specialist.

Such grammar works are, of necessity, quite voluminous. And compiling them is a huge task. Furthermore, no grammar can ever be complete. Instead new subdomains can always come under scientific scrutiny and lead to additional volumes. We therefore intend to build up these grammars incrementally, volume by volume.

A pioneering project called *Modern Grammar of Dutch*, initiated by Henk van Riemsdijk and executed by Hans Broekhuis has already resulted in 6 volumes covering the noun phrase, the prepositional phrase. the adjective phrase, and a substantial part of the verb phrase. The first of these volumes are now appearing under the heading *Syntax of Dutch* and more are to come. But other projects are also under way. In Hungary, a research group is working on a grammar of Hungarian. Similarly, Romanian linguists are working towards a grammar of Romanian. In Beijing efforts are being undertaken to set up a project to produce a Grammar of Mandarin, and plans for other languages are also being drawn up.

In view of the encyclopaedic nature of grammars, and in view of the size of the works, adequate search facilities must be provided in the form of good indices and extensive cross-referencing. Furthermore, frequent updating of such resources is imperative. The best way to achieve these goals is by making the grammar resources available in electronic format on a dedicated platform. Following current trends, the works will therefore appear in dual mode: as open access objects freely perusable by anyone interested, and as hard copy volumes to cater to those who cherish holding a real book in their hands. The scientific quality of these grammar resources will be jointly guaranteed by the series editors Henk van Riemsdijk and István Kenesei and the publishing house Amsterdam University Press.

14W32464/ T2/ 9789089646019